Third Workshop on Scholarly Document Processing 2022

Gyeongju, South Korea
12-17 October 2022

ISBN: 978-1-7138-6194-2

Printed from e-media with permission by:

Curran Associates, Inc.
57 Morehouse Lane
Red Hook, NY 12571

Some format issues inherent in the e-media version may also appear in this print version.

Printed with permission by Curran Associates, Inc. (2023)

For permission requests, please contact the Association for Computational Linguistics at the address below.

Association for Computational Linguistics
209 N. Eighth Street
Stroudsburg, Pennsylvania 18360

Phone: 1-570-476-8006
Fax: 1-570-476-0860

acl@aclweb.org

Additional copies of this publication are available from:

Curran Associates, Inc.
57 Morehouse Lane
Red Hook, NY 12571 USA
Phone: 845-758-0400
Fax: 845-758-2633
Email: curran@proceedings.com
Web: www.proceedings.com

COLING

International Conference on Computational Linguistics

Proceedings of the Conference and Workshops

COLING

Volume 29 (2022), No. 9

Proceedings of the Workshop

Third Workshop on Scholarly Document Processing

October 12 - 17, 2022
Gyeongju, Republic of Korea

Message from the SDP 2022 Organizing Committee

Welcome to the Third Workshop on Scholarly Document Processing (SDP) at COLING 2022.

The SDP workshop has existed in other forms over the years, mainly in digital libraries or information sciences venues. In recent years, we have transitioned to organizing the SDP workshop at ACL events for several reasons. First, ACL events are the premier venues for the confluence of NLP and ML, and most of the cornerstone tasks in processing scholarly documents are NLP tasks. Improving machine understanding of scholarly semantics embedded in research papers is essential to furthering many tasks and applications in scholarly document processing. Second, the clear practical importance of the scholarly literature makes it an attractive testbed and source of distinctive challenges for researchers focused more generally on computational linguistics. By co-locating with ACL events, we aimed to expand the SDP community by drawing the attention of computational linguists and NLP researchers in search of important, practical problem areas. And third, we have sought to bring together researchers and practitioners from various backgrounds focusing on different aspects of scholarly document processing. We believe that the interdisciplinary nature of the ACL venues greatly assists in encouraging submissions from a diverse set of fields.

Organizing Committee

Arman Cohan, Allen Institute for Artificial Intelligence, USA
Guy Feigenblat, Piiano Privacy Solutions, Israel
Dayne Freitag, SRI International, San Diego, USA
Tirthankar Ghosal, Institute of Formal and Applied Linguistics, Charles University, Czech Republic
Drahomira Herrmannova, Elsevier, USA
Petr Knoth, Open University, UK
Kyle Lo, Allen Institute for Artificial Intelligence, USA
Philipp Mayr, GESIS – Leibniz Institute for the Social Sciences, Germany
Michal Shmueli-Scheuer, IBM Research AI, Haifa Research Lab, Israel
Anita de Waard, Elsevier, USA
Lucy Lu Wang, Allen Institute for Artificial Intelligence and University of Washington, USA

Table of Contents

Overview of the Third Workshop on Scholarly Document Processing

Arman Cohan[a] **Guy Feigenblat**[b] **Dayne Freitag**[c]
Tirthankar Ghosal[d] **Drahomira Herrmannova**[e] **Petr Knoth**[f]
Kyle Lo[a] **Philipp Mayr**[g] **Michal Shmueli-Scheuer**[h]
Anita de Waard[e] **Lucy Lu Wang**[a,i]

Abstract

With the ever-increasing pace of research and high volume of scholarly communication, scholars face a daunting task. Not only must they keep up with the growing literature in their own and related fields, scholars increasingly also need to rebut pseudo-science and disinformation. These needs have motivated an increasing focus on computational methods for enhancing search, summarization, and analysis of scholarly documents. However, the various strands of research on scholarly document processing remain fragmented. To reach out to the broader NLP and AI/ML community, pool distributed efforts in this area, and enable shared access to published research, we held the 3rd Workshop on Scholarly Document Processing (SDP) at COLING as a hybrid event (https://sdproc.org/2022/). The SDP workshop consisted of a research track, three invited talks and five Shared Tasks: 1) MSLR22: Multi-Document Summarization for Literature Reviews, 2) DAGPap22: Detecting automatically generated scientific papers, 3) SV-Ident 2022: Survey Variable Identification in Social Science Publications, 4) SKGG: Scholarly Knowledge Graph Generation, 5) MuP 2022: Multi Perspective Scientific Document Summarization. The program was geared towards NLP, information retrieval, and data mining for scholarly documents, with an emphasis on identifying and providing solutions to open challenges.

[a]Allen Institute for AI, USA
[b]Piiano Privacy Solutions
[c]SRI International, USA
[d]ÚFAL, MFF, Charles University, Czech Republic
[e]Elsevier, USA
[f]The Open University, UK
[g]GESIS — Leibniz Institute for the Social Sciences, Germany
[h]IBM Research AI, Haifa Research Lab, Israel
[i]University of Washington, USA

1 Workshop description

Over the past several years and at various venues, the Joint Workshop on Bibliometric-enhanced IR and NLP for Digital Libraries (**BIRNDL**[1]) (Cabanac et al., 2020; Mayr et al., 2018), the **CL-SciSumm** Shared Task, and the International Workshop on Mining Scientific Publications (**WOSP**[2]) (Knoth et al., 2020) have established themselves as the principal venues for research in scholarly document processing (SDP). However, as these venues are collocated with conferences that are not focused on NLP, current solutions in this domain lag behind modern techniques generated by the greater NLP community.

In 2020, the first **SciNLP** workshop[3] was held online at the AKBC 2020 conference; the workshop brought together interested parties in a talk series focused on various aspects of scientific NLP. The first **Scholarly Document Processing** (SDP) workshop then took place in co-location with the EMNLP 2020 conference as an online workshop (see overview in Chandrasekaran et al. (2020)), and provided a dedicated venue for those working on SDP to submit and discuss their research. Following these successes and the clear appetite for venues to foster discussions around scholarly NLP, SDP 2021 co-located at NAACL, again aimed to connect researchers and practitioners from different communities working with scientific literature and data and created a premier meeting point to facilitate discussions on open problems in SDP.

Program The SDP 2022 workshop consisted of three Keynote talks, a Research Track and a Shared Task Track. The full program with links to papers, videos and posters is available at

[1]https://philippmayr.github.io/BIRNDL-WS/
[2]https://wosp.core.ac.uk/
[3]https://scinlp.org/

Proceedings of the Third Workshop on Scholarly Document Processing, pages 1–6
October 12–17, 2022.

https://sdproc.org/2022/program.html.

2 Keynotes

This year, we had 3 keynote speakers discussing a variety of recent advancements in scholarly document processing: Min-Yen Kan (National University of Singapore), Sophia Ananiadou (University of Manchester), and Andrew Head (University of Pennsylvania). More talk info provided below:

Title "Scholarly Document Processing Research in the Age of AIs".

Speaker Min-Yen Kan

Abstract Artificial Intelligence is poised to impact many fields, but how will the rise of AI impact the way that we do science and scholarly work? Thomas Kuhn, in his philosophical analyses of sciences coined the term "paradigm shift" to describe the resultant progress in science theory when the normal science of an existing paradigm collides with theory-unaccountable, replicable observations. With scientists in AI still expecting key discoveries to be made, will we expect a new paradigm to overturn current normal science in AI and other fields? Will the age of accelerations, as defined by Thomas Friedman, hold sway over how real-world contexts are either accounted for or discarded by research practitioners and scholars alike? I relate my perspective on how normal science and paradigm shifting science relate to the notion of research, fast and slow, and how scholarly document processing can facilitate the mean and variance in science discovery. I give an opinionated view of the importance of scholarly document processing, as a meta-research agenda that can either aid thoughtful slow research, or be leveraged to further exacerbate acceleration of normal science.

Title "Biomedical Text Summarisation: Methods and Challenges"

Speaker Sophia Ananiadou

Abstract Biomedical text summarization techniques are used to support users in accessing information efficiently, by retaining only the most important semantic information contained within documents. Text summarization is important in a variety of scenarios, including systematic reviews (synthesis), evidence-based medicine, clinical decision support, etc. I will discuss current trends in biomedical text summarization, the use of pre-trained language models (PLMs), benchmarks, evaluation measures and challenges faced in both extractive and abstractive methods. In particular, I will examine how to extract salient sentences by exploiting both local and global contexts and explore how the integration of fine-grained medical knowledge into PLMs can improve extractive summarisation.

Title "Exploring How Intelligent Interfaces Can Support the Reading of Scholarly Articles"

Speaker Andrew Head

Abstract In this talk, I share a vision of interactive research papers, where user interfaces surface information for readers when and where they need it. Grounded in tools that I and my collaborators have developed, I discuss what it takes to design reading interfaces that (1) surface definitions of terms where readers need them (2) explain the meaning of math notation and (3) convey the meaning of jargon-dense passages in simpler terms. In our research, we have found that effective reading support requires not only sufficient document processing techniques, but also the careful presentation of derived information atop visually complex documents. I discuss tensions and solutions in designing interactive papers, and identify future research directions that can bring about powerful augmenting reading experiences.

3 Research Track

We invited submissions from all communities demonstrating usage of and challenges associated with natural language processing, information retrieval, and data mining of scholarly and scientific documents. Relevant topics included:

1. Representation learning
2. Information extraction
3. Summarization
4. Generation
5. Question answering
6. Discourse and argumentation mining
7. Network analysis
8. Bibliometrics, scientometrics, and altmetrics
9. Reproducibility
10. Peer review
11. Search and indexing
12. Datasets and resources
13. Document parsing

14. Text mining
15. Research infrastructure, and others.

In total, we accepted 18 submissions for the research track for presentation.

4 Shared Task Track

SDP 2022 hosted five shared tasks. Each shared task had its own organizing committee consisting of several members of the SDP 2022 organizers and/or other collaborators. Shared task presentations were held online in parallel sessions to the main SDP workshop. See short descriptions of the shared tasks below. Detailed overview papers of the shared tasks are referred to and followed in the proceedings.

4.1 Multi-document Summarization for Systematic Reviews (MSLR2022)

Organizers: Lucy Lu Wang, Jay DeYoung, and Byron Wallace

Systematic literature reviews aim to comprehensively summarize evidence from all available studies relevant to a question, and provide the highest quality evidence towards clinical care. Reviews are expensive to produce manually and quickly go out of date (Shojania et al., 2007); (semi-)automation via NLP may facilitate faster evidence synthesis without sacrificing rigor. Toward this end, we provided two datasets of reviews and studies derived from the scientific literature to study the task of generating review summaries (DeYoung et al., 2021; Wallace et al., 2020). We also encouraged submissions extending our task/datasets, e.g., proposing scaffolding tasks, methods for model interpretability, and improved automated evaluation methods. We received submissions from 6 teams, with a total of 10 public submissions to the Cochrane and MS^2 subtask leaderboards. We observed modest improvements in task performance as assessed by automated evaluation metrics, and gained significant insights into the remaining challenges for this task. Systems reports submitted by 5 teams are included in the workshop proceedings along with an overview paper (Wang et al., 2022) summarizing potential directions for future work.

4.2 Detecting automatically generated scientific papers (DAGPap22)

Organizers: Yury Kashnitsky, Drahomira Herrmannova, Anita de Waard, Georgios Tsatsaronis, Catriona Fennell, and Cyril Labbé

Can we automatically distinguish machine-generated papers from those written by humans? For this challenge, we provided a corpus of over 4,000 papers that are (probably) synthetic to some extent, based on the work of Cabanac et al. (2021), as well as documents collected by our publishing and editorial teams. As a control, we provided a corpus of open access human-written papers from the same scientific domains. We also encouraged contributions that extended this dataset with other computer-generated scientific papers, or papers that propose valid metrics to assess automatically generated papers against those written by humans. The DAGPap22 overview paper is available at Kashnitsky et al. (2022).

4.3 Survey Variable Identification in Social Science Publications (SV-Ident 2022)

Organizers: Tornike Tsereteli, Yavuz Selim Kartal, Simone Paolo Ponzetto, Andrea Zielinski, Kai Eckert, Philipp Mayr

The **SV-Ident 2022**[4] task is the first shared task on survey variable identification in the Social Science domain. Social Science literature often uses and references survey datasets, which contain sometimes hundreds of items or questions, called *survey variables* or *variables*. Studies may focus on and reference only a specific subset of these variables. While survey datasets that are used in a publication are typically referenced explicitly in-text using a bibliographic citation, individual variables are often only referenced ambiguously. This lack of explicit linking limits access to research along the FAIR principles.

The dataset for SV-Ident contains 5,972 expert-annotated sentences (with and without variable mentions) that are linked to 11,356 variables of which 1,165 are unique. The shared task is divided into two sub-tasks: a) variable detection and b) variable disambiguation. The former deals with identifying sentences that contain variable mentions, while the latter focuses on linking the correct variables mentioned in a sentence. Results show that implicit variables, which require contextual knowledge, are significantly more difficult to identify. Furthermore, we find that both tasks can be conducted in a zero-shot setting using pretrained language models.

[4] https://vadis-project.github.io/sv-ident-sdp2022/

The SV-Ident overview paper is available at (Tsereteli et al., 2022).

4.4 Scholarly Knowledge Graph Generation (SKGG)

Organizers: Petr Knoth, David Pride, Ronin Wu and Drahomira Herrmannova

With the demise of the widely used Microsoft Academic Graph (MAG) (Wang et al., 2020; Herrmannova and Knoth, 2016) at the end of 2021, the scholarly document processing community faces a pressing need to replace MAG with an open source community supported service. A number of challenging data processing tasks are needed to create a comprehensive scholarly graph, i.e., a graph of entities including research papers, authors, research organisations, and research themes. This shared task aimed to evaluate three key sub-tasks of scholarly graph generation: 1) *document deduplication*, identifying and linking different versions of the same paper, 2) *extracting research themes*, and 3) *affiliation mining*, linking papers to the organisations that produced them. Unfortunately, participants only submitted results in the first subtask, using a new 50k large dataset of 36 research themes compiled based on the UK Research Excellence Framework exercise and enriched using the CORE (Knoth and Zdrahal, 2012) and the Semantic Scholar (Ammar et al., 2018) APIs. The task has created a new performance benchmark comparing traditional and state-of-the-art models under the same experimental conditions. The highest performance was achieved by a transformer-based classifier model based on BERT with the use of argumentative zoning. The SKGG overview paper is available at Óscar E. Mendoza et al. (2022).

4.5 Multi Perspective Scientific Document Summarization (MuP 2022)

Organizers: Arman Cohan, Guy Feigenblat, Tirthankar Ghosal and Michal Shmueli-Scheuer

MuP 2022 shared task is the first shared task on multi-perspective scientific document summarization. The task provides a testbed representing challenges for summarization of scientific documents, and facilitates development of better models to leverage summaries generated from multiple perspectives. We received 139 total submissions from 9 teams. We evaluated submissions both by automated metrics (i.e., ROUGE) and human judgments on faithfulness, coverage, and readability which provided a more nuanced view of the differences between the systems. Systems reports submitted by 5 teams are included in the workshop proceedings along with an overview paper summarizing results and insights.

While we observe encouraging results from the participating teams, we conclude that there is still significant room left for improving summarization leveraging multiple references. The MuP overview paper is available at Cohan et al. (2022).

5 Workshop Overview and Outlook

The organizers were gratified by both the size and breadth of the response to the third edition of SDP. The subjects of accepted papers ranged from end uses of the scholarly literature (such as search, document expansion, or writing support) to challenges associated with automated understanding (such as metadata extraction and disambiguation or argument mining), to adaptations of recent successes in the broader field of NLP. It is apparent that automated processing of the scholarly literature is a problem that meets with substantial interest. And it seems likely that we are observing the beginnings of a research community with a narrow enough focus to make rapid progress, but a broad enough set of concerns to offer ample opportunities for cross-pollination.

To a first approximation, we regard SDP as a confluence of three communities: NLP, information retrieval, and scientometrics. Given our colocation with COLING, it is perhaps not surprising that the majority of our submissions emphasized NLP. As we consider future iterations of the workshop, we are discussing ways to increase its subject diversity. With SDP 2022 we have begun to present a more varied set of shared tasks, each highlighting challenges unique to the automated processing of the scholarly literature. As we proceed with planning and advertising, a key objective will be to elicit high-quality submissions from researchers interested in the uses and metalinguistic aspects of scholarly communication.

6 Conclusion

The scholarly literature has long served as a rich source of interesting and challenging problems for computer science, and there is substantial prior work in information retrieval, scientometrics, data mining, and computational linguistics, but many important challenges remain. In many respects, our efforts to faithfully capture the semantics of scholarly communication through automated means are still in their infancy. At the same time, recent events regarding misinterpretation of scholarly information accentuate the importance of better approaches to the automated processing of scholarly literature.

By drawing attention to these problems and offering a forum for interested scientists from a range of disciplines to collaborate, we hope that this and future instances of SDP encourage the application of recent advances in relevant fields to this problem area, identify new use cases or improve our understanding of existing ones, and ultimately foster solutions that improve the practice of scholarship and serve society.

7 Program Committee

1. Akiko Aizawa, National Institute of Informatics, Japan
2. Hamed Alhoori, Northern Illinois University, USA
3. Iana Atanassova, Université de Bourgogne Franche-Comté, France
4. Premjith B, Amrita Vishwa Vidyapeetham, Coimbatore, India
5. Arie Cattan, Bar Ilan University, Israel
6. Yimeng Dai, University of Melbourne, Australia
7. Sourish Dasgupta, Dhirubhai Ambani Institute of Information and Communication Technology, India
8. Jay DeYoung, Northeastern University, USA
9. Alexander Fabbri, Salesforce, USA
10. Zheng Gao, Amazon Alexa AI, USA
11. John Giorgi, University of Toronto, Canada
12. Paul Groth, University of Amsterdam, Netherlands
13. Daisuke Ikeda, Kyushu University, Japan
14. Roman Kern, Graz University of Technology, Austria
15. Valia Kordoni, Humboldt University Berlin, Germany
16. Xiangci Li, University of Texas at Dallas, USA
17. Yoshitomo Matsubara, University of California, Irvine, USA
18. Aakanksha Naik, Carnegie Mellon University, USA
19. David Pride, The Open University, UK
20. Terry Ruas, University of Wuppertal, Germany
21. Angelo Antonio Salatino, The Open University, UK
22. Zejiang Shen, Massachusetts Institute of Technology, USA
23. Mayank Singh, Indian Institute of Technology Gandhinagar, India
24. Neil Smalheiser, University of Illinois at Chicago, USA
25. Markus Stocker, German National Library of Science and Technology, Germany
26. Wojtek Sylwestrzak, University of Warsaw, Poland
27. Rajeev Verma, Indian Institute of Technology Patna, India
28. Boris Veytsman, Chan Zuckerberg Initiative, USA
29. David Wadden, University of Washington, USA
30. Byron Wallace, Northeastern University, USA
31. Xuan Wang, University of Illinois at Urbana-Champaign, USA
32. Jian Wu, Old Dominion University, USA
33. Wuhe Zou, NetEase AI, China

Acknowledgements

We organizers wish to thank all those who contributed to this workshop series: The researchers who contributed papers, the many reviewers who generously offered their time and expertise, and the participants of the workshop.

References

Waleed Ammar, Dirk Groeneveld, Chandra Bhagavatula, Iz Beltagy, Miles Crawford, Doug Downey, Jason Dunkelberger, Ahmed Elgohary, Sergey Feldman, Vu Ha, et al. 2018. Construction of the literature graph in semantic scholar. *arXiv preprint arXiv:1805.02262*.

Guillaume Cabanac, Ingo Frommholz, and Philipp Mayr. 2020. Bibliometric-Enhanced Information Retrieval 10th Anniversary Workshop Edition. In Joemon M. Jose, Emine Yilmaz, João Magalhães, Pablo Castells, Nicola Ferro, Mário J. Silva, and Flávio Martins, editors, *Advances in Information Retrieval*, volume 12036, pages 641–647. Springer International Publishing, Cham.

Guillaume Cabanac, Cyril Labbé, and Alexander Magazinov. 2021. Tortured phrases: A dubious writing style emerging in science. evidence of critical issues affecting established journals. *arXiv preprint arXiv:2107.06751*.

Muthu Kumar Chandrasekaran, Guy Feigenblat, Dayne Freitag, Tirthankar Ghosal, Eduard Hovy, Philipp Mayr, Michal Shmueli-Scheuer, and Anita de Waard. 2020. Overview of the First Workshop on Scholarly Document Processing (SDP). In *Proceedings of the First Workshop on Scholarly Document Processing*, pages 1–6, Online. Association for Computational Linguistics.

Arman Cohan, Guy Feigenblat, Tirthankar Ghosal, and Michal Shmueli-Scheuer. 2022. Overview of the first shared task on multi perspective scientific document summarization. In *Proceedings of the Third Workshop on Scholarly Document Processing*, Gyeongju, Republic of Korea. Association for Computational Linguistics.

Jay DeYoung, Iz Beltagy, Madeleine van Zuylen, Bailey Kuehl, and Lucy Lu Wang. 2021. MS2: Multi-document summarization of medical studies. In *EMNLP*.

Óscar E. Mendoza, Wojciech Kusa, Alaa El-Ebshihy, Ronin Wu, David Pride, Petr Knoth, Drahomira Herrmannova, Florina Piroi, Gabriella Pasi, and Allan Hanbury. 2022. Benchmark for research theme classification of scholarly documents. In *Proceedings of the Third Workshop on Scholarly Document Processing*, Gyeongju, Republic of Korea. Association for Computational Linguistics.

Drahomira Herrmannova and Petr Knoth. 2016. An analysis of the microsoft academic graph. *D-Lib Magazine*, 22(9/10).

Yury Kashnitsky, Drahomira Herrmannova, Anita de Waard, Georgios Tsatsaronis, Catriona Fennell, and Cyril Labbé. 2022. Overview of the DAGPap22 shared task on detecting automatically generated scientific papers. In *Proceedings of the Third Workshop on Scholarly Document Processing*, Gyeongju, Republic of Korea. Association for Computational Linguistics.

Petr Knoth, Christopher Stahl, Bikash Gyawali, David Pride, Suchetha N. Kunnath, and Drahomira Herrmannova, editors. 2020. *Proceedings of the 8th International Workshop on Mining Scientific Publications*. Association for Computational Linguistics, Wuhan, China.

Petr Knoth and Zdenek Zdrahal. 2012. Core: three access levels to underpin open access. *D-Lib Magazine*, 18(11/12).

Philipp Mayr, Ingo Frommholz, Guillaume Cabanac, Muthu Kumar Chandrasekaran, Kokil Jaidka, Min-Yen Kan, and Dietmar Wolfram. 2018. Introduction to the Special Issue on Bibliometric-Enhanced Information Retrieval and Natural Language Processing for Digital Libraries (BIRNDL). *International Journal on Digital Libraries*, 19(2-3):107–111.

Kaveh G Shojania, Margaret Sampson, Mohammed T Ansari, Jun Ji, Steve Doucette, and David Moher. 2007. How quickly do systematic reviews go out of date? a survival analysis. *Annals of internal medicine*, 147(4):224–233.

Tornike Tsereteli, Yavuz Selim Kartal, Simone Paolo Ponzetto, Andrea Zielinski, Kai Eckert, and Philipp Mayr. 2022. Overview of the SV-Ident 2022 Shared Task on Survey Variable Identification in Social Science Publications. In *Proceedings of the Third Workshop on Scholarly Document Processing*. Association for Computational Linguistics.

Byron C. Wallace, Sayantani Saha, Frank Soboczenski, and Iain James Marshall. 2020. Generating (factual?) narrative summaries of RCTs: Experiments with neural multi-document summarization. In *AMIA Annual Symposium*.

Kuansan Wang, Zhihong Shen, Chiyuan Huang, Chieh-Han Wu, Yuxiao Dong, and Anshul Kanakia. 2020. Microsoft academic graph: When experts are not enough. *Quantitative Science Studies*, 1(1):396–413.

Lucy Lu Wang, Jay DeYoung, and Byron Wallace. 2022. Overview of MSLR2022: A shared task on multi-document summarization for literature reviews. In *Proceedings of the Third Workshop on Scholarly Document Processing*, Gyeongju, Republic of Korea. Association for Computational Linguistics.

Finding Scientific Topics in Continuously Growing Text Corpora

André Bittermann
Leibniz Institute for Psychology (ZPID), Universitätsring 15, 54296 Trier, Germany
abi@leibniz-psychology.org

Jonas Rieger
Department of Statistics, TU Dortmund University, 44221 Dortmund, Germany
rieger@statistik.tu-dortmund.de

Abstract

The ever growing amount of research publications demands computational assistance for everyone trying to keep track with scientific processes. Topic modeling has become a popular approach for finding scientific topics in static collections of research papers. However, the reality of continuously growing corpora of scholarly documents poses a major challenge for traditional approaches. We introduce RollingLDA for an ongoing monitoring of research topics, which offers the possibility of sequential modeling of dynamically growing corpora with time consistency of time series resulting from the modeled texts. We evaluate its capability to detect research topics and present a Shiny App as an easy-to-use interface. In addition, we illustrate usage scenarios for different user groups such as researchers, students, journalists, or policy-makers.

1 Introduction

In the era of "Big Literature" (Nunez-Mir et al., 2015), the exponentially growing number of research publications (Bornmann et al., 2021) poses a serious challenge to those trying to keep up with the vast amount of scientific information published every day. On the one hand, this affects scientists and students who want to stay up-do-date. Due to the accelerating effects of digitization and globalization (cf. Hilbert and López, 2011), assessing scientific developments in a timely manner has become a challenging endeavor – even for experts in their respective fields. A recent example is the plethora of research papers on COVID-19 that rapidly grew after the outbreak in 2020 (Aviv-Reuven and Rosenfeld, 2021). The exceptionally large number of researchers (Ioannidis et al., 2021) produce scientific output that is arguably too much to be reviewed by individual researchers on a case by case basis. Outside academia, on the other hand, journalists, politicians, and the general public are interested in research processes and findings as well. For instance, policy-makers need to evaluate whether a research field is moving toward the intended direction, e.g., whether funding yields scientific output as expected. Journalists who want to report the latest trends in research often depend on (potentially biased) expert opinions or conferences that take place only once per year or biennially. This hampers trend detection on a timely, large scale, and reproducible basis.

1.1 Related Work

Scientific output that is high in volume and velocity demands statistical methods and tools that assist in processing such amounts of information. One strategy to reduce the overload of information is to condense large volumes of text collections to their main topics. In recent years, bibliometrics enhanced with natural language processing (NLP) has emerged as a promising solution for handling such large text corpora (Atanassova et al., 2019). For finding scientific topics, in particular topic modeling became a standard method in scientometrics (e.g., Colavizza et al., 2021; Griffiths and Steyvers, 2004; Yau et al., 2014). Initially developed for information retrieval purposes (Blei et al., 2003), topic modeling is widely used for gaining insights into the underlying themes of text collections. It reduces high dimensional text data to a few groups of co-occurring terms which are interpreted as topics. Put differently, the goal is to "analyze the words of the original texts to discover the themes that run through them" (Blei, 2012, p. 77). By considering the document metadata, the analyses can get more fine-grained. For instance, by incorporating the date of publication into the model, the topic prevalence over time can reveal patterns of publication trends such as "hot" or "cold topics" (Griffiths and Steyvers, 2004). The main advantage of deriving topics from scholarly texts instead of using

Equal contribution.

Proceedings of the Third Workshop on Scholarly Document Processing, pages 7–18
October 12–17, 2022.

database metadata (such as subject headings or classification codes; Krampen, 2016) is their ability to detect novel topics more flexibly (Suominen and Toivanen, 2016).

In summary, NLP approaches like topic modeling can help in coping with the vast amounts of scholarly documents published every day. From a methodological point of view, however, the integration of new texts into existing models fitted on a previous set of texts poses a major challenge. In particular, it remains an open question how to continuously detect research topics in a "living" corpus of scholarly documents.

1.2 Contribution

The current paper addresses the question of how to keep track of scientific topics and trends. We apply a recent topic modeling method to an annually updated corpus of scholarly documents and present a Shiny App that makes the results accessible to users without prior knowledge of coding or topic modeling. Firstly, we describe how topic modeling works and how traditional approaches deal with the integration of new documents into the model. Secondly, we argue that RollingLDA (Rieger et al., 2021) offers the possibility of sequential modeling of dynamically growing corpora ensuring time consistency of time series resulting from the modeled texts. Thirdly, using publications from the field of psychology as a use case, we investigate whether the RollingLDA approach can detect novel topics by comparing its evolved topics to those from a single topic model fitted on a corpus of publications from the year 2020. Fourthly, we describe a Shiny App that provides a user interface for exploring and analyzing research topics. Finally, we discuss practical implications for different user groups, the assets and drawbacks of our newly presented approach as well as future directions.

2 Methodological Background

Topic modeling is used in many application domains (cf. Blei, 2012), which might be partly due to the intuitive explanation of the model idea: a corpus of documents can be described by distributions of topics over time, where each word in each of these documents is assigned to one of the topics. This in turn yields word distributions for each topic, which are thereby made interpretable.

Probably the best known model among topic models is the latent Dirichlet allocation (LDA, Blei

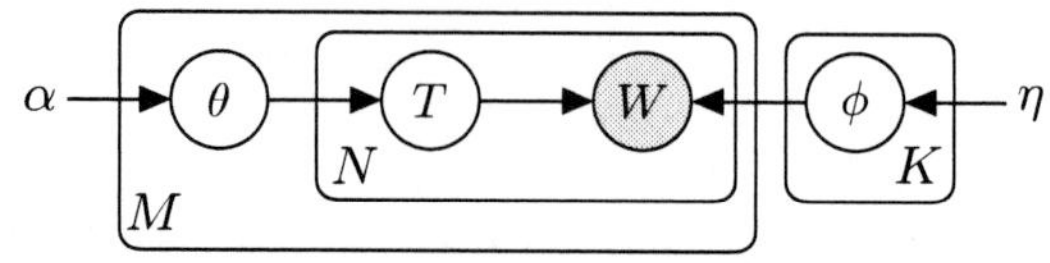

Figure 1: Schematic (plate) representation of LDA.

et al., 2003). The underlying probabilistic model (Griffiths and Steyvers, 2004) is given by

$$W_n^{(m)} \mid T_n^{(m)}, \phi_k \sim \text{Discr}(\phi_k), \quad \phi_k \sim \text{Dir}(\eta),$$
$$T_n^{(m)} \mid \theta_m \sim \text{Discr}(\theta_m), \quad \theta_m \sim \text{Dir}(\alpha),$$

where α and η are Dirichlet priors and K the number of topics to be modeled chosen by the user and each document $m = 1, \dots, M$ is considered a bag of words set $\{W_n^{(m)} \mid n = 1, \dots, N^{(m)}\}$ with observed words $W_n^{(m)} \in W = \{W_1, \dots, W_V\}$. Then, $T_n^{(m)}$ describes the corresponding topic assignment for each word. Figure 1 gives a schematic representation of LDA. The observable variable W is colored gray, latent variables encircled, while constants are not. The latent word and topic distributions are represented by ϕ and θ, respectively.

For modeling topics in scientific corpora, we use a rolling variant of the classical LDA, estimated with the Gibbs sampler (Griffiths and Steyvers, 2004), named RollingLDA (cf. Sect. 2.2). The main challenge is to update the topic model with new publications while preserving the old time series based on the topic assignments of previous models on the one hand and allowing for the creation and mutation of new topics on the other hand.

2.1 Related Methods

Traditional approaches for this kind of task include the **one model fits all** approach, which consists of assigning new documents to topics of the existing topic model. This type of model is implemented by the online LDA (Zhai and Boyd-Graber, 2013), which is computationally inexpensive but lacks ability to capture new topics.

A second possible approach is to **recalculate the complete model** on the entire corpus for each update. In this way, it is possible that the model also catches more recent themes. However, with this approach, old topics usually change strongly or become unidentifiable. In addition, the consistency of the time series based on previous models is lost. Examples for this type of model are topics over time (Wang and McCallum, 2006) or continuous time dynamic topic model (Wang et al., 2008).

Both methods use information of future documents for modeling past documents.

Instead of calculating the new model on the entire data, it is possible to calculate **separate models** for each time period. In this way, past topics remain consistently interpretable, while the temporal interpretability of topics is lost, so that topics from different time intervals have to be matched in a complex (and tricky) way (cf. Niekler and Jähnichen, 2012) to get a minimum of interpretability.

One way to deal with the aforementioned drawbacks is the **restricted memory** approach. The temporal LDA (Wang et al., 2012), which can be used for monitoring writing styles of individual authors, or the streaming LDA (Amoualian et al., 2016), which is rather suitable for thematically narrower corpora due to a dependence structure between consecutive documents, are specialized models that implement this concept. For the given use case, the RollingLDA (Rieger et al., 2021) implements a more flexible version of the online LDA, whereby knowledge about previous documents is forgotten as time passes, thus allowing for mutations and new topics to be created. For the reasons mentioned above, we use RollingLDA for regular annual updates of the model.

We do not perform a qualitative comparison of the RollingLDA and (for instance) the online LDA, as there is no established evaluation metric for the quality of topic segmentation for the given application. Rather, there is a need for further research that defines task-based evaluation metrics and evaluates their usefulness, cf. Doogan and Buntine (2021); Ethayarajh and Jurafsky (2020) - for example, regarding correlation with human perception of meaningful structured topics, cf. Chang et al. (2009); Hoyle et al. (2021).

2.2 RollingLDA

The rolling version of LDA we use is initially based on one special LDA taken from an user defined initialization period (parameter `init`). Up to this date, a highly reliable run is selected from a set of LDA runs using the LDAPrototype method (Rieger et al., 2022a). Then, RollingLDA models the incoming data in minibatches (parameter `chunks`). For this, only a restricted time directly before each minibatch is considered as `memory`. Based on the topic assignments of the documents within the memory, the topics are reinitialized for each minibatch. By forgetting topic assignments from documents before the memory period, the model allows evolving topics or weakly populated topics to mutate strongly. This allows current topics to be captured by the model as well.

As long as topics are continuously populated, i.e., that there is no extraordinary drop in the topic's frequency, the initialization of the following minibatch ensures that existing topics are preserved. This prevents the problem of matching topics over time (cf. Niekler and Jähnichen, 2012). By the same property, the gradual evolution of topics is made possible by updating the topic initialization with only the most recent documents for every minibatch. In contrast, very weakly populated topics may be replaced by newly emerging topics due to the model architecture.

3 Framework

In order to explore the feasibility of RollingLDA for bibliometric purposes, the goals of the current study are threefold

- to compare the evolved RollingLDA topics to a topic model fitted on a specific year only,
- to show an efficient way of top term lifting in RollingLDA, and
- to illustrate how RollingLDA can be integrated into a Shiny App.

We investigate the eligibility of RollingLDA for topic identification in scholarly documents by setting different temporal lengths for model initialization as well as different numbers of topics and compare their evolved topics of 2020 to an individual LDA model fitted on the 2020 corpus only. We propose a method for time restricted top term weighting that offers additional insights into the evolution of topics. Moreover, we illustrate the integration of RollingLDA in a topic app. Leveraging R Shiny (Chang et al., 2021), we present an easy-to-use interface to the topic model that, among other things, visualizes topic trends and topic evolution, i.e., the change of topic terms over time.

We utilize the approach to the field of psychology as a use case, as psychological research is in most parts empirical, but also comprises theoretical and methodological contributions. This variety in study methodology should favor generalizability of our topic detection approach to other scientific disciplines.

3.1 Data

We extracted publication data from PSYNDEX, the comprehensive reference database for psychology publications from the German-speaking countries. PSYNDEX (`www.psyndex.de/en`) is produced by the Leibniz Institute for Psychology (ZPID) in Germany and has a field structure analogous to the international PsycInfo database, produced by the American Psychological Association. PSYNDEX is accessible for free via PubPsych (`www.pubpsych.eu`). The database was queried in November 2021, including a total of 360,009 publication references (titles, abstracts, and metadata) from the years 1980 to 2021.

3.2 Preprocessing

For finding scientific topics, we build a text corpus that consists of English language titles, abstracts, and standardized keywords. These keywords are the controlled terms of the American Psychological Association (Tuleya, 2007), a thesaurus of central concepts in psychological research similar to the MeSH terms of the National Library of Medicine. In contrast to author keywords, such standardized vocabulary represent the main concepts of the publications while reducing variance due to spelling variants or synonyms. This is especially relevant for methodological terms, as methods like "linear regression" are only indexed with the respective keyword, if the method itself was in focus of the publication, not a mere application for analyzing the data. Abstracts and titles are lemmatized and tokenized, while the keywords are left in their initial form due to their standardization. As suggested by Maier et al. (2018), we transformed all text to lowercase and removed punctuation as well as the stop words of scholarly abstracts provided by Christ et al. (2019) and Bittermann and Klos (2019a).

3.3 Study Design

For selecting a model variant with appropriate parameters, we first build a reliable reference model based only on the data from 2020, aiming for a RollingLDA variant which has a topic structure of the evolved topics in 2020 that is most similar to that of the reference model. In addition, the selected RollingLDA model should satisfy traditional topic quality criteria.

3.3.1 Reference Model for 2020

In order to determine the "actual" topics of 2020, we fit a topic model to documents published in 2020 only. Multiple LDA runs lead to different results, stressing the importance of topic reliability (Maier et al., 2018). We address this issue by applying LDAPrototype (Rieger et al., 2022a), which computes several LDA models and determines the one being the most similar to the other LDA models. For different numbers of topics K, we run 25 replications. Based on Bittermann and Fischer (2018) who found 500 topics in a psychology corpus spanning 37 years, we assume that a single year will have a significantly smaller number of topics. Hence, we inspect $K = 150, 175, \ldots, 300$. We set the number of iterations to 500, $\alpha = 0.0001$ and $\eta = 1/K$ (package default), to create a few high probability topics and a lot of close-to-zero probability topics per publication. In order to reduce computation time (Strubell et al., 2019) and most likely without lack of quality (Maier et al., 2020), we exclude terms appearing in less than 15 publications.

To determine the optimal number of topics K, we follow the recommendations of Maier et al. (2018) and focus on topic interpretability. As proposed by Roberts et al. (2014), we jointly use two statistical metrics of topic quality: Semantic coherence as defined by Mimno et al. (2011) and topic exclusivity using LDAvis relevance score with $\lambda = 0$ (Sievert and Shirley, 2014). Subsequently, we manually inspect top words and the most representative documents of the three models with highest quality, leading to a final 2020 reference model with 250 topics.

3.3.2 RollingLDA Candidate Models

For RollingLDA, three model-specific parameters have to be set: `chunks`, `memory`, and a threshold for vocabularies to be considered, `vocab.limit`. The memory parameter determines how much information from prior years is used to model the documents from the new publication year. Setting memory to a larger value has the effect of topics remaining rather stable, while smaller values let topic terms vary more from year to year. For the present corpus, years are the smallest available unit of time. Fixing all other parameters for RollingLDA, we inspect the results of setting `memory` to the last two years, the last year, and a random sample of 30% of last year's documents. While the random sample produce topics that are hard to interpret, using the documents from the last two years yield only minor changes in topic terms over time. Hence, as we were looking for flexibility while preserving the overall topic structure over time, we decide to use all last year's publications as memory for the RollingLDA topic assignments.

The vocabulary threshold controls which new terms are integrated into the overall vocabulary: Words that occur more than `vocab.limit` times in a minibatch are added, otherwise discarded for modeling the topics of the new publication year. We set it to ten, as we find this to be the best compromise of flexibility and computation time (after inspecting thresholds ranging from 5 to 25, cf. Strubell et al., 2019; Maier et al., 2020). The `chunks` parameter cuts the corpus into intervals, which is set to yearly updates in the present case. We inspect $K = 200, 250, \ldots, 500$ (cf. Bittermann and Fischer, 2018), taking into account that modeling topic evolution will result in a lower total number of psychology topics in the RollingLDA model. The remaining parameters (α, η, and number of iterations) are set analogously to the LDAPrototype model for 2020 (cf. Sect. 3.3.1).

Another important parameter for the model evaluation is the date until which the documents are used for the initial model, because the RollingLDA updates are based on these initial topic structures. For a continuous tracking of scientific topics, we evaluate whether the topics evolve correctly in the long term. If the initial model is based on too little data, the RollingLDA might not be able to incorporate future changes adequately. Indeed, this is especially true when a scientific discipline has broadened its thematic spectrum over the years – which might be the case for psychology from the German-speaking countries: In PSYNDEX, the number of documents is rather low in the 1980s (cf. Bittermann, 2022, Fig. 14). This suggests that taking only documents from this period of time into consideration for the initial model won't provide enough information to let the RollingLDA evolve to the "actual" topics of 2020. Hence, we test several variants for the initial model, i.e., different starting points for RollingLDA, namely $1990, 1995, \ldots, 2015$. All initial models start with the publication year 1980 and include terms that appear in at least 25 publications.

3.3.3 Model Comparisons

In total, we try seven values for K and six different starting years. The resulting $7 \times 6 = 42$ RollingLDAs are evaluated using the following criteria:

- Cosine similarity to the reference model,
- topic quality metrics, and
- external topic validation.

We consider similarity to the 2020 reference model as the most crucial factor, as it helps to assess whether sequential modeling can lead to topic results comparable to static modeling. Specifically, we compute the mean cosine similarity between all possible pairwise combinations of word distributions of the topics from the 2020 reference model and each rolling variant's 2020 topics. We decide to use cosine similarity as Rieger et al. (2021) propose this measure to be superior to other metrics for monitoring topic stability or topic self-similarities. In order to emphasize this first criterion, we select the five most similar RollingLDA model variants for subsequent analysis of topic quality and external validation of topic contents.

Despite being able to reflect the semantic contents of the "actual" 2020 topics, high quality topics are still an important issue. Hence, for topic quality metrics, we calculate semantic coherence and topic exclusivity (cf. Sect. 3.3.1). Maier et al. (2018) stresses the importance of topic validity. While intra-topic semantic validity (Quinn et al., 2010) via inspecting the top terms and most representative documents for each of the model variants is not feasible (especially w.r.t. change of top terms over time), we employ a strategy of external validation. Here, we use the concordance of topics with the database classification system (cf. Griffiths and Steyvers, 2004). For each topic, we determine the share of the APA classification categories (`https://www.apa.org/pubs/databases/training/class-codes`) in those publications where the topic was the overall most dominant one (i.e., document's topic probability > 0.5). By doing so, we retrieve a distribution of classification category shares for each topic, which we then correlate with the actual frequency distribution of these categories in the corpus metadata: The higher the resulting correlation coefficient, the more similar the category distributions of the RollingLDA variants are to the actual distributions. For determining the overall best fitting model, we standardize all values to z-scores and calculate the mean for each RollingLDA variant.

3.4 Shiny App, Term Lifting, and Topic Labels

Building upon the LDA-based Shiny App developed by Bittermann (2019), we design a novel

Start	K	Similarity*	Coherence	Exclusivity	Correlation**	Mean (of z-scores)
2010	**200**	0.623 898	−123.997 870	4.137 017	0.960 064	**0.188 719**
2005	200	0.621 397	−123.516 668	3.949 559	0.962 599	−0.054 622
1995	200	0.621 219	−123.226 158	3.881 941	0.966 658	0.176 869
2010	300	0.621 108	−123.386 484	4.320 748	0.946 135	−0.008 355
2015	200	0.620 810	−123.740 794	4.410 456	0.944 504	−0.302 611

Table 1: Comparison of RollingLDA model variants. The reference model for 2020 (cf. Sect. 3.3.1) comprised 250 topics. The best fitting model variant is printed in bold. Notes: *mean cosine similarity to the topics of the reference model. **correlations between actual classification category frequencies and classification shares in the topics (external validation).

user interface that visualizes RollingLDA topics while keeping it reasonably simple. In order to be both easy-to-use by novices and adaptable by the research community, we find R Shiny (Chang et al., 2021) to be a suitable solution: A slim user interface allows even users without programming skills to explore the topics, and the widespread R programming language (Muenchen, 2019) lets data analysts easily modify the app to their needs. Our topic app "PsychTopics" is updated quarterly, licensed as open source software, and made available on GitHub (`https://github.com/leibniz-psychology/psychtopics`).

In topic modeling, topics are characterized by groups of words that tend to co-occur. These so-called global top terms are determined according to the occurrence probabilities of the words over the entire time horizon. In addition, the RollingLDA approach lets topic terms vary over the years. In the PsychTopics app, we call these year-specific words evolution terms. Here, the occurrence probabilities of the words in the topic are determined for a specific year and weighted for disproportional occurrences in this topic compared to other topics (cf. Rieger et al., 2022a, Formula 9), which allows mapping particularly characteristic topic alignments in individual years. By distinguishing between global and year-specific evolution top terms, it is possible both to classify them in the global topic structure and to identify temporary shifts.

Since the absolute frequency and the exclusivity of a word for a specific topic can vary greatly, determining the overall theme of a topic is not trivial. To facilitate topic interpretation, we manually assign labels to the topics by adopting best-practice recommendations by Maier et al. (2018). Specifically, two researchers independently inspected the evolution of top terms, the most representative publications, and the most frequent journals that published

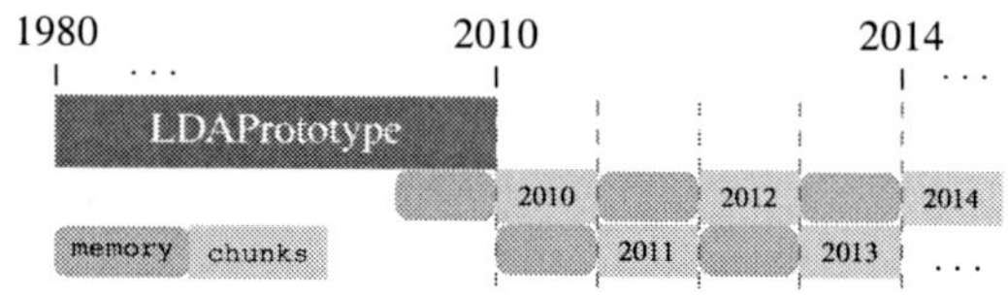

Figure 2: PsychTopics modeling scheme for the best fitting model (start = 2010).

articles on this topic. In addition, for each topic we take the most frequently observed classification categories into account. In case of topic shifts, i.e., new or diverging contents in the topic starting in a specific year, we assign arrows to the label. For instance, the topic label "Miscellaneous Disorders → Trauma" indicates that over the years, a rather broad topic on psychological disorders became specialized on trauma.

4 Analysis

The five model variants with highest cosine similarity to the reference model (cf. Sect. 3.3.2 and 3.3.3) comprise either 200 or 300 topics, while their RollingLDA starting years ranged from 1995 to 2015. Table 1 shows the metrics used for comparison. The cosine similarities are rather close, but the variants differ in topic quality metrics (especially exclusivity) and correlations with the metadata classification categories. The five models' overall high correlation coefficients (0.95 to 0.97) underline their high external validity. The mean z-scores indicate that the variant with $K = 200$ topics and the starting year of 2010 for RollingLDA is the overall best fitting model (cf. Figure 2), so we choose this for integration in the topic app. All analysis scripts were executed in R (R Core Team, 2022) and can be found in the supplementary material.

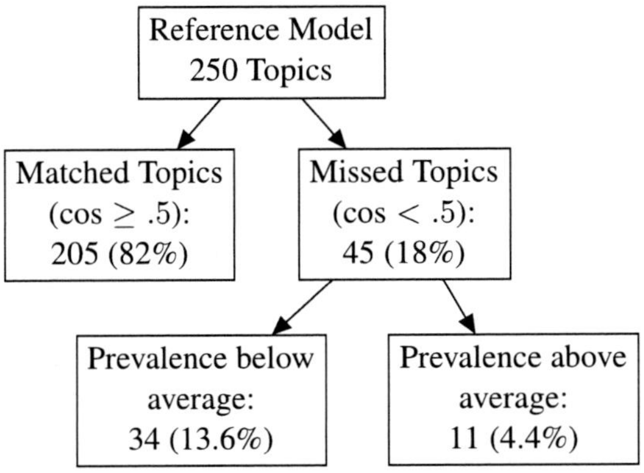

Figure 3: Matched and missed topics of the reference model for the best fitting model ($K = 200, \text{start} = 2010$).

4.1 Matched and Missed Topics

The best fitting model ($K = 200, \text{start} = 2010$) is not perfectly aligned to the reference model ($\cos = .62$), which is not surprising, as the number of topics in the models differ (200 vs. 250) and as the variants are initialized with data from 1980 to 2009. The individual topic similarities range from .30 to .91 ($\sigma = .13$, $x_{0.25} = .52$, $x_{0.5} = .62$, $x_{0.75} = .72$). Of the 250 topics in the reference model, 45 (18%) get a similarity value of less than .5, realizing prevalences $\theta_{m,k}$ ranging from .19% to .46%, with 11 topics having a prevalence above the model's average ($1/K = 1/250 = 0.4\%$). That is, 205 (82%) topics can be detected satisfactorily by the RollingLDA, whereas eleven (4.4%) of the more prevalent topics in 2020 are missed as individual topics (cf. Figure 3). Despite being not matched satisfactorily, characteristic terms of these topics (e.g., dreams, climate, tinnitus) can be found in other topics, so these themes are not lost, but just less prevalent. The remaining 34 (13.6%) topics are negligible due to their low prevalence in the reference model.

A moderate correlation between cosine similarity and topic prevalence in the reference model ($r = .34$) indicates that topics without match in the variant model (i.e., low similarity) have the tendency to be less prevalent. Indeed, nine of the ten most common topics in the reference model (e.g., psychotherapy, psychoanalysis, mental disorders, memory, group therapy), can be matched to the most similar variant topics (ranging in cosine similarity from .64 to .88). The only exception is a topic on refugee psychotherapy. The highest value of cosine similarity has a variant topic on psychotherapy. Nevertheless, six refugee-related topics are included in the variant model, however, scoring lower as they focus on refugees in context of trauma, COVID-19, social issues, or health services. In the supplementary material, we provide tables with global top terms of the reference and evolution terms of the variant model, as well as a table including the cosine similarities.

4.2 Topic Interpretability and Topic Shifts

Focusing on the variant's 200 topics, there is one topic to be too diverse for a coherent interpretation (global top terms: "theory, social, process, model, concept, behavior, development, psychology, group, system"). These are rather generic terms in psychological research, which is why we regard this as a "background topic". For 20 (10%) topics, top terms vary within an overarching theme (e.g., "Miscellaneous Disorders") and/or within a specific period in time (e.g., "Miscellaneous Disorders → Trauma"). In total, shifts are found for 34 (17%) topics, while the remaining 83% of all topics evolve within the same semantic scope. In nine cases (4.5%), topic shifts are limited to a relatively close semantic space (e.g., "Child Psychopathology → Trauma") or refined the topic (e.g., "Experimental Psychology → Decision Making"). Eight (4%) topics "disappear", as their top terms over time become too diverse for coherent interpretation (e.g., "Learning Environments → Miscellaneous"). Interestingly, for 17 topics "hard shifts" can be detected, as their their top terms change drastically (e.g., "Psychoanalysis → COVID-19"). Such shifts reflect the RollingLDA model's ability to integrate rising topics (e.g., COVID-19) and to neglect declining topics. This finding does not mean that these topics became irrelevant to the scientific community; rather, they are subsumed under broader topics or they no longer contribute to the main research topics of the field.

4.3 Topic App

Our associated app is called "PsychTopics" (`https://abitter.shinyapps.io/psychtopics/`) and features

- "Start" – a general overview of the overall most prevalent topics as well as the preliminary topics of the current year,
- "Browse Topics" – a detailed list of topic characteristics (such as the number of essential publications or the share of empirical research within these publications),

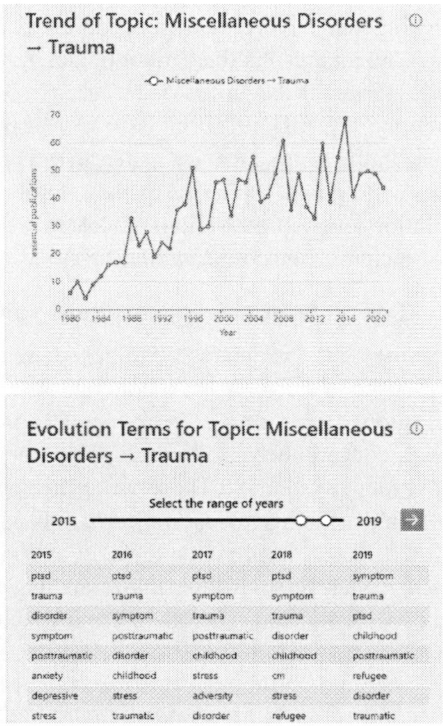

Figure 4: Screenshot of the evolution for topic "Miscellaneous Disorders → Trauma".

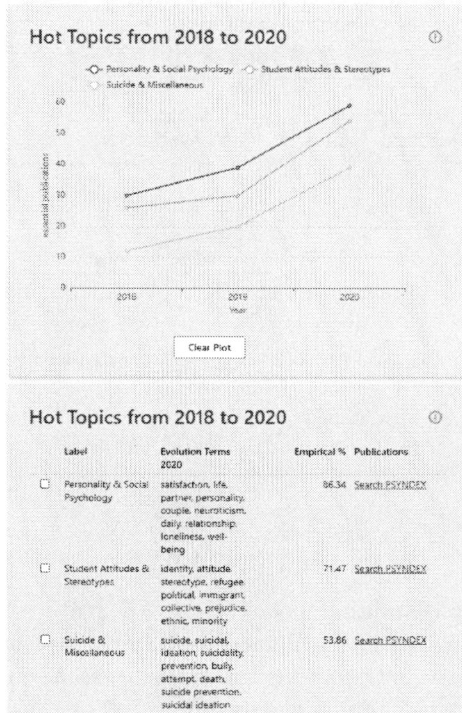

Figure 5: "Hot" topics with the greatest publication gradient between 2018 and 2020.

- "Popular by Year" – the most prevalent topics for a specific year,
- "Hot/Cold" – the topics with the largest increase or decrease in publications,
- "Topic Evolution" – the evolution of lifted top terms across publication years, and
- "Methods" – describing technical details and links to further literature.

Figure 4 shows a screenshot of the "Topic Evolution" view with the example of the topic "Miscellaneous Disorders → Trauma". The line chart depicts the number of essential publications (i.e., $\theta_{m,k} > .5$) for this topic over time. The table below the chart lists the "evolution terms" for the years 2015 to 2019. The topic is less prevalent in the 1980s and at the same time more characterized by publications addressing neurological conditions, schizophrenia, and depression in a more general way. Over the years, and especially from 2001 onwards, there has been a greater specialization of the topic. This topic shift is accompanied by a more prominent appearance of the terms "posttraumatic", "PTSD" and "trauma", from 2012 additionally "childhood" and from 2018 additionally "refugee". In the German-speaking countries, psychology has increasingly addressed the topic of "flight and migration" as a result of the so-called "refugee crisis" in 2015 (Bittermann and Klos, 2019b). A time lag in the appearance of the topic can be explained by a "publication lag" between the initial study idea and the publication of the paper (cf. Björk and Solomon, 2013).

Besides inspecting the evolution of topics, another way to use PsychTopics is to examine trends in the research literature. The "Hot/Cold" view in Figure 5 shows the topics with the strongest rising and the strongest falling linear trend (cf. Griffiths and Steyvers, 2004). Here it can be seen that between the years 2018 and 2020 "Personality & Social Psychology" is the hottest topic. By clicking on the respective points of the lines in the diagram, details of the topics can be accessed. Moreover, clicking the "Search PSYNDEX" link automatically queries the evolution terms in the PubPsych portal and provides relevant publication references.

5 Discussion

In this paper, we applied RollingLDA to a continuously growing corpus of scholarly documents. Using the field of psychology as an use case, we found that RollingLDA is capable of integrating the annual updates of the database to meaningful topics. The framework can be easily applied to any scientific discipline or even to multiple fields. For this, the text input should at least consist of titles and abstracts. In addition, we recommend controlled keywords (e.g., MeSH terms), as they provide the main contents of the articles in a standardized manner. Regarding metadata, we used the year of publication, the classification category, and the study methodology (e.g., empirical research, theoretical discussion). This allows to analyze temporal trends, to validate topic contents, and to highlight topics that might be suitable for meta-analyses. However, our approach is not limited to these metadata and many other additions are conceivable. For instance, the share of open access articles or study preregistrations over time could be compared between topics and research fields. The model is implemented as a Shiny App that lets users explore and analyze the topics and trends without the need of programming skills, while the open source code facilitates the mentioned modifications to the PsychTopics app.

5.1 Practical Implications

The PsychTopics app encourages exploration and thus provides an overview of the variety of scientific publications to researchers, students, policymakers, and the interested public. For journalists and policy-makers, it might be of interest to determine the extent to which publications address topics of social relevance. A corresponding topic in PsychTopics is "Psychology & Society", which is increasingly dedicated to climate change from 2019. The hyperlink to the free literature search in PSYNDEX helps students in finding reading material for class. Furthermore, PsychTopics lists the three journals that have published the most on the topics. This can guide early career researchers in finding suitable journals for their own research papers. In addition, the proportion of empirical studies indicates topics that be suitable for quantitative research syntheses (meta-analyses). In particular, hot topics with very high publication activity and a large share of primary studies may be of relevance for living research syntheses (e.g., Burgard et al., 2022) to keep the meta-analytic evidence as up-to-date as possible.

5.2 Limitations and Further Research

Like most topic modeling techniques, the presented approach focuses on texts written in the English language, but is easily adaptable to other monolingual corpora. In contrast, multilingualism in topic modeling can lead to different topics despite the same content (e.g., English "Therapy" topic and German "Therapie" topic) or lower the semantic coherence of topics (Mimno et al., 2011). Hence, the handling of multilingual text input in sequential modeling of dynamically growing corpora represents a target for future research (e.g., based on Mimno et al., 2009; Vulić et al., 2015).

Topic shifts, i.e., changes in top terms over the years that imply the ending of the prior and the beginning of a new topic, were detected manually and indicated in the topic labels using an arrow symbol. For instance, "Experimental Psychology $\rightarrow$ Decision Making" means that the topic became more specialized over the years. Topics with an abrupt shift to completely different contents (e.g., "Psychoanalysis $\rightarrow$ COVID-19") are split into separate topics in the app. In this way, misleading interpretations of topic names are avoided (such as psychoanalysis became concerned with COVID-19). However, the different types of changes (e.g., abrupt, flowing) remain to be investigated. Moreover, the current manual detection of shifts is labor intensive. This process could be automated by change detection within topics (cf. Rieger et al., 2022b).

It is methodologically interesting to split topics including shifts into two temporal topics, so that the model would have a dynamic number of topics over time. Naturally, it is reasonable to assume that some years of research lead to more different topics, others to less. An approach for a dynamic number of topics might be to delete topics from the initialization of a following minibatch that are characterized by both few document assignments and incoherent top words. This specific topic would end, and the empty topic "slot" could develop a new topic. Unless this newly emerged topic develops a coherent context in the following minibatch, the topic would be neglected. However, as soon as it develops its own meaning, it is taken up as a new topic and also detached from the previous meaning, so that it is considered as an individual topic for the interpretation.

We tested a total of 42 RollingLDA variants, using different settings for the number of topics and starting years of the sequential RollingLDA modeling. We found 200 topics and an initialization model for the publication years 1980 to 2019 yielding the best results in terms of evolving to topics in 2020 comparable to a single 2020 reference model. As we argued, our corpus shows a strong increase in publication volume during the 1980s with a steady increase onwards (cf. Bittermann, 2022, Fig. 14). Other research fields might show a different pattern in publication activity over the years, making different parameters necessary. Thus, the generalizability of the specific model parameters presented might be limited, but our framework and model selection procedure can give guidance to find the best parameters for an application to other corpora of scholarly documents.

The transfer of the framework to other domains requires the major manual effort for the initial preparation of the model. During the routine updates there is some monitoring effort (e.g., whether new subtopics have emerged, whether topics have strongly mutated), which can be kept to a minimum by automated procedures. Optimal model parameters (in particular K, `init`, `memory`) for other domains will depend on the publication volume over time, the desired update intervals and the topical variety of the modeled texts. With our proposed procedure for finding the optimal parameters (cf. Sect. 3.3.3 and Table 1), the resulting manual effort can also be kept to a minimum.

5.3 Conclusion

Taken together, RollingLDA is a suitable method for an ongoing monitoring of scientific topics. It is capable of reducing information overload by summarizing a plethora of publications by means of their main topics. A major benefit of the presented framework is the high degree of automation once the initial model is created. Updates can be produced efficiently and thus timely with regard to runtime and manual effort. Importantly, the model integrates new publications while keeping time series of topic trends consistent. This, in contrast to standard LDA methods, can help various stakeholders like researchers or policy makers to evaluate how fields of research evolve over time. The presented topic app makes these insights easily accessible.

Acknowledgements

The present study is partly supported by the Dortmund Center for data-based Media Analysis (DoCMA) at TU Dortmund University.

References

Hesam Amoualian, Marianne Clausel, Eric Gaussier, and Massih-Reza Amini. 2016. Streaming-LDA: A copula-based approach to modeling topic dependencies in document streams. In *Proceedings of the 22nd SIGKDD-Conference*, pages 695–704. ACM.

Iana Atanassova, Marc Bertin, and Philipp Mayr. 2019. Editorial: Mining scientific papers: NLP-enhanced bibliometrics. *Frontiers in Research Metrics and Analytics*, 4(2).

Shir Aviv-Reuven and Ariel Rosenfeld. 2021. Publication patterns' changes due to the COVID-19 pandemic: a longitudinal and short-term scientometric analysis. *Scientometrics*, 126:6761–6784.

André Bittermann. 2019. Development of a user-friendly app for exploring and analyzing research topics in psychology. In *Proceedings of the 17th Conference of the International Society for Scientometrics and Informetrics*, pages 2634–2635. Edizioni Efesto.

André Bittermann. 2022. Publikationstrends der Psychologie zu Themen gesellschaftlicher und fachlicher Relevanz: Juni 2022. *ZPID Science Information Online*, 22(2).

André Bittermann and Andreas Fischer. 2018. How to identify hot topics in psychology using topic modeling. *Zeitschrift für Psychologie*, 226(1):3–13.

André Bittermann and Eva Maria Klos. 2019a. Code zu: "Ist die psychologische Forschung durchlässig für aktuelle gesellschaftliche Themen? Eine szientometrische Analyse am Beispiel Flucht und Migration mithilfe von Topic Modeling". *PsychArchives*.

André Bittermann and Eva Maria Klos. 2019b. Ist die psychologische Forschung durchlässig für aktuelle gesellschaftliche Themen? *Psychologische Rundschau*, 70(4):239–249.

Bo-Christer Björk and David Solomon. 2013. The publishing delay in scholarly peer-reviewed journals. *Journal of Informetrics*, 7(4):914–923.

David M. Blei. 2012. Probabilistic Topic Models. *Communications of the ACM*, 55(4):77–84.

David M. Blei, Andrew Y. Ng, and Michael I. Jordan. 2003. Latent Dirichlet allocation. *Journal of Machine Learning Research*, 3:993–1022.

Lutz Bornmann, Robin Haunschild, and Rüdiger Mutz. 2021. Growth rates of modern science: a latent piecewise growth curve approach to model publication numbers from established and new literature databases. *Humanities and Social Sciences Communications*, 8(224).

Tanja Burgard, Michael Bosnjak, and Robert Studtrucker. 2022. Psychopen cama: Publication of community-augmented meta-analyses in psychology. *Research Synthesis Methods*, 13(1):134–143.

Jonathan Chang, Jordan Boyd-Graber, Sean Gerrish, Chong Wang, and David M. Blei. 2009. Reading tea leaves: How humans interpret topic models. In *NIPS: Advances in Neural Information Processing Systems*, volume 22, pages 288–296. Curran Associates Inc.

Winston Chang, Joe Cheng, JJ Allaire, Carson Sievert, Barret Schloerke, Yihui Xie, Jeff Allen, Jonathan McPherson, Alan Dipert, and Barbara Borges. 2021. *shiny: Web Application Framework for R*. R package version 1.7.1.

Alexander Christ, Marcus Penthin, and Stephan Kröner. 2019. Research general stop words for: Big data and digital aesthetic, arts and cultural education: Hot spots of current quantitative research. *PsychArchives*.

Giovanni Colavizza, Rodrigo Costas, Vincent A. Traag, Nees Jan van Eck, Thed van Leeuwen, and Ludo Waltman. 2021. A scientometric overview of CORD-19. *PLOS ONE*, 16.

Caitlin Doogan and Wray Buntine. 2021. Topic model or topic twaddle? re-evaluating semantic interpretability measures. In *Proceedings of the 2021 NAACL-Conference*, pages 3824–3848. ACL.

Kawin Ethayarajh and Dan Jurafsky. 2020. Utility is in the eye of the user: A critique of NLP leaderboards. In *Proceedings of the 2020 EMNLP-Conference*, pages 4846–4853. ACL.

Thomas L. Griffiths and Mark Steyvers. 2004. Finding scientific topics. *Proceedings of the National Academy of Sciences*, 101(suppl 1):5228–5235.

Martin Hilbert and Priscila López. 2011. The world's technological capacity to store, communicate, and compute information. *Science*, 332(6025):60–65.

Alexander Hoyle, Pranav Goel, Andrew Hian-Cheong, Denis Peskov, Jordan Lee Boyd-Graber, and Philip Resnik. 2021. Is automated topic model evaluation broken? The incoherence of coherence. In *NeurIPS: Advances in Neural Information Processing Systems*.

John P. A. Ioannidis, Maia Salholz-Hillel, Kevin W. Boyack, and Jeroen Baas. 2021. The rapid, massive growth of COVID-19 authors in the scientific literature. *Royal Society open science*, 8(9).

Günter Krampen. 2016. Scientometric trend analyses of publications on the history of psychology: Is psychology becoming an unhistorical science? *Scientometrics*, 106:1217–1238.

Daniel Maier, Andreas Niekler, Gregor Wiedemann, and Daniela Stoltenberg. 2020. How document sampling and vocabulary pruning affect the results of topic models. *Computational Communication Research*, 2(2).

Daniel Maier, A. Waldherr, P. Miltner, G. Wiedemann, A. Niekler, A. Keinert, B. Pfetsch, G. Heyer, U. Reber, T. Häussler, H. Schmid-Petri, and S. Adam. 2018. Applying LDA topic modeling in communication research: Toward a valid and reliable methodology. *Communication Methods and Measures*, 12(2-3):93–118.

David Mimno, Hanna M. Wallach, Jason Naradowsky, David A. Smith, and Andrew McCallum. 2009. Polylingual topic models. In *Proceedings of the 2009 EMNLP-Conference*, pages 880–889. ACL.

David Mimno, Hanna M. Wallach, Edmund Talley, Miriam Leenders, and Andrew McCallum. 2011. Optimizing Semantic Coherence in Topic Models. In *Proceedings of the 2011 EMNLP-Conference*, pages 262–272. ACL.

Robert A. Muenchen. 2019. The popularity of data science software [blog post]. Accessed 2022-07-04.

Andreas Niekler and Patrick Jähnichen. 2012. Matching results of latent Dirichlet allocation for text. In *Proceedings of ICCM*, pages 317–322.

Gabriela C. Nunez-Mir, Basil V. Iannone III, Keeli Curtis, and Songlin Fei. 2015. Evaluating the evolution of forest restoration research in a changing world: a "big literature" review. *New Forests*, 46:669–682.

Kevin M. Quinn, Burt L. Monroe, Michael Colaresi, Michael H. Crespin, and Dragomir R. Radev. 2010. How to analyze political attention with minimal assumptions and costs. *American Journal of Political Science*, 54(1):209–228.

R Core Team. 2022. *R: A Language and Environment for Statistical Computing*. R Foundation for Statistical Computing, Vienna, Austria.

Jonas Rieger, Carsten Jentsch, and Jörg Rahnenführer. 2021. RollingLDA: An update algorithm of latent Dirichlet allocation to construct consistent time series from textual data. In *Findings Proceedings of the 2021 EMNLP-Conference*, pages 2337–2347. ACL.

Jonas Rieger, Carsten Jentsch, and Jörg Rahnenführer. 2022a. LDAPrototype: A model selection algorithm to improve reliability of latent Dirichlet allocation. *Preprint available at Research Square*.

Jonas Rieger, Kai-Robin Lange, Jonathan Flossdorf, and Carsten Jentsch. 2022b. Dynamic change detection in topics based on rolling LDAs. In *Proceedings of the Text2Story'22 Workshop*, volume 3117 of *CEUR-WS*, pages 5–13.

Margaret E. Roberts, Brandon M. Stewart, Dustin Tingley, Christopher Lucas, Jetson Leder-Luis, Shana Kushner Gadarian, Bethany Albertson, and David G. Rand. 2014. Structural topic models for open-ended survey responses. *American Journal of Political Science*, 58(4):1064–1082.

Carson Sievert and Kenneth Shirley. 2014. LDAvis: A method for visualizing and interpreting topics. In *Proceedings of the Workshop on Interactive Language Learning, Visualization, and Interfaces*, pages 63–70. ACL.

Emma Strubell, Ananya Ganesh, and Andrew McCallum. 2019. Energy and policy considerations for deep learning in NLP. In *Proceedings of the 57th ACL-Conference*, pages 3645–3650. ACL.

Arho Suominen and Hannes Toivanen. 2016. Map of science with topic modeling: Comparison of unsupervised learning and human-assigned subject classification. *Journal of the Association for Information Science and Technology*, 67(10):2464–2476.

Lisa Gallagher Tuleya, editor. 2007. *Thesaurus of psychological index terms*, 11th edition. American Psychological Association.

Ivan Vulić, Wim De Smet, Jie Tang, and Marie-Francine Moens. 2015. Probabilistic topic modeling in multilingual settings: An overview of its methodology and applications. *Information Processing & Management*, 51(1):111–147.

Chong Wang, David M. Blei, and David Heckerman. 2008. Continuous time dynamic topic models. In *Proceedings of the 24th UAI-Conference*, pages 579–586. AUAI.

Xuerui Wang and Andrew McCallum. 2006. Topics over time: A non-markov continuous-time model of topical trends. In *Proceedings of the 12th SIGKDD-Conference*, pages 424–433. ACM.

Yu Wang, Eugene Agichtein, and Michele Benzi. 2012. TM-LDA: Efficient online modeling of latent topic transitions in social media. In *Proceedings of the 18th SIGKDD-Conference*, pages 123–131. ACM.

Chyi-Kwei Yau, Alan Porter, Nils Newman, and Arho Suominen. 2014. Clustering scientific documents with topic modeling. *Scientometrics*, 100:767–786.

Ke Zhai and Jordan Boyd-Graber. 2013. Online latent Dirichlet allocation with infinite vocabulary. In *Proceedings of the 30th ICML-Conference*, Proceedings of Machine Learning Research, pages 561–569. PMLR.

A Supplementary Material

The analysis code and the mentioned topic and similarity tables are provided on GitHub (`https://github.com/abitter/sdp22_supplements`)

Large-scale Evaluation of Transformer-based Article Encoders on the Task of Citation Recommendation

Zoran Medić and **Jan Šnajder**
Text Analysis and Knowledge Engineering Lab
Faculty of Electrical Engineering and Computing, University of Zagreb
Unska 3, 10000 Zagreb, Croatia
{zoran.medic, jan.snajder}@fer.hr

Abstract

Recently introduced transformer-based article encoders (TAEs) designed to produce similar vector representations for mutually related scientific articles have demonstrated strong performance on benchmark datasets for scientific article recommendation. However, the existing benchmark datasets are predominantly focused on single domains and, in some cases, contain easy negatives in small candidate pools. Evaluating representations on such benchmarks might obscure the realistic performance of TAEs in setups with thousands of articles in candidate pools. In this work, we evaluate TAEs on large benchmarks with more challenging candidate pools. We compare the performance of TAEs with a lexical retrieval baseline model BM25 on the task of citation recommendation, where the model produces a list of recommendations for citing in a given input article. We find out that BM25 is still very competitive with the state-of-the-art neural retrievers, a finding which is surprising given the strong performance of TAEs on small benchmarks. As a remedy for the limitations of the existing benchmarks, we propose a new benchmark dataset for evaluating scientific article representations: **M**ulti-**D**omain **C**itation **R**ecommendation dataset (**MDCR**), which covers different scientific fields and contains challenging candidate pools.

1 Introduction

The introduction of large pre-trained language models (LMs) (Devlin et al., 2019; Radford et al., 2019; Lewis et al., 2020; Raffel et al., 2020) based on the transformer architecture (Vaswani et al., 2017) has improved performance on numerous NLP tasks. The adaptation of LMs to scientific corpora (Beltagy et al., 2019; Luu et al., 2021; Gupta et al., 2022; Lee et al., 2020) laid the foundation for applying transformer-based LMs to various scholarly document processing (SDP) tasks, such as named-entity recognition (Naseem et al., 2020), article summarization (Cai et al., 2022), scientific fact-checking (Wadden et al., 2020), describing relationships between articles (Luu et al., 2021), and citation recommendation (CR) (Nogueira et al., 2020; Gu et al., 2022), among others.

While some of the SDP tasks rely on word- or sentence-level representations, others, such as CR and article summarization, require document-level representations. To obtain such representations, recent work has proposed various transformer-based article encoders (TAEs), i.e., LMs that are finetuned using citation or co-citation information as a training signal, such as SPECTER (Cohan et al., 2020), ASPIRE (Mysore et al., 2021a), and SciNCL (Ostendorff et al., 2022). Representations obtained with these models can then be used in various downstream recommendation tasks where a user searches for articles that are in some way relevant to a given query article.

To date, article representations obtained with TAEs have been evaluated against recommendation benchmarks such as SCIDOCS (Cohan et al., 2020), RELISH, (Brown et al., 2019) or TREC-COVID (Voorhees et al., 2021). While SCIDOCS focuses mainly on the field of computer science, RELISH and TRECCOVID cover articles from the biomedical field. These benchmarks contain a set of query articles, where each query is paired with a candidate pool consisting of both relevant and irrelevant articles for that query. The difference between the benchmarks, apart from the domains they cover, is how the candidate pools are constructed: RELISH and TRECCOVID contain expert-annotated relevance labels for each candidate in a pool, while SCIDOCS uses random sampling of negative candidates for pool construction. However, they all contain relatively small candidate pools (e.g., 25 in SCIDOCS). Such small and, in some cases, randomly sampled candidate pools do not resemble typical use-case scenarios in which query articles are compared to millions of candidate articles from

Proceedings of the Third Workshop on Scholarly Document Processing, pages 19–31
October 12–17, 2022.

public databases. Thus, evaluating TAEs on such benchmarks can lead to an overly optimistic performance estimation as the candidate pool does not constitute a representative sample of the population of candidate articles in realistic use cases.

In this work, we turn to a more realistic evaluation of TAEs and evaluate them on large (≥200k) candidate pools and across different scientific fields. Although emulating such a realistic setup has so far been avoided due to the prohibitive computational cost of nearest neighbor search on millions of embeddings, research on GPU-based nearest neighbor (NN) search (Johnson et al., 2019) has given rise to efficient techniques that enable embedding-based search in large-scale setups. To make use of fast NN search, we focus on the bi-encoder models (Lin et al., 2021), that can be easily coupled with fast GPU-based NN search. We evaluate TAEs on the task of CR, in which a model outputs a list of articles as recommendations for citing in a given article. Alongside TAEs, we evaluate the traditional lexical retrieval model BM25 (Robertson and Walker, 1994), which, in spite of its simplicity, still stands as a hard-to-beat baseline in many retrieval tasks. Our evaluation shows that BM25 performs on par with TAEs in this setup, especially as candidate pools grow.

Building on the results of our large-scale evaluation of TAEs, we then construct a new benchmark dataset for evaluating scientific article representations on the task of CR. Our Multi-Domain CR-based benchmark dataset (MDCR), albeit comparable in size to previous benchmarks, spans different scientific fields and consists of challenging candidate pools. More precisely, candidate pools in MDCR contain different candidate types, ranging from those obtained from the large-scale evaluation of state-of-the-art TAEs to candidates from the citation graph neighborhood.

To summarize, the contribution of our work is twofold: (1) we conduct a large-scale evaluation of state-of-the-art TAEs on pools of varying sizes, and (2) present a new and challenging multi-domain benchmark dataset for evaluating scientific article representations that contains challenging candidates identified in the large-scale evaluation.[1]

The rest of the paper is organized as follows. In Section 2, we describe the models we evaluate and give an overview of the existing benchmarks for scientific article recommendation. Section 3 presents the results of a large-scale evaluation of TAEs and BM25 in two evaluation setups. In Section 4 we describe the construction of a new and more challenging multi-domain benchmark and present the initial results for the models we considered. Section 5 concludes the paper and proposes future work.

2 Models and Benchmarks

2.1 Transformer-based Article Encoders

As a baseline TAE, we consider **SciBERT** (Beltagy et al., 2019), a variant of BERT (Devlin et al., 2019), trained on a corpus of scientific articles with masked language modeling objective. Next, we include **SPECTER** (Cohan et al., 2020), a SciBERT-based TAE trained with a contrastive learning objective that minimizes the L2 distance between embeddings of citing-cited article pairs. Further, we consider **SciNCL** (Ostendorff et al., 2022), another SciBERT-based TAE that uses citation graph embeddings for a more informative selection of negative examples with the same contrastive learning objective as SPECTER. Finally, we also evaluate **ASPIRE** (Mysore et al., 2021a), a TAE that uses a co-citation signal to make sentence embeddings of co-cited articles similar.

Among these four TAEs, only SciBERT is trained without any inter-article (i.e., citation or co-citation) training signal. We thus consider it as a baseline to investigate how well LMs pre-trained on domain's corpora can be used in retrieval scenarios without any finetuning. On the other hand, the rest of the TAEs differ both in the type of inter-article training signal used (co-citation for ASPIRE vs. citation for SPECTER and SciNCL) and in the granularity of representation used for article matching (sentence embeddings for ASPIRE vs. document embeddings for SPECTER and SciNCL). All the considered TAEs are *bi-encoders* (Lin et al., 2021), i.e., they produce dense representations of a single input article, which allows them to be easily employed in large-scale setups when coupled with fast nearest neighbor search methods. The alternative are the *cross-encoders*, which take two concatenated articles as the input and output the relevance matching score. Although the cross-encoders often outperform bi-encoders, we do not consider them here as they are not compatible with nearest neighbor search methods and therefore not suitable for

[1]Our code, the data splits and the new benchmark data are publicly available at the following link: `https://github.com/zoranmedic/mdcr`.

large-scale retrieval. [2]

All the considered TAEs produce scientific article representations using the article's title and abstract as input. Since the title and abstract serve as a condensed overview of an article, it is clear that not all possible relationships between a pair of articles can be detected using such input only. However, we consider the title and abstract a reliable proxy for otherwise complex and computationally expensive processing of the whole article's content.

2.2 Existing Benchmarks

Scientific article recommendation benchmarks that TAEs were evaluated on so far were designed for domain-specific retrieval evaluation across small-sized and, in some cases, randomly sampled candidate pools. Each benchmark consists of a set of queries, where each query (title and abstract or a free-form text) is paired with a corresponding *candidate pool*, i.e., a set of query-relevant (*positive*) and query-irrelevant (*negative candidates*) articles. We review the most commonly used benchmarks below.

SCIDOCS (Cohan et al., 2020): A collection of datasets for the evaluation of classification and retrieval tasks that use abstract-level article representations. In retrieval tasks, each query article is paired with a candidate pool of 5 positive and 25 randomly sampled negative candidates.

RELISH (Brown et al., 2019): A collection of query and candidate articles expert-annotated for relevance. Query articles are from the field of biomedicine, each paired with a set of 60 candidates.

TRECCOVID (Voorhees et al., 2021): A TREC-style benchmark consisting of various queries related to COVID-19. Each query is paired with around 300 candidate articles annotated for relevance by medical experts.

CSFCUBE (Mysore et al., 2021b): An expert-annotated dataset of 50 computer science articles annotated at sentence-level for aspect-based relevance with candidate articles. The average candidate pool size is 125.

[2]We thus only consider TS-ASPIRE model in our work and leave out OT-ASPIRE, a variant that uses optimal transport over sentence embeddings, whose computational complexity prohibits its use in large-scale retrieval scenarios.

Three of these benchmarks (RELISH, TREC-COVID, CSFCUBE) are single-domain by design, while SCIDOCS is constructed with queries from different scientific fields. However, the majority of SCIDOCS queries (over 70%) come from a single domain (computer science), making it a predominantly computer science-oriented benchmark.

Existing benchmarks also differ in how the candidate pools in each of them were constructed. While RELISH, TRECCOVID, and CSFCUBE contain expert-annotated candidate pools, meaning that field experts annotated the relevance of each candidate to the query, candidate pools for retrieval tasks in SCIDOCS are made of negative candidates randomly sampled from a set of articles that are not related to the query. For example, in the case of the "Cite" task in SCIDOCS, each query article is paired with a pool of 5 articles cited in the query, and 25 negative candidates are randomly sampled from a held-out set of articles not cited in the query article. An obvious advantage of random candidate pools over expert-annotated pools is that they are less expensive to construct. However, a downside is that random candidate pools might contain many candidates that are entirely unrelated to the query and lead to overly optimistic performance estimates that are not representative of realistic large-scale retrieval scenarios.

3 Large-Scale Evaluation

We performed the large-scale evaluation in two setups: dataset- and field-level. Dataset-level evaluation resembles a basic evaluation setup – a random sampling of both queries and articles in the candidate pool. The field-level evaluation focuses on specific scientific fields using queries and candidate pools comprised of articles from specific fields.

In both setups, we evaluated the chosen models on the task of global CR, in which a model is trained to produce a list of articles as recommendations for citing in a given query article. Although CR is not the only task on which TAEs can be evaluated, it is arguably the most accessible among the article retrieving tasks. Whereas other tasks (e.g., user activity tasks) might require data that is typically not publicly available (e.g., search engine logs), CR datasets are easily obtained through parsing reference lists of publicly available articles. Previous research on global CR has proposed many features that could be used to represent the input articles (Bhagavatula et al., 2018; Ali et al., 2021).

However, in this work, we only use the article's title and abstract as input, as our focus is not on improving the state-of-the-art in global CR but rather on evaluating the TAE-produced article representations in a retrieval scenario. For a detailed overview of the various tasks and methods in CR, we refer the reader to (Medić and Šnajder, 2020).

For each TAE that we consider, the input was constructed by concatenating the input article's title and abstract (separated with a `[SEP]` token). For SciBERT, SPECTER, and SciNCL, we used the final layer's `[CLS]` token embedding as input article's representation, while for ASPIRE we mean-pooled token embeddings across all layers for each sentence in the input. We used HuggingFace's[3] implementations of TAEs, while for BM25 we used Lucene's implementation, i.e., its Python toolkit `pyserini`.[4] For nearest neighbor search across article embeddings, we used Faiss (Johnson et al., 2019).[5]

We used the S2ORC dataset (Lo et al., 2020) in all our experiments. S2ORC is a recently released large dataset of 81.1M scientific articles covering dozens of scientific fields. Together with the metadata and article's title and abstract, the dataset contains citation links between the articles. Therefore, we consider it appropriate for the large-scale evaluation, not just due to its size and coverage but recency as well. We perform initial filtering of articles and remove all those with (1) empty publication year field, (2) empty title field, (3) abstract shorter than 30 characters, or (4) less than three citations in S2ORC. This filtering leaves us with a *prefiltered set* of around 16M articles that we use for both sampling of queries and candidate pool construction in both evaluation setups.

For both evaluation setups, we report the standard metrics used in prior work on scientific article recommendation: MAP, nDCG, and R@30. We set k in R@k to 30, since on average there are 29 positives (cited articles) for each query in the query set. All metrics range from 0 to 1, where higher is better. Although defined differently, all the metrics yield higher values when relevant articles are positioned higher in the list of retrieved articles.

[3]https://github.com/huggingface/transformers

[4]https://github.com/castorini/pyserini

[5]https://github.com/facebookresearch/faiss

3.1 Dataset-level

We start by describing the dataset-level setup in which we evaluated how TAEs perform when asked to provide recommendations over a large candidate pool for random queries from S2ORC.

First, we sampled a random set of 3800 query articles[6] from the prefiltered set of articles. We left out the query articles used in the training sets of SPECTER and SciNCL.[7] Next, we sampled candidate pools of various sizes: 200k, 500k, 1M, and 2M. Each candidate pool contained all the articles cited in the query articles, while the remaining candidates were randomly sampled from the prefiltered set. To make the setup more realistic, we considered the publication years of both query and candidate articles: queries were sampled from the articles published in 2019, while candidate articles' year of publication was 2019 or earlier. Year-based sampling ensures that no article published after the query article can be recommended for citing in that article. Although such year-based sampling still allows for the articles published after the citing (later in 2019) to be included as candidates, it reduces such possibility compared to other benchmarks (e.g., SciDocs) that do not account for it.[8] For each candidate pool size, we repeat the pool sampling procedure three times and report the mean values of the metrics.

Dataset-level results are given in Table 1. We retrieved the top 500 ranked candidates for each model and reported MAP, nDCG, and recall at 30 averaged over three runs for each pool size. For ASPIRE, we used its "BioMed" variant, i.e., the one trained on articles from the biomedicine field.[9] We optimized BM25's parameters b and k_1 on separate validation sets constructed in the same way as test sets. A detailed description of the BM25 formula and the role of the two parameters is given in the Appendix A.

We observe that the best performing model on the pool sizes of 200k and 500k is SciNCL, with

[6]In field-level setup, we sampled 200 queries for each of the 19 MAG fields. To keep the total number of queries the same over both setups, we sampled 3800 total queries in the dataset-level setup as well.

[7]At the time of writing, ASPIRE's training set was not publicly available, so we did not account for that overlap.

[8]Since S2ORC only provides publication years (and not the dates) for articles it contains, filtering can at most be year-based. Additionally, excluding from the candidate pools articles that were published in the same year as the citing would considerably reduce the pool size in some fields.

[9]The other available ASPIRE model, trained on computer science articles, obtained worse results.

Pool sizes →	200k			500k			1M			2M		
Models ↓	MAP	NDCG	R@30	MAP	NDCG	R@30	MAP	NDCG	R@30	MAP	NDCG	R@30
BM25	40.4	73.8	43.0	32.8	68.9	36.4	**27.4**	**64.9**	31.6	**22.5**	**60.8**	**26.9**
SCIBERT	5.5	40.3	5.6	4.6	38.5	3.9	4.1	37.3	3.0	3.8	36.5	2.2
SPECTER	37.4	72.0	40.9	29.5	66.5	33.9	24.1	62.1	28.7	19.2	57.8	23.8
SCINCL	**42.5**	**75.2**	**45.2**	**33.4**	**69.3**	**37.6**	27.1	64.6	**31.9**	21.6	60.0	26.5
ASPIRE-BM	41.4	74.7	43.3	32.6	68.9	35.9	25.7	63.5	30.5	20.4	59.0	25.2

Table 1: Results on different pool sizes in the dataset-level setup for BM25 and three considered TAEs. Values in **bold** indicate the best-performing model for a combination of pool size and metric.

ASPIRE and BM25 not far behind. However, with larger pool sizes of 1M and 2M, BM25 performs better than TAEs for most metrics (except R@30 in the 1M pool, where SCINCL outperforms BM25). Given the slight difference in performance between BM25 and SCINCL, our results demonstrate that traditional lexical retrieval is still very competitive in large-scale retrieval scenarios. These results are in line with those of (Reimers and Gurevych, 2021), who also compared the performance of sparse and dense retrieval models on varying pool sizes and found that the performance of the dense retrieval models decreases quicker for the increasing pool sizes compared to sparse methods. Looking at differences between TAEs, the results show clear benefits of finetuning TAEs with inter-article training signal – both SPECTER and SCINCL outperform SCIBERT.

We also observed a significant drop in performance for all the evaluated TAEs compared to their performance on the "Cite" task in SCIDOCS (results on SCIDOCS are given in Appendix A). For example, MAP for SCIBERT in the "Cite" task of SCIDOCS was 48.3 (Cohan et al., 2020), while in a large-scale setup, it ranges from 5.5 in the case of 200k pool size to 3.8 with a 2M pool size. This difference supports our hypothesis that small-scale evaluation is not indicative of the performance of a model in a realistic, large-scale setup. However, our large-scale evaluation results are consistent with some other findings from the evaluation on SCIDOCS, as reported in (Ostendorff et al., 2022): SCINCL's careful sampling of negatives for the training set leads to a clear improvement in retrieval performance, with SCINCL outperforming SPECTER for all candidate pool sizes.

3.2 Field-level

In the field-level evaluation, we evaluate TAEs on a set of queries and candidate pools from specific scientific fields. Such an evaluation setup resembles a more realistic and also more challenging large-scale retrieval scenario: in a real-world application, given a query article as input, a retrieval model is expected to detect the query article's field and narrow the candidate pool to articles from that field.

To determine the article's field, we used Microsoft Academic Graph (MAG) labels provided in S2ORC. We sampled 200 query articles for each of the 19 distinct MAG fields from S2ORC. As in the dataset-level setup, we used year-based splits and sample query articles published in 2019. Next, for each scientific field, we constructed a candidate pool of size 100k that contains all the articles cited in the query articles alongside field-specific negative candidates. To obtain field-specific negative candidates, we randomly sampled the remaining pool articles (up to 100k) from a set of field-cited articles, i.e., a set of articles cited in all S2ORC articles labeled with a specific MAG field. For example, when sampling negative candidates for the Medicine field, we first filtered all articles labeled with Medicine in their S2ORC's MAG field. We then went through all the articles that they cite and included those in the newly created set of field-cited articles, from which we then sampled negative candidates. As in dataset-level evaluation, we repeat the candidate sampling procedure three times for all the fields where the field-cited article set is larger than 100k (all except Art, History, and Philosophy) and report the mean values of the metrics.

Field-level results in terms of MAP are shown in Table 2 (the NDCG and R@30 results are included in Appendix A; the best performing models are the same in all cases except R@30 for the Bio field). As with dataset-level evaluation, we retrieve the top 500 candidates and report results on these sets. In this setup, we also include ASPIRE-CS, i.e., ASPIRE variant trained on computer science articles.

BM25 achieves the highest mean MAP across

	Art	Bio	Bus	Ch	CS	Eco	Eng	ES	Geog	Geol	His	MS	Mat	Med	Phi	Phy	PS	Psy	Soc	AVG
BM25	**36.1**	44.3	**21.2**	**42.6**	35.6	**26.4**	**34.2**	**27.5**	**29.2**	**32.1**	**32.8**	**34.9**	**35.6**	46.3	**25.0**	**35.8**	**21.2**	31.9	**17.7**	**32.1**
SciBERT	6.2	6.7	3.2	6.7	4.2	4.7	4.6	4.8	4.8	4.7	5.3	4.4	4.9	5.4	3.5	5.5	2.8	5.0	3.0	4.8
Specter	25.1	37.0	18.0	35.4	33.7	22.6	28.5	22.6	20.1	20.3	17.4	29.0	31.5	48.6	16.2	27.5	14.4	32.0	14.3	26.0
SciNCL	26.9	42.2	18.7	39.6	**37.8**	23.4	31.5	25.5	23.7	22.7	20.7	30.9	33.5	**52.4**	18.7	31.4	16.5	**34.1**	15.7	28.7
Aspire-BM	26.8	**44.7**	19.3	39.9	35.3	24.3	29.7	24.5	23.3	22.9	20.1	29.8	33.1	52.1	17.2	30.0	15.9	33.1	14.3	28.2
Aspire-CS	25.8	37.1	20.0	34.9	35.8	23.5	30.2	21.9	21.7	20.1	18.4	27.5	34.2	46.5	17.1	29.0	15.3	32.7	15.7	26.7

Table 2: Results in terms of MAP in the "field-level" evaluation setup. Values in **bold** indicate the best performing model per field. Table with field-abbreviation mapping is given in Table 5 in Appendix A.

all fields, again demonstrating the robust performance of lexical retrieval. SciNCL performs close to BM25, performing best on CS, Med, and Psy fields. While SciNCL's strong performance in CS and Med fields could be explained by a high percentage of SciNCL training queries from those fields (~16% and ~25.3% of SciNCL train queries come from Med and CS fields, respectively), a high MAP value in Psy field is unexpected given the small percentage of Psy queries in SciNCL's train set (~4.1%). Analyzing performance across fields, models perform quite well in some fields (e.g., Med and Bio) and worse in others (e.g., Soc, Bus, PS). Regarding these differences, we note that training sets of most of the TAEs (Specter, SciNCL, Aspire-BM) have a highly skewed distribution toward Med, Bio, and CS fields. However, another possible explanation might be the different levels of interdisciplinarity in particular fields, which could lead to a richer vocabulary than in mono-disciplinary fields. We leave the investigation of the performance across fields for future work.

Comparing TAEs between each other supports our dataset-level results: SciNCL performs slightly better than Aspire (BM), but both outperform Specter, which in turn surpasses SciBERT. Just as in dataset-level evaluation, this ordering is expected given the differences in the training objectives and the training signal used. When comparing different TAEs across fields, we observe that Aspire performs especially well in the fields on which it was originally trained: Aspire-BM outperformed other TAEs in Bio and Ch fields, which shows that field-specific sentence-level encoders might be more successful than other TAEs for other fields as well. Field-level evaluation results also confirm the need for large-scale evaluation of TAEs – their performance is again much worse than in small-scale benchmark evaluation scenarios, such as SciDocs.

To sum up, both of our setups demonstrated (1) a strong performance of a lexical retrieval model BM25, which either surpassed (field-level) or performed competitively to TAEs (dataset-level) in large-scale evaluation scenarios, and (2) a large decrease in performance of all the evaluated TAEs compared to previous small-scale benchmark setups (SciDocs). Although we argue that large-scale evaluation is mandatory for more realistic performance estimates, we also recognize the benefits of standardized evaluation benchmarks as they enable the research community to track the improvement on a task easily. However, even when evaluation is not performed on a large scale, we argue that to keep the benchmark-obtained performance estimation as realistic as possible, small benchmarks should contain realistic candidate pools with challenging negatives. With this in mind, in the next section, we describe the construction of a small but more realistic benchmark for evaluating article representations.

4 Multi-Domain Citation Recommendation Benchmark

We now present our newly constructed **M**ulti-**D**omain **C**itation **R**ecommendation benchmark – **MDCR**. As queries in MDCR, we use the same 200 queries per field as in the field-level evaluation setup (§3.2). For the candidate pools, we start with a random sampling of 5 articles cited in the query article and then select negative candidates.

4.1 Benchmark Construction

To construct challenging candidate pools, we used four different candidate selection strategies: (1) model-based, (2) graph neighbors-based, (3) citation count-based, and (4) random selection. Each candidate strategy produces different candidate types that can be used for a more detailed evaluation of the model's performance. We outline the selection strategies below.

Model-based selection. This strategy aims to capture difficult candidates for the models evaluated in the large-scale setup. As these candidates are difficult for current models, we expect at least some of these candidates to be challenging for some of the future models. Brown et al. (2019) used a similar method for candidate pool construction in RELISH, where candidates were selected using three different retrieval models and then annotated for relevance by the field experts. In MDCR, we do not provide expert-level annotations for candidates but instead, rely on citations as proxy signals for relevance.

We started with compiling lists of the top 200 candidates per query obtained with each model on the candidate pool from the field-level setup. As we evaluate models that are both trained and used differently, it is reasonable to expect each model to have difficulties with different negative candidates. With this in mind, we intended to select those candidates that are difficult for different models. To determine the degree to which the models' top candidates overlap, we calculated the average Jaccard index between the highest-ranked negative candidates of different model pairs. The models that obtained a low average Jaccard index tend to make different mistakes (i.e., rank different negative candidates highly) than other models. We chose the three models with the lowest average Jaccard index for selecting negative candidates in this strategy: BM25, SciNCL, and SPECTER. For each query and each of the three selected models, we randomly sampled ten negative candidates from the top 200 highest ranked candidates by the model and added them to the query's candidate pool. We call these candidate types `BM25`, `SPECTER`, and `SciNCL` for candidates obtained from the respective models.

Graph neighbors-based selection. Research on citation-seeking behavior states that scientists often traverse citation graphs to find articles relevant to their needs (Belter, 2016; Hinde and Spackman, 2015). This suggests that challenging articles should be sampled from the same source, i.e., from a set of articles that either cite or are cited in the articles relevant to the query.

To include such candidates in our pools, we employed the following procedure over the citation graph. Let q be a query article and $OC_q = \{c_1, ..., c_n\}$ a set of articles that are cited in q (i.e., *outgoing* citations). For each $c_i \in OC_q$, we constructed corresponding OC_{c_i} and $IC_{c_i} = \{i_1, ..., i_m\}$ sets, where i_j represents an article that cites c_i (i.e., *incoming* citations). Using such sets, we calculated the overlap similarity as $O_{q,c_i} = |OC_q \cap (OC_{c_i} \cup IC_{c_i})|/|OC_q|$, which represents the similarity between q's outgoing citations and c_i's incoming and outgoing citations. The high O_{q,c_i} value suggests a considerable overlap in citation links between q and c_i, which indicates that these articles are highly topically related.

We calculated O_{q,c_i} for all the query articles and their cited articles. We then sorted the cited articles by their O_{q,c_i} values, starting from the highest (highly topically relevant) to the lowest (slightly topically related). Since we wanted to make our candidate pool challenging, we started with the c_i that has the highest O_{q,c_i} value and added to the query's candidate pool all the articles from its $OC_{c_i} \cup IC_{c_i}$ set that are not in OC_q (i.e., cited in the query article). We repeated this procedure until ten negative candidates were added to the pool. We call this candidate type `Graph`.

Citation count-based selection. In this selection strategy, we created a list of the top 200 most cited articles in each scientific field. We used S2ORC's MAG field to detect articles from each field and sorted them by the citation counts in descending order. We then randomly sampled ten candidate articles for each query article based on the query article's MAG field and added these articles to the candidate pool. This type of candidates is called `Most cited`.

Random selection. Finally, as a less challenging and baseline candidate set, we settled for a random selection strategy, where we randomly sampled ten candidates from the prefiltered set of S2ORC articles. We call this candidate type `Random`.

4.2 Benchmark Size

Overall, MDCR contains 200 queries per each of the 19 MAG fields, where each query is paired with a set of 60 negative candidates and five cited articles, totalling 247,000 query-candidate pairs that need to be evaluated. Compared to SciDocs, where 1,000 queries are paired with candidate pools of size 25 (a total of 25,000 query-candidate pairs), MDCR is almost ten times bigger. While this growth in size increases the computational complexity when using MDCR compared to other smaller benchmarks, it arguably makes the results more realistic. In addition, we also note that since

MDCR is split across different scientific fields, models can be evaluated on specific fields only, which reduces the number of query-candidate pairs to be evaluated.

4.3 Results

Results of evaluation on MDCR are given in Table 3. We report MAP and R@5 (each query is coupled with five positive candidates) across all pairs of the scientific fields and evaluated the model. We evaluate the same set of models as in the field-level large-scale evaluation.

Results demonstrate, yet again, a strong performance from BM25, which outperformed all other models in terms of average metric scores across all fields. Interestingly, when evaluated on MDCR's small-sized pools, the difference in performance between SciBERT and other TAEs (e.g., SciNCL) is smaller than in large-scale evaluation (11.7 in MAP on MDCR vs. 37 in MAP on dataset-level, 200k pool size). Such a difference in results confirms the benefits of evaluating TAEs on larger pools to obtain more realistic results. Another observation is a similar average performance between SciNCL and Aspire, despite Aspire variants being trained only on the articles from specific fields (biomedicine and computer science). As in the field-level evaluation, competitive results from Aspire indicate that sentence-level representations might be able to capture a more informative signal between related articles than document-level ones.

Although BM25 outperforms other models in most fields, TAEs obtain the best scores in some cases when looking at performance in specific fields. Specifically, Aspire-BM is the top-performing model in the Bio, Med, and Soc fields (and Psy in MAP value), which is not surprising as it was trained on articles from the biomedicine field. Similar goes for Aspire-CS and its performance in the Mat field, although it does not yield the best results in the field it was trained on (CS). However, when analyzing Aspire's performance, it is worth noting that we did not account for the overlap of Aspire training queries with our new benchmark since Aspire's training set was not publicly available at the time of writing. For this reason, the results of both Aspire variants might be too optimistic if the train-test overlap is significant.

4.4 Performance across Candidate Types

To analyze the difficulty of candidate types that we introduced in §4.1, we evaluate the models on subsets of candidate pools consisting of 5 cited articles and all negative candidates from specific candidate type. Evaluation across candidate types allows us to analyze how difficult each candidate type is for each model. As the candidates obtained via model-based selection are chosen precisely because they were difficult for the particular models, we do expect these models to not perform well on such candidates. However, such evaluation can reveal interesting insights into the differences across the evaluated models, e.g., whether the same candidate types are difficult for all neural-based models.

Results of this evaluation are presented in Table 4. Unsurprisingly, `Random` candidates are the easiest candidate type for all the evaluated models. Candidates from the `Most cited` type are also relatively easy for the models, with on average >90 score in MAP. On average, the most challenging candidate type is the `Graph` candidates subset, with an average MAP score of 55.9. Interestingly, the best-performing model on the `Graph` candidates subset is SciNCL, which explicitly uses citation graph embeddings in selecting training examples. Such a training strategy seems to help the model distinguish between relevant and irrelevant graph neighbors.

The performance on the candidate types obtained with the model-based selection strategy differs between TAEs and BM25, which is somewhat expected given the difference between neural (TAEs) and non-neural (BM25) models. As expected, negative candidates from the `BM25` type are the most difficult for BM25 itself since those were sampled from a set of top candidates provided by BM25. On the other hand, TAEs (SciBERT excluded) all perform similarly well on the `BM25` candidate type. Likewise, `SPECTER` and `SciNCL` candidates are the most difficult for SPECTER and SciNCL, respectively, while BM25 performs better than TAEs on these candidate types. It is interesting to note the difference in the performance of SciNCL on `SPECTER` candidates compared to the performance of SPECTER on `SciNCL` candidates. While SciNCL outperforms SPECTER on `SPECTER` candidates with more the 10 points in the absolute value (for both metrics), SPECTER improves over SciNCL on `SciNCL` candidates with only 3.7 absolute points. These results again confirm that the way in which negative candidates are sampled when training the models with the contrastive learning objective is important. As for

Models →	BM25		SciBERT		SPECTER		SciNCL		Aspire-BM		Aspire-CS	
Fields ↓	MAP	R@5	MAP	R@5	MAP	R@5	MAP	R@5	MAP	R@5	MAP	R@5
Art	**38.2**	**32.3**	22.4	16.6	34.1	28.8	34.7	29.2	34.0	27.7	34.1	28.0
Bio	38.3	33.6	20.4	14.0	34.6	30.0	36.8	32.3	**38.7**	**33.7**	35.7	29.9
Bus	28.1	22.5	19.1	13.1	27.5	21.8	28.5	**24.6**	28.5	23.4	**29.6**	23.1
Ch	**38.0**	**32.6**	20.0	13.7	33.7	29.3	36.5	31.5	36.5	31.0	34.1	28.3
CS	34.8	30.5	19.5	12.7	35.6	30.4	**37.2**	**32.2**	35.4	30.4	35.4	30.1
Eco	**30.5**	**26.0**	21.4	15.4	27.3	21.9	28.3	23.2	29.3	24.3	28.0	22.7
Eng	**34.6**	**29.3**	20.5	13.9	31.3	27.3	34.2	28.0	32.7	27.7	33.4	28.1
ES	**31.6**	**26.2**	21.3	15.1	30.1	24.2	31.5	25.5	30.8	24.7	29.9	23.7
Geog	**31.8**	**27.8**	21.9	16.7	26.4	22.2	29.5	23.8	30.3	26.0	28.4	22.2
Geol	**33.1**	**28.0**	19.5	13.9	24.8	20.1	25.7	19.9	28.5	23.5	25.8	21.4
His	**38.1**	**32.9**	20.8	15.2	27.1	20.6	30.9	23.9	31.0	24.2	28.5	22.1
MS	**36.1**	**30.7**	22.1	15.5	34.1	28.2	35.8	29.6	35.8	29.8	34.0	29.2
Mat	35.3	28.3	22.8	18.3	34.2	28.9	34.9	30.1	36.2	31.0	**36.9**	**32.2**
Med	38.6	32.5	22.0	16.4	41.4	36.3	42.7	36.5	**44.0**	**37.8**	41.7	36.7
Phi	**30.2**	**25.7**	19.2	13.3	27.1	21.1	29.9	23.5	28.7	24.1	29.1	23.3
Phy	**35.1**	30.2	23.9	18.1	30.8	26.3	34.5	**30.3**	32.9	27.7	32.9	28.7
PS	**28.6**	**23.1**	19.4	14.0	24.2	18.0	26.4	21.7	25.9	21.2	26.8	21.7
Psy	32.5	28.9	20.3	16.2	32.3	28.1	34.2	**30.5**	**34.3**	29.4	34.2	28.3
Soc	26.8	20.5	20.2	15.8	25.2	20.5	26.7	21.9	**27.3**	**22.2**	26.7	**22.2**
AVG	**33.7**	**28.5**	20.9	15.2	30.6	25.5	32.6	27.3	32.7	27.4	31.8	26.4

Table 3: Results in terms of MAP and R@5 on MDCR. Values in **bold** indicate the best performing model for a combination of field and metric.

Candidate types →	BM25		SPECTER		SciNCL		Graph		Most cited		Random	
Models ↓	MAP	R@5	MAP	R@5	MAP	R@5	MAP	R@5	MAP	R@5	MAP	R@5
BM25	52.2	39.0	68.8	57.5	68.0	56.9	58.0	46.7	90.3	82.2	93.0	86.3
SciBERT	50.5	39.1	47.6	36.0	49.0	37.7	47.2	36.1	79.6	69.3	84.9	75.8
SPECTER	67.4	56.3	51.1	38.7	57.8	45.8	57.3	46.3	92.8	86.5	99.0	97.1
SciNCL	68.3	57.6	61.2	49.8	54.1	42.1	58.1	47.3	94.0	88.3	99.0	97.2
Aspire-BM	66.7	55.6	57.7	46.5	59.3	47.5	57.3	46.5	93.6	87.6	99.1	97.2
Aspire-CS	66.0	54.9	55.7	43.8	58.5	46.8	57.2	46.6	94.3	88.7	98.9	96.8
AVG	61.8	50.4	57.0	45.4	57.8	46.1	55.9	44.9	90.8	83.8	95.7	91.7

Table 4: Results in terms of MAP and R@5 for different candidate types on MDCR.

the Aspire variants and candidate types obtained with the model-based strategy, Aspire variants perform better on the BM25 candidate type than on the SPECTER or SciNCL type. We hypothesize that such difference is due to TAEs being similar neural models and therefore prone to similar errors regarding semantic vs. lexical matching of texts. In contrast, BM25, a purely lexical model, makes different errors. We leave the analysis of the differences in performance between neural and non-neural models for future work.

5 Conclusion

We evaluated transformer-based article encoders in large-scale citation recommendation scenarios across different scientific fields and candidate pool sizes. Together with transformer-based encoders, we evaluated the performance of a robust lexical retrieval baseline BM25 and demonstrated that it still performs competitively with recent neural-based models. In the case of large field-specific candidate pools, BM25 outperformed transformer-based models in most fields.

Furthermore, to promote a more realistic and a more diverse evaluation across different fields in comparison to the existing benchmarks used for evaluating scientific article representations, we presented a new multi-domain benchmark dataset based on citation recommendation task, which we call MDCR. Evaluation on MDCR demonstrated the difficulty of specific candidate types and set the ground for evaluating future scientific article encoders.

Our evaluation demonstrated the varying performance across scientific fields, which we believe should be analyzed in future work to improve encoders' performance across all fields, not just those prevailing in the datasets. Given that our benchmark dataset is not expert-annotated but rather based on citations as relevance signals, we propose constructing an expert-annotated dataset with articles from different scientific fields. We hope our contributions will stimulate the community to work on more realistic and challenging evaluation setups of scientific article recommendation models.

Acknowledgments

This research was supported by the grant AIDWAS KK.01.2.1.02.0285. The first author has been supported by a grant from the Croatian Science Foundation (HRZZ-DOK-2018-09).

References

Zafar Ali, Guilin Qi, Khan Muhammad, Pavlos Kefalas, and Shah Khusro. 2021. Global Citation Recommendation Employing Generative Adversarial Network. *Expert Systems with Applications*, 180:114888.

Iz Beltagy, Kyle Lo, and Arman Cohan. 2019. SciBERT: A Pretrained Language Model for Scientific Text. In *Proceedings of the 2019 Conference on Empirical Methods in Natural Language Processing and the 9th International Joint Conference on Natural Language Processing (EMNLP-IJCNLP)*, pages 3615–3620, Hong Kong, China. Association for Computational Linguistics.

Christopher W Belter. 2016. Citation Analysis as a Literature Search Method for Systematic Reviews. *Journal of the Association for Information Science and Technology*, 67(11):2766–2777.

Chandra Bhagavatula, Sergey Feldman, Russell Power, and Waleed Ammar. 2018. Content-Based Citation Recommendation. In *Proceedings of the 2018 Conference of the North American Chapter of the Association for Computational Linguistics: Human Language Technologies, Volume 1 (Long Papers)*, pages 238–251, New Orleans, Louisiana. Association for Computational Linguistics.

Peter Brown, Aik-Choon Tan, Mohamed A El-Esawi, Thomas Liehr, Oliver Blanck, Douglas P Gladue, Gabriel MF Almeida, Tomislav Cernava, Carlos O Sorzano, Andy WK Yeung, et al. 2019. Large Expert-curated Database for Benchmarking Document Similarity Detection in Biomedical Literature Search. *Database*, 2019.

Xiaoyan Cai, Sen Liu, Libin Yang, Yan Lu, Jintao Zhao, Dinggang Shen, and Tianming Liu. 2022. COVIDSum: A Linguistically Enriched SciBERT-based Summarization Model for COVID-19 Scientific Papers. *Journal of Biomedical Informatics*, 127:103999.

Arman Cohan, Sergey Feldman, Iz Beltagy, Doug Downey, and Daniel Weld. 2020. SPECTER: Document-level Representation Learning using Citation-informed Transformers. In *Proceedings of the 58th Annual Meeting of the Association for Computational Linguistics*, pages 2270–2282, Online. Association for Computational Linguistics.

Jacob Devlin, Ming-Wei Chang, Kenton Lee, and Kristina Toutanova. 2019. BERT: Pre-training of Deep Bidirectional Transformers for Language Understanding. In *Proceedings of the 2019 Conference of the North American Chapter of the Association for Computational Linguistics: Human Language Technologies, Volume 1 (Long and Short Papers)*, pages 4171–4186, Minneapolis, Minnesota. Association for Computational Linguistics.

Nianlong Gu, Yingqiang Gao, and Richard H. R. Hahnloser. 2022. Local Citation Recommendation with Hierarchical-Attention Text Encoder and SciBERT-Based Reranking. In *Advances in Information Retrieval*, pages 274–288, Cham. Springer International Publishing.

Tanishq Gupta, Mohd Zaki, NM Krishnan, et al. 2022. MatSciBERT: A Materials Domain Language Model for Text Mining and Information Extraction. *npj Computational Materials*, 8(1):1–11.

Sebastian Hinde and Eldon Spackman. 2015. Bidirectional Citation Searching to Completion: an Exploration of Literature Searching Methods. *Pharmacoeconomics*, 33(1):5–11.

Jeff Johnson, Matthijs Douze, and Hervé Jégou. 2019. Billion-scale Similarity Search with GPUs. *IEEE Transactions on Big Data*, 7(3):535–547.

Jinhyuk Lee, Wonjin Yoon, Sungdong Kim, Donghyeon Kim, Sunkyu Kim, Chan Ho So, and Jaewoo Kang. 2020. BioBERT: A Pre-trained Biomedical Language Representation Model for Biomedical Text Mining. *Bioinformatics*, 36(4):1234–1240.

Mike Lewis, Yinhan Liu, Naman Goyal, Marjan Ghazvininejad, Abdelrahman Mohamed, Omer Levy, Veselin Stoyanov, and Luke Zettlemoyer. 2020. BART: Denoising Sequence-to-Sequence Pre-training for Natural Language Generation, Translation, and Comprehension. In *Proceedings of the 58th Annual Meeting of the Association for Computational Linguistics*, pages 7871–7880, Online. Association for Computational Linguistics.

Jimmy Lin, Rodrigo Nogueira, and Andrew Yates. 2021. Pretrained Transformers for Text Ranking: BERT and Beyond. *Synthesis Lectures on Human Language Technologies*, 14(4):1–325.

Aldo Lipani, Mihai Lupu, Allan Hanbury, and Akiko Aizawa. 2015. Verboseness Fission for BM25 Document Length Normalization. In *Proceedings of the 2015 International Conference on the Theory of Information Retrieval*, pages 385–388.

Kyle Lo, Lucy Lu Wang, Mark Neumann, Rodney Kinney, and Daniel Weld. 2020. S2ORC: The Semantic Scholar Open Research Corpus. In *Proceedings of the 58th Annual Meeting of the Association for Computational Linguistics*, pages 4969–4983, Online. Association for Computational Linguistics.

Kelvin Luu, Xinyi Wu, Rik Koncel-Kedziorski, Kyle Lo, Isabel Cachola, and Noah A. Smith. 2021. Explaining Relationships Between Scientific Documents. In *Proceedings of the 59th Annual Meeting of the Association for Computational Linguistics and the 11th International Joint Conference on Natural Language Processing (Volume 1: Long Papers)*, pages 2130–2144, Online. Association for Computational Linguistics.

Yuanhua Lv and ChengXiang Zhai. 2011. Adaptive Term Frequency Normalization for BM25. In *Proceedings of the 20th ACM international conference on Information and knowledge management*, pages 1985–1988.

Zoran Medić and Jan Šnajder. 2020. A Survey of Citation Recommendation Tasks and Methods. *Journal of computing and information technology*, 28(3):183–205.

Sheshera Mysore, Arman Cohan, and Tom Hope. 2021a. Multi-Vector Models with Textual Guidance for Fine-Grained Scientific Document Similarity.

Sheshera Mysore, Tim O'Gorman, Andrew McCallum, and Hamed Zamani. 2021b. CSFCube - A Test Collection of Computer Science Research Articles for Faceted Query by Example. In *Thirty-fifth Conference on Neural Information Processing Systems Datasets and Benchmarks Track (Round 2)*.

Usman Naseem, Katarzyna Musial, Peter Eklund, and Mukesh Prasad. 2020. Biomedical Named-entity Recognition by Hierarchically Fusing BioBERT Representations and Deep Contextual-level Word-embedding. In *2020 International Joint Conference on Neural Networks (IJCNN)*, pages 1–8. IEEE.

Rodrigo Nogueira, Zhiying Jiang, Kyunghyun Cho, and Jimmy Lin. 2020. Evaluating Pretrained Transformer Models for Citation Recommendation. In *CEUR Workshop Proceedings*, volume 2591, pages 89–100. CEUR-WS.

Malte Ostendorff, Nils Rethmeier, Isabelle Augenstein, Bela Gipp, and Georg Rehm. 2022. Neighborhood Contrastive Learning for Scientific Document Representations with Citation Embeddings. *arXiv preprint arXiv:2202.06671*.

Alec Radford, Jeff Wu, Rewon Child, David Luan, Dario Amodei, and Ilya Sutskever. 2019. Language Models are Unsupervised Multitask Learners.

Colin Raffel, Noam Shazeer, Adam Roberts, Katherine Lee, Sharan Narang, Michael Matena, Yanqi Zhou, Wei Li, and Peter J. Liu. 2020. Exploring the Limits of Transfer Learning with a Unified Text-to-Text Transformer. *Journal of Machine Learning Research*, 21(140):1–67.

Nils Reimers and Iryna Gurevych. 2021. The Curse of Dense Low-Dimensional Information Retrieval for Large Index Sizes. In *Proceedings of the 59th Annual Meeting of the Association for Computational Linguistics and the 11th International Joint Conference on Natural Language Processing (Volume 2: Short Papers)*, pages 605–611, Online. Association for Computational Linguistics.

Stephen E Robertson and Steve Walker. 1994. Some Simple Effective Approximations to the 2-poisson Model for Probabilistic Weighted Retrieval. In *SIGIR'94*, pages 232–241. Springer.

Ashish Vaswani, Noam Shazeer, Niki Parmar, Jakob Uszkoreit, Llion Jones, Aidan N Gomez, Ł ukasz Kaiser, and Illia Polosukhin. 2017. Attention is All you Need. In *Advances in Neural Information Processing Systems*, volume 30. Curran Associates, Inc.

Ellen Voorhees, Tasmeer Alam, Steven Bedrick, Dina Demner-Fushman, William R. Hersh, Kyle Lo, Kirk Roberts, Ian Soboroff, and Lucy Lu Wang. 2021. TREC-COVID: Constructing a Pandemic Information Retrieval Test Collection. *SIGIR Forum*, 54(1).

David Wadden, Shanchuan Lin, Kyle Lo, Lucy Lu Wang, Madeleine van Zuylen, Arman Cohan, and Hannaneh Hajishirzi. 2020. Fact or Fiction: Verifying Scientific Claims. In *Proceedings of the 2020 Conference on Empirical Methods in Natural Language Processing (EMNLP)*, pages 7534–7550, Online. Association for Computational Linguistics.

A Appendix

A.1 BM25

Here we provide details about the relevance score function used by BM25 (Robertson and Walker, 1994). Before calculating relevance scores for pairs of articles, article texts are first transformed into bag-of-words vectors. Given a query Q, containing terms $q_1, ..., q_n$, and a document D, BM25 calculates relevance score s as follows:

$$\mathrm{s}(Q, D) = \sum_{i=1}^{n} \mathrm{IDF}(q_i) \cdot \frac{f(q_i, D) \cdot (k_1 + 1)}{f(q_i, D) + k_1 \cdot \left(1 - b + b \cdot \frac{|D|}{\mathrm{avgdl}}\right)}$$

where $f(q_i, D)$ is the frequency q_i in document D, $|D|$ is the length of D in words, avgdl is the average document length, and k_1 and b are parameters that can be tuned for a specific document collection. $\mathrm{IDF}(q_i)$ is the inverse document frequency for q_i, and is typically calculated as:

$$\mathrm{IDF}(q_i) = \ln \left(\frac{N - n(q_i) + 0.5}{n(q_i) + 0.5} + 1 \right)$$

where N is the total number of documents in the collection and $n(q_i)$ is the number of documents containing the term q_i.

Intuitively, s will output higher scores for a document D that contains many terms as Q, that also do not appear often in other documents. When it comes to parameters b and k_1, b controls to what degree the length of a document will affect the final score (Lipani et al., 2015), while k_1 controls to what degree an additional occurrence of a term affects the final score (Lv and Zhai, 2011).

A.2 Field Abbreviations

Table 5 shows the abbreviations for MAG fields.

A.3 Evaluation on SciDocs

Table 6 shows the results of evaluation of SciBERT, SPECTER, SciNCL, and ASPIRE on SciDocs benchmark, as reported in the previous work.

A.4 Field-level Evaluation Results

Results for "field-level" evaluation setup in terms of NDCG and recall@30 are given in Tables 7 and 8, respectively. Best scoring combinations of model and field are mostly the same as in case of MAP (reported in Table 2), with the exception of recall@30 in Bio field, where BM25 yields the best result (as opposed to ASPIRE-BM in case of MAP).

MAG field	Abbreviation
Art	Art
Biology	Bio
Business	Bus
Chemistry	Ch
Computer Science	CS
Economics	Eco
Engineering	Eng
Environmental Science	ES
Geography	Geog
Geology	Geol
History	His
Materials Science	MS
Mathematics	Mat
Medicine	Med
Philosophy	Phi
Physics	Phy
Political Science	PS
Psychology	Psy
Sociology	Soc

Table 5: Abbreviations for MAG fields that we use in the field-level evaluation and in the new benchmark.

Model	MAP	NDCG
SciBERT	48.3	71.7
SPECTER	88.3	94.9
SciNCL	93.6	97.3
TS-ASPIRE	91.0	95.0

Table 6: Results of different TAEs evaluated on SciDocs's "Cite" task. Values as reported in (Cohan et al., 2020), (Mysore et al., 2021a), and (Ostendorff et al., 2022).

Model	Art	Bio	Bus	Ch	CS	Eco	Eng	ES	Geog	Geol	His	MS	Mat	Med	Phi	Phy	PS	Psy	Soc	AVG
BM25	**64.2**	78.8	**56.9**	**76.2**	69.3	**65.0**	**68.0**	**62.6**	**64.5**	**69.2**	**62.7**	**69.8**	**70.1**	77.8	**56.9**	**70.1**	**56.2**	70.2	**54.0**	**66.5**
SciBERT	33.2	45.8	33.6	43.7	36.0	39.6	36.4	36.8	37.6	39.6	32.9	37.3	37.9	39.8	31.2	39.5	32.1	40.9	32.9	37.2
Specter	53.5	74.2	53.9	71.8	67.7	61.9	63.6	58.2	56.5	59.2	47.0	65.6	66.5	79.2	48.6	63.8	49.2	70.5	49.9	61.1
SciNCL	55.3	77.5	54.1	74.0	**70.3**	62.5	66.0	60.7	59.6	61.2	50.5	67.0	68.0	**81.1**	50.8	67.1	51.4	**71.7**	51.3	63.1
Aspire-BM	55.6	**79.2**	55.2	74.4	69.1	63.5	64.8	60.0	59.4	61.5	50.1	66.2	68.1	81.0	50.1	66.2	50.6	70.9	49.8	62.9
Aspire-CS	54.8	74.2	56.1	71.1	69.4	62.9	65.0	57.7	57.8	59.0	48.1	64.3	69.1	77.9	49.6	65.5	50.4	70.8	51.4	61.8

Table 7: Results in terms of nDCG in the "field-level" evaluation setup. Values in **bold** indicate the best performing model per field.

Model	Art	Bio	Bus	Ch	CS	Eco	Eng	ES	Geog	Geol	His	MS	Mat	Med	Phi	Phy	PS	Psy	Soc	AVG
BM25	**46.5**	**38.9**	**27.5**	**41.7**	43.1	**29.7**	**42.7**	**35.3**	**34.6**	**34.2**	**42.7**	**39.5**	**42.2**	48.2	**34.0**	**40.9**	**28.3**	32.0	**24.0**	**37.2**
SciBERT	9.0	4.8	2.1	5.8	5.0	3.3	5.5	5.1	5.0	3.9	8.0	4.1	6.0	4.8	3.8	6.6	1.6	3.4	2.4	4.8
Specter	35.5	33.4	24.7	35.3	41.9	25.7	36.4	30.3	24.3	23.4	24.8	34.2	38.5	49.0	24.1	33.4	19.9	32.6	19.8	30.9
SciNCL	38.9	36.8	25.4	39.3	**46.4**	26.0	39.5	33.0	28.0	25.5	28.2	35.5	40.2	**52.0**	26.4	37.1	23.0	**34.7**	21.5	33.5
Aspire-BM	34.9	38.2	25.1	38.6	42.5	27.3	37.0	31.5	27.5	25.3	28.0	34.5	39.9	51.6	25.0	35.2	22.2	32.3	19.2	32.4
Aspire-CS	34.9	33.0	25.5	34.7	42.1	25.9	37.5	29.4	25.6	23.2	25.3	33.0	40.1	47.3	24.7	34.5	21.4	32.2	20.1	31.1

Table 8: Results in terms of recall@30 in the "field-level" evaluation setup. Values in **bold** indicate the best performing model per field.

Investigating the detection of Tortured Phrases in Scientific Literature

Puthineath Lay[1], Martin Lentschat[1], and Cyril Labbé[1]

[1] Univ. Grenoble Alpes, CNRS, Grenoble INP, LIG, 38000 Grenoble, France
puthineath.lay@cadt.edu.kh, martin.lentschat@univ-grenoble-alpes.fr

Abstract

With the help of online tools, unscrupulous authors can today generate a pseudo-scientific article and attempt to publish it. Some of these tools work by replacing or paraphrasing existing texts to produce new content, but they have a tendency to generate nonsensical expressions. A recent study introduced the concept of "tortured phrase", an unexpected odd phrase that appears instead of the fixed expression. E.g. *counterfeit consciousness* instead of *artificial intelligence*. The present study aims at investigating how tortured phrases, that are not yet listed, can be detected automatically. We conducted several experiments, including non-neural binary classification, neural binary classification and cosine similarity comparison of the phrase tokens, yielding noticeable results.

1 Introduction

Scientific texts generated by computer programs can be meaningless, and fake generated papers are served and sold by various publishers with the estimation of 4.29 documents every one million reports (Cabanac and Labbé, 2021). But generated texts are also meaningful: with the inputs of a thousand articles, new books are now produced (e.g. Beta Writer, 2019). Despite the ability of text-generators to produce counterfeit publications, meaningless generated papers can be easily spotted by both machines and humans (Cabanac et al., 2021). Texts produced by neural language models are more difficult to spot (Hutson et al., 2021). These neural language models can produce paraphrased texts that are closer to human-written texts (Brown et al., 2020), and therefore machine-paraphrased texts are harder to differentiate from the human-written texts.

Online tools such as Spinbot, and Spinner Chief are used to paraphrase texts. However the capacity of a paraphrasing software to assist a writer can be harmful to the scientific literature. Cabanac et al. (2021) screened recent publications (e.g. in the journal *Microprocessors and Microsystems*) and discovered over 500 meaning less phrases in those scientific papers. They called it "tortured phrases", unexpected odd phrases replacing the lexicalised expression, such as *counterfeit consciousness* instead of *artificial intelligence* (i.e., the expected phrase). The database of tortured phrases, and articles that contain them, have since been expanded to over 9000 publications in different domains such as Computer Sciences, Biology or Medicine.

In this paper, we investigate strategies to automatically detect new (i.e. unlisted) tortured phrases. Focusing solely on tortured phrases detection, and not paraphrased text in general, we will use recent machine learning techniques and state-of-the-art language models. Our methods were trained on a corpus composed of 141 known tortured phrases, taking their sentences as contexts, and aims at detecting never-seen-before tortured phrases. All code and corpus used are available online.

2 Related Works

Up to now, no dataset has been built for the automatic detection of tortured phrases. In Cabanac et al. (2021), authors and contributors collected a set of tortured phrases and their expected phrases that we will use as dataset. Wahle et al. (2021) used Spinbot and Spinnerchief to paraphrase original data from several sources such as an arXiv test sets, graduation theses, and Wikipedia articles. Their study aims at detecting whether a paragraph is machine-paraphrased or not. The authors tested classic machine learning approaches and neural language models based on the Transformer architecture (Vaswani et al., 2017), such as BERT (Devlin et al., 2018), RoBERTa (Liu et al., 2019), ALBERT (Lan et al., 2019), Longformer (Beltagy et al., 2020), and others. They showed that such approaches can complement text-matching software, such as PlagScan and Turnitin, which often fail to

Proceedings of the Third Workshop on Scholarly Document Processing, pages 32–36
October 12–17, 2022.

notice machine-paraphrased plagiarism.

Because paraphrasing tools like Spinbot and Spinnerchief can generate tortured phrases, the dataset created by Wahle et al. (2021) surely contains such phrases. But the task we aim at, i.e. detecting new tortured phrases, is more specific than detecting paraphrased text. Thus, we investigated three supervised machine learning classifiers: Random Forest, Perceptron, and Transfomer-based model. Random Forest classifier (Breiman, 2001) is an ensemble learning method that builds decision trees and classifies each data according to the most selected class. Perceptron (Rosenblatt, 1958) is a linear classifier used to classify vectors of numbers. Term Frequency-Inverse Document Frequency (TF-IDF), GloVe (Pennington et al., 2014), and BERT (Devlin et al., 2018) were used for word vector representation. These models were chosen for their state-of-the-art performances and to compare how a model with fixed vectors (i.e. GloVe) compares with a model using dynamic ones (i.e. BERT).

3 Building datasets of tortured phrases

This experiment uses two data sources: the tortured phrases (Cabanac et al., 2021) database and the contexts containing tortured phrases from Wahle et al. (2021). We automatically extracted the context of known tortured phrases from the corpus of Wahle et al. (2021) to build a training set.

Tortured phrases identified by Cabanac et al. (2021) consists of 558 tortured phrases (e.g. Table 1). These phrases were annotated by the authors and other contributors in several media (e.g. PubPeer, Twitter) in 2021-2022. After pre-processing, we retained 545 tortured phrases.

Tortured phrases	Expected phrases
innocent Bayes	naive Bayes
ghostly grouping	spectral clustering
Unused Britain	New England
Joined together states	United States
immature nations	developing countries

Table 1: Example of tortured and expected phrases.

The dataset of Wahle et al. (2021) is constituted of 193, 646 paragraphs, paraphrased using Spinbot and Spinnerchief. 65, 433 original data were retrieved from several sources: arXiv, graduation theses of ESL students at the Mendel University in Brno (Czech Republic) and Wikipedia articles.

We extracted the paragraphs containing tortured phrases (Cabanac et al., 2021) to build a training and evaluation corpus. This resulted in 1, 104 paragraphs with tortured phrases and 1, 668 paragraphs without tortured phrases (randomly extracted from the non-paraphrased original data).

Data augmentation: five-grams extraction To increase the training data, we extracted the n-grams (i.e. sequences of n adjacent tokens) of each sentence, with $n = 5$, as it is the maximum length of the known tortured phrases. A five-gram is considered positive if a complete tortured phrase appears in that five-gram.This produced 38, 397 five-grams, 5, 024 positive five-grams (in the '1' class) and 33, 373 negative five-grams (in the '0' class).

4 Experiment and Result

We investigated binary classifiers to check the difference between paragraphs or five-grams containing tortured phrases in several settings. The paragraphs and five-grams containing tortured phrases are considered positives, with label '1', while negative paragraphs are labeled as '0'. Accuracy, precision, recall, and F-measure are used to evaluate the classification performances.

Classifiers: Random Forest and Perceptron In this experiment, five-grams data are used in the classification. The five-grams are converted to a numerical representation using Sklearn TF-IDF count vectorizer and split randomly 80% for training and 20% for testing. We used the Scikit Learn library for the Random Forest and Perceptron with the default value of all parameters.

The result in Table 2 shows an accuracy for the Random Forest classifier of .98 and the Perceptron of .94. The precision, recall, and F1-score of the Random Forest classifier are high, especially in class 0, and the results in class 1 is slightly lower than in class 0. The precision, recall, and F1-score of the Perceptron method is slightly lower than that of the Random Forest classifier, but it is still comparable for class 0. In class 1, Perceptron results are significantly lower compared to the results of Random Forest classifier. We also observe results higher in class 0 than in class 1, this might be due to the data imbalance.

After observing the accuracy, precision, recall, and F1-score, we see that the models perform well based on TF-IDF vector representation. However, it is believable that the models learned to classify five-grams based solely on specific words: since the training and test data were split randomly, a tortured phrase can be present in both sub-sets.

Transformer-based classifier on paragraphs Here, we seek at detecting paragraphs containing at least one tortured phrase. The data are split 67% for training and 33% for test set. The architecture of this model is based on the Transformer technique. Pre-trained transformers from Huggingface, `distilbert-base-uncased` model (Sanh et al., 2019), was chosen for its lightness and speed. We applied transfer learning by adding one linear layer for classification purposes. In that linear layer, the number of input features was set to 768 with an output size of 2, indicating class 0 and class 1. The model was trained on 10 epochs.

The results in Table 2 show an accuracy of .86. The .92 precision on class 1 is higher than on class 0. For the recall and F1-score, class 0 gets a better result than class 1. Since the amount of paragraph data are small, we suspect that only a few tokens constitute the tortured phrases, and that the rest of the token's paragraph affect the performance.

Transformer-based classifier on five-grams The data of class '1' was split 79% for training and 21% for testing by filtering the test set with tortured phrases not present in the training set. In this experiment, two versions of the model were trained: one using the entire dataset and one with a proportion of data balanced in both classes.

The training data are made of $28,995$ five-grams ($25,029$ in class '0' and $3,966$ in class '1'). The test data are made of $9,402$ five-grams ($8,344$ and $1,058$). Table 2 shows an accuracy of .88. Precision, recall, and F1-score on class '1' are exceptionally low compared to the '0' class.

Regarding the classifier with balanced data, the size of the training set is $7,932$ five-grams ($3,966$ in each class) and the size of the testing set is $2,116$ five-grams ($1,058$ in each class). The accuracy is .71, and the precision, recall, and F1-score are around .70 in both classes (cf. bold values in Table 2). In this experiment, the balance of the classes induces a greater reliability of the results and we believe this approach presents the best applicability. The model focuses on the tortured phrases in five-grams rather than tortured phrases in the whole paragraph, so the model can learn to generalize the five-grams containing tortured phrases or not.

4.1 Cosine similarity comparison

We studied the cosine similarity between tokens in the tortured phrases compared to the similarity of tokens in the expected phrases. Cabanac et al. (2021) annotated a dataset of tortured phrases, and their respective expected phrases, from several media such as PubPeer during 2021-2022.

We intuitively expect that the cosine score of the tokens in the phrases could yield noticeable results, useful to differentiate tortured and expected phrases due to the similarity, or non-similarity, of adjacent tokens. The expected phrases are idioms (i.e. multi-word-expression forming a lexical and semantic unit) and, as such, we hypothesize that the semantic score defined by the cosine of the vectors between their terms should be higher than for the tortured phrases, which words are less likely to be semantically related or frequently associated. If validated, such observation could help distinguish tortured phrases from legitimate ones. For this experiment, only the similarity of two-tokens phrases were computed, using two kinds of word embedding models: GloVe and BERT.

Cosine similarity on phrases using BERT In this study, we used BERT (Devlin et al., 2018) as the word embedding model. We followed the architecture of McCormick (2019) by summing the last four layers of 12 layers of BERT to get one-word vectors with 768 values.

Since the BertTokenizer will separate unknown words into sub-words (e.g. *vitality utilize* becomes *vital*, *#ity*, and *utilize*), it can be complicated to compute their cosine similarity. We chose to discard tortured phrases containing words unknown by the model. We retained 82 tortured phrases after the tokenization process.

The scores obtained from cosine computation between word pairs in tortured and expected phrases present slight differences, as shown in Figure 1. The median scores of expected and tortured phrases are .51 and .49, respectively. The absence of significant differences can be explained by the nature of the BERT model: a two-word context is probably not sufficient to differentiate tortured and expected phrases using cosine similarity.

Cosine similarity on phrases using GloVe For this experiment, we computed the cosine similarity of token pairs in tortured and expected phrases. We used the pre-trained GloVe word embedding (Pennington et al., 2014)

Classifiers	Data type	Accuracy	Precision		Recall		F1-score	
class			0	1	0	1	0	1
Random Forest	Random five-grams	.98	.99	.92	.99	.91	.99	.92
Perceptron	Random five-grams	.94	.96	.84	.98	.69	.97	.75
Transformer	Paragraph	.86	.82	.92	.94	.77	.87	.84
Transformer	Random five-grams	.88	.89	.42	.99	.03	.93	.06
Transformer	Balanced five-grams	**.71**	**.67**	**.75**	**.79**	**.62**	**.73**	**.68**

Table 2: Classification results.

(`glove.6B.200d.txt`)which was trained on Wikipedia 2014 and Gigaword. Unlike BERT, GloVe is a context-free model, meaning that each word in this pre-trained model is assigned to one constant vector. However, GloVe vocabulary is limited and thus some tokens in the phrases might not appear in this model. For this issue, we padded the out-of-vocabulary word with 0. For the phrases in which both words do not appear in the model, the cosine similarity is 0. We discarded the phrases whose scores were lower than or equal to 0 ($cosine\_score \leq 0$). As a result, 139 phrases are used for this experiment.

The Figure 1 indicates that the cosine similarity scores of tortured phrases tend to be smaller than those of expected phrases when using GloVe. The median score of expected phrases is .3 and the median score of tortured phrases is .12.

Figure 1: Comparison of cosine score of phrases using BERT and GloVe.

These results indicate that the cosine score between terms could be employed to differentiate tortured phrases from legitimate ones. Since Bert relies on embeddings, it is overly influenced by the phrase contexts to yields useful results. With Glove, or another language model with static vectors, one could chose a threshold to classify phrases, e.g. as legitimate, tortured, or requiring human expertise.

5 Conclusions

In this research, we aimed at detecting new tortured phrases. We studied different classification approaches and examined the characteristics of tortured phrases using cosine similarity. The result of Perceptron and Random Forest classifier are high, but we intuitively suspect they are not reliable due to the word representation using TF-IDF vectorization. The Transformer-based classifier model with paragraph data provided the best result among Transformer models. However, we suspect that the model learned to classify paragraphs based only on a few tokens, and classifying paragraphs is not sufficient to detect the exact tortured phrases. Thus, the Transformer-based classifier model five-gram data yields the best result with balanced classes (i.e. results above .70 for all metrics).

We also studied the use of cosine similarity between the phrase tokens to identify new tortured phrase. This showed that language model with fixed vectors (e.g. Glove) could be used to classify part of the phrases.

Future research should include more human evaluation of tortured phrases and a bigger dataset tortured phrases with their context. To improve the classification, future work could investigate Support Vector Machine (SVM) and Naïve Bayes model (NB): SVM performs better with a small dataset and binary class, while NB can provide probabilities of a prediction.Finally, computing the cosine similarity of the tortured phrase and expected phrase pairs within the whole context to see tortured phrases' performance.

Acknowledgments

The NanoBubbles project has received Synergy grant funding from the European Research Council (ERC), within the European Union's Horizon 2020 program, grant agreement no. 951393.

References

Iz Beltagy, Matthew E Peters, and Arman Cohan. 2020. Longformer: The long-document transformer. *arXiv preprint arXiv:2004.05150.*

Lithium-Ion Beta Writer. 2019. *a Machine-Generated Summary of Current Research/Beta Writer.* Springer International Publishing.

Leo Breiman. 2001. Random forests. *Machine learning*, 45(1):5–32.

Tom Brown, Benjamin Mann, Nick Ryder, Melanie Subbiah, Jared D Kaplan, Prafulla Dhariwal, Arvind Neelakantan, Pranav Shyam, Girish Sastry, Amanda Askell, et al. 2020. Language models are few-shot learners. *Advances in neural information processing systems*, 33:1877–1901.

Guillaume Cabanac and Cyril Labbé. 2021. Prevalence of nonsensical algorithmically generated papers in the scientific literature. *Journal of the Association for Information Science and Technology*, 72(12):1461–1476.

Guillaume Cabanac, Cyril Labbé, and Alexander Magazinov. 2021. Tortured phrases: A dubious writing style emerging in science. evidence of critical issues affecting established journals. *CoRR*, abs/2107.06751.

Jacob Devlin, Ming-Wei Chang, Kenton Lee, and Kristina Toutanova. 2018. Bert: Pre-training of deep bidirectional transformers for language understanding. *arXiv preprint arXiv:1810.04805.*

Matthew Hutson et al. 2021. Robo-writers: the rise and risks of language-generating ai. *Nature*, 591(7848):22–25.

Zhenzhong Lan, Mingda Chen, Sebastian Goodman, Kevin Gimpel, Piyush Sharma, and Radu Soricut. 2019. Albert: A lite bert for self-supervised learning of language representations. *arXiv preprint arXiv:1909.11942.*

Yinhan Liu, Myle Ott, Naman Goyal, Jingfei Du, Mandar Joshi, Danqi Chen, Omer Levy, Mike Lewis, Luke Zettlemoyer, and Veselin Stoyanov. 2019. Roberta: A robustly optimized bert pretraining approach. *arXiv preprint arXiv:1907.11692.*

Chris McCormick. 2019. Bert word embeddings tutorial.

Jeffrey Pennington, Richard Socher, and Christopher D. Manning. 2014. Glove: Global vectors for word representation. In *Empirical Methods in Natural Language Processing (EMNLP)*, pages 1532–1543.

Frank Rosenblatt. 1958. The perceptron: a probabilistic model for information storage and organization in the brain. *Psychological review*, 65(6):386.

Victor Sanh, Lysandre Debut, Julien Chaumond, and Thomas Wolf. 2019. Distilbert, a distilled version of bert: smaller, faster, cheaper and lighter.

Ashish Vaswani, Noam Shazeer, Niki Parmar, Jakob Uszkoreit, Llion Jones, Aidan N Gomez, Łukasz Kaiser, and Illia Polosukhin. 2017. Attention is all you need. *Advances in neural information processing systems*, 30.

Jan Wahle, Terry Ruas, Tomas Foltynek, Norman Meuschke, and Bela Gipp. 2021. Identifying machine-paraphrased plagiarism.

Lightweight Contextual Logical Structure Recovery

Po-Wei Huang, Abhinav Ramesh Kashyap, Yanxia Qin, Yajing Yang, Min-Yen Kan*
National University of Singapore
{huangpowei,abhinav,qinyx,yang0317,kanmy}@comp.nus.edu.sg

Abstract

Logical structure recovery in scientific articles associates text with a semantic section of the article. Although previous work has disregarded the surrounding context of a line, we model this important information by employing line-level attention on top of a transformer-based scientific document processing pipeline. With the addition of loss function engineering and data augmentation techniques with semi-supervised learning, our method improves classification performance by 10% compared to a recent state-of-the-art model. Our parsimonious, text-only method achieves a performance comparable to that of other works that use rich document features such as font and spatial position, using less data without sacrificing performance, resulting in a lightweight training pipeline.

1 Introduction

Logical structure recovery in scientific document processing (SDP) provides fundamental information about scientific documents. The logical structure of a document is "*the hierarchy of logical labels that indicates the construction of the document*" (Mao et al., 2003; Luong et al., 2010). Recovering the logical structure gives insight into the structure of a long scientific document and aids further SDP tasks such as abstractive summarization, metadata extraction, and information extraction, etc.

Logical structure recovery classifies the lines of a scientific document into predefined semantic categories that represent its role in the document (*cf.* Table 1). Previous work considered this classification in isolation, without considering the context of the line (Ramesh Kashyap and Kan, 2020). Some works have tried to alleviate this problem by providing better context by including feature-rich information such as font type, text position (Luong et al., 2010; Rahman and Finin, 2019). However, we have to rely on external systems (such as Optical Character Recognition, OCR) to obtain such features, which makes the process cumbersome and error-prone. *Can we obtain similar performance on logical structure recovery without relying on feature-rich information?*

We answer this challenge by creating a parsimonious but robust model that operates on purely textual data without incorporating such features. Instead, we rely on better context modeling of surrounding lines, identifying the continuity of logical structure of the document, and making use of abundant unlabeled data.

First, we consider multiple lines of marginally breaked text as context (cross-line context) and use attention (Yang et al., 2016; Beltagy et al., 2020) on top of transformer models (Vaswani et al., 2017; Devlin et al., 2019) to obtain context-sensitive sentence embeddings of lines. Second, we employ semi-supervised learning (Xie et al., 2020; Sohn et al., 2020) over the abundance of unlabeled data to address the lack of labeled data in the recovery of logical structures. Lastly, we employ elements of loss engineering from recent semi-supervised learning frameworks such as UDA (Xie et al., 2020) without the use of unlabeled data to increase performance under a supervised training regime to deploy a lightweight training pipeline.

Although only plain text is used for training, our model achieves results close to the current state-of-the-art (SOTA) compared to models based on rich text features. Furthermore, we show that semi-supervised learning helps improve SOTA for logical structure recovery by 10% on macro-F1.

2 Related Work

Aside from the text of scientific papers, previous work extracts rich text information — such as font size, font style, paragraphing — as rich text information is a primary factor in discerning the logical structure of a document (Rahman and Finin,

* Corresponding Author

Proceedings of the Third Workshop on Scholarly Document Processing, pages 37–48
October 12–17, 2022.

Text	Label
Lightweight Contextual Logical Structure Recovery	`title`
Po-Wei Huang, Abhinav Ramesh Kashyap, Yanxia Qin, Yajing Yang, Min-Yen Kan*	`author`
National University of Singapore	`affiliation`
{huangpowei,abhinav,qinyx,yang0317,kanmy}@comp.nus.edu.sg	`email`
Abstract	`sectionHeader`
Logical structure recovery in scientific articles	`bodyText`
associates text with a semantic section of the ar-	`bodyText`

Table 1: Sample Logical Structure Classification

2019). For example, SectLabel (Luong et al., 2010) extracts rich text information from scientific documents using OCR, then subsequently applying Conditional Random Fields (CRF; Lafferty et al. 2001) to classify the extracted text into predetermined labels. Tao et al. (2014) extends this approach further, combining the usage of spatial measures, typesetting, and minimal text patterns with contextual meaning into a 2D CRF model for classification. Koreeda and Manning (2021)'s work involves using remnant visual cues extracted from text data including line breaks, indentation, and text alignment to augment logical structure extraction while using random forest as their primary model.

Other work focus on the usage of layout itself to discern such logical structures, utilizing deep object detection models such as R-CNN models (Ren et al., 2015; He et al., 2017; Cai and Vasconcelos, 2018) to capture logical structures, taking "screenshots" of the PDF document as input. LayoutLM models (Xu et al., 2020, 2021; Huang et al., 2022) combine object detection models with textual transformers (Vaswani et al., 2017) along with positional embeddings of logical structures on the page to form multimodal models, while Document Image Transformers (DiT; Li et al. 2022) use Vision Transformers (ViT; Dosovitskiy et al. 2021) as backbone models for further image-based detections of the logical structures.

Although rich text information is usually incorporated, there are models, such as the SciWING toolkit (Ramesh Kashyap and Kan, 2020), for logical structure recovery that operate only on plain text. Our work is in line with such lightweight text-only methods, which benefit from the simple and streamlined input without redundant metadata. In contrast to SciWING's simple text representation for each line, we aim to incorporate richer textual information from the cross-line context and make use of abundant unlabeled data available.

3 Contextual Model Construction

We attempt the task of logical structure classification, as proposed by Luong et al. (2010), and label each line in scientific papers to represent its logical structure. We address this task in a purely textual method, employing modern NLP model architectures and training techniques to achieve our goal of creating a more lightweight and streamlined approach. We consider this task as a line-based classification problem as we want to preserve the notion of margin breaks without having to include layout or spatial information. Given a document $\mathcal{D}_n$ of length n, we have the following:

$$\mathcal{D}_n = \{\ell_1, \ell_2, \ldots, \ell_n\}, \quad (1)$$

where ℓ_i refers to the ith line extracted by a PDF text extractor. Our objective is to construct a model $\mathcal{M}$ that classifies each line ℓ_i into one of 23 predefined categories $\mathcal{C}$ defined by Luong et al. (2010)[1].

3.1 Baseline Model

We use Ramesh Kashyap and Kan (2020)'s logical structure classification model from the SciWING toolkit as a baseline, as the toolkit takes only pure text data as input. SciWING's model produces contextual sentence embeddings for each line individually via ELMo (Peters et al., 2018) and biLSTMs (Hochreiter and Schmidhuber, 1997; Graves and Schmidhuber, 2005) for linear classification.

3.2 Line-Level Attention

In contrast to the baseline, we propose a model that considers the context of neighboring lines, as

[1]Luong et al. (2010) classify each document line into the following 23 classes: `address`, `affiliation`, `author`, `bodyText`, `category`, `construct`, `copyright`, `email`, `equation`, `figure`, `figureCaption`, `footnote`, `keyword`, `listItem`, `note`, `page`, `reference`, `sectionHeader`, `subsectionHeader`, `subsubsectionHeader`, `table`, `tableCaption`, and `title`.

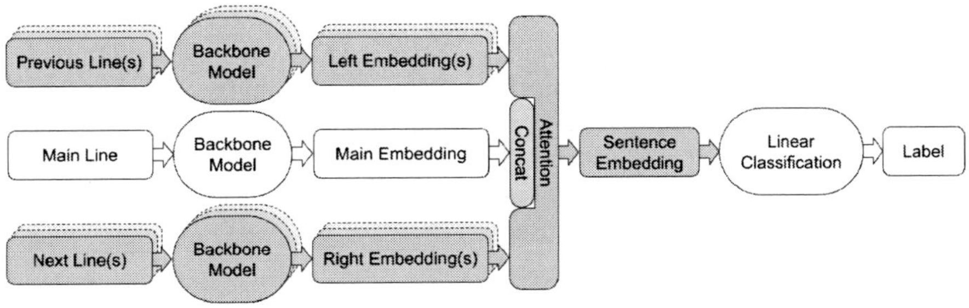

Figure 1: Our proposed architecture which considers cross-line context with an inserted attention layer and contextual modeling.

logical structures tend to span multiple consecutive lines. Inclusion of such context reduces misclassifications in the middle of large logical structures. We refine the current neural models for logical structure classification by adapting Hierarchical Attention Networks (HAN; Yang et al. 2016). By selecting context-sensitive embedders, we forgo word-level encoding and word-level attention layers and generate contextual sentence embeddings directly. We then add a line-level attention layer between the encoder and the classification layer to account for cross-line context (Figure 1).

To account for cross-line context, without increasing the runtime quadratically in proportion to the document length, we introduce a similar method to the sliding window attention model used in Longformers (Beltagy et al., 2020) for the line-level attention layer. Longformers replace the expensive global self-attention mechanism with a local version that is based on sliding windows and allows building representations from neighboring lines. In our case, for each target sentence to be labeled, we take into account the contextual information of neighboring lines, the amount of which depends on the size of the sliding window. Taking the surrounding context of d lines upward and downward as the key K and value V matrices and the target line ℓ_i as the query matrix Q as input to the attention layer, we obtain the sentence embedding ℓ'_i as follows:

$$K = V = \text{Stack}(\{\ell_{i-d}, \ldots, \ell_{i-1}, \ell_{i+1}, \ldots, \ell_{i+d}\}), \tag{2}$$

$$\ell'_i = \text{Concat}(\ell_i, \text{MultiHead}(Q = \ell_i, K, V)). \tag{3}$$

3.3 Sentence Embeddings with Transformers

We also improve the quality of contextual sentence embeddings using pretrained transformer models such as BERT (Devlin et al., 2019), SciBERT (Beltagy et al., 2019), Sentence-BERT (Reimers and Gurevych, 2019), and RoBERTa (Liu et al., 2019). Sentence embeddings are generated from transformer outputs by either:

1. Using the embedding of special classification token `[CLS]` that signals the beginning of the sentence (Devlin et al., 2019). Upon fine-tuning for downstream tasks, such tokens model the input's contextual meaning;

2. Obtaining the mean pooling of the output subword embeddings, which Reimers and Gurevych (2019) concluded produced more accurate sentence embeddings, and can be further enhanced with finetuning, or;

3. Obtaining an attentively pooled embedding by adding an extra attention layer, similar to the hierarchical attention structure that of Yang et al. (2016), using the `[CLS]` as the query matrix and the remaining subword embeddings as the key and value matrices.

4 Semi-Supervised Learning

Supervised learning can be used to produce accurate models when adequate labeled data are provided. While unlabeled data is easy to obtain, labeled data are scarce, particularly in the SDP domain. Semi-supervised learning (SSL) methods address this problem using both labeled and unlabeled data, resulting in better performance compared to purely supervised means.

4.1 Preliminaries

Notations. Prior to discussing SSL frameworks, we define some necessary notation. Let $\mathcal{X} = \{(x_b, y_b) : b \in (1, \ldots, B)\}$ be a batch of B labeled data samples with x_b being the input sample and y_b being the ground-truth label. We let

$\mathcal{U} = \{u_b : b \in (1, \dots, \mu B)\}$ be a batch of μB unlabeled data samples. We denote $\hat{y}(x)$ as the predicted class distribution of the sample x made by the model. Further, we also denote $H(q, p)$ as the standard cross-entropy loss of predicted distribution p and target distribution q, and $D(q||p)$ as the Kullback–Leibler divergence between distributions p and q. We denote $\mathcal{A}(\cdot)$ and $\alpha(\cdot)$ as "strong" and "weak" data augmentations, respectively. We discuss the difference between strong and weak augmentations in the next section.

Data Augmentation. Recent semi-supervised learning frameworks for image classification such as MixMatch (Berthelot et al., 2019), ReMixMatch (Berthelot et al., 2020), and FixMatch (Sohn et al., 2020) use both "strong" and "weak" augmentations as a form of robust data augmentation. Weak augmentations refer to simple flip-and-crops of the input image, while strong augmentations contain more complex operations such as RandAugment (Cubuk et al., 2020) and CTAugment (Berthelot et al., 2020), which perform multifold image transformations to inject *valid* yet *diverse* noise into the input data (Xie et al., 2020).

In the text domain, we employ back-translation (Sennrich et al., 2016; Edunov et al., 2018) as a form of strong augmentation as proposed by Xie et al. (2020). The use of back-translation retains the contextual meaning of the text (*validity*), and reorganizes the text into different writing (*diversity*). Although there is no counterpart for weak augmentation in current semi-supervised learning frameworks, we follow the spirit of the flip-and-crop and apply Easy Data Augmentation (EDA; Wei and Zou 2019) to simulate the effects of weak augmentation. EDA employs synonym replacement, random insertion, random swap, and random deletion of words in a sentence at random, augmenting the sentence in a way that may not be grammatically correct or human-readable but contextually similar and sufficient for sentence embedding generation.

4.2 SSL Frameworks

We now review some SSL frameworks we use in our work (Figure 2).

Unsupervised Data Augmentation (UDA; Xie et al. 2020) is an SSL framework that uses consistency training in conjunction with data augmentation on unlabeled data to regularize the model to be invariant to noise in classification tasks. Labeled data are used to compute cross-entropy loss (Equation 4), similar to supervised training, while unlabeled data are used to compute consistency loss against its strongly augmented version generated by back-translation (Equation 5). The training objective would be minimizing the loss term $\mathcal{L}$:

$$\mathcal{L}_s = \frac{1}{B}\sum_{b=1}^{B} H(y_b, \hat{y}(x_b)), \tag{4}$$

$$\mathcal{L}_u = \frac{1}{\mu B}\sum_{b=1}^{\mu B} D(\hat{y}(\mathcal{A}(u_b))||\hat{y}(u_b)), \tag{5}$$

$$\mathcal{L} = \mathcal{L}_s + \lambda \mathcal{L}_u, \tag{6}$$

where λ is a hyperparameter to scale the relative weight of the unsupervised loss.

FixMatch (Sohn et al., 2020) is a simplified SSL framework for image classification that combines elements from MixMatch (Berthelot et al., 2019) and UDA (Xie et al., 2020). Like UDA, FixMatch also employs data augmentation on unlabeled data to increase robustness, but replaces the consistency training of UDA with a cross-entropy loss on a pseudo-label. For supervised learning, the FixMatch algorithm trains on a weakly augmented version of the labeled data against its label (Equation 7); while for unsupervised learning, it infers a pseudo-label from the weakly augmented data, and obtains the cross-entropy loss of the strong augmented data against the pseudo-label (Equation 8). The training objective would be minimizing the loss term $\mathcal{L}$:

$$\mathcal{L}_s = \frac{1}{B}\sum_{b=1}^{B} H(p_b, p_m(y, \alpha(x_b)), \tag{7}$$

$$\begin{aligned}\mathcal{L}_u =& \frac{1}{\mu B}\sum_{b=1}^{\mu B} \mathbb{1}(\max(p_m(y|\alpha(u_b)) > \tau)\cdot \\ & H(\arg\max(p_m(y, \alpha(u_b)), p_m(y, \mathcal{A}(u_b)),\end{aligned} \tag{8}$$

$$\mathcal{L} = \mathcal{L}_s + \lambda \mathcal{L}_u, \tag{9}$$

where λ is a hyperparameter to scale the relative weight of the unsupervised loss and τ is a threshold to which we retain the pseudo-label.

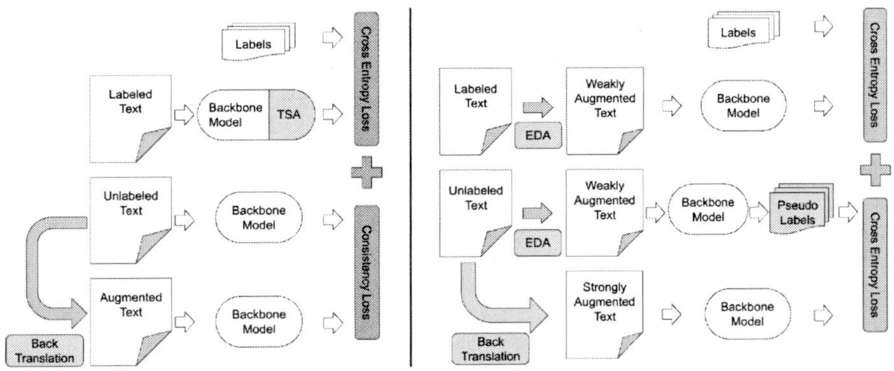

Figure 2: Frameworks Used for Semi-Supervised Training (Left: UDA (Xie et al., 2020), Right: FixMatch (Sohn et al., 2020))

4.3 Loss Engineering as a Supervised Training Strategy

While semi-supervised training does indeed increase training accuracy and robustness, SSL frameworks such as UDA often employ techniques that regulate the loss term for better training, begging the question: *Does employing such loss term engineering techniques improve training under a supervised setting?*

4.3.1 Training Signal Annealing

We focus first on Training Signal Annealing (TSA), a technique originally used in Xie et al. (2020)'s UDA framework (omitted for simplicity in the previous section) as a method to reduce overfitting on the training data. TSA employs a moving ceiling η_t on the probabilities of the model prediction:

$$\eta_t = \alpha_t \cdot \left(1 - \frac{1}{K}\right) + \frac{1}{K}, \tag{10}$$

where K is the number of label classes, and α_t is a schedule function in accordance to three schedules with training progress percentile t as a variable:

- Exponential: $\alpha_t = \mathrm{e}^{5(t-1)}$,
- Linear: $\alpha_t = t$,
- Logarithmic: $\alpha_t = 1 - \mathrm{e}^{-5t}$.

Each sample is only added to the calculation of the loss function if the highest probabilities of the prediction are lower than the ceiling η_t. This allows the model to select non-confident samples for training, to improve the robustness of the training process. We then get the loss term:

$$\mathcal{L}_{TSA} = \frac{\sum_{b=1}^{B} H(y,b,\hat{y}(x_b))\cdot\mathbb{1}(\max(\hat{y}(x_b))<\eta_t)}{\max\left(1, \sum_{b=1}^{B} \mathbb{1}(\max(\hat{y}(x_b))<\eta_t)\right)}. \tag{11}$$

We noted that the selection of non-confident samples for training during the early stages of the training can be beneficial to training on imbalanced datasets, as classes that have fewer instances are computed into the loss function more. As training progresses, the full dataset can still be trained as the ceiling for the prediction certainty based on the loss increases, adding more samples for loss function computation. Due to the continuous nature of the training data and the importance of cross-line context, we employ TSA as a method to combat performance degradation caused by an imbalanced dataset, as other discrete techniques such as SMOTE (Chawla et al., 2002) may not be easy to leverage due to its lack of lexical versions of such methods.

4.3.2 Supervised Data Augmentation

We also employ UDA (Xie et al., 2020) in a supervised setting, which we denote here as SDA (Supervised Data Augmentation; Figure 3). We simulate the usage of unlabeled data from the unsupervised consistency training component by stripping the labels from our labeled data. We pass both the original labeled data and the augmented version of the text simultaneously into the model and run the consistency loss training for augmented data against the labeled text alongside the original cross-entropy loss for the text and label within the same batch, returning the sum of both losses as the loss term. We also employ the usage of TSA on top of

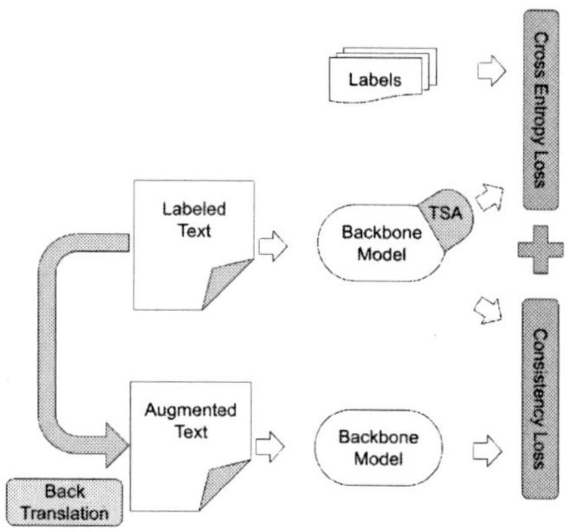

Figure 3: Our Proposed Supervised Data Augmentation Framework

the cross-entropy loss, resulting in the loss term $\mathcal{L}$:

$$\mathcal{L}_{Aug} = \frac{1}{B}\sum_{b=1}^{B} D(\hat{y}(\mathcal{A}(x_b))||\hat{y}(x_b)), \quad (12)$$

$$\mathcal{L} = \mathcal{L}_{TSA} + \mathcal{L}_{Aug}, \quad (13)$$

where $\mathcal{L}_{TSA}$ is the same loss term as Equation 11.

5 Experiments

Dataset. We use the dataset that contains 20 ACL and 20 ACM articles from various years collected and labeled by Luong et al. (2010), which we refer to as the *SectLabel dataset*. Each line of the dataset included the original text, as well as formatted versions of the rich context information of that particular line. The version of the dataset we use is the one used to train the contextual models in SciWING, where the contextual data are discarded, and only the raw data and the label remain. The SectLabel dataset in SciWING randomly splits each individual line into the training, validation, and test dataset without considering neighboring lines. However, due to our need to feed consecutive lines into the model with the inclusion of a sliding window attention, we needed to reconstruct the train–validation–test split in the dataset by randomly select 4 papers each to form the validation and test dataset, training the model on the remaining 32 papers only, to cleanly separate the splits to avoid data snooping.

Furthermore, to scale the performance to a slightly outside of domain setting for the evaluation of the inference performance, we constructed an independent test dataset in addition to the test dataset partitioned from the SectLabel data, which we refer to as the *extended test dataset*. We manually label 20 randomly selected papers from *ACL 2020*, assigning each extracted text line to a particular label with the help of the original PDF file to ensure that the labels are correct. The text extraction engine and manual labeling differ from the SectLabel dataset, allowing this dataset to have a slight out-of-domain property that tests the model's ability to generalize.

For semi-supervised training, we assembled a new corpus of unlabeled training data consisting of 570 long articles from *ACL 2021* and 1895 articles from *NeurIPS 2021*, which we refer to as the *unlabeled dataset*. The unlabeled dataset is then augmented by data augmentation techniques such as EDA (Wei and Zou, 2019) and back-translation (Sennrich et al., 2016; Edunov et al., 2018) to form the unlabeled dataset used for semi-supervised training. (See Table 2 for sample augmentations.)

Evaluation Metric. As categories such as `bodyText` and `reference` comprise most of the text in scientific articles, our data are extremely skewed and unbalanced, requiring us to utilize the *macro F1* score.

Results. Table 3 presents the main performance results, where we take the SciWING logical structure classification engine (Ramesh Kashyap and Kan, 2020) as our baseline model. Our best model increases SOTA performance in plain text-based logical structure recovery networks by 10%. Among architecture types, we find that the RoBERTa-Sliding Attention model *(RoBERTa-Attn)* performs well, outperforming SciWING by 7% in the SectLabel test dataset. We note that these results are not directly comparable as the training data are sampled differently.

When we further incorporate TSA and UDA, we find that the performance grows even more, with SDA improving performance on the SectLabel test dataset by 10%, and UDA increasing the generalizability of the model and increasing performance on the extended test dataset.

6 Analysis

We analyze in detail both the architectural changes (§6.1, 6.2) and training techniques (§6.3, 6.4). We employ an iterative alteration of models in our experiments, starting with SciWING's SectLabel

Original	Once upon a midnight dreary, while I pondered, weak and weary,
Synonym Replacement (EDA)	**Erstwhile** upon a midnight dreary, while I pondered, weak and weary,
Random Insertion (EDA)	Once upon a midnight dreary, while I pondered, weak and **once** weary,
Random Swap (EDA)	Once upon **I** midnight dreary, while **a** pondered, weak and weary,
Random Delete (EDA)	Once upon a ␣ dreary, while I pondered, ␣ and weary,
Back Translation	Once at midnight it was bleak while I was thinking, weak and tired,

Table 2: Sample Augmentation of EDA and Back Translations

	SectLabel		Extended	
Model	Macro F1	Micro F1	Macro F1	Micro F1
SciWING (Ramesh Kashyap and Kan, 2020)	0.732	0.900	-	-
RoBERTa-Attn Model (OURS)	0.806	0.904	0.596	0.870
RoBERTa-Attn Model + UDA_{log} †	0.784	0.906	**0.669**	**0.887**
RoBERTa-Attn Model + SDA_{log} †	**0.832**	**0.929**	0.623	0.886
SectLabel (Luong et al., 2010)‡	***0.847***	***0.934***	-	-

* Bold text indicates SOTA performance.
† The subscript refers to the logarithmic Training Signal Annealing schedule used in training (§ 4.3.1).
‡ Uses rich text information in addition to plain text.

Table 3: Abridged Comparison of Our Models and Other Relevant Models

Window	SectLabel Test		Extended Test	
Size	Macro	Micro	Macro	Micro
1†	0.693	0.869	0.446	0.791
3	0.770	0.907	0.531	0.855
5	0.779	0.909	0.579	0.871
7	0.778	0.907	0.564	0.876
5 (dilated)	0.758	0.900	0.539	0.856

* The model architecture for this experiment follows SciWING in using ELMo-biLSTM as the backbone sentence embedder model.
† Using a window size of 1 reduces the model back to the SciWING baseline.

Table 4: Effects of Sliding Window Size

model as our baseline, and iteratively adding techniques experimentally proven to be beneficial to act as the baseline of the next batch of experiments.

6.1 Sliding Window Attention

For better context modeling, we incorporate a sliding window attention layer to account for neighboring lines. We study the effect of varying window size 1, 3, 5, 7, and 5 (dilated) in Table 4. Here, a window size of 1 reduces the model back to the baseline, while a dilated sliding window skips every other line in the window.

With the inclusion of sliding window attention, the model is less prone to misclassify lines in the middle of a large logical structure (Table 5). We observe, however, with the increase of window size from 1 to 3, some categories in which single line contextual information suffices to determine the label such as `address` and `email` drops in performance slightly, but recover when the window size increases to 5. Taking a window size of 7, we find that the categories that exist within the boundaries of the document, such as `title`, `affiliation`, have dropped in performance, while other categories of the spanned text, such as `listItem` and `footnote` have also dropped, possibly due to the window size being too large and including too much "noise".

For the dilated window size of 3, although such a setting is able to include a larger span of context, we find that although most categories perform slightly worse for the dilated version, `title` and `author` performed particularly badly. We believe the overall decrease in performance is because some logical structures only span one line and using a dilated window skips over such logical structures and lowers the continuity of the contextual information.

Overall, we consider the window size of 5 to have the best performance in total and we use such a window size on further experiments.

	Baseline	Sliding Window 5
Matthew E Peters, Mark Neumann, Mohit Iyyer, Matt	*author*	reference
Gardner, Christopher Clark, Kenton Lee, and Luke	reference	reference
Zettlemoyer. Deep contextualized word representa-	*bodyText*	reference
tions. arXiv preprint arXiv:1802.05365, 2018.	reference	reference

Table 5: Sample Classification Result of Sliding Window on Consecutive Lines (Citation of Peters et al. (2018))

Extended Test (Macro-F1)	`[CLS]`	Mean	Attention
BERT (uncased)	0.506	0.485	0.511
BERT (cased)	0.546	0.581	0.580
SciBERT (uncased)	0.493	0.514	0.505
SciBERT (cased)	0.581	0.571	0.568
S-BERT	0.074	0.381	0.117
RoBERTa	0.555	0.564	0.596

* Sliding window attention of size 5 is employed.

Table 6: Training Results of Different Pretrained Transformers

Macro F1	UDA			FixMatch	
	Exp	Linear	Log	No Aug	w/EDA
SectLabel	0.781	0.818	0.784	0.796	**0.820**
Extended	0.499	0.627	**0.669**	0.570	0.642

* Backbone model is the RoBERTa model with a sliding window of size 5 employed.

Table 7: Training Results of Different SSL Frameworks

6.2 BERT and Pooling

We test the three different pooling methods for producing sentence embeddings (`[CLS]` token, mean pooling, and attention pooling), cross-examining the results with the following pre-trained transformer models: BERT (Devlin et al., 2019), SciBERT (Beltagy et al., 2019), Sentence-BERT (SBERT) (Reimers and Gurevych, 2019), and RoBERTa (Liu et al., 2019) in Table 6.

We observe that uncased models underperform, returning worse results than the SciWING baseline model. In particular, categories that require capitalization to convey context such as `address`, `sectionHeader`, `title`, etc, underperform.

Furthermore, as Sentence-BERT models are trained specifically to produce sentence embeddings of entire sentences, it may not be suitable for our purposes, as the stripped lines in our training data are broken into lines on a typesetting basis rather than a contextual basis that takes contextual completeness into account.

In contrast, among BERT variants, RoBERTa produces the best result when applying attention pooling. Our further analysis found no performance correlation between the model and the pooling technique used.

6.3 Semi-Supervised Learning

We train our model in a semi-supervised setting in hopes of increasing performance levels due to the limited amount of labeled data. We also attempt to increase the robustness of the model in terms of out-of-domain data, and evaluate on the extended test dataset.

We experimented with all three Training Signal Annealing (TSA) training schedules in conjunction with Unsupervised Data Augmentation (UDA). For FixMatch, we also attempt a version where weak augmentation is not employed, performing cross-entropy loss on the labeled data directly for supervised learning. The results in Table 7 show that FixMatch is able to achieve the highest performance in the partitioned data set, which is in line with the results reported by (Sohn et al., 2020) in image classification. In addition, we see that UDA with a logarithmic TSA schedule is able to increase robustness of the model most, as exemplified on the performance of the out-of-domain extended test dataset.

With FixMatch, we see that the weakly augmented version has increased performances on both the SectLabel and extended test data, which validates Sohn et al. (2020)'s explanation that removing weak augmentation may lead to overfitting on the guessed pseudo-labels. As seen from the results of the extended test data, the model reinforces its inference and fails to generalize without the use of weak augmentation on the training data.

Turning our discussions to UDA, although the exponential schedule should in theory work well in a semi-supervised setting due to the need to regulate the release of training signals slowly to avoid overfitting the labeled data, we observe that such a schedule underperforms (Xie et al., 2020). Observ-

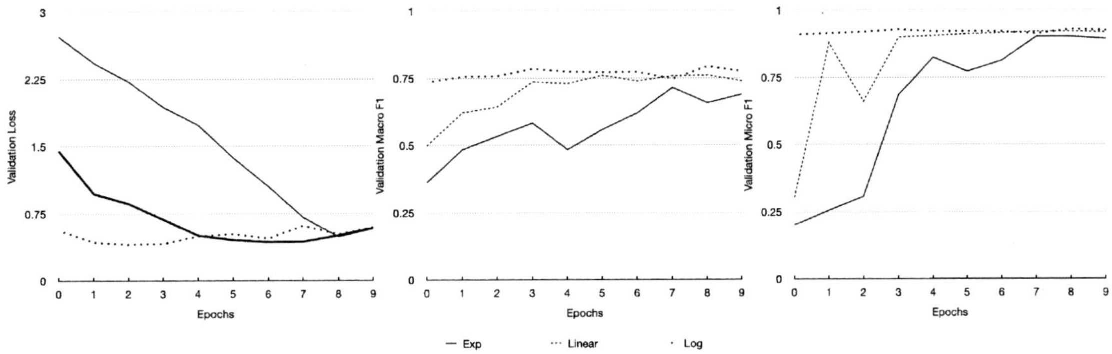

Figure 4: Training Progress of UDA (Semi-Supervised) under Different Annealing Schedules

ing the validation metrics in Figure 4, we see that convergence is slow and conclude that this may be due to the minimal release of training signals early in the training, allowing initial errors to amplify themselves in the unsupervised consistency loss.

On the other hand, we find that the logarithmic schedule limits the amount of training signals of the supervised data, hence placing more emphasis on the unlabeled data during training. This can lead to a more robust model, given that the unlabeled data are diverse enough. We expect this property to be useful when dealing with cross-domain training.

While semi-supervised learning does increase performance, ultimately it does not improve the accuracy of minority classes by much, due to the inherent reinforcement of noisy model prediction. As the unlabeled data are pseudo-labeled according to the predictions of the model, they contain the model's biases from the labeled data (Kim et al., 2020; Wei et al., 2021). The result is that the minority classes' performance are only improved a bit as the majority classes still have an outsized influence on the overall accuracy.

6.4 Loss Engineering

We now attempt to optimize the training process by engineering the training loss term and observe whether this is enough to improve training without the requirement of additional unlabeled data and the lengthy training procedure of semi-supervised techniques. This includes the integration of elements of UDA (Xie et al., 2020) – TSA to counter the imbalanced dataset, and training our model with a supervised version of UDA (SDA).

Regarding the annealing schedules for the TSA function α_t, we believe that under a supervised background, due to the large difference in the amount of training signals released in the first half of the training process, the distribution of data differs greatly from schedule to schedule and would greatly affect performance.

Macro F1		Exp	Linear	Log
SectLabel Test	TSA	0.790	0.824	0.819
	SDA	0.761	0.819	**0.836**
Extended Test	TSA	0.568	0.608	**0.632**
	SDA	0.548	0.606	0.623

* Backbone model is the RoBERTa model with a sliding window of size 5 employed.

Table 8: Training Results of Loss Engineering Techniques

Table 8 shows convex annealing schedules (exponential) perform worse than the baseline, likely due to there being insufficient training signals to properly train the data, as observed from the slow loss convergence in Figure 5. On the other hand, non-convex annealing schedules (linear and logarithmic) generally perform better, due to an earlier increase in the moving ceiling η_t, so the model can emphasize more training on non-confident samples while still retaining enough training signals.

We find that the inclusion of consistency loss enhances the effects of the TSA schedule itself, returning a worse performance on the exponential schedule, while improving performance on the logarithmic schedule. However, judging from the extended testing data, such an addition of the consistency loss may run a risk of overfitting as a result of using two loss terms on the same sample, as the performance decreased with such an inclusion.

From the experimental results, we observe that utilizing training signal annealing is indeed able to mitigate negative effects brought by data skewness and improve model performance, even exceeding

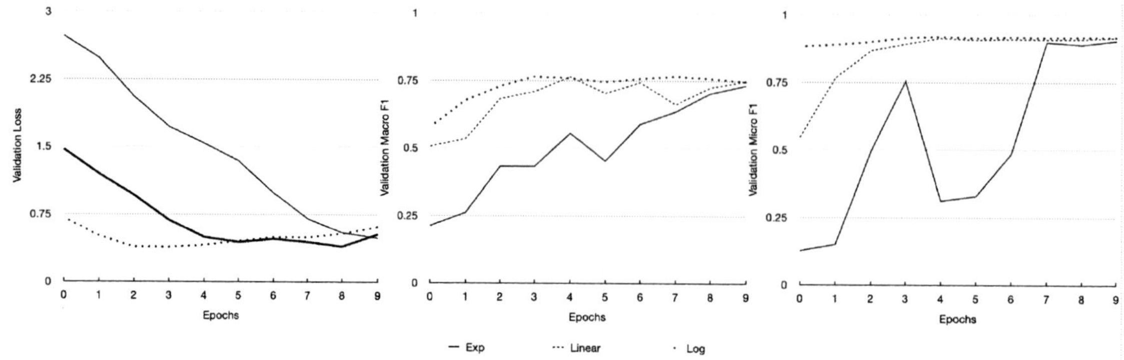

Figure 5: Training Progress of Supervised Learning Under Different Annealing Schedules

	Parameters	Modality	Image Embedding
BERT	110M	T	×
RoBERTa	125M	T	×
LayoutLM			
Vanilla	113M	T+L	×
+ Image	160M	T+L+I	ResNet101
LayoutLMv2	200M	T+L+I	ResNeXt101

Table 9: Comparison of Selected Text-Only and Multimodal (with Layout and Image) Transformers

	Batch Size
BERT/RoBERTa w/Sliding Attention	32
BERT/RoBERTa w/Sliding Attention + SSL	16
LayoutLM w/ResNet	8
LayoutLM w/ResNet + Sliding Attention	4
LayoutLMv2	MemoryError

Table 10: Batch Sizes of Transformer Models Compared on a Single Nvidia RTX3090

that of the semi-supervised training results. However, as it still utilizes fewer training data, under out-of-domain conditions, the model is not as robust as that of the semi-supervised training.

6.5 Comparison With Multimodal Models

We conclude our discussion with a brief mention of multimodal models that can be used for logical structure recovery. Related works such as LayoutLM (Xu et al., 2020) and LayoutLMv2 (Xu et al., 2021) use positional coordinates and image embeddings to encode the position and font attributes of text in the embedding. The addition of image embeddings not only increases the model size (as shown in Table 9, but also lengthens the inference timing, as multimodal models like the LayoutLM series are, in essence, ensemble models, requiring the finetune/inference timing to include both the main transformer model and the image embedding model. Furthermore, the batch size of the input must be similarly reduced, as the input now includes the full image albeit compressed.

A preliminary testing of corresponding largest batch sizes on a 24GB RAM Nvidia RTX3090 is shown in Table 10. On the other hand, while image-based models such as the Document Image Transformer (DiT; Li et al. 2022) are not as hard to train, we find the subsequent need of employing OCR engines to such models to be an extra inference dependency that can increase error. Given the high amount of resources needed to train a multimodal model, our work provides a purely contextual model that serves as a lightweight and accessible alternative.

7 Conclusion

This paper shows that, with effective use of multiline context, the results of plain text logical structure recovery models are comparable with other models that use rich text information. We achieve this by employing transformers to produce high-quality sentence embeddings, applying sliding window attention to consider cross-line context, and further optimizing by engineering loss functions such as employing training signal annealing, incorporating consistency loss, and/or training under a semi-supervised regime.

Further work on purely contextual models may extend to solving the class imbalance problem of logical structures, which is further amplified due to the usage of semi-supervised training. Given the importance of neighboring context, one cannot simply rebalance the dataset. These issues require other methods to decrease such biases.

References

Iz Beltagy, Kyle Lo, and Arman Cohan. 2019. SciBERT: A pretrained language model for scientific text. In *Proceedings of the 2019 Conference on Empirical Methods in Natural Language Processing and the 9th International Joint Conference on Natural Language Processing (EMNLP-IJCNLP)*, pages 3615–3620, Hong Kong, China. Association for Computational Linguistics.

Iz Beltagy, Matthew E. Peters, and Arman Cohan. 2020. Longformer: The long-document transformer.

David Berthelot, Nicholas Carlini, Ekin D. Cubuk, Alex Kurakin, Kihyuk Sohn, Han Zhang, and Colin Raffel. 2020. ReMixMatch: Semi-supervised learning with distribution matching and augmentation anchoring. In *International Conference on Learning Representations*.

David Berthelot, Nicholas Carlini, Ian Goodfellow, Nicolas Papernot, Avital Oliver, and Colin A Raffel. 2019. MixMatch: A holistic approach to semi-supervised learning. In *Advances in Neural Information Processing Systems*, volume 32. Curran Associates, Inc.

Zhaowei Cai and Nuno Vasconcelos. 2018. Cascade r-cnn: Delving into high quality object detection. In *Proceedings of the IEEE Conference on Computer Vision and Pattern Recognition (CVPR)*.

Nitesh V. Chawla, Kevin W. Bowyer, Lawrence O. Hall, and W. Philip Kegelmeyer. 2002. SMOTE: Synthetic minority over-sampling technique. *J. Artif. Int. Res.*, 16(1):321–357.

Ekin Dogus Cubuk, Barret Zoph, Jon Shlens, and Quoc Le. 2020. RandAugment: Practical automated data augmentation with a reduced search space. In *Advances in Neural Information Processing Systems*, volume 33, pages 18613–18624. Curran Associates, Inc.

Jacob Devlin, Ming-Wei Chang, Kenton Lee, and Kristina Toutanova. 2019. BERT: Pre-training of deep bidirectional transformers for language understanding. In *Proceedings of the 2019 Conference of the North American Chapter of the Association for Computational Linguistics: Human Language Technologies, Volume 1 (Long and Short Papers)*, pages 4171–4186, Minneapolis, Minnesota. Association for Computational Linguistics.

Alexey Dosovitskiy, Lucas Beyer, Alexander Kolesnikov, Dirk Weissenborn, Xiaohua Zhai, Thomas Unterthiner, Mostafa Dehghani, Matthias Minderer, Georg Heigold, Sylvain Gelly, Jakob Uszkoreit, and Neil Houlsby. 2021. An image is worth 16x16 words: Transformers for image recognition at scale. In *International Conference on Learning Representations*.

Sergey Edunov, Myle Ott, Michael Auli, and David Grangier. 2018. Understanding back-translation at scale. In *Proceedings of the 2018 Conference on Empirical Methods in Natural Language Processing*, pages 489–500, Brussels, Belgium. Association for Computational Linguistics.

Alex Graves and Jürgen Schmidhuber. 2005. Framewise phoneme classification with bidirectional LSTM and other neural network architectures. *Neural Networks*, 18(5):602–610. IJCNN 2005.

Kaiming He, Georgia Gkioxari, Piotr Dollar, and Ross Girshick. 2017. Mask R-CNN. In *Proceedings of the IEEE International Conference on Computer Vision (ICCV)*.

Sepp Hochreiter and Jürgen Schmidhuber. 1997. Long Short-Term Memory. *Neural Computation*, 9(8):1735–1780.

Yupan Huang, Tengchao Lv, Lei Cui, Yutong Lu, and Furu Wei. 2022. Layoutlmv3: Pre-training for document ai with unified text and image masking.

Jaehyung Kim, Youngbum Hur, Sejun Park, Eunho Yang, Sung Ju Hwang, and Jinwoo Shin. 2020. Distribution aligning refinery of pseudo-label for imbalanced semi-supervised learning. In *Advances in Neural Information Processing Systems*, volume 33, pages 14567–14579. Curran Associates, Inc.

Yuta Koreeda and Christopher Manning. 2021. Capturing logical structure of visually structured documents with multimodal transition parser. In *Proceedings of the Natural Legal Language Processing Workshop 2021*, pages 144–154, Punta Cana, Dominican Republic. Association for Computational Linguistics.

John D. Lafferty, Andrew McCallum, and Fernando C. N. Pereira. 2001. Conditional random fields: Probabilistic models for segmenting and labeling sequence data. In *Proceedings of the Eighteenth International Conference on Machine Learning*, ICML '01, page 282–289, San Francisco, CA, USA. Morgan Kaufmann Publishers Inc.

Junlong Li, Yiheng Xu, Tengchao Lv, Lei Cui, Cha Zhang, and Furu Wei. 2022. DiT: Self-supervised pre-training for document image transformer.

Yinhan Liu, Myle Ott, Naman Goyal, Jingfei Du, Mandar Joshi, Danqi Chen, Omer Levy, Mike Lewis, Luke Zettlemoyer, and Veselin Stoyanov. 2019. RoBERTa: A robustly optimized BERT pretraining approach.

Minh-Thang Luong, Thuy Dung Nguyen, and Min-Yen Kan. 2010. Logical structure recovery in scholarly articles with rich document features. *Int. J. Digit. Library Syst.*, 1(4):1–23.

Song Mao, Azriel Rosenfeld, and Tapas Kanungo. 2003. Document structure analysis algorithms: a literature survey. In *Document Recognition and Retrieval X*, volume 5010, pages 197 – 207. International Society for Optics and Photonics, SPIE.

Matthew E. Peters, Mark Neumann, Mohit Iyyer, Matt Gardner, Christopher Clark, Kenton Lee, and Luke Zettlemoyer. 2018. Deep contextualized word representations. In *Proceedings of the 2018 Conference of the North American Chapter of the Association for Computational Linguistics: Human Language Technologies, Volume 1 (Long Papers)*, pages 2227–2237, New Orleans, Louisiana. Association for Computational Linguistics.

Muhammad Mahbubur Rahman and Tim Finin. 2019. Unfolding the structure of a document using deep learning.

Abhinav Ramesh Kashyap and Min-Yen Kan. 2020. SciWING– A software toolkit for scientific document processing. In *Proceedings of the First Workshop on Scholarly Document Processing*, pages 113–120, Online. Association for Computational Linguistics.

Nils Reimers and Iryna Gurevych. 2019. Sentence-BERT: Sentence embeddings using Siamese BERT-networks. In *Proceedings of the 2019 Conference on Empirical Methods in Natural Language Processing and the 9th International Joint Conference on Natural Language Processing (EMNLP-IJCNLP)*, pages 3982–3992, Hong Kong, China. Association for Computational Linguistics.

Shaoqing Ren, Kaiming He, Ross Girshick, and Jian Sun. 2015. Faster R-CNN: Towards real-time object detection with region proposal networks. In *Advances in Neural Information Processing Systems*, volume 28. Curran Associates, Inc.

Rico Sennrich, Barry Haddow, and Alexandra Birch. 2016. Improving neural machine translation models with monolingual data. In *Proceedings of the 54th Annual Meeting of the Association for Computational Linguistics (Volume 1: Long Papers)*, pages 86–96, Berlin, Germany. Association for Computational Linguistics.

Kihyuk Sohn, David Berthelot, Nicholas Carlini, Zizhao Zhang, Han Zhang, Colin A Raffel, Ekin Dogus Cubuk, Alexey Kurakin, and Chun-Liang Li. 2020. FixMatch: Simplifying semi-supervised learning with consistency and confidence. In *Advances in Neural Information Processing Systems*, volume 33, pages 596–608. Curran Associates, Inc.

Xin Tao, Zhi Tang, Canhui Xu, and Yongtao Wang. 2014. Logical labeling of fixed layout pdf documents using multiple contexts. In *2014 11th IAPR International Workshop on Document Analysis Systems*, pages 360–364.

Ashish Vaswani, Noam Shazeer, Niki Parmar, Jakob Uszkoreit, Llion Jones, Aidan N Gomez, Ł ukasz Kaiser, and Illia Polosukhin. 2017. Attention is all you need. In *Advances in Neural Information Processing Systems*, volume 30. Curran Associates, Inc.

Chen Wei, Kihyuk Sohn, Clayton Mellina, Alan Yuille, and Fan Yang. 2021. CReST: A class-rebalancing self-training framework for imbalanced semi-supervised learning. In *2021 IEEE/CVF Conference on Computer Vision and Pattern Recognition (CVPR)*, pages 10852–10861.

Jason Wei and Kai Zou. 2019. EDA: Easy data augmentation techniques for boosting performance on text classification tasks. In *Proceedings of the 2019 Conference on Empirical Methods in Natural Language Processing and the 9th International Joint Conference on Natural Language Processing (EMNLP-IJCNLP)*, pages 6382–6388, Hong Kong, China. Association for Computational Linguistics.

Qizhe Xie, Zihang Dai, Eduard Hovy, Thang Luong, and Quoc Le. 2020. Unsupervised data augmentation for consistency training. In *Advances in Neural Information Processing Systems*, volume 33, pages 6256–6268. Curran Associates, Inc.

Yang Xu, Yiheng Xu, Tengchao Lv, Lei Cui, Furu Wei, Guoxin Wang, Yijuan Lu, Dinei Florencio, Cha Zhang, Wanxiang Che, Min Zhang, and Lidong Zhou. 2021. LayoutLMv2: Multi-modal pre-training for visually-rich document understanding. In *Proceedings of the 59th Annual Meeting of the Association for Computational Linguistics and the 11th International Joint Conference on Natural Language Processing (Volume 1: Long Papers)*, pages 2579–2591, Online. Association for Computational Linguistics.

Yiheng Xu, Minghao Li, Lei Cui, Shaohan Huang, Furu Wei, and Ming Zhou. 2020. LayoutLM: Pre-training of text and layout for document image understanding. In *Proceedings of the 26th ACM SIGKDD International Conference on Knowledge Discovery & Data Mining*, KDD '20, page 1192–1200, New York, NY, USA. Association for Computing Machinery.

Zichao Yang, Diyi Yang, Chris Dyer, Xiaodong He, Alex Smola, and Eduard Hovy. 2016. Hierarchical attention networks for document classification. In *Proceedings of the 2016 Conference of the North American Chapter of the Association for Computational Linguistics: Human Language Technologies*, pages 1480–1489, San Diego, California. Association for Computational Linguistics.

Citation Context Classification: Critical vs Non-critical

Sonita Te[1], Amira Barhoumi[1], Martin Lentschat[1], Frédérique Bordignon[2,3], Cyril Labbé[1], and François Portet[1]

[1]Univ. Grenoble Alpes, CNRS, Grenoble INP, LIG, 38000 Grenoble, France
sonita.te@cadt.edu.kh , *{firstName.lastName}@univ-grenoble-alpes.fr*
[2]Ecole des Ponts, Marne-la-Vallée, France
[3]LISIS, CNRS, INRAE, Univ Gustave Eiffel, Marne-la-Vallée, France
frederique.bordignon@enpc.fr

Abstract

Recently, there have been numerous research in Natural Language Processing on citation analysis in scientific literature. Studies of citation behavior aim at finding how researchers cited a paper in their work. In this paper, we are interested in identifying cited papers that are criticized. Recent research introduces the concept of *Critical citations* which provides a useful theoretical framework, making criticism an important part of scientific progress. Indeed, identifying critics could be a way to spot errors and thus encourage self-correction of science. In this work, we investigate how to automatically classify the critical citation contexts using Natural Language Processing (NLP). Our classification task consists of predicting critical or non-critical labels for citation contexts. For this, we experiment and compare different methods, including rule-based and machine learning methods, to classify critical vs. non-critical citation contexts. Our experiments show that fine-tuning pretrained transformer model *RoBERTa* achieved the highest performance among all systems.

1 Introduction

In scientific papers, citations acknowledge the sources and help the reader to find more information about the citation context. Citations are also an important indicator exploited to identify significant publications in a specific scientific field (Aragón, 2013). They are used for different purposes, e.g. referring to state of the art, to a specific method or result, and they reflect how authors frame their work and this diversity impacts future academics' adoption (Jurgens et al., 2018).

According to Bordignon (2022), the study of critical citation appears to give an applicable theoretical framework, making criticism a vital phenomenon for scientific development. We believe that classifying citation contexts into critical/non-critical categories could be essential to downstream process, such as identifying scientific claims or observing controversial papers.

Bordignon (2022) identifies three different functions for *Critical citation context* : "to criticize," "to compare," and "to question" where :

- "to criticize" function refers when the citing paper points out a weakness or a fault in the cited paper. For instance, *"X1 method did not work well, although they reported 80% accuracy in (Y1 and Y2, 2002)."*
- "to compare" function refers to a link made between two studies with the indication that one research is superior to another, without necessarily including one's own work. One must have the criticizing meaning in the citation contexts. For example, *"(Y1 and Y2, 2008) outperformed (Y3 and Y4, 2007).".*
- "to question" function refers to a citation made by the citing paper to raise concerns, doubts, and uncertainty about the cited paper. For instance, *"Thus, the full model proposed by Y1 (2002) has remained empirically unproven."*

There have been numerous researches on citation analysis in NLP, with for instance determining citation sentiments (Athar, 2011; Liu, 2017). In addition to citation sentiment, there have been research to define citation function which refers to the specific purpose a citation plays with respect to the citing paper (Bakhti et al., 2018; Jurgens et al., 2016; Pride et al., 2019; Yu et al., 2020). These researches have been conducted to find the real reason behind the citation. Nevertheless, how citation might be utilized to point out criticism and encourage correction have not been studied yet.

Given a set of citation contexts, our work aims at determining critical ones using NLP methods.

Proceedings of the Third Workshop on Scholarly Document Processing, pages 49–53
October 12–17, 2022.

First, we present the construction process of the corpus, which contains citation contexts annotated with critical and non-critical labels. Then, we experiment different methods to classify citation contexts into critical/non-critical labels using our constructed corpus. Indeed, we compare and discuss rule-based methods and machine learning ones.

2 Related Works

In this section, we present different existing works for citation analysis. Some of them are rule-based methods, while others are based on machine learning methods.

Since 2000, several researches on automation citation classification have been using rule-based approaches (Garzone and Mercer, 2000; Nanba et al., 2000; Pham and Hoffmann, 2003). The rule creation process is generally composed of 2 steps. In the first step, cue words/phrases are extracted from dataset samples. In the second step, rules are created based on the extracted cue words/phrases. These rules are the bases to classify citation contexts. For instance, in (Avanço, 2020) a rule-based method is used to identify negative or contradictory citation contexts. The authors built *CitaNeg* corpus (Table 1) and created functions (linguistic patterns) grouped by category: 13 functions for weakness category (WF), 5 functions for compare category (CF), 4 functions for background category (BF), 6 functions for hedges category (HF) and 14 for additional category (GF). However, only WF and CF categories were used for evaluation giving a precision of 0.72 and a recall of 0.69.

More recently, several approaches relying on machine learning have been proposed. For example, Teufel et al. (2006) used IBk, a form of K-Nearest Neighbor (kNN), to classify citation contexts into 4 polarities (Weakness, Positive, Contrast and Neutral) and obtained an f1-score of 0.61 using *Athar* corpus (Table 1). Jurgens et al., 2016, 2018 introduced a representative corpus containing nearly 2 000 citations annotated with 6 labels (background, motivation, extension, use, contrast or future) and reached an f1-score of 0.53 with a Random Forest classifier on their data and a portion of CFC (cf. Table 1). Raza et al. (2019) conducted citation sentimental analysis and citation function analysis by experimenting six machine learning models (Naïve-Bayes, Support Vector Machine, Logistic Regression, Decision Tree, K-Nearest Neighbors and Random Forest). Using *CFC* corpus, the SVM model gave the best performance with an f1-score of 0.88. Using deep learning techniques, Nicholson et al. (2021) developed a *smart citation index* called *scite*, which classifies citations based on their contexts. It indicates whether the context mentions, supports or contrasts the citation. *Scite* is trained on more than 880 million labeled citation contexts, but this data is proprietary and not publicly available. Recently, Karim et al. (2022) evaluated convolutional neural network (CNN) for citation sentiment analysis using different pre-trained word embeddings such as fastText and GloVe. With GloVe embeddings, their CNN model obtained a precision of 0.94 on the *Athar* corpus. Finally, Visser and Dunaiski (2022) used the pre-trained transformer model RoBERTa for citation sentimental analysis and obtained an accuracy of 0.89 on *Athar*.

Table 1 regroups different existing citation context corpora available to the community.

Type	Name	Size
Citation sentiment	Athar (Athar, 2011)	8 736
	Liu (Liu, 2017)	3 581
	CitaNeg (Avanço, 2020)	19 309
	Critical corpus [1]	1 690
Citation function	CFC (Teufel et al., 2006)	2 829
	Concit (Hernández and Gómez, 2015)	2 195
	IMS (Jochim and Schütze, 2012)	2 008
	DFKI (Dong and Schäfer, 2011)	1 768

Table 1: Available citation context corpora (the Size column contains the number of citation contexts).

3 Experimental setup

We present our methods used for critical/non critical classification in section 3.1. Then, we describe our corpus in section 3.2.

3.1 Methods

We experimented different classification methods to predict critical/non-critical classes. Two rule-based methods (RB and RB+) and 3 machine learning ones (LR, CNN and F-Roberta) were tested.

[1]Critical corpus is provided by LISIS and LIGM and will be published soon

- **RB** represents the rule-based method proposed by (Avanço, 2020). It is considered as a baseline in this work.
- **RB+** represents the improved version of RB method after analyzing and selecting only the rule functions corresponding to the definition of critical citation in Bordignon (2022).
- **LR** refers to Logistic Regression using Tf-Idf for n-grams in range of 1 and 3 grams
- **CNN** represents an inspiration of Karim et al. (2022) using CNN with Glove embeddings.
- **F-RoBERTa** represents a Fine-tuning RoBERTa (Visser and Dunaiski, 2022).In this model, we assigned the class weights of the training set to the model during training in order to deal with imbalance dataset[2].

3.2 Corpus

In order to build a corpus containing critical and non-critical citation contexts, we used available existing annotated datasets presented in Table 1. For the critical class, we used *Critical* corpus which contains 1 690 critical citation contexts. The non-critical citation contexts have been selected from *CitaNeg* dataset based on the definitions of citation functions. In fact, we kept only citation functions that don't contain critical meaning in their definitions. Our final corpus contains 2 413 citation contexts: 1 464 critical citation contexts and 949 non-critical citation contexts. The dataset was randomly split into training and test sets of 75% and 25%, respectively. Table 4 shows the number of citation contexts in the training and test sets.

	Train	Test	Overall
Critical	1098	366	2643
Non-critical	711	238	

Table 2: Train and test sets with numbers of citation contexts

4 Results and Discussion

Table 3 exhibits the performances of the models on the test set. It can be seen that *F-RoBERTa* outperformed all other models. Foremost, we observe that machine learning based approaches systematically outperform rule-based ones.

The confusion matrix in Figure 1 shows that the rule-based system *RB+* has some difficulties in the prediction of critical class (119 are misclassified

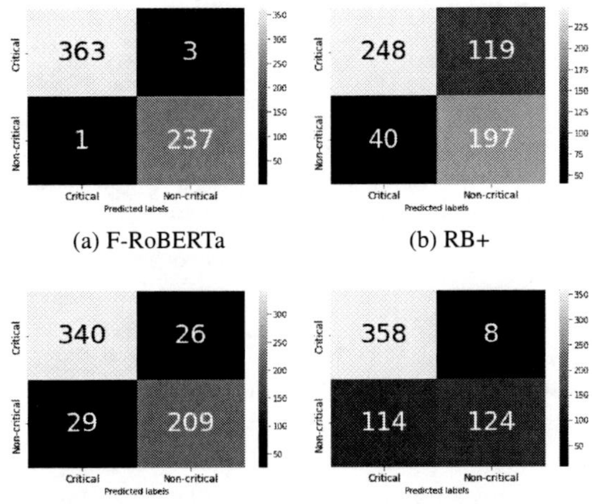

(a) F-RoBERTa (b) RB+

(c) CNN (d) LR

Figure 1: Confusion matrix of the methods

among 366 critical citation contexts). To improve the quality of the *RB+* system, we need to add more rules to identify critical citation contexts. For instance, we could analyze in depth the grammar or cue words/phrases to define more patterns for critical citation contexts. We could also analyze the concept "to question" of critical citation context that has not been taken into account by our rule-based system *RB+* yet.

If we take a look at confusion matrix of *LR* and *CNN* systems in Figure 1d and Figure 1c respectively, the number of misclassified non-critical examples is greater than the number of misclassified critical ones. It could be explained by imbalanced training set. Indeed, critical class represents around 60% of the training set. Being aware of imbalanced training set, we might enhance *CNN* and *LR* performances by assigning class weights while training. However, the *CNN* model does not exhibits a strong bias towards a particular class, so it is likely that a class weighting strategy would have a marginal impact on the performance.

F-RoBERTa (Figure 1a) predicts well non-critical examples, only 1 non-critical and 3 critical examples are misclassified. This could be explained by the class weights' assignment while training *F-RoBERTa* in order to deal with class imbalance. To go further, we analysed these 4 misclassified examples. One of them is *"It is based on modal logic and owes much to the work of Blackburn 1994."* has been classified critical while it should not. If we check out the linguistic aspect of the citation context above, the use of the

[2]We tested RoBERTa model without/with class weights. We reported in this paper the best results obtained with RobERTa with class weights assignment (F-RoBERTa)

Approach	Method	Accuracy (%)	Precision (%)	Recall (%)	F1-score (%)
Rule-based	RB	73.50	86.31	67.02	75.46
	RB+	74.33	86.30	68.66	76.47
Machine Learning	LR	80.00	75.84	97.81	85.44
	CNN	91.00	88.93	87.81	88.37
	F-RoBERTa	**98.84**	**98.73**	**98.31**	**98.52**

Table 3: Evaluation results of experimented methods

word *"owes"* may reflect critical citation aspect. But, we still can argue if *"owes"* here did not be used to criticize the cited paper, it seems like an incomplete context. In this case, we might need more investigation of corpus. The misclassified critical citation contexts are reported in Table 4. Such miss-classification by *F-RoBERTa* could be explained by the existence of positive and negative words in the same citation context. For example in *Doc_2*, *"perform very well"* is positive and *"dramatically fails"* is negative. To go further, we will use attention mechanism to determine relevant words participating in the prediction.

Critical citation contexts
Doc_1: The morphological processing in PairClass (Minnen et al., 2001) is more sophisticated than in Turney (2006).
Doc_2: In particular, we showed that using a general purpose machine translation (MT) system such as SYSTRAN, or a general purpose parallel corpus - both of which perform very well for news stories (Peters, 2003) - dramatically fails in the medical domain.
Doc_3: In particular, these problems affect the processing of predicate argument structures annotated in PropBank (Kingsbury and Palmer, 2002) or FrameNet (Fillmore, 1982).

Table 4: Misclassified critical examples by *F-RoBERTa*

5 Conclusion and Future work

In this paper, we were interested in identifying critical citation contexts in scientific papers. We proposed and tested five methods for citation context classification into critical/non-critical labels. The methods *RB* and *RB+* were rule-based. The three others, *LR*, *CNN* and *F-RoBERTa*, were machine learning based. We also built a corpus to evaluate and compare these methods. Our task-specific corpus was composed of 2643 citation contexts labeled as being critical or non-critical.

Machine learning based systems outperformed rule-based ones. The best system *F-RoBERTa* gave 98.84% of accuracy and 98.52% of F1-score. The performances could be explained by the use of transfer learning in *F-RoBERTa*. Class weight assignment while training might also explain the good accuracy of *F-RoBERTa*'s performance compared to other systems, since our training set was imbalanced.

Some improvements can be made to the proposed systems. In particular, we will assign class weights while model training to solve imbalanced datasets. Moreover, we could operate the data itself (and not the model) to balance the corpus by applying sampling methods either oversampling or undersampling. Dealing with scientific documents, It could be crucial to train our best system *F-RoBERTa*, initially trained on standard corpora, on scientific texts by using for example SciBERT embeddings (Beltagy et al., 2019). Another perspective consists on expanding corpus. To go further, we would extend this work of identifying critical citation contexts in NLP field and study field portability. Indeed, we would identify critical citations in other fields, such as biology or medicine.

Acknowledgments

This work has been undertaken within the *NanoBubbles* project which has received Synergy grant funding from the European Research Council (ERC), within the European Union's Horizon 2020 program, grant agreement no. 951393. It has also been partially supported by MIAI@Grenoble Alpes (ANR-19-P3IA-0003).

References

Alejandro M Aragón. 2013. A measure for the impact of research. *Scientific reports*, 3(1):1–5.

Awais Athar. 2011. Sentiment analysis of citations using sentence structure-based features. In *Proceedings of the ACL 2011 Student Session*, pages 81–87,

Portland, OR, USA. Association for Computational Linguistics.

Karla Fernanda F. C Avanço. 2020. *Typologie des citations négatives dans les publications scientifiques.*

Khadidja Bakhti, Zhendong Niu, Abdallah Yousif, and Ally Nyamawe. 2018. *Citation Function Classification Based on Ontologies and Convolutional Neural Networks*, pages 105–115.

Iz Beltagy, Kyle Lo, and Arman Cohan. 2019. Scibert: Pretrained language model for scientific text. In *EMNLP*.

Frederique Bordignon. 2022. Critical citations in knowledge construction and citation analysis: from paradox to definition. *Scientometrics*, 127(2):959–972.

Cailing Dong and Ulrich Schäfer. 2011. Ensemble-style self-training on citation classification. In *Proceedings of 5th International Joint Conference on Natural Language Processing*, pages 623–631, Chiang Mai, Thailand. Asian Federation of Natural Language Processing.

Mark Garzone and Robert E. Mercer. 2000. Towards an automated citation classifier. In *Advances in Artificial Intelligence*, pages 337–346, Berlin, Heidelberg. Springer Berlin Heidelberg.

Myriam Hernández and José M. Gómez. 2015. Concit-corpus: Context citation analysis to learn function, polarity and influence.

Charles Jochim and Hinrich Schütze. 2012. Towards a generic and flexible citation classifier based on a faceted classification scheme. In *Proceedings of COLING 2012*, pages 1343–1358, Mumbai, India. The COLING 2012 Organizing Committee.

David Jurgens, Srijan Kumar, Raine Hoover, Dan McFarland, and Dan Jurafsky. 2018. Measuring the Evolution of a Scientific Field through Citation Frames. *Transactions of the Association for Computational Linguistics*, 6:391–406.

David Jurgens, Srijan Kumar, Raine Hoover, Daniel A. McFarland, and Dan Jurafsky. 2016. Citation classification for behavioral analysis of a scientific field. *CoRR*, abs/1609.00435.

Musarat Karim, Malik Muhammad Saad Missen, Muhammad Umer, Saima Sadiq, Abdullah Mohamed, and Imran Ashraf. 2022. Citation context analysis using combined feature embedding and deep convolutional neural network model. *Applied Sciences*, 12(6).

Haixia Liu. 2017. Sentiment analysis of citations using word2vec. *CoRR*, abs/1704.00177.

Hidetsugu Nanba, Noriko Kando, and Manabu Okumura. 2000. Classification of research papers using citation links and citation types: Towards automatic review article generation. *Advances in Classification Research Online*, 11(1):117–134.

Josh Nicholson, Milo Mordaunt, Patrice Lopez, Ashish Uppala, Dominic Rosati, Neves Rodrigues, Peter Grabitz, and Sean Rife. 2021. Scite: A smart citation index that displays the context of citations and classifies their intent using deep learning. *Quantitative Science Studies*, 2:1–38.

Son Bao Pham and Achim Hoffmann. 2003. A new approach for scientific citation classification using cue phrases. In *Australasian Joint Conference on Artificial Intelligence*, pages 759–771. Springer.

David Pride, Petr Knoth, and Jozef Harag. 2019. Act: An annotation platform for citation typing at scale. In *2019 ACM/IEEE Joint Conference on Digital Libraries (JCDL)*, pages 329–330.

Hassan Raza, M. Faizan, Ahsan Hamza, Ahmed Mushtaq, and Naeem Akhtar. 2019. Scientific text sentiment analysis using machine learning techniques. *International Journal of Advanced Computer Science and Applications*, 10(12).

Simone Teufel, Advaith Siddharthan, and Dan Tidhar. 2006. Automatic classification of citation function. In *Proceedings of the 2006 Conference on Empirical Methods in Natural Language Processing*, pages 103–110, Sydney, Australia. Association for Computational Linguistics.

Ruan Visser and Marcel Dunaiski. 2022. Sentiment and intent classification of in-text citations using bert. EasyChair Preprint no. 7593.

Wenhao Yu, Mengxia Yu, Tong Zhao, and Meng Jiang. 2020. Identifying referential intention with heterogeneous contexts. pages 962–972.

Incorporating the Rhetoric of Scientific Language into Sentence Embeddings using Phrase-guided Distant Supervision and Metric Learning

Kaito Sugimoto[1]
[1]The University of Tokyo
Tokyo, Japan
kaito_sugimoto@is.s.u-tokyo.ac.jp

Akiko Aizawa[2,1]
[2]National Institute of Informatics
Tokyo, Japan
aizawa@nii.ac.jp

Abstract

Communicative functions are an important rhetorical feature of scientific writing. Sentence embeddings that contain such features are highly valuable for the argumentative analysis of scientific documents, with applications in document alignment, recommendation, and academic writing assistance. Moreover, embeddings can provide a possible solution to the open-set problem, where models need to generalize to new communicative functions unseen at training time. However, existing sentence representation models are not suited for detecting functional similarity since they only consider lexical or semantic similarities. To remedy this, we propose a combined approach of distant supervision and metric learning to make a representation model more aware of the functional part of a sentence. We first leverage an existing academic phrase database to label sentences automatically with their functions. Then, we train an embedding model to capture similarities and dissimilarities from a rhetorical perspective. The experimental results demonstrate that the embeddings obtained from our model are more advantageous than existing models when retrieving functionally similar sentences. We also provide an extensive analysis of the performance differences between five metric learning objectives, revealing that traditional methods (e.g., softmax cross-entropy loss and triplet loss) outperform state-of-the-art techniques.[1]

1 Introduction

Scientific articles explain new ideas or discoveries and attempt to convince readers of their validity and importance. A key characteristic that distinguishes these articles from other texts is their specific rhetorical structures. The most well-known example is the main section of a paper, organized

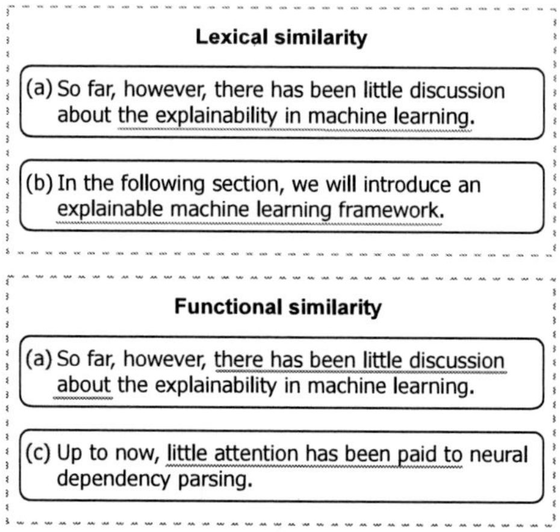

Figure 1: The upper panel shows an example of lexically similar sentences. Sentence (a) conveys the communicative function of "showing lack of previous work", whereas (b) conveys a different function, "showing the outline of the paper". In contrast, the lower panel shows a pair of functionally similar sentences.

as Introduction, Methods, Results, and Discussion. Several attempts have also been made to identify argumentative roles within a section (Swales, 1990; Teufel et al., 1999; Lauscher et al., 2018). For example, a sentence in a paper beginning with "little attention has been paid to ..." shows the background of the research, or more specifically, the lack of previous research on that topic. In our work, we collectively refer to this rhetorical aspect of scientific writing as a *communicative function*, following Kanoksilapatham (2005).

Although previous studies have mainly focused on classifying sentences into a predefined set of communicative-function labels (Hirohata et al., 2008; Fisas et al., 2015; Cohan et al., 2019; Brack et al., 2022), we shift the focus to developing a sentence representation model for communicative functions. In other words, we consider sentence embeddings that can handle **functional similarity**, as opposed to lexical or semantic similarities

[1]Our code, data and trained models are publicly available at https://github.com/kaisugi/rhetorical_aspect_embeddings

Proceedings of the Third Workshop on Scholarly Document Processing, pages 54–68
October 12–17, 2022.

(Figure 1). There are two main reasons to prefer this approach: (i) The embedding model serves as an off-the-shelf tool to discover the most similar sentences to a query from a rhetorical perspective, which is beneficial for practical applications, including scientific document alignment (Zhou et al., 2020) and aspect-based scientific paper recommendation (Kobayashi et al., 2018; Chan et al., 2018). Such models can also contribute to writing assistance systems (Liu et al., 2016; Shioda et al., 2017) by suggesting sentences that have the same rhetorical feature as a query. (ii) Embeddings obtained from neural networks have shown the generalization ability to deal with the cases in which training and test sets do not share the same labels (i.e., open-set settings) (Musgrave et al., 2020; Geng et al., 2021). We argue that models for scholarly document processing (SDP) should perform well in open-set settings and generalize to unseen communicative functions, because there is no prepared list that covers all functional categories used in scientific articles.

In this paper, we introduce a new method for training a sentence representation model to capture functional similarity. We first address the scarcity of fine-grained datasets with communicative-function labels. Inspired by the success of distant supervision on low-resource natural language processing (Hedderich et al., 2021), we retrieve sentences from the Semantic Scholar Open Research Corpus (S2ORC) (Lo et al., 2020) and annotate labels based on simple text matching using an academic phrase dictionary, Academic Phrasebank (Davis and Morley, 2018). The resulting dataset, dubbed the Communicative-Function-labeled Semantic Scholar Sentence Dataset (CFS3), contains 100,016 sentences, classified into 77 function labels. We use this dataset to fine-tune SciBERT (Beltagy et al., 2019) with a metric learning loss so that functionally similar sentences come close together and dissimilar sentences are separated. As several recent studies (Musgrave et al., 2020; Boudiaf et al., 2020; Coria et al., 2020) have claimed that the performance of conventional metric learning losses (e.g., softmax cross-entropy loss) is comparable to or even better than that of state-of-the-art methods (e.g., ArcFace loss (Deng et al., 2019)), we also investigate whether these findings are valid in our settings.

We evaluate the trained model, named SCITORICSBERT[2], on sentence retrieval tasks designed to assess the rhetorical aspects of sentence representations. The experimental results show that our model is more suitable for retrieving functionally similar sentences than existing sentence representation models. We also observe that, in most cases, softmax cross-entropy loss yields better performance than other state-of-the-art methods. Furthermore, we train the same model using a limited number of communicative-function labels to better understand the generalizability of the trained models in open-set settings. The results reveal that the performance gain of conventional methods becomes even larger when the number of labels used for training becomes smaller.

Our contributions are as follows:

- We release CFS3, a distantly-labeled sentence dataset that includes 100K+ samples with 77 communicative-function labels.
- We present sentence embeddings that focus on the functional part of a sentence. Our model outperforms existing models in retrieving functionally similar sentences.
- We empirically demonstrate that the state-of-the-art metric learning methods do not improve performance on learning task-specific sentence embeddings.

2 Related Work

2.1 Argumentative Analysis of Scientific Texts

There is a large body of literature on assessing the argumentative status of scientific articles. Some notable schemes include move analysis (Swales, 1990) and argumentative zoning (Teufel et al., 1999). Another area of study is the annotation of communicative-function labels in abstracts using structured abstracts (Dernoncourt and Lee, 2017) or through crowdsourcing (Cohan et al., 2019; Huang et al., 2020).

Machine learning algorithms, such as conditional random fields (Hirohata et al., 2008), logistic regression, and support vector machines (Fisas et al., 2015), have been used to automatically classify sentences into function labels. Recently, SciBERT, a pre-trained language model on scientific texts, has pushed the limits of the classification accuracy (Cohan et al., 2019; Huang et al., 2020).

[2]The term SCITORICS was coined by Lauscher et al. (2018) to represent the rhetorical aspects of scientific writing.

2.2 Sentence Representation Models

Work on sentence embeddings can be divided into unsupervised and supervised methods. Conventional unsupervised models produce sentence embeddings by averaging each word or subword embedding from static or contextualized language models. This approach allows us to assess the lexical similarity of two sentences based on the distributional hypothesis (Harris, 1954). Recent supervised models trained on natural language inference (NLI) datasets (Conneau et al., 2017; Reimers and Gurevych, 2019; Gao et al., 2021) have shown significant improvements in semantic textual similarity (STS) tasks. These models can compute the semantic similarity of two sentences more faithfully than unsupervised models.

To the best of our knowledge, Iwatsuki et al. (2022) is the only study that investigated sentence representations for functional similarity. Their approach assigns different weights to word embeddings in the functional and non-functional parts of a sentence, whereas our proposed model eliminates the need to identify the functional part in advance.

2.3 Metric Learning

Metric learning (Kaya and Bilge, 2019) aims to learn a new mapping function from samples to vectors to reduce the distance between similar samples while increasing the distance between dissimilar samples. This training procedure is also called contrastive learning when the training data are annotated with pairwise labels (positive and negative pairs denote similar and dissimilar samples, respectively).

Triplet loss (or triplet margin loss) is one of the most studied learning methods. Neural networks associated with a triplet loss are known as "triplet networks", and they have been used in several applications, such as face recognition (Schroff et al., 2015), person re-identification (Hermans et al., 2017), sentence-level similarity learning (Ein Dor et al., 2018; Reimers and Gurevych, 2019), and document-level similarity learning (Cohan et al., 2020). Another classical approach is softmax cross-entropy loss. Although this loss is typically chosen for classification tasks, several studies have used it to train embedding models (Sun et al., 2014; Boudiaf et al., 2020).

Recently, much research has been devoted to designing loss functions to learn effective visual representations (Musgrave et al., 2020). These loss functions have been successfully applied to learning textual information, such as sentences (Yan et al., 2021; Giorgi et al., 2021; Kim et al., 2021; Gao et al., 2021), dialogues (Liu et al., 2021a), social media behaviors (Andrews and Bishop, 2019), and biomedical entities (Liu et al., 2021b). However, some studies have also shown that state-of-the-art loss functions do not necessarily outperform classical methods (Musgrave et al., 2020; Boudiaf et al., 2020; Coria et al., 2020).

3 Methods

Our approach can be roughly divided into two parts: phrase-guided distant supervision (Sections 3.1 and 3.2) and metric learning (Section 3.3), as illustrated in Figure 2.

3.1 Acquisition of Labeled N-gram List

Academic Phrasebank[3] is an online public database of generic academic phrases (Davis and Morley, 2018). Based on the observation that specific (formulaic) phrases serve as key markers for communicative functions (Swales, 1990), the database identifies 80 functions according to the main sections of a paper and samples approximately 20 phrases for each.

Our motivation is to utilize Academic Phrasebank for annotating sentences with communicative functions. Prior research has also leveraged this database to label sentences (Iwatsuki and Aizawa, 2021). However, their study relied on manual phrase extraction and annotation to maintain the quality of the labeling process. In contrast, we pursue a fully automated approach to create a larger, finer-grained dataset.

As the number of phrases in Academic Phrasebank is relatively small, we first perform data augmentation on the entire database using PPDB 2.0 (Pavlick et al., 2015) by randomly paraphrasing one noun, adjective, or adverb in a phrase. This results in a total of 30,505 phrases, which is approximately 20 times larger than the original.

The augmented phrases themselves are unsuitable for annotating sentences, because most of them are too lengthy to include specific content words that are irrelevant to communicative functions (e.g., "metabolism" in the phrase "X plays a vital role in the metabolism of ..."). We therefore extract every n-gram from the phrases. In

[3] https://www.phrasebank.manchester.ac.uk/

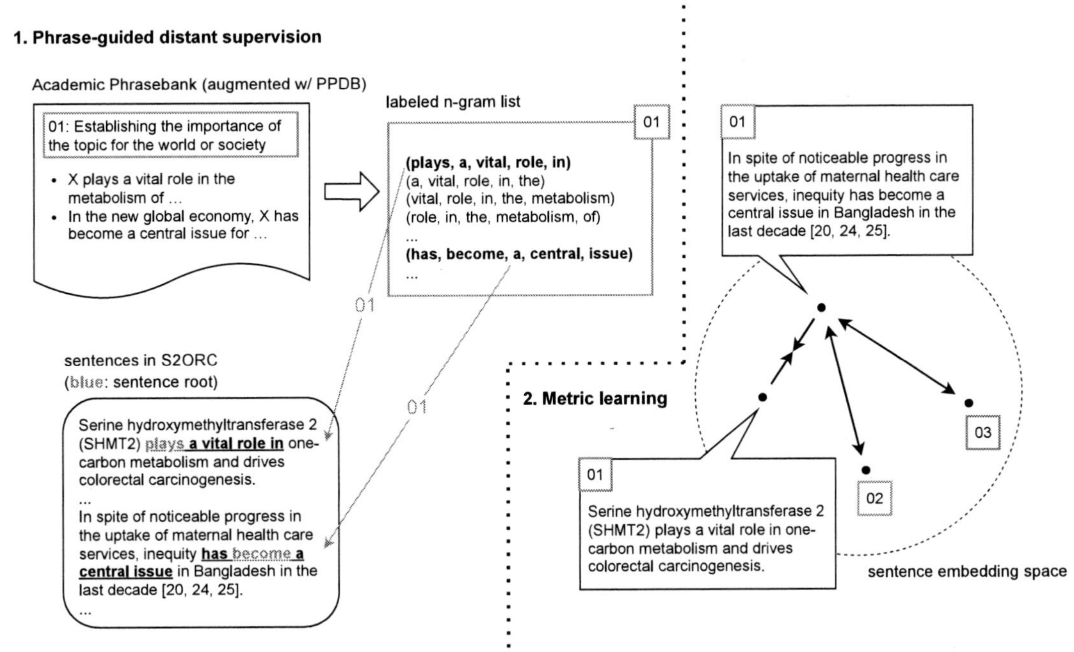

Figure 2: Overview of a combined approach of phrase-guided distant supervision and metric learning.

this study, we set $n = 5$.[4] We exclude from the list the lemmatized n-grams that have more than one label. As a result, we obtain 68,242 pairs of n-grams and their corresponding function labels. Although some of the n-grams (e.g., "vital role in the metabolism") still include content words, we find that they are negligible because such n-grams rarely retrieve sentences in Section 3.2.

3.2 Automatic Annotation of Sentences

We use the S2ORC (Lo et al., 2020) dataset to draw example sentences that contain specific n-grams. First, we randomly sample approximately 1M papers from S2ORC. Some are excluded during the preprocessing phase (see Appendix A for details). Then, we split each paper's abstract and body text into sentences using the NLTK tokenizer (Bird et al., 2009). This process produces approximately 19M sentences. Subsequently, for each labeled n-grams in Section 3.1, we inherit the same label for a sentence that satisfies the following constraints: (i) the sentence includes the n-gram, and (ii) the n-gram includes a root word in the dependency tree. The latter condition is derived from the observation that the functional part of a sentence often contains a sentence root (Iwatsuki et al., 2022). We use the spaCy (Honnibal et al., 2020) dependency parser to confirm whether the n-gram includes the root. This automatic annotation provides us with 100,016 labeled sentences.

Of the 80 function classes in Academic Phrasebank, three classes are assigned to no sentence; thus, the sentences are categorized into 77 classes. We name our dataset the Communicative-Function-labeled Semantic Scholar Sentence Dataset (CFS3). Table 1 contains randomly selected samples from CFS3. We find that the automatically-annotated sentences have expected function labels overall, except that, in the third sentence, the phrase "is interesting to note that" is not necessarily connected to the label "restating the result or one of several results", causing an annotation error.

3.3 Training with Metric Learning Loss

We train our embedding model using a metric learning framework to create a vector space in which sentences with similar functions have smaller distances, and those with different functions have longer ones. This trained model is referred to as SCITORICSBERT.

We begin from the pre-trained checkpoint of SciBERT (Beltagy et al., 2019) and take 768-dimensional embeddings from the `[CLS]` token

[4] We empirically determine that $n = 5$ is optimal. As we observe, for the case of $n < 5$, n-grams (e.g., "has been shown to") tend to be too generic to convey a specific communicative function. For the case of $n > 5$, on the other hand, n-grams often fail to retrieve any sentence.

in the last layer as the output. Then, we train the model with one of the five metric learning objectives mentioned below (the first two losses are conventional methods, while the rest are state-of-the-art methods that have been initially introduced in computer vision but also applied to natural language processing):

Softmax Cross-entropy Loss Let $\mathbf{x}_i \in \mathbb{R}^d$ denotes the output embeddings of the i-th sample, which belongs to the y_i-th communicative-function label ($1 \leq y_i \leq n$). Here, d is set to 768. We then minimize the following loss function:

$$\mathcal{L}_1 = -\frac{1}{N}\sum_{i=1}^{N} \log \frac{\exp(\mathbf{W}_{y_i}^\top \mathbf{x}_i + b_{y_i})}{\sum_{j=1}^{n} \exp(\mathbf{W}_j^\top \mathbf{x}_i + b_j)}, \tag{1}$$

where $\mathbf{W}_j$ is the j-th column vector of the linear matrix, $\mathbf{W} \in \mathbb{R}^{d \times n}$, and b_j is the j-th element of the bias term, $\mathbf{b} \in \mathbb{R}^n$. N denotes the batch size.

Triplet Loss Triplets $\{a_i, p_i, n_i\}_{i=1}^N$ are collected from a training batch, provided that p_i has the same label as a_i, and that n_i has a different label.[5] We denote by $\mathbf{x}_i^a, \mathbf{x}_i^p, \mathbf{x}_i^n \in \mathbb{R}^d$ the corresponding model outputs. Triplet loss is formulated as follows:

$$\mathcal{L}_2 = \frac{1}{K}\sum_{i=1}^{N} \max\left(\|\mathbf{x}_i^a - \mathbf{x}_i^p\|_2 - \|\mathbf{x}_i^a - \mathbf{x}_i^n\|_2 + m, 0\right), \tag{2}$$

where margin m denotes a hyperparameter, and K denotes the number of cases in which $\|\mathbf{x}_i^a - \mathbf{x}_i^p\|_2 - \|\mathbf{x}_i^a - \mathbf{x}_i^n\|_2 + m > 0$.

ArcFace Loss ArcFace loss (or additive angular margin loss) (Deng et al., 2019; Andrews and Bishop, 2019) modifies the softmax cross-entropy loss to make the learned embeddings more discriminative between classes.

We define $\mathbf{x}_i \in \mathbb{R}^d$ and $\mathbf{W}_j \in \mathbb{R}^d$ ($1 \leq j \leq n$), which is similar to softmax cross-entropy loss. Let $\theta_j = \arccos\left(\frac{\mathbf{W}_j^\top \mathbf{x}_i}{\|\mathbf{W}_j\|_2 \|\mathbf{x}_i\|_2}\right)$ be the angle between the output vector and the j-th column vector of the weight matrix. Then, ArcFace loss is defined as follows:

$$\mathcal{L}_3 = -\frac{1}{N}\sum_{i=1}^{N} \log \frac{\exp(s \cos \theta'_{y_j})}{\sum_{j=1}^{n} \exp(s \cos \theta'_j)}, \quad \text{s.t. } \theta'_j = \begin{cases} \theta_j + m & (j = y_i) \\ \theta_j & (j \neq y_i) \end{cases}, \tag{3}$$

where angular margin m and scale s are hyperparameters.

MS Loss Multi-similarity (MS) loss (Wang et al., 2019; Liu et al., 2021b) considers multiple types of similarities for a pair, aiming to generalize previous loss functions.

Let $\mathbf{S} \in \mathbb{R}^{N \times N}$ be a similarity matrix whose

Examples
Optical Flow: The estimation of optical flow is a classic problem in computer vision [18, 24] . **(02: Establishing the importance of the topic for the discipline)**
Initial and final nutrient concentrations, and significance between time points within each treatment group (t-test, p < 0.05) are shown in Figure 1 . **(48: Referring to data in a table or chart)**
It is interesting to note that one obtains Re J = 0 if cos ŏ3b1 e = 0 and U 0 is tri-bimaximal (t a = 1, **(63: Restating the result or one of several results)**
Method: A total of 104 participants (44 SZ patients and 60 age-and gender-matched healthy controls (HC)) were recruited for this study. **(36: Describing the characteristics of the sample)**
It has been suggested that dietary Zn is mostly absorbed in the duodenum, ileum, and jejunum by active transport through ZIP4 [48] . **(22: Previous research: what has been established or proposed)**
It has been suggested that bacteria may use hemolysin to obtain nutrients from the host cells (e.g., irons released from lysed red blood cells) [35] . **(22: Previous research: what has been established or proposed)**
This finding is consistent with other analyses, indicating that Tu-138 cells are more sensitive to E2F-1-induced apoptosis than are Tu-167 cells. **(65: Comparing the result: supporting previous findings)**
The modified QPM and the Delta method were used to analyse the data for each calendar month. **(47: Referring back to the research aims or procedures)**
It has been argued that the purposeful inclusion of social work values in social work research is one of its distinguishing features (Shaw et al., 2006) . **(22: Previous research: what has been established or proposed)**
Statistical analysis was performed using unpaired two-tailed Student's t-test where *P<0.05; **P<0.01. **(45: Describing the process: statistical procedures)**

Table 1: Ten randomly-selected examples from the CFS3 dataset. Function labels and corresponding n-grams are shown in bold and underlined, respectively.

[5] In our work, all possible triplets are used for training without negative sampling.

Datasets		#sentences	#labels
CF-labeled	Introduction	773	11
	Methods	468	6
	Results	521	6
	Discussion	781	9
CSAbstruct		1,349	5
PubMed-RCT		30,135	5

Table 2: Dataset statistics.

(i,j)-th element satisfies $\mathbf{S}_{ij} = \frac{\mathbf{x}_i^\top \mathbf{x}_j}{\|\mathbf{x}_i\|_2 \|\mathbf{x}_j\|_2}$, where $\mathbf{x}_i$ is the i-th model output in a N-sized training batch.

We regard a pair of two in-batch samples with the same label to be positive, and otherwise negative. We denote the sets of indices of positive and negative pairs by $\mathcal{P}$ and $\mathcal{N}$, respectively. The training objective is formulated as follows:

$$\mathcal{L}_4 = \frac{1}{N}\sum_{i=1}^{N}\left\{\frac{1}{\alpha}\log\left[1 + \sum_{\substack{j=1,\\(i,j)\in\mathcal{P}}}^{N} \exp(-\alpha(\mathbf{S}_{ij} - \lambda))\right] + \frac{1}{\beta}\log\left[1 + \sum_{\substack{j=1,\\(i,j)\in\mathcal{N}}}^{N} \exp(\beta(\mathbf{S}_{ij} - \lambda))\right]\right\}, \tag{4}$$

where α, β, and λ are hyperparameters.

NT-Xent Loss Normalized temperature-scaled cross-entropy (NT-Xent) loss (Chen et al., 2020; Giorgi et al., 2021) takes a form similar to softmax cross-entropy loss, but it differs in that it maximizes the similarity of a positive pair.

We define $\mathbf{S} \in \mathbb{R}^{N\times N}, \mathcal{P}, \mathcal{N}$ in the same manner as MS loss. NT-Xent loss can be expressed as follows:

$$\mathcal{L}_5 = -\frac{1}{|\mathcal{P}|}\sum_{(i,j)\in\mathcal{P}} \log \frac{\exp(\mathbf{S}_{ij}/T)}{\exp(\mathbf{S}_{ij}/T) + \sum_{\substack{k=1,\\(i,k)\in\mathcal{N}}}^{N} \exp(\mathbf{S}_{ik}/T)}, \tag{5}$$

where temperature T is a hyperparameter.

4 Experiments

4.1 Settings

Task Description We conduct sentence retrieval tasks on communicative-function labeled datasets to see how successfully SCITORICSBERT contains rhetorical features. This task begins by converting all the sentences in a dataset into embeddings using a given representation model. We select one sentence as a query and regard the others as references. We then retrieve the nearest neighbors of the query and evaluate whether the extracted sentences have the same label as the query.[6] This procedure is repeated for the entire dataset, and the performance scores are averaged.

Evaluation Datasets We employ three datasets: **the CF-labeled sentence dataset** (Iwatsuki and Aizawa, 2021), **CSAbstruct** (Cohan et al., 2019), and **PubMed-RCT** (Dernoncourt and Lee, 2017). The CF-labeled sentence dataset is manually annotated with communicative-function labels for each section of papers from multiple disciplines. The other two datasets collect sentences from the abstracts of the computer science and biomedical domains, respectively. We report the dataset statistics in Table 2. Note that with CSAbstruct and PubMed-RCT, sentences in scientific abstracts are classified into one of the five categories {BACKGROUND, OBJECTIVE, METHOD, RESULT, CONCLUSION (OTHER)}, the granularity of which is much coarser than that of the CF-labeled sentence dataset (32 labels total).

Evaluation Metrics We use two evaluation metrics: precision at 1 (P@1) and mean average precision at R (MAP@R) (Musgrave et al., 2020). Whereas P@1 focuses on the top retrieval result, MAP@R measures the overall retrieval quality.[7] For SCITORICSBERT, we report the average results from five trained models with different random seeds.

Baselines We compare SCITORICSBERT with unsupervised language models, including average GloVe embeddings (Pennington et al., 2014), BERT (Devlin et al., 2019), and RoBERTa (Liu et al., 2019). Other baselines include domain-specific language models, such as SciBERT (Beltagy et al., 2019) and PubMedBERT (Gu et al., 2020).[8] We also compare SCITORICSBERT with SRoBERTa (Reimers and Gurevych, 2019) and (supervised) SimCSE-RoBERTa (Gao et al., 2021), which are both fine-tuned RoBERTa models on NLI datasets.

Training Details To train SCITORICSBERT, we split our CFS3 dataset into a training and validation set at a ratio of 4:1. As the dataset is imbalanced,

[6] All the embeddings are L2 normalized beforehand.

[7] R denotes the total number of references with the same label as the query.

[8] Regarding transformer-based unsupervised models, we take the average of their last hidden layers.

Model	Introduction		Methods		Results		Discussion		Avg.	
	P@1	MAP	P@1	MAP	P@1	MAP	P@1	MAP	P@1	MAP
GloVe avg.	.391	.073	.462	.089	.484	.125	.325	.058	.415	.086
$BERT_{base}$ avg.	.523	.099	.434	.099	.511	.140	.361	.063	.457	.100
$RoBERTa_{base}$ avg.	.507	.106	.451	.102	.557	.152	.392	.068	.477	.107
SciBERT avg.	<u>.604</u>	.151	<u>.526</u>	<u>.117</u>	<u>.612</u>	.156	<u>.483</u>	<u>.093</u>	<u>.556</u>	<u>.129</u>
PubMedBERT avg.	.547	.134	.521	.108	.570	.140	.435	.078	.518	.115
$SRoBERTa_{base}$	.422	.099	.325	.075	.501	.148	.335	.072	.396	.099
$SimCSE\text{-}RoBERTa_{base}$	.551	<u>.165</u>	.429	.095	.511	<u>.162</u>	.403	.088	.474	.128
SciToricsBERT (Softmax loss)	.857	**.537**	.765	.375	**.866**	**.501**	**.741**	**.334**	**.807**	**.437**
SciToricsBERT (Triplet loss)	**.858**	.514	**.776**	.368	.855	.494	.734	.329	.806	.426
SciToricsBERT (ArcFace loss)	.840	.513	.741	.378	.845	.462	.708	.301	.783	.414
SciToricsBERT (MS loss)	.829	.485	.721	.354	.832	.475	.684	.314	.767	.407
SciToricsBERT (NT-Xent loss)	.839	.511	.741	**.385**	.838	.494	.708	.312	.781	.425

Table 3: Precision@1 and MAP@R scores for sentence retrieval tasks on the CF-labeled sentence dataset. The best-performing scores are highlighted in bold. The underlined scores are the highest among the baseline scores.

Model	CS		PubMed	
	P@1	MAP	P@1	MAP
GloVe avg.	.445	.124	.627	.167
BERT avg.	.553	.166	.681	.196
RoBERTa avg.	.523	.159	.681	.185
SciBERT avg.	<u>.563</u>	.169	<u>.700</u>	.204
PubMedBERT avg.	.553	<u>.169</u>	.694	<u>.213</u>
SRoBERTa	.480	.136	.566	.143
SimCSE-RoBERTa	.529	.164	.646	.187
SciToricsBERT				
(Softmax loss)	**.616**	**.226**	**.761**	**.325**
(Triplet loss)	.599	.214	.760	.324
(ArcFace loss)	.576	.205	.748	.307
(MS loss)	.583	.191	.739	.300
(NT-Xent loss)	.591	.216	.752	.324

Table 4: Precision@1 and MAP@R scores in sentence retrieval tasks on CSAbstruct and PubMed-RCT.

we follow stratified random sampling to ensure that both sets have similar label distributions. We measure the MAP@R score in the validation dataset for each epoch and select the best-performing model. The maximum number of epochs is set to five. See Appendix B for further detailed configurations.

4.2 Overall Results

We present the evaluation results for the CF-labeled sentence dataset in Table 3 and the other two datasets in Table 4.

Among the baseline models, SciBERT and PubMedBERT achieve the highest average scores. These domain-specific models consistently outperform BERT, indicating that pre-training on scientific texts provides *distributional functions* (i.e., words that occur in similar contexts have similar functions). As for supervised models, both SRoBERTa and SimCSE-RoBERTa perform poorly, sometimes even worse than RoBERTa. This suggests that semantic similarity does not help compare sentences from a rhetorical perspective.

Turning to our proposed method, we find that SciToricsBERT yields substantial improvements over the baselines in all the datasets. On the CF-labeled sentence dataset, the model achieves approximately 0.25 points gain in P@1 and 0.30 points gain in MAP@R over the best baseline. This result is not surprising because the labels in the CF-labeled sentence dataset are similar to those in our CFS3. More importantly, SciToricsBERT also outperforms on CSAbstruct and PubMed-RCT, although these datasets are generated from abstracts and are thus annotated with more coarse-grained function labels than CFS3.

Regarding the metric learning loss, there is no clear evidence that state-of-the-art methods are more competitive than conventional methods. Although triplet and NT-Xent losses achieve slightly better performance on some subsets of the CF-labeled sentence dataset, softmax cross-entropy loss outperforms all other methods in CSAbstruct and PubMed-RCT.

To illustrate the efficacy of our method, we compare the sentences retrieved by SciBERT and SciToricsBERT on the Introduction subset of the CF-labeled sentence dataset in Table 5. As the examples show, SciToricsBERT successfully suggests similar sentences based on the functional part of the query sentence. Additional examples are presented in Appendices C and D.

Query sentence			The main **question addressed in this paper concerns** whether it is possible to achieve a comparable or even better accuracy using just a small and non-redundant set of subtrees.
(Query function)			(Showing the outline of the paper)
SciBERT avg.		#1	The main challenge is the search problem, which is to find an optimal parse tree among all that can be constructed with any word choice and order from the set of input words.
	✓	#2	Another **issue addressed in this paper is** automatic construction of a lexicon for verbs related to activities and events.
		#3	Thus, the aim of this paper is to find an appropriate level of comparison for the combinatorial properties of music and language, ideally, in a way that is independent of controversies specific to one or the other field.
SciToricsBERT (ours)	✓	#1	The third **issue addressed in this paper concerns** the nature of the category to be formed.
	✓	#2	The **problem addressed in this paper is** how to model and capture temporal contexts and how to enhance NED with this novel asset.
	✓	#3	Another **issue addressed in this paper is** automatic construction of a lexicon for verbs related to activities and events.
Query sentence			Second, **it remains unclear under which circumstances** higher inertia of positive emotions (PE) is maladaptive.
(Query function)			(Showing limitation or lack of past work)
SciBERT avg.		#1	However, the notion of automaticity has been challenged by subsequent studies.
		#2	Consequently, narrowing down which constructs are tied to ego depletion will help in solving the current controversy surrounding the effect.
	✓	#3	Currently, **little is known about how** auditory distraction impacts upon metacognitive regulation of memory responses as captured by the [CITATION] framework.
SciToricsBERT (ours)	✓	#1	However, despite the success of NNLMs on large datasets ([CITATION], [CITATION], [CITATION]), **it remains unclear whether** their advantages transfer to scenarios with extremely limited amounts of data.
	✓	#2	**It remains unclear whether** similar enhancements in creativity can be observed if negatively arousing music is used.
	✓	#3	However, the molecular mechanism of NTP-induced cancer cell death **remains unclear**.

Table 5: Examples of top-3 sentences retrieved by SciBERT and SciToricsBERT. ✓ stands for the same function label as the query. For ease of comparison, we show phrases that appear to accord with the function in bold.

4.3 Generalizability Analysis

We now investigate whether SciToricsBERT generalizes across scientific documents or only memorizes specific phrasal patterns that accord with the communicative functions in our CFS3 dataset. We randomly sample 10, 20, or 40 of the 77 function labels in CFS3, train the model using only those data, and measure the average P@1 and MAP@R scores on the CF-labeled sentence dataset.[9] We hypothesize that models that have good generalizability can successfully retrieve similar sentences when trained on a portion of CFS3.

The results are shown in Figures 3 and 4. We see that all the models show strong performance over the best baseline, even if they are trained with only ten labels. This suggests that SciToricsBERT can, to some extent, handle functional similarity in general. We also observe that P@1 scores keep higher values than MAP@R when training labels are reduced, indicating that the model uses clues to find the most similar sentence, which is easy to learn and generalizes well.

Notably, conventional softmax cross-entropy and triplet losses perform even better than the other methods when the number of training labels decreases. This contradicts our expectation as the other methods have achieved state-of-the-art results on the open-set image recognition tasks, where training and test sets do not share the same labels. One possible explanation is that the number of labels in our CFS3 is too small to train state-of-the-art methods effectively, considering that those

[9] To align the number of training samples, we vary the maximum training epoch in inverse proportion to the number of training labels. We report the average results from five trained models with different training labels and random seeds.

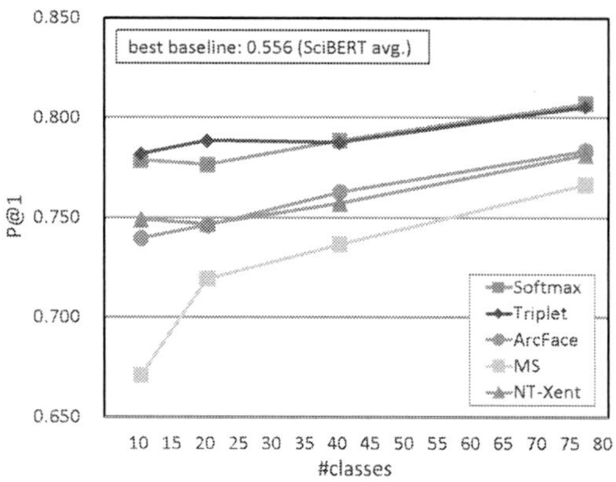

Figure 3: Effect of the number of classes on Precision@1 scores in the CF-labeled sentence dataset.

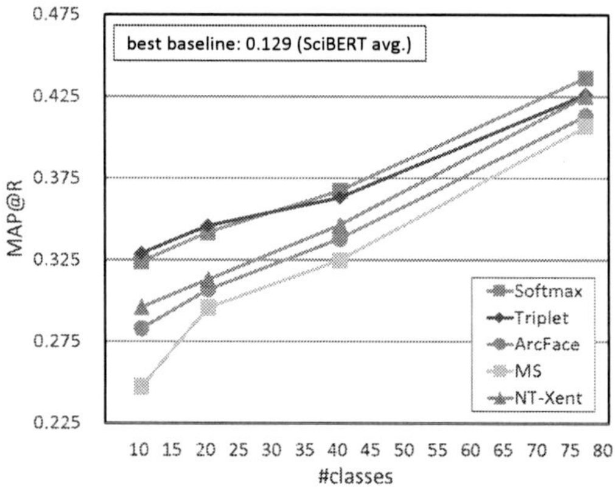

Figure 4: Effect of the number of classes on MAP@R scores in the CF-labeled sentence dataset.

methods are usually trained on a large-scale face recognition dataset containing thousands or millions of labels (e.g., the MS1MV2 dataset (Deng et al., 2019) contains 85K labels).

5 Conclusions and Future Work

This paper presents SCITORICSBERT, a sentence representation model that recognizes the rhetorical aspects of scientific writing. The proposed model achieves more successful results than existing representation models in retrieving functionally similar sentences. We also provide empirical evidence that softmax cross-entropy loss is a strong baseline for learning task-specific sentence embeddings, which has practical implications for other studies on representation learning.

Future work should focus on improving our training methods using hard negatives (e.g., functionally dissimilar but lexically similar samples) and investigating our model in downstream applications.

Acknowledgements

We would like to thank the anonymous reviewers for their valuable comments. We are also grateful to Saku Sugawara for his insightful comments on an earlier version of the manuscript. This work was (partly) supported by JST, AIP Trilateral AI Research, Grant Number JPMJCR20G9, Japan.

References

Nicholas Andrews and Marcus Bishop. 2019. Learning invariant representations of social media users. In *Proceedings of the 2019 Conference on Empirical Methods in Natural Language Processing and the 9th International Joint Conference on Natural Language Processing (EMNLP-IJCNLP)*, pages 1684–1695.

Iz Beltagy, Kyle Lo, and Arman Cohan. 2019. SciBERT: A pretrained language model for scientific text. In *Proceedings of the 2019 Conference on Empirical Methods in Natural Language Processing and the 9th International Joint Conference on Natural Language Processing (EMNLP-IJCNLP)*, pages 3615–3620.

Steven Bird, Ewan Klein, and Edward Loper. 2009. *Natural Language Processing with Python*. O'Reilly.

Malik Boudiaf, Jérôme Rony, Imtiaz Masud Ziko, Eric Granger, Marco Pedersoli, Pablo Piantanida, and Ismail Ben Ayed. 2020. A unifying mutual information view of metric learning: Cross-entropy vs. pairwise losses. In *Computer Vision - ECCV 2020 - 16th European Conference, Glasgow, UK, August 23-28, 2020, Proceedings, Part VI*, volume 12351 of *Lecture Notes in Computer Science*, pages 548–564.

Arthur Brack, Anett Hoppe, Pascal Buschermöhle, and Ralph Ewerth. 2022. Cross-domain multi-task learning for sequential sentence classification in research papers. In *JCDL '22: The ACM/IEEE Joint Conference on Digital Libraries in 2022, Cologne, Germany, June 20 - 24, 2022*, pages 34:1–34:13.

Joel Chan, Joseph Chee Chang, Tom Hope, Dafna Shahaf, and Aniket Kittur. 2018. SOLVENT: A mixed initiative system for finding analogies between research papers. *Proc. ACM Hum. Comput. Interact.*, 2(CSCW):31:1–31:21.

Ting Chen, Simon Kornblith, Mohammad Norouzi, and Geoffrey E. Hinton. 2020. A simple framework for contrastive learning of visual representations. In *Proceedings of the 37th International Conference on Machine Learning, ICML 2020, 13-18 July 2020, Virtual Event*, volume 119 of *Proceedings of Machine Learning Research*, pages 1597–1607.

Arman Cohan, Iz Beltagy, Daniel King, Bhavana Dalvi, and Dan Weld. 2019. Pretrained language models for sequential sentence classification. In *Proceedings of the 2019 Conference on Empirical Methods in Natural Language Processing and the 9th International Joint Conference on Natural Language Processing (EMNLP-IJCNLP)*, pages 3693–3699.

Arman Cohan, Sergey Feldman, Iz Beltagy, Doug Downey, and Daniel Weld. 2020. SPECTER: Document-level representation learning using citation-informed transformers. In *Proceedings of the 58th Annual Meeting of the Association for Computational Linguistics*, pages 2270–2282.

Alexis Conneau, Douwe Kiela, Holger Schwenk, Loïc Barrault, and Antoine Bordes. 2017. Supervised learning of universal sentence representations from natural language inference data. In *Proceedings of the 2017 Conference on Empirical Methods in Natural Language Processing*, pages 670–680.

Juan Manuel Coria, Sahar Ghannay, Sophie Rosset, and Hervé Bredin. 2020. A metric learning approach to misogyny categorization. In *Proceedings of the 5th Workshop on Representation Learning for NLP*, pages 89–94.

Mary Davis and John Morley. 2018. Facilitating learning about academic phraseology: teaching activities for student writers. *Journal of Learning Development in Higher Education*.

Jiankang Deng, Jia Guo, Niannan Xue, and Stefanos Zafeiriou. 2019. Arcface: Additive angular margin loss for deep face recognition. In *IEEE Conference on Computer Vision and Pattern Recognition, CVPR 2019, Long Beach, CA, USA, June 16-20, 2019*, pages 4690–4699.

Franck Dernoncourt and Ji Young Lee. 2017. PubMed 200k RCT: a dataset for sequential sentence classification in medical abstracts. In *Proceedings of the Eighth International Joint Conference on Natural Language Processing (Volume 2: Short Papers)*, pages 308–313.

Jacob Devlin, Ming-Wei Chang, Kenton Lee, and Kristina Toutanova. 2019. BERT: Pre-training of deep bidirectional transformers for language understanding. In *Proceedings of the 2019 Conference of the North American Chapter of the Association for Computational Linguistics: Human Language Technologies, Volume 1 (Long and Short Papers)*, pages 4171–4186.

Liat Ein Dor, Yosi Mass, Alon Halfon, Elad Venezian, Ilya Shnayderman, Ranit Aharonov, and Noam Slonim. 2018. Learning thematic similarity metric from article sections using triplet networks. In *Proceedings of the 56th Annual Meeting of the Association for Computational Linguistics (Volume 2: Short Papers)*, pages 49–54.

Beatriz Fisas, Horacio Saggion, and Francesco Ronzano. 2015. On the discoursive structure of computer graphics research papers. In *Proceedings of The 9th Linguistic Annotation Workshop*, pages 42–51.

Tianyu Gao, Xingcheng Yao, and Danqi Chen. 2021. SimCSE: Simple contrastive learning of sentence embeddings. In *Proceedings of the 2021 Conference on Empirical Methods in Natural Language Processing*, pages 6894–6910.

Chuanxing Geng, Sheng-Jun Huang, and Songcan Chen. 2021. Recent advances in open set recognition: A survey. *IEEE Trans. Pattern Anal. Mach. Intell.*, 43(10):3614–3631.

John Giorgi, Osvald Nitski, Bo Wang, and Gary Bader. 2021. DeCLUTR: Deep contrastive learning for unsupervised textual representations. In *Proceedings of the 59th Annual Meeting of the Association for Computational Linguistics and the 11th International Joint Conference on Natural Language Processing (Volume 1: Long Papers)*, pages 879–895.

Yu Gu, Robert Tinn, Hao Cheng, Michael Lucas, Naoto Usuyama, Xiaodong Liu, Tristan Naumann, Jianfeng Gao, and Hoifung Poon. 2020. Domain-specific language model pretraining for biomedical natural language processing. *CoRR*, abs/2007.15779.

Zellig S Harris. 1954. Distributional structure. *Word*, 10(2-3):146–162.

Michael A. Hedderich, Lukas Lange, Heike Adel, Jannik Strötgen, and Dietrich Klakow. 2021. A survey on recent approaches for natural language processing in low-resource scenarios. In *Proceedings of the 2021 Conference of the North American Chapter of the Association for Computational Linguistics: Human Language Technologies*, pages 2545–2568.

Alexander Hermans, Lucas Beyer, and Bastian Leibe. 2017. In defense of the triplet loss for person reidentification. *CoRR*, abs/1703.07737.

Kenji Hirohata, Naoaki Okazaki, Sophia Ananiadou, and Mitsuru Ishizuka. 2008. Identifying sections in scientific abstracts using conditional random fields. In *Proceedings of the Third International Joint Conference on Natural Language Processing: Volume-I*.

Matthew Honnibal, Ines Montani, Sofie Van Landeghem, and Adriane Boyd. 2020. spaCy: Industrial-strength Natural Language Processing in Python.

Ting-Hao Kenneth Huang, Chieh-Yang Huang, Chien-Kuang Cornelia Ding, Yen-Chia Hsu, and C. Lee Giles. 2020. CODA-19: Using a non-expert crowd to annotate research aspects on 10,000+ abstracts in the COVID-19 open research dataset. In *Proceedings of the 1st Workshop on NLP for COVID-19 at ACL 2020*.

Kenichi Iwatsuki and Akiko Aizawa. 2021. Communicative-function-based sentence classification for construction of an academic formulaic expression database. In *Proceedings of the 16th Conference of the European Chapter of the Association for Computational Linguistics: Main Volume*, pages 3476–3497.

Kenichi Iwatsuki, Florian Boudin, and Akiko Aizawa. 2022. Extraction and evaluation of formulaic expressions used in scholarly papers. *Expert Syst. Appl.*, 187:115840.

Budsaba Kanoksilapatham. 2005. Rhetorical structure of biochemistry research articles. *English for Specific Purposes*, 24(3):269–292.

Mahmut Kaya and Hasan Sakir Bilge. 2019. Deep metric learning: A survey. *Symmetry*, 11(9):1066.

Taeuk Kim, Kang Min Yoo, and Sang-goo Lee. 2021. Self-guided contrastive learning for BERT sentence representations. In *Proceedings of the 59th Annual Meeting of the Association for Computational Linguistics and the 11th International Joint Conference on Natural Language Processing (Volume 1: Long Papers)*, pages 2528–2540.

Diederik P. Kingma and Jimmy Ba. 2015. Adam: A method for stochastic optimization. In *3rd International Conference on Learning Representations, ICLR 2015, San Diego, CA, USA, May 7-9, 2015, Conference Track Proceedings*.

Yuta Kobayashi, Masashi Shimbo, and Yuji Matsumoto. 2018. Citation recommendation using distributed representation of discourse facets in scientific articles. In *Proceedings of the 18th ACM/IEEE on Joint Conference on Digital Libraries, JCDL 2018, Fort Worth, TX, USA, June 03-07, 2018*, pages 243–251.

Anne Lauscher, Goran Glavaš, and Kai Eckert. 2018. ArguminSci: A tool for analyzing argumentation and rhetorical aspects in scientific writing. In *Proceedings of the 5th Workshop on Argument Mining*, pages 22–28.

Mike Lewis, Yinhan Liu, Naman Goyal, Marjan Ghazvininejad, Abdelrahman Mohamed, Omer Levy, Veselin Stoyanov, and Luke Zettlemoyer. 2020. BART: Denoising sequence-to-sequence pre-training for natural language generation, translation, and comprehension. In *Proceedings of the 58th Annual Meeting of the Association for Computational Linguistics*, pages 7871–7880.

Che Liu, Rui Wang, Jinghua Liu, Jian Sun, Fei Huang, and Luo Si. 2021a. DialogueCSE: Dialogue-based contrastive learning of sentence embeddings. In *Proceedings of the 2021 Conference on Empirical Methods in Natural Language Processing*, pages 2396–2406.

Fangyu Liu, Ehsan Shareghi, Zaiqiao Meng, Marco Basaldella, and Nigel Collier. 2021b. Self-alignment pretraining for biomedical entity representations. In *Proceedings of the 2021 Conference of the North American Chapter of the Association for Computational Linguistics: Human Language Technologies*, pages 4228–4238.

Yinhan Liu, Myle Ott, Naman Goyal, Jingfei Du, Mandar Joshi, Danqi Chen, Omer Levy, Mike Lewis, Luke Zettlemoyer, and Veselin Stoyanov. 2019. Roberta: A robustly optimized BERT pretraining approach. *CoRR*, abs/1907.11692.

Yuanchao Liu, Xin Wang, Ming Liu, and Xiaolong Wang. 2016. Write-righter: An academic writing assistant system. In *Proceedings of the Thirtieth AAAI Conference on Artificial Intelligence, February 12-17, 2016, Phoenix, Arizona, USA*, pages 4373–4374.

Kyle Lo, Lucy Lu Wang, Mark Neumann, Rodney Kinney, and Daniel Weld. 2020. S2ORC: The semantic scholar open research corpus. In *Proceedings of the 58th Annual Meeting of the Association for Computational Linguistics*, pages 4969–4983.

Kevin Musgrave, Serge J. Belongie, and Ser-Nam Lim. 2020. A metric learning reality check. In *Computer Vision - ECCV 2020 - 16th European Conference, Glasgow, UK, August 23-28, 2020, Proceedings, Part XXV*, volume 12370 of *Lecture Notes in Computer Science*, pages 681–699.

Ellie Pavlick, Pushpendre Rastogi, Juri Ganitkevitch, Benjamin Van Durme, and Chris Callison-Burch. 2015. PPDB 2.0: Better paraphrase ranking, fine-grained entailment relations, word embeddings, and style classification. In *Proceedings of the 53rd Annual Meeting of the Association for Computational Linguistics and the 7th International Joint Conference on Natural Language Processing (Volume 2: Short Papers)*, pages 425–430.

Jeffrey Pennington, Richard Socher, and Christopher Manning. 2014. GloVe: Global vectors for word representation. In *Proceedings of the 2014 Conference on Empirical Methods in Natural Language Processing (EMNLP)*, pages 1532–1543.

Nils Reimers and Iryna Gurevych. 2019. Sentence-BERT: Sentence embeddings using Siamese BERT-networks. In *Proceedings of the 2019 Conference on Empirical Methods in Natural Language Processing and the 9th International Joint Conference on Natural Language Processing (EMNLP-IJCNLP)*, pages 3982–3992.

Florian Schroff, Dmitry Kalenichenko, and James Philbin. 2015. Facenet: A unified embedding for face recognition and clustering. In *IEEE Conference on Computer Vision and Pattern Recognition, CVPR 2015, Boston, MA, USA, June 7-12, 2015*, pages 815–823.

Kent Shioda, Mamoru Komachi, Rue Ikeya, and Daichi Mochihashi. 2017. Suggesting sentences for ESL using kernel embeddings. In *Proceedings of the 4th Workshop on Natural Language Processing Techniques for Educational Applications (NLPTEA 2017)*, pages 64–68.

Yi Sun, Xiaogang Wang, and Xiaoou Tang. 2014. Deep learning face representation from predicting 10, 000 classes. In *2014 IEEE Conference on Computer Vision and Pattern Recognition, CVPR 2014, Columbus, OH, USA, June 23-28, 2014*, pages 1891–1898.

John Swales. 1990. *Genre analysis: English in academic and research settings*. Cambridge University Press.

Simone Teufel, Jean Carletta, and Marc Moens. 1999. An annotation scheme for discourse-level argumentation in research articles. In *Ninth Conference of the European Chapter of the Association for Computational Linguistics*, pages 110–117.

Xun Wang, Xintong Han, Weilin Huang, Dengke Dong, and Matthew R. Scott. 2019. Multi-similarity loss with general pair weighting for deep metric learning. In *IEEE Conference on Computer Vision and Pattern Recognition, CVPR 2019, Long Beach, CA, USA, June 16-20, 2019*, pages 5022–5030.

Yuanmeng Yan, Rumei Li, Sirui Wang, Fuzheng Zhang, Wei Wu, and Weiran Xu. 2021. ConSERT: A contrastive framework for self-supervised sentence representation transfer. In *Proceedings of the 59th Annual Meeting of the Association for Computational Linguistics and the 11th International Joint Conference on Natural Language Processing (Volume 1: Long Papers)*, pages 5065–5075.

Xuhui Zhou, Nikolaos Pappas, and Noah A. Smith. 2020. Multilevel text alignment with cross-document attention. In *Proceedings of the 2020 Conference on Empirical Methods in Natural Language Processing (EMNLP)*, pages 5012–5025.

A Preprocessing in Dataset Construction

We conduct preprocessing before extracting texts from the S2ORC dataset. This phase proceeds in three steps. First, we exclude papers that lack venue or journal information in their metadata. Second, we exclude papers that do not contain body texts. Finally, we remove papers that are collected in one of the following corpora: *ACL anthology*, *Molecules*, *Oncotarget*, and *Frontiers in Psychology*. These four corpora are also used in the CF-labeled sentence dataset (Iwatsuki and Aizawa, 2021); thus, we consider that including them could cause data leakage. Note that the other two evaluation datasets contain papers in the computer science and biomedical domains, but we do not exclude them from the training data as some baselines such as SciBERT (Beltagy et al., 2019) and PubMedBERT (Gu et al., 2020) are already pre-trained on massive texts in those domains.

B Training Details

We use the Adam optimizer (Kingma and Ba, 2015) with a learning rate of 2e-5. The batch size is set to 64. Following Hermans et al. (2017) and Musgrave et al. (2020), we adopt PK-style batches that first randomly sample P classes and then K instances for each class. We set $P = 64$ and $K = 1$ for Softmax and ArcFace losses and $P = 8$ and $K = 8$ for the others.

We conduct a hyperparameter search with fixed random seeds using the validation dataset, except for softmax cross-entropy loss. Table 6 lists hyperparameter configurations for each metric learning objective.

C Retrieval Examples by SciToricsBERT

Table 7 shows the retrieval examples by SciToricsBERT on the Introduction subset of the CF-labeled sentence dataset.

D A Case Study on Document Alignment

We showcase the utility of SciToricsBERT in the scenario of comparing different scientific papers. Specifically, we consider Devlin et al. (2019) and Lewis et al. (2020), which propose BERT and BART, respectively. We first retrieve texts from PDF files using S2ORC-doc2json (Lo et al., 2020), and split them into sentences using the NLTK tokenizer (Bird et al., 2009). Then, for each sentence

Loss	Hyperparameters
Triplet	$m \in \{0.025, 0.05^{\bullet}, 0.1, 0.2, 0.4\}$
ArcFace	$m \in \{0.1, 0.3, 0.5^{\bullet}\}, s \in \{16^{\bullet}, 32, 64\}$
MS	$\alpha \in \{1, 2^{\bullet}\}, \beta \in \{30, 40^{\bullet}, 50\}, \lambda \in \{0.5, 0.75^{\bullet}, 1.0\}$
NT-Xent	$T \in \{0.0125, 0.025, 0.05, 0.1^{\bullet}, 0.2\}$

Table 6: Values tested during the hyperparameter search. $^{\bullet}$ denotes those used for reporting the results.

in Lewis et al. (2020), we retrieve the most similar one from Devlin et al. (2019) using SCITORICS-BERT. We present a few selected examples in Table 8.

Query sentence			Dystrophin is an important protein for cytoskeletal structure and normal muscle function and plays a vital role in membrane stability and signaling [[CITATION]].
(Query function)			(Showing the importance of the topic)
SCITORICSBERT (ours)	✓	#1	VEGF is a major modulator of endothelial cell function, such as blood vessel formation during embryonic development, and plays a vital role in the proliferation, migration, and invasion of vascular endothelial cells [[CITATION]].
	✓	#2	Thrombin is an extracellular serine protease that plays a crucial role in the blood coagulation cascade, thrombosis, and hemostasis [[CITATION], [CITATION]].
	✓	#3	Copper is an essential element which plays a critical role in human metabolism.
Query sentence			From a computational standpoint, the main challenge is to ensure that the model scales well as the number of languages increases.
(Query function)			(Showing the main problem in the field)
SCITORICSBERT (ours)	✓	#1	, the main challenge is to detect the pattern without being distracted by background noise from other events.
	✓	#2	The main challenge is to maintain the continuity and coherence of the original text.
	✓	#3	The main challenge is to create a lexicon of dialect word forms and their associated probability maps.
Query sentence			Thus, in this paper we describe, for the first time, a straightforward synthesis of novel 1-(2'-α-O-D-glucopyranosyl ethyl) 2-arylbenzimidazoles via one-pot glycosylation of hydroxyethyl arylbenzimidazole aglycones and 2,3,4,6-tetra-O-benzyl 1-hydroxylglucose employing the Appel-Lee reagent [[CITATION], [CITATION]].
(Query function)			(Showing the importance of the research)
SCITORICSBERT (ours)		#1	The theoretical analysis developed in this paper aims to contribute to existing stage models of decision-making ([CITATION] [CITATION] [CITATION] [CITATION] [CITATION]).
		#2	Considering this, and in order to propose a greener route to fully epoxidized oligo-isosorbide glycidyl ethers, this paper reports a new protocol of heterogeneous ultrasound-assisted epoxidation in the presence of atomized sodium hydroxide.
	✓	#3	We argue for the first time that discourse parsing should be viewed as an extension of, and be performed in conjunction with, constituency parsing.
Query sentence			Recently, there has been a breakthrough in cancer immunotherapy against various cancer types by employing immune checkpoint blockade, particularly using antibodies directed against programmed death-ligand 1 (PD-L1) pathway members [[CITATION]].
(Query function)			(Showing brief introduction to the methodology)
SCITORICSBERT (ours)		#1	In recent years, there has been an increasing interest in controlled environment (CE) plant production which reduces variation related to climate, soil, and nutrition [[CITATION], [CITATION], [CITATION]], decreases contamination of samples by weeds, insects, and foreign matter [[CITATION]] and enhances the standardization of secondary metabolite production [[CITATION]].
		#2	In recent years, there has been an increasing interest in lichens as a potential source of pharmacologically bioactive agents for therapeutic treatments [[CITATION], [CITATION], [CITATION]].
	✓	#3	Non-human animal consciousness research has also witnessed groundbreaking advances in the study of contents of consciousness by employing perceptual rivalry paradigms and elucidating the effect of reversible thalamic and cortical inactivations.

Table 7: Examples of top-3 sentences retrieved by SCITORICSBERT. ✓ stands for the same function label as the query.

Query sentence from Lewis et al. (2020)	Retrieved sentence from Devlin et al. (2019)
We present BART, a denoising autoencoder for pretraining sequence-to-sequence models.	We introduce a new language representation model called BERT, which stands for Bidirectional Encoder Representations from Transformers.
The most successful approaches have been variants of masked language models, which are denoising autoencoders that are trained to reconstruct text where a random subset of the words has been masked out.	To pretrain word embedding vectors, left-to-right language modeling objectives have been used (Mnih and Hinton, 2009) , as well as objectives to discriminate correct from incorrect words in left and right context.
BART uses a standard Tranformer-based neural machine translation architecture which, despite its simplicity, can be seen as generalizing BERT (due to the bidirectional encoder), GPT (with the left-to-right decoder), and many other more recent pretraining schemes (see Figure 1) .	Model Architecture BERT's model architecture is a multi-layer bidirectional Transformer encoder based on the original implementation described in Vaswani et al.
A key advantage of this setup is the noising flexibility; arbitrary transformations can be applied to the original text, including changing its length.	The advantage of these approaches is that few parameters need to be learned from scratch.
In total, BART contains roughly 10% more parameters than the equivalently sized BERT model.	By contrast, BERT BASE contains 110M parameters and BERT LARGE contains 340M parameters.
Unlike existing denoising autoencoders, which are tailored to specific noising schemes, BART allows us to apply any type of document corruption.	Unlike left-toright language model pre-training, the MLM objective enables the representation to fuse the left and the right context, which allows us to pretrain a deep bidirectional Transformer.
Because BART has an autoregressive decoder, it can be directly fine tuned for sequence generation tasks such as abstractive question answering and summarization.	As a result, the pre-trained BERT model can be finetuned with just one additional output layer to create state-of-the-art models for a wide range of tasks, such as question answering and language inference, without substantial taskspecific architecture modifications.
Similar to BERT (Devlin et al., 2019), we use concatenated question and context as input to the encoder of BART, and additionally pass them to the decoder.	We use a gelu activation (Hendrycks and Gimpel, 2016) rather than the standard relu, following OpenAI GPT.
Following RoBERTa , we use a batch size of 8000, and train the model for 500000 steps.	We use a batch size of 32 and fine-tune for 3 epochs over the data for all GLUE tasks.
We mask 30% of tokens in each document, and permute all sentences.	In all of our experiments, we mask 15% of all WordPiece tokens in each sequence at random.
The most directly comparable baseline is RoBERTa, which was pre-trained with the same resources, but a different objective.	The most comparable existing pre-training method to BERT is OpenAI GPT, which trains a left-to-right Transformer LM on a large text corpus.
BART reduces the mismatch between pre-training and generation tasks, because the decoder is always trained on uncorrupted context.	BERT alleviates the previously mentioned unidirectionality constraint by using a "masked language model" (MLM) pre-training objective, inspired by the Cloze task (Taylor, 1953) .
Code and pre-trained models for BART are available at https://github.com/pytorch/fairseq and https://huggingface.co/transformers	The code and pre-trained models are available at https://github.com/google-research/bert.

Table 8: Example of document alignment using SCITORICSBERT.

Identifying Medical Paraphrases in Scientific versus Popularization Texts in French for Laypeople Understanding

Ioana Buhnila[1]
[1]LiLPa UR 1339 - Linguistique, Langues, Parole, University of Strasbourg, France
ioana.buhnila@etu.unistra.fr

Abstract

Scientific medical terms are difficult to understand for laypeople due to their technical formulas and etymology. Understanding medical concepts is important for laypeople as personal and public health is a lifelong concern. In this study, we present our methodology for building a French lexical resource annotated with paraphrases for the simplification of monolexical and multiword medical terms. In order to find medical paraphrases, we automatically searched for medical terms and specific lexical markers that help to paraphrase them. We annotated the medical terms, the paraphrase markers, and the paraphrase. We analysed the lexical relations and semantico-pragmatic functions that exists between the term and its paraphrase. We computed statistics for the medical paraphrase corpus, and we evaluated the readability of the medical paraphrases for a non-specialist coder. Our results show that medical paraphrases from popularization texts are easier to understand (62.66%) than paraphrases extracted from scientific texts (50%).

1 Introduction

Understanding medical terms is a challenge for laypeople of all ages and education level. In this study, we concentrated on adults that are not professionals of the medical field but are interested in understanding medical knowledge and research. Medical language is difficult to understand due to, partially, the large number of medical terms. The *term* represents a lexical unit that expresses concepts specific to a field of knowledge, recognised and shared by members of a community of specialists (Costa, 2005). The *term* belongs to an autonomous "subsystem" of the language with the goal of communicating technical or scientific knowledge (Contente, 2005). Medical terms are particularly difficult to understand because of their Greek and/or Latin etymology (Grabar and Hamon, 2015). They can be composed of a mix of prefixes/suffixes from these two ancient languages together with morphemes of the modern language. Laypeople have difficulties in understanding the meaning of medical terms such as "cholecystectomy", which is formed with two Greek basis, "chole" (=bile) and "ectomy" (=surgical removal), and in the middle of these, a Latin basis, "cystis" (=bladder) (Grabar and Hamon, 2015). We can simplify medical terms by using synonyms from the common language, but it is sometimes difficult to find the right synonym. In this paper, we explore the medical paraphrases as means of simplification of medical terms in French. *Paraphrasing* is the process of rewriting in order to explain or simplify a word, sentence, or phrase, while keeping the same meaning.

In this paper, we worked on scientific medical texts in French that treat a certain medical concept (diseases, treatments, medical procedures) and on their versions written for laypeople. We looked for paraphrases of these concepts created with simpler words and expressions from the common language. We evaluated the level of difficulty of these medical paraphrases for adult lay readers.

The annotated paraphrases will constitute a corpus of medical paraphrases that could be used as a textual resource in Natural Language Processing (NLP) and deep learning tasks.

Section 2 presents the medical corpus exploited and in Section 3 we describe the methodology we used to identify medical terms and paraphrase markers, and thus, the medical paraphrase. We continue with the annotation process in Section 4. Section 5 describes the evaluation of the medical paraphrases and their readability level according to a non-expert coder whose native language is

Proceedings of the Third Workshop on Scholarly Document Processing, pages 69–79
October 12–17, 2022.

French. We conclude with the potential use of our annotated corpus for scientific medical term simplification (in Section 6).

2 Related Work

In this section, we present several studies on the themes that our research is related to: paraphrases, medical paraphrase corpus, paraphrase markers, medical terms, and automatic paraphrase identification in French.

2.1 Paraphrases

In linguistics, *paraphrasing* represents the process of rewriting in order to explain or simplify a concept or phrase. There are multiple studies on the concept of paraphrase (Gühlich and Kotschi, 1983; Fuchs, 1994; Rossari, 1990; Vassiliadou, 2013; Grabar and Eshkol-Taravella, 2016; Eshkol-Taravella and Grabar, 2017; Steuckardt, 2018; Fuchs, 2020; Pennec, 2020; Vassiliadou, 2020), from which we highlight:

- The concept of *paraphrasing* as the process of preserving the meaning and intending to get close to a semantic equivalence (Fuchs, 2020; Pennec, 2020; Vassiliadou, 2020);
- *Subphrastic paraphrase* (Bouamor, 2012), composed of words or groups of words that are semantically tied and are integrated in a sentence;
- *Subphrastic paraphrasing,* defined as the process of intra-lingual translation (translation with elements of the same language system, keeping the same meaning) that does not exceed the length of a sentence (our definition);
- *The classical paraphrase*, which expresses an equivalence based on a common semantic core (Fuchs, 1982; Bouamor, 2012; Kampeera, 2013; Pennec, 2020).

In this study, we chose to work on the large concept of *paraphrasing*, as our goal was to identify the largest sequence of words that are semantically equivalent. As we searched for paraphrases that coexist with the medical term in the same sentence, we worked exclusively on *subphrastic paraphrases*. We looked for any paraphrase that can be used to explain and simplify medical terms. The goal of our project was to build a corpus of medical paraphrases that can be used as a database for simplifying scientific medical concepts and adapting medical knowledge to laypeople (Cardon, 2021; Grabar and Hamon, 2015; Grabar and Hamon, 2016).

2.2 Paraphrase Markers

The classical way of identifying paraphrases is through specific markers. *The paraphrase markers* are linguistic elements that help to identify paraphrases in texts. They can be lexical, grammatical, or orthographic markers or cues of paraphrase (Fuchs, 2020; Steuckardt, 2018). Several studies on French focused on paraphrase markers based on the verb *dire* (to say), such as *c'est-à-dire* (that is), *ça veut dire* (that means), *pour dire autrement* (to say otherwise), *autrement dit* (otherwise said) (Vassiliadou, 2013; Grabar and Eshkol-Taravella, 2016; Steuckardt, 2018; Magri, 2018). These markers can have a narrative or paraphrastic role. Vassiliadou (2013) considers the marker *c'est-à-dire* (that is) as the typical paraphrase marker. Grabar and Eshkol-Taravella (2016) worked on specific markers for lexical paraphrases (*c'est-à-dire* (that is), *disons* (let's say), *ça veut dire* (it means)) using a rule-based system and manual annotations. Their study aimed at automatically classifying phrases with and without paraphrases. To identify paraphrases, Grabar and Eshkol-Taravella (2016) looked for the syntagmatic structure "S1 marker S2", where S1 is the paraphrased element and S2 is the paraphrase. These two parts are linked by the paraphrase markers cited above. Their study was conducted on two general oral language corpora and a medical forum corpus.

In our work, we also took into consideration the possibility of the *absence* of the paraphrase marker. We looked for *paraphrase cues* specific to the medical domain, as a scientific and specialized type of text. We classified the *paraphrase cues* into three types:

- *General language cues* that, through their semantics and use in discourse, refer to the simplification, definition, or explanation of concepts: *définition* (definition), *défini/e* (defined), etc.;
- *Grammatical cues* that announce a list of hyponyms of the medical term: *comme* (such as), *par exemple* (for example);

- *Cues specific to the medical domain* which are hypernyms of the medical terms: *maladie* (disease), *affection* (affection), *trouble* (disorder).

We manually analysed the corpus to find more paraphrases without markers or lexical cues. We found other markers, such as the *typographical cues* (parentheses or commas) (Steuckardt, 2018). Unlike Grabar and Eshkol-Taravella (2016), who worked on medical forum texts (which contain text that are very similar to oral written speech), we analysed written medical texts (scientific and popular articles) in order to create a set of sentences that contain medical paraphrases in natural language context (and not only in a lexicon). For this purpose, we used markers analysed in other similar works, but we also added additional markers and cues of paraphrase, presented in section 3.2.

2.3 Scientific Medical Terms and their Paraphrases

In order to locate the paraphrase, we first identified the medical term that is paraphrased. The aim of paraphrasing medical terms is to propose a meaning equivalent to the sequence of words from the common language, adapted to non-specialist readers, such as patients, students, or laypeople in general (Leroy et al., 2013; Brouwers et al., 2012; Pecout, Tran and Grabar, 2019).

Several different methods were experimented to identify medical terms and their paraphrases, for example searching for Latin or Greek prefixes and suffixes, using medical ontologies (Grabar and Hamon, 2016) or with term detection tools with n-gram patterns (Buhnila, 2018). Grabar and Hamon (2016) searched for medical terms in a corpus of Wikipedia articles using medical terminologies (Snomed International (Côté, 1996) and the French part of UMLS (*Unified Medical Language System*) (Donald et al., 1993). Their study focused on paraphrases that appear in free contexts, meaning that the technical terms and their paraphrases can be separated by several words. In the same study, they used the French morphological analyser DériF (Namer, 2009) to extract words in modern French from medical terms of Greek or Latin origin. For example, the term "myocardique" contains the modern French words "muscle" / muscle (myo) and "cœur" / heart (carde). The authors looked for these words in the corpora and extracted 2,596 definitory contexts automatically.

In this paper, we focused on simple and multiword medical terms and we used the SNOMED-3.5VF medical ontology (Côté, 1996) for scientific term extraction.

2.4 Medical Paraphrase Corpus for French

We can mention the study of Cardon and Grabar (2021) on 4,596 pairs of parallel sentences extracted from the CLEAR corpus (Grabar and Cardon, 2018), a medical corpus of popularization and scientific texts. The goal of the study was to automatically simplify biomedical texts using neural networks. Cardon and Grabar (2021) used several resources: the parallel phrases of the CLEAR corpus, a lexicon that matches complex medical terms with paraphrases easy to understand to laypeople (7,580 paraphrases for 4,516 medical terms) and 297,494 parallel sentences in the common language from WikiLarge (Zhang and Lapata, 2017). The WikiLarge corpus was automatically translated from English to French. Their experiments proved that using a medical lexicon of paraphrases and medical simplified phrases helped simplify biomedical texts.

The goal of our study was to build an annotated corpus of sentences that contain medical paraphrases in a natural language context and that can be used for the simplification of medical texts and scientific medical concepts. We present our method in Section 3.

3 Methodology

For this study, we worked on the CLEAR corpus which is composed of French scientific medical texts and medical texts adapted for laypeople (Grabar and Cardon, 2018). Our method consisted of automatically identifying simple and multiword medical terms with the SIFR-BioPortal annotator (Tchechmedjiev et al., 2018). We also tested other annotators for French, such as Bio-YODIE (Gorrell et al., 2018) and PyMedTermino (Lamy et al., 2015), but SIFR-BioPortal proved to be the most intuitive to use. SIFR-BioPortal works by parsing texts for medical terms from the SNOMED-3.5VF medical ontology (Côté, 1996) (released by ASIP Santé). This ontology contains 150,906 scientific medical concepts in French. In order to identify specific markers for the medical domain, we looked for words that collocate with a term and the relations that this term may have with other elements of the sentence. More precisely, we run a

Perl script to identify relation markers (Condamines, 2018) that link a medical term to its paraphrase (Ramadier, 2016), such as hypernymy, hyponymy, synonymy, meronymy.
We expected to find paraphrases in the context of the medical term in the same sentence. After the automatic identification of the medical terms and paraphrase markers, we manually annotated the sentences to find out whether the paraphrases are correct or not. We also annotated the paraphrases for the lexical relations and semantico-pragmatic functions, such as definition, explanations, etc. (presented in detail in section 4.2 and 4.3). We present each step of the methodology in detail as it follows.

3.1 Corpus of Study

Our corpus of study was the CLEAR Cochrane corpus, which is a part of the CLEAR corpus (Grabar and Cardon, 2018). CLEAR is a comparable corpus composed of *scientific texts from the medical field* designed for experts and *simplified texts* written for laypeople. The texts were written by researchers of the Cochrane Foundation. Grabar and Cardon (2018) collected a number of 8,789 texts in November 2017, of which 3,815 were duplicates of the same medical concept: asthma, arthritis, motor neuron disease, etc. The expert corpus contains 2,840,003 tokens and the laypeople corpus counts 1,515,051 tokens.

CLEAR Cochrane	N° of texts	Same theme texts	Size (token)
Expert (EX)	8,789	3,815	2,840,003
Laypeople (GP)			1,515,051

Table 1: Size of the CLEAR Cochrane corpus by text type (Grabar and Cardon, 2018).

The CLEAR Cochrane corpus is built with comparable texts on the same theme, where a scientific text is followed by its simplified version. For our study, we decided to separate expert and laypeople texts in two sub-corpora: scientific corpus written for experts (CLEAR EX) and general public corpus (CLEAR GP). Our hypothesis is that scientific texts have more medical terms while general public texts contain more synonyms, paraphrases, or explanations in the common language. We split the texts into sentences using end-of-line characters (. ; ! ; ?) to display one sentence per line. Once the corpus was cleaned and aligned, we proceeded to automatically identify the medical terms (see Table 1).

3.2 Automatic Annotation of Medical Terms and Paraphrase Markers

We identified the medical terms in our corpus with the help of a Perl script and the French version of the SIFR-BioPortal annotator (Tchechmedjiev et al., 2018). The annotator provides 28 medical terminologies in French. We chose the SNOMED-3.5VF ontology because it contains a wide variety of medical concepts: administrative and treatments, agents, anatomy, diagnoses, drugs, symptoms, disease, procedures, etc. This large panel of medical concepts and the search by lemma helped us tag a large number of medical terms in our corpus of study.

As for the *paraphrase markers*, we listed the most frequent ones from the literature, to which we added markers according to our own observations from the corpus:

- Markers formed on the French verb *dire* (to say) (*c'est-à-dire* (it means), *ça veut dire / veut dire* (meaning), *pour dire autrement* (to say otherwise), *autrement dit* (in other words) (Vassiliadou, 2013; Vassiliadou, 2016; Grabar and Eshkol-Taravella, 2016; Steuckardt, 2018; Magri, 2018);

- Markers derived from the verbs *désigner* (to designate) and *signifier* (to signify) (Péry-Woodley and Rebeyrolle, 1998; Charolles and Coltier, 1986);

- Markers derived from the verb *être* (to be) with its different morphological forms, *est un/une/des* (is a), *sont un/une/des* (are a/some) (Meyer, 2001; Grabar and Hamon, 2016) followed by hypernyms from the medical domain such as "disease", "affection" and "disorder";

- Markers that are specific to our corpora, such as the ones formed on the verb *appeler* (to call) (*qu'on appelle, ce que l'on appelle* (what it's called), *est aussi appelé / aussi appelé* (is also called / also called) and others, such as *doit être compris comme* (must be understood as), *au sens de* (in the sense of).

These paraphrase markers are domain-independent (except medical hypernyms) and can indicate different types of relations between the medical term and its paraphrase (further details in Section 4.2).

4 Paraphrase Annotation Process

In this section we present different levels of the annotation process of the medical paraphrases. This annotation was manually done in order to assess the quality of the paraphrases that were automatically identified with previous tasks. In this paper we annotated the status of the paraphrase, the lexical relations and the semantico-pragmatic relations that exists between the medical term and its paraphrase.

4.1 Status of the Paraphrase

We chose five different possible values for the status of the paraphrase, as follows:

- *yes*: the sentence contains a correct paraphrase;
- *yes<rev>*: the sentence contains a reversed paraphrase (the paraphrase is found before the medical term);
- *yes<2+>*: there are two or more correct paraphrases in the same sentence;
- *yes<2+><rev>*: there are two or more correct paraphrases in the same sentence, with at least one reversed paraphrase;
- *no*: the sentence does not contain a correct paraphrase.

4.2 Lexical Relations

We classified the lexical relations that exist between the paraphrase and the corresponding medical term: synonymy, hyponymy, hypernymy, meronymy. Medical hypernyms (Săpoiu, 2013) have an important role in the classification of scientific medical concepts (e.g. "scrub typhus") into wide classes that are easier to understand for laypeople, such as "bacterial disease" (Grabar and Hamon, 2015). For instance, in the case of hyponymy, the term "antibiotics" is the hypernym, and the paraphrase simplifies the meaning of the term by using hyponyms such as "chloramphenicol, tetracycline and doxycycline".

4.3 Semantico-pragmatic Functions

The semantico-pragmatic functions express the reasons that motivate the writer to use paraphrases (such as definition, designation, exemplification, explanation, rephrasing) (Eshkol-Taravella and Grabar, 2017). In this study, we adapted this taxonomy, originally created on oral texts of common language, to written texts in the medical domain. We defined these functions as follows:

- *Definition*: the term is given a definition because it is considered to be too technical or domain specialised, thus difficult to understand;
- *Designation*: the term is paraphrased using another word or term;
- *Exemplification*: the paraphrase is a list of examples (several entities of the same type) that help to illustrate the meaning of the term;
- *Explanation*: the term is explained through a particular situation or procedure;
- *Rephrasing*: the meaning of the term is expressed with simpler words;

Definitive contexts are marked by specific lexical cues: *définition* (definition), *défini/e* (defined), *défini/e comme* (defined as). The phrases *tel/lle/s/lles que* (such as) and *par exemple* (for example) announce the paraphrase through an exemplification.

4.4 Readability Level of Paraphrases

Paraphrases can be easier or more difficult to understand by laypeople. The complexity is given by the use of technical words. For instance, the medical term "antibiotics" could be simpler to understand than "chloramphenicol". In this sense, we asked a coder who is not a specialist in the field of medicine to evaluate a sample of correct medical paraphrases. We evaluated the level of comprehension of paraphrases through the manual annotation of a sample of correct paraphrases. We selected a sample of 300 paraphrases that were labelled as correct by our two coders (both not specialists in medicine), 150 from each type of corpus (scientific and for laypeople). We evaluate the comprehension of the paraphrases by three levels:

- *Level 1* – easy to understand: the paraphrase is easier to understand than the term (there are words from the common language in the paraphrase);
- *Level 2* – same complexity: same level of complexity or technicity between the term and the paraphrase, meaning that both the term and the paraphrase are difficult to understand;
- *Level 3* – difficult to understand: the paraphrase is more complex or technical than the term.

The annotation is done by a French native speaker, who is studying Linguistics at a Masters 2 degree level. The student annotated the paraphrases identified by the other coder of the study (ourselves). We present the results of this evaluation in the next section.

5 Results and Data Evaluation

The automatic extraction of the sentences containing both the medical terms annotated by SIFR-BioPortal and occurrences of markers or paraphrase indicators is done with Perl scripts. We adapted our scripts to identify all morphological forms and to automatically annotate medical terms and markers/cues. We obtained 4,681 sentences for the corpus of scientific texts (CLEAR EX) and 3,975 sentences for the corpus of medical texts for the general public (CLEAR GP). These sentences were therefore analysed manually by two coders. We present the results and statistics of these annotations in the tables below.

5.1 Coder Agreement

We computed the agreement between two coders, ourselves, and a French native speaker, Master-level student. We computed the Kappa annotator agreement (Cohen, 1960), the precision and recall of paraphrases identified. We show in Table 2 and 3 the number of paraphrases that were identified as correct medical paraphrases by both coders, the number of paraphrases that received the same "status" tag ("yes", "yes-rev", "no"), in both corpora. We also computed the number of paraphrases tagged differently by both coders. We decided to not include "yes<2+>" and "yes<2+><rev>" tags in this study, as these paraphrases appear in a small number. We will analyse them in future studies.

CLEAR EX		
Statistics	**Coder 1**	**Coder 2**
Paraphrases with ***yes***	1321	1714
Paraphrases with ***yes-rev***	37	50
Paraphrases with ***no***	3323	2917
Different tag paraphrases - ***total***	**948**	
Same tag paraphrases - ***yes***	1059	
Same tag paraphrases - ***yes-rev***	7	
Same tag paraphrases - ***no***	2667	
Same tag paraphrases - ***total***	**3733**	
Total number of paraphrases	**4681**	

Table 2: Coder data statistics on CLEAR EX

As for the general public corpus, we analysed only the annotated sentences (1,903 out of 3,975). We calculated the precision, the recall, and the relative frequencies in order to interpret data equally.

CLEAR GP		
Statistics	**Coder 1**	**Coder 2**
Paraphrases with ***yes***	671	707
Paraphrases with ***yes-rev***	55	22
Paraphrases with ***no***	1177	1174
Different tag paraphrases - ***total***	**291**	
Same tag paraphrases - ***yes***	552	
Same tag paraphrases - ***yes-rev***	17	
Same tag paraphrases - ***no***	1043	
Same tag paraphrases - ***total***	**1612**	
Total number of paraphrases	**1903**	

Table 3: Coder data statistics on CLEAR GP

We calculated the recall as the number of paraphrases tagged with "yes" or "no" by both coders, divided by the number of paraphrases tagged with "yes" or "no" by coder 1 and respectively by coder 2. We considered one annotation as the gold standard and then we changed the other way around (in Tables 4 and 5, the recall is computed with coder 1, and coder 2 respectively, as reference).

$$Recall = \frac{common\ paraphrases\ Coder1\&\ Coder2}{paraphrases\ Coder1}$$

Figure 1: Coder recall formula

CLEAR EX		
Measures	**Coder 1**	**Coder 2**
Precision - *yes*	0.29	0.38
Precision - *yes - average*	**0.34**	
Precision - *no*	0.71	0.62
Precision - *no - average*	**0.67**	
Precision - *same tag*	**0.80**	
Recall - *yes*	0.78	0.60
Recall - *yes - average*	**0.69**	
Recall - *no*	0.80	0.91
Recall - *no - average*	**0.86**	
Recall - *total average*	**0.78**	
Kappa annotator score	**0.55**	

Table 5: Statistics on CLEAR EX

CLEAR GP		
Measures	**Coder 1**	**Coder 2**
Precision - *yes*	0.38	0.38
Precision - *yes - total*	**0.38**	
Precision - *no*	0.62	0.62
Precision - *no - average*	**0.62**	
Precision - *same tag*	**0.85**	
Recall - *yes*	0.84	0.80
Recall - yes - *total*	**0.82**	
Recall - *no*	0.89	0.89
Recall - *no - average*	**0.89**	
Recall - *total average*	**0.86**	
Kappa annotator score	**0.68**	

Table 7: Statistics on CLEAR GP

The big differences in the number of "yes" tag paraphrases were due to different decisions of the coders, as the coder 1 decided not to consider *abbreviations* as *paraphrases*, while the coder 2 considered them as paraphrases. We intend to automatically annotate abbreviations in future studies for further analysis and conduct new analysis with and without abbreviations as paraphrases. Results proved that precision, recall, and *Cohen's Kappa* annotator are higher for the general public corpus than for the expert corpus. We also used the *ReCal tool* (Freelon, 2013) to do ordinal, interval, and ratio-level scores on both annotations. We gave numeric values to our tags, 1 for "yes", 2 for "yes-rev" and 3 for "no". The highest agreement score was the ordinal one, with **0.707** for the general public corpus and of **0.566** for the expert corpus.

We assume that these score differences were due to the higher level of technicity of the expert corpus, thus making it more difficult to assess the same tags for the paraphrases by both coders, while in the general public corpus the paraphrases were easier to analyse and evaluate.

Data	CLEAR EX	CLEAR GP
File size	23405 bytes	9515 bytes
N° coders	2	2
N° cases	4681	1903
N° decisions	9362	3806

Table 4: Corpus data for the ReCal Tool

ReCal Tool	EX	GP
Measures	**Score**	**Score**
Krippendorff's alpha (nominal)	0.552	0.688
Krippendorff's alpha (ordinal)	**0.566**	**0.707**
Krippendorff's alpha (interval)	0.565	0.705
Krippendorff's alpha (ratio)	0.562	0.701

Table 6: Measure scores obtained with ReCal

We analysed the absolute and relative frequencies of lexical relations and semantico-pragmatic functions for both corpora. We compared the average relative frequencies of both annotations, and we observed that the lexical relation of hypernymy is the most frequent in both corpora with a score of **63.32%** for the expert corpus and a score of **62.39%** for the general public corpus. We observed that the semantic-pragmatic function of definition had similar scores (**49.95%** and **52.28%** respectively). This can be justified by the fact that the definitory context has, most of the time, the following syntax:

medical term – paraphrase marker – medical hypernym – paraphrase

Semantico-pragmatic functions	CLEAR EX			CLEAR GP		
	A.F C1	**A.F C2**	**Av R.F**	**A.F C1**	**A.F C2**	**Av R.F**
Definition	723	342	**49.95 %**	356	239	**52.28 %**
Designation	30	152	8.53 %	18	83	8.87 %
Exemplifica-tion	242	222	**21.76 %**	128	113	**21.17 %**
Explanation	28	209	11.11 %	30	97	11.15 %
Rephrasing	43	141	8.63 %	37	37	6.50 %
N° phrases	**1066**		**100%**	**569**		**100%**

Table 8: Lexical relations between medical terms and their paraphrases (A.F=absolute frequency; Av R.F=average relative frequency; C1=coder 1; C2=coder 2; N° phrases: phrases with "yes" and "yes-rev" in common for both coders)

In the example: *La bronchectasie est une maladie respiratoire chronique* (Bronchiectasis is a chronic respiratory disease), the term "La bronchectasie" is paraphrased in a definitory sentence introduced by the medical hypernym "une maladie".

Lexical relations	CLEAR EX			CLEAR GP		
	A.F C1	A.F C2	Av R.F	A.F C1	A.F C2	Av R.F
Synonymy	86	162	11.63 %	57	83	12.30 %
Hyponymy	245	218	**21.71 %**	128	114	**21.26 %**
Hypernymy	668	682	**63.32 %**	339	371	**62.39 %**
Meronymy	67	4	3.33%	45	1	4.04 %
N° phrases	**1066**		**100%**	**569**		**100%**

Table 9: Semantico-pragmatic functions between medical terms and their paraphrases (A.F=absolute frequency; Av R.F=average relative frequency; C1=coder 1; C2=coder 2; N° phrases: phrases with "yes" and "yes-rev" in common for both coders)

We observed the same situation for the lexical relation of hyponymy and the semantico-pragmatic function of exemplification, as they have almost the same scores (21.71% and 21.76% for CLEAR EX and 21.26% and 21.17% for CLEAR GP), meaning that they were annotated as appearing in the same context.

5.2 Complexity for Laypeople

The manual annotation of the level of comprehension of paraphrases showed that paraphrases from CLEAR GP are easier to understand (**62.66%** in comparison with **50%** for the scientific corpus). Meanwhile, the number of opaque paraphrases (where the paraphrase is as difficult to understand as the medical term because few words from the common language are used) is higher in the scientific corpus (**42%** compared to **27.33%** for the simplified version). This can be explained by the bigger number of scientific terms used as paraphrases in the expert texts.

Level	CLEAR EX		CLEAR GP	
	Abs F	Rel F	Abs F	Rel F
1: Easy to understand	75	**50%**	94	**62.66 %**
2: Same level of complexity	63	42%	41	27.33 %
3: Difficult to understand	12	8%	15	10%
Paraphrases	**150**		**150**	

Table 10: Assessment of the level of comprehension of medical paraphrases (Abs F=absolute frequency; Rel F=relative frequency)

6 Conclusion and further research

Our study has shown that medical paraphrases are present in both scientific and popularization texts. There is a higher number of paraphrases in the general corpus and are also easier to understand, both for annotation tasks and for lay readers comprehension. The analysis and evaluation of lexical relations and semantico-pragmatic functions that can be identified between the medical term and its paraphrase highlighted relations such as hyponymy and hyponymy help to identify more correct paraphrases. The same result is observed with the semantico-pragmatic functions of definition and exemplification. In further studies we will also conduct quantitative and qualitative analyses of paraphrase markers (or their absence) and compare them in scientific and popular texts. We could also evaluate the level of readability of each type of lexical relation and semantico-pragmatic function and assess which type of simplifications are easier to understand for laypeople. Further analysis could focus on whether the identified paraphrases are scientifically accurate and allow laypeople to be correctly informed about medical topics.

Here we created a corpus of **1,635 paraphrases of scientific medical terms in French** and an **annotated corpus of 6,584 phrases** that contain scientific medical terms and paraphrase markers. Once the annotation process is finished, the annotated corpora will be shared with the scientific community on the github repository. We are currently using the corpus for Natural Language Processing (NLP) tasks such as generating medical paraphrases for scientific terms and binary classification with deep learning and neural networks such as *OpenNMT* (Klein et al., 2020) and *APT* (Adversarial Paraphrasing Task) (Nighojkar et Licato, 2021).

Our method and experiences can also be applied on other Romance languages close to French, such as Romanian (Buhnila, 2021). Our corpus of medical paraphrases can constitute a useful lexical resource for scientific medical texts simplification system for adult lay readers or patients.

References

Houda Bouamor. 2012. *Etude de la paraphrase sous-phrastique en traitement automatique des langues*. Université Paris Sud - Paris XI. Français. ⟨NNT: 2012PA112100⟩. ⟨tel-00717702⟩.

Laetitia Brouwers, Delphine Bernhard, Anne-Laure Ligozat and Thomas François. 2012. *Simplification syntaxique de phrases pour le français (syntactic simplification for french sentences) [in French]. In Actes de la conférence conjointe JEP-TALN-RECITAL 2012, 2 : TALN* :211–224. Grenoble, France : ATALA/AFCP.

Ioana Buhnila. 2018. *Simplification lexicale entre les textes scientifiques et les textes de vulgarisation du domaine de la médecine.* Mémoire de Master, Université de Strasbourg, Strasbourg, France.

Ioana Buhnila. 2021. *Building a Corpus of Medical Paraphrases in Romanian. In Proceedings of the The 16th Edition of the International Conference on Linguistic Resources and Tools for Natural Language Processing – ConsILR-2021*, Iasi, 139-152.

Rémi Cardon. 2021. *Simplification automatique de textes techniques et spécialisés. Informatique et langage [cs.CL].* Université de Lille. Français. ⟨NNT: 2021LILUH007⟩. ⟨tel-03343769v2⟩.

Rémi Cardon and Natalia Grabar. 2021. *Simplification automatique de textes biomédicaux en français : lorsque des données précises de petite taille aident (French Biomedical Text Simplification : When Small and Precise Helps). In Actes de la 28e Conférence sur le Traitement Automatique des Langues Naturelles. Volume 1 : conférence principale*, 275–277, Lille, France. ATALA.

Michel Charolles and Danielle Coltier. 1986. Le contrôle de la compréhension dans une activité rédactionnelle : l'exemple des paraphrases paraphrastiques. Pratiques 49 (1): 51 66. https://doi.org/10.3406/prati.1986.2450.

Jacob Cohen. 1960. *A coefficient of agreement for nominal scales*. Educ. Psychol. Meas., 20, 27-46.

Condamines, A. 2018). Nouvelles perspectives pour la terminologie textuelle. J. Altmanova; M. Centrella; K.E. Russo. Terminology and Discourse, Peter Lang, 1-13. 978-3-0343-2415-1. ff10.3726/978-3-0343-2414-4ff. ffhalshs-01899150f.

Madalena Contente. 2005. *Termes et textes : la construction du sens dans la terminologie médicale. Actes des septièmes Journées scientifiques du réseau de chercheurs Lexicologie Terminologie Traduction*, 453 65. Bruxelles, Belgique.

Rute Costa. 2005. *Texte, terme et contexte. Actes des septièmes Journées scientifiques du réseau de chercheurs Lexicologie Terminologie Traduction*, 79-88. Bruxelles, Belgique.

Réné Côté. 1996. *Répertoire d'anatomopathologie de la SNOMED internationale*, v3.4. Université de Sherbrooke, Sherbrooke, Québec.

Deen Freelon. 2013. *ReCal OIR: Ordinal, Interval, and Ratio Intercoder Reliability as a Web Service. International Journal of Internet Science. 8 (1)*, 10-16.

Iris Eshkol-Taravella and Natalia Grabar. 2017. *Taxinomie dans les paraphrases du point de vue de la linguistique de corpus.* Syntaxe et Sémantique, vol. 18, no. 1, 149-184.

Iris Eshkol-Taravella and Natalia Grabar. 2018. *Paraphrases : de l'étude outillée dans les corpus disponibles vers leur détection automatique.* Langages N° 212 (4), 5-16.

Catherine Fuchs. 1982. *La Paraphrase*. PUF, Paris, 184 pages.

Catherine Fuchs. 1994. *Paraphrase et énonciation.* Editions OPHRYS, 185 pages.

Catherine Fuchs. 2020. Paraphrase et paraphrase : un chassé-croisé entre deux notions. Autour de la paraphrase, 36, Droz, Coll. Recherches et Rencontres, 978-2-600-06051-6, 41-55.

Genevieve Gorrell, Xingyi Song and Angus Roberts. 2018. Bio-YODIE: A Named Entity Linking System for Biomedical Text. arXiv:1811.04860 [cs], http://arxiv.org/abs/1811.04860 , p. 1-5.

Natalia Grabar and Iris Eshkol-Taravella. 2016. *Disambiguation of occurrences of paraphrase markers c'est-à-dire, disons, ça veut dire. JADT 2016 : 13ème Journées internationales d'Analyse statistique des Données Textuelles*, 1-13. Nice, France.

Natalia Grabar and Thierry Hamon. 2015. *Extraction automatique de paraphrases grand public pour les termes médicaux. 22ème Traitement Automatique des Langues Naturelles*, 14. Caen, France.

Natalia Grabar and Thierry Hamon. 2016. *Exploitation de la morphologie pour l'extraction automatique de paraphrases grand public des termes médicaux. Traitement Automatique des Langues, Varia*, 57 (1), 85 109.

Natalia Grabar and Rémi Cardon. 2018. CLEAR - Simple Corpus for Medical French. In *Proceedings of the 1st Workshop on Automatic Text Adaptation (ATA). Tilburg, the Netherlands: Association for Computational Linguistics*. https://doi.org/10.18653/v1/W18-7002, 3–9.

Elisabeth Gühlich and Thomas Kotschi. 1983. *Les marqueurs de la paraphrase paraphrastique*. Cahiers de Linguistique française 5, 305-351.

Wannachai Kampeera. 2013. *Analyse linguistique et formalisation pour le traitement automatique de la paraphrase*. Linguistique. Université de Franche-Comté. Français. ⟨NNT: 2013BESA1011⟩. ⟨tel-01288926⟩.

Guillaume Klein, François Hernandez, Vincent Nguyen, and Jean Senellart. 2020. *The OpenNMT Neural Machine Translation Toolkit*: 2020 Edition. AMTA 2020.

Anaïs Koptient and Natalia Grabar. 2020. *Rated Lexicon for the Simplification of Medical Texts. The Fifth International Conference on Informatics and Assistive Technologies for Health-Care*, Medical Support and Wellbeing HEALTHINFO 2020, Porto, Portugal.

Jean-Baptiste Lamy, Alain Venot and Catherine Duclos. 2015. PyMedTermino: an open-source generic API for advanced terminology services. *Studies in Health Technology and Informatics*, IOS Press, 2015, 210, pp.924-8. ⟨hal-03650024⟩.

Gondy Leroy, David Kauchak and Mouradi Obay. 2013. *A user-study measuring the effects of lexical simplification and coherence enhancement on perceived and actual text difficulty*. Int J Med Inform, 82(8), 717–730.

Donald A. B. Lindberg, Betsy Humphreys and Alexa Mccray. 1993. *The Unified Medical Language System*, Methods Inf Med, vol. 32, no 4, 281-291.

Mounica Maddela, Fernando Alva-Manchego and Wei Xu. 2020. *Controllable text simplification with explicit paraphrasing*. arXiv preprint arXiv:2010.11004.

Véronique Magri. 2018. *Marqueurs de paraphrase : exploration outillée et contrastive dans deux corpus narratifs*. Langages N° 212 (4), 35-50.

Ingrid Meyer. 2001. *Extracting Knowledge-Rich Contexts for Terminography: A conceptual and methodological framework*. Dans D. Bourigault, C. Jacquemin, & M.-C. L'Homme (Éds), Recent Advances in Computational Terminology, 279-302, Amsterdam: John Benjamins.

Fiammetta Namer. 2009. *Morphologie, Lexique et TAL : l'analyseur DériF*. TIC et Sciences cognitives, Hermes Sciences Publishing, London.

Animesh Nighojkar and John Licato. 2021. *Improving Paraphrase Detection with the Adversarial Paraphrasing Task*. In *Proceedings of the 59th Annual Meeting of the Association for Computational Linguistics and the 11th International Joint Conference on Natural Language Processing (Volume 1: Long Papers)*, pages 7106–7116, Online. Association for Computational Linguistics.

Anaïs Pecout, Tran, Thi M. and Natalia Grabar. 2019. *Améliorer la diffusion de l'information sur la maladie d'Alzheimer : étude pilote sur la simplification de textes médicaux*. Ela. Etudes de linguistique appliquée N° 195 (3): 325 41.

Blandine Pennec. 2020. *Les paraphrases : des formes méta-énonciatives par excellence. Spécificités et introducteurs*. Autour de la paraphrase, 36, Droz, Coll. Recherches et Rencontres, 57-75.

Marie-Paule Péry-Woodley and Josette Rebeyrolle. 1998. *Domain and genre in sublanguage text: definitional microtexts in three corpora*, LREC, 987-992.

Lionel Ramadier. 2016. *Indexation et apprentissage de termes et de relations à partir de comptes rendus de radiologie*. Informatique. Université Montpellier, Français. ⟨NNT: 2016MONTT298⟩. ⟨tel-01479769v2⟩.

Corinne Rossari. 1990. *Projet pour une typologie des opérations de paraphrase*. Cahiers de linguistique française 11, 345-359.

Camelia Săpoiu. 2013. *Hiponimia în terminologia medicală*. Modalităţi de abordare în semantică şi lexicografie. Piteşti, Editura Trend, 199 pages.

Agnès Steuckardt. 2018. *Les marqueurs de paraphrase formés sur dire : exploration outillée*. Langages N° 212 (4), 17-34.

Andon Tchechmedjiev, Amine Abdaoui, Vincent Emonet, Stella Zevio et Clement Jonquet. 2018. *SIFR annotator: ontology-based semantic annotation of French biomedical text and clinical notes*. BMC bioinformatics, 19(1), 405.

Hélène Vassiliadou. 2013. C'est-à-dire (que) : embrayeur d'énonciation. Semen. Revue de sémio-linguistique des textes et discours, no 36 (octobre). 1-14. http://journals.openedition.org/semen/9684. https://doi.org/10.4000/semen.9684.

Hélène Vassiliadou. 2016. *Mouvements de réflexion sur le dire et le dit : c'est-à-dire, autrement dit, ça veut dire.* Histoires de dire. Petit glossaire des marqueurs formés sur le verbe dire, L. Rouanne & J.-C. Anscombre (éds), Bern/Berlin/Bruxelles/New York/Oxford/Wien, Peter Lang, 339-364.

Hélène Vassiliadou. 2020. *Peut-on aborder la notion de "paraphrase" autrement que par la typologie des marqueurs ?* Pour une analyse sémasiologique et onomasiologique. Olga Inkova. Autour de la Paraphrase, Droz, 978-2-600-06051-6, 77-94.

Seid M. Yimam and Chris Biemann. 2018. *Par4Sim-Adaptive Paraphrasing for Text Simplification.* arXiv preprint arXiv:1806.08309.

Xingxing Zhang and Mirella Lapata. 2017. *Sentence simplification with deep reinforcement learning.* In *Proceedings of the 2017 Conference on Empirical Methods in Natural Language Processing*, 584–594, Copenhagen, Denmark: Association for Computational Linguistics.

Multi-objective Representation Learning for Scientific Document Retrieval

Mathias Parisot
Zeta Alpha
parisot@zeta-alpha.com

Jakub Zavrel
Zeta Alpha
zavrel@zeta-alpha.com

Abstract

Existing dense retrieval models for scientific documents have been optimized for either retrieval by short queries, or for document similarity, but usually not for both. In this paper we explore the space of combining multiple objectives to achieve a single representation model that presents a good balance between both modes of dense retrieval, combining the relevance judgements from MS MARCO with the citation similarity of SPECTER, and the self-supervised objective of independent cropping. We also consider the addition of training data from document co-citation in a sentence context and domain-specific synthetic data. We show that combining multiple objectives yields models that generalize well across different benchmark tasks, improving up to 73% over models trained on a single objective.

1 Introduction

With the explosive growth of the volume of scientific publications, researchers increasingly rely on sophisticated discovery and recommendation tools to find relevant literature and related work (Ammar et al., 2018; Fadaee et al., 2020). In particular, the development of neural information retrieval (Lin et al., 2021) has led to a quest for dense document representations that capture the semantics of documents better than the previous generation of keyword-based retrieval methods. Such representations are typically achieved by specializing pre-trained large language models for the retrieval task. In this paper, we focus on the case of the bi-encoder (Humeau et al., 2019), where at indexing time documents are embedded as dense vector representations and stored in a fast approximate nearest neighbor system, and at retrieval time queries are encoded using the same model and similarity search is performed in the vector space.

The data set that has powered a lot of advances in this area is MS MARCO (Bajaj et al., 2016), which consists of user queries combined with human relevance judgements for documents and passages. Models trained on this data set are the current state of the art for retrieval based on queries, though the discussion is still ongoing about their effectiveness in terms of out-of-domain generalization (Thakur et al., 2021). As Table 1 shows, models based on this data set tend to perform less well on benchmarks that test document-to-document retrieval. In (Cohan et al., 2020), a scientific document retrieval model called SPECTER was introduced that is specifically optimized for document-to-document similarity, based on exploiting the signal in the citation graph between documents. Model trained for document representations tend to perform less well than MS MARCO based models on query-to-document retrieval tasks such as those presented in the BEIR data set (Table 1).

	BEIR subset	SciDocs	ICLR 2022
Single objective			
MS MARCO	0.270	68.72	0.260
SPECTER	0.207	79.75	0.407
Multi-objective			
ICrop+context2doc	0.285	78.29	0.450
Δ*MS MARCO*	+5.6%	+13.9%	+73.1%
Δ*SPECTER*	+37.7%	-1.8%	+10.6%
AllObj-Alt	0.278	79.44	0.424
Δ*MS MARCO*	+3.0%	+15.6%	+63.1%
Δ*SPECTER*	+34.3%	-0.4%	+4.2%

Table 1: Single objective compared to multi-objective training. Metrics are ndcg@10 for BEIR and ICLR2022 (doc2doc dataset), and average over all tasks for SciDocs. Δ +/- percentages represent the relative improvement compared to single objective models for the given benchmark. ICrop+context2doc is a model trained on independent cropping and finetuned on unarXiv context2doc. AllObj-Alt is trained alternating batches of independent cropping, SPECTER, and MS MARCO .

Additional evidence suggests that self-

Proceedings of the Third Workshop on Scholarly Document Processing, pages 80–88
October 12–17, 2022.

supervised tasks, such as the Inverse Cloze Task (Lee et al., 2019) or Independent Cropping (Izacard et al., 2021) can make document representations more robust and improve retrieval relevance (Chang et al., 2020; Izacard et al., 2021). Also, in-domain synthetic data has been explored to enhance retrieval effectiveness in new domains (Bonifacio et al., 2022).

So far, however, no systematic study were performed on the combination of multiple objectives for scientific document representation learning. In this paper, we explore several methods to combine different data sets and training objectives and study the effectiveness of these training strategies on a number of scientific document retrieval benchmarks. In addition to this, we introduce and make available a new data set that emphasises document-to-document similarity. By doing this, we try to answer the following research question:

How can we best combine multiple data sets and task objectives to train a scientific document retriever that can be queried both using short queries and documents?

Although in practice a retrieval system could use multiple different document embeddings for multiple tasks, a single multi-purpose document representation offers great advantages in terms of storage space, computational resources, and operational efficiency.

The main contributions of this paper are the following:

1. We train a dense retriever that performs well on both query2doc and doc2doc retrieval;
2. We introduce a new way to use citation context to generate semi-supervision signal for scientific documents;
3. We release a scientific document to document data set with 1844 human annotations among which 441 are positive relevance judgements; and
4. We publish the code and data sets used for our experiments at `https://github.com/zetaalphavector/multi-obj-repr-learning`

2 Related work

Document retrieval. Multiple recent papers focus on learning representations for scientific documents and dense neural document retrieval (Tan et al., 2022; Zhang et al., 2022; Ostendorff et al., 2022a). (Cohan et al., 2020) presents how to use weak supervision from the scientific citation graph to train a dense retrieval model (SPECTER) and introduces SciDocs, a benchmark to evaluate document representations. (Ostendorff et al., 2022b) improves on SPECTER by using a graph embedding model to sample positive and negative documents and create better training triplets. (Abolghasemi et al., 2022) combines a ranking and representation loss to train a query by document retriever. (Althammer et al., 2022) proposes a method to disregard the input length restriction of transformer-based models by using a paragraph aggregation retrieval model. In our own work, we build on (Cohan et al., 2020) and use the same framework but explore how adding multiple training objectives can improve the performance of a document retriever.

citation context. Earlier work by (Colavizza et al., 2017) already shows that co-citation of documents, especially at the sentence level, is a strong signal for semantic relatedness of documents. (Mysore et al., 2022) explores co-citation context supervision for document representation learning, and applies it to aspect matching. We add this signal to our mix of potentially useful constraints in a multi-objective learning setting, and focus on document representation and training models which can be used for both query to document and document to document retrieval. Moreover, we introduce a new co-citation supervision by using the citing sentence context as a query for the documents cited.

3 Method

3.1 Bi-encoder and losses

We focus on dense retrieval using a bi-encoder architecture (Humeau et al., 2019) with a shared encoder E for the query q (here q can be a short query or a document query) and document d. The model E encodes the query and document into representations $E_q = E(q)$ and $E_d = E(d) \in R^n$ respectively. Note that, in our case, the encoder E is a transformer-based model (Vaswani et al., 2017) which means that its output is a sequence of token representations. We aggregate this sequence into a single representation using mean pooling (we also experimented with using the $[CLS]$ token representation without success over mean pooling). The relevance between the query and document is expressed using a distance metric, cosine similarity in our case, between the two representations: $s(q, d) = dist(E_q, E_d)$.

To train the model, we use data sets of triples of the form: (q, d^+, d^-) where d^+ and d^- are documents that are respectively relevant and not relevant for the query q. When possible, we concatenate the title and abstract of a document as follow: $E_d = E(d_{title}[SEP]d_{abstract})$

We experiment with two losses: Multiple Negative Ranking Loss (MNRL) and Triplet Loss (TL). With MNRL, the single negative document d^- is enriched into a set of negative documents D^- composed of the positive and negative documents from the other triples in the training batch.

$$MNRL(q, D) = -\log \frac{\exp(s(q, d^+))/\tau}{\sum_{d \in D} \exp(s(q, d))/\tau} \tag{1}$$

Where $D = D^- \cup \{d^+\}$ is the set of all positive and negative documents of all the queries in the batch. With TL, each query uses exactly one positive and one negative document.

$$TL(q, d^+, d^-) = \max\{d(q, d^+) - d(q, d^-) + \epsilon, 0\} \tag{2}$$

Where $d(q, d) = ||E_q - E_d||_2$ is the L2 norm between the representations of the query and document. While several works (Cohan et al., 2020; Ostendorff et al., 2022b) use TL as their loss function,in most of our experiments, MNRL performed better across different data sets and domains. All the presented results in this paper use MNRL.

3.2 Multi-objective training (multiple types of supervision and domain)

Multi-task learning (Caruana, 1993) has shown good results to improve the generalization of language models. Tasks can be machine translations, next-word predictions, information retrieval, and others. Following those advances, we focus here on a single task (information retrieval) but are interested in combining several types of supervision objectives, data sets, and data domains with the goal to increase the amount of useful training signals and to train a more general-purpose dense retriever.

We experiment with multiple types of supervision: fully supervised data, weakly supervised, and self-supervised training. We also explore two domains: online question answering and scientific document representation for finding related documents. The goal of those experiments is to study whether combining multiple objectives can improve performance across the board. Here, an objective refers to a type of supervision combined with a domain.

We start by considering the following three objectives:

- **MS MARCO data** as fully supervised out-of-domain (question answering) data.
- **Scientific citation graph data** as weakly supervised data, automatically extracted from the scientific literature. There are several ways to use the citation graph as supervision signals. A common approach to derive relevance information is to use cited documents as positive examples (Cohan et al., 2020). We also explore other ways such as using co-cited documents within a given citation context and using the context as the query for the documents that it cites.
- **Unsupervised data** generated via independent-cropping (Izacard et al., 2021) on a scientific corpus. Given a document, independent-cropping samples two independent spans of tokens (which can overlap) forming the query and the positive document. The negative document is sampled similarly from another document in the corpus. The original authors suggest that the overlap between query and documents encourages the model to learn lexical matching between query and document. In our implementation, both the query and document spans contain at least ten tokens.

3.3 Combining objectives

This subsection describes three ways to combine objectives.

In-batch mixing. One way to combine objectives is in-batch objective mixing. Here, data from different objectives are randomly mixed within the same batch. Each of the N objectives is assigned a weight w_i ($\sum_{n=1}^{N} w_i = 1$). A batch of B instances is composed of $w_i \times B$ instances on average of a given objective i. We experiment with multiple weighting configurations. When using MNRL, because the negative documents are shared within the batch, in-batch mixing negatives are more diverse compared to the two other ways to combine objectives.

Alternate batch mixing. Another way to combine objectives is to change the objective for each training iteration. Overall, the training data is equally distributed across the objectives, but there is no mix within a given batch. As opposed to in-batch mixing, the set of negative documents comes from the same objective.

Finetuning. The last way we explore is finetuning. For a given objective A, we train a model on A until convergence and then finetune it on a target objective B. The training on the second objective is shorter and commonly uses a lower learning rate.

4 Experimental Setups

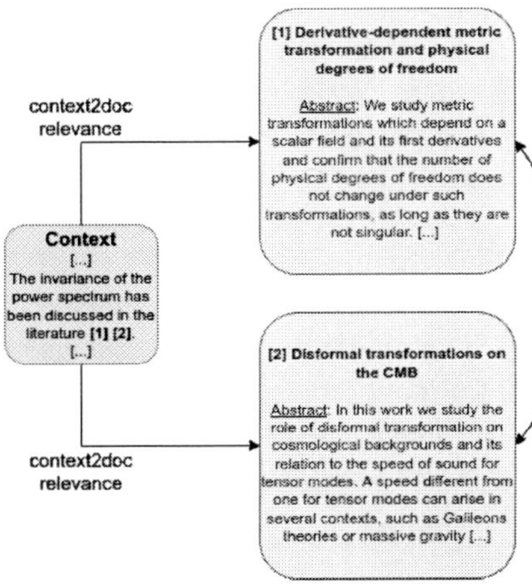

Figure 1: Descriptions of two ways to extract relevant pairs of text for citation contexts. doc2doc uses citation contexts to associated co-cited documents. context2doc uses the context as the query for a cited document.

This section describes details about our experimental setups. We discuss the training and evaluation data sets as well as our choice of hyperparameters.

4.1 Training data

MS MARCO (Bajaj et al., 2016) is a large-scale information retrieval data set created from Bing's search query logs. Sentence-BERT (Reimers and Gurevych, 2019) provides a data set of hard negatives[1] mined from dense models for this data set. We create triplets (q, p, n) where q is the query, p is the annotated positive document, and n is a negative document sampled from the data set. For our experiments, we mined 5 negative documents per system, all with a cross-encoder score of 3.0 or less.

[1]https://huggingface.co/datasets/sentence-transformers/msmarco-hard-negatives

SPECTER, a data set extracted from the Semantic Scholar corpus (Ammar et al., 2018), a data set of scientific papers. We train our models with the subset of the corpus used by Cohan et al.. The data set is composed of triplets (q, p, n) where q is the query paper, p is a paper cited by p, and n is a paper not cited by q but cited by a paper cited by the query paper q. The data set contains 684,100 training triplets and 145,375 validation triplets.

unarXiv (Saier and Färber, 2020) is a large scholarly data set with annotated in-text citations. From it, we extract all one-sentence contexts containing at least two arXiv papers and only select the contexts with citing papers that are posted on arXiv (with an associated arXiv identifier). Our final data set contains a collection 343,578 one-sentence context citing a total of 300,736 arXiv papers across multiple scientific fields (see Figure 2). The contexts and documents contain respectively 29.8 and 152.5 words on average. We use unarXiv for 2 tasks (see Figure 1). First, we use the co-cited documents as positive examples in a document-to-document retrieval setup (we refer to this objective as *doc2doc*). Then, we use the context as the query for any of the documents it cites. We refer to this objective as *context2doc* short for context to document. Our version of the dataset is available here [2].

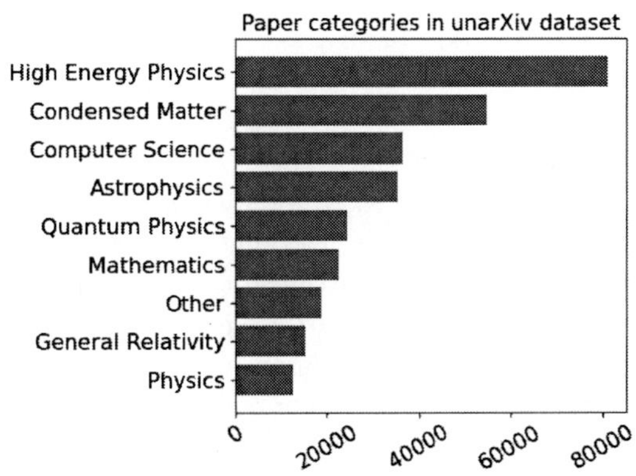

Figure 2: Counts of ArXiv categories for the documents in unarXiv collection. Categories with less than 10,000 documents are grouped into "Other".

InPars (Bonifacio et al., 2022) is a recent method to generate synthetic training data sets for information retrieval tasks. The idea is to use large language models, such as GPT-3 (Brown et al., 2020), to generate queries that are relevant to a

[2][github link]

given document. Bonifacio et al. generated synthetic data for all the data sets present in BEIR. We combine all the synthetic data sets [3] into one and use it as training data. We only experiment with this data set for finetuning models pre-trained on other objectives.

4.2 Evaluation

BEIR (Thakur et al., 2021) is a benchmark containing 15 information retrieval tasks. We select 5 openly available long document data sets from the benchmark: SciDocs (Cohan et al., 2020); NFCorpus (Boteva et al., 2016) a medical information retrieval data set of 3,244 queries and 9,964 documents; SciFact (Wadden et al., 2020) a scientific fact-checking data set of 300 queries and 5,183 documents; TREC-COVID (Voorhees et al., 2020) a pandemic information retrieval data set of 50 queries and 171,332 documents; ArguAna (Wachsmuth et al., 2018) a counter-argument data set of 1,406 queries and 8,670 documents. Except for ArguAna, where queries have 192.98 words on average, all the other selected BEIR data sets are short queries to document retrieval tasks. The selected data set with the longest queries is SciFact with 12.37 words per query on average.

SciDocs (Cohan et al., 2020) is a framework evaluating scientific paper embeddings. It is composed of 4 tasks: document classification, citation prediction, user activity, and recommendation. Note that the SciDocs task presented above in the BEIR benchmark is only a subtask.

ICLR2022 . Furthermore, we introduce a new specialized document to document retrieval data set of artificial intelligence scientific papers. We create our corpus from all the 1094 papers presented at ICLR 2022 [4]. We randomly sample 40 of those papers and use them as our queries. We index the corpus using FAISS (Johnson et al., 2019) library and retrieve a list of 10 documents with cosine similarity using multiple models. We distribute the query-document pairs across 4 in-house annotators and manually annotate the pairs using 3-scale relevance judgements: 0 not-relevant, 1 relevant and 2 very relevant. Removing the duplicate pairs across the ranking lists of different models, the data set contains 1,844 relevance judgements out of which 358 are relevant and 83 are very relevant. The dataset is available here [5].

4.3 Hyper-parameters and training details

We use a pre-trained MiniLM-L6[6] Transformer model as a basis, and train each of our models from this for a maximum of 200,000 steps or until convergence of the validation loss with a patience of 2. Each training batch contains 16 triplets and we accumulate the gradients during 2 steps. When multiple objectives are combined during training, the convergence metric is the average of the validation losses of the training objectives. The optimizer is AdamW (Loshchilov and Hutter, 2017) with a learning rate of 2×10^{-5}, no weight decay and $\epsilon = 10^{-8}$. The learning rate follows a linear schedule without warmup. When finetuning models on a target objective, we train the model on a single epoch of the target data set using a learning rate of 10^{-5}. The rest of the optimizer and scheduler parameters stay the same.

All the experiments were run on a single NVDIA Titan RTX GPU with 24GB GDDR6. The use of the MiniLM-L6 model means that we were able to do fast experiments, but also that the results we report in this paper are not directly comparable to the state-of-the-art achieved using much larger models.

5 Results and Discussion

Single vs. Multi-objective training. We first study the impact of adding supervision signals from multiple sources compared to a single training objective. Table 1 presents the results of *ICrop. + context2doc* and *AllObj-Alt* two multi-objective models compared to the best single-objective models on each of the 3 evaluation metrics. Both multi-objective models manage to outperform the baseline model trained on MS MARCO for all metrics with at least 3% and up to 38% improvement on single metrics. The multi-objective models reached performance on SciDocs close to the baseline model trained on SPECTER while toping its score on BEIR and ICLR2022 . We take those results as empirical evidence that multi-objective training leads to models that generalize better across multiple domains.

Combining objectives. We study the impact of the four combining methods: in-batch mixing,

[3]https://github.com/zetaalphavector/inPars

[4]https://iclr.cc/Conferences/2022

[5][link to dataset]

[6]https://huggingface.co/nreimers/MiniLM-L6-H384-uncased

Training objectives	Combining	BEIR-subset (ndcg@10)	SciDocs (avg.)	ICLR2022 (ndcg@10)
2 objectives				
(1) MS MARCO , (2) ICrop.	in batch mix	0.269	74.93	0.342
	alternate	0.282	74.51	0.341
	finetune 1 → 2	0.262	74.27	0.343
	finetune 2 → 1	**<u>0.324</u>**	**75.09**	**0.396**
(1) SPECTER, (2) MS MARCO	in batch mix	0.230	78.90	0.396
	alternate	0.258	**79.25**	0.381
	finetune 1 → 2	**0.307**	75.08	0.330
	finetune 2 → 1	0.265	78.91	**0.419**
(1) SPECTER, (2) ICrop.	in batch mix	0.127	78.85	0.413
	alternate	0.239	78.57	0.384
	finetune 1 → 2	0.242	75.78	0.375
	finetune 2 → 1	**0.248**	**79.40**	**<u>0.471</u>**
3 objectives				
MS MARCO , SPECTER, ICrop.	in batch mix	0.244	77.78	0.389
	alternate	**0.278**	**<u>79.44</u>**	**0.424**

Table 2: Comparison of combining objectives methods. BEIR subset is the average ndcg of the 5 tasks, SciDocs avg is the average metric of all the tasks. Results in bold are the best result given a set of objectives, underlined results are the best overall.

alternate, and finetuning in both directions. To do so we combine three objectives: MS MARCO , SPECTER, and independent cropping. The results are presented in Table 2. When using only two data sets, finetuning is a better option than both in-batch mixing and alternating between batches. The results are consistent across the 3 pairs of objectives. There is no clear preference between alternating batches and in-batch mixing for two objectives. The models trained with the latter perform best on SciDocs and ICLR2022 while the models trained with alternate batches perform best on BEIR. Maybe the diverse domains of the BEIR data sets create negatives that are too easy to spot, while the domains of SciDocs and ICLR2022 are relatively similar making the negative harder and forcing the model to learn better representations. When using three objectives, alternating between batches performs well across the three evaluation metrics and seems like the best compromise.

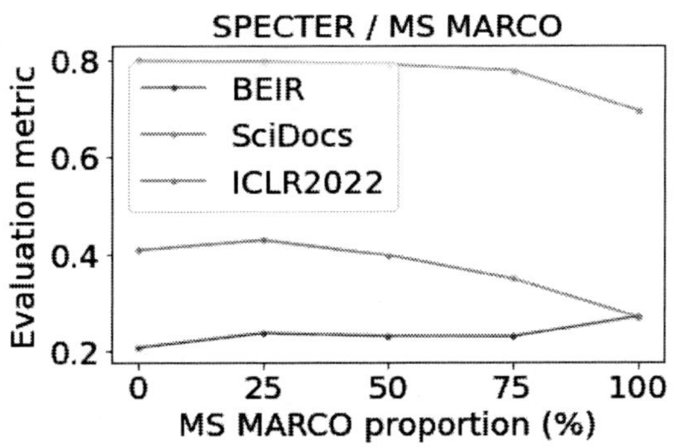

Figure 3: Performance on SciDocs, BEIR, and ICLR2022 when combining SPECTER and MS MARCO objectives with in-batch mixing and varying the proportion of data instances coming from MS MARCO . When MS MARCO proportion is 25% the split is 75%-25%. The evaluation metric for SciDocs is divided by 100 for clarity.

Split proportion. We analyze the effect of the split proportion when combining 2 objectives using in-batch mixing. Figure 3 presents the performances of a model trained using in-batch mixing on MS MARCO and SPECTER objectives. We explore 5 split-proportions going from a model trained on only SPECTER data (0% MS MARCO) to one trained using 100% MS MARCO data. The figure shows that only adding a small proportion of MS MARCO data results in better performance on BEIR while maintaining high performance on SciDocs and ICLR2022 (25% MS MARCO gives the highest score on ICLR2022). As expected, training on a larger proportion of MS MARCO increases the performance on BEIR but the trade-off is not interesting as the document representation and document retrieval performance suffer significantly.

Training	BEIR-subset (ndcg@10)	SciDocs (avg.)	ICLR2022 (ndcg@10)
ICrop.	0.244	74.93	0.370
MS MARCO	0.270	68.72	0.260
ICrop. + MS MARCO	**0.324**	**75.09**	**0.396**
SPECTER	0.207	**79.75**	0.407
ICrop. + SPECTER	**0.248**	79.40	**0.471**
unarXiv doc2doc	0.170	75.42	0.378
ICrop. + unarXiv doc2doc	**0.251**	**78.19**	**0.467**
unarXiv context2doc	0.252	75.08	0.379
ICrop. + unarXiv context2doc	**0.285**	**78.29**	**0.450**

Table 3: Comparison of training on a single objective versus using independent croping (ICrop) and finetuning on the target objective (Ind. Crop. + {target}). BEIR subset is the average ndcg of the 5 tasks, SciDocs avg is the average metric of all the tasks. Results in bold are the best result given a target objective.

Independent cropping. Furthermore, we study how well self-supervised pre-training on an information retrieval task performs. In this experiment, we train a model using independent cropping and finetune it on four target objectives. Table 3 presents the results when finetuning on MS MARCO , SPECTER, unarXiv document to document, and unarXiv context to document objectives. We find that independent cropping is an effective pre-training method. For every one of the target objectives (except SPECTER on the SciDocs benchmark), pre-training using the self-supervised method leads to an increase in performance compared to only training on the target objective. The results are consistent across the three evaluation metrics for all the target objectives except SPECTER (the performance on SciDocs is slightly less but similar).

Using citation contexts as semi-supervised signal. In addition, we make use of citation contexts to extract semi-supervised relevance signals. In particular, we study two ways to define relevancy: the first is co-occurring documents within a citation context (*unarXiv doc2doc*), and the second uses the context as the query for any document appearing in it (*unarXiv context2doc*). The last four rows in Table 3 presents the doc2doc in context vs. context2doc. Using unarXiv doc2doc as a single training objective does not perform well across the three evaluation metrics but using it as a target objective after training on independent cropping improves the performance but does not compare to finetuning on SPECTER which gets similar results on BEIR but higher results on SciDocs and ICLR2022 . One explanation could be the difference in data set size: SPECTER training set contains 684,100 triplets and unarXiv doc2doc only contains 456,766. Using citation context as queries (unarXiv context2doc) is a better alternative. When pre-trained on independent cropping and finetuned on unarXiv context2doc, our model performs well on the three evaluation metrics. In particular, the model performs well on the subset of BEIR whose tasks contain mostly short queries. We find that using citation contexts, which are shorter than documents (on average 29.8 words per context), is an effective way to introduce query to document supervision for the scientific document domain.

Pre-train data	BEIR	SciDocs	ICLR 2022
Baselines			
MSMARCO	0.270	68.72	0.260
SPECTER	0.207	79.75	0.407
ICrop.	0.244	74.93	0.370
Finetuning on InPars			
MSMARCO	0.300	69.70	0.248
SPECTER	0.304	74.88	0.300
ICrop	0.313	75.12	0.341

Table 4: Finetuning models on InPars synthetic data. The first 3 rows are models trained on a single objective. Metrics are ndcg@10 for BEIR and ICLR2022 , and average over all tasks for SciDocs.

Using synthetic data. Finally, following (Bonifacio et al., 2022), we experimented with InPars, the introduction of in domain synthetic data (query document pairs generated using GPT-3 (Brown et al., 2020)). Table 4 presents the results of finetuning on InPars data compared to single objective training. We find that InPars significantly improves the performance on BEIR regardless of the pre-training objective. The performance on SciDocs increases when for both MS MARCO and independent cropping pre-training. The results are mitigated when finetuning a model trained on SPECTER, the performance on BEIR increases by 50% with the cost of 6.1% and 11.1% decrease on SciDocs and ICLR2022 respectively. The synthetic data contains mostly short queries, therefore the increase in performance on BEIR, which contains a majority of short query to document tasks, is expected. Future work could explore generating long query synthetic data.

6 Conclusion

We explored multi-objective dense retrieval training as a way to optimize models for both short queries and document queries. We study three ways to combine objectives (in-batch mixing, alternating between batches, and finetuning). We find that using multiple objectives is a way to train dense retrievers that perform well for short and long query retrieval. Considering the performances across a subset of BEIR, SciDocs and ICLR2022 our best models achieve an average relative improvement between 13.4 and 19.2% compared to the best single objective models. Our work here focused on bi-encoders, and future work could explore whether multi-objective training is also beneficial for a cross-encoder architecture (Lin et al., 2021).

Furthermore, we find that pre-training a model using independent cropping and finetuning it on a target objective consistently improves the retrieval performance compared to only training on the target objective.

We also introduced context-to-document, a new weakly supervised training objective using the citation context sentence as the query for the cited document. This signal outperforms the co-cited relevance signal and improves the model performance on short query retrieval. For future work, we would like to explore how to pre-filter citation contexts that do not contain useful information to identify a relevant document, thus removing potential noise from the training data.

Finally, we released a new document to document retrieval data set composed of ICLR 2022 papers and 1,844 human relevance judgement.

All our experiments were conducted using a MiniLM-L6 (22.7 million parameters) model which is more than 10 times smaller than BERT (Devlin et al., 2019) (345 million parameters). Future work should consider how multi-objective training scales to larger models.

With this work, we hope to make a step in the direction of a multi-purpose document representation to reduce storage space, computational resources, and increase the operational efficiency of scientific retrieval systems.

Acknowledgements

We thank Andrew Yates, Assistant Professor in the Information Retrieval Lab at the University of Amsterdam, for assistance and feedback with the methodology and experiments.

References

Amin Abolghasemi, Suzan Verberne, and Leif Azzopardi. 2022. Improving bert-based query-by-document retrieval with multi-task optimization.

Sophia Althammer, Sebastian Hofstätter, Mete Sertkan, Suzan Verberne, and Allan Hanbury. 2022. Parm: A paragraph aggregation retrieval model for dense document-to-document retrieval.

Waleed Ammar, Dirk Groeneveld, Chandra Bhagavatula, Iz Beltagy, Miles Crawford, Doug Downey, Jason Dunkelberger, Ahmed Elgohary, Sergey Feldman, Vu Ha, Rodney Kinney, Sebastian Kohlmeier, Kyle Lo, Tyler Murray, Hsu-Han Ooi, Matthew E. Peters, Joanna Power, Sam Skjonsberg, Lucy Lu Wang, Chris Wilhelm, Zheng Yuan, Madeleine van Zuylen, and Oren Etzioni. 2018. Construction of the literature graph in semantic scholar. *CoRR*, abs/1805.02262.

Payal Bajaj, Daniel Campos, Nick Craswell, Li Deng, Jianfeng Gao, Xiaodong Liu, Rangan Majumder, Andrew McNamara, Bhaskar Mitra, Tri Nguyen, Mir Rosenberg, Xia Song, Alina Stoica, Saurabh Tiwary, and Tong Wang. 2016. Ms marco: A human generated machine reading comprehension dataset.

Luiz Bonifacio, Hugo Abonizio, Marzieh Fadaee, and Rodrigo Nogueira. 2022. Inpars: Data augmentation for information retrieval using large language models.

Vera Boteva, Demian Gholipour, Artem Sokolov, and Stefan Riezler. 2016. A full-text learning to rank dataset for medical information retrieval.

Tom Brown, Benjamin Mann, Nick Ryder, Melanie Subbiah, Jared D Kaplan, Prafulla Dhariwal, Arvind Neelakantan, Pranav Shyam, Girish Sastry, Amanda Askell, Sandhini Agarwal, Ariel Herbert-Voss, Gretchen Krueger, Tom Henighan, Rewon Child, Aditya Ramesh, Daniel Ziegler, Jeffrey Wu, Clemens Winter, Chris Hesse, Mark Chen, Eric Sigler, Mateusz Litwin, Scott Gray, Benjamin Chess, Jack

Clark, Christopher Berner, Sam McCandlish, Alec Radford, Ilya Sutskever, and Dario Amodei. 2020. Language models are few-shot learners.

Rich Caruana. 1993. Multitask learning: A knowledge-based source of inductive bias. In *Proceedings of the Tenth International Conference on Machine Learning*, pages 41–48.

Wei-Cheng Chang, Felix X. Yu, Yin-Wen Chang, Yiming Yang, and Sanjiv Kumar. 2020. Pre-training tasks for embedding-based large-scale retrieval.

Arman Cohan, Sergey Feldman, Iz Beltagy, Doug Downey, and Daniel S. Weld. 2020. SPECTER: Document-level Representation Learning using Citation-informed Transformers. In *ACL*.

Giovanni Colavizza, Kevin W. Boyack, Nees Jan van Eck, and Ludo Waltman. 2017. The closer the better: Similarity of publication pairs at different co-citation levels.

Jacob Devlin, Ming-Wei Chang, Kenton Lee, and Kristina Toutanova. 2019. Bert: Pre-training of deep bidirectional transformers for language understanding.

Marzieh Fadaee, Olga Gureenkova, Fernando Rejon Barrera, Carsten Schnober, Wouter Weerkamp, and Jakub Zavrel. 2020. A new neural search and insights platform for navigating and organizing ai research.

Samuel Humeau, Kurt Shuster, Marie-Anne Lachaux, and Jason Weston. 2019. Poly-encoders: Transformer architectures and pre-training strategies for fast and accurate multi-sentence scoring.

Gautier Izacard, Mathilde Caron, Lucas Hosseini, Sebastian Riedel, Piotr Bojanowski, Armand Joulin, and Edouard Grave. 2021. Unsupervised dense information retrieval with contrastive learning.

Jeff Johnson, Matthijs Douze, and Hervé Jégou. 2019. Billion-scale similarity search with GPUs. *IEEE Transactions on Big Data*, 7(3):535–547.

Kenton Lee, Ming-Wei Chang, and Kristina Toutanova. 2019. Latent retrieval for weakly supervised open domain question answering.

Jimmy Lin, Rodrigo Nogueira, and Andrew Yates. 2021. Pretrained transformers for text ranking: Bert and beyond.

Ilya Loshchilov and Frank Hutter. 2017. Fixing weight decay regularization in adam. *CoRR*, abs/1711.05101.

Sheshera Mysore, Arman Cohan, and Tom Hope. 2022. Multi-vector models with textual guidance for fine-grained scientific document similarity.

Malte Ostendorff, Till Blume, Terry Ruas, Bela Gipp, and Georg Rehm. 2022a. Specialized document embeddings for aspect-based similarity of research papers.

Malte Ostendorff, Nils Rethmeier, Isabelle Augenstein, Bela Gipp, and Georg Rehm. 2022b. Neighborhood contrastive learning for scientific document representations with citation embeddings.

Nils Reimers and Iryna Gurevych. 2019. Sentence-bert: Sentence embeddings using siamese bert-networks. In *Proceedings of the 2019 Conference on Empirical Methods in Natural Language Processing*. Association for Computational Linguistics.

Tarek Saier and Michael Färber. 2020. unarXive: A Large Scholarly Data Set with Publications' Full-Text, Annotated In-Text Citations, and Links to Metadata. *Scientometrics*, 125(3):3085–3108.

Shicheng Tan, Shu Zhao, and Yanping Zhang. 2022. Coherence-based distributed document representation learning for scientific documents.

Nandan Thakur, Nils Reimers, Andreas Rücklé, Abhishek Srivastava, and Iryna Gurevych. 2021. BEIR: A heterogeneous benchmark for zero-shot evaluation of information retrieval models. In *Thirty-fifth Conference on Neural Information Processing Systems Datasets and Benchmarks Track (Round 2)*.

Ashish Vaswani, Noam Shazeer, Niki Parmar, Jakob Uszkoreit, Llion Jones, Aidan N. Gomez, Lukasz Kaiser, and Illia Polosukhin. 2017. Attention is all you need.

Ellen M. Voorhees, Tasmeer Alam, Steven Bedrick, Dina Demner-Fushman, William R. Hersh, Kyle Lo, Kirk Roberts, Ian Soboroff, and Lucy Lu Wang. 2020. TREC-COVID: constructing a pandemic information retrieval test collection. *CoRR*, abs/2005.04474.

Henning Wachsmuth, Shahbaz Syed, and Benno Stein. 2018. Retrieval of the best counterargument without prior topic knowledge. In *Proceedings of the 56th Annual Meeting of the Association for Computational Linguistics (Volume 1: Long Papers)*, pages 241–251, Melbourne, Australia. Association for Computational Linguistics.

David Wadden, Shanchuan Lin, Kyle Lo, Lucy Lu Wang, Madeleine van Zuylen, Arman Cohan, and Hannaneh Hajishirzi. 2020. Fact or fiction: Verifying scientific claims. In *EMNLP*.

Shunyu Zhang, Yaobo Liang, Ming Gong, Daxin Jiang, and Nan Duan. 2022. Multi-view document representation learning for open-domain dense retrieval.

Visualization Methods for Diachronic Semantic Shift

Raef Kazi and **Alessandra Amato** and **Shenghui Wang** and **Doina Bucur**
Unversity of Twente
Drienerlolaan 5, 7522 NB Enschede, The Netherlands
{r.kazi,a.amato}@student.utwente.nl
{shenghui.wang,d.bucur}@utwente.nl

Abstract

The meaning and usage of a concept or a word changes over time. These diachronic semantic shifts reflect the change of societal and cultural consensus as well as the evolution of science. The availability of large-scale corpora and recent success in language models have enabled researchers to analyze semantic shifts in great detail. However, current research lacks intuitive ways of presenting diachronic semantic shifts and making them comprehensive. In this paper, we study the PubMed dataset and compute semantic shifts across six decades. We develop three visualization methods that can show, given a root word: the temporal change in its linguistic context, word re-occurrence, degree of similarity, time continuity, and separate trends per geographic location. We also propose a taxonomy that classifies visualization methods for diachronic semantic shifts with respect to different purposes.

1 Introduction

Diachronic semantic shift or concept drift studies how a language (the meaning and usage of words) evolve over time (Wang et al., 2011). Studying such semantic shifts is valuable for researchers who are interested in either the societal and cultural evolution, or the development of scientific research. In the latter case, innovations and groundbreaking discoveries often introduce new concepts, bring new meanings to existing ones, or shift existing meanings completely. Automatically identifying and understanding diachronic semantic shifts is thus desirable.

The availability of large-scale corpora (Hilpert and Gries, 2008) and recent success in language models (Tum, 2020) have enabled researchers to analyze semantic shifts in great detail (Jatowt and Duh, 2014; Hamilton et al., 2016; Azarbonyad et al., 2017; Gonen et al., 2020). Most of the research focuses on discovering general trends in semantic shifts, tracing the dynamics of the relationships between words, and elaborates on the methods used to detect such a shift (Kutuzov et al., 2018). Little research has explored the visual representation of such semantic shifts to help understand them intuitively. The visuals used across multiple studies include word graphs (Wijaya and Yeniterzi, 2011; Li et al., 2021), scatterplots (Kulkarni et al., 2015; Mahmood et al., 2016), and storylines (Mahmood et al., 2016). However, these methodologies currently fail in explicitly showing the temporal changes of a word and require the user to have some domain knowledge to fully comprehend the drifts. There is a strong need for further exploring the nature of this semantic shift by employing new visualization methods to make the semantic shift understandable, explainable, and explorable.

The goal of the this study, therefore, is to present a classification of visualization methods for a word's semantic shift based on the type of concept the user wishes to analyze, which leads us to the following objectives:

(a) Introduce intuitive methods for visualizing diachronic semantic shifts

(b) Propose a taxonomy that classifies visualization methods for diachronic shifts based on the type of concept one wishes to visualize

In this paper, we compute diachronic semantic shifts in PubMed across six decades, and propose three visualization methods utilising radial bars, spiral lines and word-cloud maps that can show, given a root word: the temporal change in its linguistic context, word re-occurrence, degree of similarity, time continuity, and separate trends per geographic location. We compare different visualization methods and propose a taxonomy that classifies methods for visualizing diachronic semantic shift.

Proceedings of the Third Workshop on Scholarly Document Processing, pages 89–94
October 12–17, 2022.

2 Data

Our study is based on PubMed (National Library of Medicine, 2022), a large, long-term corpus of citations and abstracts of biomedical literature. We include articles from 1970 onward (when abstracts are available). We randomly sample 106 out of the available 1114 `xml` data files, to keep the data relatively balanced over the 52 years, enough to create a word embedding for each decade. We then divide the corpus into six decades, from the 1970s to the 2020s. Table 1 shows the distribution of articles per decade.

Decade	No. articles	Decade	No. articles
1970s	222771	2000s	434448
1980s	258171	2010s	458802
1990s	247961	2020s	426790

Table 1: **PubMed**: the distribution of articles per decade

The biomedical abstracts have all their punctuation removed, and are tokenized into words which are then lowercased and lemmatized, with numerals and stop words also removed. On this preprocessed corpus, concept drift can be measured.

3 Method

3.1 Quantifying semantic drift

Inspired by Gonen et al. (2020), word embeddings are computed per decade (so the six decades are treated separately). We use the Continuous Bag of Words (CBOW) model of word2vec (Mikolov et al., 2013) with window size 10 to train each decade, and store the resulting embeddings. Then, the top $k = 50$ neighbours of a word in the embedded space make up the "linguistic context" of the word. Parameter k is tunable; Li et al. (2021) also showed that this model generally produces stable similarity scores across the corpus, when varying k. To measure concept drift, we look at the similarity of its contexts across time. The Jaccard index measures the context similarity of any word between any two decades. Let C_1 and C_2 be two different word contexts of the same word related to two different decades, the Jaccard index is defined as follows:

$$J(C_1, C_2) = \frac{|C_1 \cap C_2|}{|C_1 \cup C_2|} = \frac{|C_1 \cap C_2|}{|C_1| + |C_2| - |C_1 \cap C_2|}$$

3.2 Visualizing semantic drift

Using the word embeddings and contexts, we propose three **visualization methods**. The features of these visualization methods are summarized in Table 2, and compared to those of the related work. These features were chosen to help visualize at a glance the change of a word over time. The *similar words* and the *degree of similarity* are standard measures of closeness of a word or change in meaning. The *continuity* of a word is able to show precisely how its meaning changes over time. The *word re-occurrence* informs a user whether a linguistic shift has occurred or not, and *geography* adds an extra dimension to study the context of concept drift.

Table 2 also forms a taxonomy that classifies visualization methods for diachronic semantic shifts with respect to different purposes. While all related work is focused on showing the top similar words and the degree of similarity with the root word, our methods also capture a combination of word re-occurrence and continuity through time, so the temporal factor becomes clearer. We also add a geographic dimension in the word-cloud map.

Radial bar chart This visualization shows the concept drift of a *root word* over time periods at a glance. A circle is divided into time slices (here, per decade). In each slice, the k words in the context of that time period are arranged. Their order is informative, so the words are sorted twice: first by their *re-occurrence* (whether the word is present in the context of any other decade), and then by their *similarity* to the root word (their closeness in embedded space). The length of the bar shows this degree of similarity. The bars have one of two colours: orange if re-occurring and blue otherwise. The proportion of colours and the length of the bars provide a *global* picture of the concept drift over time. The user can then also read the individual words to understand the *local* context.

Spiral line chart This visualization focuses on showing the continuity of a context word across time. Per root word, each context word is represented as a line that runs through each decade. A spiral (rather than line) shape is chosen to compress multiple time periods and words in a small space. The spiral starts in summary: a bar chart with the root word's aggregate context over all time periods (taller bars mark context words which re-occur in the context of the root word). The spiral then continues through time periods. The continuity of a context word through time is seen in the continuity of its line through the spiral. A segment is present in a time period only if the respective word occurs in the word embedding for that particular decade.

	top similar words	word re-occurrence	degree of similarity	continuity	geography
Radial bar chart (this work)	✓	✓	✓		
Spiral line chart (this work)	✓	✓		✓	
Word-cloud map (this work)	✓		✓		✓
Word graph	✓		✓		
Scatterplot	✓		✓		
Storyline chart	✓			✓	

Table 2: **Features of visualizations compared with related work**: word graphs (Li et al., 2021; Wijaya and Yeniterzi, 2011), scatterplots (Kulkarni et al., 2015; Mahmood et al., 2016), storyline charts (Mahmood et al., 2016)

This visualization is similar to storyline visualization (Mahmood et al., 2016), but has the added benefit of determining, at a glance, the words that are a closest match to and retain the context of the root word.

Word-cloud map This visualization tracks changes geographically, as well as across time periods, in a word cloud of the top $k = 100$ neighbours (with k tunable). Kulkarni et al. (2015) performed studies on tracking geographic changes, but they use a scatterplot which doesn't make geographic differences explicit. The geographic data here is the home country of the journal publishing the work.

4 Results

First, the Jaccard index (the context similarity of any word between any two decades) shows a clear trend for each combination of decades, and various root words. Namely, many root words have a Jaccard similarity close to 0 (they exhibit a near-total change in their context across the time periods). However, these root words are not common scientific terms. The distribution of Jaccard index values has a long tail towards the maximum value 1, and the more interesting terms (such as those presented in the next examples) lie on this tail.

Figure 1 shows the radial bar charts for the terms "anxiety", "cigarette", "coronavirus", and "misinformation". We see that the context around "anxiety" and "cigarette" stay relatively stable, but the difference is that the context of "anxiety" is much stronger than that of "cigarette" as the length of the bars does not change much among the top 50 contextual words.

The lower left radial bar chart shows that the context of "coronavirus" (especially in the 2020s) has changed dramatically, suggesting how the research around coronavirus has shifted its focus due to the ongoing Covid-19 pandemic. For the relatively modern word "misinformation", interesting patterns are visualized. From being nearly completely missing in the 1970s, its context has largely changed, with quite different degrees of similarity. Words such as "journalist" and "trump" show up in the 2010s, owing to the rise of the "fake news" phenomena that was prevalent at the time, and words like "twitter", "antivaccination", "netizens", "celebrity", "socialmedia", "facebook", and "instagram" in the 2020s, signifying social media and the internet as primary modes through which information, or in this case misinformation, is being disseminated.

In Figure 2, we track the continuity of the word "anxiety" over time. We have manually annotated the category a word may belong to and assigned a colour to each of them. The continuity of the word can be seen if the line corresponding to the word is present in all the decades. Some words, such as "alienation" and "apprehension" are only present in a single decade, while "fear" is present in the initial few decades, moves out of the word context, and is present in the later decades again. Words such as "anger", "mood", and "selfesteem" are present across all decades and can be seen as uninterrupted lines across all the time periods.

Figure 3 shows the geography of the word "divorce" over three pairs of decades, respectively 1970s/1980s, 1900s/2000s and 2010s/2020s. The countries selected are USA, UK and The Netherlands and the choice was motivated by the large volume of articles that they presented in the dataset. As can be observed from the picture, an interesting pattern is identified; during the 1970s and 1980s divorce had context words related to social status and level of education. However, in more recent years, the word seems to be more associated to the negative consequences that divorce itself can cause, such as increased criminal behaviour, violence and self-harm. This phenomenon is more apparent in the USA and The Netherlands, but is not as evident in the UK, where divorce is still closely related to paternity and motherhood.

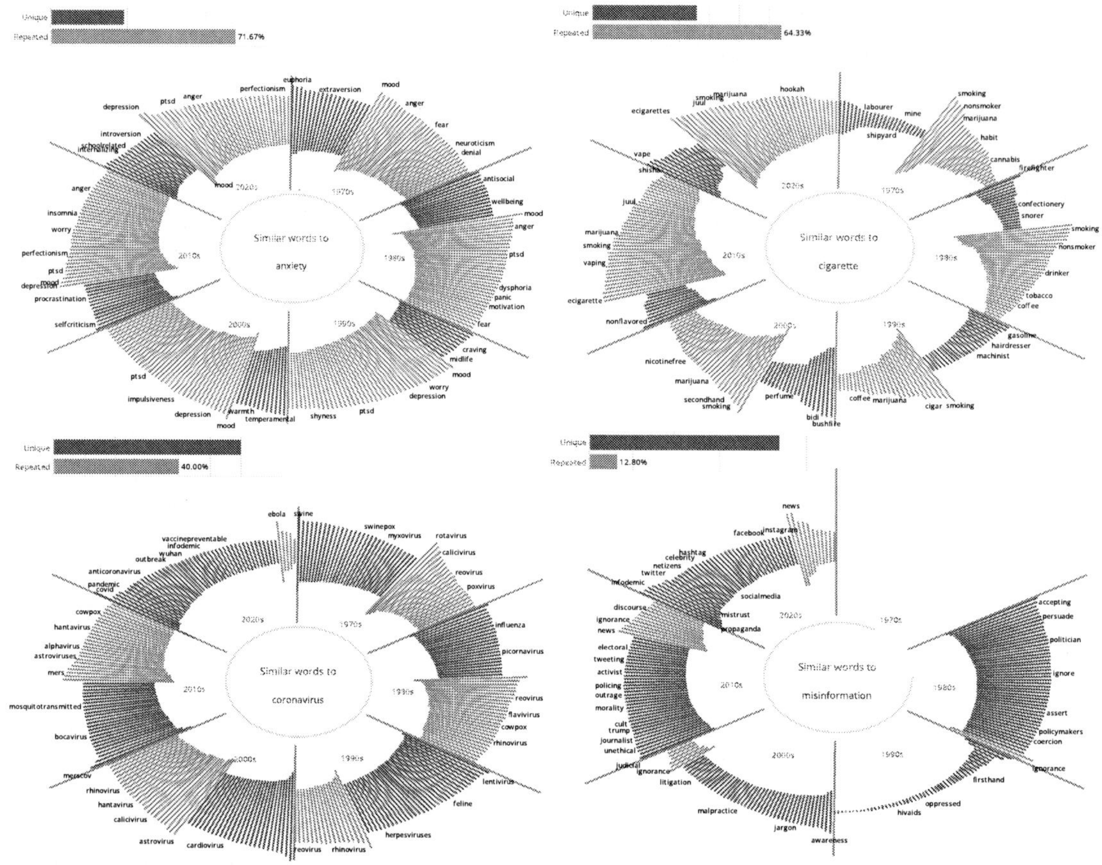

Figure 1: **Radial bar charts** ($k = 50$) for the terms "anxiety", "cigarette", "coronavirus", and "misinformation". Interactive versions online (Raef Kazi, 2022a).

5 User Study

To test the usability of these visualizations and measure whether they provide the desired benefit, we conducted a user study incorporating a self-assessment questionnaire. This study was conducted using the "VisEngage" questionnaire developed for interactive visualizations by (Hung and Parsons, 2017). Our questionnaire consisted of 11 questions which were grouped together based on type of characteristics they were meant to measure, which were, **aesthetics**, **ease of finding information**, **usability**, and **user engagement**. For each question, participants provide their response on a seven-point Likert scale, ranging from strongly disagree (1) to strongly agree (7).

Our study consisted of 5 visualizations, including previous visualization techniques from related work, the proposed methods in this paper, and the same information in tabular data for a comparison of usability. For each visualization, the study consisted of 2 task-related questions whose answers could be found within the visualization, the questionnaire for measuring the categories, and an open feedback form for the user to share their opinion on the visualization.

The results of this study from 8 participants have been summarized Figure 4. The heatmap shows that the average scores of the proposed Radial Bar Chart and Spiral Line Chart are *4.96* and *4.43* respectively, both above a *"neutral"* score (4), whereas, from the related work, only the Word Graph (4.7) scores above a *"neutral"* score, with the Scatterplot scoring a *3.74* and plain tabular data scoring *3.77*. The Radial Bar Chart performs best in categories of **aesthetics**, **usability**, and **user engagement**, and is second to the Word Graph in **ease of finding information**. We see that the Word Graph performs better overall compared to the Spiral Line Chart (except in the **aesthetics** category), and is a close second to the Radial Bar Chart overall, allowing it to also be a viable option for visualizing semantic shifts.

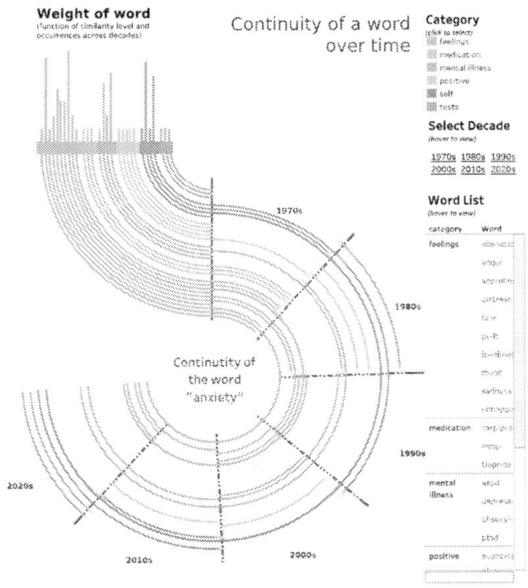

Figure 2: **Spiral line chart** for the word "anxiety". Interactive versions online ((Raef Kazi, 2022b)).

Figure 3: **Word-cloud maps** ($k = 100$) for the word "divorce" by the publisher location (UK, The Netherlands, and USA)

These scores from the study, taken in conjunction with the features visualized by each chart from Table 2, can aid in the selection of the right chart to use to best visualize a concept.

6 Conclusion

In this paper we have studied the diachronic semantic shift of words over time and have proposed methods to visualize these shifts. We perform a user study to test the usability of the proposed methods. Our interactive visualization tool helps users explore and understand these semantic shift. We also study previous visualization methods by other researchers and compare them to our proposed methods with a classification taxonomy.

In the future, we will study the complete PubMeb dataset and apply different methods to identify semantic shifts. More metrics need to be developed to further quantify the semantic shift so that highly dynamic words can be identified automatically. Furthermore, instead of manually annotating radial bar charts and selecting words for storylines, we will explore different possibilities of automatic annotation and selection.

This method does not capture the context of multiple words occurring together. For example, the meaning of the words "vaccine" and "news" may stay the same throughout time, but the context in which these words occur together can differ across time periods (these 2 words could have different neighbours if considered during the coronavirus pandemic). We will also develop additional ways of visualizing diachronic semantic shift.

	Question	Scatterplot	Word Graph	Radial Bar Chart	Tabular Data	Spiral Line Chart
Aesthetics	A	3.88	4.50	5.75	3.00	5.00
	B	3.75	4.00	5.63	3.38	4.63
	C	2.75	3.88	4.63	3.13	4.75
Ease of finding information	D	3.50	5.50	5.13	3.75	4.25
	E	3.50	5.38	4.63	3.75	4.25
Usability	F	4.38	5.13	5.38	4.63	4.38
	G	4.13	6.00	5.38	4.25	4.75
	H	3.00	4.63	4.13	3.38	4.00
User Engagement	I	4.25	4.00	4.88	4.75	4.38
	J	3.50	4.63	4.25	4.00	4.25
	K	4.50	5.13	4.88	3.50	4.13

Score Legend				
2.00	3.00	4.00	5.00	6.00

Figure 4: Heatmap of average scores for each question of each item across 5 visualizations. Values 1 and 7 have been removed from the score legend as they were never used by the participants. Sections have been superimposed for discussion purposes.

References

Hosein Azarbonyad, Mostafa Dehghani, Kaspar Beelen, Alexandra Arkut, Maarten Marx, and Jaap Kamps. 2017. Words are malleable: Computing semantic shifts in political and media discourse. In *Proceedings of the 2017 ACM on Conference on Information and Knowledge Management*, pages 1509–1518.

Hila Gonen, Ganesh Jawahar, Djamé Seddah, and Yoav Goldberg. 2020. Simple, interpretable and stable method for detecting words with usage change across corpora. In *Proceedings of the 58th Annual Meeting of the Association for Computational Linguistics*, pages 538–555, Online. Association for Computational Linguistics.

William L. Hamilton, Jure Leskovec, and Dan Jurafsky. 2016. Diachronic word embeddings reveal statistical laws of semantic change. In *Proceedings of the 54th Annual Meeting of the Association for Computational Linguistics (Volume 1: Long Papers)*, pages 1489–1501, Berlin, Germany. Association for Computational Linguistics.

Martin Hilpert and Stefan Th. Gries. 2008. Assessing frequency changes in multistage diachronic corpora: Applications for historical corpus linguistics and the study of language acquisition. *Literary and Linguistic Computing*, 24(4):385–401.

Ya-Hsin Hung and Paul Parsons. 2017. Assessing user engagement in information visualization. In *Proceedings of the 2017 CHI Conference Extended Abstracts on Human Factors in Computing Systems*, pages 1708–1717.

Adam Jatowt and Kevin Duh. 2014. A framework for analyzing semantic change of words across time. In *IEEE/ACM Joint Conference on Digital Libraries*, pages 229–238. IEEE.

Vivek Kulkarni, Bryan Perozzi, and Steven Skiena. 2015. Freshman or fresher? quantifying the geographic variation of internet language. *arXiv preprint arXiv:1510.06786*.

Andrey Kutuzov, Lilja Øvrelid, Terrence Szymanski, and Erik Velldal. 2018. Diachronic word embeddings and semantic shifts: a survey. In *Proceedings of the 27th International Conference on Computational Linguistics*, pages 1384–1397, Santa Fe, New Mexico, USA. Association for Computational Linguistics.

Ruiyuan Li, Pin Tian, and Shenghui Wang. 2021. Study concept drift in 150-year english literature. In *CEUR workshop proceedings of the First Workshop on AI + Informetrics*, volume 2871, pages 153–163.

Salman Mahmood, Rami Al-Rfou, and Klaus Mueller. 2016. Visualizing linguistic shift. *arXiv preprint arXiv:1611.06478*.

Tomas Mikolov, Ilya Sutskever, Kai Chen, Greg Corrado, and Jeffrey Dean. 2013. Distributed representations of words and phrases and their compositionality. In *Proceedings of the 26th International Conference on Neural Information Processing Systems - Volume 2*, NIPS'13, page 3111–3119, Red Hook, NY, USA. Curran Associates Inc.

National Library of Medicine. 2022. PubMed. `https://pubmed.ncbi.nlm.nih.gov`. Accessed 2022.

Raef Kazi. 2022a. Radial bar chart (concept drift). `https://public.tableau.com/app/profile/raef6267/viz/RadialBarChartConceptDrift/RadialBarChartConceptDrift`. Accessed 2022.

Raef Kazi. 2022b. Spiral line chart (concept drift). `https://public.tableau.com/app/profile/raef6267/viz/SpiralLineChartConceptDrift/SpiralLineChart`. Accessed 2022.

Phylypo Tum. 2020. A survey of the state-of-the-art language models up to early 2020. https://medium.com/@phylypo/a-survey-of-the-state-of-the-art-language-models-up-to-early-2020-aba824302c6.

Shenghui Wang, Stefan Schlobach, and Michel Klein. 2011. Concept drift and how to identify it. *Journal of Web Semantics*, 9(3):247–265. Semantic Web Dynamics Semantic Web Challenge, 2010.

Derry Tanti Wijaya and Reyyan Yeniterzi. 2011. Understanding semantic change of words over centuries. In *Proceedings of the 2011 international workshop on DETecting and Exploiting Cultural diversiTy on the social web*, pages 35–40.

Unsupervised Partial Sentence Matching for Cited Text Identification

Kathryn Ricci* **Haw-Shiuan Chang*** **Purujit Goyal** **Andrew McCallum**
[1]CICS, University of Massachusetts, Amherst
kathryn.d.ricci@gmail.com, hschang@cs.umass.edu
purujitgoyal@umass.edu, mccallum@cs.umass.edu

Abstract

Given a citation in the body of a research paper, cited text identification aims to find the sentences in the cited paper that are most relevant to the citing sentence. The task is fundamentally one of sentence matching, where affinity is often assessed by a cosine similarity between sentence embeddings. However, (a) sentences may not be well-represented by a single embedding because they contain multiple distinct semantic aspects, and (b) good matches may not require a strong match in all aspects. To overcome these limitations, we propose a simple and efficient unsupervised method for cited text identification that adapts an asymmetric similarity measure to allow partial matches of multiple aspects in both sentences. On the CL-SciSumm dataset we find that our method outperforms a baseline symmetric approach, and, surprisingly, also outperforms all supervised and unsupervised systems submitted to past editions of CL-SciSumm Shared Task 1a.

1 Introduction

The goal of a sentence-matching task is to extract a sentence that is most relevant to the query sentence from a collection of candidate sentences. In addition to information retrieval (IR) methods, a common unsupervised approach to sentence-matching tasks is to represent the query and candidate sentences by dense vectors, each computed by averaging the (contextualized) word embeddings corresponding to all constituent words in the sentence (Milajevs et al., 2014; Arora et al., 2017).

In this way, all semantic aspects of each sentence are collapsed into a single embedding representing the entirety of its semantics. By applying a cosine similarity to each query-candidate pair of these embeddings to evaluate affinity, the implicit assumption is that the most similar pair of sentences should contain exactly the same set of semantic aspects.

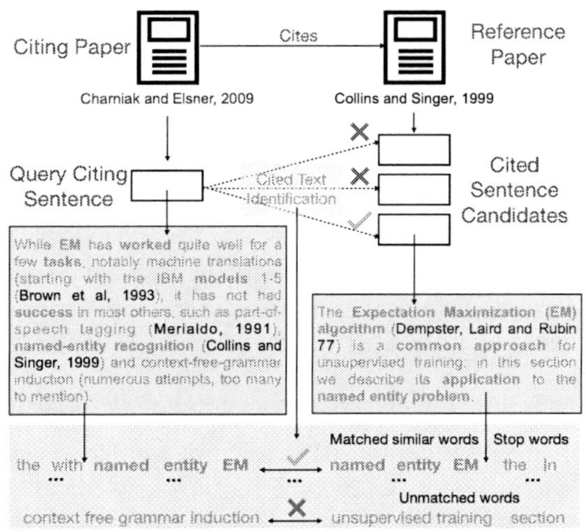

Figure 1: A sample query citing sentence and gold cited sentence from the CL-SciSumm dataset illustrating how shared semantic aspects, emphasized in the figure, may be accompanied by additional aspects in both sentences.

However, this approach is suboptimal for some applications, such as the task of identifying the "target" cited sentence(s) from a reference academic paper given a "query" citing sentence. As the example in Figure 1 shows, the target matching cited sentence may contain extra semantic aspects in addition to those that are shared, perhaps providing further details. Similarly, the query citing sentence might contain extra aspects referring to other work or to the relation of the cited information to the citing paper.

Motivated by this observation, we propose a simple and efficient unsupervised method that can accommodate extra semantic aspects in both query and candidates in the cited sentence identification task. To achieve this, our method employs an asymmetric sentence similarity measure to ignore words in the candidate that have little similarity to any query words, and we introduce a scaling function that de-emphasizes the unmatched words in the query citing sentence as well.

* Equal contribution

Proceedings of the Third Workshop on Scholarly Document Processing, pages 95–104
October 12–17, 2022.

On F1 of CL-SciSumm Shared Task 1a (Chandrasekaran et al., 2019, 2020), our method outperforms the corresponding symmetric similarity baseline, a strong unsupervised IR approach (Aumiller et al., 2020), and the best supervised approach among the past submissions between 2018 and 2020, which ensembles four BERT-based models (Chai et al., 2020).

2 Method

Figure 2 illustrates our similarity estimation method given a pair of sentences. In Section 2.1, we ignore the details in the cited sentence candidate and only consider its matched words. In Section 2.2, we softly remove the stop words because the similarity score should not consider the number of matched stop words. Finally, we reduce the influence of irrelevant words in the query citing sentence and let the similarity score be determined more by the exactly matched words in Section 2.3.

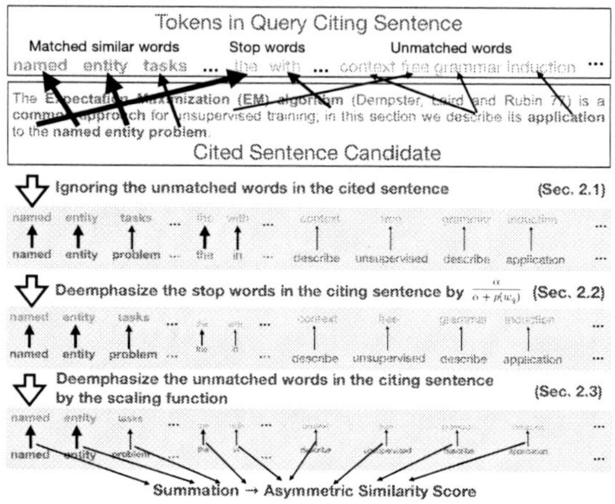

Figure 2: Illustration of our asymmetric similarity estimation. Smaller font sizes or arrows indicate smaller contribution to the output similarity score. Our method can extract the partially matched cited sentence candidates by decreasing the influence of unmatched words and stop words to highlight the matched semantic words.

2.1 Asymmetric Sentence Similarity Measure

Kobayashi et al. (2015) perform extractive summarization by extracting the summary sentences that cover the original document best. Inspired by their work, we extract the cited sentences that cover the query citing sentence best, which means not penalizing the details or extra words in the cited sentences.

Specifically, we represent the query citing sentence as a multiset of the word embeddings. For each token in the query citing sentence, we find the most similar word in the extracted sentence candidate, and compute the asymmetric similarity score $\text{sim}(S_q, S_c)$ as

$$\sum_{w_q \in S_q} W(w_q) \max_{\boldsymbol{w}_c \in S_c} \sigma(\boldsymbol{w}_q^T \boldsymbol{w}_c), \quad (1)$$

where $\boldsymbol{w}_q$ are the embeddings of the constituent words w in the query sentence S_q and $\boldsymbol{w}_c$ are the word embeddings from the cited sentence candidate S_c. The word embeddings are normalized by their l^2-norms so that the dot product between two word embeddings is their cosine similarity. $W(w_q)$ is the weight of word w_q and σ is a scaling function, which are detailed in Section 2.2 and Section 2.3, respectively.

We output the top K sentences S_c with the highest similarities to the query citing sentence $\text{sim}(S_q, S_c)$. We find that this optimization method is better than the greedy selection for extractive summarization proposed in Kobayashi et al. (2015). See Appendix C.1 for details.

2.2 Inverse Frequency Weighting

Unlike Kobayashi et al. (2015) which treats each word equally, we assign a lower weight to a common word (e.g., a stop word) in the query citing sentence because a high-frequency word is naturally more likely to be matched to irrelevant sentences in the cited paper.

Following Arora et al. (2017), we set the weight of the word w_q in Equation 1 as

$$W(w_q) = \frac{\alpha}{\alpha + p(w_q)}, \quad (2)$$

where frequency probabilities $p(w_q)$ are computed by $\frac{f(w_q)}{N}$, $f(w_q)$ is the frequency of words, and N is total number of words in the corpus. We let $\alpha = 10^{-4}$, which is a typical value suggested by Arora et al. (2017).

2.3 Scaling Function for Word Similarities

In Figure 2, the correct sentence pair only shares a few terms, such as *named entity*, while there are several unmatched words in the query citing sentence, such as *context free*. To let the matching terms in the query contribute more to the final similarity score than the unmatched words, we set the scaling function in Equation 1 to be

$$\sigma(x) = x^d, \quad (3)$$

where $d > 0$ is a fixed hyperparameter.

When d is large, our method effectively ignores the cosine similarities that are smaller than 1, which means it only considers the exact lexical matching words. In contrast, a small d encourages the cited sentences to contain more words that are topically related to the words in the query. We can tune d to balance the hard matching and soft matching.

3 Experiments

We evaluate our method on the CL-SciSumm dataset (Chandrasekaran et al., 2019), comparing our results to past submissions to Shared Task 1a. In the official evaluation, performance is measured based on sentence overlap F1 and ROUGE-S*[1] (Lin and Och, 2004), both micro-averaged over all sentences selected by all annotators.

We train 300-dimensional word embeddings using Word2Vec skip-gram (Mikolov et al., 2013). We use the ACL Anthology Reference Corpus Version 2 (Bird et al., 2008) as our training corpus, because the papers in CL-SciSumm are sampled from the computational linguistics domain. For each query citing sentence in the corpus, we select the top $K = 2$ sentences from our candidate ranking to submit for evaluation. All the hyperparameters are experimentally chosen to maximize average F1 scores on the training set.

3.1 Preprocessing

We use a regular expression to remove citation markers (e.g., of the form (*Author, Year*)) from the word-embedding training corpus, citing sentences, and candidate sentences. These markers do not contribute to the semantics of the sentences, yet the weights of these low-frequency markers in Equation 2 are high and the markers may erroneously match with words in our similarity computations. Our ablation study in Appendix C.2 finds that omitting this preprocessing step indeed significantly degrades performance.

Our objective function in Equation 1 encourages the selected cited sentence candidates to cover the query citing sentence. The method has a preference for selecting longer sentences because the asymmetric similarity measurement does not penalize the unmatched details in the cited sentences, and more words in each candidate tend to cover the query sentence better (Kobayashi et al., 2015).

[1]We discover that the official evaluation script outputs ROUGE-S* rather than ROUGE-SU4.

Best-Performing Model Configuration (and Tuning Range)		
Asymmetry Direction:	Candidate Covers Query	(or Reverse)
Word Similarity:	Cosine	(or Dot Product)
Optimization:	Top K	(or Greedy)
Extracted Sent. Num. K:	2	(or 1-10)
Weights of Query Words:	Arora et al. (2017)	(or Uniform)
Scaling Function Power (d):	4	(or 1-10)
Citation Markers:	Remove	(or Keep)
Truncation:	After 100 Tokens	(or 50 or None)
Casing:	Cased	(or Uncased)
Word2Vec Min. Word Count:	35	(or 50 or 100)

Table 1: Configuration of our best-performing Word2Vec-based model, **Asymm (d=4)**, on CL-SciSumm training set. The hyperparameters in parentheses are the ranges we tested.

Our scaling function alleviates the problem by emphasizing the exactly matched words. To further alleviate the issue, we truncate sentences to a chosen maximum length under the assumption that most of the relevant semantic aspects occur at the beginning of a long citing or candidate sentence.

3.2 Model and Baselines

We consider the following methods (see Appendix C.2 for more ablation baselines).

- **Asymm (d=4)**: Our proposed asymmetric method with the configuration in Table 1, the best-performing Word2Vec-based configuration on the training set. d refers to the power of our scaling function in Equation 3.

- **Asymm (d=1)**: Same configuration as **Asymm (d=4)** but using the trivial scaling function $\sigma(x) = x$.

- **Symm**: The symmetric method that computes a cosine similarity between average word embeddings (Milajevs et al., 2014). Our best **Symm** configuration removes stop words and does not employ the inverse frequency weighting of Arora et al. (2017), which we found to lower performance in our experiments.

- **Asymm SciBERT (d=4)**: Replacing Word2Vec in **Asymm (d=4)** with SciBERT (Beltagy et al., 2019).

- **BERT ensemble**: Best-performing submission to Shared Task 1a from 2018-2020 (Chai et al., 2020). The supervised approach creates an ensemble of four SciBERT-based models. They also set the number of output sentences $K = 2$.

- **BM25 ensemble**: An unsupervised retrieval

method proposed by Aumiller et al. (2020)[2] that considers the exact term overlap using BM25 (Robertson and Walker, 1994). The approach, which achieves the second-best F1 score on Shared Task 1a of all 2018-2020 submissions, is an ensemble of two search configurations with additional preprocessing steps to remove citation markers, as we do, and to mask math-like text.

Notice that both **BERT ensemble** and **BM25 ensemble** utilize the position information of the candidate sentence within the reference text, while all of our methods do not make any assumption on the position of extracted sentences.

3.3 Main Result

The results in Table 2 show that, according to F1, **Asymm (d=4)** outperforms **Asymm (d=1)** and **Symm**. On the test set, **Asymm (d=4)** outperforms **BERT ensemble** and **BM25 ensemble** in terms of F1, with the latter's reported F1 and ROUGE scores similar to those of **Asymm (d=1)**. This demonstrates that the unsupervised approach for cited text identification can outperform supervised approach due to the small training dataset size.

We observe that the performance of **Asymm SciBERT (d=4)** is inconsistent on training and test data. On the test set, Word2Vec significantly outperforms SciBERT. One reason might be that the keywords in ACL papers are less ambiguous compared to other text domains such as news. The result also highlights the advantages of the non-contextualized word embeddings: we can easily weight or mask individual word embeddings when matching the sentences. It is also much more efficient to train Word2Vec on a new corpus and encode a new sentence into their word embeddings.

4 Related Work

A variety of unsupervised approaches to sentence-matching tasks have been proposed. A traditional method uses an average (contextualized) word embedding as a sentence representation and computes a cosine similarity between query and candidate embeddings (Milajevs and Purver, 2014; Arora et al., 2017). Another approach solves optimal transportation to match the words between two sentences (Kusner et al., 2015). In addition, Skip-Thought (Kiros et al., 2015), BERT (Devlin et al., 2019), and SimCSE (Gao et al., 2021) encode the sentence into a single embedding to predict the nearby sentences or augmented original sentence. These methods assume that all the semantic aspects in a sentence should be matched and lack a way to emphasize the matched aspects.

[2] Aumiller et al. (2020) also propose a two-stage re-ranking approach using a BERT re-ranker, but the second stage does not improve the result.

Method	Training Set			Test Set		
	Recall	F1	R-S*	Recall	F1	R-S*
Symm	15.5	13.5	12.0	18.0	12.4	9.6
Asymm (d=1)	18.0	15.6	10.2	23.1	16.0	11.3
Asymm (d=4)	18.8	16.4	11.2	**25.1**	**17.4**	12.9
Asymm SciBERT (d=4)	**19.5**	**17.0**	**12.2**	22.1	15.3	11.4
BM25 ensemble†	–	–	–	–	16.1	11.3
BERT ensemble♮♯	–	–	–	24.6	17.2	**14.7**

Table 2: Results of evaluation on the CL-SciSumm training and test sets. All scores are reported as percentages. ♮ a supervised method. † results taken from Aumiller et al. (2020). ♯ results taken from Chai et al. (2020).

Kobayashi et al. (2015) propose an asymmetric similarity measure to be used in unsupervised extractive summarization. BERTScore (Zhang et al., 2020) automatically evaluates generated text using similar asymmetric similarity scores. The coverage score from the generation to reference is its recall, and the score with the reverse direction is its precision. However, they do not use the asymmetric similarity to solve partial sentence matching tasks such as cited text identification.

There are also many supervised approaches for estimating the relevancy of two sentences. For example, the approaches built on BERT include the cross-encoder model (Devlin et al., 2019), bi-encoder model (Sentence-BERT) (Reimers and Gurevych, 2019), and the model that maximizes the coverage score from the retrieved document to the query (ColBERT) (Khattab and Zaharia, 2020). Although effective, these approaches often require a large training dataset to learn a good sentence-matching. Thus, such methods might not perform well in scientific sentence-matching tasks where annotations are very limited and expensive.

5 Conclusion

We observe that many target cited sentences and query citing sentences are only partially matched, which motivates us to propose a simple asymmetric sentence similarity measurement that down-weights or masks the unmatched words, stop words, and citation markers. With only a few training labels, learning the prior weighting on contextualized word embeddings could be challenging, and we suspect that this is the main reason that our simple unsupervised approach could outperform a well-tuned BERT-based supervised approach.

6 Acknowledgement

We thank Kaivankumar Shah and Anjali Ramaprasad for their preliminary exploration of this project. We also thank Gully Burns and Boris Veytsman for their constructive feedback. This work was supported in part by the Center for Data Science and the Center for Intelligent Information Retrieval, in part by the Chan Zuckerberg Initiative under the project Scientific Knowledge Base Construction, in part by the IBM Research AI through the AI Horizons Network, in part using high performance computing equipment obtained under a grant from the Collaborative R&D Fund managed by the Massachusetts Technology Collaborative, and in part by the National Science Foundation (NSF) grant numbers IIS-1922090 and IIS-1763618. Any opinions, findings, conclusions, or recommendations expressed in this material are those of the authors and do not necessarily reflect those of the sponsor.

7 Ethical and Broader Impact

There are several potential applications of our approach. For example, it could be used to accelerate the labeling process, trace the claims made by the citing sentence to verify their correctness, or serve as a baseline for future supervised cited text identification approaches.

One potential risk of our approach is that its assumptions might not be always valid and might create biases in downstream applications. For example, we assume that high-frequency words or unmatched words are less important in cited text identification tasks. This assumption could bias our method toward outputting longer sentences with more low-frequency words, which might be less comprehensible to users.

References

Sanjeev Arora, Yingyu Liang, and Tengyu Ma. 2017. A simple but tough-to-beat baseline for sentence embeddings. In *International conference on learning representations*.

Dennis Aumiller, Satya Almasian, Philip Hausner, and Michael Gertz. 2020. UniHD@CL-SciSumm 2020: Citation extraction as search. In *Proceedings of the First Workshop on Scholarly Document Processing*, pages 261–269, Online. Association for Computational Linguistics.

Iz Beltagy, Kyle Lo, and Arman Cohan. 2019. Scibert: A pretrained language model for scientific text. In *Proceedings of the 2019 Conference on Empirical Methods in Natural Language Processing and the 9th International Joint Conference on Natural Language Processing (EMNLP-IJCNLP)*, pages 3615–3620.

Steven Bird, Robert Dale, Bonnie Dorr, Bryan Gibson, Mark Joseph, Min-Yen Kan, Dongwon Lee, Brett Powley, Dragomir Radev, and Yee Fan Tan. 2008. The ACL Anthology reference corpus: A reference dataset for bibliographic research in computational linguistics. In *Proceedings of the Sixth International Conference on Language Resources and Evaluation (LREC'08)*, Marrakech, Morocco. European Language Resources Association (ELRA).

Ling Chai, Guizhen Fu, and Yuan Ni. 2020. NLP-PINGAN-TECH @ CL-SciSumm 2020. In *Proceedings of the First Workshop on Scholarly Document Processing*, pages 235–241, Online. Association for Computational Linguistics.

Muthu Kumar Chandrasekaran, Guy Feigenblat, Eduard Hovy, Abhilasha Ravichander, Michal Shmueli-Scheuer, and Anita de Waard. 2020. Overview and insights from the shared tasks at scholarly document processing 2020: Cl-scisumm, laysumm and longsumm. In *Proceedings of the first workshop on scholarly document processing*, pages 214–224.

Muthu Kumar Chandrasekaran, Michihiro Yasunaga, Dragomir Radev, Dayne Freitag, and Min-Yen Kan. 2019. Overview and results: Cl-scisumm shared task 2019. In *In Proceedings of Joint Workshop on Bibliometric-enhanced Information Retrieval and NLP for Digital Libraries (BIRNDL 2019)*.

Jacob Devlin, Ming-Wei Chang, Kenton Lee, and Kristina Toutanova. 2019. BERT: Pre-training of deep bidirectional transformers for language understanding. In *Proceedings of the 2019 Conference of the North American Chapter of the Association for Computational Linguistics: Human Language Technologies, Volume 1 (Long and Short Papers)*, pages 4171–4186, Minneapolis, Minnesota. Association for Computational Linguistics.

Tianyu Gao, Xingcheng Yao, and Danqi Chen. 2021. Simcse: Simple contrastive learning of sentence embeddings. In *Proceedings of the 2021 Conference on Empirical Methods in Natural Language Processing*, pages 6894–6910.

Gautier Izacard, Mathild Caron, Lucas Hosseini, Sebastian Riedel, Piotr Bojanowski, Armand Joulin, and Edouard Grave. 2021. Unsupervised dense information retrieval with contrastive learning. *arXiv preprint arXiv:2112.09118*.

Kokil Jaidka, Michihiro Yasunga, Muthu Chandrasekaran, Dragomir Radev, and Min-Yen Kan.

2018. The cl-scisumm shared task 2018: Results and key insights. In *BIRNDL @ SIGIR 2018*.

Omar Khattab and Matei Zaharia. 2020. ColBERT: Efficient and effective passage search via contextualized late interaction over bert.

Ryan Kiros, Yukun Zhu, Russ R Salakhutdinov, Richard Zemel, Raquel Urtasun, Antonio Torralba, and Sanja Fidler. 2015. Skip-thought vectors. In *Advances in Neural Information Processing Systems*, volume 28. Curran Associates, Inc.

Hayato Kobayashi, Masaki Noguchi, and Taichi Yatsuka. 2015. Summarization based on embedding distributions. In *Proceedings of the 2015 conference on empirical methods in natural language processing*, pages 1984–1989.

Matt Kusner, Yu Sun, Nicholas Kolkin, and Kilian Weinberger. 2015. From word embeddings to document distances. In *International conference on machine learning*, pages 957–966. PMLR.

Chin-Yew Lin and Franz Josef Och. 2004. Automatic evaluation of machine translation quality using longest common subsequence and skip-bigram statistics. In *Proceedings of the 42nd Annual Meeting of the Association for Computational Linguistics (ACL-04)*, pages 605–612.

Tomas Mikolov, Ilya Sutskever, Kai Chen, Greg Corrado, and Jeffrey Dean. 2013. Distributed representations of words and phrases and their compositionality. In *NeurIPS*.

Dmitrijs Milajevs, Dimitri Kartsaklis, Mehrnoosh Sadrzadeh, and Matthew Purver. 2014. Evaluating neural word representations in tensor-based compositional settings. In *EMNLP*.

Dmitrijs Milajevs and Matthew Purver. 2014. Investigating the contribution of distributional semantic information for dialogue act classification. In *Proceedings of the 2nd Workshop on Continuous Vector Space Models and their Compositionality (CVSC)*, pages 40–47, Gothenburg, Sweden. Association for Computational Linguistics.

Ori Ram, Gal Shachaf, Omer Levy, Jonathan Berant, and Amir Globerson. 2022. Learning to retrieve passages without supervision. In *NAACL*.

Nils Reimers and Iryna Gurevych. 2019. Sentence-BERT: Sentence embeddings using Siamese BERT-networks. In *Proceedings of the 2019 Conference on Empirical Methods in Natural Language Processing and the 9th International Joint Conference on Natural Language Processing (EMNLP-IJCNLP)*, pages 3982–3992, Hong Kong, China. Association for Computational Linguistics.

Stephen E Robertson and Steve Walker. 1994. Some simple effective approximations to the 2-poisson model for probabilistic weighted retrieval. In *SIGIR'94*, pages 232–241. Springer.

sbert.net. 2021. `sentence-transformers all-mpnet-base-v2`.

David Wadden, Shanchuan Lin, Kyle Lo, Lucy Lu Wang, Madeleine van Zuylen, Arman Cohan, and Hannaneh Hajishirzi. 2020. Fact or fiction: Verifying scientific claims. In *Proceedings of the 2020 Conference on Empirical Methods in Natural Language Processing (EMNLP)*, pages 7534–7550.

Tianyi Zhang, Varsha Kishore, Felix Wu, Kilian Q. Weinberger, and Yoav Artzi. 2020. BERTScore: Evaluating text generation with bert. In *International Conference on Learning Representations*.

A Appendix Overview

In the appendix, we list our main contributions in Appendix B, conduct more experiments and analyses in Appendix C, provide more details of CL-SciSumm Shared Task 1a in Appendix D, provide more details of computing our objective function in Appendix E, and discuss some potential future work in Appendix F.

B Main Contributions

- Inspired by Kobayashi et al. (2015), we propose a sentence-matching model that allows both query sentence and retrieved sentence to contain unmatched semantic aspects.
- We discover that some preprocessing steps such as removing the citation markers are crucial in a cited text identification task.
- Our extensive experiments on CL-SciSumm Shared Task 1a show that a simple, efficient, and unsupervised method based on Word2Vec can achieve slightly higher F1 score than the state-of-the-art supervised method that ensembles multiple BERT-based models.

C More Experimental Results

We describe our baselines for our ablation study in Appendix C.1, analyze the results of the ablation study in Appendix C.2, test different d values in our scaling function and reverse the asymmetry direction in Appendix C.3, compare the average length of extracted sentences in Appendix C.4, and report the Recall@K in Appendix C.5.

C.1 Ablation Study Setup

We start from **Asymm (d=4)**, which uses the best Word2Vec-based configuration reported in Table 1, and change one design choice or hyperparameter at a time. In addition, we test a few variants of **Asymm SciBERT**.

Kobayashi et al. (2015) theoretically show that a greedy optimization is effective for maximizing Equation 1. Hence, we also tried to greedily select the kth cited sentence S_c^k such that the selected sentence candidates up to this point $\cup_{i=1}^{k}\{S_c^i\}$ best cover the query citing sentence: $\arg\max_{S_c^k} \text{sim}(S_q, \cup_{i=1}^{k}\{S_c^i\})$. This baseline is called **Greedy Optimization**.

To confirm the effectiveness of our word weighting described in Section 2.2, we set the weights $W(w_q)$ in Equation 2 to be always 1 and call this

Method	Training Set F1	Training Set R-S*	Test Set F1	Test Set R-S*
Asymm (d=4)	16.4	11.2	**17.4**	**12.9**
Word Similarity: Dot Product	13.0	9.1	15.1	11.4
Greedy Optimization	13.8	10.0	15.3	12.0
Unif. Weights	9.5	7.1	8.9	6.9
Unif. Weights, No Stop Words	14.1	10.4	15.3	11.4
Keep Citation Markers	11.0	8.2	13.1	9.1
No Truncation	16.3	10.9	17.2	12.8
Truncate after 50 Tokens	15.9	10.9	**17.4**	12.7
Uncased	16.2	10.3	**17.4**	12.8
Word2Vec Min. Word Count: 100	15.7	11.1	16.7	12.5
Word2Vec Min. Word Count: 50	15.9	11.1	**17.4**	12.8
Asymm SciBERT (d=4)	**17.0**	12.2	15.3	11.4
Asymm SciBERT (d=1)	16.8	**12.5**	15.0	11.6
Asymm SciBERT (d=4), Unif. Weights	15.1	11.6	13.4	10.1

Table 3: Results of the ablation study. We report F1 (%) and ROUGE-S* (%) on training and test sets. See Table 1 for the configuration of **Asymm (d=4)**.

baseline **Unif. Weights**. In addition to this, **Unif. Weights, No Stop Words** sets $W(w_q)$ as 0 if the word w_q is in our stop word list and as 1 otherwise.

Finally, to decrease the vocabulary size, we map the words to the [UNK] token if the word frequency is below a threshold. By default, the threshold is set to be 35, and we also try 50 and 100 in **Word2Vec Min. Word Count: 50 or 100**.

C.2 Ablation Study Results

Table 3 reports the results of our ablation study on both training and test sets. When using Word2Vec embeddings, we find that the following ablation baselines significantly degrade the performance measured by F1: (1) using a dot product instead of cosine similarity to compute word similarity (**Word Similarity: Dot Product**), (2) using greedy optimization, (3) removing the inverse frequency weighting of Arora et al. (2017) (**Unif. Weights**), and (4) omitting citation marker removal (**Keep Citation Markers**). Changing the truncation or casing configuration, or raising the minimum word count, only slightly decreases scores on the training set and results in little or no decrease in F1 on the test set.

We additionally find that the greedy sentence selection used in Kobayashi et al. (2015) is less effective than ranking sentences by their individual similarity scores when using our method for this task. We hypothesize that the effectiveness discrepancy comes from the length of the query. In the extractive summarization, the query is a long document, so we usually want the extracted next sentence to cover the aspects of query documents that are not covered by the previously extracted sentences. In contrast, the query in cited text identification is much shorter, so the first citing sentences often can cover the important keywords of the query. As a result, the greedy method might extract the incorrect second cited sentence that does not mention these important keywords in the query citing sentences.

Furthermore, the ablation study shows that simply removing the stop words from a list (**Unif. Weights, No Stop Words**) is significantly worse than the inverse frequency weighting (**Asymm (d=4)**). This means that non-stop high-frequency words often carry less semantic information and thus, their matches should also be counted with smaller weights.

When using SciBERT embeddings, we also observe that removing inverse frequency weighting degrades performance, but the difference is smaller than the difference between **Asymm (d=4)** and **Unif. Weights**. This might highlight the difficulty of weighting the contextualized embeddings of individual words.

We note that the effect on F1 and ROUGE scores of setting $d = 1$ in the scaling function is mixed for **Asymm SciBERT**. A possible reason for this is that when using contextualized embeddings, an exact lexical match of two words does not yield a cosine similarity of 1, which makes a higher d also decrease the similarity scores between the exactly matched words from the sentence pair.

C.3 Varying the Power Hyperparameter in our Scaling Function and Reversing the Asymmetry Direction

Figure 3 plots the F1 score of **Asymm** on training and test sets against the value of the power hyperparameter d in our proposed method's scaling function. They plot the same quantity for the method that has the same configuration but reverses the standard direction of asymmetry such that the query aspects must cover the candidate aspects (**Asymm Reverse**). That is, we select the top 2 citation sentences with the highest $\text{sim}(S_c, S_q)$. **Symm**, **BERT ensemble**, and **BM25 ensemble** are also represented.

Reversing the direction of the asymmetry is an inherently challenging approach: the variability in candidate sentence length causes the system to prefer the longest candidates, as there are more terms in the summation over query words in Equation 1.

However, Figure 3 shows that, on the training set, the F1 score of **Asymm Reverse** becomes closer to that of **Asymm** as d is increased. Furthermore, on the test set, the F1 score of **Asymm Reverse** approaches that of **BM25 ensemble**, as does the score of **Asymm** after surpassing that of **BM25 ensemble** for more moderate values of d.

This observation is consistent with the intuition that as the power is increased, the mechanism of the asymmetric method approaches that of an exact word-matching method. The figure further suggests that an optimal value of d (on the training set, it is 4) might allow our method to strike a balance between a soft matching method that considers all query words and an exact matching method that considers only query words with a lexical match in the candidate, leading to improved performance over both these approaches.

Method	Selected Sentence Avg. Length
Symm	39.3
Asymm (d=1)	47.0
Asymm (d=4)	41.0
Asymm Reverse (d=1)	132.5
Asymm Reverse (d=4)	56.4

Table 4: Average sentence length of the top $K = 2$ sentences selected for all citing sentences in the training set.

C.4 Retrieved Sentence Lengths

Table 4 contains the average length of the top $K = 2$ sentences selected by each of the listed methods for the training set. An expected effect of our proposed method is to decrease the tendency of the basic asymmetric method with $d = 1$ to select longer sentences, noted in Section 3.1. From the table it is evident that adding the scaling function with $d = 4$ indeed leads to the selection of shorter sentences on average, reducing the average selected sentence length by 6 tokens to more closely approach the corresponding figure for our symmetric baseline, **Symm**.

The same effect is apparent when the standard direction of asymmetry in the similarity measure is reversed such that the query must cover the candidate (**Asymm Reverse**). In this case, we see that **Asymm Reverse (d=1)** generally selects very long candidate cited sentences, as expected due to the variability in candidate length, noted in Appendix C.3. However, increasing the power of the scaling function to $d = 4$ more than halves the average selected sentence length, likely by de-

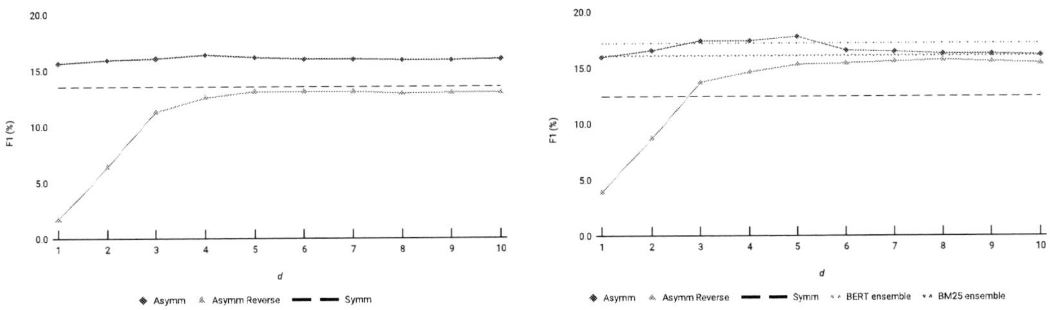

Figure 3: Training (Left) and test (Right) set F1 score of our proposed asymmetric method, **Asymm**, and the same method with the direction of asymmetry reversed (**Asymm Reverse**), as the hyperparameter d of the scaling function is varied. Scores for **Symm**, **BERT ensemble**, and **BM25 ensemble** are drawn from Table 2 for comparison where available.

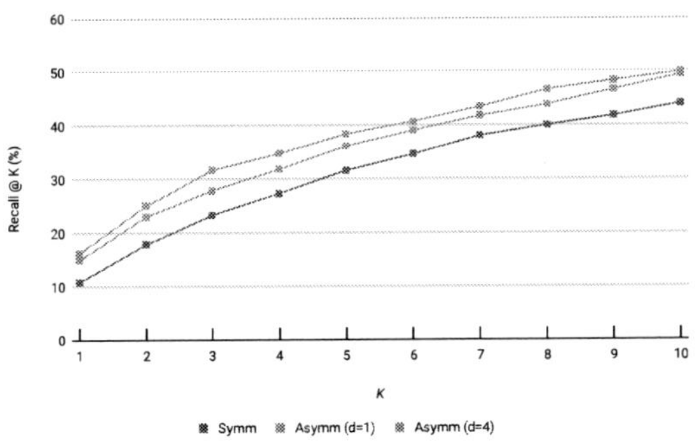

Figure 4: Recall on the test set as the number of selected sentences, K, is increased from 1 to 10.

emphasizing irrelevant words in relatively long candidates. Figure 3 show that this effect is accompanied by a drastic improvement in performance, although **Asymm Reverse** continues to be outperformed by **Asymm** for all choices of d in our experiments.

C.5 Recall@K

Figure 4 plots the test set recall performance of **Symm**, **Asymm (d=1)**, and our best-performing Word2Vec-based configuration, **Asymm (d=4)**. **Asymm (d=4)** consistently outperforms the two baselines as the number of selected sentences K is increased from 1 to 10. Within 10 predictions out of possibly 200 sentence candidates in a reference paper, the ability of our method to identify around 50% of all cited sentences selected by annotators indicates its practicality to a user who wishes to identify relevant sentences within the cited text.

	Training	Test
Num. Annotators per Citing Sentence	1	3
Num. Reference Papers	40	20
Avg. Num. Citing Sentences per Reference Paper	18.8	19.2
Num. (citing sentence,{gold cited sentences}) Pairs	753	1149

Table 5: CL-SciSumm corpus statistics.

D Experiment Details

The CL-SciSumm Shared Task was last held in 2020, and in that year the official task overview (Chandrasekaran et al., 2020) reported results for Task 1a from up to five runs from each of eight participants. Previous task offerings in 2018 (Jaidka et al. (2018); 10 participants) and 2019 (Chandrasekaran et al. (2019); 9 participants) evaluated submissions using the same blind test set, which is now public.

The dataset includes manual annotations for each citing sentence, each consisting of up to five spans from the reference paper that best reflect the citing sentence. The task statistics are reported in Table 5. We use the official evaluation script used in past editions of the Shared Task 1a to obtain our micro-averaged sentence overlap and ROUGE results.

E Method Details

Word2Vec training. The ACL Anthology Reference Corpus Version 2 (ACL ARC 2), used as our Word2Vec training corpus, contains 86M tokens. We train embeddings of dimension 300 using the Gensim library[3].

Word-frequency statistics. When our method is used with Word2Vec embeddings, the query word

[3]https://radimrehurek.com/gensim/

weights of Arora et al. (2017) are computed from word-count statistics collected from the training corpus. When our embeddings are contextualized embeddings from SciBERT, we similarly use the ACL ARC 2 corpus to compute word frequencies, but do so after WordPiece tokenization using the SciBERT tokenizer.

Stop words. We use the following lowercased stop word list: @-@, =, <eos>, <unk>, disambiguation, etc, etc., –, @card@, ∼, -, _, @, ^, &, *, <, >, (,), \, |, {, },], [, :, ;, ', ", /, ?, !, „ ., 't, 'd, 'll, 's, 'm, 've, *a, about, above, after, again, against, all, am, an, and, any, are, aren, as, at, be, because, been, before, being, below, between, both, but, by, can, cannot, could, couldn, did, didn, do, does, doesn, doing, don, down, during, each, few, for, from, further, had, hadn, has, hasn, have, haven, having, he, her, here, here, hers, herself, him, himself, his, how, how, i, if, in, into, is, isn, it, it, its, itself, let, me, more, most, mustn, my, myself, no, nor, not, of, off, on, once, only, or, other, ought, our, ours, ourselves, out, over, own, same, she, should, shouldn, so, some, such, than, that, the, their, theirs, them, themselves, then, there, these, they, this, those, through, to, too, under, until, up, very, was, wasn, we, were, weren, what, when, where, which, while, who, whom, why, with, won, would, wouldn, you, your, yours, yourself, yourselves*.

F Future Work

How to combine our approach with contextualized word embeddings more effectively is a promising research direction. For example, we can pretrain BERT on ACL papers as in Chai et al. (2020) after removing the citation markers. Furthermore, all of our experiments are done on CL-SciSumm Shared Task 1a, and we hope to also test our methods on other datasets such as SCIFACT (Wadden et al., 2020).

Recently, Gao et al. (2021) propose SimCSE, an effective unsupervised sentence similarity estimation method. Izacard et al. (2021) and Ram et al. (2022) propose unsupervised dense IR approaches. We are curious about the effectiveness of these approaches on partial sentence-matching tasks such as cited text identification. Furthermore, training Sentence-BERT (Reimers and Gurevych, 2019) on various kinds of similar sentences results in a general-purpose sentence similarity model (sbert.net, 2021). We leave the comparison with these approaches for future work.

Multi-label Classification of Scientific Research Documents Across Domains and Languages

Autumn Toney-Wails
Georgetown University
autumn.toney@georgetown.edu

James Dunham
Georgetown University
james.dunham@georgetown.edu

Abstract

Automatic organization of scholarly literature is a challenging but essential task. In particular, assigning key concepts to scientific publications allows researchers, policymakers, and the general public to search for and discover relevant research. But any meaningful organization of scientific publications must evolve with new research, requiring up-to-date and scalable text classification models. Additionally, scientific research publications benefit from multi-label classification, particularly with more fine-grained sub-domains. Prior work has focused on classifying scientific publications from one research area (e.g., computer science), referencing static concept descriptions, and implementing English-only classification models. We propose a multi-label classification model that can be implemented in non-English languages, across all scientific literature, with dynamic concepts.

1 Introduction

Maintaining an up-to-date organization of scientific literature in any domain requires an automated approach—a comprehensive and real-time solution for a constant influx of text data. Specifically, research publications require characterization or indexing in order to be searchable and accessible to researchers, policymakers, and the public. Many academic databases and publishers maintain a taxonomy that authors or editors reference in order to manually assign topics, research fields, or concepts to scientific publications. Yet, manual labeling is notoriously laborious and error-prone. Automation is necessary to accurately label documents with taxonomy concepts in a timely manner.

Here, we focus on scientific publication classification based on Microsoft Academic Graph's field of study taxonomy (Shen et al., 2018). This taxonomy contains a hierarchy of scientific concepts (fields of study) to organize scholarly literature. Our objective is to design an **updatable** and **scalable** multi-label classification model that is independent of manual annotation or input language. We experiment with scientific research documents in English and Chinese, as these are by far the two most frequent languages for publications in our database.

Our work leverages a multi-lingual knowledge base, Wikipedia, in order to obtain up-to-date concept descriptions in English and other languages. Using MediaWiki's API, we first locate an English concept's Wikipedia page and are then able to find the corresponding page in other languages (MediaWiki, 2022). Hence, a multi-lingual knowledge base provides multi-lingual concept descriptions without requiring any direct translating of the concept taxonomy or concept descriptions.

We represent both the concept descriptions and research publications text data in embedding form. By using vector space representations of text (word embeddings) we can compute the cosine similarities between concept embeddings and publication embeddings, with the cosine similarity score indicating the relevance of a concept to a publication. In this way, we are able to compute either one top field (most similar) or multiple fields of study that are relevant (determined by a similarity score threshold for the task at hand) to a given publication. A multi-label classification model is a practical approach to scientific publication classification, as most scientific research publications are relevant to more than one field of study, particularly at the more granular level of fields. For example, a publication can be relevant to *natural language processing* and *machine learning*.

We implement our multi-label classification model in English and Chinese, generating field descriptions, embeddings, and field-to-publication similarity scores in each language. Our database of scholarly literature contains more than 184 million documents in English and more than 44 million

Proceedings of the Third Workshop on Scholarly Document Processing, pages 105–114
October 12–17, 2022.

documents in Chinese, which serve both as input text for word embeddings and as target publications for classification. Applying our scientific publication word embeddings and field of study descriptions from Wikipedia, we compute field embeddings for 313 different fields of study, and publication embeddings for the scientific research publications in English and Chinese.

Because we do not have a manually annotated, ground-truth dataset with field labels assigned to publications, we provide extensive evaluations of our results and include a case study on artificial intelligence and machine learning publications.

The contributions of the paper are summarized as follows: 1) word embeddings in English and Chinese, trained on a comprehensive set of scholarly literature, 2) a scientific text classification model not restricted to the English language, and 3) a Python library for updating field embeddings and models in sync with changes to underlying field definitions (from Wikipedia articles and the sources they cite), to address conceptual drift. All results and code will be made public in our GitHub repository[1].

2 Related Work

Classifying text according to a defined taxonomy is applied across a wide range of domains, such as patents, news articles, and scientific literature, using numerous machine learning approaches. Text classification for scientific literature typically involves text extraction, topic modeling, or citation graphs to cluster related documents (Aljaber et al., 2010; Tsai et al., 2013; Yau et al., 2014; Kim and Gil, 2019). Prior research that uses a predefined taxonomy for multi-label classification is generally limited to one broad area of research, and selecting a dataset with annotated publication data (i.e., a dataset limited to a classification scheme).

Santos and Rodrigues reference the Association for Computing Machinery (ACM) Concept Classification System (CCS) to assign multiple concept labels to computer science papers (Santos and Rodrigues, 2009). The authors crawl relevant web pages to identify concept-related descriptive text and implement three different classification models: Binary Relevance, Label Powerset, and Multi-Label k-Nearest Neighbors (Santos and Rodrigues, 2009). Similarly, Mustafa et al. reference the ACM CCS, but use Word2Vec embeddings to represent scientific research publication text and cosine similarity to compute a similarity score and determine concept assignment (Mustafa et al., 2021).

Shen et al. generate a six-level scientific document taxonomy for all of science. Using Word2Vec and term frequency-inverse document frequency (TF-IDF) embeddings trained on scientific publication titles and abstracts, Shen et al. generate field of study embeddings and publication embeddings. Each scientific publication is assigned multiple field labels using cosine similarity between the publication embedding and the field embeddings (Shen et al., 2018).

3 Data

We use three datasets in our model: 1) scientific research documents, 2) a scientific research field of study taxonomy, and 3) a knowledge base.

3.1 Scientific Research Documents

In this work, we use a comprehensive set of scientific research documents that we compiled from six scholarly literature databases: Clarivate's Web of Science (WOS), Digital Science's Dimensions[2] (DS), Microsoft Academic Graph (MAG), arXiv, Papers with Code (PWC) and the Chinese National Knowledge Infrastructure[3] (CNKI). There is no common publication identifier across these six datasets, so we deduplicate publications to generate a merged corpus of scholarly literature.

We deduplicate documents in a two-step process illustrated in Figure 1. In step one, we extract six document identifiers (DOI, citations, normalized abstract, normalized author names, normalized title, and publication year) for each document. To normalize the document abstracts, author names, and titles, we implement the Normalization Form Compatibility Composition standard, which decomposes Unicode characters by compatibility and recomposes them by canonical equivalence. We de-accent letters, strip copyright signs, HTML tags, punctuation, non-alphanumeric characters, and numbers, and remove white space from the strings. If any three identifiers between documents are equal, we assign those documents a

[1] `https://github.com/georgetown-cset/scientific-field-classification`

[2] Data sourced from Dimensions, an inter-linked research information system provided by Digital Science `http://www.dimensions.ai`

[3] All China National Knowledge Infrastructure content is furnished for use in the United States by East View Information Services, Minneapolis, MN, USA

unique merged ID.

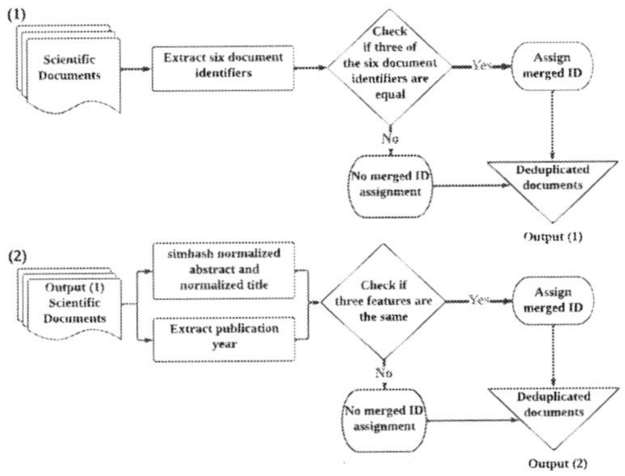

Figure 1: Scientific document de-duplication process.

In step two, we use the SimHash fuzzy matching algorithm with a rolling window of three characters in order to match articles that were published in the same year and have similar abstracts and titles (Manku et al., 2007). Articles matched in step two are also assigned a merged ID. Articles that do not have a distinct merged ID assigned in either deduplication step are included in the final corpus as unique documents.

From the deduplicated set of scientific research documents, we generate a set of English documents, EN-PUBLICATIONS (184,381,319 publications), and a set of Chinese documents, ZH-PUBLICATIONS (44,166,696 publications), using Chromium Compact Language Detector 2 (CLD2). Each document is represented by the text available from the title and abstract; if both title and abstract are present then the text is concatenated.

3.2 Field of Study Taxonomy

We use MAG's Field of Study (FoS) taxonomy, which contains six levels (0 through 5) of fields. Level 0 ("L0") represents the most broad fields, such as *computer science* and *medicine*, and Level 5 ("L5") represents the most granular fields, such as *key clustering* and *gene density.* FoS L0 and L1 were derived from Science-Metrix classification scheme[4] and refined manually by the authors, whereas and L2-L5 were automatically identified (Shen et al., 2018).

In this study, we select the 19 L0 and the 294 L1 FoS as our target classification scheme; L1 FoS are sub-domains of L0. In Table 1 we display all 19 L0 FoS with several examples of their L1 child FoS. We denote the total number of L1 FoS under each L0 in parentheses next to their label. *Medicine* has the most L1 child FoS, with 45, followed by *engineering* with 44 and *economics* with 40.

The FoS taxonomy we reference in this study defines the fields: their names and parent/child relations. All FoS in this taxonomy are provided in English only.

3.3 Knowledge Base

For our knowledge base we use Wikipedia, an open-collaboration online encyclopedia accessible for free, with articles published in 327 languages (Wikipedia, 2022). We access Wikipedia articles through MediaWiki's API (MediaWiki, 2022). Given the English Wikipedia page title for a field (if known) or otherwise the field name in English, we query the Mediawiki API for metadata on any such page in English Wikipedia. Specifically, we request its `langlinks` property, which describes corresponding pages in other languages/Wikipedias. In this way, the English FoS can be linked to any language of interest without manual translation, making Wikipedia an ideal knowledge base for our multilingual classification model.

In Figure 2 we display a portion of the Wikipedia articles for *natural language processing*, in English and Chinese. We use the full-body text in the article, as well as the publication titles and abstracts listed in the "References" section.

4 Field of Study Classification Model

Our field of study multi-label classification model is adapted from MAG's scientific publication classification scheme, with key design modifications. In Shen et al.'s model, the descriptive text used to generate L0 and L1 FoS embeddings are titles and abstracts from sets of scientific publications for each field, in which the publications are selected from a sample of unknown journals and conferences (Shen et al., 2018). For one of their embeddings set the authors generate Word2Vec vectors.

We use Wikipedia article text and reference publications for L0 and L1 FoS descriptive text. In this way, field descriptions can be replicated, extended to languages other than English, and updated as the fields evolve. We describe in this section the project workflow to process our data and design our field of study classification model. Figure 3 shows the high-level pipeline to produce the field

[4] `http://science-metrix.com/en/classification`

Art (displaying 6 of 6 L1)
Aesthetics, Art History, Classics, Humanities, Literature, Visual Arts

Biology (displaying 7 of 32 L1)
Anatomy, Animal Science, Bioinformatics, Botany, Genetics, Immunology, Zoology

Business (displaying 6 of 13 L1)
Accounting, Actuarial Science, Commerce, Finance, International Trade, Marketing

Chemistry (displaying 5 of 21 L1)
Biochemistry, Food Science, Mineralogy, Organic Chemistry, Radiochemistry

Computer Science (displaying 5 of 34 L1)
Algorithm, Artificial Intelligence, Database, Internet Privacy, Parallel Computing

Economics (displaying 5 of 40 L1)
Accounting, International Trade, Management, Political Economy, Socioeconomics

Engineering (displaying 5 of 44 L1)
Aeronautics, Control Theory, Nuclear Engineering, Simulation, Systems-Engineering

Environmental Science (displaying 4 of 8 L1)
Agricultural Science, Agroforestry, Environmental Planning, Environmental Protection

Geography (displaying 6 of 11 L1)
Archaeology, Cartography, Forestry, Geodesy, Meteorology, Regional Science

Geology (displaying 6 of 18 L1)
Climatology, Earth Science, Geophysics, Hydrology, Oceanography, Petrology

History (displaying 6 of 7 L1)
Ancient History, Archaeology, Classics, Economic History, Ethnology, Genealogy

Materials Science (displaying 5 of 7 L1)
Ceramic Materials, Composite Material, Metallurgy, Nanotechnology, Optoelectronics

Mathematics (displaying 6 of 20 L1)
Algebra, Combinatorics, Geometry, Mathematical Optimization, Statistics, Topology

Medicine (displaying 7 of 45 L1)
Audiology, Cancer Research, Nursing, Orthodontics, Pediatrics, Surgery, Virology

Philosophy (displaying 6 of 7 L1
Aesthetics, Epistemology, Humanities, Linguistics, Religious Studies, Theology

Physics (displaying 5 of 27 L1)
Astronomy, Geophysics, Nuclear Physics, Quantum Mechanics, Thermodynamics

Political Science (displaying 3 of 3 L1)
Law, Public Administration, Public Relations

Psychology (displaying 5 of 14 L1)
Cognitive Science, Criminology, Neuroscience, Psychiatry, Social Psychology

Sociology (displaying 5 of 13 L1)
Anthropology, Demography, Ethnology, Gender Studies, Media Studies, Political Economy

Table 1: The 19 L0 Fields of Study and a sample of their child fields (L1). Next to each field is the number of L1 FoS displayed and the total number of child fields.

and document embedding outputs necessary for our classification model.

We describe each step in our classification model pipeline as follows:

Step 1: To normalize the scientific publication text, we remove all punctuation and numeric tokens. For languages that are case-sensitive, we set all text to lowercase. For example "COVID-19" is transformed to "covid19" in English. The normalized texts are used as inputs for the TF-IDF and fastText embeddings in Step 2.

Step 2: With the normalized scientific publication text (from Step 1) as input, we produce TF-IDF embeddings using `TfIdfTransformer` from gensim and 250-dimensional fastText word embeddings using the skipgram model (Rehurek and Sojka, 2011; Bojanowski et al., 2017). TF-IDF provides a measurement of how important a word is to a document based on the word's occurrences in the entire document. FastText word embeddings encode n-grams in a vector space that represents semantics. Since both vector representations of words (TF-IDF and fastText) are determined by the input corpus, it is necessary to use a representative corpus for the task at hand.

Step 3: For each of the 19 L0 and 294 L1 FoS, we retrieve the corresponding associated text (page content and reference publications) in Wikipedia, which we refer to as descriptive field text. Combining the Wikipedia page text and scientific publication text we aim to capture both definitions and exemplar research for a given field.

Step 4: We compute field TF-IDF and fastText embeddings using the embedding sets from Step

English

Natural language processing

From Wikipedia, the free encyclopedia

Natural language processing (**NLP**) is a subfield of linguistics, computer science, and artificial intelligence concerned with the interactions between computers and human language, in particular how to program computers to process and analyze large amounts of natural language data. The goal is a computer capable of "understanding" the contents of documents, including the contextual nuances of the language within them. The technology can then accurately extract information and insights contained in the documents as well as categorize and organize the documents themselves.

Challenges in natural language processing frequently involve speech recognition, natural language understanding, and natural language generation.

Chinese

自然语言处理 [编辑]

维基百科，自由的百科全书

自然语言处理（英语：**Natural Language Processing**，缩写作 **NLP**）是人工智能和语言学领域的分支学科。此领域探讨如何处理及运用自然语言；自然语言处理包括多方面和步骤，基本有认知、理解、生成等部分。

自然语言认知和理解是让电脑把输入的语言变成有意思的符号和关系，然后根据目的再处理。自然语言生成系统则是把计算机数据转化为自然语言。

历史 [编辑]

自然语言处理大体是从1950年代开始，虽然更早期也有作为。1950年，图灵发表论文"计算机器与智能"，提出现在所谓的"图灵测试"作为判断智能的条件。

1954年的乔治城-IBM实验涉及全部自动翻译超过60句俄文成为英文。研究人员声称三到五年之内即可解决机器翻译的问题。[1]不过实际进展远低于预期，1966年的ALPAC报告发现十年研究未达预期目标，机器翻译的研究经费遭到大幅削减。一直到1980年代末期，统计机器翻译系统发展出来，机器翻译的研究才得以更上一层楼。

References [edit]

^ Robertson, Adi (2022-04-06). "OpenAI's DALL-E AI image generator can now edit pictures, too". *The Verge*. Retrieved 2022-06-07.

^ "The Stanford Natural Language Processing Group". *nlp.stanford.edu*. Retrieved 2022-06-07.

^ Coyne, Bob; Sproat, Richard (2001-08-01). "WordsEye: an automatic text-to-scene conversion system". *Proceedings of the 28th annual conference on Computer graphics and interactive techniques*. SIGGRAPH '01. New York, NY, USA: Association for Computing Machinery: 487–496. doi:10.1145/383259.383316. ISBN 978-1-58113-374-5.

^ "Previous shared tasks | CoNLL". *www.conll.org*. Retrieved 2021-01-11.

^ "Cognition". *Lexico*. Oxford University Press and Dictionary.com. Retrieved 6 May 2020.

^ "Ask the Cognitive Scientist". *American Federation of Teachers*. 8 August 2014. "Cognitive science is an interdisciplinary field of researchers from Linguistics, psychology, neuroscience, philosophy, computer science, and anthropology that seek to understand the mind."

^ Robinson, Peter (2008). *Handbook of Cognitive Linguistics and Second Language Acquisition*. Routledge. pp. 3–8. ISBN 978-0-805-85352-0.

^ Goldberg, Yoav (2016). "A Primer on Neural Network Models for Natural Language Processing". *Journal of Artificial Intelligence Research*. **57**: 345–420. arXiv:1807.10854. doi:10.1613/jair.4992. S2CID 8273530.

^ Goodfellow, Ian; Bengio, Yoshua; Courville, Aaron (2016). *Deep Learning*. MIT Press.

^ Jozefowicz, Rafal; Vinyals, Oriol; Schuster, Mike; Shazeer, Noam; Wu, Yonghui (2016). *Exploring the Limits of Language Modeling*. arXiv:1602.02410. Bibcode:2016arXiv160202410J.

^ Choe, Do Kook; Charniak, Eugene. "Parsing as Language Modeling". *Emnlp 2016*. Archived from the original on 2018-10-23. Retrieved 2018-10-22.

Figure 2: Sample Wikipedia article on Natural Language Processing

2 and the descriptive field text from Step 3. We follow the procedure in "Algorithm 1" to generate TF-IDF and fastText embeddings for each FoS.

Algorithm 1 Full Text to Single Embedding

Input: Word embedding dictionary, E
Text, t
Output: Single text vector, $\vec{t}$

```
procedure EMBED_TEXT(t, E)
    V = []                          ▷ Empty array to store word vectors
    for word in t do
        if word in E.keys() then
            w⃗ = E[word]
            V.append(w⃗)
        end if
    end for
    t⃗ = sum(V, axis=0)
    l2 = linalg.norm(t⃗, 2, axis=0)
    if l2 == 0 then return t⃗
    else t⃗ = t⃗ / l2
    end if
    return t⃗                        ▷ The text vector is t⃗
end procedure
```

Step 5: Separate from FoS embeddings in Step 4, we compute entity embeddings. We generate these for a FoS or publication as the average over the embeddings of each FoS mention in its text.

Step 6: Using "Algorithm 1", we compute document embeddings for each scientific research publication in our corpus.

Step 7: We use cosine similarity to compute a similarity score for each document compared to each FoS, for each embedding set (TF-IDF and fastText). Our similarity score is the average of the two cosine similarities. The cosine similarity between two vectors is defined as:

$$\cos(\vec{f}, \vec{d}) = \frac{\mathbf{f} \cdot \mathbf{d}}{||\mathbf{f}||||\mathbf{d}||} \quad (1)$$

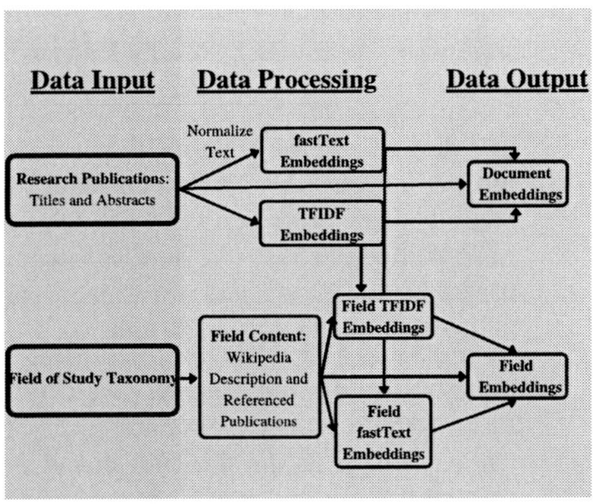

Figure 3: Process to generate document embeddings and three sets of FoS embeddings

Here, $\vec{f}$ represents a FoS embedding and $\vec{d}$ represents a document embedding. Cosine similarity returns a value between 0 and 1, with 0 indicating no similarity and 1 indicating perfect similarity. By computing cosine similarity for all FoS and document pairs, we can choose if we want to label a document with only one field (the most similar FoS), or set a similarity score threshold and assign multiple fields. This is particularly useful with more granular fields. For example, a publication can be relevant to *computer vision* and *machine learning* L1 FoS.

5 Experiments

We perform Steps 1-7 on EN-PUBLICATIONS and ZH-PUBLICATIONS. Text normalization and embedding generation (Steps 1-2) may require different tools and packages depending on the choice of non-English languages; we use `jieba` for Chinese text processing.

For knowledge base information retrieval (Step 3), we reference MAG's FoS metadata for field ID, field name, field level, and field Wikipedia page. The field of study attributes metadata includes English Wikipedia URLs for all fields. We query MediaWiki with the assigned Wikipedia pages for each FoS in English to store the descriptive text and search for the corresponding page in Chinese. This results in several outcomes that we detail below for non-English implementations of our model:

1. **The Wikipedia page does not exist** (maybe it once did; maybe not). We fall back to searching Wikipedia for this term (in a second API request), in case there exists a near match. We store these "near-match" results for manual review to ensure they are accurate.

2. **The desired English Wikipedia page exists but the `langlinks` property does not include a link to a corresponding page on Chinese Wikipedia.** We store the English page name and page ID, and leave the Chinese page fields blank to flag for manual review.

3. **We find the desired English page and a linked Chinese page**. We store each page name and page ID, for the English and Chinese results.

With the completed links between FoS and Wikipedia pages, we are able to retrieve the descriptive text from Wikipedia pages and the text from referenced publications. At this stage in the process, the Chinese implementation is self-contained and no longer relies on any data linkages in English, which would be the case for any non-English language implementation.

We generate document embeddings for each scientific document in EN-PUBLICATIONS and ZH-PUBLICATIONS, and we generate FoS embeddings and entity embeddings for our English and Chinese

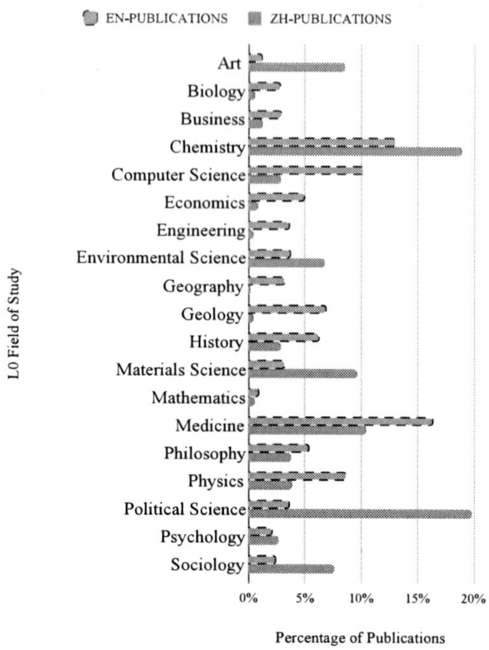

Figure 4: Percentage of papers in EN-PUBLICATIONS and ZH-PUBLICATIONS by the top L0 FoS label

results, respectively (Steps 4-6). We then compute the cosine similarity between every document and FoS embedding pair in both languages (Step 7).

6 Results and Evaluation

Evaluating our results is particularly challenging without a ground-truth dataset that contains publications and their corresponding field of study labels. Because of this limitation, we offer several methods of evaluation that do not require annotation (to limit human bias and error) and can be replicated. Our evaluation methods compare results at the FoS level and the publication level in order to measure our taxonomy representation results (FoS embeddings) and our publication classification results.

6.1 Top Field of Study Labels

With each publication in EN-PUBLICATIONS and ZH-PUBLICATIONS having cosine similarity scores for the L0 and L1 FoS, we first analyze the top L0 field assignments (i.e., the L0 field with the highest cosine similarity score). Figure 4 displays the percentage of papers from EN-PUBLICATIONS and ZH-PUBLICATIONS with each top L0 field label. In EN-PUBLICATIONS, *medicine*, *chemistry*, and *computer science* have the most top field labels,

Corpus	Computer Science	Economics	Medicine	Sociology
EN-PUBLICATIONS	1. **Data Science** 2. Machine Learning 3. Internet Privacy 4. Computer Network 5. Computer Security	1. Economic Growth 2. **Economy** 3. Microeconomics 4. International Econ. 5. Economic Policy	1. Cancer Research 2. Surgery 3. Cardiology 4. Virology 5. Medical Physics	1. Media Studies 2. Socioeconomics 3. **Gender Studies** 4. Communication 5. Criminology
ZH-PUBLICATIONS	1. Algorithm 2. **Data Science** 3. Simulation 4. Real-time Computing 5. Software Engineering	1. Commerce 2. **Economy** 3. Monetary Econ. 4. Macroeconomics 5. Financial System	1. Pharmacology 2. Immunology 3. Audiology 4. Oncology 5. Family Medicine	1. Regional Science 2. **Gender Studies** 3. Law & Economics 4. Social Science 5. Anthropology

Table 2: Top five L1 fields of study for computer science, economics, medicine, and sociology L0 fields. L1 fields in bold font indicate that they appear in both the English and Chinese top five results for the same L0 field.

whereas in ZH-PUBLICATIONS *political science*, *medicine*, and *chemistry* have the most.

Next, we analyze the top L1 FoS (child) for each L0 FoS (parent). In Table 2, we present results from four representative L0 FoS (*computer science*, *economics*, *medicine*, and *sociology*) and list the top five L1 FoS from EN-PUBLICATIONS and ZH-PUBLICATIONS. We bold the fields that appear in both the English and Chinese top five L1 results; medicine has no overlapping top five L1 fields.

6.2 L0-to-L0 Similarities

Each FoS has a unique vector representation, calculated in Step 4; thus we can evaluate how similar FoS are to each other using cosine similarity. In Figure 5, we compare all L0 FoS embeddings using their cosine similarity scores; we present the results for English (left) and Chinese (right).

The diagonal represents the cosine similarity score for each L0 FoS to itself, which is 1. We find that the results in English are stronger than the results in Chinese. For example, in English, we see high similarities between L0 FoS we know are related: [*computer science*, *engineering*]; [*political science*, *sociology*]. Additionally, we see low similarities between L0 FoS that are unrelated: [*biology*, *political science*], [*chemistry*, *political science*], [*materials science*, *philosophy*]. In Chinese, we find L0 FoS pairs with high similarities that we would expect, such as [*political science*, *economics*] and [*mathematics*, *physics*]. However, we also find L0 pairs with high similarities that do not align with field relatedness, such as [*chemistry*, *economics*] and [*history*, *physics*].

6.3 L0-to-L1 Field Similarities

We evaluate the parent-child relationship between L0 and L1 FoS. For each L0 FoS, we generate a t-Distributed Stochastic Neighbor Embedding (t-SNE) plot with its corresponding L1 FoS. Using t-SNE, we implement dimensionality reduction on our 250-dimensional embeddings and plot the FoS embeddings in a 2-D space. In this way, we can visualize the organization of the parent FoS to its children. Figure 6 shows our results in both languages; the L0 FoS (parent) is highlighted in yellow.

We display the same four representative FoS (economics, computer science, medicine, and sociology) from Section 6.1 in Figure 6, but all L0 FoS graphs will be available in our GitHub repository. The t-SNE plots allow us to see how the L1 FoS are represented in the embedding space, and they highlight similarities and differences between the results in English and Chinese. For example, in computer science the L1 FoS have different groupings, such as data science and data mining in English, and pattern recognition and computer vision in Chinese. Alternatively, in economics, both languages have strong similarities between finance and actuarial science.

The t-SNE plots also help us compare the L1 field embeddings to their L0 (parent) field embeddings. We find that the English results for *economics* and *medicine* show the L0 fields as more central, with the L1 fields tightly clustered, as opposed to the *computer science* and *sociology* results. The Chinese graphs highlight that the L1 fields are not as tightly clustered as the English L1 fields.

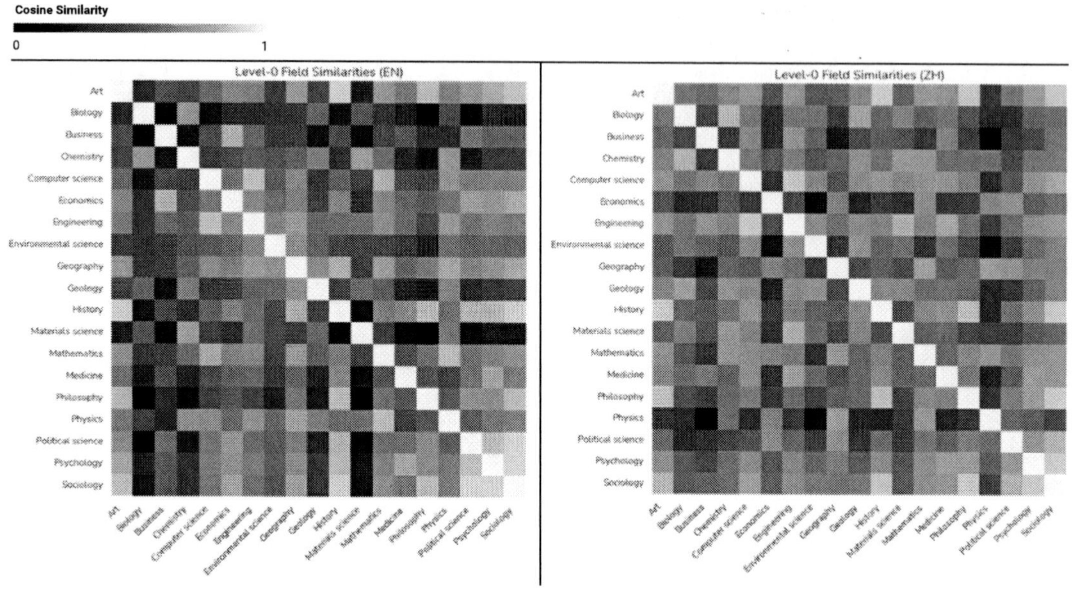

Figure 5: L0 Fields of Study cosine similarity heatmaps.

6.4 Case Study: Publication Field of Study Labels in Artificial Intelligence and Machine Learning

In order to evaluate how well our model assigns field labels to scientific research publications, we select publications from 13 top artificial intelligence (AI) and machine learning (ML) conferences identified by CSRankings[5]:

1. AAAI Conference on Artificial Intelligence
2. International Joint Conference on Artificial Intelligence
3. IEEE Conference on Computer Vision and Pattern Recognition
4. European Conference on Computer Vision
5. IEEE International Conference on Computer Vision
6. International Conference on Machine Learning
7. International Conference on Knowledge Discovery and Data Mining
8. Neural Information Processing Systems
9. Annual Meeting of the Association for Computational Linguistics
10. North American Chapter of the Association for Computational Linguistics
11. Conference on Empirical Methods in Natural Language Processing
12. International Conference on Research and Development in Information Retrieval
13. International Conference on World Wide Web.

There are 127,257 publications in EN-PUBLICATIONS that were published in a top AI/ML conference; this evaluation is limited to EN-PUBLICATIONS. We find that 57% of these publications have *computer science* as the top L0 FoS, with *physics* coming in second with 27%. Additionally, we check for the number of L0 FoS that are children of *computer science* and find that 59% of the publications have a top L1 FoS that is a child of *computer science*.

7 Conclusion and Future Work

Organizing scholarly literature is necessary for accessibility and usefulness of scientific research publications. Prior work has focused on a few broad areas of research, English-only research publications and taxonomies, and static taxonomy descriptions. In this paper, we implement a multi-label classification model that encompasses research fields from all of science, can be updated using a comprehen-

[5] www.csrankings.org

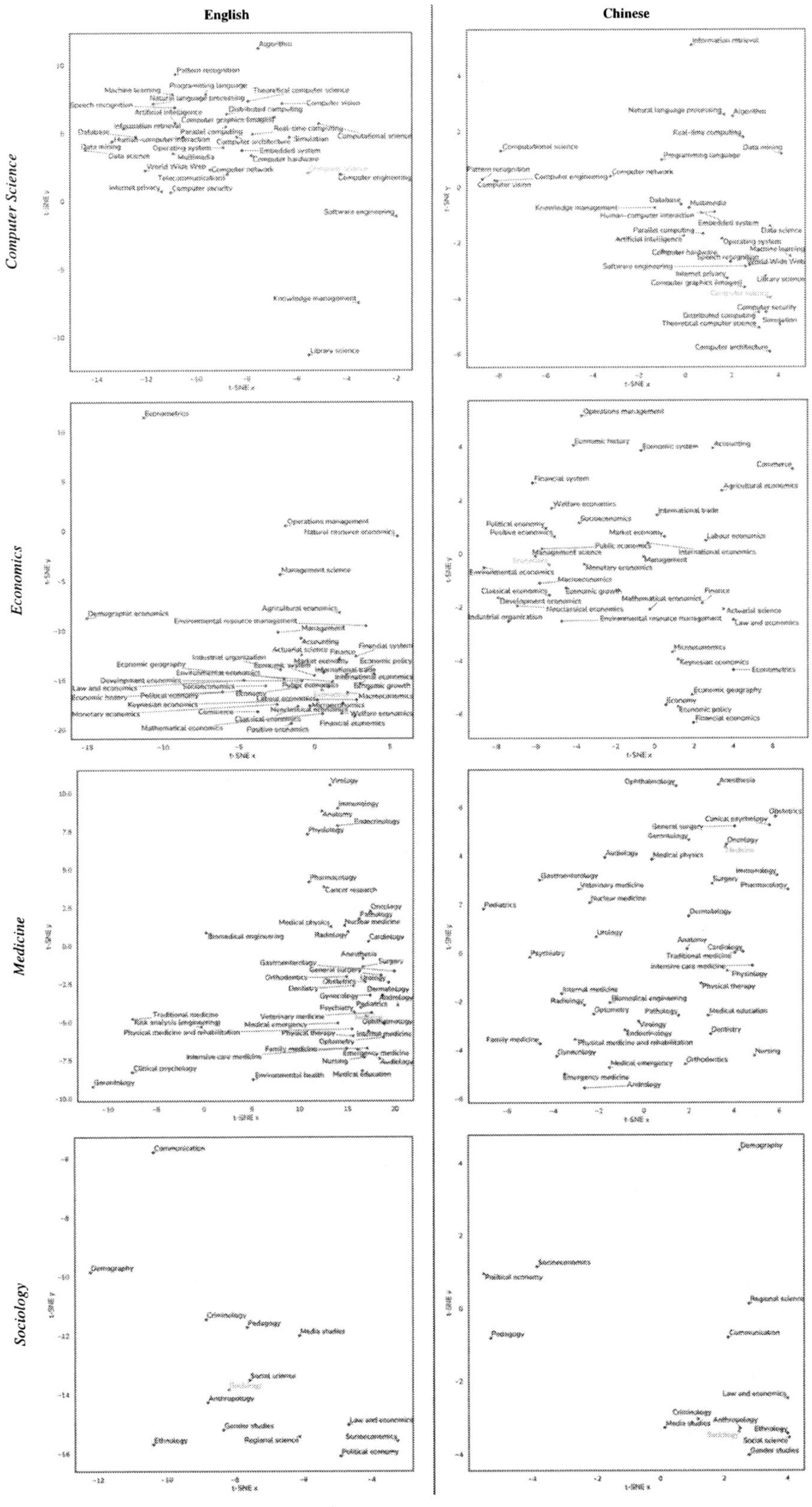

Figure 6: English and Chinese L1 embedding t-SNE plots for Economics, Computer Science, Medicine, and Sociology L0 fields of study

sive, online knowledge base, and is not restricted to the English language.

In future work, we plan to expand to additional languages and explore the longitudinal dynamics of fields: how their relative positions have shifted, within and between languages, as Wikipedia article text and references have changed.

References

Bader Aljaber, Nicola Stokes, James Bailey, and Jian Pei. 2010. Document clustering of scientific texts using citation contexts. *Information Retrieval*, 13(2):101–131.

Piotr Bojanowski, Edouard Grave, Armand Joulin, and Tomas Mikolov. 2017. Enriching word vectors with subword information. *Transactions of the Association for Computational Linguistics*, 5:135–146.

Sang-Woon Kim and Joon-Min Gil. 2019. Research paper classification systems based on tf-idf and lda schemes. *Human-centric Computing and Information Sciences*, 9(1):1–21.

Gurmeet Singh Manku, Arvind Jain, and Anish Das Sarma. 2007. Detecting near-duplicates for web crawling. In *Proceedings of the 16th international conference on World Wide Web*, pages 141–150.

MediaWiki. 2022. Api:main page — mediawiki,. [Online; accessed 1-July-2022].

Ghulam Mustafa, Muhammad Usman, Lisu Yu, Muhammad Sulaiman, Abdul Shahid, et al. 2021. Multi-label classification of research articles using word2vec and identification of similarity threshold. *Scientific Reports*, 11(1):1–20.

Radim Rehurek and Petr Sojka. 2011. Gensim–python framework for vector space modelling. *NLP Centre, Faculty of Informatics, Masaryk University, Brno, Czech Republic*, 3(2).

António Paulo Santos and Fátima Rodrigues. 2009. Multi-label hierarchical text classification using the acm taxonomy. In *14th Portuguese Conference on Artificial Intelligence (EPIA)*, volume 5, pages 553–564. Springer Berlin.

Zhihong Shen, Hao Ma, and Kuansan Wang. 2018. A web-scale system for scientific knowledge exploration. In *Proceedings of ACL 2018, System Demonstrations*, pages 87–92.

Chen-Tse Tsai, Gourab Kundu, and Dan Roth. 2013. Concept-based analysis of scientific literature. In *Proceedings of the 22nd ACM international conference on information & knowledge management*, pages 1733–1738.

Wikipedia. 2022. Wikipedia:about. Online; accessed 22-June-2022.

Chyi-Kwei Yau, Alan Porter, Nils Newman, and Arho Suominen. 2014. Clustering scientific documents with topic modeling. *Scientometrics*, 100(3):767–786.

Investigating Metric Diversity for Evaluating Long Document Summarisation

Cai Yang*
Australian National University
Canberra, Australia
`cai.yang@anu.edu.au`

Stephen Wan
CSIRO Data61
Sydney, Australia
`stephen.wan@data61.csiro.au`

Abstract

Long document summarisation, a challenging summarisation scenario, is the focus of the recently proposed LongSumm shared task. One of the limitations of this shared task has been its use of a single family of metrics for evaluation (the ROUGE metrics). In contrast, other fields, like text generation, employ multiple metrics. We replicated the LongSumm evaluation using multiple test set samples (vs. the single test set of the official shared task) and investigated how different metrics might complement each other in this evaluation framework. We show that under this more rigorous evaluation, (1) some of the key learnings from Longsumm 2020 and 2021 still hold, but the relative ranking of systems changes, and (2) the use of additional metrics reveals additional high-quality summaries missed by ROUGE, and (3) we show that SPICE is a candidate metric for summarisation evaluation for LongSumm[1].

1 Introduction

Text summarisation is an increasingly sought-after capability that is required by corporations and governments for productivity gains. For such use-cases, long documents with complex structures are often used as the input data. However, work on summarizing long documents into detailed summaries has not dominated the summarisation research field. There have been some exceptions to this, for example, work on government reports (Huang et al., 2021; Cao and Wang, 2022) and PubMed literature (Gupta et al., 2021). In contrast, most of the text summarisation work focuses on shorter documents or generating shorter summaries (for example, Wikipedia data (Gholipour Ghalandari et al., 2020), scientific articles (Teufel and Moens, 2002; Cohan et al., 2018), and news summarisation (See et al., 2017))).

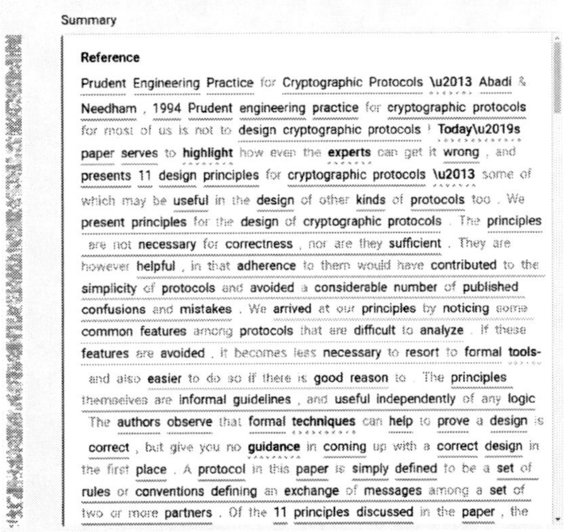

Figure 1: An example of a long document abstractive summary from the LongSumm data set, presented using SUMMVis (Vig et al., 2021).

To bridge this gap, the shared task of summarizing long scientific articles (LongSumm) was proposed, where the system should produce a detailed and informative technical summary of a source article. This shared task was introduced in the 2020 Scholarly Document Processing workshop (Chandrasekaran et al., 2020). The shared task includes an extractive and abstractive version of the problem. The former is based on the TalkSumm dataset (Lev et al., 2020), an alignment of presentation transcripts to the publication. The latter is captured using a data set of technical blogs and publications (Chandrasekaran et al., 2020).

The abstractive data set is interesting in that summaries must provide both high-level and low-level details. An example is provided in Figure 1, where the summary is a blog "walkthrough" of the main points of a paper (presented using the SUMMVis tool (Vig et al., 2021), showing colored alignments of content to the source material).

The 2020/2021 LongSumm shared tasks resulted

*Work done during the internship at CSIRO Data61.

[1]Our code is available at `https://github.com/caiyangcy/SDP-LongSumm-Metric-Diversity`

Proceedings of the Third Workshop on Scholarly Document Processing, pages 115–125
October 12–17, 2022.

in a couple of key learnings for abstractive summarisation: (1) that there was no clear difference in performance between extractive and abstractive methods; and (2) approaches that focus on the representation of long documents, such as the Bigbird (Zaheer et al., 2020) and Pegasus (Zhang et al., 2020a) combination outperformed simpler abstractive methods like BART (Lewis et al., 2020).

One potential weakness of the LongSumm shared tasks is that they were limited to the ROUGE family of metrics (Lin, 2004), including recall of unigrams (ROUGE-1), bigrams (ROUGE-2), and longest common subsequences (ROUGE-LCS). In contrast, current trends in Natural Language Generation (NLG), for example, the E2E evaluation (Dušek et al., 2020), and Image Caption Generation (ICG), for example, the MS Coco evaluation (Chen et al., 2015), employ multiple metrics.

There are also issues with the application of ROUGE to new data sets. For example, ROUGE has been shown to be problematic when used on text types other than news, like microblogs (Mackie et al., 2014), meeting summaries, (Liu and Liu, 2008) and online review text (Tay et al., 2019).[2]

Given that it is not clear that ROUGE is necessarily the best metric for this new domain, we take the approach that diversity of metrics is key. We thus employ the metrics from NLG E2E shared task and MS Coco evaluation scripts. We also add some of the new metrics from these fields, such as SPICE (Anderson et al., 2016), a metric considering semantic graphs that has been demonstrated to improve image captioning evaluation, and BERTScore (Zhang et al., 2020b), a metric that utilizes BERT contextual embeddings to better capture lexical and structural semantics and which is increasingly used in evaluating text summarisation.[3] These metrics can be seen as covering a range of linguistic phenomena. We provide more detail on the metrics in Section 4.

To consider the role of the different metrics for the LongSumm evaluation, we use a spectrum of different system approaches, including oracle methods, baselines, and state-of-the-art approaches. In addition, where the original LongSumm evaluation uses a single test set, we repeat our experiments multiple times with different training-testing data set splits to account for variance.

Our contributions are as follows. (I) We retest key outcomes from the earlier shared tasks, e.g, (i) abstractive and extractive methods perform similarly on the LongSumm abstractive data set, and (ii) the relative performance of tested algorithms. (II) We show that the informativeness of ROUGE might be affected by stopword matching. (III) We show that SPICE agrees somewhat with ROUGE and BERTScore, offering a complementary view on summarisation quality.

The remainder of the paper is structured as follows. In Section 2, we outline related work. Section 3 describes the different summarisation methods and baseline approaches. We outline our experimental procedure in Section 4. In Section 5, we describe our experimental results that address the research questions above. Section 6 presents qualitative analysis and future work. We present concluding remarks in Section 7.

2 Related Work

In this section, we outline some of the highlights in which the NLP community has critically examined evaluation methodology. We provide more details on shared task data, leading approaches, and metrics examined in subsequent sections.

We note that the field of machine translation has been a source of inspiration for other NLP fields. Indeed, the ROUGE metric is itself inspired by the BLEU metric from translation research. This field has shown that reliance on intrinsic metrics and reference summaries is problematic. For example, the BLEU metric may not correlate with human judgments (Callison-Burch et al., 2006). Indeed, in recent years, machine translation has turned to the research topic of Quality Estimation (QE) (Specia and Astudillo, 2018), the task of estimating run-time translation quality without ground truth data. Our work has some superficial similarities to QE methodology, in examining summary rankings and high and low-quality quartiles. However, our analysis differs from the core focus of QE, as we investigate the utility of multiple metrics.

Within the NLG community, BLEU has been used as an evaluation metric even though it is problematic. For example, it has been shown not to correlate with human judgments (for example, (Belz and Reiter, 2006) and (Cahill, 2009)). The use of these metrics is further called into doubt when we

[2]Note: the ROUGE metric was originally designed for the DUC 2001 data set of news articles at a time when extractive summarisation methods were the dominant method. For more information about DUC 2001, visit https://duc.nist.gov/pubs.html#2001

[3]Indeed, BERTScore is an official metric of the LongSumm 2022 shared task.

see that n-gram matching metrics like BLEU are also not suitable for evaluating text simplification (Sulem et al., 2016), a closely related task to text summarisation. This has led to the research in new metrics (for example, GLEU (Mutton et al., 2007) and BLEURT (Das and Parikh, 2019)). In this work, we follow the NLG and ICG best practice, which is to use a combination of metrics, knowing that each individual metric may have its failings.

There have been some recent works on evaluating summarisation metrics (Bhandari et al., 2020; Fabbri et al., 2021), which highlights the limitation of current metrics and the need for upgrading evaluation protocols. We note that other metrics exist to overcome some of the limitations of ROUGE (Schluter, 2017), such as needing to account for multiple judgments of content saliency as in the Pyramid method (Nenkova and Passonneau). A linear ensemble of diverse metrics has also been shown to be able to outperform metrics in isolation (Kasai et al., 2022). The NLG community has tended to report human quality assessments, for example, collecting judgments for *quality* and *naturalness* (Novikova and Rieser, 2018). In this respect, our work is again complementary in that we use SUMMVis (Vig et al., 2021) to inspect the quality of the system summaries.

3 Baselines and Approaches

3.1 Oracles

To estimate an upper bound on performance for the metrics, we employ a series of "oracle" methods, so-called because they use the reference summaries to approximate a perfect content selection mechanism. The oracle methods are:

(Or-TopK) Oracle-Top K Sentences Matching For each sentence from the reference summary, we extract the k most similar sentence from the document. Similarity is measured through the longest contiguous matching subsequence by using `SequenceMatcher` from `difflib`.

(Or-TopK-SS) Oracle-Surrounding Sentences The process is similar to Oracle-Single Sentence Matching, except the preceding and subsequent sentence of the most similar sentence will also be selected.

(Or-TopK-PM) Oracle-Paragraph Matching Instead of finding the most similar sentence, paragraphs are chosen and included in the summary. We do this by selecting the paragraph to which the most similar sentence belongs.

(Or-SW) Oracle-only Stopwords This entry only includes stopwords in the summaries. We do this by selecting stopwords from the reference summaries and including them in the summary.

3.2 Baseline Text Summarizers

The baseline summarisation methods are:

(RandN) Randomly select n sentences and include them in the summary.

(LeadN) Select the first n sentences. This is known to be a strong baseline for other data sets.

3.3 2020/2021 Best Published Methods

For this study, we take the extractive and abstractive entries from the 2020 (Chandrasekaran et al., 2020) and 2021 (Ying et al., 2021a) LongSumm shared tasks. For each method tested, we use the authors' public code repository and use system parameters as described in the original published works.

The published performance of these methods is presented in Table 1. The extractive methods ranking using ROUGE-LCS is: DGCNN > SummaRuNNer > BERTSum-Multi. The abstractive methods ranking is: Bigbird-Pegasus > BART.

3.3.1 DGCNN

Dilated Gated Convolutional Neural Networks (DGCNN) have been used for extractive summarisation (Ying et al., 2021b). It is based on Conv1D layers with residual connections and different dilation rates. The sentences from each document are passed through RoBERTa and the output from the last hidden layers with average pooling is used as the feature representations. These are passed into the DGCNN layers to output a binary label for sentence selection.[4]

3.3.2 SummaRuNNer

SummaRuNNer (Nallapati et al., 2017) is an extractive model consisting of a two-layer bi-directional GRU. The first layer operates on the word level to produce hidden state representations of words while the second layer operates on the sentence level to encode sentence representations. A document representation is obtained through a non-linear transformation of the sentence representations. Selection (binary) classification is made on

[4]https://aclanthology.org/2021.sdp-1.12

	Recall			F-measure		
	ROUGE-1	ROUGE-2	ROUGE-L	ROUGE-1	ROUGE-2	ROUGE-L
BERTSum-Multi (Sotudeh Gharebagh et al., 2020)	0.5460	0.1728	0.2090	0.5311	0.1677	0.2034
SummaRuNNer (Ghosh Roy et al., 2020)	0.4390	0.1498	0.1898	0.4938	0.1686	0.2138
DGCNN (Ying et al., 2021a)	0.5275	0.1711	0.2209	0.2262	0.1747	0.5415
Bigbird-Pegasus (Ying et al., 2021a)	0.5080	0.1740	0.2156	0.1634	0.4755	0.2016
BART (Ying et al., 2021a)	0.1921	0.0533	0.1062	0.1122	0.0310	0.0620

Table 1: Top-performing entries reported by SDP-2020 and SDP-2021 and their reported performance.

sentences, which considers the content, document context, salience and novelty. Ghosh Roy et al. (2020) apply this method in LongSumm.[5] [6]

3.3.3 BERTSum-Multi

BERTSum-Multi (Sotudeh Gharebagh et al., 2020; Sotudeh et al., 2021) is a variant of extractive summarisation approach BERTSum (Liu and Lapata, 2019). The variant, proposed for the LongSumm shared task, uses joint task training to select sentences and predict section labels for each sentence. It outperforms the standard BERTSum algorithm for LongSumm data (Sotudeh Gharebagh et al., 2020; Sotudeh et al., 2021).[7]

3.3.4 Bigbird-Pegasus

The Bigbird-Pegasus approach (Ying et al., 2021a) is an abstractive model proposed for the LongSumm shared task. It incorporates Bigbird (Zaheer et al., 2020), a sparse attention mechanism that overcomes the quadratic complexity in the encoder, which is designed to capture more context at the document level. This document representation is then used with Pegasus, an abstractive summarisation approach that is pretrained through gap sentences generation and masked language modeling (Zhang et al., 2020a).[8][9]

3.3.5 BART

BART (Lewis et al., 2020) is an abstractive model whose pretrained objective is to denoise the input text, which is corrupted by token deletion, token masking, sentence permutation, text infilling and document rotation. It was proposed for use in LongSumm by (Ying et al., 2021a).[10][11]

[5] https://github.com/sayarghoshroy/Summaformers

[6] model: https://github.com/hpzhao/SummaRuNNer

[7] github.com/Georgetown-IR-Lab/ExtendedSumm

[8] aclanthology.org/2021.sdp-1.12

[9] Pretrained model: summarisation/arxiv. See console.cloud.google.com/storage/browser/bigbird-transformer/summarisation/arxiv/pegasus

[10] Pretrained model: *"facebook/bart-large"*.

[11] huggingface.co/docs/transformers/model_doc/bart

4 Experimental Procedure

4.1 Data

In this work, we use the abstractive subset of the LongSumm data set for evaluation purposes. As the public release of this data set does not have a specified test set, we are required to create our own training, development, and testing partitions.

4.2 Evaluation conditions

We randomly sample 22 test cases from the public data set as held out data, repeating this procedure 10 times, ensuring disjoint training and testing sets. Summaries are limited to 600 words for evaluation, following the LongSumm shared task.

4.3 Evaluation Metrics

In this work, we use a diverse set of evaluation metrics, following best practices from the NLG and ICG communities. Unless otherwise specified, we use the implementation from the E2E shared task.[12]

Our categories of metrics are (with the dominant metrics used in that community in bold):

- Translation: **BLEU**, NIST, METEOR
- Summarisation: **ROUGE** family of metrics
- Image Captioning: CIDEr, **SPICE**
- Semantic: **BERTScore**, METEOR, SPICE

4.3.1 BLEU

BLEU (Papineni et al., 2002) was originally proposed for machine translation. It is based on the product of modified n-gram precision and brevity penalty that penalizes short sentences. BLEU weights each n-gram equally.

4.3.2 NIST

Adapted from BLEU, NIST (Doddington, 2002) pays more attention to less frequent n-grams. It uses the arithmetic mean as opposed to the geometric mean in BLEU for the modified n-gram

[12] github.com/tuetschek/e2e-metrics

precision and weights each n-gram by its frequency in the references.

4.3.3 ROUGE*

ROUGE family of metrics (Lin, 2004) is based on n-gram overlap between system-generated summaries and reference summaries. Following the SDP workshops, we use ROUGE-1 , ROUGE-2 and ROUGE-LCS as our evaluation metrics.

4.3.4 CIDEr

CIDEr (Vedantam et al., 2015) was first proposed for image captioning tasks to capture consensus. CIDEr computes the cosine similarity using Term Frequency Inverse Document Frequency (TF-IDF) vectors for each n-gram. We use a variant of CIDEr with Gaussian penalty (named CIDEr-D) introduced to reduce the effects of word repetition.

4.3.5 METEOR

METEOR (Banerjee and Lavie, 2005) aligns the system output and references based on exact word matching and morphological variations such as stems, synonyms, and paraphrases of words. METEOR is calculated as the harmonic mean of precision and recall, along with a penalty factor to favour longer matching sequences.

4.3.6 SPICE

Metrics mentioned above are sensitive to n-gram overlap. However, n-gram overlap is neither necessary nor sufficient for two sentences to convey the same meaning (Giménez and i Villodre, 2007). SPICE is based on the hypothesis that semantic propositional content is an important component of image caption human evaluation (Anderson et al., 2016). SPICE constructs scene graphs based on input text processed via semantic parsing. It computes precision, recall and F1 score based on the binary matching of logical tuples, which contains objects, attributes and relations from the scene graphs.

Although SPICE is designed to operate on a system generated and reference caption, we adapt it to the summarisation scenario, and use a full system generated and reference summaries as input.[13] While the captioning scenario corresponds to a comparison of two sentences, our usage is a comparison of sets of sentences. We show that even this simple adaptation shows agreement with ROUGE and BERTScore metrics.

[13] github.com/tylin/coco-caption

4.3.7 BERTScore

N-gram models can under-estimate performance on semantically-correct matched phrases (Zhang et al., 2020b) and fail to penalize semantically-critical ordering changes (Isozaki et al., 2010). To overcome such issues, BERTScore (Zhang et al., 2020b) maps tokens to BERT contextual embeddings (Devlin et al., 2019) and computes precision, recall and F-measure through cosine similarity of word tokens, optionally weighted by the inverse document frequency to emphasize rare tokens.[14]

5 Results

5.1 Agreement of Metrics on Baselines

We begin by examining how the metrics score the oracle and baseline methods. These will provide some insights on upper bounds in performance (oracle methods), performance due to chance (random methods), and performance due to trivial generation (stopword baseline).

We present the baseline and oracle methods in Table 2. We see that the best oracle method is one that takes the best matching source document sentence (that is aligned with a reference sentence), and that adding additional context, whether by paragraph or surrounding sentences, does not improve performance (e.g., Or-TopK=1-PM does not improve on Or-TopK=1). Similarly, returning the top 3-5 aligned sentences does not help. This may be due to lexical divergences between the reference and system summaries, so matches are predominantly in the first sentence.

Interestingly, there is not a large difference in scores between random and lead methods; both increase as more sentences are selected. Note, BERTScore measures for baselines and oracle methods have a narrow range of 2-3 points.

We note that stopwords account for a large proportion of lexical correspondences in ROUGE, as evidenced by the high ROUGE-1 and ROUGE-2 scores for Or-SW, which are in the same range as the SOTA scores in Table 3. This suggests yet another weakness; namely, word recall may be overly dominated by non-content words like stopwords.

5.2 Agreement of Metrics on Systems

We present the results of system comparisons in Table 3. It is clear that the best systems outperform the baseline methods in every case. However, there

[14] pypi.org/project/bert-score/

system	BLEU	NIST	ROUGE-1-F1	ROUGE-2-F1	ROUGE-LCS-F1	CIDEr	METEOR	SPICE	BERTScore
Or-TopK=1	**0.2739**(0.0432)	**6.2682**(0.5135)	**0.5439**(0.0233)	**0.2453**(0.0336)	0.3430(0.0299)	**0.2207**(0.1656)	**0.2456**(0.0141)	**0.3061**(0.0387)	**0.8521**(0.0057)
Or-TopK=3	0.1403(0.0216)	4.5371(0.1952)	0.4959(0.0193)	0.1828(0.0196)	0.2281(0.0132)	0.0324(0.0342)	0.1973(0.0090)	0.2225(0.0184)	0.8380(0.0044)
Or-TopK=1-PM	0.0937(0.0115)	3.6976(0.1293)	0.4256(0.0165)	0.1233(0.0110)	0.1802(0.0118)	0.0446(0.0398)	0.1732(0.0049)	0.1719(0.0117)	0.8218(0.0035)
Or-TopK=1-SS	0.1241(0.0150)	4.1964(0.1516)	0.4668(0.0176)	0.1553(0.0150)	0.1979(0.0126)	0.0346(0.0358)	0.1848(0.0071)	0.1969(0.0160)	0.8285(0.0036)
Or-SW	0.0134(0.0020)	0.0314(0.0084)	0.4959(0.0090)	0.1484(0.0058)	-	0.0001(0.0002)	0.0885(0.0032)	0.0063(0.0025)	0.7378(0.0039)
RandN=3	0.0001(0.0001)	0.0000(0.0000)	0.1360(0.0174)	0.0265(0.0069)	0.0809(0.0093)	0.0003(0.0008)	0.0252(0.0029)	0.0577(0.0077)	0.8067(0.0028)
RandN=5	0.0016(0.0009)	0.0002(0.0004)	0.1993(0.0182)	0.0405(0.0070)	0.1049(0.0080)	0.0008(0.0011)	0.0414(0.0040)	0.0822(0.0090)	0.8103(0.0032)
RandN=10	0.0158(0.0032)	0.1156(0.0876)	0.3054(0.0118)	0.0630(0.0067)	0.1348(0.0050)	0.0016(0.0037)	0.0776(0.0057)	0.1166(0.0057)	0.8144(0.0030)
LeadN=3	0.0001(0.0001)	0.0000(0.0000)	0.1695(0.0125)	0.0470(0.0046)	0.1019(0.0060)	0.0004(0.0010)	0.0303(0.0021)	0.0850(0.0059)	0.8236(0.0042)
LeadN=5	0.0018(0.0010)	0.0001(0.0002)	0.2424(0.0111)	0.0673(0.0075)	0.1315(0.0071)	**0.0081**(0.0140)	0.0495(0.0037)	0.1145(0.0087)	**0.8262**(0.0038)
LeadN=10	**0.0202**(0.0040)	**0.1399**(0.0928)	**0.3279**(0.0142)	**0.0837**(0.0088)	**0.1539**(0.0080)	0.0032(0.0054)	**0.0864**(0.0044)	**0.1321**(0.0080)	0.8204(0.0041)
Best Oracle	0.2739	6.2682	0.5439	0.2453	0.4857	0.2207	0.2456	0.3061	0.8521
Best Baseline	0.0202	0.1399	0.3279	0.0837	0.1539	0.0032	0.0864	0.1321	0.8204
δ(Oracle-Baseline)	0.2537	6.1283	0.2160	0.1616	0.3318	0.2175	0.1592	0.1740	0.0317

Table 2: Baselines and Non-trivial Measurement, where N=number of sentences in the ground truth summary. Each cell contains the average score across the 10 test sets (with standard deviation in brackets). Best values are in bold.

system	BLEU	NIST	ROUGE-1-F1	ROUGE-2-F1	ROUGE-LCS-F1	CIDEr	METEOR	SPICE	BERTScore
SummaRuNNer	**0.0840**(0.0130)	3.2979(0.2287)	*0.4205*(0.0236)	*0.1204*(0.0175)	*0.1772*(0.0161)	0.0119(0.0140)	0.1508(0.0066)	**0.1619**(0.0148)	*0.8230*(0.0051)
DGCNN	0.0783(0.0164)	3.3395(0.2509)	0.3975(0.0240)	0.1075(0.0151)	0.1613(0.0109)	0.0135(0.0180)	0.1606(0.0078)	0.1522(0.0139)	0.8145(0.0036)
BERTSum-Multi	0.0757(0.0089)	**3.4014**(0.2060)	0.4204(0.0200)	0.1050(0.0078)	0.1644(0.0089)	*0.0140*(0.0219)	**0.1819**(0.0067)	0.1570(0.0104)	0.8207(0.0031)
BART	*0.0642*(0.0078)	*2.3875*(0.5556)	**0.4248**(0.0249)	**0.1256**(0.0119)	**0.1845**(0.0109)	**0.0173**(0.0185)	*0.1406*(0.0064)	*0.1559*(0.0118)	**0.8304**(0.0046)
Bigbird-Pegasus	0.0285(0.0041)	2.0301(0.4101)	0.3438(0.0162)	0.0662(0.0055)	0.1551(0.0063)	0.0064(0.0095)	0.1161(0.0070)	0.1113(0.0092)	0.8023(0.0030)
Best Extractive	0.0840	3.4014	0.4205	0.1204	0.1772	0.0140	0.1819	0.1619	0.8230
Best Abstractive	0.0642	2.3875	0.4248	0.1256	0.1845	0.0173	0.1406	0.1559	0.8304
Ex vs Ab Winner	(ex)	(ex)	(ab)	(ab)	(ab)	(ab)	(ex)	(ex)	(ab)

Table 3: Extractive or Abstractive models. Each cell contains the average score across the 10 test sets (with standard deviation in brackets). Best values in bold, second best in italics.

is still a considerable margin between the oracle methods (an estimate of an upper bound) and the best system, suggesting that there is still plenty of room for improvement for the task of selecting the content for the generated summary.

As we use multiple test set samples, our results are not exactly the same as the published results displayed in Table 1, however the scores are roughly in the same neighbourhood as the published results. Using ROUGE-LCS F1, our ranking of extractive systems in this replication of LongSumm results is SummerRuNNer > BERTSum-Multi > DGCNN. Curiously, the best-placed extractive method is now ranked last based on ROUGE-LCS alone. For the abstractive systems, we note that Bigbird-Pegasus performed worse than BART, and that the BART ROUGE performance was very different from published results. We suspect the difference is in part due to our use of multiple test sets, which will account for variance in the test data.

Rankings by other metrics are different again. However, the three methods which were repeatedly ranked first were SummaRuNNer, BERTSum-Multi, and BART. The translation metrics ranked extractive approaches best. ROUGE metrics ranked the BART system first. CIDER and SPICE, favour different systems, BART and SummaRuNNer, respectively. For the semantic metrics, the METEOR and SPICE systems ranked extractive methods highest, and BERTScore ranked BART best. Note that only differences measured by BERTScore and METEOR were statistically significant.

We also find that there is no clear winner between the extractive and abstractive methods on this data set, when evaluating with the multiple metrics. If we group together all ROUGE metrics, extractive and abstractive methods are tied on 4 metrics apiece (last row, Table 3).

We thus conclude that our replication weakly agrees with prior published results. We observe, as in prior work, that extractive and abstractive methods perform similarly on the abstractive data set. However, the ranking of methods differs slightly.

5.3 Inspecting top and bottom ranks per metric

We explore the notion of the complementarity of the metrics by examining the top and bottom n ranked generated summaries, as ranked by each of the different metrics. Due to space constraints, we present and discuss a subset of the results here, limiting the discussion to the dominant community metrics (BLEU, ROUGE-LCS (hereafter ROUGE), SPICE, and BERTScore), and considering only output from the three systems that had some agreement across the metrics as performing well (SummaRuNNer, BERTSumm-Multi, and BART).

In Table 4, we present a summary of the sim-

Comparisons	BART	SummaRunner	BERTSum	Avg.
RL. vs BS.	0.62(0.19)/0.64(0.12)	0.70(0.13)/0.56(0.15)	0.72(0.13)/0.62(0.11)	0.67(0.15)/0.61(0.13)
RL. vs BL.	0.34(0.13)/0.46(0.22)	0.30(0.18)/0.44(0.15)	0.28(0.16)/0.40(0.15)	0.31(0.16)/0.43(0.17)
RL. vs SP.	0.60(0.15)/0.70(0.10)	0.64(0.15)/0.74(0.04)	0.56(0.15)/0.74(0.20)	0.60(0.15)/0.73(0.11)
BS. vs BL.	0.26(0.18)/0.36(0.22)	0.22(0.17)/0.38(0.14)	0.26(0.13)/0.46(0.20)	0.25(0.16)/0.40(0.18)
BS. vs SP.	0.56(0.15)/0.68(0.13)	0.68(0.13)/0.60(0.18)	0.52(0.10)/0.62(0.17)	0.59(0.13)/0.63(0.16)
BL. vs SP.	0.44(0.20)/0.44(0.20)	0.30(0.18)/0.44(0.15)	0.38(0.11)/0.60(0.18)	0.37(0.16)/0.49(0.18)
Avg.	0.47(0.17)/0.55(0.17)	0.47(0.16)/0.53(0.14)	0.45(0.13)/0.57(0.17)	0.46(0.15)/0.55(0.16)

Table 4: Agreement in the top and bottom quartiles of test cases, as ranked by the BLEU (BL), ROUGE-LCS (RL), SPICE (SP), and BERTScore (BS) metrics.

ilarities in rankings in a pairwise comparison of metrics, across different systems. Specifically, we examine the top and bottom quartiles of a test set of 22 documents (where we take the top and bottom 5 ranked documents).[15] Each cell in the table shows two numbers, one for the agreement of test case ids in the top quartile and the corresponding agreement of the bottom quartile.[16]

We note that the agreement of the bottom quartile is usually higher than the top quartile. This is because this quartile contains the difficult test cases to score automatically, which will tend to be the same for all metrics. The difficulty lies, for example, in the fact that the reference summaries are very short (leaving less opportunity to match the content that might well be reasonable).

Curiously, there are some summaries that are in the top quartile for some metrics which are in the bottom quartile for others. Occasionally, BLEU will place summaries judged to be in the top quartile by another metric into its bottom quartile. We assume this relates to critiques of using BLEU for NLG, where novel text differing from the reference will be penalized.

Most interesting is the diversity of summaries selected in the top quartile. When looking at the average agreement for each metric pair (last column of Table 4), we note that ROUGE and BERTScore have the best agreement of all pairs of metrics, which is constant across different summarisation systems. SPICE metric has the second-best agreement when paired with either ROUGE-LCS or BERTScore. The BLEU metric has the lowest agreement with the others. These results indicate that one should consider the use of SPICE as a summarisation metric.

[15]We use a test set with a size of 22 documents as in the official evaluation.

[16]The values are the mean across over 10 test sets, and the standard deviation is in brackets

6 Discussion

6.1 Qualitative Analysis of Metric Complementarity

The results in Table 4 raise an interesting question. When utilizing a diverse set of metrics, what are the complementary qualities of a system summary that might be captured by the metrics? That is, do the summaries ranked highly by SPICE and BLEU represent quality summaries that are neglected by ROUGE and BERTScore? For this manual analysis, there are 3 test cases agreed upon by ROUGE and BERTscore, and 4 complementary test cases ranked highly by SPICE and BLEU. Upon inspection of these summaries manually, we find that all seven summaries are generally reasonable.

For insight, we examine the source-summary alignments generated SUMMVis for the 3 test cases that ROUGE and BERTScore agree upon, and the 4 complementary, presented in Figure 3. We note that the last 4, representing the complementary summaries, seem to share the property that content is selected later in the source document. That is 3 summaries ranked highly by ROUGE/BERTScore summaries seem "top-heavy" and the complementary set seem "bottom-heavy", with respect to where content from the source is drawn from.

We present an example of the ROUGE/BERTScore highly-ranked summary and an example from the complementary set in Figure 2. Upon inspection, the leftmost summary seems to rely heavily on copying and rewriting content from the source document, as indicated by the SUMMVis color-coding of long common sequences. In contrast, the complementary summary (rightmost) seems to exhibit shorter fragments, possibly from novel sentences.

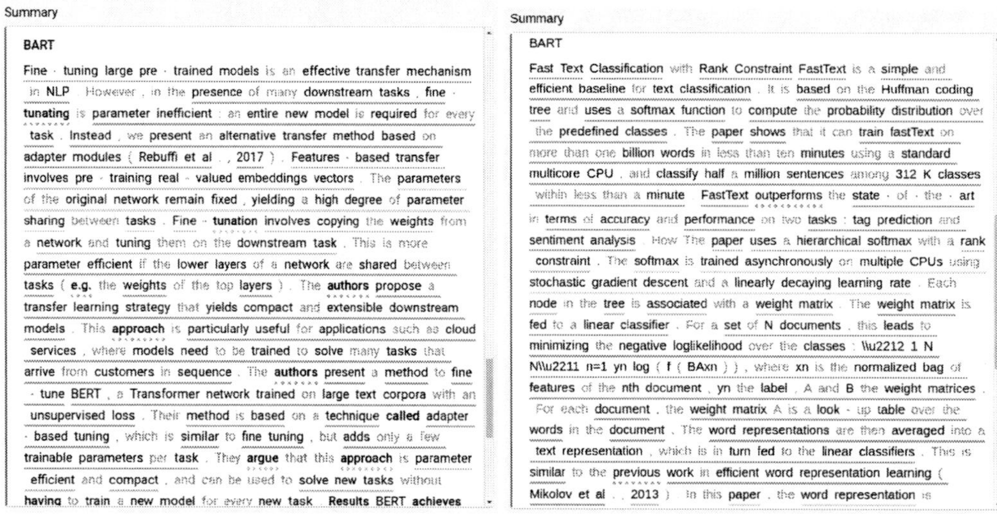

Figure 2: BART summaries in the ROUGE top quartile (left) and the SPICE top quartile (right).

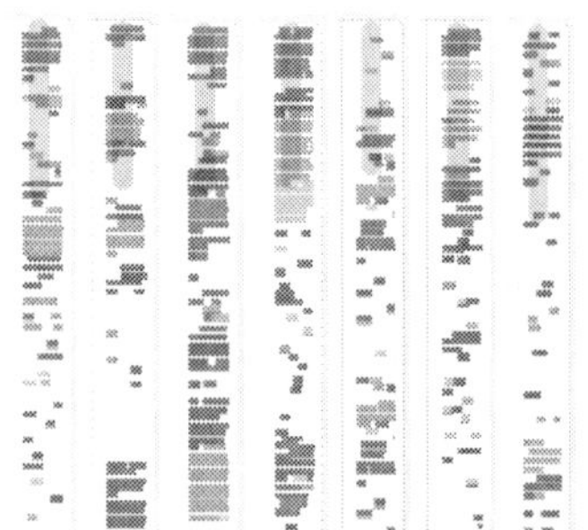

Figure 3: The first three images are ROUGE and BERTSCORE common test cases in the top quartile. The last four images are complementary high-quality summaries in top quartile suggested by SPICE and BLEU. The figures depict portions of the source document that align with the system-generated summary.

6.2 Future Work

Our results show that using multiple metrics may be beneficial in identifying summaries that are of a similar high calibre. In future work, we aim to investigate how the multiple metrics might be used in concert to evaluate systems and provide incremental intrinsic measures of progress.

We also intend to investigate how metrics like SPICE might be used to identify high-quality novel sentences, and to see if the graph comparison underpinnings allows SPICE to make qualitatively different judgments to metrics like BERTScore. Finally, we will explore other adaptations of SPICE accounting for multiple sentences in texts.

7 Conclusions

We present a detailed evaluation of multiple text summarisation metrics for long document summarisation. Utilising a oracle, baseline and state-of-the-art systems, we show that a diverse suite of metrics can capture work in a complementary fashion, so that an evaluation framework is not subject to the limitations of a single metric. In a rigorous analysis over 10 repeated trials, we show that performance of the tested approaches is roughly the same as published results. However, while some findings from the LongSumm shared task can be replicated, we find the ranking of methods in our experiments differs from prior results. When we examine the top and bottom quartiles of summarisation performance, we show that ROUGE and BERTScore are often in agreement. Further diversity in evaluation may be obtained using the metrics commonly used natural language generation and image captioning. In particular, we present preliminary results that show that the SPICE metric, which considers graph comparisons of semantic information, also agrees with the ROUGE and BERTScore metrics. We see that SPICE can identify other situations in which summarisation systems are performing well, complementing the insights gained from ROUGE and BERTScore.

8 Acknowledgement

Cai Yang is supported by Undergraduate Vacation Studentship from CSIRO. We sincerely thank both reviewers for their efforts and valuable comments in helping us improve the manuscript.

References

Peter Anderson, Basura Fernando, Mark Johnson, and Stephen Gould. 2016. Spice: Semantic propositional image caption evaluation. In *ECCV*.

Satanjeev Banerjee and Alon Lavie. 2005. Meteor: An automatic metric for mt evaluation with improved correlation with human judgments. In *IEEvaluation@ACL*.

Anja Belz and Ehud Reiter. 2006. Comparing automatic and human evaluation of NLG systems. *EACL 2006 - 11th Conference of the European Chapter of the Association for Computational Linguistics, Proceedings of the Conference*, pages 313–320.

Manik Bhandari, Pranav Narayan Gour, Atabak Ashfaq, Peng fei Liu, and Graham Neubig. 2020. Re-evaluating evaluation in text summarization. *ArXiv*, abs/2010.07100.

Aoife Cahill. 2009. Correlating human and automatic evaluation of a German surface realiser. *ACL-IJCNLP 2009 - Joint Conf. of the 47th Annual Meeting of the Association for Computational Linguistics and 4th Int. Joint Conf. on Natural Language Processing of the AFNLP, Proceedings of the Conf.*, (August):97–100.

Chris Callison-Burch, Miles Osborne, and Philipp Koehn. 2006. Re-evaluating the role of Bleu in machine translation research. In *11th Conference of the European Chapter of the Association for Computational Linguistics*, pages 249–256, Trento, Italy. Association for Computational Linguistics.

Shuyang Cao and Lu Wang. 2022. Hibrids: Attention with hierarchical biases for structure-aware long document summarization. In *ACL*.

Muthu Kumar Chandrasekaran, Guy Feigenblat, Eduard Hovy, Abhilasha Ravichander, Michal Shmueli-Scheuer, and Anita de Waard. 2020. Overview and insights from the shared tasks at scholarly document processing 2020: CL-SciSumm, LaySumm and LongSumm. In *Proceedings of the First Workshop on Scholarly Document Processing*, pages 214–224, Online. Association for Computational Linguistics.

X Chen, H Fang, T Y Lin, R Vedantam, S Gupta, P Dollár, and C L Zitnick. 2015. Microsoft COCO Captions: Data Collection and Evaluation Server. *arXiv:1504.00325*.

Arman Cohan, Franck Dernoncourt, Doo Soon Kim, Trung Bui, Seokhwan Kim, Walter Chang, and Nazli Goharian. 2018. A discourse-aware attention model for abstractive summarization of long documents. *NAACL HLT 2018 - 2018 Conference of the North American Chapter of the Association for Computational Linguistics: Human Language Technologies - Proceedings of the Conference*, 2:615–621.

Dipanjan Das and Ankur P Parikh. 2019. BLEURT: Learning Robust Metrics for Text Generation.

Jacob Devlin, Ming-Wei Chang, Kenton Lee, and Kristina Toutanova. 2019. Bert: Pre-training of deep bidirectional transformers for language understanding. *ArXiv*, abs/1810.04805.

George R. Doddington. 2002. Automatic evaluation of machine translation quality using n-gram co-occurrence statistics.

OndDušek, Jekaterina Novikova, and Verena Rieser. 2020. Evaluating the {{State}}-of-the-{{Art}} of {{End}}-to-{{End Natural Language Generation}}: {{The E2E NLG Challenge}}. *Computer Speech \& Language*, 59:123–156.

A. R. Fabbri, Wojciech Kryscinski, Bryan McCann, Richard Socher, and Dragomir Radev. 2021. Summeval: Re-evaluating summarization evaluation. *Transactions of the Association for Computational Linguistics*, 9:391–409.

Demian Gholipour Ghalandari, Chris Hokamp, Nghia The Pham, John Glover, and Georgiana Ifrim. 2020. A Large-Scale Multi-Document Summarization Dataset from the Wikipedia Current Events Portal. pages 1302–1308.

Sayar Ghosh Roy, Nikhil Pinnaparaju, Risubh Jain, Manish Gupta, and Vasudeva Varma. 2020. Summaformers @ LaySumm 20, LongSumm 20. In *Proceedings of the First Workshop on Scholarly Document Processing*, pages 336–343, Online. Association for Computational Linguistics.

Jesús Giménez and Lluís Màrquez i Villodre. 2007. Linguistic features for automatic evaluation of heterogenous mt systems. In *WMT@ACL*.

Vivek Gupta, Prerna Bharti, Pegah Nokhiz, and Harish Karnick. 2021. Sumpubmed: Summarization dataset of pubmed scientific articles. In *ACL*.

Luyang Huang, Shuyang Cao, Nikolaus Nova Parulian, Heng Ji, and Lu Wang. 2021. Efficient attentions for long document summarization. In *NAACL*.

Hideki Isozaki, Tsutomu Hirao, Kevin Duh, Katsuhito Sudoh, and Hajime Tsukada. 2010. Automatic evaluation of translation quality for distant language pairs. In *EMNLP*.

Jungo Kasai, Keisuke Sakaguchi, Ronan Le Bras, Lavinia Dunagan, Jacob Morrison, Alexander R. Fabbri, Yejin Choi, and Noah A. Smith. 2022. Bidimensional leaderboards: Generate and evaluate language hand in hand. In *NAACL*.

Guy Lev, Michal Shmueli-Scheuer, Jonathan Herzig, Achiya Jerbi, and David Konopnicki. 2020. Talk-Summ: A dataset and scalable annotation method for scientific paper summarization based on conference talks. *ACL 2019 - 57th Annual Meeting of the Association for Computational Linguistics, Proceedings of the Conference*, pages 2125–2131.

Mike Lewis, Yinhan Liu, Naman Goyal, Marjan Ghazvininejad, Abdelrahman Mohamed, Omer Levy, Veselin Stoyanov, and Luke Zettlemoyer. 2020. BART: Denoising Sequence-to-Sequence Pre-training for Natural Language Generation, Translation, and Comprehension. pages 7871–7880.

Chin-Yew Lin. 2004. {ROUGE}: A Package for Automatic Evaluation of Summaries. In *Text Summarization Branches Out*, pages 74–81, Barcelona, Spain. Association for Computational Linguistics.

Feifan Liu and Yang Liu. 2008. Correlation between rouge and human evaluation of extractive meeting summaries. *ACL-08: HLT - 46th Annual Meeting of the Association for Computational Linguistics: Human Language Technologies, Proceedings of the Conference*, (June):201–204.

Yang Liu and Mirella Lapata. 2019. Text summarization with pretrained encoders. In *Proceedings of the 2019 Conference on Empirical Methods in Natural Language Processing and the 9th International Joint Conference on Natural Language Processing (EMNLP-IJCNLP)*, pages 3730–3740, Hong Kong, China. Association for Computational Linguistics.

Stuart Mackie, Richard McCreadie, Craig Macdonald, and Iadh Ounis. 2014. On choosing an effective automatic evaluation metric for microblog summarisation. *Proceedings of the 5th Information Interaction in Context Symposium, IIiX 2014*, pages 115–124.

A. Mutton, M. Dras, S. Wan, and R. Dale. 2007. GLEU: Automatic evaluation of sentence-level fluency. In *ACL 2007 - Proceedings of the 45th Annual Meeting of the Association for Computational Linguistics*.

Ramesh Nallapati, Feifei Zhai, and Bowen Zhou. 2017. Summarunner: A recurrent neural network based sequence model for extractive summarization of documents. In *AAAI*.

Ani Nenkova and Rebecca Passonneau. Evaluating Content Selection in Summarization : The Pyramid Method.

Jekaterina Novikova and Verena Rieser. 2018. Findings of the E2E NLG Challenge. 17:322–328.

Kishore Papineni, Salim Roukos, Todd Ward, and Wei-Jing Zhu. 2002. Bleu: a method for automatic evaluation of machine translation. In *ACL*.

Natalie Schluter. 2017. The limits of automatic summarisation according to ROUGE. *15th Conference of the European Chapter of the Association for Computational Linguistics, EACL 2017 - Proceedings of Conference*, 2(1):41–45.

Abigail See, Peter J Liu, and Christopher D Manning. 2017. Get To The Point: Summarization with Pointer-Generator Networks. *CoRR*, abs/1704.0.

Sajad Sotudeh, Arman Cohan, and Nazli Goharian. 2021. On generating extended summaries of long documents. In *The AAAI-21 Workshop on Scientific Document Understanding (SDU 2021)*.

Sajad Sotudeh Gharebagh, Arman Cohan, and Nazli Goharian. 2020. GUIR @ LongSumm 2020: Learning to generate long summaries from scientific documents. In *Proceedings of the First Workshop on Scholarly Document Processing*, pages 356–361, Online. Association for Computational Linguistics.

Lucia Specia and F Astudillo. 2018. Findings of the WMT 2018 Shared Task on Quality Estimation. 2:689–709.

Elior Sulem, Omri Abend, and Ari Rappoport. 2016. BLEU is Not Suitable for the Evaluation of Text Simplification.

Wenyi Tay, Aditya Joshi, Xiuzhen Zhang, Sarvnaz Karimi, and Stephen Wan. 2019. Red-faced ROUGE: Examining the Suitability of ROUGE for Opinion Summary Evaluation. *Proceedings of the The 17th Annual Workshop of the Australasian Language Technology Association*, pages 52–60.

Simone Teufel and Marc Moens. 2002. Summarizing scientific articles: Experiments with relevance and rhetorical status. *Computational Linguistics*, 28(4):409–445.

Ramakrishna Vedantam, C. Lawrence Zitnick, and Devi Parikh. 2015. Cider: Consensus-based image description evaluation. *2015 IEEE Conference on Computer Vision and Pattern Recognition (CVPR)*, pages 4566–4575.

Jesse Vig, Wojciech Kryściński, Karan Goel, and Nazneen Fatema Rajani. 2021. SummVis: Interactive Visual Analysis of Models, Data, and Evaluation for Text Summarization.

Senci Ying, Zheng Yan Zhao, and Wuhe Zou. 2021a. LongSumm 2021: Session based automatic summarization model for scientific document. In *Proceedings of the Second Workshop on Scholarly Document Processing*, pages 97–102, Online. Association for Computational Linguistics.

Senci Ying, Zheng Yan Zhao, and Wuhe Zou. 2021b. LongSumm 2021: Session based automatic summarization model for scientific document. pages 97–102.

Manzil Zaheer, Guru Guruganesh, Kumar Avinava Dubey, Joshua Ainslie, Chris Alberti, Santiago Ontanon, Philip Pham, Anirudh Ravula, Qifan Wang, Li Yang, and others. 2020. Big bird: Transformers for longer sequences. *Advances in Neural Information Processing Systems*, 33.

Jingqing Zhang, Yao Zhao, Mohammad Saleh, and Peter J. Liu. 2020a. PEGASUS: Pre-Training with extracted gap-sentences for abstractive summarization. *37th International Conference on Machine Learning, ICML 2020*, PartF16814:11265–11276.

Tianyi Zhang, Varsha Kishore, Felix Wu, Kilian Q. Weinberger, and Yoav Artzi. 2020b. Bertscore: Evaluating text generation with bert. In *International Conference on Learning Representations*.

Exploiting Unary Relations with Stacked Learning for Relation Extraction

Yuan Zhuang[1], Ellen Riloff[1], Kiri L. Wagstaff[2], Raymond Francis[2], Matthew Golombek[2], Leslie Tamppari[2]

[1]School of Computing, Univeristy of Utah

[2]Jet Propulsion Laboratory, California Institute of Technology

{yyzhuang, riloff}@cs.utah.edu

wkiri@wkiri.com

{raymond.francis, matthew.p.golombek, leslie.k.tamppari}@jpl.nasa.gov

Abstract

Relation extraction models typically cast the problem of determining whether there is a relation between a pair of entities as a single decision. However, these models can struggle with long or complex language constructions in which two entities are not directly linked, as is often the case in scientific publications. We propose a novel approach that decomposes a binary relation into two unary relations that capture each argument's role in the relation separately. We create a stacked learning model that incorporates information from unary and binary relation extractors to determine whether a relation holds between two entities. We present experimental results showing that this approach outperforms several competitive relation extractors on a new corpus of planetary science publications as well as a benchmark dataset in the biology domain.

1 Introduction

For many scientific domains, information extraction (IE) systems can play a valuable role in harvesting information from the scientific literature to automatically populate knowledge bases. Our work is motivated by the goal of populating a Mars knowledge base by extracting information from the planetary science literature about observations made by the rovers on Mars. Specifically, we seek to extract information about the composition and properties of named "Targets" (rocks, soils, dunes, etc.) on the surface of Mars. Figure 1 shows an example sentence from this domain.

Several hypotheses could explain the abundance of potassium feldspar observed by CheMin X-ray diffraction of the Windjana drill sample.

Figure 1: Example sentence from the planetary science domain with a CONTAINS relation between Target *Windjana* and Component *potassium feldspar*.

Our IE task requires identification of three types of entities (Components, Properties, and Targets) and two types of relations (CONTAINS and HASPROPERTY). The Component entities can be minerals or elements. The sentence in Figure 1 mentions one Target (*Windjana*) and one Component (*potassium feldspar*), which participate in a CONTAINS relation. Intuitively, this relation means that potassium feldspar was detected at the Windjana site on Mars [1].

Typically, relation extraction (RE) systems determine whether a pair of entities participate in a relation. In many scientific domains, relation extraction can be challenging because of complex language constructions that do not directly link two relevant entities, even when they occur in the same sentence. For example, the relation in Figure 1 derives from the following complex path: *potassium feldspar was observed by X-ray diffraction ... diffraction of a drill sample ... a drill sample taken at the Windjana site.* This type of sentence structure is challenging for NLP systems to recognize, both lexically and syntactically.

However, even in long or complex sentences, our intuition is that local context is often sufficient to recognize *one* argument of a relation, even when recognizing both arguments simultaneously is difficult. To explore this hypothesis, our research decomposes two-argument (binary) relations into a pair of one-argument *unary* relations and trains separate unary relation extractors for each argument. For example, let us revisit Figure 1 and the CONTAINS relation. We can decompose the binary relation CONTAINS(X,Y) into two unary relations: CONTAINER(X) and CONTAINEE(Y). In Figure 1, the phrase *potassium feldspar observed* strongly suggests the unary relation CONTAINEE(*potassium feldspar*) (i.e., potassium feldspar is part of the

[1]The sentence refers to the result of X-ray diffraction by the CheMin instrument (on the Mars Science Laboratory rover) applied to a drill sample at the Windjana site.

Proceedings of the Third Workshop on Scholarly Document Processing, pages 126–137
October 12–17, 2022.

composition of something). The phrase *Windjana drill sample* suggests the unary relation CONTAINER(*Windjana*) (i.e., Windjana was studied (drilled) for its composition).

When the local context around one argument is compelling, the unary relation extractor can provide a strong signal that the full binary relation may also exists. But challenges remain with unary relation extractors alone: (1) only one argument may be recognized, and (2) it can be challenging to pair up the individual unary relations correctly. Consequently, we expect that unary relations can be most useful when considered alongside other features to accurately extract binary relations.

In this paper, we present a stacked learning architecture for relation extraction that uses a traditional binary relation extraction model alongside new information from unary relation extractors and features about the entity pair (Section 4). In our stacked learning framework, a meta-classifier makes a decision about a pair of entities based on two perspectives of the sentence context: the broad perspective of the binary relation extraction model and the local perspectives of the corresponding unary relation extractors. As a result, the meta-classifier can be more robust then either approach on its own. We evaluate this stacked learning model on relation extraction tasks for two scientific domains: the Mars mission planetary science domain and a biology domain (chemical-protein interactions) (Section 5). We find that our stacked learning model consistently outperforms traditional binary relation extraction models in both domains.

2 Related Work

Many relation extraction models have used feature-based or kernel-based approaches, such as (Zelenko et al., 2003; Bunescu and Mooney, 2005; Nguyen et al., 2015). Recent relation extraction models often use deep learning methods to learn representations of entities and their contexts and avoid the need for manual feature engineering (e.g., Socher et al., 2012; Zhang and Wang, 2015; Verga et al., 2018; Wang et al., 2019; Christopoulou et al., 2018; Zhang et al., 2018). Many of these methods also fine-tune pretrained language models to better capture contextual information. Such models include BERT (Devlin et al., 2019), SciBERT (Beltagy et al., 2019), which is pretrained over scientific publications, and LinkBERT (Yasunaga et al., 2022), which is pretrained to also capture dependencies between documents.

Pipeline architectures have been widely used for relation extraction, which perform entity recognition as the first stage and then extract relations among the detected entities (e.g., Kambhatla, 2004; Chan and Roth, 2011; Zhong and Chen, 2021). Another approach is to perform entity recognition and relation extraction jointly, which aims to eliminate the problem of error propagation that can occur with pipelines (e.g., Miwa and Bansal, 2016; Zhang et al., 2017; Luan et al., 2019; Wadden et al., 2019; Dixit and Al-Onaizan, 2019; Lin et al., 2020).

Nearly all previous systems make decisions about a relation based on all arguments at the same time. One exception that bears some similarity to our work is (Wei et al., 2020), which trains a classifier to recognize the first argument ("subject") of a relation before trying to detect its second argument ("object"). However, their classifier uses information about the subject to identify the object, and then uses both arguments to make its final decision. In contrast, our unary models completely decouple the tasks of recognizing the first and second arguments of a binary relation.

There has been growing interest in information extraction from scientific publications across a variety of domains (e.g., Gupta and Manning, 2011; Tsai et al., 2013; Tateisi et al., 2014; Li et al., 2016a, 2017; Verga et al., 2018; Watanabe et al., 2019). However, relatively little work has been done for planetary science. The GeoDeepDive project extracts information about rock formations and stratigraphy on Earth from geology publications (Zhang et al., 2013). The Mars Target Encyclopedia project (Wagstaff et al., 2018) extracts named entities (targets, minerals, and elements) and compositional relations from planetary science publications. Their relation extraction component used jSRE (Giuliano et al., 2006), an SVM classifier based on shallow parsing features. We included their data (covering one Mars mission and one relation, CONTAINS) in our experiments, and we augmented it with three more missions, hundreds of additional documents, and a new relation, HASPROPERTY (see Section 5.1). We compare the performance of jSRE models with our relation extraction models in Section 5.4.

3 Mars Target Relations

Our study focuses on relation extraction tasks in the planetary science domain. Rovers and landers have been exploring the surface of Mars for decades, and the science teams directing their activities have identified and named thousands of individual observation targets (rocks, soils, dunes, etc.). These targets are mentioned in subsequent scientific publications in conference and journal venues.

Our goal is to construct a relation extraction system that can successfully identify statements about the composition and properties of Mars targets. We assume that entities of type Target, Component (element or mineral), and Property (e.g., "layers", "dusty", "pits") have already been identified within the text, and the relation extraction system must determine which pairs of entities exhibit a given relation. We study two relations of interest: CONTAINS(*Target, Component*) and HASPROPERTY(*Target, Property*). An example of the CONTAINS relation was shown in Figure 1.

The sentence below includes three instances of the HASPROPERTY relation.

> *The dark rocks such as Barnacle Bill are more silica-rich, while the Bright Rocks such as Yogi and Wedge are more sulfur-rich and probably more weathered.*

The complete set of relations includes:

HASPROPERTY(*Barnacle Bill*, *dark*),

HASPROPERTY(*Yogi*, *weathered*),

HASPROPERTY(*Wedge*, *weathered*),

CONTAINS(*Barnacle Bill*, *silica*),

CONTAINS(*Yogi*, *sulfur*), and

CONTAINS(*Wedge*, *sulfur*).

It is common in this domain for multiple Targets to share a relation with the same Property (or the same Component in the CONTAINS relation). Conversely, it is also common for multiple Properties or Components to share a relation with a single Target. Relation extraction for this domain can be quite complex even when focusing on a single sentence. Additional challenges arise from the use of abbreviations for mineral names (e.g., Fe for iron), locally defined shorthand such as *BB* for *Barnacle Bill*, complex grammar with multiple clauses per sentence, and "hedging language" (Lakoff, 1972) that captures the uncertainty about properties of targets on another planet. Examples of hedging occur as the words "likely" and "possibly" in this sentence:

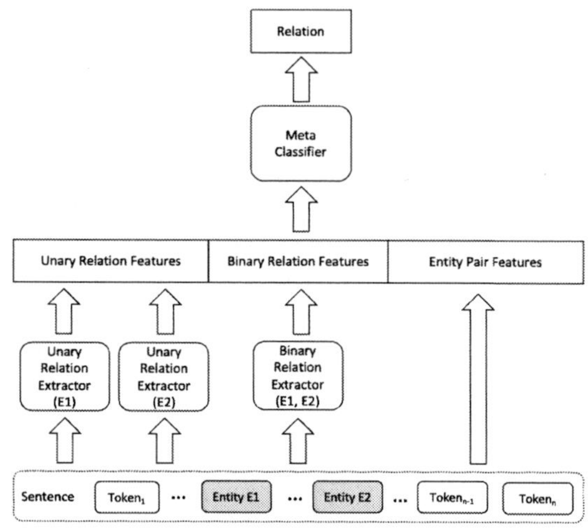

Figure 2: Stacked Learning Model

> *The Big Sky tailings were spectrally flat (similar to Telegraph Peak) likely from the presence of magnetite, and include a weak downturn > 750 nm, possibly from minor hematite.*

This complex sentence entails two relations:
CONTAINS(*Big Sky*, *magnetite*) and
CONTAINS(*Big Sky*, *hematite*).

4 Stacked Learning with Unary Relation Extractors

Our task is to perform within-sentence relation extraction given pre-specified ("gold") entities. We propose a stacked RE system in which a meta-classifier employs the output of a traditional binary relation extractor as well as two unary relation extractors, as shown in Figure 2. At a high level, the binary relation extractor captures the context spanning two arguments, while each unary relation extractor captures local information for one argument of the relation. The meta-classifier also includes features that describe the pair of entities under consideration. We utilize existing models from prior work for the binary relation extraction models. In this section, we present the design of our new unary relation extraction models and the meta-classifier.

4.1 The Stacked Learning Model

4.2 Unary Relation Extraction

A novel contribution of this work is the focus on *unary* relations. Each binary relation $\mathcal{R}(E_1, E_2)$ that applies to two entities can be decomposed into unary relations $\mathcal{R}_1(E_1)$ and $\mathcal{R}_2(E_2)$. Unary relations operate on a single entity to predict whether that entity acts as the appropriate argument for the relevant binary relation. For example, the sentence "*X provided guidance for Y's university studies*" includes an instance of the binary relation ADVISES(*Person, Person*) in the form of ADVISES(*X, Y*). This relation can be decomposed into ADVISOR(*Person*) and ADVISEE(*Person*) which can be separately evaluated for each of *X* and *Y*. Local context may lead us to infer ADVISOR(*X*) and ADVISEE(*Y*), indicating their argument status and differentiating *X* and *Y* despite their identical entity types.

For the planetary science domain, we decompose CONTAINS(*Target, Component*) into two unary relations: (1) the CONTAINER unary relation focuses on Target entities that contain an unspecified component (i.e., CONTAINS(*Target*, *)), and (2) the CONTAINEE unary relation focuses on Component entities that are part of an unspecified Target's composition (i.e., CONTAINS(*, *Component*)).[2] Similarly, we decompose the HASPROPERTY(*Target, Property*) relation into (1) PROPERTYHOLDER, which corresponds to HASPROPERTY(*Target*, *), and (2) PROPERTYHELD, which corresponds to HASPROPERTY(*, *Property*). All of our unary relation extractors share the same model architecture, which is explained in the following section.

4.2.1 Unary Relation Extractors

Each unary relation extractor takes an entity along with its sentence as input and predicts whether the entity participates in a specific unary relation. We define the input sentence S to consist of n tokens $S_1, S_2, \ldots, S_n$ and represent the entity of interest, e, with its beginning and ending indices, *BGN(e)* and *END(e)* respectively. Following prior work (Zhong and Chen, 2021), we insert a begin marker $\langle B \rangle$ and an end marker $\langle /B \rangle$ around e in the sentence to highlight the entity of interest:

$$S' = ..., \langle B \rangle, S_{BGN(e)}, ..., S_{END(e)}, \langle /B \rangle, ...$$

We use a pre-trained language model to encode S' and produce a contextual representation for the sentence. We then use the representation of the start marker $\langle B \rangle$ as the entity representation, denoted as E. Intuitively, we expect the representation of the start marker to encode the relevant contextual evidence around the entity (e.g., "*an increase in potassium*"). We pass E into a ReLU activation layer, a dropout layer, and finally a single-layer neural network to produce a predicted probability for whether the entity participates in the unary relation.

4.2.2 Training the Unary Models

The positive training instances for unary relation $\mathcal{R}_i(T)$ consist of all annotated instances of entity type T that participate as argument i in a binary relation of type $\mathcal{R}$. Negative training instances consist of all instances of T that do not participate as argument i of a relation of type $\mathcal{R}$. We trained the extraction models by fine-tuning a pre-trained language model with cross-entropy loss: $L(\theta) = \sum_{\text{x, y}\in\text{train}} logP(y|x, \theta)$, where x is an instance, $y \in \{0, 1\}$ is the unary relation label, and θ are the model parameters. We experimented with several different language models, which we will discuss in Section 5.

We create one stacked model for each relevant pair of entity types (e.g., one model to extract relations for (*Target, Component*) and another for (*Target, Property*)). Each model takes a pair of entities (E_1, E_2) of types (T_1, T_2) in a sentence as input and produces a prediction for whether a relation of type $\mathcal{R}$ exists between E_1 and E_2 (see Figure 2). We represent each pair of entities with a feature vector based on three sets of features: unary relation features, binary relation features, and entity pair features.

4.2.3 Unary Relation Features

The unary relation features consist of the outputs (confidence scores) of both unary relation extractors and a "unary pairing" feature. The latter feature is true if either entity $E_i \in \{E_1, E_2\}$ satisfies the following two criteria: 1) E_i receives a confidence score of at least 50% for a unary relation $\mathcal{R}_i(T_i)$, and 2) E_i is the closest entity of type T_i relative to the other entity in the pair. Intuitively, this rule hypothesizes a probable binary relation when at least one of the entities is predicted to participate in a unary relation and no other entity of the same type is closer to the other entity.

More generally, if there are $k > 1$ relations for the same kind of entity pairs (e.g., ADVISES(*Person, Person*) or MARRIED(*Person, Person*)), the unary relation features consist of $2{*}k$ confidence scores and k unary pairing features.

[2] We use the asterisk (*) symbol to indicate when an argument is unspecified.

4.2.4 Binary Relation Features

The binary relation feature is the output (confidence score) of the binary relation extractor. If there are $k > 1$ relations, a multi-class binary relation extractor is used to generate k posterior probabilities for the feature vector.

4.2.5 Entity Pair Features

The entity pair features capture general information about the context in which the entities occur.

Negation: Negation may suggest that there is no relation, so we create a binary feature to indicate if there is a negation word between E_1 and E_2.[3]

Order of Entities: One binary feature indicates the relative order of the two entities in the sentence.

Number of Entity Pairs: We count the number of entity pairs of type (T_1, T_2) in the sentence, and then bucket the counts into five bins $([1, 2), [2, 4), [4, 10), [10, \infty))$.

Nearest Entity: One binary feature indicates whether E_1 is the closest entity of type T_1 to E_2. Similarly, another binary feature indicates whether E_2 is the closest entity of type T_2 to E_1.

Entity Distribution: We hypothesize that the distribution of entities around E_1 and E_2 affects the likelihood that a relation exists between them. For example, a relation may be less likely if other entities occur between E_1 and E_2. So we develop two binary features to capture whether there is an entity of type T_2 to the left or to the right of E_1. Similarly, we develop two features to capture the same information for E_2 with type T_1.

Distance: Capturing the distance between two entities has shown to be useful in previous work. We create a distance feature by binning the number of words between the entities into q quantile bins, where the quantiles are computed over the distances observed in the training set. We explore different values (2, 5, 10, 15, 20) for q (the number of bins), and choose the one that performs best on the development set.

4.2.6 Meta-classifier

The input to the meta-classifier is a sentence with two entities marked. We then create a feature vector based on the three aforementioned feature sets, and feed it into the meta-classifier to predict a relation. While the model choice is flexible, we used a linear SVM in our experiments.

[3]The negation words we use are: no, not, none, nothing, never, nowhere, hardly, barely, scarcely.

	Count
Documents	602
Targets	5,140
Components	15,826
Properties	14,895
CONTAINS	3,045
HASPROPERTY	2,764

Table 1: Annotation statistics for LPSC corpus.

5 Experiments

We conducted experiments to evaluate the stacked relation extraction approach on the planetary science document collection as well as a benchmark data set to compare directly with recent prior work. We release the dataset and codes at `https://github.com/yyzhuang1991/StackedLearningWithUnaryModels`.

5.1 Planetary Science (LPSC) Data Set

We used a total of 602 documents that were manually annotated by three planetary scientists from the Jet Propulsion Laboratory, who are also co-authors of this work, to indicate the presence of relevant entities (Target, Component, Property) and relationships between them as CONTAINS(Target, Component) or HASPROPERTY(Target, Property). The corpus consists of text extracted from publicly available two-page extended abstracts that were published at the Lunar and Planetary Science Conference (LPSC). We started with a public collection of 117 documents from 2015 and 2016 that were annotated with CONTAINS relations for targets from the Mars Science Laboratory mission (Francis and Wagstaff, 2017). To expand the collection size and have more than one relation to study, we annotated almost 500 additional documents from 1998 to 2020 for targets from three more Mars missions: Mars Pathfinder, Mars Phoenix Lander, and the MER-A (Spirit) Mars Exploration Rover (Wagstaff et al., 2022). We also added the new relation HASPROPERTY. Table 1 shows the total number of annotated entities and relations.

5.2 Planetary Science Domain Methodology

We randomly selected 25% of the documents (151 documents) for a development set to tune hyperparameters and performed 5-fold cross validation over the other 451 documents. We report the precision, recall, and F1 score averaged across the 5 runs. All of our relation extraction models take gold (manually annotated) entities as input.

To populate a knowledge base, it is sufficient to store each relation once. The planetary science domain experts who annotated the corpus had this mindset, so they did not always annotate duplicate instances of the same relation within a document. For example, if CONTAINS(*Windjana, potassium feldspar*) occurs three times in a document, they may have only annotated it once. Therefore, we report precision, recall, and F1 score by comparing the set of distinct predicted relations in a document against the set of distinct annotated relations, a metric that has been used in other RE work (Li et al., 2016b). Specifically, for each document and relation $\mathcal{R}$, we compiled the unique occurrences of entity pairs (E_1, E_2) annotated with relation $\mathcal{R}$ as the set of annotated relations. This approach ignores (and therefore does not require) duplicate occurrences of the same relation found in different sentences of a document.

5.3 Relation Extraction Models

We compared the performance of the stacked learning model to that of existing binary relation extractors as well as unary relation extraction alone. For binary relation extraction, we experimented with fine-tuning pre-trained language models (LMs) on our planetary science data, since previous work (Gu et al., 2022; Yasunaga et al., 2022) has found this approach to work quite well. We created models with BERT (Devlin et al., 2019), which has been widely used across many NLP tasks and domains, as well as SciBERT (Beltagy et al., 2019) and LinkBERT (Yasunaga et al., 2022), which have proven to be beneficial for other scientific domains.[4]

Specifically, each binary relation extraction system is a pre-trained language model with an additional classification layer on top. The input is a sentence with exactly two entities marked as relevant. The sentence is encoded by the language model, and its representation (as captured by the special [CLS] token) is then fed into a single layer feedforward network that produces a probability distribution over the set of possible relations.[5] For hyperparameters, we used a batch size of 10 and a dropout rate of 0.1.[6] We then performed a grid search over all combinations of learning rates (1e-5, 2e-5) and epochs (4, 5, 10) and used the values which performed best on the development set.

To our knowledge, the only previous work on relation extraction for the planetary science domain was reported by Wagstaff et al. (2018), for the CONTAINS relation only. They used jSRE (Giuliano et al., 2006), which employs an SVM classifier to predict the presence of a relation between two entities given features derived from a shallow parser. For comparison with that earlier work in this domain, we also trained a jSRE model for each of our binary relations. For hyperparameter-tuning, we explored every possible combination of SVM kernels (LC, GC, SL) and window sizes (1, 2, 5, 10, 15, 20), choosing the values that performed best on the development set.

We also created a binary relation extraction system that uses *only* unary relation extractors. The challenge for this approach is how to recover binary relations from the unary predictions, particularly because multiple entities are often predicted for each unary relation. After exploring several strategies, the best approach seemed to be aggressively pairing each entity predicted to be in a unary relation with *all* other entities of the appropriate type in the sentence. For example, to produce the CONTAINS(Target, Component) relation, we pair each predicted CONTAINER(Target) with all Component entities, and likewise we pair each predicted CONTAINEE(Component) with all Target entities. We refer to this approach as the **Paired Unary (PU)** Model.

The logic behind this approach is that one unary relation can have strong local evidence, while the other may not. For example, this model performs well in situations where (say) two Targets are correctly recognized as CONTAINERS but the mineral detected at those sites is not recognized as being in a CONTAINEE context. We found that this heuristic worked fairly well in the planetary science domain, with substantially higher recall but lower precision. But an advantage of stacked learning is that it avoids the need to manually create heuristics because the meta-classifier learns what will work well in different domains and for different relations.

[4]We used $\text{BERT}_{\text{base-uncased}}$, $\text{SciBERT}_{\text{scivocab-uncased}}$, and $\text{LinkBERT}_{\text{base}}$.

[5]The [CLS] token is used in language models of BERT variants for classification tasks.

[6]We found that different batch sizes did not impact performance much, and a dropout rate of 0.1 consistently outperformed other rates from 0.1 to 0.5 with increments of 0.1.

Model	Pr	Rec	F1
jSRE	**69.1**	75.8	72.3
$PU_{SciBERT}$	59.6	94.1	72.6
$PU_{LinkBERT}$	59.3	**95.1**	72.7
PU_{BERT}	60.2	94.6	73.2
$BR_{SciBERT}$	68.6	83.9	74.7
BR_{BERT}	66.5	87.9	75.0
$BR_{LinkBERT}$	68.4	86.6	**76.0**

Table 2: Results for the CONTAINS relation (LPSC)

Model	Pr	Rec	F1
jSRE	56.3	60.8	58.3
$PU_{LinkBERT}$	54.0	**97.1**	69.1
$PU_{SciBERT}$	55.4	95.8	69.8
PU_{BERT}	56.0	94.2	70.0
BR_{BERT}	74.5	75.0	74.6
$BR_{SciBERT}$	**76.0**	76.9	76.2
$BR_{LinkBERT}$	74.4	79.9	**76.9**

Table 3: Results for the HASPROPERTY relation (LPSC)

5.4 Results for Binary Relation Extraction

Table 2 shows the experimental results for jSRE, the Binary Relation (BR) extraction models, and the Paired Unary (PU) model for the CONTAINS relation. We fine-tuned the BERT, SciBERT, and LinkBERT language models for the planetary science domain for the PU and BR extractors.

The jSRE model achieved the highest precision but the lowest F1 score. All Paired Unary models slightly outperformed jSRE, but the Binary Relation models performed the best. Of the language models, BERT performed best for the PU models but LinkBERT performed best for the BR models.

Table 3 shows the results for the HASPROPERTY relation. The jSRE model performs substantially worse than for CONTAINS, and the performance of the PU models is lower too. However, the BR models achieve similar F1 scores, albeit with higher precision and lower recall than for CONTAINS. For both relations, LinkBERT is the best language model for binary relation extraction.

5.5 Results for Stacked Learning

For our stacked learning approach, we created a meta-classifier by training a linear SVM using the scikit-learn package (Pedregosa et al., 2011). We created three different stacked learning models consisting of fine-tuned component models (unary and binary extractors) that all employed either BERT, SciBERT, or LinkBERT. For the SVM meta-classifier, we explored different values for the regularization parameter C within the set (0.001, 0.005, 0.01, 0.05, 0.1, 0.5, 1, 5) and used the best value based on the development set.

Model	Pr	Rec	F1
$Stacked_{SciBERT}$	67.5	86.9	75.6
$Stacked_{BERT}$	68.4	**89.3**	77.2
$Stacked_{LinkBERT}$	**72.1**	86.3	**78.5**

Table 4: Stacked learning results for CONTAINS.

Model	Pr	Rec	F1
$Stacked_{BERT}$	68.8	**86.2**	76.5
$Stacked_{SciBERT}$	71.2	85.0	77.4
$Stacked_{LinkBERT}$	**74.1**	82.8	**78.1**

Table 5: Stacked learning results for HASPROPERTY.

Tables 4 and 5 show the results for stacked learning for the CONTAINS and HASPROPERTY relations respectively. The results are remarkably consistent. In every case, the stacked model that uses language model L performs better than the binary relation extractor that uses language model L. The best models use LinkBERT, where stacking improves performance from 76.0% → 78.5% for CONTAINS and from 76.9% → 78.1% for HASPROPERTY. These results demonstrate the value of combining unary and binary relation extractors in a stacked ensemble.

As a concrete example of the benefits of including unary relation extractors in the stacked model, consider the following sentence. It contains three CONTAINS relations between Target *Home Plate* and *Px* (an abbreviation for the mineral pyroxene), *Mt* (magnetite), and *npOx* (nanophase oxides). However, *Home Plate* does not contain *Ol* (olivine), which is a false positive for the $BR_{LinkBERT}$ model, but a true negative for $Stacked_{LinkBERT}$, which had access to the unary extractor and correctly predicted no CONTAINEE(*Ol*) relation.

> *Vesicular basalts investigated in the vicinity of Home Plate such as the rock Esperanza have the same Fe mineralogical composition as eastern Home Plate: rich in Px and Mt, no Ol and little npOx.*

5.6 Experiments on Chemprot Data

To assess the effectiveness of our approach in other domains, we conducted another experiment on the Chemprot task (Taboureau et al., 2010). The Chemprot task is designed to extract chemical-protein relations (CPR) from PubMed abstracts. In the dataset, five chemical-protein relations are used for evaluation (CPR:3, CPR:4, CPR:5, CPR:6 and CPR:9). We used code provided by Yasunaga et al. (2022) to obtain and preprocess the training, development, and test sets.[7] $\text{LinkBERT}_{\text{BioLinkBERT-base}}$ after fine-tuning is reported to achieve the best performance on this data set, so we used it as the pre-trained language model in unary extractors. The unary extractors and stacked model were trained as described in Section 5.3. A single stacked model is sufficient since all Chemprot relations operate on (*Chemical, Protein*) pairs. The binary relation features were generated by $\text{LinkBERT}_{\text{BioLinkBERT-base}}$ predictions kindly released by Yasunaga et al. (2022).

Table 6 shows the performance of different models, reported as precision, recall and F1 scores, micro-averaged and macro-averaged across the five relations. The Paired Unary model achieves the lowest overall performance due to its extremely low precision. It allows an entity to be mistakenly extracted by **multiple** unary relations in Chemprot. This emphasizes that heuristic rules to construct full relations using only the unary relation extractors may not work well for different domains.

The following rows show results reported by Gu et al. (2022) for competitive binary relation extractors produced by fine-tuning different language models.[8] Among these methods, LinkBERT achieves the best performance. The bottom row shows that our stacked model based on LinkBERT improves upon LinkBERT alone and achieves state-of-the-art performance on this task. Specifically, the micro-F1 score increases from 77.6% to 78.3% and the macro-F1 score from 76.8% to 77.9%. According to the precision-recall breakdown, the stacked model achieves a substantial increase in precision (by 3.2% absolute points in micro-average, and 5.7% in macro-average) although at the expense of some recall.

[7]The source code can be found at https://github.com/michiyasunaga/LinkBERT.

[8]For most binary extractors, only the micro-F1 score was reported.

Model	Micro Average			Macro Average		
	P	R	F1	P	R	F1
$\text{PU}_{\text{LinkBERT}}$	36.3	**88.5**	51.5	34.5	**87.6**	49.4
Binary Extractors						
BERT†	-	-	71.8	-	-	-
SciBERT†	-	-	75.2	-	-	-
BioBERT†	-	-	76.1	-	-	-
PubMedBERT†	-	-	77.2	-	-	-
LinkBERT	76.6	78.5	77.6	75.6	76.1	76.8
Stacked Model						
$\text{SVM}_{\text{LinkBERT}}$	**79.8**	76.8	**78.3**	**81.3**	75.0	**77.9**

Table 6: Performance of relation extraction models on Chemprot. †: Scores reported by Gu et al. (2022).

Dataset	FULL	w/o UNARY	w/o EP	w/o BINARY
LPSC				
CONTAINS	78.5	77.5	77.2	75.3
HASPROPERTY	78.1	76.9	77.0	76.5
Chemprot				
CPR:3	75.6	74.5	75.6	65.5
CPR:4	81.8	81.7	81.8	78.6
CPR:5	81.3	78.2	81.6	67.3
CPR:6	82.6	82.9	81.3	75.1
CPR:9	68.2	67.6	68	62.9
Micro-AVG	78.3	77.6	78.2	72.7
Macro-AVG	77.9	77.0	77.6	70.0

Table 7: F1 scores of the stacked model $\text{SVM}_{\text{LinkBERT}}$ in ablation experiments.

6 Analysis

We performed additional manual analyses to better understand the behavior of our stacked models.

We performed ablation experiments to assess the contributions of different components of the stacked ensemble by separately removing the Unary Relation Features (UNARY), Binary Relation Features (BINARY), and Entity Pair Features (EP) from the best stacked model $\text{SVM}_{\text{LinkBERT}}$. Table 7 shows the F1 score for each relation within the LPSC and Chemprot data sets. For LPSC, removing any feature set reduces performance, so they are all valuable. For Chemprot, however, only BINARY and UNARY are important; excluding EP does not significantly impact the overall performance. Looking at individual CPR relations, we find that including unary relation features benefits CPR:3, CPR:5, and CPR:6 the most. This result suggests that those relations have more local contextual cues that are associated with one or the other side of the relation.

Next, we examined whether the stacked model extracts relations from sentences with more entities better. Figure 3 shows a graph that plots the F1 scores of $\text{SVM}_{\text{LinkBERT}}$ and LinkBERT against the number of entity pairs in a sentence for the

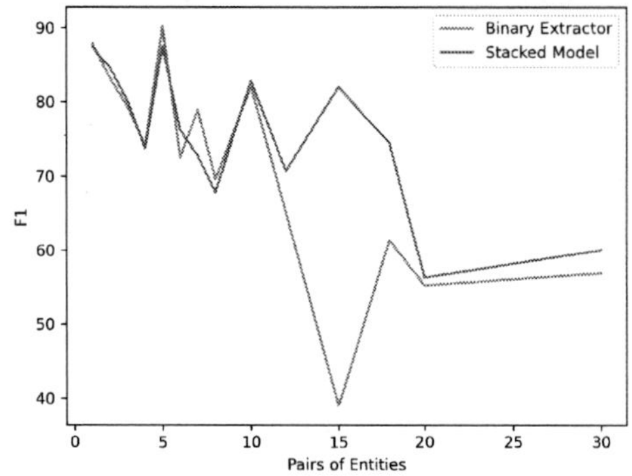

Figure 3: F1 scores versus the number of entity pairs (Target, Component) in a sentence for the CONTAINS relation. The binary relation extractor is LinkBERT and the stacked model is $SVM_{LinkBERT}$. Scores are averaged across the 5-fold cross validation.

Missed ⟶ Extracted
1. An APXS analysis of the "*Hula*" sample (Figs.3, 4) shows elevated MgO (11wt%), SO3 (33wt%), and Ni (900 ppm), suggestive of Mg-*Nickel* sulfate.
2. The *Hematite* abundance (8 wt%) is significantly more than observed in other samples from Gale Crater: 0.8, 0.6, 0.7, and 0.6 wt% for Rocknest, John Klein , Cumberland , and *Windjana*, respectively[4, 5].
Falsely Extracted
3. At this time there is not enough data, experimental and petrologic, to suggest whether or not *Humphrey* contains cumulate *Olivine*.
4. Rock Humphrey shows similar *Phosphorus* contents in RU and RB and a decrease in RR , whereas for rock *Mazatzal* the highest P concentration is measured in its weathering rind of RB[5].

Table 8: Examples of correct and incorrect extraction by the stacked model, $SVM_{LinkBERT}$, for the CONTAINS relation. Components are highlighted in blue and Targets are highlighted in green.

CONTAINS relation. The stacked model performs comparably to the binary relation extractor over sentences with fewer entity pairs, but it consistently outperforms the binary relation extractor over sentences with more than 10 pairs of entities. We hypothesize that it is important to filter out entities that do not participate in any unary relation when there are many entities in a sentence. By recognizing unary relations, the stacked model is able to handle the complexity of a large number of entity pairs.

Finally, Table 8 shows some correct and incorrect cases extracted by $SVM_{LinkBERT}$. In the top portion, we show examples of the CONTAINS relation that the binary relation extractor, LinkBERT, missed but the stacked model correctly extracted. We found that a lot of these cases contain strong local cues (such as "*suggestive of*" in 1), and "*abundance*" in 2)) that signify relevant unary relations. The bottom portion of Table 8 shows some false positive examples where the stacked model incorrectly extracted the CONTAINS relation. 3) is a challenging case where the local context is misleading (e.g., "*Humphrey* contains cumulate *Olivine*") and it is important to understand the more global contexts *"there is not enough data"*. 4) is a common error we have observed, where both the Target and the Component entities are in the relevant unary relations but they do not participate in the same binary relation.

7 Conclusions and Future Work

The goal of this work is to perform an automated analysis of scientific publications that enables the construction of domain-specific knowledge bases. We focused on the planetary science discipline, which to date has not received much attention from automated information extraction work. The complex grammar often employed in scientific publications can pose problems for state-of-the-art relation extraction systems. We proposed the use of unary relation extractors to enable specialization for each argument of a relation, within a stacked learning framework. Our approach performed well both in this domain and the Chemprot benchmark (biology) data set. In future work, we plan to expand the scope of this approach to include relations that cross sentences, which is a major challenge for current relation extraction systems and for which local unary relation modeling is especially well suited.

Acknowledgements

We thank the NASA Planetary Data Archiving, Restoration, and Tools (PDART) program (19-PDART19_2-0077) for funding this project. Part of this research was carried out at the Jet Propulsion Laboratory, California Institute of Technology, under a contract with the National Aeronautics and Space Administration.

References

Iz Beltagy, Kyle Lo, and Arman Cohan. 2019. Scibert: Pretrained language model for scientific text. In *Proceedings of the 2019 Conference on Empirical Methods in Natural Language Processing and the 9th International Joint Conference on Natural Language Processing (EMNLP-IJCNLP)*,.

Razvan Bunescu and Raymond Mooney. 2005. A shortest path dependency kernel for relation extraction. In *Proceedings of Human Language Technology Conference and Conference on Empirical Methods in Natural Language Processing*, pages 724–731, Vancouver, British Columbia, Canada. Association for Computational Linguistics.

Yee Seng Chan and Dan Roth. 2011. Exploiting syntactico-semantic structures for relation extraction. In *Proceedings of the 49th Annual Meeting of the Association for Computational Linguistics: Human Language Technologies*, pages 551–560, Portland, Oregon, USA. Association for Computational Linguistics.

Fenia Christopoulou, Makoto Miwa, and Sophia Ananiadou. 2018. A walk-based model on entity graphs for relation extraction. In *Proceedings of the 56th Annual Meeting of the Association for Computational Linguistics (Volume 2: Short Papers)*, pages 81–88, Melbourne, Australia. Association for Computational Linguistics.

Jacob Devlin, Ming-Wei Chang, Kenton Lee, and Kristina Toutanova. 2019. BERT: Pre-training of deep bidirectional transformers for language understanding. In *Proceedings of the 2019 Conference of the North American Chapter of the Association for Computational Linguistics: Human Language Technologies, Volume 1 (Long and Short Papers)*, pages 4171–4186, Minneapolis, Minnesota. Association for Computational Linguistics.

Kalpit Dixit and Yaser Al-Onaizan. 2019. Span-level model for relation extraction. In *Proceedings of the 57th Annual Meeting of the Association for Computational Linguistics*, pages 5308–5314, Florence, Italy. Association for Computational Linguistics.

Raymond Francis and Kiri L. Wagstaff. 2017. Mars Target Encyclopedia - LPSC abstracts labeled data set (Version 1.0.0 [Data set]). Presented at the Thirtieth Annual Conference on Innovative Applications of Artificial Intelligence (IAAI), `https://doi.org/10.5281/zenodo.1048419`.

Claudio Giuliano, Alberto Lavelli, and Lorenza Romano. 2006. Exploiting shallow linguistic information for relation extraction from biomedical literature. In *Proceedings of the 11th Conference of the European Chapter of the Association for Computational Linguistics (EACL 2006)*, pages 401–408.

Yuxian Gu, Robert Tinn, Hao Cheng, Michael R. Lucas, Naoto Usuyama, Xiaodong Liu, Tristan Naumann, Jianfeng Gao, and Hoifung Poon. 2022. Domain-specific language model pretraining for biomedical natural language processing. *ACM Transactions on Computing for Healthcare (HEALTH)*, 3:1 – 23.

Sonal Gupta and Christopher Manning. 2011. Analyzing the dynamics of research by extracting key aspects of scientific papers. In *Proceedings of 5th International Joint Conference on Natural Language Processing*, pages 1–9, Chiang Mai, Thailand. Asian Federation of Natural Language Processing.

Nanda Kambhatla. 2004. Combining lexical, syntactic, and semantic features with maximum entropy models for information extraction. In *Proceedings of the ACL Interactive Poster and Demonstration Sessions*, pages 178–181, Barcelona, Spain. Association for Computational Linguistics.

George Lakoff. 1972. *The Semantics of Natural Language*, chapter Linguistics and natural logic. D. Reidel Publishing Company, Dordrecht, Holland.

Fei Li, Meishan Zhang, Guohong Fu, and Donghong Ji. 2017. A neural joint model for entity and relation extraction from biomedical text. *BMC Bioinformatics*, 18.

Jiao Li, Yueping Sun, Robin Johnson, Daniela Sciaky, Chih-Hsuan Wei, Robert Leaman, Allan Peter Davis, Carolyn Mattingly, Thomas Wiegers, and Zhiyong lu. 2016a. Biocreative v cdr task corpus: a resource for chemical disease relation extraction. *Database*, 2016:baw068.

Jiao Li, Yueping Sun, Robin J. Johnson, Daniela Sciaky, Chih-Hsuan Wei, Robert Leaman, Allan Peter Davis, Carolyn J. Mattingly, Thomas C. Wiegers, and Zhiyong Lu. 2016b. BioCreative V CDR task corpus: a resource for chemical disease relation extraction. *Database*, 2016. Baw068.

Ying Lin, Heng Ji, Fei Huang, and Lingfei Wu. 2020. A joint neural model for information extraction with global features. In *Proceedings of the 58th Annual Meeting of the Association for Computational Linguistics*, pages 7999–8009, Online. Association for Computational Linguistics.

Yi Luan, Dave Wadden, Luheng He, Amy Shah, Mari Ostendorf, and Hannaneh Hajishirzi. 2019. A general framework for information extraction using dynamic span graphs. In *Proceedings of the 2019 Conference of the North American Chapter of the Association for Computational Linguistics: Human Language Technologies, Volume 1 (Long and Short Papers)*, pages 3036–3046, Minneapolis, Minnesota. Association for Computational Linguistics.

Makoto Miwa and Mohit Bansal. 2016. End-to-end relation extraction using LSTMs on sequences and tree structures. In *Proceedings of the 54th Annual Meeting of the Association for Computational Linguistics (Volume 1: Long Papers)*, pages 1105–1116, Berlin, Germany. Association for Computational Linguistics.

Thien Huu Nguyen, Barbara Plank, and Ralph Grishman. 2015. Semantic representations for domain adaptation: A case study on the tree kernel-based method for relation extraction. In *Proceedings of the 53rd Annual Meeting of the Association for Computational Linguistics and the 7th International Joint Conference on Natural Language Processing (Volume 1: Long Papers)*, pages 635–644, Beijing, China. Association for Computational Linguistics.

F. Pedregosa, G. Varoquaux, A. Gramfort, V. Michel, B. Thirion, O. Grisel, M. Blondel, P. Prettenhofer, R. Weiss, V. Dubourg, J. Vanderplas, A. Passos, D. Cournapeau, M. Brucher, M. Perrot, and E. Duchesnay. 2011. Scikit-learn: Machine learning in Python. *Journal of Machine Learning Research*, 12:2825–2830.

Richard Socher, Brody Huval, Christopher D. Manning, and Andrew Y. Ng. 2012. Semantic compositionality through recursive matrix-vector spaces. In *Proceedings of the 2012 Joint Conference on Empirical Methods in Natural Language Processing and Computational Natural Language Learning*, pages 1201–1211, Jeju Island, Korea. Association for Computational Linguistics.

Olivier Taboureau, Sonny Kim Nielsen, Karine Audouze, Nils Weinhold, Daniel Edsgärd, Francisco S Roque, Irene Kouskoumvekaki, Alina Bora, Ramona Curpan, Thomas Skøt Jensen, et al. 2010. Chemprot: a disease chemical biology database. *Nucleic Acids Research*, 39(suppl_1):D367–D372.

Yuka Tateisi, Yo Shidahara, Yusuke Miyao, and Akiko Aizawa. 2014. Annotation of computer science papers for semantic relation extrac-tion. In *Proceedings of the Ninth International Conference on Language Resources and Evaluation (LREC'14)*, pages 1423–1429, Reykjavik, Iceland. European Language Resources Association (ELRA).

Chen-Tse Tsai, Gourab Kundu, and Dan Roth. 2013. Concept-based analysis of scientific literature. In *Proceedings of the 22nd ACM International Conference on Information & Knowledge Management*, page 1733–1738, New York, NY, USA. Association for Computing Machinery.

Patrick Verga, Emma Strubell, and Andrew McCallum. 2018. Simultaneously self-attending to all mentions for full-abstract biological relation extraction. In *Proceedings of the 2018 Conference of the North American Chapter of the Association for Computational Linguistics: Human Language Technologies, Volume 1 (Long Papers)*, pages 872–884, New Orleans, Louisiana. Association for Computational Linguistics.

David Wadden, Ulme Wennberg, Yi Luan, and Hannaneh Hajishirzi. 2019. Entity, relation, and event extraction with contextualized span representations. In *Proceedings of the 2019 Conference on Empirical Methods in Natural Language Processing and the 9th International Joint Conference on Natural Language Processing (EMNLP-IJCNLP)*, pages 5784–5789, Hong Kong, China. Association for Computational Linguistics.

Kiri L. Wagstaff, Raymond Francis, Matthew Golombek, Leslie Tamppari, and Steven Lu. 2022. Mars Target Encyclopedia - Labeled LPSC abstracts for four Mars missions (Version 1.0.0 [Data set]). `https://doi.org/10.5281/zenodo.7066107`.

Kiri L. Wagstaff, Raymond Francis, Thamme Gowda, You Lu, Ellen Riloff, Karanjeet Singh, and Nina L. Lanza. 2018. Mars Target Encyclopedia: Rock and soil composition extracted from the literature. In *Proceedings of the Thirtieth Annual Conference on Innovative Applications of Artificial Intelligence*, pages 7861–7866.

Haoyu Wang, Ming Tan, Mo Yu, Shiyu Chang, Dakuo Wang, Kun Xu, Xiaoxiao Guo, and Saloni Potdar. 2019. Extracting multiple-relations in one-pass with pre-trained transformers. In *Proceedings of the 57th Annual Meeting of the Association for Computational Linguistics*, pages 1371–1377, Florence, Italy. Association for Computational Linguistics.

Taiki Watanabe, Akihiro Tamura, Takashi Ninomiya, Takuya Makino, and Tomoya Iwakura. 2019. Multitask learning for chemical named entity recognition with chemical compound paraphrasing. In *Proceedings of the 2019 Conference on Empirical Methods in Natural Language Processing and the 9th International Joint Conference on Natural Language Processing (EMNLP-IJCNLP)*, pages 6244–6249, Hong Kong, China. Association for Computational Linguistics.

Zhepei Wei, Jianlin Su, Yue Wang, Yuan Tian, and Yi Chang. 2020. A novel cascade binary tagging framework for relational triple extraction. In *Proceedings of the 58th Annual Meeting of the Association for Computational Linguistics*, pages 1476–1488, Online. Association for Computational Linguistics.

Michihiro Yasunaga, Jure Leskovec, and Percy Liang. 2022. Linkbert: Pretraining language models with document links. In *Association for Computational Linguistics (ACL)*.

Dmitry Zelenko, Chinatsu Aone, and Anthony Richardella. 2003. Kernel methods for relation extraction. *Joural of Machine Learning Research*, 3:1083–1106.

Ce Zhang, Vidhya Govindaraju, Jackson Borchardt, Tim Foltz, Christopher Ré, and Shanan Peters. 2013. GeoDeepDive: Statistical inference using familiar data-processing languages. In *Proceedings of the 2013 ACM SIGMOD International Conference on Management of Data*, pages 993–996.

Dongxu Zhang and Dong Wang. 2015. Relation classification via recurrent neural network. Preprint on arXiv, `https://arxiv.org/abs/1508.01006v2`.

Meishan Zhang, Yue Zhang, and Guohong Fu. 2017. End-to-end neural relation extraction with global optimization. In *Proceedings of the 2017 Conference on Empirical Methods in Natural Language Processing*, pages 1730–1740, Copenhagen, Denmark. Association for Computational Linguistics.

Yuhao Zhang, Peng Qi, and Christopher D. Manning. 2018. Graph convolution over pruned dependency trees improves relation extraction. In *Proceedings of the 2018 Conference on Empirical Methods in Natural Language Processing*, pages 2205–2215, Brussels, Belgium. Association for Computational Linguistics.

Zexuan Zhong and Danqi Chen. 2021. A frustratingly easy approach for entity and relation extraction. In *Proceedings of the 2021 Conference of the North American Chapter of the Association for Computational Linguistics: Human Language Technologies*, pages 50–61, Online. Association for Computational Linguistics.

Mitigating Data Shift of Biomedical Research Articles for Information Retrieval and Semantic Indexing

Nima Ebadi[1], **Anthony Rios,**[2] **and Paul Rad**[1,2]
[1]Department of Computer Science
[2]Department of Information Systems and Cyber Security
University of Texas at San Antonio
{nima.ebadi, anthony.rios, peyman.najafirad>}@utsa

Abstract

Researchers have explored novel methods for both semantic indexing and information retrieval of biomedical research articles. Moreover, most solutions treat each task independently. However, both tasks are related. For instance, semantic indexes are generally used to filter results from an information retrieval system. Hence, one task can potentially improve the performance of models trained for the other task. Thus, this study proposes a unified retriever-ranker-based model to tackle the tasks of information retrieval (IR) and semantic indexing (SI). Particularly, our proposed model can adapt to rapid shifts in scientific research. Our results show that the model effectively leverages task similarity to improve the robustness to dataset shift. For SI, the Micro f1 score increases by 8% and the LCA-F score improves by 5%. For IR, the MAP increases by 5% on average.

1 Introduction

The pandemic caused the rapidly evolving curation of scientific publications about COVID-19, resulting in an information crisis (Roberts et al., 2020). As a result, healthcare practitioners, policymakers, and other individuals fighting against COVID-19 require specialized information retrieval (IR) and semantic indexing (SI) systems to keep track of the ever-evolving literature landscape (Esteva et al., 2020; Wang et al.). Researcher's methods to address these tasks have generally focused on one task, IR or SI (Zhang et al., 2020; Colic et al., 2020).

IR and SI are related. For example, IR addresses the question, "what are the most relevant research papers, and why are they deemed relevant?" SI is essential to facilitate easy browsing and filtering of IR-retrieved manuscripts. For instance, if a user finds all relevant papers related to the question, "What vaccines are the most effective for COVID-19?", they can use SI to filter papers associated with a specific COVID-19 variant, e.g., MeSH terms on PubMed (Lipscomb, 2000). Hence, this paper proposes a novel architecture that jointly addresses both tasks.

There has been an array of research in IR and SI of biomedical documents. For instance, since 2012, there has been an annual competition where researchers compete to develop more accurate biomedical IR and SI methods (BioASQ[1]). The competition is essential to improve the National Library of Medicine's (NLM) infrastructure, which provides IR and SI systems for biomedical scientists and healthcare professionals to search for biomedical research articles. NLM manually indexes biomedical research articles with Medical Subject Headings (MeSH). MeSH terms are used for biomedical SI purposes (e.g., filtering search results), to facilitate hypothesis generation by biomedical scientists, and to help general knowledge discovery. Unfortunately, there are over 29 thousand MeSH terms. Thus manually identifying the subset of terms applicable to each article is difficult and expensive to complete in a timely manner. Hence, the competition has helped researchers introduce various methods for automated MeSH coding. For instance, many researchers have trained linear models, which still result in strong baselines (Liu et al., 2014; Rios and Kavuluru, 2015). For example, Liu et al. (2014) combined linear models with a learning-to-rank framework, which is still used today in combination with neural networks (Dai et al., 2020).

Similarly, BioASQ had a part in advancing biomedical IR systems. For instance, Pappas et al. (2020) used convolutional neural networks for biomedical snippet retrieval. Similar to BioASQ, recent IR efforts have focused on COVID-related IR as part of the annual TREC competition (TREC-COVID) (Roberts et al., 2020). For example, Soni and Roberts (2021) evaluated two commercial deep

[1]http://www.bioasq.org/

Proceedings of the Third Workshop on Scholarly Document Processing, pages 138–151
October 12–17, 2022.

learning IR systems on the TREC-COVID dataset, showing that both systems underperformed the expected results. Researchers have proposed other models beyond the commercial systems, including pre-trained transformer models for text ranking (Lin et al., 2020), along with zero-shot retrieval systems for COVID (MacAvaney et al., 2020). Some researchers have recently explored combining IR and SI. As an example, researchers have used an IR system as part of a KNN-based component of an ensemble model to improve MeSH identification (Liu et al., 2014; Dai et al., 2020). Nevertheless, to the best of our knowledge, no prior work has used SI to improve IR systems, especially in IR systems for COVID-related retrieval.

There are four major technical challenges with developing COVID-related IR and SI systems: sparse datasets, shifts in the data distribution, scale, and interpretability. The limited amount of labeled data and dynamic changes in the COVID-19 landscape has made it challenging to generalize IR and SI methods beyond the datasets used to train them (Shokraneh and Russell-Rose, 2020). Because information is quickly becoming outdated in research articles, understanding what is relevant is difficult for current IR methods. For example, expert human judgments did not identify 70% of the retrieved results as relevant (Voorhees et al., 2021). However, the manual assessment process is time-consuming. Therefore, it is important to improve current models and provide textual evidence for "why" it detected a document as relevant to facilitate easier manual assessments by human experts (Xun et al., 2019)—providing answers to "why" is useful, especially if we develop systems that work to help experts. For instance, Jin et al. (2018) shows that human indexers at NLM become significantly more efficient and accurate if they are provided semantically sensible associations between the input text and system outputs.

To address the technical challenges, we propose a specialized IR and SI approach that combines interpretability, multi-task learning, and a mechanism of using unlabeled data via self-supervised learning to improve model robustness. Overall, our model will allow for quick adaptation and robustness to the dataset shift problem, becoming suitable for the context of the pandemic. We summarize the major contributions of this paper below: **(1.)** We propose a novel interpretable, self-supervised, multi-task learning method to tackle the tasks of IR and SI COVID-19-related research articles. We devise a mechanism to train a unified retriever-ranker on a self-supervised *masked language modeling (MLM)*, SI, and an IR task. This joint training framework enables inter-document representation learning, quick adaptation to new changes in the data distribution, and interpretability, which we demonstrate to be important for the context of the pandemic. To the best of our knowledge, this is the first study to show the utility of joint training of SI and IR tasks—showing both tasks complement each other in a single model, not just one task helping the other one. **(2.)** We introduce a novel output layer transformation method that allows us to predict new concepts as they appear over time *without* retraining the model. **(3.)** Our study provides detailed quantitative and qualitative analysis of our model's interpretability and transfer learning components that highlight the dataset shift challenges of IR and SI tasks during a health crisis.

2 Related Work

Biomedical Semantic Indexing. NLM has collected biomedical literature from the last 150 years. As of 2020, the PubMed database contains about 30 Million biomedical journal citations. This number has risen from 12 Million citations in 2004 to 30 Million citations in 2020, having a growth rate of 4% per year. Through a laborious process, NLM curators fully examine every document and annotate it with a set of hierarchically organized terminologies developed by NLM called Medical Subject Headings (MeSH[2]) along with supplementary concepts for more fine-grained categorization (Papagiannopoulou et al., 2016). In 2019, more than 900K biomedical citations were added to PubMed and manually indexed to more than 29K MeSH concept categories[3].

Researchers have been trying to address biomedical natural language processing problems effectively for more than a decade, e.g. BioASQ (Tsatsaronis et al., 2015c), which has led to introduction of many models for IR and SI (Jin et al., 2018; Peng et al., 2016; Müller et al., 2017; Zavorin et al., 2016; Xun et al., 2019). A successful group of submissions involves deep learning models with substantial hand-coded features and supervision. DeepMesh (Peng et al., 2016), the best performing model in the BioASQ challenge, combines docu-

[2] https://www.nlm.nih.gov/mesh/meshhome.html

[3] https://www.nlm.nih.gov/pubs/techbull/mj18/brief/mj18_updates_2018_baseline_stats.html

ment to vector models with crafted features from the document and MeSH indexes, along with ensemble models fed by those features. Other deep learning approaches include UIMA concept extractor links (Peng et al., 2016), and AUTH, which also uses a document-to-vector approach with an ensemble of machine learning classifier (SVM) fed with document-MeSH features (Papagiannopoulou et al., 2016). Jin et al. (2018) and Xun et al. (2019) combined retrieval systems with deep recurrent neural networks and attention mechanism and also provide explainability for MeSH indexing decisions. The amount of hand-crafted features and supervision required for these models make it difficult to scale up as the biomedical databases change during pandemic crises (Foroughi Pour et al., 2020).

Most SI models are developed to perform well in normal situations across a broad range of biomedical concepts. Researchers evaluate SI models based on their overall performance on all major MeSH indices (Nentidis et al., 2019). In the pandemic situation, however, the focus of the literature has drastically shifted toward the specific concepts and subconcepts related to the current Coronavirus disease. The number of published documents related to Coronavirus has risen from a few articles per month to more than 10K articles in June 2020—roughly 1 out of every 11.5 citations are about Coronavirus these days. Chen et al. (2020) The rapidly growing and evolving literature on COVID-19 causes challenges for automatic SI models (Shokraneh and Russell-Rose, 2020). Previously introduced SI models are based on supervised learning approaches and heavily hand-coded features. Therefore, they require large amounts of labeled data for a specific concept to perform well. They also have challenges scaling up to newly introduced terminologies and sub-concepts. Hence, they are unsuitable for emergencies, like the ongoing health crisis. In this paper, we focus on measuring and improving shifts in this setting.

Biomedical Information Retrieval. As previously mentioned, BioASQ challenge (Tsatsaronis et al., 2015a) is the largest challenge for SI and IR. Since 2015. BioASQ have shared a set of question—answering-related datasets every year. IR systems work in two phases. First, a broad (simple) method is used to retrieve the initial candidate's articles, and the second stage is to re-rank the candidates using a more complex method. The re-ranking model is usually based on the cross-attention model and fine-tuned for the binary classification task (Nentidis et al., 2020). For the first stage, many researchers use BM25 (Rosso-Mateus et al., 2018; Almeida and Matos, 2020; Kazaryan et al., 2020; Pappas et al., 2020). Likewise, several methods have been developed for the second stage. Rosso-Mateus et al. (2020) developed a system that takes as input learns distance metric to match question-passage pairs. Specifically, they use siamese and triplet networks to create a novel similarity learning method using a max-margin approach.

To the best of our knowledge, our study is the first to combine the two specific tasks of extraction of semantic indexes (which is essentially a multi-label text classification into a set of pre-defined, hierarchically organized semantic indexes) and IR (ranking a list of documents based on their relatedness to a query)—two tasks for which high-quality annotation by human experts exists compared to other domains. Other multi-task learning benchmarks mostly combine text problems that take a single piece of text as input rather than multiple documents, such as masked language modeling, NLU, and text classification (Raffel et al., 2019; McCann et al., 2018). Semantic search studies use the pre-trained models on such single input text problems, then fine-tune and use the representation of the document along with a similarity function or task-specific layers to compute the similarity between mid-level representations from the pre-trained encoder. These approaches cause discrepancies between the operations required for pre-text and downstream tasks. Therefore, they may not leverage the transfer learning (Ratner et al., 2018) effectively.

The most similar work to this paper is by Liu et al. (2019) which combines binary text classification with an information retrieval task via a multi-task learning framework. However, our work differs from Liu et al. (2019) in three major ways. First, we focus on semantic indexing, which is multi-label and contains more than 29k classes. Hence, rather than assigning a binary class to an instance (yes vs. no), our method must be able to assign a set of classes. Moreover, training large-scale multi-label models requires substantially different methodological choices beyond what binary classification needs. Second, their work does not focus on the biomedical domain, particularly biomedical-related scientific documents. Third, most of their work focuses on single sentences rather than complete documents. Because of the sequence length limitation of BERT (Beltagy et al., 2020) multi-document and long-document analysis is only feasible by truncating the text. Hence, our approach can scale beyond sentence-level tasks.

3 Datasets

This paper uses three datasets: BioASQ Tasks 8a and 8b dataset, CORD-19 (Wang et al., 2020), and TREC-COVID. We describe each dataset below:

BioASQ 8a and 8b. First, we use the SI and IR datasets that were part of the BioASQ 8a and 8b competitions. Specifically, we use the PubMed articles from BioASQ's (Tsatsaronis et al., 2015b) Task 8a dataset, which includes almost 15 million article abstracts and titles. We select 8M recent articles published from 2007 to 2019.

For IR, we use BioASQ's Task 8b dataset, which includes 3,243 questions paired with related article abstracts. We use validation sets for each task for hyperparameter tuning. We also use the validation dataset as a pretraining procedure for the COVID-19-related corpora. But, we ensure there is no overlap between these general sets and their corresponding COVID-19 datasets.

CORD-19. The models are trained and/or evaluated on the following three COVID-19 datasets corresponding to the three tasks: SI, IR, and Masked Language Modeling (MLM). For our Semantic Indexing task, we use CORD-19 dataset (Wang et al., 2020) which includes 200K research articles about Coronavirus published in peer-reviewed venues and archival services such as bioRxiv[4] and medRxiv[5]. We select CORD-19 articles whose MeSH indexes are manually annotated in PubMed. We crawl and collect each article's MeSH indexes. The COVID-related SI dataset contains 17K articles which we chronologically sort and split into 13.6K for training (the oldest 80%) and 3.4K for testing (the latest 20%)—the number of articles is less than 200k because NLM has not yet indexed many articles.

During a data crisis, such as what is occurring with COVID-19, it is likely that we will collect unlabeled data quickly. However, it is unclear how to best use the unlabeled data. In response to this issue, we add an unsupervised task of incorporating COVID-related information into our models. Specifically, we perform a self-supervised pre-text task similar to Masked Language Modeling in (Devlin et al., 2019) to introduce knowledge about the pandemic. The masked article is treated as a query, and masked tokens are selected from a list of COVID-19-related terms[6]. The model attempts to detect articles that include the masked term(s), which allows our model to learn context matching using intra- and inter-document information (Cohan et al., 2020). To train this task, we use the entire CORD-19 training dataset, even the articles that have not been indexed yet at the time of the experiments.

TREC-COVID (Information Retrieval). As for the COVID-19-specific IR task, we use the TREC-COVID dataset (Roberts et al., 2020), which is an IR dataset for question answering similar to BioASQ QA task 8b. TREC-COVID includes 50 topics as queries represented by (concept, question, narrative) tuples. It also includes a dataset of 191K candidate documents from CORD-19. Experts manually evaluated the relevance of 69,317 topic-document pairs and annotated with three labels: unrelated, partially related, and related. Our task is to return a list of related articles, which include the target answer using the topic assigned to each question and given question as a query. This task structure is the same as used in BioASQ IR task 8b.

4 Methods

Intuitively, our method reformulates the semantic indexing task as IR such that we can train a single model—with a single output layer—that can perform both indexing and retrieval. Furthermore, our method does not require learning class-level parameters, thus allowing it to adapt easily to changes in the data distribution. Specifically, our method has three main phases: 1. Given an input document, we query all similar PubMed articles using a robust IR approach (combining BM25 and document embeddings). 2. We generate document embeddings that combine information from the input document (query) with each candidate (similar) document returned in step 1 (the initial retrieval phase) 3. Finally, given the query-candidate joint embeddings, we introduce a novel output layer that can apply to both the Semantic Indexing (classification) and

[4] https://www.biorxiv.org

[5] https://www.medrxiv.org

[6] We have used the list of related terms published by NLM https://www.nlm.nih.gov/pubs/techbull/nd20/nd20_mesh_covid_terms.html

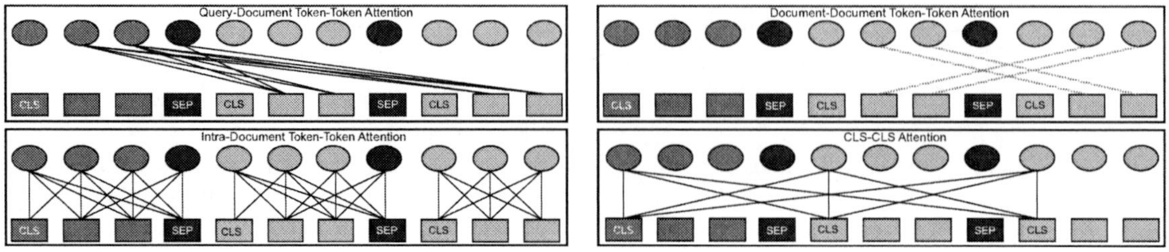

Figure 1: Intuitive attention modification diagram between the query Q (i.e., the purple items in the Figure) and candidates D (i.e., the orange items). The candidates (document-document) attentions are masked in our model.

IR tasks. Given the novel output layer, we take advantage of multi-task learning, jointly training the model for SI, IR, and additional tasks (self-supervised learning) to improve performance further. We describe each step in the following subsections.

Initial Retrieval. For the first stage, we use an initial retrieval system to identify a subset of related articles along with their task-specific annotations (for example, for extraction of semantic indexes, the task annotations include each candidate article's MeSH terms). Our initial retrieval system combines a document-level embedding model of SPECTER (Cohan et al., 2020) with a Bag-of-Words representation fused with BM25 following the schema of (Jin et al., 2018) and (Esteva et al., 2020). We initialize sPECTER with SciBERT (Beltagy et al., 2019) and trained on a bipartite graph of citations to capture document-level relatedness and minimize a triplet loss between related articles and maximize over unrelated ones. We further pre-train SPECTER on PubMed articles and fine-tune it on the COVID-19 dataset only. In addition, we use a BM25 weighted sum of article tokens to compute a keyword-based representation as well.

Formally, the input query and each candidate document are described as sequences of word tokens, denoted as $Q = \{q_i\}_{i=1}^{n}$ and $D = \{d_j\}_{j=1}^{m}$, respectively. For every candidate article, we also track associated metadata such as manually assigned MeSH terms defined as $L_D = \{l_j\}_{j=1}^{U_D}$, where U_D is the total number of MeSH terms assigned to candidate document C. We represent every article as an embedding $\mathbf{c} \in \mathbb{R}^z$ defined as

$$\mathbf{c}_d = \frac{\sum_{i=1}^{n} \text{Score}(w_i, D) \cdot \mathbf{v}_{w_i}}{\sum_{i=1}^{n} \text{Score}(w_i, D)} \quad (1)$$

where z is the size of the SPECTER embedding, n is the number of tokens in document D, Score() $\in \mathbb{R}$ represents a token-level BM25 score, w_i is the i-th word in article d, and $\mathbf{v}_{w_i} \in \mathbb{R}^z$ is the token-level embeddings from the pre-trained model. Equation 1 is used to represent every document D which is used to represent both query $\mathbf{d}_Q$ and candidate $\mathbf{d}_D$ documents.

Next, we use the cosine similarity scores between each input query representation $\mathbf{d}_Q$ and every candidate article representation $\mathbf{d}_D$ in our database to find the top K most relevant articles $\mathcal{C} = \{D_1, \ldots, D_K\}$.

Transformer-based Representations and Reranking Next, given a query document Q and a set of candidate documents $\mathcal{C} = \{D_1, \ldots, D_K\}$, we use a BERT-like transformer model to rerank each candidate document D_i with respect to the input query. Specifically, we first concat the query Q with each candidate D_i to form a long sequence $[\text{CLS}, Q, \text{SEP}, \text{CLS}, D_1, \ldots, \text{SEP}, \text{CLS}, D_K]$, where each candidate is separated with a CLS and SEP token. Next, we predict a score for each candidate $\hat{y}_i = \sigma(\text{CLS}_{D_i})$, where σ represents a sigmoid function and CLS_{D_i} represents the CLS token directly preceding the start of candidate D_i's sequence of tokens.

At each level of the BERT representation, our input structure provides the ability to interpret that model in three unique ways using attention scores: token-to-token, token-to-document, and document-to-document. A high-level depiction of the attention scores is shown in Figure 1. First, the token-to-token scores between words within each query Q or within each candidate document D (i.e., the self-attention scores in Figure 1) calculates the importance of each word. For instance, the model can learn that the word "the" is unimportant for the downstream task. The *token-to-token* scores are also calculated between the tokens in the query and each candidate document (i.e., the token-to-token cross-attention scores in Figure 1), which can be interpreted as a similarity between the two words across two documents regarding the downstream tasks.

Given that we care about relations between the query and candidates, but we do not care about token-to-token relations between two candidates, we mask the attention weights at each level of the BERT representation such that they are ignored. Next, the *CLS-to-token* attention is calculated between each token within a query or candidate document and the CLS representing each other document, which can be interpreted as the importance of how similar that token is regarding the topical content of another document. Finally, the *CLS-to-CLS* attention scores can be interpreted as a similarity score between each document—either between the query and each candidate or between each candidate, respectively. For instance, for semantic indexing of MeSH terms, the model should learn to give large CLS-to-CLS attention scores (for attention scores between the query and each candidate) to candidate documents with many MeSH terms that should be assigned to the query. Finally, because of the input sequence size, we use the Longformer model (Beltagy et al., 2020).

Output Layer Transformation. The output of the reranker transformer model is a set of sigmoid scores representing similarities between each candidate document and the input query. However, while these scores can directly be used to train the IR models to detect relevant documents for reranking purposes, we propose to use these identical scores to generate other types of output, such as MeSH code predictions for semantic indexing. Specifically, we propose a simple output layer transformation and training procedure to handle this task. Intuitively, our model is a Transformer-weighted k-NN, where scores of the scores for each "neighbor" is learned and contextual.

Formally, given a candidate score $\hat{y}_i$ for each candidate $D_j \in \mathcal{C}$, we generate a score for MeSH term as

$$\hat{l}_i = \sum_{j=1}^{K} \hat{y}_j \cdot \mathbb{1}[l_i \in L_j]$$

where $\hat{y}_j$ represents the sigmoid score for candidate $D_j \in \mathcal{C}$, l_i represents the j-th MeSH code, L_j represents the set of MeSH codes assigned to candidate D_j, and $\hat{l}_i$ is the final prediction score for MeSH code l_i with respect to the input query Q. At inference time, we optimize the thresholds to maximize the micro-f1 score (Pillai et al., 2013).

For the SSL task, we generate scores for each of the COVID-related terms that are masked within the candidate documents.

To train the model, we first sample a task randomly, then sample training instances for the task, apply the output transformation, and train using Binary Cross-Entropy loss. For instance, for MeSH prediction, we train the model as

$$L = \sum_{i=1}^{U} l_i \log(\hat{l}_i) + (1 - l_i) \log(1 - \hat{l}_i)$$

where l_i represents the ground-truth label (1 or 0) for the i-th MeSH term and $\hat{l}_i$ is the prediction for the i-th term.

Note that for the IR task, we also train on relevance using binary cross-entropy. Hence, instead of using l_i as the ground-truth and $\hat{l}_i$ as the prediction, we use $\hat{l}_j$ and l_j, where $\hat{l}_j$ is the sigmoid output described in Section 4 that scores the relevance between the query and the j-th candidate and l_j is the ground-truth relevance (1 if relevant, 0 otherwise). Overall, this output transformation procedure has two major advantages. First, we do not need to learn any label-specific parameters. Many MeSH terms appear infrequently. As new MeSH terms are added, models must be retrained to predict them. However, our method can hypothetically predict terms as soon as new terms are used to annotate existing documents *without* retraining the model. Second, the output layer can predict any meta-data manually assigned or computed (as is the case for the SSL task) to the candidate database instances.

5 Results

Evaluation Metrics. To evaluate the performance of SI we use two sets of evaluation measures; i) flat measures such as micro- and macro-f1 scores, and ii) hierarchical measures such as Lowest Common Ancestor F-measure (LCA-F) (Kosmopoulos et al., 2015) for which we leverage BioASQ suggested algorithm[7].

For evaluation of IR tasks, we leverage *trec_eval*, the evaluation metrics and algorithms provided by TREC-COVID [8]. The evaluation metrics include normalized discounted cumulative gain (nDCG@N), P@N, Mean Average Precision

[7] https://github.com/BioASQ/Evaluation-Measures/tree/master/hierarchical

[8] https://trec.nist.gov/trec_eval/

Model	Micro F1
Medical Text Indexer (MTI) (default)	.658
MTI (first line indes)	.649
Average top score	**.714**
R+TR (base) (full attention)	.553
R+TR (base) (w/o multi-task)	.660
R+TR (base) (w/ multi-task)	.667
R+TR (large) (w/o multi-task)	.698
R+TR (large) (w/ multi-task)	**.705**

(a)

Model	MAP
Average top score	**.464**
R+TR (base) (full attention)	.191
R+TR (base) (w/o multi-task)	.328
R+TR (base) (w/ multi-task)	.344
R+TR (large) (w/o multi-task)	.355
R+TR (large) (w/ multi-task)	**.410**

(b)

Table 1: Semantic Indexing (a) and Information Retrieval (b) performances of our models, Retriever and Transformer-based Ranker (R+TR), along with the baselines (best performing models of BioASQ Task 8a for SI, and Task 8b Phase A for IR). The baseline scores are the average of their provided Micro F1 and Mean Average Persision (MAP) for IR and SI, respectively. The results are averaged across all test batches. Our model Retriever and Transformer-based Ranker is abbreviated as R+TR.

(MAP), and Binary preference (Bpref) (Esteva et al., 2020).

Baselines. We compare to three baseline models: the default MTI, MTI first line index, and the top models from the BioASQ competition. We explore MTI with base and "first line" parameters. MTI is a pre-trained model that is for SI of biomedical articles by the US National Library of Medicine. The first line version is the current version used by NLM that partially automates the standard indexing process at the US National Library of Medicine before human annotators further fine tune the indexes. We also report the scores for the best BioASQ team in each batch as "Average top score". Finally, to compare state-of-the-art methods on the COVID data, we retrain Attention MeSH (Grishchenko et al., 2020).

Hyperparameters and Model Variations. We optimize hyperparameters using a held-out validation dataset. For the SI experiments, K (i.e., the number of relevant articles retrieved) is set to 512. For the IR experiments, we set K to 1024. We use two versions of our re-ranker, a longformer base version (4 layers, 256 hidden size, 8 heads) and a large version (6 layers, 512 hidden size, 8 heads). Furthermore, we evaluate different attention mechanism on the base model. We also experiment with a naïve full attention mechanism (R+TR (full attention)) to compare the effect of the specific attention mechanism suggested by (Beltagy et al., 2020)[9]. All hyperparameters were chosen using the validation data. Refer to the Appendix for a comprehensive list of hyperparameters we searched over in our experiments.

	All Training Data				Micro F1			
Model	**LCA-F**	**MiF**	**MaF**	**Accu.**	**0%**	**5%**	**10%**	**20%**
MTI (default)	.563	.730	.506	.491	.222	.332	.459	.564
MTI (first line indes)	.553	.722	.501	.507	.218	.309	.462	.578
Attention MeSH	.579	**.764**	.529	.558	.271	.396	.504	.619
R+TR (base) (w/o ssl & mt)	.540	.700	.492	.485	.307	.433	.504	.591
R+TR (base) (w/ ssl)	.552	.728	.506	.510	.380	.486	.616	.663
R+TR (base) (w/ ssl & mt)	.563	.755	.511	.523	**.485**	.592	.656	**.724**
R+TR (large) (w/o ssl & mt)	.562	.742	.502	.523	.363	.474	.559	.595
R+TR (large) (w/ ssl)	.597	**.777**	.532	.569	**.490**	.619	**.698**	**.733**
R+TR (large) (w/ ssl & mt)	.612	**.810**	.558	.586	**.564**	**.676**	**.741**	**.789**

Table 2: Semantic indexing performance of our proposed models in comparison with baselines and ablation studies. For ablation, we experiment with (w/) and without (w/o) self-supervised learning (ssl) and multi-task learning (mt). For evaluation, we use Micro F1 (MiF) and Macro F1 (MaF). The second half of the table shows the MiF score based on the size of the COVID-19 training dataset, ranging from 0% (zero-shot) to 20% (few-shot).

BioASQ Experiments (Non-COVID). We analyze several design decisions for our transformer-based ranking system, such as the effect of multi-task learning on the general datasets and experimentally compare our use of the masked attention mechanisms. We report the results of each design decision in Table 5aa for BioASQ SI Task 8a, and Table 1bb for the BioASQ IR Task 8b, respectively. Our model Retriever and Transformer-based Ranker is abbreviated as R+TR.

Overall, for both IR and SI, we find that the full attention mechanism requires truncating the input documents, resulting in poor performance. The multi-task learning improves the performance of IR without affecting the SI's performance. Such improvement is expected not only because of the ef-

[9] R+TR (full attention) requires truncation of the input documents, resulting in poor performance. However, Longformer uses *dilated sliding window* attention to avoid truncation. Dilation and window sizes are the target hyperparameters here. See the appendix for results with various dilation parameters.

fect of transfer learning but also because the SI task improves retrieval and reinforces the latent space to be closer to those of the semantic indexes which human experts believed to be a better representation. For the IR results, we find that the multi-task improvement is higher for larger versions of our ranker (.328→.344 vs. .355→.410), showing that the knowledge transfer capability increases with the size of the transformer model. We do not report the effect of the self-supervision results here because it is only for COVID-19 datasets and disregarded in our ablation analysis on the general data. However, its effect is analysed in the following sections. Overall, the SI results in match the top contestants in the BioASQ competition (.714 vs .705). This is substantial given the submissions use ensemble methods while we are just training a single model. Similarly, for the IR task, we do not match the best contestants. However, we will show in the next results sections our model generalizes better to out of domain data related to COVID-19.

COVID-19 Semantic Indexing Experiments. Table 2 shows the SI performance of our models and baselines on the COVID-19 SI test set. Results on the left side (All Training Data) show the performance of the models once trained on the entire COVID-19 SI training set. The baselines are similarly fine-tuned with the training data for fair comparison. Our proposed "R+TR(large) w/o SSL & MT" model (i.e., without self-supervied learning and without multi-task learning) performs similar to the state-of-the-art baselines without leveraging the proposed self-supervised task and multi-task learning with IR (.742 Micro F1 vs .764). However, when combined, each of these transfer learning techniques substantially improves the SI performance. Leveraging the self-supervised learning task contributes and multi-task learning (SI + IR) helps because R+TR models gets acquainted with the context of the novel pandemic and its distributions, improving the Micro F1 score to 0.810. Overall, this experiment supports our hypothesis that IR tasks with SI improves model performance, particularly for COVID-related data.

The right side of Table 2 shows the performances based on the size of the COVID-specific training data. We chronologically sort the data and train the SI models with a proportion of them from the beginning. As shown in Table 2 the partitions include:0% which represents the zero shot learning ability, 5%, 10%, and 20% denoting the few-shot learning. 0% represents a model only trained on the original BioASQ dataset (i.e., no COVID-specific data). Our large R+TR's zero-shot micro-f1 score is significantly higher than the baselines, by 0.32 on average. It achieves 97% of its optimum performance by using only 20% of the training data. Again, providing evidence that our SI + IR multi-task learning framework can adapt better across domains.

Model	nDCG@20	P@20	Bpref	MAP
top score	**.850**	**.876**	**.638**	**.473**
ranke#1 in nCDG@20	**.850**	**.876**	.637	.472
ranke#1 in P@20	**.850**	**.876**	.637	.472
ranke#1 in Bpref	.850	.870	**.638**	**.473**
ranke#1 in MAP	.850	.870	**.638**	**.473**
R+TR (base) (w/o ssl & mt)	.792	.838	.602	.455
R+TR (base) (w/ ssl)	.821	.856	.626	.468
R+TR (base) (w/ ssl & mt)	**.857**	.870	**.642**	.464
R+TR (large) (w/o ssl & mt)	.805	.849	.620	.457
R+TR (large) (w/ ssl)	.830	.861	.633	.475
R+TR (large) (w/ ssl & mt)	**.889**	**.891**	**.657**	**.492**
R+TR (base) (w/ ssl & mt) (w/ f.t.)	**.899**	**.915**	**.664**	**.506**
R+TR (large) (w/ ssl & mt) (w/ f.t.)	**.924**	**.946**	**.691**	**.523**

Table 3: Information retrieval performance of our model with and without pre-training on self-supervised and semantic extraction tasks.

Information Retrieval on COVID-19 Experiments.

Table 3 shows the IR performance of our models evaluated on TREC-COVID round 5 dataset.[10]. Our model trained without SSL and Multi-Task learning (R+TR (base) (w/o ssl & mt) was only trained on the BioASQ QA dataset (i.e., No COVID-specific data), hence, it shows inferior performance which is because of the inconsistencies between two tasks. However, leveraging SSL and multi-task learning, our base model beats the top nDCG@20 and Bpref scores. This shows how the proposed transfer learning framework improves model's ability to scale up to a new domain. Our large R+RT achieves significantly superior performance in every metric score.

To analyze the zero- and few-shot learning ability of our model, we fine-tune our SSL multi-task learning models with TREC-COVID dataset. We choose round 3 dataset for training which has 40 topics identical to the first 40 topics in round 5. This is because the competition stated from 30 topics in round 1 and every time added 5 topics for the next round. We leave the last 10 topics of round 5 for evaluation.

[10]See for other baselines `https://ir.nist.gov/covidSubmit/archive.html`

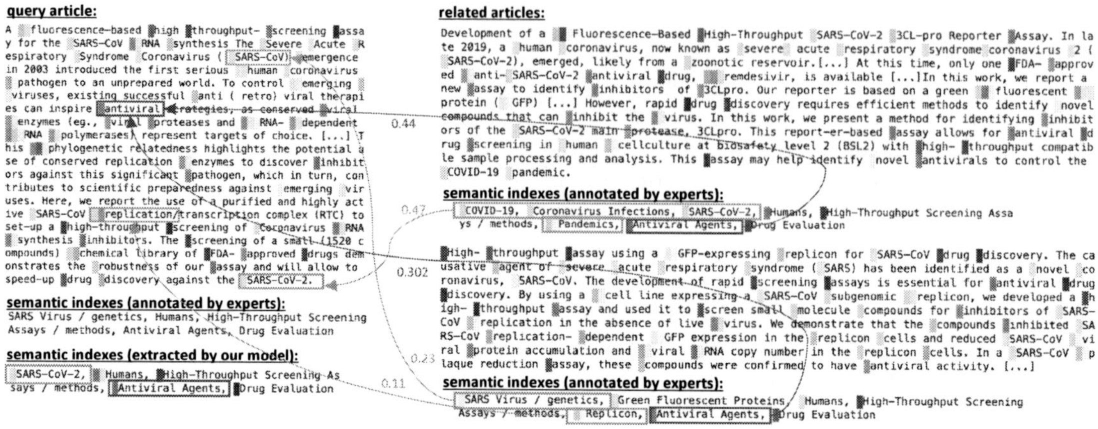

Figure 2: Illustration of attention weights between the input query and candidate articles along with the extracted outputs. The intensity and the color of the highlights denotes attention weights' values which is averaged and set to three scalar between the highly correlated terms.

We also expand the 40 samples of *(topic , set of candidate documents)* to 1,530 samples by randomly selecting a subset of 128 candidate documents for every given topic rather than 1024. As shown in the bottom of Table 3, our base and large model can leverage such fine-tuning and achieve significantly better scores than the top ones, by 0.05 MAP score. Note that in TREC-COVID challenge also participants could use results from previous rounds.

Interpretability.

As mentioned in Section 1, if our models improve human productivity, it is important for them to be interpretable. The interpretability can help human experts comprehend the decision making of a model and what has caused a mistaken output. As shown in Figure 2, the local-global attention of our model can assist human experts even when it makes an error by providing evidence for the mistaken output and suggesting other alternatives. The model extract the semantic index of SARS-CoV-2 while the manual annotator believes the article is about the general SARS viruses rather than a specific variant. Highlights in the figure show the global attention between the related articles and the query article, and the local attention within the query article. The weights are averaged and set to three scalar values, following (Sarker et al., 2019), to make the visualization simple (Lei et al., 2017). As depicted by Figure 2, the extraction of SARS-CoV-2 is because of the highly matched context about COVID-19 (the top related article) and the last sentence. However, the global attention provides another related article along with suggestions for the correct index. Knowing these, one can quickly identify and fix the error.

The interpretability can also help to understand the performance of the model in mitigating the challenges of COVID-19 infodemic. Please refer to A for more interpretability analysis.

6 Conclusion

In this study, we have unified the tasks of IR for question answering with the extraction of semantic indexes and with a self-supervised pre-text task. Our approach allows us to *simultaneously* train on downstream tasks and unlabeled data to maximize the advantages of transfer learning in addressing the data efficiency, generalization, and dataset shift issues. Compared to benchmarks, our model learns with less labeled data (it does not even need to learn class-specific parameters) and shows a substantially higher zero-shot (out-of-domain) performance. Overall, our study brings focus towards state-of-the-art remedies to the current challenges of the pandemic, which opens up new doors to a more systematic analysis of each of these challenges and more sophisticated algorithms.

As future research, we will look to combine more IR and SI-related tasks as more data is being annotated and prepared for the domain-specific environment of the pandemic. To better evaluate the performance of the global-local interpretability, we plan to perform qualitative analysis by providing this tool to human experts. The goal is for the tool to improve their time efficiency and performance when they are performing manual indexing of biomedical research articles.

References

Tiago Almeida and Sérgio Matos. 2020. Bit. ua at bioasq 8: Lightweight neural document ranking with zero-shot snippet retrieval. In *CLEF (Working Notes)*.

Iz Beltagy, Kyle Lo, and Arman Cohan. 2019. Scibert: A pretrained language model for scientific text. *arXiv preprint arXiv:1903.10676*.

Iz Beltagy, Matthew E Peters, and Arman Cohan. 2020. Longformer: The long-document transformer. *arXiv preprint arXiv:2004.05150*.

Q. Chen, A. Allot, and Z. Lu. 2020. Keep up with the latest coronavirus research. *Nature*, 579(7798):193.

Arman Cohan, Sergey Feldman, Iz Beltagy, Doug Downey, and Daniel S Weld. 2020. Specter: Document-level representation learning using citation-informed transformers. In *Proceedings of the 58th Annual Meeting of the Association for Computational Linguistics*, pages 2270–2282.

Nico Colic, Lenz Furrer, and Fabio Rinaldi. 2020. Annotating the pandemic: Named entity recognition and normalisation in covid-19 literature. In *Proceedings of the 1st Workshop on NLP for COVID-19 (Part 2) at EMNLP 2020*.

Suyang Dai, Ronghui You, Zhiyong Lu, Xiaodi Huang, Hiroshi Mamitsuka, and Shanfeng Zhu. 2020. Fullmesh: improving large-scale mesh indexing with full text. *Bioinformatics*, 36(5):1533–1541.

Jacob Devlin, Ming-Wei Chang, Kenton Lee, and Kristina Toutanova. 2019. BERT: Pre-training of deep bidirectional transformers for language understanding. In *Proceedings of the 2019 Conference of the North American Chapter of the Association for Computational Linguistics: Human Language Technologies, Volume 1 (Long and Short Papers)*, pages 4171–4186, Minneapolis, Minnesota. Association for Computational Linguistics.

Andre Esteva, Anuprit Kale, Romain Paulus, Kazuma Hashimoto, Wenpeng Yin, Dragomir Radev, and Richard Socher. 2020. Co-search: Covid-19 information retrieval with semantic search, question answering, and abstractive summarization. *arXiv preprint arXiv:2006.09595*.

Ali Foroughi Pour, Maciej Pietrzak, Lori A Dalton, and Grzegorz A Rempała. 2020. High dimensional model representation of log-likelihood ratio: binary classification with expression data. *BMC bioinformatics*, 21:1–27.

Ivan Grishchenko, Artsiom Ablavatski, Yury Kartynnik, Karthik Raveendran, and Matthias Grundmann. 2020. Attention mesh: High-fidelity face mesh prediction in real-time. *arXiv preprint arXiv:2006.10962*.

Zhiwen Hu, Zhongliang Yang, Qi Li, and An Zhang. 2020. The covid-19 infodemic: Infodemiology study analyzing stigmatizing search terms. *Journal of medical Internet research*, 22(11):e22639.

Qiao Jin, Bhuwan Dhingra, William Cohen, and Xinghua Lu. 2018. Attentionmesh: Simple, effective and interpretable automatic mesh indexer. In *Proceedings of the 6th BioASQ Workshop A challenge on large-scale biomedical semantic indexing and question answering*, pages 47–56.

Ashot Kazaryan, Uladzislau Sazanovich, and Vladislav Belyaev. 2020. Transformer-based open domain biomedical question answering at bioasq8 challenge. In *CLEF (Working Notes)*.

Aris Kosmopoulos, Ioannis Partalas, Eric Gaussier, Georgios Paliouras, and Ion Androutsopoulos. 2015. Evaluation measures for hierarchical classification: a unified view and novel approaches. *Data Mining and Knowledge Discovery*, 29(3):820–865.

Tao Lei et al. 2017. *Interpretable neural models for natural language processing*. Ph.D. thesis, Massachusetts Institute of Technology.

Jimmy Lin, Rodrigo Nogueira, and Andrew Yates. 2020. Pretrained transformers for text ranking: Bert and beyond. *arXiv preprint arXiv:2010.06467*.

Carolyn E Lipscomb. 2000. Medical subject headings (mesh). *Bulletin of the Medical Library Association*, 88(3):265.

Ke Liu, Junqiu Wu, Shengwen Peng, Chengxiang Zhai, and Shanfeng Zhu. 2014. The fudan-uiuc participation in the bioasq challenge task 2a: The antinomyra system. In *CEUR Workshop Proceedings*, volume 1180, pages 1311–1318. CEUR-WS.

Xiaodong Liu, Pengcheng He, Weizhu Chen, and Jianfeng Gao. 2019. Multi-task deep neural networks for natural language understanding. *arXiv preprint arXiv:1901.11504*.

Sean MacAvaney, Arman Cohan, and Nazli Goharian. 2020. Sledge: A simple yet effective zero-shot baseline for coronavirus scientific knowledge search. In *Proceedings of the 2020 Conference on Empirical Methods in Natural Language Processing (EMNLP)*, pages 4171–4179.

Bryan McCann, Nitish Shirish Keskar, Caiming Xiong, and Richard Socher. 2018. The natural language decathlon: Multitask learning as question answering. *arXiv preprint arXiv:1806.08730*.

Bernd Müller, Christoph Poley, Jana Pössel, Alexandra Hagelstein, and Thomas Gübitz. 2017. Livivo–the vertical search engine for life sciences. *Datenbank-Spektrum*, 17(1):29–34.

Anastasios Nentidis, Konstantinos Bougiatiotis, Anastasia Krithara, and Georgios Paliouras. 2019. Results of the seventh edition of the bioasq challenge. In

Joint European Conference on Machine Learning and Knowledge Discovery in Databases, pages 553–568. Springer.

Anastasios Nentidis, Anastasia Krithara, Konstantinos Bougiatiotis, and Georgios Paliouras. 2020. Overview of bioasq 8a and 8b: Results of the 8th edition of the bioasq tasks a and b. In *CLEF(Working Notes)*.

Toan Q Nguyen and Julian Salazar. 2019. Transformers without tears: Improving the normalization of self-attention. *arXiv preprint arXiv:1910.05895*.

Eirini Papagiannopoulou, Yiannis Papanikolaou, Dimitris Dimitriadis, Sakis Lagopoulos, Grigorios Tsoumakas, Manos Laliotis, Nikos Markantonatos, and Ioannis Vlahavas. 2016. Large-scale semantic indexing and question answering in biomedicine. In *Proceedings of the Fourth BioASQ workshop*, pages 50–54.

Dimitris Pappas, Petros Stavropoulos, and Ion Androutsopoulos. 2020. Aueb-nlp at bioasq 8: Biomedical document and snippet retrieval. In *CLEF (Working Notes)*.

Shengwen Peng, Ronghui You, Hongning Wang, Chengxiang Zhai, Hiroshi Mamitsuka, and Shanfeng Zhu. 2016. Deepmesh: deep semantic representation for improving large-scale mesh indexing. *Bioinformatics*, 32(12):i70–i79.

Ignazio Pillai, Giorgio Fumera, and Fabio Roli. 2013. Threshold optimisation for multi-label classifiers. *Pattern Recognition*, 46(7):2055–2065.

Colin Raffel, Noam Shazeer, Adam Roberts, Katherine Lee, Sharan Narang, Michael Matena, Yanqi Zhou, Wei Li, and Peter J Liu. 2019. Exploring the limits of transfer learning with a unified text-to-text transformer. *arXiv preprint arXiv:1910.10683*.

Alex Ratner, Braden Hancock, Jared Dunnmon, Roger Goldman, and Christopher Ré. 2018. Snorkel metal: Weak supervision for multi-task learning. In *Proceedings of the Second Workshop on Data Management for End-To-End Machine Learning*, pages 1–4.

Anthony Rios and Ramakanth Kavuluru. 2015. Analyzing the moving parts of a large-scale multi-label text classification pipeline: Experiences in indexing biomedical articles. In *2015 International Conference on Healthcare Informatics*, pages 1–7. IEEE.

Kirk Roberts, Tasmeer Alam, Steven Bedrick, Dina Demner-Fushman, Kyle Lo, Ian Soboroff, Ellen Voorhees, Lucy Lu Wang, and William R Hersh. 2020. Trec-covid: Rationale and structure of an information retrieval shared task for covid-19. *Journal of the American Medical Informatics Association*.

Andrés Rosso-Mateus, Fabio A. González, and Manuel Montes-y Gómez. 2018. MindLab neural network approach at BioASQ 6B. In *Proceedings of the 6th BioASQ Workshop A challenge on large-scale biomedical semantic indexing and question answering*, pages 40–46, Brussels, Belgium. Association for Computational Linguistics.

Andrés Rosso-Mateus, Fabio A. González, and Manuel Montes-y Gómez. 2020. A deep metric learning method for biomedical passage retrieval. In *Proceedings of the 28th International Conference on Computational Linguistics*, pages 6229–6239, Barcelona, Spain (Online). International Committee on Computational Linguistics.

Abeed Sarker, Ari Z Klein, Janet Mee, Polina Harik, and Graciela Gonzalez-Hernandez. 2019. An interpretable natural language processing system for written medical examination assessment. *Journal of biomedical informatics*, 98:103268.

Farhad Shokraneh and Tony Russell-Rose. 2020. Lessons from covid-19 to future evidence synthesis efforts: first living search strategy and out of date scientific publishing and indexing industry (submitted). *Journal of Clinical Epidemiology*.

Sarvesh Soni and Kirk Roberts. 2021. An evaluation of two commercial deep learning-based information retrieval systems for covid-19 literature. *Journal of the American Medical Informatics Association*, 28(1):132–137.

G. Tsatsaronis, Georgios Balikas, Prodromos Malakasiotis, Ioannis Partalas, M. Zschunke, M. Alvers, Dirk Weissenborn, Anastasia Krithara, Sergios Petridis, D. Polychronopoulos, Y. Almirantis, John Pavlopoulos, Nicolas Baskiotis, P. Gallinari, T. Artières, A. N. Ngomo, N. Heino, Éric Gaussier, L. Barrio-Alvers, M. Schroeder, Ion Androutsopoulos, and G. Paliouras. 2015a. An overview of the large-scale biomedical semantic indexing and question answering competition. *BMC Bioinformatics*, 16.

George Tsatsaronis, Georgios Balikas, Prodromos Malakasiotis, Ioannis Partalas, Matthias Zschunke, Michael R Alvers, Dirk Weissenborn, Anastasia Krithara, Sergios Petridis, Dimitris Polychronopoulos, Yannis Almirantis, John Pavlopoulos, Nicolas Baskiotis, Patrick Gallinari, Thierry Artieres, Axel Ngonga, Norman Heino, Eric Gaussier, Liliana Barrio-Alvers, Michael Schroeder, Ion Androutsopoulos, and Georgios Paliouras. 2015b. An overview of the bioasq large-scale biomedical semantic indexing and question answering competition. *BMC Bioinformatics*, 16:138.

George Tsatsaronis, Georgios Balikas, Prodromos Malakasiotis, Ioannis Partalas, Matthias Zschunke, Michael R Alvers, Dirk Weissenborn, Anastasia Krithara, Sergios Petridis, Dimitris Polychronopoulos, et al. 2015c. An overview of the bioasq large-scale biomedical semantic indexing and question answering competition. *BMC bioinformatics*, 16(1):138.

Ellen Voorhees, Tasmeer Alam, Steven Bedrick, Dina Demner-Fushman, William R. Hersh, Kyle Lo, Kirk

Roberts, Ian Soboroff, and Lucy Lu Wang. 2021. Trec-covid: Constructing a pandemic information retrieval test collection. *SIGIR Forum*, 54(1).

Jingqi Wang, Huy Anh, Frank Manion, Masoud Rouhizadeh, and Yaoyun Zhang. Covid-19 signsym– a fast adaptation of general clinical nlp tools to identify and normalize covid-19 signs and symptoms to omop common data model. *ArXiv*.

Lucy Lu Wang, Kyle Lo, Yoganand Chandrasekhar, Russell Reas, Jiangjiang Yang, Darrin Eide, Kathryn Funk, Rodney Michael Kinney, Ziyang Liu, William. Merrill, Paul Mooney, Dewey A. Murdick, Devvret Rishi, Jerry Sheehan, Zhihong Shen, Brandon Stilson, Alex D. Wade, Kuansan Wang, Christopher Wilhelm, Boya Xie, Douglas M. Raymond, Daniel S. Weld, Oren Etzioni, and Sebastian Kohlmeier. 2020. Cord-19: The covid-19 open research dataset. *ArXiv*.

Guangxu Xun, Kishlay Jha, Ye Yuan, Yaqing Wang, and Aidong Zhang. 2019. Meshprobenet: a self-attentive probe net for mesh indexing. *Bioinformatics*, 35(19):3794–3802.

Ilya Zavorin, James Mork, and Dina Demner-Fushman. 2016. Using learning-to-rank to enhance nlm medical text indexer results. In *Proceedings of the Fourth BioASQ workshop*, pages 8–15.

Edwin Zhang, Nikhil Gupta, Raphael Tang, Xiao Han, Ronak Pradeep, Kuang Lu, Yue Zhang, Rodrigo Nogueira, Kyunghyun Cho, Hui Fang, et al. 2020. Covidex: Neural ranking models and keyword search infrastructure for the covid-19 open research dataset. *arXiv preprint arXiv:2007.07846*.

A Interpretability

As a case study, to analyze the performance of our model in handling the shift in the topics and terminologies of COVID-19 related literature, we look at attention weights between the various stigmatized and standard terms for the novel Coronavirus over the time. The stigmatized terms include those which have been used prior to the provisional standard term “2019-nCoV”, such as “Wuhan Coronavirus,” “Chinese Virus,” “Wuhan Novel Pneumonia” to name a few (Hu et al., 2020). We use the aggregated weights[11] when these terms attend to or get attended by the standard ones (i.e. COVID-19 and SARS-CoV-2). We use the chronologically sorted dataset and looked at the weights as the model gets trained over the different time frames.

As shown in Figure 3, as the distribution of terminologies changes over time, the attention mechanism learns to relate to the well-established terms mitigating the effect of the dataset shift. In the beginning, the model shows high attention weights toward SARS-CoV as it is another variant of Coronavirus, which has also originated from China. This finding shows that the model matches the new context. Specifically, the model quickly relates stigmatized terms even prior to introducing their standard terms. With the standard terms, the model pays less attention to stigmatized and provisional terms. The attention over SARS-CoV-1 and other related variants decreases as the model dissolves the confusion between them.

[11]Summed and averaged over all sample queries and candidate articles, using both local and global attentions.

Hyperparameter	**Value(s)**
$\|V\|$	20M, **30M**
K	128, 256 , **512**, 1024
w (sliding window size)	32,..., 512, **inc**[32 : 512], dec[32 : 512]
dilation	0, 1, 2, 3, **inc**[0 : 3]
dilation heads	1, **2**, 3
dorpout	0.1, **0.2**, 0.3, **0.4***
batch size	8, **16**, 32, 64 (gpu memory limit)
output vector size	512, **1024**, 2048
w.e. size	128, **256**, **512***
hidden size	128, **256**, **512***
#layers	**4**, 5, **6***, 7, 8
learning rate	0.001, **0.0005**, 0.00025, **0.0001**

Table 4: Hyperparameter values. w.e.: embedding size for initial retrieval step. We use bold text for the optimal ones among all tried values. * refer to those for large ranker. Best dilation size is achieved by increasing it by 1 from first layer to the last.

B Hyperparameters

In Table 4, we list all of the hyperparameters we search over in this study. The best hyperparameters we found on the validation dataset are marked via bold and an asterisk (*). When training the transformer reranker model, we use a dropout value of 0.2, batch size of 16, 2 dilation heads, with a dilation varying from 0 to 3 from the first to last layer of the Longformer (increasing or decreasing every/every other layer).

C Dilation Results

In Table 5, we experiment with the longformer dilation parameter w, fixing it at 230, varying it from size 32 to 512 from the first to last layer, varying it from 512 to 32 from the first to last layer (i.e., in reverse), using dilation on two heads, and combining global dilation with dialated sliding windows. See Beltagy et al. (2020) for more details on the dilation parameters. Overall, we find that the combination of global and dilated sliding window

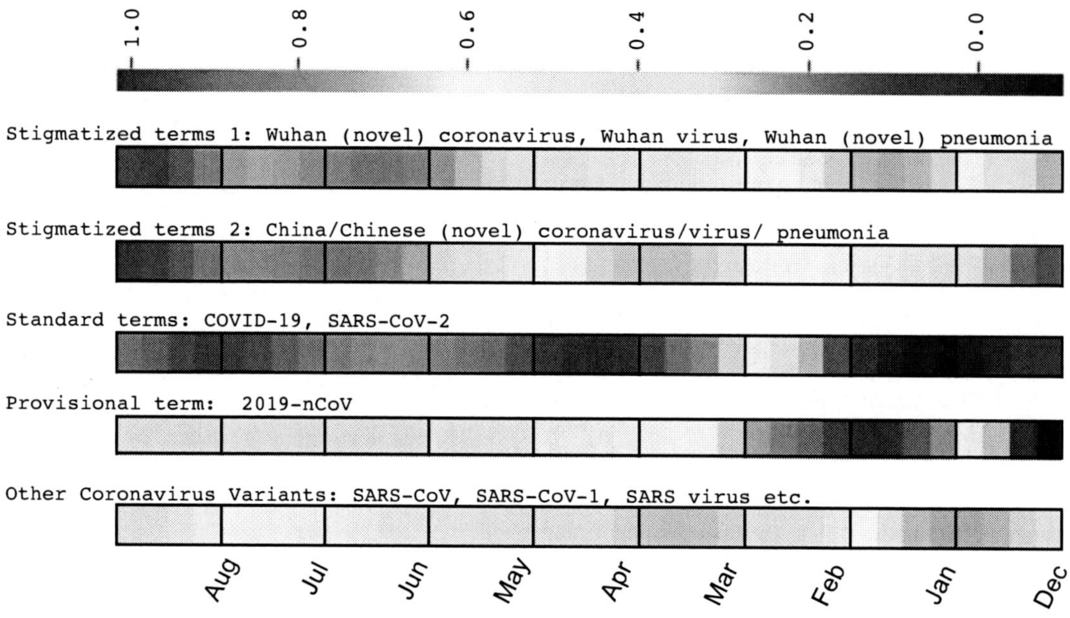

Figure 3: Attention weights of terms attending to COVID-19 and SARS-CoV-2 over different time frames. These weights are normalized for visualization purpose, following (Nguyen and Salazar, 2019)

with increasing window size shows better performance than other combinations in both IR and SI. However, the performance still does not match our custom attention filtering as shown in Tables 5a and 1b.

Model	Micro F1
R+TR (base) (full attention)	.553
R+TR (increasing w) (from 32-512)	.628
R+TR (fixed w) (=230)	.614
R+TR (decreasing w) (from 512-32)	.600
R+TR (increasing w) (dilation on 2 heads)	.633
R+TR (global + dilated sliding window*)	.660

(a)

Model	MAP
R+TR (base) (full attention)	.191
R+TR (increasing w) (from 32-512)	.293
R+TR (fixed w) (=230)	.280
R+TR (decreasing w) (from 512-32)	.258
R+TR (increasing w) (dilation on 2 heads)	.303
R+TR (global + dilated sliding window*)	.328

(b)

Table 5: Semantic Indexing (a) and Information Retrieval (b) performances of our models, Retriever and Transformer-based Ranker (R+TR), along with the baselines (best performing models of BioASQ Task 8a for SI, and Task 8b Phase A for IR). The baseline scores are the average of their provided Micro F1 and Mean Average Persision (MAP) for IR and SI, respectively. The results are averaged across all test batches. Our model Retriever and Transformer-based Ranker is abbreviated as R+TR.

A Japanese Masked Language Model for Academic Domain

Hiroki Yamauchi[1] **Tomoyuki Kajiwara**[1] **Marie Katsurai**[2]
Ikki Ohmukai[3,4] **Takashi Ninomiya**[1]
[1]Ehime University [2]Doshisha University [3]University of Tokyo
[4]National Institute of Informatics
{yamauchi@ai.,kajiwara@,ninomiya@}cs.ehime-u.ac.jp
katsurai@mm.doshisha.ac.jp, i2k@l.u-tokyo.ac.jp

Abstract

We release a pretrained Japanese masked language model for an academic domain. Pretrained masked language models have recently improved the performance of various natural language processing applications. In domains such as medical and academic, which include a lot of technical terms, domain-specific pretraining is effective. While domain-specific masked language models for medical and SNS domains are widely used in Japanese, along with domain-independent ones, pretrained models specific to the academic domain are not publicly available. In this study, we pretrained a RoBERTa-based Japanese masked language model on paper abstracts from the academic database CiNii Articles. Experimental results on Japanese text classification in the academic domain revealed the effectiveness of the proposed model over existing pretrained models.

1 Introduction

Academic papers in various fields and languages are accumulating daily on the Web. For example, more than 76k papers in the field of natural language processing (NLP) are currently available on the ACL Anthology.[1] Since the cost for humans to exhaustively learn from these large numbers of academic papers is immeasurable, scholarly document processing by NLP (Cohan and Goharian, 2015; Singh et al., 2018; Mohammad, 2020) is promising.

In NLP based on deep learning, which is currently the mainstream, supervised learning with a large-scale labeled corpus is effective. However, in domains where technical terms are frequently used, such as in academic fields, hiring professional annotators is very expensive. Therefore, the low-resource problem is a serious issue in various languages, domains, and tasks.

In recent NLP, finetuning of pretrained masked language models on large-scale raw corpora, such as BERT (Devlin et al., 2019) and RoBERTa (Liu et al., 2019), has been widely employed to address the low-resource problem. Especially in domains such as medical (Alsentzer et al., 2019) and academic (Beltagy et al., 2019; Lee et al., 2020), the effectiveness of domain-specific pretraining has been reported. Similar to these previous studies in English, domain-specific masked language models for medical (Kawazoe et al., 2021) and SNS[2] are widely used in Japanese, along with domain-independent masked language models.[3,4] However, there are no publicly available pretrained Japanese models that are specific to the academic domain.

In this study, we pretrained a RoBERTa-based Japanese masked language model (Liu et al., 2019) using 6.28M sentences of paper abstracts from a scholarly article database CiNii Articles[5] to improve the performance of scholarly document processing in Japanese. Experimental results on Japanese text classification in the academic domain revealed the effectiveness of the proposed model, which is specific to the academic domain, compared to the domain-independent masked language models. Our model (Academic RoBERTa) will be available on GitHub[6] when this paper is published.

2 Related Work

Finetuning of pretrained Transformer (Vaswani et al., 2017) achieves excellent performance on many NLP tasks (Wang et al., 2018). BERT (Devlin et al., 2019), a typical pretraining model, trains the Transformer encoder by multi-task learning of masked language modeling and next sentence pre-

[1]https://aclanthology.org/

[2]https://github.com/hottolink/hottoSNS-bert

[3]https://huggingface.co/cl-tohoku/bert-base-japanese

[4]https://huggingface.co/nlp-waseda/roberta-base-japanese

[5]https://ci.nii.ac.jp/

[6]https://github.com/hirokiyamauch/AcademicRoBERTa

Proceedings of the Third Workshop on Scholarly Document Processing, pages 152–157
October 12–17, 2022.

diction. RoBERTa (Liu et al., 2019) outperforms BERT by pretraining only masked language modeling, through dynamic masking and increasing batch size and number of training steps. This study conducts powerful RoBERTa-based pre-training to develop a Japanese masked language model specific to the academic domain.

The effectiveness of domain-specific pretraining to address technical terms and style-specific expressions has been reported. In English, domain-specific masked language models are publicly available for various domains, including medical (Alsentzer et al., 2019), academic (Beltagy et al., 2019; Lee et al., 2020), and SNS (Nguyen et al., 2020). Domain-specific masked language models have also been developed in Japanese, such as UTH-BERT (Kawazoe et al., 2021) for the medical domain and hottoSNS-BERT[2] for the SNS domain. However, no pretraining Japanese model specific to the academic domain has been released.

3 Methods

To improve the performance of scholarly document processing in Japanese, we release a Japanese masked language model specific to the academic domain. First, in Section 3.1, we create a Japanese corpus consisting of paper abstracts. Then, in Section 3.2, we use this corpus to conduct pretraining based on RoBERTa (Liu et al., 2019).

3.1 Corpus

We use CiNii Articles,[5] a scholarly article database, to create a Japanese corpus specific to the academic domain. We extracted 1.27 million abstracts of academic papers included in CiNii Articles as of March 2022, containing Japanese characters (hiragana or katakana). Then, a corpus of approximately 6.28 million sentences (about 180 million words) was created by applying the five-step preprocessing shown in Table 1.

Deletion of Fixed Expressions Paper abstracts extracted from CiNii Articles contain noise due to automatic information extraction, such as "論文タイプ || 研究ノート" (paper type || research notes). To exclude these fixed expressions from the corpus, we remove them when the same document appears more frequently than a threshold. Since there were cases where the same document appeared 5 or 6 times due to ID registration errors, we set the threshold as 7 or more times.

Preprocess	Corpus size
Number of paper abstracts	1.27 M docs.
1. Deletion of fixed expressions	1.15 M docs.
2. Segmentation into sentences	7.31 M sents.
3. Extraction of Japanese sentences	6.68 M sents.
4. Deletion of duplicate sentences	6.33 M sents.
5. Limitation of sentence length	6.28 M sents.

Table 1: Change in corpus size due to preprocessing.

Segmentation into Sentences For 1.15 million documents obtained by the previous preprocessing, sentence segmentation is performed. Approximately 7.31 million sentences were obtained by rule-based sentence segmentation.[7]

Extraction of Japanese Sentences To clean our Japanese corpus, we remove sentences written in languages other than Japanese. Since technical terms are often expressed in other languages, sentences in which the characters above the threshold are Japanese (hiragana or katakana or kanji) are extracted. In this study, this threshold was set at 50%, resulting in about 6.68 million Japanese sentences.

Deletion of Duplicate Sentences To prevent bias caused by high-frequency expressions, sentences that occur frequently in specific fields, such as "下腹部痛を主訴に来院。" (Visited the hospital with a chief complaint of lower abdominal pain.) and fixed form sentences in academic papers, such as "その結果を以下に示す。" (The results are shown below.) are removed. In the case of sentence duplication, the sentence was left in the corpus only once and the others were deleted, resulting in a corpus of about 6.33 million unique sentences.

Limitation of Sentence Length Finally, extremely short and long sentences are removed to completely eliminate errors in fixed expressions and sentence segmentation. Sentences of less than 10 characters often contained expressions such as "（編集委員会作成）" (prepared by the editorial board) that would not be included in the actual paper abstracts. Therefore, in this study, we created a corpus of approximately 6.28 million sentences by extracting sentences with between 10 and 200 characters.

[7]`https://github.com/wwwcojp/ja_sentence_segmenter`

3.2 Pretraining

The corpus created in Section 3.1 is used to pretrain masked language modeling equivalent to RoBERTa (Liu et al., 2019). Subword segmentation by SentencePiece[8] (Kudo and Richardson, 2018) with a vocabulary size of 32,000 was performed for tokenization. Our model is a Transformer (Vaswani et al., 2017) with the same structure as the `roberta-base`, implemented by the fairseq toolkit.[9] (Ott et al., 2019) That is, our masked language model consists of 12 layers of 768 dimensions with 12 self-attention heads. We set the maximum number of tokens per input instance to 512, the batch size to 64 sentences, and the dropout rate to 0.1. We used Adam (Kingma and Ba, 2015) with learning rate scheduling by polynomial decay as the optimizer and we set the maximum learning rate to 0.0001 and the warmup step to 10,000. The number of training steps was set to 700,000 for a fair comparison with a previous study.[4] Our model was pretrained on two CPUs (Intel Xeon GOLD 5115) with 192 GB RAM and four GPUs (RTX A6000 48 GB).

4 Evaluation

To evaluate the effectiveness of our masked language model (Academic RoBERTa) specific to the academic domain, we empirically compare our model with existing domain-independent masked language models through experiments on Japanese text classification in the academic domain.

4.1 Baselines

In this experiment, BERT (Tohoku BERT)[3] and RoBERTa (Waseda RoBERTa)[4], which are domain-independent masked language models for Japanese, are employed as baseline models. Both baselines are Transformer models (Vaswani et al., 2017) with the same structure as Academic RoBERTa and have the same size vocabulary. However, they differ in the corpus used for pretraining, its preprocessing, and the hyperparameters during pretraining. We used HuggingFace Transformers (Wolf et al., 2020) to implement our baseline models.

Tohoku BERT is a BERT model (Devlin et al., 2019) pretrained on Japanese Wikipedia. Morphological analysis with MeCab (IPADIC) (Kudo et al., 2004) and subword segmentation with WordPiece (Wu et al., 2016) were used as preprocessing. The maximum number of tokens per input instance is 512, the batch size is 256 sentences, and 1 million steps of pretraining is performed.

Waseda RoBERTa is a RoBERTa model (Liu et al., 2019) pretrained on both Japanese Wikipedia and the Japanese part of CC100 (Wenzek et al., 2020). Morphological analysis with Juman++ (Tolmachev et al., 2020) and subword segmentation with SentencePiace (Kudo and Richardson, 2018) are used as preprocessing. The maximum number of tokens per input instance is 128, the batch size is 256 sentences ($\times$8 GPUs), and 700,000 steps of pretraining is performed.

4.2 Tasks

As evaluation tasks in the academic domain, we experiment with two types of Japanese text classification on the titles of research projects funded by Grants-in-Aid for Scientific Research (KAKENHI). KAKENHI is a competitive research fund in Japan that covers scientific research in all fields. For this experiment, we collected 73,000 KAKENHI proposals from 2013 to 2017. We designed two evaluation tasks: an author identification task to estimate whether the principal investigator is the same or not from pairs of research project titles, and a category classification task to estimate the research fields from research project titles. In both tasks, each masked language model is automatically evaluated by the accuracy of its classification.

Author Identification This task is a sentence-pair classification task that performs a binary classification of whether the principal investigators of two research projects are identical or not. In this experiment, a total of 120,000 pairs, 50,000 positive examples consisting of research project titles proposed by the same principal investigator and 70,000 negative examples consisting of those proposed by different principal investigators, were paired and randomly split for training, validation, and evaluation as shown in the top row of Table 2. Two sentences were input simultaneously into the masked language model with a special token of `[SEP]` in between.

Category Classification This task is a sentence classification task to estimate research fields from the titles of research projects. KAKENHI employs a four-level hierarchical structure of research fields, which include 4, 14, 77, and 318 categories, in

[8]https://github.com/google/sentencepiece

[9]https://github.com/facebookresearch/fairseq

	Author indentification	Category classificaton			
# examples for Train/Valid/Test	100k / 10k / 10k	70k / 1.5k / 1.5k			
# classes	2	4	14	77	318
Tohoku BERT	95.1	83.7	69.6	53.3	40.3
Waseda RoBERTa	97.1	83.9	71.9	55.4	42.7
Academic RoBERTa	**98.7**	**84.7**	**72.9**	**58.8**	**44.6**

Table 2: Accuracy of academic text classification in Japanese.

descending order from the largest categories. In this experiment, each level of classification was performed independently. That is, the classification results for the larger categories do not affect the classification of the smaller categories.

4.3 Finetuning

The corpus described in Section 4.2 was used to finetune the masked language models. As a preprocessing, subword segmentation was performed for each model using the same settings as in the pretraining. For finetuning, the batch size was 256 sentences, the dropout rate was set to 0.1, and Adam (Kingma and Ba, 2015) was used as the optimizer with a maximum learning rate of $5e^{-5}$. Finetuning was terminated when the accuracy in the validation dataset did not improve for 10 epochs as early stopping.

4.4 Results

Table 2 shows the experimental results. RoBERTa consistently achieved better performance than BERT, and Academic RoBERTa, which is specific to the academic domain, showed the best performance on all tasks. In particular, the proposed method showed significant performance improvement in classifying minor categories (*i.e.*, 77-class and 318-class classifications), which require more detailed expertise than major categories (*i.e.*, 4-class and 14-class classifications).

There is no difference in model structure or number of training steps between Waseda RoBERTa and Academic RoBERTa. In addition, since Tohoku BERT and Waseda RoBERTa are pretrained using corpora of approximately 17 million and 4 billion sentences, respectively, our approximately 6.28 million sentences have no advantage in terms of corpus size. Therefore, the performance improvement of our model can be attributed only to its specialization in the academic domain.

4.5 Discussion

We analyze the vocabulary of the domain-specific model. We found that 49.4% of the tokens in Academic RoBERTa's vocabulary are not included in that of existing masked language models.[10] Examples of characteristic tokens that only Academic RoBERTa has include phrases that frequently appear in academic papers in any field, such as "であることが確認された" (It was confirmed that the ...) and technical terms that frequently appear in certain fields, such as "ニューラルネットワーク" (neural networks). Our model may have achieved high performance for text classification in the academic domain because our vocabulary includes many such domain-specific tokens.

5 Conclusion

In this study, we released Academic RoBERTa, a Japanese masked language model specific to the academic domain, pretrained on abstracts of academic papers included in CiNii Articles. Experimental results on Japanese text classification in the academic domain revealed that our model consistently outperforms existing domain-independent masked language models. Detailed analysis confirmed the effectiveness of domain-specific pretraining, as many domain-specific expressions were included in the vocabulary and the accuracy of text classification improved significantly for more detailed categories requiring more expertise.

Our future work includes making Japanese text generation models such as GPT-2 (Radford et al., 2019) and BART (Lewis et al., 2020) specific to the academic domain. These models could contribute to summarization and grammatical error correction in the academic domain.

[10]The vocabulary of the existing masked language model refers to the following union sets: the vocabulary of Tohoku BERT, the vocabulary of Waseda RoBERTa, and the vocabulary when training the subword segmentation of SentencePiece on Japanese Wikipedia with a vocabulary size of 32,000.

Acknowledgment

This work was supported by JSPS KAKENHI Grant Number JP20H04484 and ROIS NII Open Collaborative Research 2020 (20S0405).

References

Emily Alsentzer, John Murphy, William Boag, Wei-Hung Weng, Di Jindi, Tristan Naumann, and Matthew McDermott. 2019. Publicly Available Clinical BERT Embeddings. In *Proceedings of the 2nd Clinical Natural Language Processing Workshop*, pages 72–78.

Iz Beltagy, Kyle Lo, and Arman Cohan. 2019. SciBERT: A Pretrained Language Model for Scientific Text. In *Proceedings of the 2019 Conference on Empirical Methods in Natural Language Processing and the 9th International Joint Conference on Natural Language Processing*, pages 3615–3620.

Arman Cohan and Nazli Goharian. 2015. Scientific Article Summarization Using Citation-Context and Article's Discourse Structure. In *Proceedings of the 2015 Conference on Empirical Methods in Natural Language Processing*, pages 390–400.

Jacob Devlin, Ming-Wei Chang, Kenton Lee, and Kristina Toutanova. 2019. BERT: Pre-training of Deep Bidirectional Transformers for Language Understanding. In *Proceedings of the 2019 Conference of the North American Chapter of the Association for Computational Linguistics: Human Language Technologies*, pages 4171–4186.

Yoshimasa Kawazoe, Daisaku Shibata, Emiko Shinohara, Eiji Aramaki, and Kazuhiko Ohe. 2021. A Clinical Specific BERT Developed Using a Huge Japanese Clinical Text Corpus. *PLOS ONE*, 16(11):1–11.

Diederik P. Kingma and Jimmy Lei Ba. 2015. Adam: A Method for Stochastic Optimization. In *Proceedings of the 3rd International Conference for Learning Representations*.

Taku Kudo and John Richardson. 2018. SentencePiece: A Simple and Language Independent Subword Tokenizer and Detokenizer for Neural Text Processing. In *Proceedings of the 2018 Conference on Empirical Methods in Natural Language Processing: System Demonstrations*, pages 66–71.

Taku Kudo, Kaoru Yamamoto, and Yuji Matsumoto. 2004. Applying Conditional Random Fields to Japanese Morphological Analysis. In *Proceedings of the 2004 Conference on Empirical Methods in Natural Language Processing*, pages 230–237.

Jinhyuk Lee, Wonjin Yoon, Sungdong Kim, Donghyeon Kim, Sunkyu Kim, Chan Ho So, and Jaewoo Kang. 2020. BioBERT: A Pre-trained Biomedical Language Representation Model for Biomedical Text Mining. *Bioinformatics*, 36(4):1234–1240.

Mike Lewis, Yinhan Liu, Naman Goyal, Marjan Ghazvininejad, Abdelrahman Mohamed, Omer Levy, Veselin Stoyanov, and Luke Zettlemoyer. 2020. BART: Denoising Sequence-to-Sequence Pre-training for Natural Language Generation, Translation, and Comprehension. In *Proceedings of the 58th Annual Meeting of the Association for Computational Linguistics*, pages 7871–7880.

Yinhan Liu, Myle Ott, Naman Goyal, Jingfei Du, Mandar Joshi, Danqi Chen, Omer Levy, Mike Lewis, Luke Zettlemoyer, and Veselin Stoyanov. 2019. RoBERTa: A Robustly Optimized BERT Pretraining Approach. *arXiv:1907.11692*.

Saif M. Mohammad. 2020. NLP Scholar: A Dataset for Examining the State of NLP Research. In *Proceedings of the 12th Language Resources and Evaluation Conference*, pages 868–877.

Dat Quoc Nguyen, Thanh Vu, and Anh Tuan Nguyen. 2020. BERTweet: A Pre-trained Language Model for English Tweets. In *Proceedings of the 2020 Conference on Empirical Methods in Natural Language Processing: System Demonstrations*, pages 9–14.

Myle Ott, Sergey Edunov, Alexei Baevski, Angela Fan, Sam Gross, Nathan Ng, David Grangier, and Michael Auli. 2019. fairseq: A Fast, Extensible Toolkit for Sequence Modeling. In *Proceedings of the 2019 Conference of the North American Chapter of the Association for Computational Linguistics (Demonstrations)*, pages 48–53.

Alec Radford, Jeff Wu, Rewon Child, David Luan, Dario Amodei, and Ilya Sutskever. 2019. Language Models are Unsupervised Multitask Learners. *Technical Report, OpenAI*, pages 1–24.

Mayank Singh, Pradeep Dogga, Sohan Patro, Dhiraj Barnwal, Ritam Dutt, Rajarshi Haldar, Pawan Goyal, and Animesh Mukherjee. 2018. CL Scholar: The ACL Anthology Knowledge Graph Miner. In *Proceedings of the 2018 Conference of the North American Chapter of the Association for Computational Linguistics: Demonstrations*, pages 16–20.

Arseny Tolmachev, Daisuke Kawahara, and Sadao Kurohashi. 2020. Design and Structure of The Juman++ Morphological Analyzer Toolkit. *Journal of Natural Language Processing*, 27(1):89–132.

Ashish Vaswani, Noam Shazeer, Niki Parmar, Jakob Uszkoreit, Llion Jones, Aidan N Gomez, Łukasz Kaiser, and Illia Polosukhin. 2017. Attention is All you Need. In *Advances in Neural Information Processing Systems*, pages 5998–6008.

Alex Wang, Amanpreet Singh, Julian Michael, Felix Hill, Omer Levy, and Samuel Bowman. 2018. GLUE: A Multi-Task Benchmark and Analysis Platform for Natural Language Understanding. In *Proceedings of the 2018 EMNLP Workshop BlackboxNLP: Analyzing and Interpreting Neural Networks for NLP*, pages 353–355.

Guillaume Wenzek, Marie-Anne Lachaux, Alexis Conneau, Vishrav Chaudhary, Francisco Guzmán, Armand Joulin, and Edouard Grave. 2020. CCNet: Extracting High Quality Monolingual Datasets from Web Crawl Data. In *Proceedings of the 12th Language Resources and Evaluation Conference*, pages 4003–4012.

Thomas Wolf, Lysandre Debut, Victor Sanh, Julien Chaumond, Clement Delangue, Anthony Moi, Pierric Cistac, Tim Rault, Remi Louf, Morgan Funtowicz, Joe Davison, Sam Shleifer, Patrick von Platen, Clara Ma, Yacine Jernite, Julien Plu, Canwen Xu, Teven Le Scao, Sylvain Gugger, Mariama Drame, Quentin Lhoest, and Alexander Rush. 2020. Transformers: State-of-the-Art Natural Language Processing. In *Proceedings of the 2020 Conference on Empirical Methods in Natural Language Processing: System Demonstrations*, pages 38–45.

Yonghui Wu, Mike Schuster, Zhifeng Chen, Quoc V. Le, Mohammad Norouzi, Wolfgang Macherey, Maxim Krikun, Yuan Cao, Qin Gao, Klaus Macherey, Jeff Klingner, Apurva Shah, Melvin Johnson, Xiaobing Liu, Łukasz Kaiser, Stephan Gouws, Yoshikiyo Kato, Taku Kudo, Hideto Kazawa, Keith Stevens, George Kurian, Nishant Patil, Wei Wang, Cliff Young, Jason Smith, Jason Riesa, Alex Rudnick, Oriol Vinyals, Greg Corrado, Macduff Hughes, and Jeffrey Dean. 2016. Google's Neural Machine Translation System: Bridging the Gap between Human and Machine Translation. *arXiv:1609.08144*.

Named Entity Inclusion in Abstractive Text Summarization

Sergey Berezin
École des Mines de Nancy
LORIA, UMR 7503,
Université de Lorraine, CNRS, Inria,
54000 Nancy, France
sergeyberezin123@gmail.com

Tatiana Batura
A. P. Ershov Institute of Informatics Systems
630090 Novosibirsk, Russia
tatiana.v.batura@gmail.com

Abstract

We address the named entity omission - the drawback of many current abstractive text summarizers. We suggest a custom pretraining objective to enhance the model's attention on the named entities in a text. At first, the named entity recognition model RoBERTa is trained to determine named entities in the text. After that, this model is used to mask named entities in the text and the BART model is trained to reconstruct them. Next, the BART model is fine-tuned on the summarization task. Our experiments showed that this pretraining approach improves named entity inclusion precision and recall metrics.

1 Introduction

Current state-of-the-art abstractive summarization methods achieved significant progress, yet they are still prone to hallucinations and substitution of the named entities with vague synonyms or omitting mention of some of them at all (Kryscinski et al., 2020a), (Maynez et al., 2020a), (Gabriel et al., 2021). Such inconsistencies in the summary limit the practicability of abstractive models in real-world applications and carry a danger of misinformation. Example in Table 1 demonstrates the difference that named entity inclusion could make in the generated summary.

Scientific texts are especially vulnerable to this issue. Omitting or substituting the name of the metric used or the method applied can make a summary useless or, in the worst case scenario, totally misleading for a reader.

We make the following contributions:

- present a new method for pretraining a summarization model to include domain-specific named entities in the generated summary;
- show that the BART model with the Masked Named Entity Language Model (MNELM) pretraining procedure is able to achieve higher precision and recall metrics of named entity inclusion.

Without named entities	With named entities
Famous North-American scientist suggested a new way of training AI algorithms.	**Andrew Ng** from **Stanford** suggested a new way of training **feed-forward neural networks**.

Table 1: Example of NE omission

2 Related work

For automatic summarization, one of the important issues is extrinsic entity hallucinations, when some entities appear in summary, but do not occur in the source text (Maynez et al., 2020b; Pagnoni et al., 2021). A number of studies have been devoted to this problem, such as fixing entity-related errors (Nan et al., 2021), ensuring the factual consistency of generated summaries (Cao et al., 2020), and task-adaptive continued pertaining (Gururangan et al., 2020). In our paper, we address the problem of named entity awareness of the summarization model by first training it on the NER task before final finetuning to make the model entity aware.

The idea of utilizing named entities during the pretraining phase first was described back in (Zhang et al., 2019), where the authors proposed the usage of knowledge graphs by randomly masking some of the named entity alignments in the input text and asking the model to select the appropriate entities from the graphs to complete the alignments. One of the disadvantages of that approach is the need for a knowledge base, which is extremely difficult to build. Only a limited number of domain-specific knowledge bases exist, and none of them can be considered complete.

The study (Kryscinski et al., 2020b) addresses the problem of the factual consistency of a generated summary by a weakly-supervised, model-

Proceedings of the Third Workshop on Scholarly Document Processing, pages 158–162
October 12–17, 2022.

based approach for verifying factual consistency and identifying conflicts between source documents and a generated summary. Training data is generated by applying a series of rule-based transformations to the sentences of the source documents.

A similar approach is suggested by the authors of the paper (Mao et al., 2020) who try to preserve the factual consistency of abstractive summarization by specifying tokens as constraints that must be present in the summary. They use a BERT-based keyphrase extractor model to determine the most important spans in the text (akin to the extractive summarization) and then use these spans to constrain a generative algorithm. The big drawback of this approach is the vagueness of the keyphrases and the limited amount of training data. Also, the use of the BERT model leaves room for improvement.

The analogous solution uses (Narayan et al., 2021), where the authors suggest entity-level content planning, i.e. prepending target summaries with entity chains – ordered sequences of entities that should be mentioned in the summary. But, as the entity chains are extracted from the reference summaries during the training, this approach cannot be used in an unsupervised manner, like MNELM, proposed in this work.

3 Method

We propose a three-step approach that aims to avoid all the aforementioned drawbacks: 1) at the first step the NER model is trained on a domain-specific dataset; 2) then the trained NER model is used for the MLM-like unsupervised pretraining of a language model; 3) the pretrained model is finetuned for the summarization task.

By following these steps, we can use a large amount of unlabeled data for the pretraining model to select domain-specific named entities and therefore to include them in the generated summary. In comparison with a regular MLM pretraining, the suggested approach helps the model converge faster, shows an increased number of entities included in the generated summary, and drastically improves the avoiding of hallucinations, i.e. eliminates named entities that did not appear in the original text.

4 Datasets and evaluation metrics

In this work, we use two datasets: SCIERC (Luan et al., 2018) for training named entity extraction model and ArXiv (Cohan et al., 2018) dataset for pretraining and training of the summarization model. The SCIERC dataset includes annotations for scientific entities for 500 scientific abstracts. These abstracts are taken from 12 AI conference/workshop proceedings in four AI communities from the Semantic Scholar Corpus. These conferences include general AI (AAAI, IJCAI), NLP (ACL, EMNLP, IJCNLP), speech (ICASSP, Interspeech), machine learning (NIPS, ICML), and computer vision (CVPR, ICCV, ECCV) conferences. The dataset contains 8.089 named entities and defines six types for annotating scientific entities: Task, Method, Metric, Material, Other-Scientific-Term and Generic. SCIERC utilizes a greedy annotation approach for spans and always prefers the longer span whenever ambiguity occurs. Nested spans are allowed when a subspan has a relation/coreference link with another term outside the span.

The second dataset is the Arxiv dataset which takes scientific papers as an example of long documents and their abstracts are used as ground-truth summaries. Authors of the dataset removed the documents that are excessively long or too short, or do not have an abstract or some discourse structure. Figures and tables were removed using regular expressions to only preserve the textual information. Also, math formulae and citation markers were normalized with special tokens. Only the sections up to the conclusion section of the document were kept for every paper.

This dataset contains 215,912 scientific papers with the average length of 4,938 words and the average summary length of 220 words. To evaluate the performance of the model we used ROUGE-1, ROUGE-2, and ROUGE-L metrics.

For scoring the occurrence of named entities and their soundness and completeness we use named-entity-wise precision and recall:

$$NE\ precision = \frac{correct\ NE\ in\ summary}{number\ of\ NE\ in\ summary}$$

$$NE\ recall = \frac{correct\ NE\ in\ summary}{number\ of\ NE\ in\ source}$$

5 Experiments

The training procedure of our model consists of the three main stages, illustrated in Figure 1.

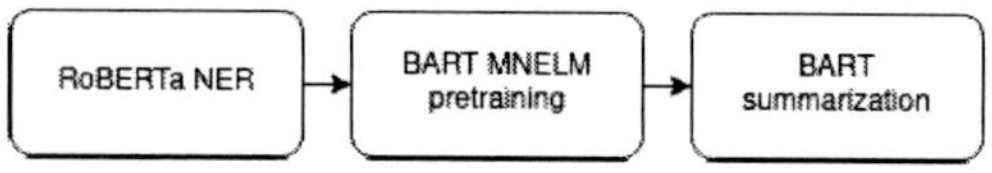

Figure 1: Training sequence

5.1 NER preparation

To start our pipeline, we trained the Named Entity Recognition model. For this purpose, we used the RoBERTa (Liu et al., 2019) language model. After the training for 7 epochs, we obtained an F1 macro score of 0.51 on the test dataset.

5.2 Custom LM pretraining

BART (Lewis et al., 2020) uses the standard sequence-to-sequence Transformer architecture (Vaswani et al., 2017) and it is pretrained by corrupting documents and then optimizing a reconstruction loss – the cross-entropy between the decoder's output and the content of the original document. Unlike most of the existing denoising autoencoders, which are tailored to specific noising schemes, BART allows us to apply any type of document corruption. In the extreme case, where all information about the source is lost, BART is equivalent to a regular language model.

This unique ability opens the road to usage of our previously trained NER model. We use it to find named entities in scientific texts from the ArXiv dataset and substitute them with [mask] tokens. This way, we bring the model's attention to the named entities instead of just random words, most of which might be from a general domain. In our experiments, we used a 0.5 probability of masking.

This approach was inspired by the original BART paper, in the conclusion of which authors encourage further experiments with noising functions: "Future work should explore new methods for corrupting documents for pre-training, perhaps tailoring them to specific end tasks" (Lewis et al., 2020).

We pretrained on 215,912 scientific articles on a single epoch starting with a learning rate of $5 * 10^{-5}$ and a linear scheduler with gamma = 0.5 every 10,000 steps.

	MNELM	MLM
NE Precision	**0.93**	0.86
NE Recall	**0.39**	0.38

Table 2: Named Entity inclusion scores.

		MNELM	MLM
	F1	**0.36**	0.35
ROUGE-1	precision	**0.51**	0.49
	recall	0.29	0.29
	F1	**0.13**	0.12
ROUGE-2	precision	**0.21**	0.19
	recall	0.10	0.10
	F1	**0.32**	0.31
ROUGE-L	precision	**0.45**	0.43
	recall	**0.26**	0.25

Table 3: Summarization scores. MNELM was trained for 20k steps, MLM was trained for 25k steps.

5.3 Summarization training

After pretraining the BART model, we finetuned it on a summarization task. Because BART has an autoregressive decoder, it can be directly fine-tuned for sequence generation tasks such as abstractive question answering and summarization. In both of these tasks, information is copied from the input, but manipulated, which is closely related to the denoising pre-training objective. Here, we trained BART with a batch size of 1 for a single epoch. We figured out that the model easily overfits, so we had to use a learning rate scheduled every 5,000 steps with gamma = 0.5. The initial learning rate was set to be $2 * 10^{-5}$. For training we used NVIDIA Tesla K80 GPU, the training took around 30 hours.

6 Results

Our model shows higher precision and recall in named entity inclusion in comparison to the same architecture, which was pretrained using regular masked language model objective - results of both models can be found in Table 2. Examples of generated summaries are shown in Appendix A.

7 Discussion

During the training of our model, we noticed that increase in common metrics for text summarization causes a decrease in named entity inclusion. We believe the reason for this is the limited length of the generated summary - one can have only so many named entities, before they will displace other words from the original text, causing the model to reformulate sentences and miss more words from the source. Therefore, during training, we tried to find the optimum point, at which the model will have high ROUGE scores and will still have high NE inclusion. At this point the MNELM-pretrained model, while keeping higher NE inclusion, converges faster than a regular MLM (in terms of ROUGE metrics). The comparison can be found in Table 3. Obtained summarization scores are inferior to the recently published state of the art models like PRIMER (Xiao et al., 2022) (ROUGE-1 = 47.6; ROUGE-2 = 20.8) or Deep-Pyramidon (Pietruszka et al., 2022) (ROUGE-1 = 47.2; ROUGE-2 = 20), but their ability to preserve named entities in text is yet to be determined.

8 Conclusion

In this work, we described the task of preserving named entities in an automatically generated summary and presented the Masked Named Entity Language Model (MNELM) pretraining task. We show that with the MNELM pretraining procedure the BART model can achieve higher precision and recall of named entity inclusion.

Pretraining with the MNELM task helps the model concentrate on domain-specific words, whereas MLM learns to reconstruct mostly common words. This leads to stronger attention on named entities, more likely preserving them in a generated text. The suggested model shows solid results in summarization metrics in comparison to the regular approach and converges faster.

In further research, we plan to improve the quality of the pretraining by masking a sequence of named entities with a single mask – the step that could help the model, according to the original BART paper (Lewis et al., 2020). Also, we plan to conduct more experiments with different hyperparameters (such as masking probability), on more datasets, including PubMed (Cohan et al., 2018) and to train an even better NER model. In addition, we plan to improve the proposed model by overcoming the internal limitation on the number of input tokens (currently, it only has access to 1024 tokens).

References

Meng Cao, Yue Dong, Jiapeng Wu, and Jackie Chi Kit Cheung. 2020. Factual error correction for abstractive summarization models. In *Proceedings of the 2020 Conference on Empirical Methods in Natural Language Processing (EMNLP)*, pages 6251–6258, Online. Association for Computational Linguistics.

Arman Cohan, Franck Dernoncourt, Doo Soon Kim, Trung Bui, Seokhwan Kim, Walter Chang, and Nazli Goharian. 2018. A discourse-aware attention model for abstractive summarization of long documents. In *Proceedings of the 2018 Conference of the North American Chapter of the Association for Computational Linguistics: Human Language Technologies, Volume 2 (Short Papers)*, pages 615–621, New Orleans, Louisiana. Association for Computational Linguistics.

Saadia Gabriel, Asli Celikyilmaz, Rahul Jha, Yejin Choi, and Jianfeng Gao. 2021. GO FIGURE: A meta evaluation of factuality in summarization. In *Findings of the Association for Computational Linguistics: ACL-IJCNLP 2021*, pages 478–487, Online. Association for Computational Linguistics.

Suchin Gururangan, Ana Marasović, Swabha Swayamdipta, Kyle Lo, Iz Beltagy, Doug Downey, and Noah A. Smith. 2020. Don't stop pretraining: Adapt language models to domains and tasks. In *Proceedings of the 58th Annual Meeting of the Association for Computational Linguistics*, pages 8342–8360, Online. Association for Computational Linguistics.

Wojciech Kryscinski, Bryan McCann, Caiming Xiong, and Richard Socher. 2020a. Evaluating the factual consistency of abstractive text summarization. In *Proceedings of the 2020 Conference on Empirical Methods in Natural Language Processing (EMNLP)*, pages 9332–9346, Online. Association for Computational Linguistics.

Wojciech Kryscinski, Bryan McCann, Caiming Xiong, and Richard Socher. 2020b. Evaluating the factual consistency of abstractive text summarization. In *Proceedings of the 2020 Conference on Empirical Methods in Natural Language Processing (EMNLP)*, pages 9332–9346, Online. Association for Computational Linguistics.

Mike Lewis, Yinhan Liu, Naman Goyal, Marjan Ghazvininejad, Abdelrahman Mohamed, Omer Levy, Veselin Stoyanov, and Luke Zettlemoyer. 2020. BART: Denoising sequence-to-sequence pre-training for natural language generation, translation, and comprehension. In *Proceedings of the 58th Annual Meeting of the Association for Computational Linguistics*, pages 7871–7880, Online. Association for Computational Linguistics.

Yinhan Liu, Myle Ott, Naman Goyal, Jingfei Du, Mandar Joshi, Danqi Chen, Omer Levy, Mike Lewis, Luke Zettlemoyer, and Veselin Stoyanov. 2019. Roberta: A robustly optimized bert pretraining approach. *ArXiv*, abs/1907.11692.

Yi Luan, Luheng He, Mari Ostendorf, and Hannaneh Hajishirzi. 2018. Multi-task identification of entities, relations, and coreference for scientific knowledge graph construction. In *Proceedings of the 2018 Conference on Empirical Methods in Natural Language Processing*, pages 3219–3232, Brussels, Belgium. Association for Computational Linguistics.

Yuning Mao, Xiang Ren, Heng Ji, and Jiawei Han. 2020. Constrained abstractive summarization: Preserving factual consistency with constrained generation. *ArXiv*, abs/2010.12723.

Joshua Maynez, Shashi Narayan, Bernd Bohnet, and Ryan McDonald. 2020a. On faithfulness and factuality in abstractive summarization. In *Proceedings of the 58th Annual Meeting of the Association for Computational Linguistics*, pages 1906–1919, Online. Association for Computational Linguistics.

Joshua Maynez, Shashi Narayan, Bernd Bohnet, and Ryan McDonald. 2020b. On faithfulness and factuality in abstractive summarization. In *Proceedings of the 58th Annual Meeting of the Association for Computational Linguistics*, pages 1906–1919, Online. Association for Computational Linguistics.

Feng Nan, Ramesh Nallapati, Zhiguo Wang, Cicero Nogueira dos Santos, Henghui Zhu, Dejiao Zhang, Kathleen McKeown, and Bing Xiang. 2021. Entity-level factual consistency of abstractive text summarization. In *Proceedings of the 16th Conference of the European Chapter of the Association for Computational Linguistics: Main Volume*, pages 2727–2733, Online. Association for Computational Linguistics.

Shashi Narayan, Yao Zhao, Joshua Maynez, Gonçalo Simões, Vitaly Nikolaev, and Ryan McDonald. 2021. Planning with learned entity prompts for abstractive summarization. *Transactions of the Association for Computational Linguistics*, 9:1475–1492.

Artidoro Pagnoni, Vidhisha Balachandran, and Yulia Tsvetkov. 2021. Understanding factuality in abstractive summarization with frank: A benchmark for factuality metrics. In *NAACL-HLT*, pages 4812–4829.

Michał Pietruszka, Łukasz Borchmann, and Łukasz Garncarek. 2022. Sparsifying transformer models with trainable representation pooling. In *Proceedings of the 60th Annual Meeting of the Association for Computational Linguistics (Volume 1: Long Papers)*, pages 8616–8633, Dublin, Ireland. Association for Computational Linguistics.

Ashish Vaswani, Noam M. Shazeer, Niki Parmar, Jakob Uszkoreit, Llion Jones, Aidan N. Gomez, Lukasz Kaiser, and Illia Polosukhin. 2017. Attention is all you need. *ArXiv*, abs/1706.03762.

Wen Xiao, Iz Beltagy, Giuseppe Carenini, and Arman Cohan. 2022. PRIMERA: Pyramid-based masked sentence pre-training for multi-document summarization. In *Proceedings of the 60th Annual Meeting of the Association for Computational Linguistics (Volume 1: Long Papers)*, pages 5245–5263, Dublin, Ireland. Association for Computational Linguistics.

Zhengyan Zhang, Xu Han, Zhiyuan Liu, Xin Jiang, Maosong Sun, and Qun Liu. 2019. ERNIE: Enhanced language representation with informative entities. In *Proceedings of the 57th Annual Meeting of the Association for Computational Linguistics*, pages 1441–1451, Florence, Italy. Association for Computational Linguistics.

A Appendix

Below is the comparison of the generated summaries. Named entities are in bold. First text is generated by the MNELM-pretrained model, second text is produced by the MLM-pretrained model:

1. "the problem of **admission control** for **web - based applications** is typically considered as a problem of **system sizing** : enough resources are to be provisioned to meet **quality of service** requirements under a wide range of operating conditions. while this **approach** is beneficial in making the **site** performance satisfactory in the most common working situations, it still leaves the site incapable to face sudden and unexpected surges of traffic. in this context , it is impossible to predict the intensity of the **overload**. this work is motivated by the need to formulate a fast **reactive and autonomous approach** to **admission control**. in particular, we propose an original **self- * overload control policy** (soc) which enables some fundamental self - * properties such as **self - configuration, self - optimization, self - protection**."

2. "we propose an autonomous **approach** to **admission control** in **distributed web systems**. the proposed **policy** is based on **self - configuration, self - optimization,** and **self - protection**. in particular, the proposed **system** is capable of self - configuring its **component level parameters** according to performance requirements, while at the same time it optimizes its own responsiveness to **overload**. at **session granularity** , it does not require any prior knowledge on the incoming traffic and can be applied to **non - session based** traffic as well."

MNELM model scores: NE precision = 0.91; NE recall = 0.49. MLM model scores: NE precision = 0.71; NE recall = 0.20.

Named Entity Recognition Based Automatic Generation of Research Highlights

Tohida Rehman
Jadavpur University, India
tohida.rehman@gmail.com

Debarshi Kumar Sanyal
Indian Association for the Cultivation of Science
debarshisanyal@gmail.com

Prasenjit Majumder
TCG CREST, India
prasenjit.majumder@gmail.com

Samiran Chattopadhyay
TCG CREST; Jadavpur University, India
samirancju@gmail.com

Abstract

A scientific paper is traditionally prefaced by an abstract that summarizes the paper. Recently, research highlights that focus on the main findings of the paper have emerged as a complementary summary in addition to an abstract. However, highlights are not yet as common as abstracts, and are absent in many papers. In this paper, we aim to automatically generate research highlights using different sections of a research paper as input. We investigate whether the use of named entity recognition on the input improves the quality of the generated highlights. In particular, we have used two deep learning-based models: the first is a pointer-generator network, and the second augments the first model with coverage mechanism. We then augment each of the above models with named entity recognition features. The proposed method can be used to produce highlights for papers with missing highlights. Our experiments show that adding named entity information improves the performance of the deep learning-based summarizers in terms of ROUGE, METEOR and BERTScore measures.

1 Introduction

Every research domain has an overabundance of textual information, with new research articles published on a daily basis. The number of scientific papers is increasing at an exponential rate (Bornmann et al., 2021). According to reports, the number of scientific articles roughly doubles every nine years (Van Noorden, 2014). For a researcher, keeping track of any research field is extremely difficult even in a narrow sub-field. Nowadays, many publishers request authors to provide a bulleted list of research highlights along with the abstract and the full text. It can help the reader to quickly grasp the main contributions of the paper.

Automatic text summarization is a process of shortening a document by creating a gist of it. It encapsulates the most important or relevant information from the original text. Scientific papers are generally longer documents than news stories and have a different discourse structure. Additionally, there are less resources available on scholarly documents to train text summarization systems. There are two broad approaches used in automatic text summarization (Luhn, 1958; Radev et al., 2002): Extractive summarization and abstractive summarization. Extractive summarization generally copies whole sentences from the input source text and combines them into a summary, discarding irrelevant sentences from the input (Jing and McKeown, 2000; Knight and Marcu, 2002). But recent trends use abstractive summarization which involves natural language generation to produce novel words and capture the salient information from the input text (Rush et al., 2015; Nallapati et al., 2016). Our aim is to generate research highlights from a research paper using an abstractive approach. But an abstractive summarizer using a generative model like a pointer-generator network (See et al., 2017) sometimes generates meaningless words in the output. In particular, for named entities which are multi-word strings, incorrect generation of a single word within the string (e.g., suppose instead of generating 'artificial neural network', it generates 'artificial network') may corrupt the meaning of the whole entity and its parent sentence. So we propose to perform named entity recognition (NER) on the input and treat a named entity as a single token before the input passes through the summarizer. This will avoid their fragmentation in the output.

The main contributions of this paper are:

1. We propose a mechanism to combine named entity recognition with pointer-generator networks having coverage mechanism to automatically generate research highlights, given the abstract of a research paper. To the best of our knowledge, this work is the first attempt to use NER in pointer-generators with coverage mechanism (See et al., 2017) to generate

Proceedings of the Third Workshop on Scholarly Document Processing, pages 163–169
October 12–17, 2022.

research highlights.

2. We analyze the performance of generating research highlights for the following different input types: (a) the input is the abstract only, (b) the input comprises the abstract and the conclusion, (c) the input comprises the introduction and the conclusion.

3. We evaluate the performance of the models using ROUGE (Lin, 2004), METEOR (Banerjee and Lavie, 2005), and BERTScore (Zhang et al., 2020b) metrics.

2 Literature survey

Early works on summarization of scientific articles include (Kupiec et al., 1995) where an extractive summarization technique is proposed and evaluated on a small dataset of 188 scientific documents, and (Teufel and Moens, 2002) which exploits the rhetorical status of assertions to summarize scientific articles. More recently, Lloret et al. (Lloret et al., 2013) have developed a new corpus of computer science papers from `arXiv.org` that contains pairs of (Introduction, Abstract). An approach proposed to generate abstracts from a research paper using Multiple Timescale model of the Gated Recurrent Unit (MTGRU) may be found in (Kim et al., 2016). Surveys on summarization of scholarly documents appears in (Altmami and Menai, 2020), (El-Kassas et al., 2021). Generating research highlights from scientific articles is not the same as document summarization. A supervised machine learning approach is proposed in (Collins et al., 2017) to identify relevant highlights from the full-text of a paper using a binary classifier. They have also contributed a new benchmark dataset containing author written research highlights for more than 10,000 documents. All documents adhere to a consistent discourse structure. Instead of a simple binary classification of sentences as highlights or not, (Cagliero and La Quatra, 2020) used multivariate regression methods to select the top-K most relevant sentences as research highlights. (Hassel, 2003) proposed a method to use appropriate weight for the named entity tagger into the SweSum summarizer for Swedish newspaper texts. (Marek et al., 2021) proposed an extractive summarization technique that determines a sentence's significance based on the density of named entities. (Rehman et al., 2021) used a pointer-generator model with coverage (See et al., 2017) to generate research highlights from abstracts. The present work, unlike the existing ones, uses NER to avoid incorrect phrases from being generated by the decoder. Note that pretrained summarization models like PEGASUS (Zhang et al., 2020a), T5 (Raffel et al., 2019), and BART (Devlin et al., 2019) are trained on generic texts. Fine-tuning them to a specific (e.g., scientific) domain requires large memory and computational resources; in this context, this paper provides a simpler alternative.

3 Methodology

We use a pointer-generator network (See et al., 2017) as our baseline model. While the pointer-generator model (See et al., 2017) first tokenizes a document using Stanford CoreNLP tokenizer and converts the tokens to word embeddings (trained with the model), the method we propose here performs NER on the input document and considers a named entity as a single token when training the model. We perform experiments with 4 variants: (1) the original pointer-generator model proposed in (See et al., 2017) (PGM), (2) pointer-generator model integrating coverage mechanism (proposed in (Tu et al., 2016)) (PGM + Cov), described in the same work (See et al., 2017), (3) NER-based pointer-generator model (NER + PGM), and (4) NER-based pointer-generator model with coverage mechanism (NER + PGM + Cov).

3.1 NER-based pointer-generator network

This model consists of an NER-based tokenizer layer and a pointer-generator network. The NER-based tokenizer layer converts the words in the input document to a sequence of tokens, thus preserving an entity name as a single token. In particular, it uses the named entity recognizer in spaCy[1] However, we do not use entity types. We do not use pretrained word embeddings as (Nallapati et al., 2016) do; in our case token embeddings are learned from scratch during training. Here, the main role of NER is that instead of directly feeding the normal tokens of the input document into the encoder, we are passing the NER-based tokens.

4 Experimental setup

4.1 Data sets

We use the data sets published by Collins et al. (Collins et al., 2017), which

[1] `https://spacy.io/usage/linguistic-features`.

Input	Model Name	ROUGE-1	ROUGE-2	ROUGE-L	METEOR	BERTScore
abstract only	PGM	35.44	11.57	29.88	25.4	83.80
	PGM + Cov	36.57	12.3	30.69	25.4	84.05
	NER + PGM	35.88	12.78	33.21	29.14	86.02
	NER + PGM + Cov	**38.13**	**13.68**	**35.11**	**31.03**	**86.3**
abstract + conclusion	PGM	29.85	8.16	25.80	19.38	83.19
	PGM + Cov	31.70	8.31	26.72	20.92	83.49
	NER + PGM	35.12	12.37	32.37	28.34	86.08
	NER + PGM + Cov	**37.48**	**13.26**	**34.95**	**28.97**	**86.64**
introduction + conclusion	PGM	29.78	7.47	25.15	19.25	83.05
	PGM + Cov	31.63	7.65	26.25	20.24	83.32
	NER + PGM	31.74	9.18	29.44	23.82	85.78
	NER + PGM + Cov	**34.24**	**9.82**	**31.92**	**25.36**	**86.1**

Table 1: Evaluation of pointer-generator type models: F1-scores for ROUGE, METEOR and BERTScore on various inputs from CSPubSumm dataset. All our ROUGE scores have a 95% confidence interval of at most ± 0.25 as reported by the official ROUGE script.

contains URLs of 10147 computer science publications from ScienceDirect (`https://www.sciencedirect.com/`). Title, abstract, author-written research highlights, a list of keywords referenced by the authors, introduction, related work, experiment, conclusion, and other important subsections as found in typical research papers are all included for each document. In our setup, every example in this data set is organised as follows: *(abstract, author-written research highlights, introduction, and conclusion)*. We use 8116 examples for training, 1017 examples for validation, and 1014 examples for testing.

4.2 Data processing

We have removed digits, punctuation, and special characters from the documents and lowercased the entire corpus. The `retokenizer.merge` method of spaCy is used to tokenize and merge several tokens into one single token based on the named entities in the document. Instead of individual tokens of "artificial", "neural", and "network", we pass all the three tokens together as a single token "artificial neural network" (referenced as vocab index 17). The data set is then reorganized in several ways to conduct various experiments. We organize the data set as *(abstract, author-written research highlights)*, *(abstract + conclusion, author-written research highlights)*, and *(introduction + conclusion, author-written research highlights)* where '+' denotes text concatenation. Since abstract and introduction usually emphasize the same aspects of the paper, we have not included them together. In this data set, the average abstract length is 186 tokens, while the average author-written-highlight length is 52 tokens. When we considered abstract and conclusion, the average length was 643. When we considered introduction and conclusion, the average length was 1234. Therefore in our model, we have set the maximum number of input tokens to 400 when the abstract is taken as the input. For all other cases, the maximum count of input tokens is set to 1500. In all cases, the generated research highlights have a maximum token count of 100. We trained all models on Tesla V100-SXM2-16GB `Colab Pro+` that supports GPU-based training. For all models, we used two bidirectional LSTMs with cell size of 256, word embeddings of dimension 128, and maximum vocabulary size of 50K tokens. We considered gradient clipping with a maximum gradient norm of 1.2. We use other hyperparameters as suggested by (See et al., 2017).

4.3 Comparison with previous works

Table 2 compares the performance of our proposed approach (NER + PGM + Cov) with other competitive baselines in the literature, on the CSPubSumm data set in terms of the ROUGE-L F1-score.

Model Name	ROUGE-L (F1)
LSTM (Collins et al., 2017)	29.50
GBR (Cagliero and La Quatra, 2020)	31.60
PGM + Cov + GloVe (Rehman et al., 2021)	29.14
NER + PGM + Cov (ours)	**35.11**

Table 2: Comparison of ROUGE-L (F1-score) of the proposed model with that of the other approaches.

Author-written research highlights: This paper studies an image collection planning problem for a korean satellite kompsat 2(korea multi purpose satellite 2). We present a binary integer programming model for this problem in a multi orbit long term planning environment. A heuristic solution approach based on the lagrangian relaxation and subgradient methods is provided.
PGM: Image collection with 2 korea 2 image acquisition [UNK] of segment square lengths as well as well as collection relaxation . Integer programming model exploiting lagrangian relaxation. Results of our computational experiment based on the lagrangian relaxation and subgradient methods.
PGM + Cov: Image collection planning problem with a multi orbit multi purpose satellite 2 korea multi purpose. A binary integer programming model for a multi orbit long term planning. A heuristic solution approach based on the lagrangian relaxation and subgradient methods. A heuristic solution approach based on the lagrangian relaxation and subgradient methods .
NER + PGM: We present a binary integer programming model for this image collection planning problem for a korean satellite kompsat. We present a binary integer programming model for this problem in a multi orbit long term planning environment. Combining the lagrangian relaxation and subgradient methods using the lagrangian relaxation and subgradient methods to solve the top problem.
NER + PGM + Cov: We present an image collection planning problem for a korean satellite kompsat. We present a binary integer programming model for image collection planning. We show the heuristic approach based on the lagrangian relaxation. We present the results on a multi orbit long term planning environment.

Figure 1: Input is only an abstract from CSPubSumm data set. Highlights produced by each of the four models are shown. Input and author-written research highlights taken `https://www.sciencedirect.com/science/article/pii/S037722171300307X`

5 Results

5.1 Comparison of pointer-generator type models

In this sub-section, we report the results of experiments on the CSPubSumm data set for various input types. Table 1 shows the F1-scores for ROUGE-1, ROUGE-2, ROUGE-L, METEOR and BERTScore metrics for various inputs from the test dataset. Among the four models, the NER-based pointer-generator network with coverage mechanism achieves the highest ROUGE, METEOR and BERTScore values. It appears that treating an entity as a single token in the input helps to learn better embeddings and results in more controlled generation of the output, thereby reducing semantically invalid words and phrases. We aim to investigate this aspect in future. The (NER + PGM + Cov) model achieves the highest scores when the input is the abstract, indicating that most of the findings reported by the research highlights are already in the abstract, and adding additional sections to the input contributes to noise for the model.

5.2 Case study

Figure 1, 2 and 3 shows sample outputs generated by our models for various input types. In all the case studies reported below, we highlight examples of factual errors , repeating words and correct named entities . Note that the NER-based models correctly generate the named entities in the output.

5.3 Manual evaluation

We selected a set of 25 papers, their author-written highlights (**A**) and their highlights from only the (NER + PGM + Cov) model (**M**). We recruited 16 human annotators (possessing or pursuing advanced degrees in software engineering at premier universities in India) to independently rate a given summary on a scale of 1(low) to 5(high) for adequacy and fluency (separately). Each rater was given the full text of a paper and *either* the author-written *or* the machine-generated highlights of the paper, but not told which one. Each summary was rated independently by two raters. On fluency, the average score for **A** was 4.02 and that for **M** was 3.3, while on adequacy, the average score for **A** was 3.82 and that for **M** was 3.12. This shows the machine-generated highlights are only slightly worse than the human-written ones.

6 Conclusion

We applied four different deep neural models to generate research highlights from a research paper. The NER-based pointer-generator model with coverage mechanism achieved the best performance in all cases. In future, we intend to investigate in detail why NER improves the generated highlights. We also aim to ensure that the generated highlights are correct in syntax and semantics.

Author-written research highlights: We present a lightweight non parametric approach to generate wrinkles for 3d facial modeling and animation. Our method represents a convenient approach for generating plausible facial wrinkles with low cost. Our method enables the reconstruction of captured expressions with wrinkles in real time.

PGM: We propose a non parametric facial modeling 3d face models from the 3d facial modeling . Synthesize the 3d face expression model with 3d depth camera is considered. Propose a non parametric face method to evaluate the performance of the 3d facial modeling . Method is provided to evaluate the performance of the proposed approach with respect to the existing method.

PGM + Cov: We propose non parametric face acquisition 3d facial modeling models. Face expression model is based on the texture synthesis of multiple subjects. Synthesis method guarantees to 3d face face acquisition. One high quality 3d face model is studied.

NER + PGM: A novel synthesis method is proposed to enhance the wrinkles using a single low cost kinect camera. The lightweight feature of the method is that it can generate plausible wrinkles using a single low cost kinect camera and one high quality 3d face model with details as the example. User specific expressions are used as blendshapes to capture facial animations in real time kinect camera and one high quality 3d face model with details.

NER + PGM + Cov: We present a lightweight non parametric method to generate wrinkles for 3d facial modeling and animation. The lightweight feature of the method is that it can generate plausible wrinkles. Our method is low cost and convenient for common users.

Figure 2: Input is (abstract + conclusion) from CSPubSumm data set. Highlights produced by each of the four models are shown. Input and author-written research highlights taken `https://www.sciencedirect.com/science/article/pii/S0010448514001857`

Author-written research highlights: We propose a novel parallel 3d delaunay meshing algorithm for large scale simulations. The model information is kept during parallel triangulation process. A 3d local non delaunay mesh repair algorithm is proposed. The meshing results can be very approaching to the model boundary. The method can achieve high parallel performance and perfect scalability.

PGM: We propose a solid model boundary preserving method for large scale parallel 3d delaunay meshing. Parallel 3d local mesh 3d delaunay meshing algorithm is proposed. Mesh reconstruction is iteratively performed to meet both the mesh and the shared interfaces . Propose a parallel 3d local mesh reconstruction algorithm to construct delaunay triangulation . Results show high performance and perfect scalability.

PGM + Cov: A new semantic parallel algorithm is proposed for large scale parallel 3d delaunay meshing. Numerical local mesh is the sampling vertices for the problem 3d delaunay meshing. Propose a parallel su based partitioning algorithm by solving the algorithm . Proposed algorithm is highly parallelized to large scale sets and high quality partition walls.

NER + PGM: We propose a solid model boundary preserving method for large scale 3d delaunay meshing. The 3d boundary representation model information is kept during the entire parallel 3d delaunay triangulation process. The 3d boundary representation model information is kept during the entire parallel 3d delaunay triangulation process . A parallel 3d local mesh optimization algorithm is presented. Experimental results demonstrate high performance and perfect scalability.

NER + PGM + Cov: We propose a solid model boundary preserving method for large scale parallel delaunay meshing. The 3d boundary representation model information is during the entire parallel 3d delaunay triangulation process. A parallel local mesh refinement algorithm to repair the non delaunay mesh is proposed. A parallel 3d delaunay mesh refinement is presented. Experimental results demonstrate scalability performance.

Figure 3: Input is (introduction + conclusion) from CSPubSumm data set. Highlights produced by each of the four models are shown. Input and author-written research highlights taken `https://www.sciencedirect.com/science/article/pii/S0010448514001821`

References

Nouf Ibrahim Altmami and Mohamed El Bachir Menai. 2020. Automatic summarization of scientific articles: A survey. *Journal of King Saud University-Computer and Information Sciences*.

Satanjeev Banerjee and Alon Lavie. 2005. METEOR: An automatic metric for mt evaluation with improved correlation with human judgments. In *Proceedings of the ACL Workshop on Intrinsic and Extrinsic Evaluation Measures for Machine Translation and/or Summarization*, pages 65–72.

Lutz Bornmann, Robin Haunschild, and Rüdiger Mutz. 2021. Growth rates of modern science: A latent piecewise growth curve approach to model publication numbers from established and new literature databases. *Humanities and Social Sciences Communications*, 8(1):1–15.

Luca Cagliero and Moreno La Quatra. 2020. Extracting highlights of scientific articles: A supervised summarization approach. *Expert Systems with Applications*, 160:113659.

Ed Collins, Isabelle Augenstein, and Sebastian Riedel. 2017. A supervised approach to extractive summarisation of scientific papers. In *Proceedings of the 21st Conference on Computational Natural Language Learning (CoNLL 2017)*, pages 195–205. Association for Computational Linguistics.

Jacob Devlin, Ming-Wei Chang, Kenton Lee, and Kristina Toutanova. 2019. BERT: Pre-training of deep bidirectional transformers for language understanding. In *Proceedings of the 2019 Conference of the North American Chapter of the Association for Computational Linguistics: Human Language Technologies, Volume 1 (Long and Short Papers)*, pages 4171–4186.

Wafaa S El-Kassas, Cherif R Salama, Ahmed A Rafea, and Hoda K Mohamed. 2021. Automatic text summarization: A comprehensive survey. *Expert Systems with Applications*, 165:113679.

Martin Hassel. 2003. Exploitation of named entities in automatic text summarization for swedish. In *NODALIDA'03–14th Nordic Conferenceon Computational Linguistics, Reykjavik, Iceland, May 30–31 2003*, page 9.

Hongyan Jing and Kathleen McKeown. 2000. Cut and paste based text summarization. In *1st Meeting of the North American Chapter of the Association for Computational Linguistics*.

Minsoo Kim, Dennis Singh Moirangthem, and Minho Lee. 2016. Towards abstraction from extraction: Multiple timescale gated recurrent unit for summarization. In *Proceedings of the 1st Workshop on Representation Learning for NLP*, pages 70–77, Berlin, Germany. Association for Computational Linguistics.

Kevin Knight and Daniel Marcu. 2002. Summarization beyond sentence extraction: A probabilistic approach to sentence compression. *Artificial Intelligence*, 139(1):91–107.

Julian Kupiec, Jan Pedersen, and Francine Chen. 1995. A trainable document summarizer. In *Proceedings of the 18th Annual International ACM SIGIR Conference on Research and Development in Information Retrieval*, pages 68–73.

Chin-Yew Lin. 2004. ROUGE: A package for automatic evaluation of summaries. In *Text Summarization Branches Out*, pages 74–81.

Elena Lloret, María Teresa Romá-Ferri, and Manuel Palomar. 2013. Compendium: A text summarization system for generating abstracts of research papers. *Data & Knowledge Engineering*, 88:164–175.

Hans Peter Luhn. 1958. The automatic creation of literature abstracts. *IBM Journal of research and development*, 2(2):159–165.

Petr Marek, Štěpán Müller, Jakub Konrád, Petr Lorenc, Jan Pichl, and Jan Šedivý. 2021. Text summarization of Czech news articles using named entities. *arXiv preprint arXiv:2104.10454*.

Ramesh Nallapati, Bowen Zhou, Caglar Gulcehre, Bing Xiang, et al. 2016. Abstractive text summarization using sequence-to-sequence rnns and beyond. *arXiv preprint arXiv:1602.06023*.

Dragomir Radev, Eduard Hovy, and Kathleen McKeown. 2002. Introduction to the special issue on summarization. *Computational Linguistics*, 28(4):399–408.

Colin Raffel, Noam Shazeer, Adam Roberts, Katherine Lee, Sharan Narang, Michael Matena, Yanqi Zhou, Wei Li, and Peter J Liu. 2019. Exploring the limits of transfer learning with a unified text-to-text transformer. *arXiv preprint arXiv:1910.10683*.

Tohida Rehman, Debarshi Kumar Sanyal, Samiran Chattopadhyay, Plaban Kumar Bhowmick, and Partha Pratim Das. 2021. Automatic generation of research highlights from scientific abstracts. In *EEKE@ JCDL*, pages 69–70.

Alexander M Rush, Sumit Chopra, and Jason Weston. 2015. A neural attention model for abstractive sentence summarization. *arXiv preprint arXiv:1509.00685*.

A. See, Peter J. Liu, and Christopher D. Manning. 2017. Get to the point: Summarization with pointer-generator networks. In *Proceedings of the 55th Annual Meeting of the Association for Computational Linguistics (Volume 1: Long Papers)*.

Simone Teufel and Marc Moens. 2002. Articles summarizing scientific articles: Experiments with relevance and rhetorical status. *Computational Linguistics*, 28(4):409–445.

Zhaopeng Tu, Zhengdong Lu, Yang Liu, Xiaohua Liu, and Hang Li. 2016. Modeling coverage for neural machine translation. In *Proceedings of the 54th Annual Meeting of the Association for Computational Linguistics*, pages 76–85.

Richard Van Noorden. 2014. Global scientific output doubles every nine years. *Nature News blog*.

Jingqing Zhang, Yao Zhao, Mohammad Saleh, and Peter Liu. 2020a. PEGASUS: Pre-training with extracted gap-sentences for abstractive summarization. In *Proceedings of the International Conference on Machine Learning (ICLR)*, pages 11328–11339. PMLR.

Tianyi Zhang, Varsha Kishore, Felix Wu, Kilian Q Weinberger, and Yoav Artzi. 2020b. BERTScore: Evaluating text generation with BERT. In *International Conference on Learning Representations*.

Citation Sentence Generation Leveraging the Content of Cited Papers

Akito Arita
Osaka Institute of Technology
m21a02@oit.ac.jp

Hiroaki Sugiyama
NTT Communication Science Laboratories
h.sugi@ieee.org

Kohji Dohsaka,Rikuto Tanaka
Akita Prefectural University
{dohsaka,B20P025}@akita-pu.ac.jp

Hirotoshi Taira
Osaka Institute of Technology
hirotoshi.taira@oit.ac.jp

Abstract

We address automatic citation sentence generation, which reduces the burden on writing scientific papers. For highly accurate citation senetence generation, appropriate language must be learned using information such as the relationship between the cited source and the cited paper as well as the context in which the paper cited. Although the abstracts of papers have been used for the generation in the past, they often contain extra information in the citation sentence, which might negatively impact the generation of citation sentences. Therefore, this study attempts to learn a highly accurate citation sentence generation model using sentences from cited articles that resemble the previous sentence to the cited location, thereby utilizing information that is more useful for citation sentence generation.

1 Introduction

In recent years, the use of such preprint servers as arXiv (McKiernan, 2000) has increased the amount of scientific literature. With this, we need a lot of citations to write a new paper and writing the related work section has become time-consuming. The development of automatic citation sentence generation system can support the writing of papers and relieve scientific researcher's burden on tracking and editing citations (Wu et al., 2021; Narimatsu et al., 2021). There have been several studies on citation sentence generation. Hoang and Kan (2010) constructed a keyword-based tree from the cited papers and utilized to generate citation sentences. Xing et al. (2020) used a multi-source pointer-generator network with cross attention mechanism to generate a single citation sentence for a single citation. Wu et al. (2021) used the Fution-in-Decoder (FiD) model (Izacard and Grave, 2021) to generate citation sentences for citing multiple papers, which is commonplace in real papers. They also consider differences in citation intent (Cohan et al., 2019). There are many different relationships between citing paper and the cited papers. The expression of the citation depends on what the intent of the citation is.

Citation intent such as background information, methods, and comparison of results which is important to improve the quality of citation sentence generation.

Citation sentence generation methods, that have been proposed in recent years, often use deep learning, which has the limitation of word sequence size. For that reason, most previous works have used abstracts of the citing and cited papers (Xing et al., 2020; Ge et al., 2021; Wu et al., 2021), that are relatively short to the entire paper, to recognize the relationship between them and generate the citation sentence.

A single sentence in the abstract is compact in length and merely expresses an overview of the characteristics of the study. However, citation sentences are often sentences that describe in detail the differences in characteristics between the citing and cited papers. The information in the sentences in the abstracts tends to be rather coarse to generate a description of those relationships, and this is one of the reasons for the lower quality of citation sentence generation.

On the other hand, in the task of generating sentences describing the relationship between two papers, which is different from citation sentence generation, Luu et al. (2021) used sentences in the introduction, rather than in the abstract of the paper, to generate high-quality, sentences describing the relationship between the two papers.

Inspired by this work, we propose a method to use all the sentences in the cited and citing papers. In order to reduce the input size to the neural network, our method retrieves and uses useful sentences for generating citation sentences from all the sentences in the cited paper with reference to

Proceedings of the Third Workshop on Scholarly Document Processing, pages 170–174
October 12–17, 2022.

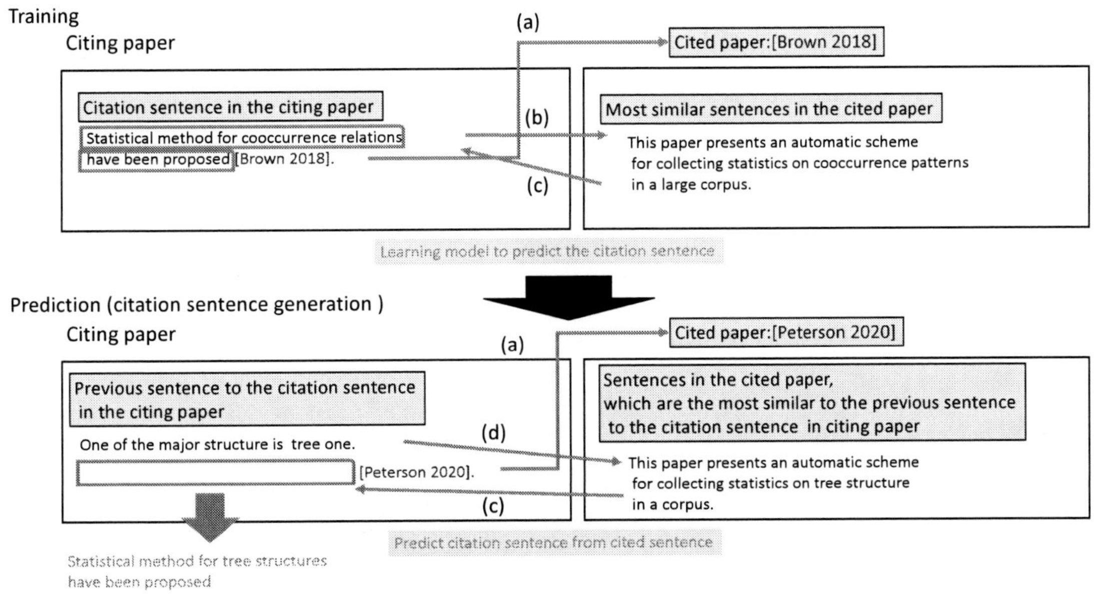

Figure 1: Overview of our method

the contents of the citing paper. The mehod finds a sentence from the cited paper, semantically similar to the previous sentence of the citation sentence to be generated, and uses it as input for generating it. Experiments with an evaluation dataset show that the method improves accuracy by about 2 points in ROUGE evaluation, compared to the method that uses only abstracts as input to generate citations.

2 Proposed Method

Citation generation is the task of generating the citation sentence to describe a cited paper under the context in a citing paper.

Figure 1 illustrates an overview of our proposed method. In the training phase, the mehod consists of three steps: a) preparing the full text of the cited papers contained in the citation sentences in the training data; b) extracting semantically similar sentences to each citation sentence from the cited papers using cosine similarity; c) learning to generate citation sentence from the semantically similar sentences.

In the prediction phase, the mehod consists of three steps: a) preparing the full text of the cited papers contained in the quoted sentences in the test data; d) extracting sentences from the cited papers that are semantically similar to the previous sentence in the target citation using cosine similarity; c) learning to generate citations from semantically similar sentences.

The major difference between training and prediction is in steps b) and d). In step b) of training phase, the system extracts sentences from the cited papers, that are similar to the citation sentence and useful for generating the citation sentence.

On the other hand, in step d) of prediction phase, the system extracts the two sentences immediately before the citation sentence, because we cannot use the citation sentence, which is the sentence itself to generate and does not exist in the phase.

To utilize the all sentences of a cited paper, excluding its abstract, the text is divided into sentences using NLTK (Loper and Bird, 2002), and we calculated the embedded representation of each sentence using SentenceBERT (Reimers and Gurevych, 2019).

In the step c), we performe fine-tuning a pre-trained model for generating citation sentences. We used T5 (Raffel et al., 2020) as a pre-trained model.

3 Experiments

We observed changes in the accuracy of the generated citation sentences by combining the citation intent, the citing paper's abstract, the citation context, the cited paper's abstract, and the cited paper's content. Then we investigated which in-

Table 1: Experimental results for each combination of inputs

Model	Citing abstract	**Citing context**	Cited abstract	**Cited content**	Citation Intent	ROUGE-1	ROUGE-2	ROUGE-L
A	✓		✓		✓	20.87	2.60	15.40
B	✓			✓	✓	21.02	2.54	14.30
C		✓	✓		✓	19.44	2.14	14.11
D		✓		✓	✓	**22.08**	**3.43**	**16.52**

formation contributes to the generation of citation sentences.

3.1 Experimental Data

We used the citation sentence generation dataset created by Xing et al. (2020) for the evaluation data. It is based on the ACL Anthology Network (AAN) corpus (Radev et al., 2013), which consists of 21,121 papers in computational linguistics and contains citation relationship information for them. The dataset is based on the assignment of pseudo-labels for all of the citations in the AAN corpus, using a model trained by 1,000 manually labeled sentences. The training data consisted of 85,652 sentences, and the test data consisted of 400 sentences. However, since we found that some of the test data were also included in the training data, we removed 103 duplicated sentences from the training data.

3.2 Experimental Settings

The input available size for the deep neural network was limited, and we could not use all sentences in the cited paper for learning to generate the citation setence. Therefore, we used the top six sentences in the cited paper, with a cosine similarity of 0.6 or more. If the number of sentences more than the threshold was less than three, we used the top three sentences. These extracted similar sentences, which were to be used as the cited paper's content,were concatenated for both training and prediction.

We used the following citation intent categories defined by Cohan et al. (2019): "Background information," "Method" and "Result comparison." Since "Result comparison" is divided into two labels, "supportive" and "not supportive," we have a total of four labels. These four citation intent categories were automatically assigned to the citation sentence by the Cohan et al. (2019) model.

We assigned a prefix token to the beginning of the text so that the citation generation model could recognize the type of data given during training. The citation intent was assigned a prefix token such as "cit_intent:".

In our experiments, we used T5-base (Raffel et al., 2020) as a pre-trained model for generating citation sentences and performed fine-tuning. We used ROUGE-1, ROUGE-2, and ROUGE-L (Lin, 2004), to calculate the abstract evaluation score.

3.3 Experimental Results

We combined the input data and show the resulting accuracy of our experiments in Table 1. We compared the two types of methods to test whether the abstracts of cited papers or their content contributed to accuracy and confirmed that the cited content only improved accuracy when combined with the citation content.

First, we compared A and B in Figure 1. A and B use the abstract as the information on the cited paper side, and A uses abstract as the information on the cited paper side, while B uses content. Compared to A , B is 0.15 points higher in the ROUGE-1 evaluation, and 0.06 points and 1.1 points lower in the ROUGE-2 and ROUGE-L evaluations. Second, we compared C and D in Figure 1. C and D use the citing context as the information on the citing paper side, and C uses abstract as the information on the cited paper side, while D uses content. Compared to C, D showed that ROUGE-1, ROUGE-2, and ROUGE-L improved by 2.64, 1.29, and 2.41 points,when the cited content was used. These results confirm that cited content alone is not particularly meaningful, and that accuracy can only be improved by using the citing and cited content.

Next, examples of the citation sentence generation results using the proposed method and a baseline method using abstracts as input, are shown in Table 2.

Our proposed method is expected to extract sen-

Table 2: Example of citation sentence generation using the proposed method

Citation intent : Background
Previous sentences to citation sentence (citation context) :
For example, whereas the first sentence of a news paper might be an effective abstract of its contents.
Of course ... identify what genre or genres a text belongs to.
Sentences in cited paper (three of sentences most similar to the citation context):
(1st) The genre of a text can also be very important
(2nd) Genres in terms of author/speaker purpose, while text types classify texts
(3rd) Which form the basis for assigning a given text to a certain genre are reflected ···
Target (ground truth):
Fortunately, there is a growing body of work on genre based text classification, including.
Baseline method's output (input both abstracts):
The resulting results are based on the results of #REFR, which is a German equivalent of the Brown corpus.
Proposed method's output (using cited paper content):
This is a problem that has been explored in previous work on genre of text categorisation.

tences that are semantically similar to the citation context in the cited paper's content. In the actual example, some similar words appear: "text," "genre," "belongings," and "assigning," indicating that keywords that are basically common to a topic.

Next we discuss a case where the most accurate citation context and the cited paper's content are used as input, based on the generation results. The proposed method's generation results show that words are generated that are synonymous with the common words discussed earlier: "genre," "text," and "categorisation." Words that are synonymous with "genre," "text," and "classification" were also generated in the actual citation sentence. The above results confirm that the characteristic keywords overlap. This suggests that the reason for the large increase in accuracy when the citation context and the cited paper's content are input as a set is that the keywords appear multiple times in both the citation context and the cited paper's content.

Next we analysed the training data by examining the proportion of words that overlap with the citations in each set of paper abstracts, citation contexts, and the cited paper's content. The results showed that the proportion of words overlapping with citations is 24% in the abstracts and 30% for the citation contexts and the cited papers's content. This is 6 points increase indicates that unnecessary information is more likely to be included in the generation of citations than in abstracts.

Finally, we discuss the generation results of our proposed method when the citation context and the cited paper's content are entered as a set, and when the baseline paper abstracts are entered. The baseline generation results are quite different compared to the actual citations that we used, because a paper's abstract summarizes an entire paper. Hence it is unclear which sentences of a given text should be focused on to generate citations. This situation resembles the results analysed above, which show that citations are more likely to contain unnecessary information.

4 Conclusion

We performed the task of generating an appropriate citation sentence from a citing paper, cited papers, and the citation context. While citation sentence generation in previous studies has been based on sentences in abstracts, we proposed citation sentence generation based on sentences in the citing paper and the cited papers. Experimental results show that our proposed method is more accurate in generating citation sentences than the conventional method of using sentences in abstracts. In the future, we will evaluate using people or other methods than ROUGE and larger citation datasets.

References

Arman Cohan, Waleed Ammar, Madeleine van Zuylen, and Field Cady. 2019. Structural scaffolds for citation intent classification in scientific publications. In *Proceedings of the 2019 Conference of the North American Chapter of the Association for Computational Linguistics: Human Language Technologies (NAACL-HLT)*, pages 3586–3596.

Yubin Ge, Ly Dinh, Xiaofeng Liu, Jinsong Su, Ziyao Lu, Ante Wang, and Jana Diesner. 2021. BACO: A background knowledge-and content-based framework for citing sentence generation. In *Proceedings of the 59th Annual Meeting of the Association for Computational Linguistics and the 11th International Joint Conference on Natural Language Processing (ACL-IJCNLP)*, pages 1466–1478.

Cong Duy Vu Hoang and Min-Yen Kan. 2010. Towards automated related work summarization. In *Proceedings of the 23rd International Conference on Computational Linguistics (COLING)*.

Gautier Izacard and Edouard Grave. 2021. Leveraging passage retrieval with generative models for open domain question answering. In *Proceedings of the 16th Conference of the European Chapter of the Association for Computational Linguistics (EACL)*, pages 874–880.

Chin-Yew Lin. 2004. ROUGE: A package for automatic evaluation of summaries. In *proceedings of the ACL-04 Workshop: Text summarization branches out*, pages 74–81.

Edward Loper and Steven Bird. 2002. NLTK: The natural language toolkit. In *Proceedings of the ACL-02 Workshop on Effective Tools and Methodologies for Teaching Natural Language Processing and Computational Linguistics*, pages 63–70.

Kelvin Luu, Xinyi Wu, Rik Koncel-Kedziorski, Kyle Lo, Isabel Cachola, and Noah A Smith. 2021. Explaining relationships between scientific documents. In *Proceedings of the 59th Annual Meeting of the Association for Computational Linguistics and the 11th International Joint Conference on Natural Language Processing (ACL-IJCNLP)*, pages 2130–2144.

Gerry McKiernan. 2000. arXiv.org: the Los Alamos National Laboratory e-print server. *International Journal on Grey Literature*, 1:127–138.

Hiromi Narimatsu, Kohei Koyama, Kohji Dohsaka, Ryuichiro Higashinaka, Yasuhiro Minami, and Hirotoshi Taira. 2021. Task definition and integration for scientific-document writing support. In *Proceedings of the Second Workshop on Scholarly Document Processing (SDP)*, pages 18–26. Association for Computational Linguistics.

Dragomir R Radev, Pradeep Muthukrishnan, Vahed Qazvinian, and Amjad Abu-Jbara. 2013. The ACL anthology network corpus. *Language Resources and Evaluation*, 47(4):919–944.

Colin Raffel, Noam Shazeer, Adam Roberts, Katherine Lee, Sharan Narang, Michael Matena, Yanqi Zhou, Wei Li, Peter J Liu, et al. 2020. Exploring the limits of transfer learning with a unified text-to-text transformer. *Journal of Machine Learning Research*, 21(140):1–67.

Nils Reimers and Iryna Gurevych. 2019. Sentence-BERT: Sentence embeddings using siamese BERT-networks. In *Proceedings of the 2019 Conference on Empirical Methods in Natural Language Processing and the 9th International Joint Conference on Natural Language Processing (EMNLP-IJCNLP)*, pages 3982–3992.

Jia-Yan Wu, Alexander Te-Wei Shieh, Shih-Ju Hsu, and Yun-Nung Chen. 2021. Towards generating citation sentences for multiple references with intent control. *arXiv preprint arXiv:2112.01332*.

Xinyu Xing, Xiaosheng Fan, and Xiaojun Wan. 2020. Automatic generation of citation texts in scholarly papers: A pilot study. In *Proceedings of the 58th Annual Meeting of the Association for Computational Linguistics (ACL)*, pages 6181–6190.

Overview of MSLR2022: A Shared Task on Multi-document Summarization for Literature Reviews

Lucy Lu Wang[1,2], **Jay DeYoung**[3], **Byron Wallace**[3]
[1]Information School, University of Washington, Seattle, WA, USA
[2]Allen Institute for AI, Seattle, WA, USA
[3]Khoury College of Computer Sciences, Northeastern University, Boston, MA, USA
lucylw@uw.edu; {deyoung.j, b.wallace}@northeastern.edu

Abstract

We provide an overview of the MSLR2022 shared task on multi-document summarization for literature reviews.[1] The shared task was hosted at the Third Scholarly Document Processing (SDP) Workshop at COLING 2022. For this task, we provided data consisting of gold summaries extracted from review papers along with the groups of input abstracts that were synthesized into these summaries, split into two summarization subtasks. In total, six teams participated, making 10 public submissions, 6 to the Cochrane subtask and 4 to the MS^2 subtask. The top scoring systems reported over 2 points ROUGE-L improvement on the Cochrane subtask, though performance improvements are not consistently reported across all automated evaluation metrics; qualitative examination of the results also suggests the inadequacy of current evaluation metrics for capturing factuality and consistency on this task. Significant work is needed to improve system performance, and more importantly, to develop better methods for automatically evaluating performance on this task.

1 Introduction

Systematic literature reviews aim to comprehensively summarize evidence from all available studies relevant to a research question. In medicine, such reviews constitute the highest quality evidence used to inform clinical care. Reviews are expensive to produce manually, taking teams of experts months to years to complete, and go out of date quickly (Shojania et al., 2007); (semi-)automation may facilitate faster evidence synthesis without sacrificing rigor. Toward this end, we initiated the MSLR2022 shared task to investigate challenges in multi-document summarization and synthesis for medical literature review. In addition to soliciting direct submissions towards the task, we encouraged work extending our task/datasets, e.g., proposing scaffolding tasks, methods for model interpretability, and improved automated evaluation methods.

We organized the task into two subtasks based on two datasets we provided: MS^2 (DeYoung et al., 2021) and Cochrane (Wallace et al., 2020). We received submissions and/or system reports from six participating groups. A selection of generated summaries from the final submissions will be sampled and subject to human annotation for quality and consistency against the gold summaries. The human annotations produced following the shared task will be released as a public dataset to encourage further work on this task and its associated automated evaluation metrics. In the rest of this overview, we provide descriptions of the shared task (Section 2), the baseline models (Section 3), submitted systems (Section 4), and a summary of insights and directions for future work (Section 5).

2 Task description

We give a brief description of the datasets, task, evaluation metrics, and submission protocol for the shared task.

Datasets We provided two datasets for model iteration and evaluation. The MS^2 dataset consists of 20k reviews (comprising 470K studies) from the literature to study the task of generating review summaries (DeYoung et al., 2021). Reviews and studies for MS^2 were collected from PubMed. Input studies were filtered from cited articles using keyword heuristics and a SciBERT-based suitability classifier trained on human annotations, and the target summary was extracted from the review abstract using a SciBERT-based sequential sentence classifier trained on manually-labeled sentences from over 200 abstracts (see DeYoung et al. (2021) for details). Target summaries in the test set were manually reviewed and corrected. In addition to the abstracts of input studies and summaries, MS^2 extracts a background section from each review as

[1]https://github.com/allenai/mslr-shared-task

Proceedings of the Third Workshop on Scholarly Document Processing, pages 175–180
October 12–17, 2022.

context for the research question.

The Cochrane dataset consists of 4.6K reviews from the Cochrane Library (Wallace et al., 2020).[2] The target summaries are the Authors' Conclusions sections of the review abstracts. The Cochrane dataset is smaller and more consistent than the MS^2 dataset since all Cochrane reviews follow a similar process. For more information on dataset construction, please refer to the original dataset papers (DeYoung et al., 2021; Wallace et al., 2020).

Task Given the abstracts of input studies pertaining to a research question (and in the case of MS^2, a background section describing that research question), the task is to produce a summary that synthesizes the information from the input studies. The synthesis of information typically results in an evidence "direction," e.g., the evidence overall suggests that the intervention studied *increases/decreases/does not change* the outcome measure for the studied population (DeYoung et al., 2020). The direction of the evidence indicated in a good generated summary should agree with that in the reference (gold) summary.

Evaluation We perform automated evaluation using ROUGE (Lin, 2004), BERTScore (Zhang et al., 2020), and the *evidence inference* (Lehman et al., 2019) divergence metric defined in Wallace et al. (2020) and modified by DeYoung et al. (2021). For ROUGE, we report ROUGE-1, ROUGE-2, and ROUGE-L. For the evidence inference-based metric, we report the average divergence (ΔEI Avg) and the Macro-F1 (ΔEI F1) computed using a model trained on the dataset provided by DeYoung et al. (2020).

For human evaluation, we developed and iterated on an annotation protocol based on the analysis conducted by Otmakhova et al. (2022b). For each annotation task, annotators are shown a gold summary and a generated summary and asked to assess the latter for (i) fluency and (ii) agreement with the gold summary in terms of the "PICO" element alignment,[3] evidence inference directional agreement, and alignment regarding the strength of the claims made in summaries. We will provide further details on human annotation results following the shared task meeting.

Submissions Leaderboards for submissions are provided for the two subtasks: MS^2[4] and Cochrane.[5] Submissions to the leaderboard are judged against the gold summaries in the test splits using the automated metrics described previously.

3 Baselines

We provide several baseline models for comparison. Baseline models from DeYoung et al. (2021) are based on the BART (Lewis et al., 2020) and Longformer (Beltagy et al., 2020) architectures. For both subtasks, we report results of the two baseline models finetuned on the subtask dataset and evaluated on the corresponding subtask test set, as well as on the opposing test set (e.g. trained on MS^2 and tested on Cochrane and vice versa).

For MS^2, we also evaluate the condition of simply providing the background section as the generated summary. This baseline performs relatively well, indicating potential limitations of the chosen automated evaluated metrics as alluded to in Otmakhova et al. (2022b).

4 Participating systems

We provide brief descriptions of all participating systems. System performance as assessed using automated evaluation metrics are given in Table 1.

ITTC (Otmakhova et al., 2022a) The team adapted PRIMERA (Xiao et al., 2022), a model based on Longformer Encoder-Decoder (Beltagy et al., 2020) that has been designed for multi-document summarization, resulting in strong performance on the MSLR Cochrane subtask. In addition to fine-tuning on the entire training sets of the MSLR shared task, the team also experimented with zero- and few- shot learning scenarios. The authors found that ROUGE did not adequately capture the performance drops observed in the zero- and 10-shot settings, where factuality of the generated summaries was poor. The team also experiment with using global attention to highlight PICO elements in the input and target texts. Though ROUGE did not vary significantly between these two settings, the authors found that when PICO spans are given global attention, the resulting summaries tended to be more abstractive.

LongT5-Pubmed (Yu, 2022) The author attempted to finetune a LongT5 model (Guo et al.,

[2]Cochrane is an international non-profit dedicated to using evidence to inform decision-making.

[3]A framework describing question important to evidence-based medicine. PICO stands for Population/Problem, Intervention, Comparator, and Outcome.

[4]https://leaderboard.allenai.org/mslr-ms2/

[5]https://leaderboard.allenai.org/mslr-cochrane/

Submitted system (Cochrane)	R-1↑	R-2↑	R-L↑	BERTScore↑	ΔEI-Avg↓	ΔEI-F1↓
SciSpace (Shinde et al., 2022)	**0.262**	0.057	**0.197**	0.859	0.223	0.301
ITTC-2 (Otmakhova et al., 2022a)	0.246	**0.069**	0.184	**0.876**	**0.220**	0.309
LED-base-16k (Giorgi et al., 2022)	0.257	0.066	0.180	0.871	0.275	0.399
ITTC-1 (Otmakhova et al., 2022a)	0.241	0.064	0.179	0.873	0.288	0.338
PuneICT (Tangsali et al., 2022)	0.247	0.055	0.173	0.859	0.271	0.379
LongT5-Pubmed (Yu, 2022)	0.113	0.015	0.090	0.786	0.467	**0.287**
Baselines						
BART-Cochrane	0.240	0.067	0.176	0.863	0.208	0.335
Longformer-Cochrane	0.239	0.066	0.176	0.864	0.235	0.332
Longformer-MS^2	0.224	0.054	0.162	0.857	0.375	0.375
BART-MS^2	0.230	0.054	0.161	0.854	0.436	0.364

Submitted system (MS^2)	R-1↑	R-2↑	R-L↑	BERTScore↑	ΔEI-Avg↓	ΔEI-F1↓
LED-base-16k (Giorgi et al., 2022)	**0.275**	**0.092**	**0.206**	**0.869**	**0.487**	0.424
PuneICT (Tangsali et al., 2022)	0.206	0.035	0.144	0.848	0.532	0.356
LongT5-Pubmed (Yu, 2022)	0.120	0.013	0.096	0.828	0.528	**0.343**
Baselines						
Longformer-MS^2	0.264	0.080	0.196	0.867	0.462	0.412
BART-MS^2	0.263	0.077	0.195	0.864	0.451	0.414
Copying background section	0.268	0.085	0.181	0.854	0.502	0.395
BART-Cochrane	0.242	0.061	0.170	0.857	0.460	0.331
Longformer-Cochrane	0.221	0.042	0.153	0.850	0.441	0.277

Table 1: System performance for the Cochrane (above) and MS^2 (below) subtasks. For baseline systems, the suffix '-MS^2' means the model is trained on the MS^2 training data, while '-Cochrane' means the model is trained on the Cochrane training data. Top scores among submitting systems are **bolded**; systems are ordered by ROUGE-L.

2022) on the MSLR datasets but found that training was cost and resource prohibitive. The final model submitted to the leaderboards is a LongT5 model pretrained on the Pubmed corpus but which had not been finetuned to the MSLR datasets.

Extract+BART-base (Obonyo et al., 2022) The team explored how input selection strategies can improve the performance of a BART-base mode. The authors fined BART-base on the summarization dataset introduced by Cohan et al. (2018). They considered several extractive techniques to reduce the size of the input sequence, comparing Text-Rank, LexRank, and models for results extraction to select salient sentences from input documents. Their results suggest that input sampling strategies are promising, though performance gains are inconsistent across the two MSLR subtasks.

PuneICT (Tangsali et al., 2022) The team experimented with finetuning BART-large, DistillBART, and T5-base for both the MS^2 and Cochrane subtasks. On the MS^2 subtask, finetuned BART-large had the highest performance of the three models based on ROUGE score; on the Cochrane subtask, DistillBART performed best.

SciSpace (Shinde et al., 2022) The team combined a BERT-based extractive method with a BigBird PEGASUS-based abstractive summarization model (Zaheer et al., 2020), leading to strong performance on the MSLR Cochrane subtask. For the extractive step, the authors use a Lecture Summarizer model to identify the most important sentences from the input documents; this method encodes input sentences using BERT, then clusters the contextual representations and selects the sentences closest to the cluster centroids. The resulting sentences are used as input into a BigBird PEGASUS model pretrained on Pubmed, which is finetuned on the MSLR training data. In analysis, the authors observed that a common error is duplication of statements in the generated summary. The model submitted by the team to the Cochrane subtask leaderboard performs best among submissions based on ROUGE-L, though the authors report that the same training strategy does not lead to good performance on the MS^2 subtask due to the much longer input sequences in MS^2.

LED-base-16k (Giorgi et al., 2022) The team fine-tuned Longformer Encoder-Decoder following a similar protocol to PRIMERA (Xiao et al., 2022), improving performance over baselines in both subtasks. Their input sequence included the titles and abstracts of up to 25 studies, separated by special tokens. No system description was submitted.

5 Insights & future directions

Though we observe modest overall improvements to task performance based on automated summarization evaluation metrics such as ROUGE and BERTScore, results are inconsistent across evaluation metrics. This is especially the case when considering the evidence inference divergence metrics introduced to measure and bolster inference direction alignments between generated and gold summaries. Further, several participant groups discovered problems with factuality, consistency, duplication, and more with generated summaries upon qualitative examination of their results (Otmakhova et al., 2022a; Shinde et al., 2022). Based on the observations of submitting teams, we summarize two key directions for future research.

Multidocument representation strategies Several submissions explored methods for input extraction and filtering to reduce the size of the input sequence and increase the saliency of the input texts. For both subtasks, a large portion of input instances extend beyond even the token limits of long-sequence transformer language models, and this is especially the case for MS^2 (the median number of input documents for MS^2 is 17, nearly twice the number for the Cochrane dataset). Obonyo et al. (2022) explored several strategies for sentence selection, including results extraction models, and found promising but inconsistent performance gains over a base model. Shinde et al. (2022) employed a sentence embedding clustering and selection approach, which led to top performance on the Cochrane subtask when combined with a powerful long-sequence trained summarization model. However, Shinde et al. (2022) noted that their methods did not extend well to MS^2 due to the larger number of input documents.

Extension of such methods would be a promising future direction. Beyond salient sentence selection, a strategy based on PICO alignment and results extraction may be more pertinent for the specific task. For example, one may only want to include the results sentence from an input document if it studies the same population and research question described in the review. Compression-based methods yielding less computationally intensive representations may also allow for full information retention, enabling salience determinations at the model-level, depending on other input studies and the review question at hand.

Evaluation metrics that better capture summary quality Unsurprisingly, our defined automated evaluation metrics are lacking, in many cases failing to capture summary quality issues identified during qualitative analysis (Otmakhova et al., 2022a; Shinde et al., 2022). Both of our task datasets are highly compressive, e.g. the average compression ratio for the Cochrane dev set is around 33 while that of the MS^2 dev set is over 100! Yet, a baseline such as copying the background section of MS^2 leads to fairly good performance when assessed using (fuzzy-)token overlap metrics such as ROUGE and BERTScore. This indicates that the task is perhaps less about summarizing and more about *synthesizing* relevant results, and hence, n-gram and token similarity-based metrics would be insufficient for capturing content similarity. These are similar concerns to those raised in single-document summarization evaluation (Fabbri et al., 2021; Deutsch et al., 2022).

We included evidence inference metrics in evaluation to offer a counterpoint to more traditional metrics, yet they bring their own challenges. The values of these metrics are not particularly comparable between the two subtask datasets, nor are the numbers easy to interpret, e.g., how much worse is a model that scores 0.4 to 0.3 ΔEI-F1 at a system level? Additionally, we currently perform evidence inference scoring for all possible PICO tuples, regardless of whether a relationship occurs between members of each tuple, which can lead to degradation in performance (where most tuples are classified as "no effect," washing out actual differences between documents; see discussion in DeYoung et al. 2021). Improvements on PICO tuple detection and alignment between documents could dramatically improve the value of evidence inference for MSLR evaluation. In addition to evidence inference-based metrics, we anticipate investigating how entailment or question-answering-based evaluation metrics for single-document summarization evaluation (Pagnoni et al., 2021) could be extended into the multi-document space for this task (and how well existing approaches fare on this specialized data and task).

Further data is needed to iterate upon model-based evaluation metrics. Towards this, we intend to collect and release a dataset of human annotations of summary quality for a sample of generations submitted to this shared task, as described in Section 2: Evaluation. Initial results will be presented at the SDP 2022 workshop.

6 Conclusion

The MSLR2022 shared task initiated further investigation into the challenging task of automatically synthesizing study results into a literature review summary. The task received submissions from six teams, leading to modest improvements on task performance and significant insights into the remaining challenges for this task. A primary challenge involves the insufficiency of automated evaluation metrics for assessing performance improvements on this task, towards which we intend to provide new datasets and methods to support and incentivize further research on this problem.

Acknowledgements

We thank John Giorgi for help in data preparation and reviewing for this shared task. This work was funded in part by the National Science Foundation (NSF) awards 2211954 and 1750978, and the National Institutes of Health (NIH) / National Library of Medicine (NLM) award R01-LM012086.

References

Iz Beltagy, Matthew E. Peters, and Arman Cohan. 2020. Longformer: The long-document transformer. *ArXiv*, abs/2004.05150.

Arman Cohan, Franck Dernoncourt, Doo Soon Kim, Trung Bui, Seokhwan Kim, Walter Chang, and Nazli Goharian. 2018. A discourse-aware attention model for abstractive summarization of long documents. In *Proceedings of the 2018 Conference of the North American Chapter of the Association for Computational Linguistics: Human Language Technologies, Volume 2 (Short Papers)*, pages 615–621, New Orleans, Louisiana. Association for Computational Linguistics.

Daniel Deutsch, Rotem Dror, and Dan Roth. 2022. Re-examining system-level correlations of automatic summarization evaluation metrics. In *Proceedings of the 2022 Conference of the North American Chapter of the Association for Computational Linguistics: Human Language Technologies*, pages 6038–6052, Seattle, United States. Association for Computational Linguistics.

Jay DeYoung, Iz Beltagy, Madeleine van Zuylen, Bailey Kuehl, and Lucy Lu Wang. 2021. MS2: Multi-document summarization of medical studies. In *EMNLP*.

Jay DeYoung, Eric Lehman, Benjamin Nye, Iain Marshall, and Byron C. Wallace. 2020. Evidence inference 2.0: More data, better models. In *Proceedings of the 19th SIGBioMed Workshop on Biomedical Language Processing*, pages 123–132, Online. Association for Computational Linguistics.

Alexander R. Fabbri, Wojciech Kryściński, Bryan McCann, Caiming Xiong, Richard Socher, and Dragomir Radev. 2021. SummEval: Re-evaluating summarization evaluation. *Transactions of the Association for Computational Linguistics*, 9:391–409.

John Giorgi et al. 2022. MSLR leaderboard: led-base-16384-ms2. https://leaderboard.allenai.org/mslr-ms2/submission/ccfknkbml1mljnftf7d0. Accessed: 2022-09-15.

Mandy Guo, Joshua Ainslie, David C. Uthus, Santiago Ontañón, Jianmo Ni, Yun-Hsuan Sung, and Yinfei Yang. 2022. Longt5: Efficient text-to-text transformer for long sequences. In *NAACL-HLT*.

Eric Lehman, Jay DeYoung, Regina Barzilay, and Byron C Wallace. 2019. Inferring which medical treatments work from reports of clinical trials. *arXiv preprint arXiv:1904.01606*.

Mike Lewis, Yinhan Liu, Naman Goyal, Marjan Ghazvininejad, Abdelrahman Mohamed, Omer Levy, Veselin Stoyanov, and Luke Zettlemoyer. 2020. BART: Denoising sequence-to-sequence pre-training for natural language generation, translation, and comprehension. In *Proceedings of the 58th Annual Meeting of the Association for Computational Linguistics*, pages 7871–7880, Online. Association for Computational Linguistics.

Chin-Yew Lin. 2004. ROUGE: A package for automatic evaluation of summaries. In *Text Summarization Branches Out*, pages 74–81, Barcelona, Spain. Association for Computational Linguistics.

Ishmael Obonyo, Silvia Casola, and Horacio Saggion. 2022. Exploring the limits of a base BART for multi-document summarization in the medical domain. In *Proceedings of the Third Workshop on Scholarly Document Processing*, Gyeongju, Republic of Korea. Association for Computational Linguistics.

Yulia Otmakhova, Hung Thinh Truong, Timothy Baldwin, Trevor Cohn, Karin Verspoor, and Jey Han Lau. 2022a. LED down the rabbit hole: exploring the potential of global attention for biomedical multi-document summarisation. In *Proceedings of the Third Workshop on Scholarly Document Processing*, Gyeongju, Republic of Korea. Association for Computational Linguistics.

Yulia Otmakhova, Karin Verspoor, Timothy Baldwin, and Jey Han Lau. 2022b. The patient is more dead than alive: exploring the current state of the multi-document summarisation of the biomedical literature. In *Proceedings of the 60th Annual Meeting of the Association for Computational Linguistics (Volume 1: Long Papers)*, pages 5098–5111, Dublin, Ireland. Association for Computational Linguistics.

Artidoro Pagnoni, Vidhisha Balachandran, and Yulia Tsvetkov. 2021. Understanding factuality in abstractive summarization with frank: A benchmark for factuality metrics. *arXiv preprint arXiv:2104.13346*.

Kartik Shinde, Trinita Roy, and Tirthankar Ghosal. 2022. An extractive-abstractive approach for multi-document summarization of scientific articles for literature review. In *Proceedings of the Third Workshop on Scholarly Document Processing*, Gyeongju, Republic of Korea. Association for Computational Linguistics.

Kaveh G Shojania, Margaret Sampson, Mohammed T Ansari, Jun Ji, Steve Doucette, and David Moher. 2007. How quickly do systematic reviews go out of date? a survival analysis. *Annals of internal medicine*, 147(4):224–233.

Rahul Tangsali, Aditya Vyawahare, Aditya Mandke, Onkar Litake, and Dipali Kadam. 2022. Abstractive approaches to multidocument summarization of medical literature reviews. In *Proceedings of the Third Workshop on Scholarly Document Processing*, Gyeongju, Republic of Korea. Association for Computational Linguistics.

Byron C. Wallace, Sayantani Saha, Frank Soboczenski, and Iain James Marshall. 2020. Generating (factual?) narrative summaries of RCTs: Experiments with neural multi-document summarization. In *AMIA Annual Symposium*.

Wen Xiao, Iz Beltagy, Giuseppe Carenini, and Arman Cohan. 2022. PRIMERA: Pyramid-based masked sentence pre-training for multi-document summarization. In *Proceedings of the 60th Annual Meeting of the Association for Computational Linguistics (Volume 1: Long Papers)*, pages 5245–5263, Dublin, Ireland. Association for Computational Linguistics.

Benjamin Yu. 2022. Evaluating pre-trained language models on multi-document summarization for literature reviews. In *Proceedings of the Third Workshop on Scholarly Document Processing*, Gyeongju, Republic of Korea. Association for Computational Linguistics.

Manzil Zaheer, Guru Guruganesh, Kumar Avinava Dubey, Joshua Ainslie, Chris Alberti, Santiago Ontañón, Philip Pham, Anirudh Ravula, Qifan Wang, Li Yang, and Amr Ahmed. 2020. Big bird: Transformers for longer sequences. *ArXiv*, abs/2007.14062.

Tianyi Zhang, Varsha Kishore, Felix Wu, Kilian Q. Weinberger, and Yoav Artzi. 2020. Bertscore: Evaluating text generation with BERT. *ArXiv*, abs/1904.09675.

LED down the rabbit hole: exploring the potential of global attention for biomedical multi-document summarisation

Yulia Otmakhova[1,*], **Hung Thinh Truong**[1,*], **Timothy Baldwin**[1,3],
Trevor Cohn[1], **Karin Verspoor**[2,1], **Jey Han Lau**[1]
[1]The University of Melbourne, [2]RMIT University, [3]MBZUAI
{yotmakhova,hungthinht}@student.unimelb.edu.au, tb@ldwin.net,
trevor.cohn@unimelb.edu.au, karin.verspoor@rmit.edu.au, jeyhan.lau@gmail.com

Abstract

In this paper we report on our submission to the Multidocument Summarisation for Literature Review (MSLR) shared task. Specifically, we adapt PRIMERA (Xiao et al., 2022) to the biomedical domain by placing global attention on important biomedical entities in several ways. We analyse the outputs of the 23 resulting models, and report patterns in the results related to the presence of additional global attention, number of training steps, and the input configuration.

1 Introduction

In this paper we describe our experiments and results on the Multidocument Summarisation for Literature Review (MSLR) shared task.[1] In particular, we attempt to improve on previous multi-document summarisation models in the biomedical domain, which have tried to integrate domain knowledge by marking important biomedical entities (Wallace et al., 2021; DeYoung et al., 2021). We hypothesise that highlighting such entities by placing global attention on them will enable better aggregation and normalisation of related entities across documents, and thus improve the factuality of the generated summaries. To explore this idea, we experiment with four different ways of modifying the global attention mechanism of PRIMERA (Xiao et al., 2022), a recent state-of-the-art model designed for multi-document summarisation (MDS). In particular, while by default the global attention tokens in Primera are used to separate documents in the input and capture their relationships, we assign global attention to important biomedical entities in input documents to create links between them. Moreover, to examine the effect of content selection on the quality of summaries produced by this underlying model, we compare results where we use the whole abstract as input vs. only the concluding sentences (which we expect to be more informative). We train and analyse models in zero-shot, few-shot (10 and 100), as well as fully fine-tuned scenarios. Overall we evaluate (using both automatic metrics and human evaluation) a total of 23 models, two of which formed our official submissions to the leaderboard.[2] Both submitted models substantially outperform the baseline approaches (DeYoung et al., 2021) in terms of automatic metrics, and one achieves the best performance in terms of BERTScore and ROUGE-2 among all submissions. Overall, our contributions in comparison to the previously published domain-specific models for MDS are the following:

- We explore the potential of using global attention as a means to highlight important biomedical entities, in order to improve aggregation across input documents.
- We examine how the amount of training data influences the quality of generated summaries, and propose several scenarios where the performance of few-shot and even zero-shot models is on par with that of fully fine-tuned ones.
- We show that in the fine-tuned scenario, the model is able to select important content without additional marking.

2 Dataset

We use the Cochrane dataset as provided in the shared task without any additional data. See Table 5 in Appendix A for dataset statistics.

2.1 Pre-processing

As the trials are collected automatically from the Cochrane library, they contain redundant metadata

*Equal contribution

[1]https://github.com/allenai/mslr-shared-task

[2]Additional results and code for all models is provided at https://github.com/joey234/PRIMER-pico-attn.

Proceedings of the Third Workshop on Scholarly Document Processing, pages 181–187
October 12–17, 2022.

such as hyperlinks, trial identifiers, funding information, copyright statements, and publication records. We perform string matching using regular expressions to remove this content. Following Wallace et al. (2021), for each review, we concatenate all corresponding documents and add a separator token to denote the end of each document.

2.2 Entity marking

The PICO framework describes several essential components of the central question in a clinical trial, including Populations (e.g. *diabetics*), Interventions (e.g. *animal insulin*), Comparators (e.g. *human insulin*), and Outcomes (e.g. *glycaemic control*) (Huang et al., 2006). We tag PICO spans in input and target documents to make the summarisation models explicitly attend to them. We train a tagger on the EBM-NLP dataset (Nye et al., 2018), which contains annotations for the P, I, and O classes[3] on abstracts of randomized controlled trials. Using this dataset, we fine-tune the BioLinkBERT model (Yasunaga et al., 2022), a BERT variant that leverages links between documents that achieve state-of-the-art results on various biomedical NLP tasks, including the PI(C)O tagging task. We adopt the same hyperparameters as in Yasunaga et al. (2022) using the BioLinkBERT$_{\text{base}}$ model, and achieve 74.06 macro-F_1 score on the EBM-NLP test set, which is comparable to the reported results in Yasunaga et al. (2022). We run the trained PIO tagger on the Cochrane dataset for both the documents and summaries. For simplicity, we only use two new special tokens ***<ent>*** and ***</ent>*** to mark the beginning and the end of each PICO span (e.g. ***<ent>*** *Magnesium sulfate* ***</ent>*** *does not have a major impact on disease progression in* ***<ent>*** *women with mild preeclampsia* ***</ent>***.).

Table 5 presents basic statistics of the Cochrane dataset used in this challenge. The average number of PIO spans in the summary and input documents is based on the output of the trained PIO tagger. Note that target summaries for the test set are not provided to participants.

3 Evaluation

For the automatic evaluation, in addition to ROUGE scores (Lin, 2004) and BERTScore[4] (Zhang et al., 2019), we report the metrics introduced in DeYoung et al. (2021), namely ΔEI which measures the distance in predicted direction of the conclusions (*increases*, *decreases*, or *no change*) in the target and generated summaries. For this metric, we report the average distance across samples and also macro-F1 score, in which the predicted direction for the target summary is treated as the correct label (ΔEI-F_1).

To estimate quality of the generated summaries, especially in terms of their factuality, we also perform human evaluation, for which we adopt the binary decision method proposed in Otmakhova et al. (2022). As we need to assess results from a large number of models, we simplify the evaluation, focusing only on factual errors and collapsing the categories of *modality* and *polarity* into a single category with five potential values (*positive*, *negative*, *no effect*, *no evidence*, *no claim*), similar to how it was done by DeYoung et al. (2021). Thus, we report if **PICO** elements used in the correct and generated summaries are aligned, if the **direction** of the findings is the same, and if the summaries are **factual**, that is, correct in these two aspects. In addition, to analyse common errors, we annotate generations as **contradictory** (i.e. containing statements with the same set of PICO elements but different polarity), **malformed** (i.e. including lexical and grammatical errors or repetitions), and **not evidential** (i.e. claiming that there is not enough evidence to determine the effect of intervention). We list some examples of contradictory, malformed and non-evidential summaries in Appendix B.

As the vast majority of the target summaries were multi-aspect — that is, contained statements regarding several groups of patients, interventions or outcomes — one of the difficulties we experienced during the evaluation was comparing them to generated summaries which were either single-aspect or contained different sets of PICO elements. We adopted a precision-based approach when evaluating such pairs of summaries: while it is not necessary for the generated summary to contain all PICO elements included in the target to be considered correct, it must not include any extra PICO elements. In the case of extra PICO elements in the generated summaries, we compared them against the *Objectives* section of the review's abstract to determine if they were truly erroneous or if the target conclusion underreported some of the elements. Moreover, in the case of multi-aspect summaries

[3]Comparators are grouped with Interventions in the dataset due to the difficulty in distinguishing them.

[4]Hash code: `roberta-large_L17_no-idf_version=0.3.11(hug_trans=3.1.0)`

Setting	Description
DocSep	The global attention is only set on the document separation token (***<doc-sep>***) as in the original PRIMERA model. The attention on ***<doc-sep>*** is used across the board in all settings described below.
EntMarkers	In addition to the ***<doc-sep>*** global attention, we set global attention on tokens which mark the beginning and end of entities (i.e. ***<ent>***, ***</ent>***).
EntMarkersSpans	In addition to the ***<ent>*** and ***</ent>*** tags, global attention is set on the tokens between them, that is, the entities themselves.
EntSpans	We only assign global attention to the entity spans. The ***<ent>*** and ***</ent>*** tokens are replaced by the padding mask token to mask them in inputs and thus do not get either global or local attention.
EntOnly	We additionally mask out all tokens outside the entity spans so they do not get either global or local attention; thus we only pass entities with global attention on them to the decoder. We test this scenario to see how well the summaries can be recovered from only the essential entities plus information collected by ***<doc-sep>*** tokens.

Table 1: Global attention settings

we consider direction to be correct only if it is correct for the corresponding set of PICO elements.

Thus though our evaluation approach is less detailed than the one proposed in Otmakhova et al. (2022), it is more strict in terms of alignment of multi-aspect summaries.

4 Experiments

4.1 Model

We base our experiments on PRIMERA (Xiao et al., 2022), which was designed for multi-document summarisation, and experiment with zero-, 10-, 100-shot, and fine-tuning scenarios with the same hyperparameters reported by the authors of the paper. We use the same random seed for all models to ensure consistency. For the baseline model (*No entity*) we use documents and summaries without any entity marking; all other models use documents with entity tags.

4.2 Entity marking and global attention

PRIMERA is based on Longformer-Encoder-Decoder (LED) (Beltagy et al., 2020), which uses sparse attention (global attention) in addition to fixed-sized window attention (local attention). Here, we experiment with employing the global attention mechanism to highlight PICO elements and aggregate them across the documents. Specifically, for the scenario with entity spans in input and target texts, we use the five settings for global attention listed in Table 1.

4.3 Manipulating inputs

As dealing with lengthy inputs is a well-known issue for multi-document summarisation, especially in scientific and biomedical domains, we experiment with several settings to control the length of individual input documents:

- *Default*: The default PRIMERA setting where LED's token budget of 4096 tokens is distributed evenly across all input documents and they are truncated to the corresponding length.
- *Last 3*: In the biomedical domain the most important information appears in conclusions at the end of the paper, so we include only the last three sentences, based on NLTK's sentence tokenizer.[5]

5 Results

Tables 2 and 3 report the results of automatic and human evaluation, correspondingly.

5.1 Models with and without global attention on entities

Though we do not see major improvements in ROUGE scores between the model without PICO entity marking (*No entity*) and the models with global attention on PICO entities (with the exception of *EntMarkers* and *EntSpans*) and even observe some decrease in factuality scores, on closer inspection the summaries generated by those systems prove to be qualitatively different. In particular, the *No entity* model is more extractive and more extensively copies the input studies, while the results of models with global attention on entities are more abstractive. For example, for review CD005963 (Table 7 in Appendix C), the *No entity* model copies the term *Mental Health Act* often mentioned in source documents but absent in target conclusions, while the other models do not.

Table 8 in Appendix D shows how the overlap with source documents decreases when the entity marking with global attention is used, thus making the summaries more abstractive. This, however comes at a cost: we notice that the models

[5] https://github.com/nltk/nltk

		R-1↑	R-2↑	R-L↑	BERTScore↑	ΔEI↓	ΔEI-F_1 ↓
Zero	Default	0.215	0.032	0.132	0.834	0.580	0.321
	Last 3	0.245	0.063	0.179	0.871	0.260	0.385
10-shot	No entity	0.229	0.037	0.147	0.857	0.269	0.328
	DocSep	0.234	0.041	0.155	0.864	0.267	0.367
	EntOnly	0.197	0.024	0.139	0.834	0.297	0.330
	EntMarkers	0.208	0.035	0.143	0.859	0.286	0.327
	EntSpans	0.235	0.036	0.155	0.854	0.307	**0.295**
	EntMarkersSpans	0.187	0.266	0.122	0.831	0.322	0.319
100-shot	No entity	**0.259**	0.052	0.171	0.864	0.302	0.376
	DocSep	0.251	0.048	0.164	0.862	0.339	0.452
	EntOnly	0.237	0.038	0.157	0.851	0.308	0.389
	EntMarkers	0.244	0.048	0.164	0.864	0.284	0.369
	EntSpans	**0.259**	0.049	0.170	0.863	0.273	0.314
	EntMarkersSpans	0.251	0.048	0.166	0.863	0.301	0.315
Full	No entity	0.256	0.064	**0.182**	0.871	0.308	0.409
	DocSep	0.234	0.060	0.170	0.869	0.337	0.373
	EntOnly	0.236	0.060	0.174	0.872	0.256	0.310
	EntMarkers	0.244	**0.066**	0.179	**0.874**	0.246	0.312
	EntSpans	0.237	0.061	0.174	**0.874**	0.251	0.302
	EntMarkersSpans	0.230	0.059	0.168	0.873	**0.244**	0.321

Table 2: Results of automatic evaluation; ↑: higher is better, ↓: lower is better

		PICO↑	Direction↑	Factual↑	Contradict.↓	Malformed↓	No evid.↓
Zero	Default	50	15	5	0	0	0
	Last 3	50	50	30	0	5	70
10-shot	No entity	25	45	10	5	30	100
	DocSep	25	50	10	15	20	95
	EntOnly	10	30	0	10	75	35
	EntMarkers	25	50	15	0	0	70
	Ent Spans	30	35	5	5	30	65
	EntMarkersSpans	20	35	10	5	70	40
100-shot	No entity	50	50	20	5	5	60
	DocSep	50	50	20	10	15	65
	EntOnly	45	35	5	5	35	45
	EntMarkers	50	45	30	25	25	85
	EntSpans	35	40	15	20	10	100
	EntMarkersSpans	60	40	25	0	0	75
Full	No entity	50	60	35	10	10	35
	DocSep	50	50	25	5	10	65
	EntOnly	30	40	20	0	5	85
	EntMarkers	35	40	20	10	0	90
	EntSpans	55	40	25	5	5	90
	EntMarkersSpans	50	40	25	5	0	100

Table 3: Results of human evaluation; ↑: higher is better, ↓: lower is better. ***Zero*** denotes the zero-shot setting.

with additional global attention produce remarkably more *no evidence* summaries, and in the fully fine-tuned scenario the number of such summaries grows with the number of tokens on which we place global attention. This is consistent with the results of another model which extensively uses global attention (DeYoung et al., 2021) which also produces a large number of *no evidence* summaries (Otmakhova et al., 2022). Another behaviour of models with extra global attention observed both in DeYoung et al. (2021) and here is that they generate sequences which are representative of biomedical text style. For example, in addition to conclusions, the summaries generated by such models contain generic sentences such as *There is a need for more studies of high methodological quality*. Thus we hypothesise that tokens with global attention tend to accumulate and reproduce information common to a large number of documents in the training set rather than information shared by a particular set of input documents. Finally, though we expected the *EntOnly* model, which only uses only PIO enti-

		R-1↑	R-2↑	R-L↑	BERTScore↑	ΔEI↓	ΔEI-F_1 ↓
Default	Zero-shot	0.215	0.032	0.132	0.834	0.580	**0.321**
	10-shot	0.229	0.037	0.147	0.857	0.269	0.328
	100-shot	**0.259**	0.052	0.171	0.864	0.302	0.376
	Full	0.256	**0.064**	**0.182**	0.871	0.308	0.409
Last 3	Zero-shot	0.245	0.063	0.179	**0.871**	**0.260**	0.385
	10-shot	0.211	0.030	0.135	0.853	0.289	0.342
	100-shot	0.250	0.046	0.164	0.862	0.341	0.424
	Full	0.239	0.061	0.171	0.870	0.279	0.382

Table 4: Results of automatic evaluation; ↑: higher is better, ↓: lower is better

ties as inputs and thus loses information about the relations between them, to perform much worse than the other models, it is very similar to them both in automatic metrics and *Direction* scores. We maintain that it shows that even if the models are able to attend to all tokens, they only reproduce PIO entities and are not able to consistently capture the relationships between them.

5.2 Zero-shot vs. few-shot vs. fully fine-tuned models

We notice that in terms of automatic metrics, zero-shot models are comparable to fine-tuned ones or even outperform them; however they perform substantially worse in terms of factuality, especially for the direction. We find that in zero-shot scenarios, PRIMERA copies spans of text from one or several of the input documents, focusing mostly on their beginnings, rather than aggregates information across documents. Thus it outputs either conclusions copied from a single document, or, more often, makes no claims at all by reporting the objectives of the review or its setup.

Another interesting finding is that the ROUGE scores tend to be the highest in the 100-shot scenario and go down for the fully fine-tuned models. We maintain that in 10-shot scenarios the models are still unable to correctly capture and reproduce important entities (which is also reflected in their low accuracy in terms of PICO), while in the fully fine-tuned models, there is a tendency to generate broader and generic entities, for example *metal-protein attenuation compounds* instead of *PBT1/PBT2* in the target summary.

Not surprisingly, the number of malformed generations decreases with increasing the number of training samples: the majority of summaries produced by *EntOnly* and *EntMarkersSpans* after 10 shots are malformed, but even 100-shot training significantly reduces this amount. On the other hand, it is surprising to see that the more the models are fine-tuned the more *no evidence* statements they produce, with some models generating only such summaries in fully fine-tuned scenario.

Lastly, we find that the 100-shot *EntMarkers* model is similar in terms of factuality to the fully fine-tuned model without entity marking (*No entity*). This is an encouraging result as high-quality multi-document summarisation data is scarce in biomedical domain, so few-shot learning is a practically important direction to explore.

5.3 *Default* vs. *Last3*

For few-shot and fine-tuned models we find no major improvements in quality when restricting the inputs to the last three sentences only (Table 4). This shows that after fine-tuning PRIMERA is able to detect most useful spans without relying on their explicit marking. On the other hand, for the zero-shot scenario, where the model tends to copy from the beginning of input documents, the quality dramatically improves when we force it to extract only from a more informative span at the end of documents. Interestingly, such an easy manipulation of inputs allows to achieve results comparable to the best 100-shot and fully fine-tuned models without any training on the in-domain dataset. Again, this is a promising direction for research considering the scarcity of high-quality data.

6 Conclusion

We tackle the problem of biomedical multi-document summarisation by incorporating PICO information into a strong summarisation model, and using global attention to enhance the representation of this information. Through automatic and human evaluations on an extensive set of experiments, we find that adding global attention to PICO spans would help in (1) generating more abstractive summaries, and (2) improving summarization quality in few-shot settings, which is especially important in the biomedical domain.

Acknowledgements

The authors would like to thank the anonymous reviewers for their comprehensive and constructive reviews. This research was undertaken using the LIEF HPC-GPGPU Facility hosted at the University of Melbourne. This Facility was established with the assistance of LIEF Grant LE170100200. This research was conducted by the Australian Research Council Training Centre in Cognitive Computing for Medical Technologies (project number ICI70200030) and funded by the Australian Government.

References

Iz Beltagy, Matthew E Peters, and Arman Cohan. 2020. Longformer: The long-document transformer. *arXiv preprint arXiv:2004.05150.*

Jay DeYoung, Iz Beltagy, Madeleine van Zuylen, Bailey Kuehl, and Lucy Wang. 2021. MS^2: Multi-document summarization of medical studies. In *Proceedings of the 2021 Conference on Empirical Methods in Natural Language Processing*, pages 7494–7513, Online and Punta Cana, Dominican Republic. Association for Computational Linguistics.

Xiaoli Huang, Jimmy Lin, and Dina Demner-Fushman. 2006. Evaluation of PICO as a knowledge representation for clinical questions. In *AMIA annual symposium proceedings*, volume 2006, page 359. American Medical Informatics Association.

Chin-Yew Lin. 2004. ROUGE: A package for automatic evaluation of summaries. In *Text Summarization Branches Out*, pages 74–81, Barcelona, Spain. Association for Computational Linguistics.

Benjamin Nye, Junyi Jessy Li, Roma Patel, Yinfei Yang, Iain Marshall, Ani Nenkova, and Byron Wallace. 2018. A corpus with multi-level annotations of patients, interventions and outcomes to support language processing for medical literature. In *Proceedings of the 56th Annual Meeting of the Association for Computational Linguistics (Volume 1: Long Papers)*, pages 197–207, Melbourne, Australia. Association for Computational Linguistics.

Yulia Otmakhova, Karin Verspoor, Timothy Baldwin, and Jey Han Lau. 2022. The patient is more dead than alive: exploring the current state of the multi-document summarisation of the biomedical literature. In *Proceedings of the 60th Annual Meeting of the Association for Computational Linguistics (Volume 1: Long Papers)*, pages 5098–5111, Dublin, Ireland. Association for Computational Linguistics.

Byron C Wallace, Sayantan Saha, Frank Soboczenski, and Iain J Marshall. 2021. Generating (factual?) narrative summaries of RCTs: Experiments with neural multi-document summarization. In *AMIA Annual Symposium Proceedings*, volume 2021, page 605. American Medical Informatics Association.

Wen Xiao, Iz Beltagy, Giuseppe Carenini, and Arman Cohan. 2022. PRIMERA: Pyramid-based masked sentence pre-training for multi-document summarization. In *Proceedings of the 60th Annual Meeting of the Association for Computational Linguistics (Volume 1: Long Papers)*, pages 5245–5263, Dublin, Ireland. Association for Computational Linguistics.

Michihiro Yasunaga, Jure Leskovec, and Percy Liang. 2022. LinkBERT: Pretraining language models with document links. In *Proceedings of the 60th Annual Meeting of the Association for Computational Linguistics (Volume 1: Long Papers)*, pages 8003–8016, Dublin, Ireland. Association for Computational Linguistics.

Tianyi Zhang, Varsha Kishore, Felix Wu, Kilian Q Weinberger, and Yoav Artzi. 2019. BERTScore: Evaluating text generation with BERT. In *International Conference on Learning Representations.*

A Dataset statistics

Table 5 reports some basic statistics of the Cochrane dataset used in this challenge. The Average number of PICO spans in the summary and the input documents (Avg. # PICO spans) are obtained using the trained PICO tagger. Note that target summaries for the test set are not provided.

	Train	Valid.	Test
# samples	3752	470	470
Avg. input length	2417	2389	2677
Avg. summary length	68	70	n/a
Avg. # PICO spans in input	213	209	236
Avg. # PICO spans in summary	4	4	n/a

Table 5: Cochrane dataset statistics.

B Examples of malformed, contradictory and non-evidential summaries

To clarify the criteria we used for evaluation, Table 6 lists some examples of contradictory, malformed and non-evidential summaries. Malformed summaries are ones containing repetitions, incomplete text or corrupted tokens. The spans of text corresponding to errors are in **bold**.

C Examples of generated summaries

Table 7 shows the examples of summaries generated for input documents for review CD005963.

Error	Summary
Contradiction	*There is* ***insufficient evidence*** *to support the use of edaravone as a therapy for acute ischemic stroke. However, it may be useful for treating other types of ischemic stroke. The current review* ***provides a rationale basis*** *for the use of edaravone as a therapy for acute ischemic stroke.* ***In the absence of evidence to support*** *the use of PBT2 in patients with severe Alzheimer's disease, clinicians and patients* ***should recommend*** *the continued use of PBT2.*
Malformed	*There is inadequate evidence to evaluate the effect of percutaneous endoscopic gastrostomy on the incidence of percutaneous wound infections. The current evidence base is limited due to the differing methodologies employed in the trials.* ***The current evidence base is limited due to the differing methodologies employed in the trials. The current evidence base is limited due to the differing methodologies employed in the trials...*** *We found no clear evidence to support the use* ***of*** *There is limited evidence to suggest that the use of* ***apleuapleuapleuapleuapleuapleua...***
No evidence	*There is insufficient evidence to support the use of metal-protein-attenuating compounds for the treatment of AD. Further trials are needed.*

Table 6: Examples of contradictory, malformed and non-evidential summaries

Setting	Summary
No entity	*... the results suggest that advance directives may be beneficial in reducing the number of people admitted to hospital under the Mental Health Act.*
DocSep	*There is insufficient evidence to support or refute the use of advance directives for people with mental illnesses.*
EntMarkers	*There is insufficient evidence to support or refute the use of advance directives for people with severe mental illness.*
EntMarkersSpans	*There is insufficient evidence to support the use of advance directives for people with severe mental illness.*
EntSpans	*There is insufficient evidence to support the use of advance directives for people with mental illness.*
EntOnly	*There is insufficient evidence to support the use of advance directives for people with severe mental illness.*

Table 7: Examples of generated summaries

D Lexical overlap with the input documents

Table 8 shows the amount of lexical overlap with the source documents in terms of ROUGE scores. The lower the score is, the less is copied from the source and the more abstractive the summary is.

		R-1↓	R-2↓	R-L↓
Full	No entity	0.052	0.022	0.040
	DocSep	0.042	0.019	0.034
	EntOnly	0.043	0.021	0.036
	EntMarkers	0.042	0.018	0.033
	EntSpans	0.040	0.017	0.032
	EntMarkersSpans	0.037	0.016	0.030

Table 8: Token overlap with the source as a measure of extractiveness; lower = more abstractive

Evaluating Pre-Trained Language Models on Multi-Document Summarization for Literature Reviews

Benjamin Yu
Georgia Tech
byu92@gatech.edu

Abstract

Systematic literature reviews in the biomedical space are often expensive to conduct. Automation through machine learning and large language models could improve the accuracy and research outcomes from such reviews. In this study, we evaluate a pre-trained LongT5 model on the MSLR22: Multi-Document Summarization for Literature Reviews Shared Task datasets. We weren't able to make any improvements on the dataset benchmark, but we do establish some evidence that current summarization metrics are insufficient in measuring summarization accuracy. A multi-document summarization web tool was also built to demonstrate the viability of summarization models for future investigators: https://ben-yu.github.io/summarizer

1 Introduction

With recent advances in natural language processing and deep learning, large language models are now capable of generating summaries of large volumes of documents that are arguably human readable and logically consistent. With the growing amount of research being published, it has become increasingly difficult to process all the available research and literature in any particular field of study. This has become exceedingly important within the biomedical field as the community has learned with the global COVID-19 pandemic. Speed of research directly impacts patient outcomes and how fast medical practitioners can respond to a constantly changing health landscape. The MSLR22: Multi-Document Summarization for Literature Reviews shared task proposes a challenging research problem that pushes current state of the art multi-document summarization models to generalize over two different datasets: MS^2 Dataset (DeYoung et al., 2021) and Cochrane Dataset (Wallace et al., 2020) We will evaluate in this research study if pre-trained summarization models can successfully solve the proposed task.

2 Related Work

Recent studies in document summarization have mostly focused on Transformer-based models, but applied to the biomedical context either through transfer learning or fine-turning on a specific biomedical dataset (Wang et al., 2021). BioBERTSum is a recent example of using such pre-training methodologies, which used a pre-trained model as an encoder and fine-tuned on a specific task (Du et al., 2020). (Moradi and Samwald, 2019) innovated in this space by applying hierarchical clustering to group contextual embeddings of sentences to select the most informative sentences from a given group to generate summaries. (Sotudeh et al., 2020) also recently proposed a mechanism to leverage domain knowledge and embed it into their SciBERT-based clinical abstractive summarization model.

Scaling such transformer models to longer input sizes has been difficult since the attention layers get exponentially larger and become computationally infeasible to train. Recent advances in model architecture like PEGASUS (Zhang et al., 2019) and Longformer (Beltagy et al., 2020) have introduced different ways around this by introducing sparse attention mechanisms like local attention which replaces the full-attention mechanism with a sparse sliding window. Researchers at Google were able to innovate on these findings further by combining pre-training strategies from PEGASUS along with a new sparse attention mechanism called Transient Global which mimics ETC's local/global attention mechanism and achieve state of the art performance on multiple summarization benchmarks. (Guo et al., 2021)

3 Data Analysis

3.1 MS^2 Dataset

The MS^2 dataset consists of 470k studies mapped to 20k reviews from PubMed (DeYoung et al., 2021). The dataset was further augmented with

Proceedings of the Third Workshop on Scholarly Document Processing, pages 188–192
October 12–17, 2022.

PICO span labels and evidence inference classes. The goal for this dataset is to generate an accurate summary given a set of multiple review abstracts.

To understand the relative difficulty of this summarization task, we measured text similarity between abstracts and their target summaries based on Term Frequency–Inverse Document Frequency (TF-IDF) and Jaccard similarity.

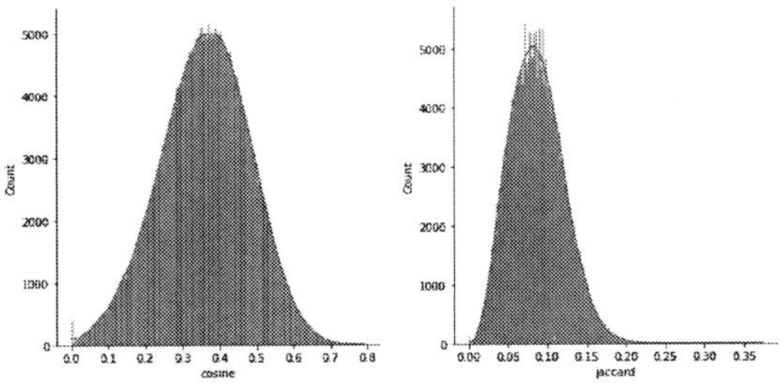

Figure 1: Distribution of MS^2 distances from abstract to target summary

The mean cosine difference was 0.4 and Jacard distance was 0.1. This indicates there was no substantial overlap between the target summaries and their source reviews.

3.2 Cochrane Dataset

This was a smaller dataset of 4.5K reviews collected from Cochrane systematic reviews (Wallace et al., 2020). This dataset was cleaner than the MS^2 dataset, but substantially smaller. The reviews on average included 10 trials each and the average abstract length of included trials was 245 words. We use the authors' conclusions subsection of the systematic review abstract as our target summary (75 words on average).

We also did a similar measurement of cosine and Jaccard distances for the Cochrane dataset:

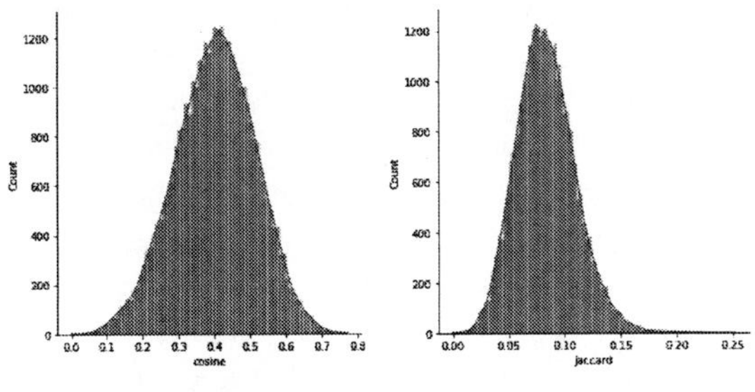

Figure 2: Distribution of Cochrane review distances from abstract to target summary

Similar to the MS^2 dataset, the cosine and Jaccard distances were normally distributed and had roughly the same average difference from their target review. This seemed to indicate that both datasets were similarly difficult and have roughly the same level of sentence overlap.

4 Experiments

The original goal of this study was to experiment with two different approaches to the MSLR22 Shared Task:

1. Fine-tune LongT5 models with both datasets
2. Evaluate existing LongT5 language models on similar datasets like PubMed (Cohan et al., 2018)

We selected the LongT5 model due to its purported state of the art performance numbers and its ability to scale its input size to up to 16384 tokens. We leveraged several cloud providers such as Google Cloud and AWS Sagemaker along with HuggingFace's transformers library for model fine tuning (Wolf et al., 2019). We also experimented with HuggingFace's AutoTrain framework to automatically search for the correct hyperparameters for training. All we had to provide was an initial training and validation datasets, and AutoTrain automated the model training and tuning process. To allow the model to train on multiple documents at once, we pre-processed the training data such that all review abstracts with the same Review ID were appended into a single input string. The single input would then be fed into our model of choice after doing some minimal input validation like checking if the input isn't more than our maximum token length of 16384. We immediately hit several limitations with cloud training including not having sufficient spend to qualify using larger GPU instances for training. HuggingFace's AutoTrain framework also never successfully completed and would often timeout after several days of training. We also attempted to fine tune our models locally, but we only had access to a single RTX 3080 10GB GPU which couldn't even fit the model and dataset even with a batch size of 1. Our conclusion from this experience has demonstrated how the trend towards larger language models might risk increasingly making this type of research inaccessible to hobbyists and practitioners. State-of-the-art model performance will likely only be achieved by researchers with access to compute power and capital unless we prioritize research into reduce model size and resource utilization.

-	Training	Training Target	Test
Characters	1745.81	435.60	1746.66
Words	299.88	68.53	301.42
Sentences	11.2	2.74	11.17

Table 1: MS^2 Dataset Properties

-	Training	Training Target	Test
Characters	1526.79	489.8	1510.42
Words	224.3	72.2	221.14
Sentences	10.2	3.4	10.09

Table 2: Cochrane Dataset Properties

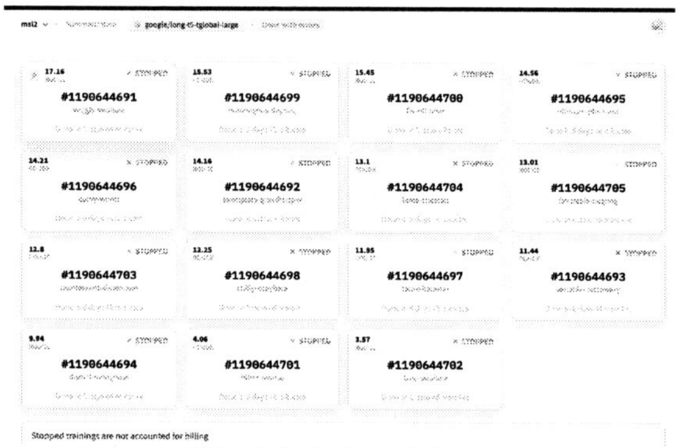

Figure 3: HuggingFace AutoTrain on LongT5

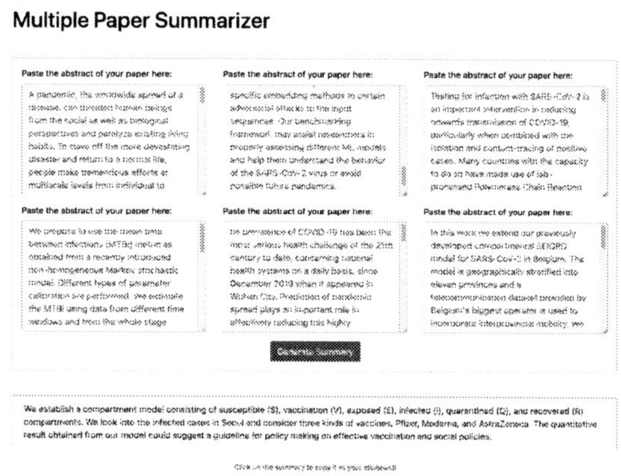

Figure 4: Multi-Document Summarization Tool with HuggingFace Inference API

For our second approach, rather than fine-tuning a base model, we wanted to evaluate if a model that was pre-trained on a similar dataset would still be able to solve this summarization task without any fine-tuning. We found a pre-trained LongT5 model on the PubMed dataset that was trained for around 3k steps (Stancl, 2022). We believed the fine-tuning should be transferable to these datasets as they largely cover the same type of biomedical content and the MS^2 dataset also gets its training data from PubMed. We leveraged Hugging-Face's Inference API for model evaluation against the MSLR22 datasets. This also restricted our ability to fine-tune the output size which probably also hindered our performance.

To aid in the model development process and also as a validation that these summarization models have a practical use, we created an online tool that allows anyone to invoke the models for any 6 paper abstracts. The tool can be found at: `https://ben-yu.github.io/summarizer`

5 Discussion

Unsurprisingly the pre-trained models were unable to exceed the dataset benchmarks on the shared task. One key failing came from our inability to configure target generation length using Hugging-Face's Accelerated Inference Text2Text Generation API. On the MS^2 Dataset our outputs only had an average sentence length of 1.1 and character count of 87.97, which significantly deviated from our target length of 2.74 sentences and 435.6 characters. This likely due to the out-of-the-box model not properly generalising over the entire PubMed dataset as the model was also only trained for about 3k steps and further training steps would have improved it's performance. The Rouge-L scores were particularly indicative, scoring sometimes up to 50% worse than the benchmarks. Increasing our model output length would have likely dramatically improved our Rouge scores. Our model didn't score that poorly in terms of a delta EI on the MS^2 dataset with only a 0.06 difference from the Long-

Model	R-1	R-2	R-L	EI↓	F1	BERT
`BART Benchmark`	0.2626	0.0770	0.1950	0.4509	0.4142	0.8636
`Longformer Benchmark`	0.2637	0.0795	0.1961	0.4621	0.4118	0.8666
`LongT5 - Pubmed`	0.1200	0.0133	0.0961	0.5280	0.3433	0.8276

Table 3: Model performance on MS^2 Dataset

Model	R-1	R-2	R-L	EI↓	F1	BERT
`BART Benchmark`	0.2397	0.0671	0.1760	0.2081	0.3348	0.8632
`Longformer Benchmark`	0.2387	0.0655	0.1755	0.2345	0.3316	0.8641
`LongT5 - Pubmed`	0.1130	0.0154	0.0903	0.4671	0.2873	0.7863

Table 4: Model performance on Cochrane Dataset

former benchmark. This could be an indicator that delta EI is a flawed metric that doesn't adequately capture the factual correctness of a summary. Recent work by (Otmakhova et al., 2022) evaluated Longformer and BART models along similar metrics and showed that both models failed to pick up and aggregate important details when manually evaluated against with expert human evaluators. Stronger metrics will likely be required in the future if there is to be significant progress in this domain.

We also found that experimenting with language models and training these large language models can be extremely cost prohibitive and potentially inaccessible to hobbyists and novice machine learning practitioners. These models are getting increasingly large and can't be built unless one has access to sufficient GPU-computing or cloud resources. Training these models can take upwards of 48 hours and there is no guarantee that your model is improving or converging at a reasonable rate.

6 Conclusion

We weren't able to improve upon existing benchmarks for either the MS^2 or Cochrane datasets. We did show there is a need for stronger summarization metrics that can capture different linguistic dimensions such as factual correctness and readability. The summaries from our pre-trained model were significantly shorter than the target summaries and often factually incorrect upon manual inspection, but this couldn't directly be inferred from our model scores outside of comparing it to task benchmarks.

References

Iz Beltagy, Matthew E. Peters, and Arman Cohan. 2020. Longformer: The long-document transformer.

Arman Cohan, Franck Dernoncourt, Doo Soon Kim, Trung Bui, Seokhwan Kim, Walter Chang, and Nazli Goharian. 2018. A discourse-aware attention model for abstractive summarization of long documents. In *Proceedings of the 2018 Conference of the North American Chapter of the Association for Computational Linguistics: Human Language Technologies, Volume 2 (Short Papers)*, pages 615–621, New Orleans, Louisiana. Association for Computational Linguistics.

Jay DeYoung, Iz Beltagy, Madeleine van Zuylen, Bailey Kuehl, and Lucy Lu Wang. 2021. Ms2: Multi-document summarization of medical studies.

Yongping Du, Qingxiao Li, Lulin Wang, and Yanqing He. 2020. Biomedical-domain pre-trained language model for extractive summarization. *Knowledge-Based Systems*, 199:105964.

Mandy Guo, Joshua Ainslie, David Uthus, Santiago Ontanon, Jianmo Ni, Yun-Hsuan Sung, and Yinfei Yang. 2021. Longt5: Efficient text-to-text transformer for long sequences.

Milad Moradi and Matthias Samwald. 2019. Clustering of deep contextualized representations for summarization of biomedical texts.

Yulia Otmakhova, Karin Verspoor, Timothy Baldwin, and Jey Han Lau. 2022. The patient is more dead than alive: exploring the current state of the multi-document summarisation of the biomedical literature. In *Proceedings of the 60th Annual Meeting of the Association for Computational Linguistics (Volume 1: Long Papers)*, pages 5098–5111, Dublin, Ireland. Association for Computational Linguistics.

Sajad Sotudeh, Nazli Goharian, and Ross W. Filice. 2020. Attend to medical ontologies: Content selection for clinical abstractive summarization.

Daniel Stancl. 2022. Longt5 large 16384 pubmed 3k step checkpoint.

Byron C. Wallace, Sayantan Saha, Frank Soboczenski, and Iain J. Marshall. 2020. Generating (factual?) narrative summaries of rcts: Experiments with neural multi-document summarization.

Benyou Wang, Qianqian Xie, Jiahuan Pei, Prayag Tiwari, Zhao Li, and Jie fu. 2021. Pre-trained language models in biomedical domain: A systematic survey.

Thomas Wolf, Lysandre Debut, Victor Sanh, Julien Chaumond, Clement Delangue, Anthony Moi, Pierric Cistac, Tim Rault, Rémi Louf, Morgan Funtowicz, Joe Davison, Sam Shleifer, Patrick von Platen, Clara Ma, Yacine Jernite, Julien Plu, Canwen Xu, Teven Le Scao, Sylvain Gugger, Mariama Drame, Quentin Lhoest, and Alexander M. Rush. 2019. Huggingface's transformers: State-of-the-art natural language processing.

Jingqing Zhang, Yao Zhao, Mohammad Saleh, and Peter J. Liu. 2019. Pegasus: Pre-training with extracted gap-sentences for abstractive summarization.

Exploring the limits of a base BART for multi-document summarization in the medical domain

Ishmael Obonyo
Universitat Pompeu Fabra
University of Nairobi
ishmaelny@gmail.com

Silvia Casola
Università degli Studi di Padova
Fondazione Bruno Kessler
scasola@fbk.eu

Horacio Saggion
Universitat Pompeu Fabra
horacio.saggion@upf.edu

Abstract

This paper is a description of our participation in the Multi-document Summarization for Literature Review (MSLR) Shared Task, in which we explore summarization models to create an automatic review of scientific results. Rather than maximizing the metrics using expensive computational models, we placed ourselves in a situation of scarce computational resources and investigate the limits of a base sequence to sequence models (thus with a limited input length) to the task. Although we explore methods to feed the abstractive model with salient sentences only (using a first extractive step), we find that the results still need some improvements.

1 Introduction

To summarize medical knowledge on specific issues, researchers undertake systematic reviews of the available literature. The process is usually long and expensive; it requires identifying appropriate studies, critically interpreting their findings, and finally synthesizing the results.

Recently, Natural Language Processing (NLP) researchers have explored the use of automatic text summarization models and tools to assist researchers with the process. Previous works by DeYoung et al. (2021); Wallace et al. (2021) have tried to model the problem as a multi-document summarization task, where several input papers (or abstracts) are summarized to generate review conclusions. Summarizing several documents is challenging, and few resources exist (DeYoung et al., 2021) compared to single-document summarization tasks.

The shared task of Multi-document Summarization for Literature Review (MSLR) adopted a similar approach and challenged participants to explore the state-of-the-art systems with two large-scale multi-document summarization datasets for literature review. To this end, instead of aiming at using very complex models to maximize the target metrics, we place ourselves in a situation of scarce computational resources and explore the limits of a base sequence-to-sequence model, BART, to the task. Our contributions to this shared task, therefore, are as follows:

- We explore the performance of a simple base transformer, namely BART, for this task.
- We explore ways to deal with the limited input size of such models, applying an extractive step before the abstractive one.
- We aim at creating general models, and explore how the two datasets can be combined during training to improve performance.

After analyzing the datasets (Section 2), we first experiment with baseline models (Section 3.1); since the model can only deal with a limited number of input tokens, we explore various strategies to reduce the input size (Section 3.2).

2 Datasets and metrics

We evaluated the models on two datasets:

Cochrane (Wallace et al., 2021): The dataset consists of 4,692 systematic reviews from the Cochrane collaboration[1]. The target is the "authors' conclusions" of the systematic review abstracts, while the input is a set of titles and abstracts of the related clinical trials.

MS^2 (DeYoung et al., 2021): is built from papers in the Semantic Scholar literature corpus (Ammar et al., 2018). It consists of 17,876 reviews. The dataset also contains some background text derived from the reviews. The dataset creation was semi-automatic: for each review, each sentence is classified as background, target or other and sentences are then aggregated.

[1] https://www.cochrane. org/

Proceedings of the Third Workshop on Scholarly Document Processing, pages 193–198
October 12–17, 2022.

Table 1 reports some statistics of the two datasets. Notice that the Cochrane dataset contains some input documents for which no abstract is provided.

Results are evaluated using:

ROUGE (Lin, 2004) (ROUGE-1, ROUGE-2, ROUGE-L): These are classical metrics for summarization, and compute the token overlap between the prediction and the gold-standard in terms of n-grams and longest common subsequence. The higher the value the better the score.

BERTScore (Zhang* et al., 2020): Instead of computing exact matches, this metric considers contextual embeddings (as generated by BERT (Devlin et al., 2019)); after computing the cosine similarity among each pair in the generated sequence and the gold standard, the maximum similarities over the gold-standard tokens (Recall) and the generated tokens (Precision) are summed and normalized; they are later used to compute f1-like metric. The higher the value the better the score.

Δ **EI** (DeYoung et al., 2021): It is a model-based metric; the disagreement of (Is, Os, EI) triplets between the input studies and the generated summary is considered, where Is are the Interventions, Os are the Outcomes and EI is Evidence Inference. The measure aims to better correlate with the factuality of the generated summary with respect to the sources. The lower the value the better the score.

3 Experiments and results

In this work, we explore the use of a simple BART base model (Lewis et al., 2020) – that we leave unchanged – for the task of multi-document summarization.

The BART model is limited to input size of 1024 sub-token. However, as figure 1 shows above, concatenating the abstracts leads to very long input sentences, that cannot be dealt with by the model. To this end, we explore if performing a previous extractive step improves performance. Since the target text summarizes the findings of previous work, we also explore the use of a classifier to extract results only from the input.

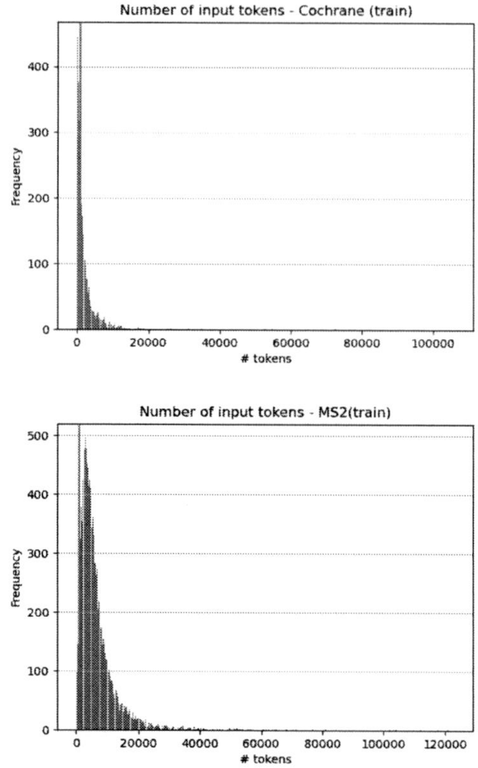

Figure 1: The number of token in the Cochraine and in the MS^2 datasets with concatenated inputs

3.1 Baselines

We train a base BART model, fine-tuned for 4 epochs on the Pubmed summarization dataset[2] (Cohan et al., 2018) to predict the target given the concatenated abstracts. Specifically, we use the concatenated abstracts as input and the target as output. We do not generally use the titles, with a few exceptions in case no abstract is present. For MS^2, we do not use any additional background information, as we want to construct models that are as general as possible. We separate the inputs using the <sep> special tokens. We do not perform any other preprocessing to the dataset text. Table 2 reports the results for our base configuration on the validation set. We report results for all metrics.

3.2 Unsupervised algorithms for decreasing the input size

Since the base model can only process a fraction of our very long input, we explore if performing an extractive step can improve performance, fol-

[2]Model *mse30/bart-base-finetuned-pubmed* from the Hugging Face model hub

	C train	C dev	C test	M train	M dev	M test
Number of input docs	40,497	5,033	5,678	323,608	5,033	5,678
Number of empty abstracts	2,611	464	470	0	0	0
Number of targets	3,752	470	470	14,188	2,021	1667
Number of docs per target (avg)	10.79	10.71	12.08	22.81	24.24	25.63
Number of tokens per abstract (avg)	224.33	222.47	14.88	299.88	302.83	301.42
Number of tokens per target (avg)	67.78	69.9	-	61.28	61.05	-

Table 1: Statistics on the Cochrane (C) and the MS^2 (M) datasets

Trained on	Eval on	R-1	R-2	R-L	BertScore	ΔEI avg	ΔEI macro
M	M	13.18	1.31	10.17	83.2	50.22	42.53
C + M (mix)	M	13.18	1.31	10.18	83.2	50.22	42.53
C, M (sequential)	M	13.23	1.35	10.18	83.14	49.33	42.55
C	C	22.48	6	16.43	86.81	31.03	38.23
C + M (mix)	C	22.86	6.03	16.82	85.1	27.85	36.44
M, C (sequential)	C	18.78	2.77	12.97	84.52	36.54	37.22

Table 2: Baseline results obtained with a base BART model on the raw input. Some models are trained on the MS^2 dataset (M) or on the Cochrane dataset (C) independently. We also trained a single model with the mixed MS^2 and Cochrane data, in random order (mix) and evaluate it on both datasets independently. Finally, we experiment with sequential fine-tunings over the two datasets (with the fine-tuning over the target dataset being the last one); for example, M, C (sequential), means that the BART model was first fine-tuned on the MS^2 dataset and then on the Cochrane dataset. All measures are obtained using the official evaluation script on the validation set.

lowing previous work (Huang et al., 2019). Specifically, we use classical unsupervised algorithms, namely TextRank (Mihalcea and Tarau, 2004) and LexRank (Erkan and Radev, 2004), that we chose since they are simple, well-studied and have a low computational cost. For each target, the extraction is performed on the whole pool of the concatenated abstracts. We also experiment with extracting sentences related to the results only from each abstract (which we then concatenate).

3.2.1 TextRank

TextRank constructs a graph using sentences as nodes and their similarity in terms of normalized number of words as edges. Then, the algorithm extracts the most central sentences according to PageRank (Page et al., 1999).

In order to extract the most important sentences only and minimize repetitions, we grouped all abstracts related to a single target and extracted the salient sentences from the whole pool of text. We used the summa library[3]; we constrained the summary obtained through TextRank to be approximately 1000 tokens (as this is the maximum number of tokens BART can process) and 500 tokens long (to experiment with even shorter salient inputs). Then, we fine-tuned a base BART model with the output data. Table 3 shows the results.

[3]https://github.com/summanlp/textrank

3.2.2 LexRank

Similarly to TextRank, LexRank constructs a graph using sentences as nodes and their similarity as edges; the similarity is computed in terms of term frequency-inverse document frequency (TF-IDF) vectors. Then most central sentences are extracted. We used the sumy[4] library for extraction and explored with outputs of a maximum of 30 sentences (as we estimate this will be compatible with BART's input constraint). Then, we fine-tuned a base BART model with the output data. Table 4 shows the results.

3.3 Extracting the abstracts' results to decrease the input size

Since a systematic review aims in assessing the knowledge in a given area, we explored extracting the results of each abstract only. To do so, we downloaded 150,000 random structured abstracts in English using the Pubmed Advanced Search Builder[5].

[4]https://github.com/miso-belica/sumy

[5]https://pubmed.ncbi.nlm.nih.gov/advanced/

Trained on	Eval on	R-1	R-2	R-L	BertScore	ΔEI avg	ΔEI macro
M - 1k tokens	M	12.7	1.15	9.79	83.02	51.98	43.32
C + M (mix) - 1k tokens	M	12.5	1.07	9.73	83.01	53.26	41.83
C + M (mix) - 500 tokens	M	13.21	1.3	10.13	83.24	49.87	42.87
C - 1k tokens	C	19.9	2.98	13.56	84.81	37.52	37.14
C + M (mix) - 1k tokens	C	22.63	6.09	16.95	86.89	31.92	38.83
M, C (sequential) - 1k tokens	C	19.47	3.4	13.75	84.94	36.63	38.43
C + M (mix) - 500 tokens	C	22.63	6.07	16.8	87	28.71	36.88

Table 3: Results obtained with a base BART model on inputs capped at around 1000 and 500 tokens extracted by TextRank algorithm. Some models are trained on the MS^2 dataset (M) or on the Cochrane dataset (C) independently. We also trained a single model with the mixed MS^2 and Cochrane data, in random order (mix) and evaluate it on both datasets independently. Finally, we experiment with sequential fine-tunings over the two datasets (with the fine-tuning over the target dataset being the last one); for example M, C (sequential), means that the BART model was first fine-tuned on the MS^2 dataset and then fine-tuned on the Cochrane dataset. All measures are obtained using the official evaluation script on the validation set.

Trained on	Eval on	R-1	R-2	R-L	BertScore	ΔEI avg	ΔEI macro
M	M	13.18	1.3	10.2	83.12	50.09	43.08
C + M (mix)	M	13.96	1.55	10.66	83.44	47.52	42.99
C	C	18.1	2.52	12.6	84.24	37.43	37.65
C + M (mix)	C	22.03	5.61	16.28	86.71	26.98	39.29

Table 4: Results obtained with a base BART model on inputs capped at around 30 sentences extracted by LexRank algorithm. Some models are trained on the M S2 dataset (M) or on the Cochrane dataset (C) independently. We also trained a single model with the mixed MS^2 and Cochrane data, in random order (mix) and evaluate it on both datasets independently. All measures are obtained using the official evaluation script on the validation set.

Trained on	Eval on	R-1	R-2	R-L	BertScore	ΔEI avg	ΔEI macro
M	M	12.97	1.27	10.02	83.09	49.59	42.48
C + M (mix)	M	12.61	1.61	9.69	82.96	52.36	41.98
C	C	22.42	5.84	16.59	86.82	30.05	38.02
C + M (mix)	C	22.95	6.17	16.9	86.94	28.43	36.97

Table 5: Results on the development set for the BART model after extracting the results only with a classifier. Some models are trained on the M S2 dataset (M) or on the Cochrane dataset (C) independently. We also trained a single model with the mixed MS^2 and Cochrane data, in random order (mix) and evaluate it on both datasets independently. All measures are obtained using the official evaluation script on the validation set.

Structured abstracts are divided into a number of sections with a related label (e.g., AIM, METHOD, CONCLUSIONS). We used regular expressions to divide the abstract into sections and extract the related label (we identified a label as a cased word or set of words at the start of a line followed by columns) and considered a section containing results as any section having as label CONCLUSION(S), CONCLUDING *, RESULT(S), SIGNIFICANCE, IMPORTANCE, RECOMMENDATION(S). We constructed a dataset assigning the positive label to sentences in such section and the negative label to sentences in the others. Since the negative instances were more than an order of magnitude more common than the positive ones, we balanced the dataset and obtained a sample of 700 negative sentences and 524 positive sentences. Then, we trained a Roberta base model to classify the sentences according to their labels. We used the dataset to extract sentences from the abstracts that have at least a 0.4 log prob of belonging to the positive class (we prefer to increase recall over accuracy, as the summarization step will remove pleonastic content). Then, we fine-tuned a BART base model with the concatenated results. Table 5 shows the obtained results.

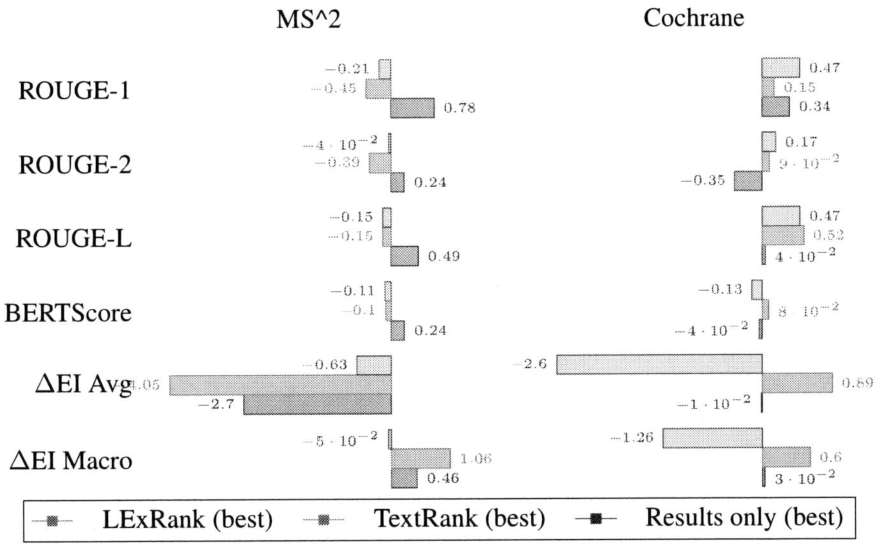

Figure 2: Effect of the extractive step. For each dataset, we consider the base model trained and evaluated on the target dataset as our baseline, and show the relative difference in performance when compared to the best model for each extractive algorithm. For LexRank, we considered the model trained on M+C mixed data, after extracting the salient sentences with LexRank. For TextRank, we considered the model trained on M+C mixed data, after extracting the salient sentences (500 tokens long for MS^2 and 1000 for Cochrane); for the Results only, we considered the model fine-tuned on MS^2 only for MS^2 and the mixed one for Cochrane.

4 Conclusions

We have explored a number of base BART models for the task of generating systematic reviews in the medical domain. Given the limited number of tokens BART can handle, we adopted several simple extractive strategies to retrieve salient sentences to the abstractive model; we also trained a model from the abstract results sentences only.

Generally, we found results on the Cochrane datasets are much more encouraging than those on the MS^2 and we believe that using the background info might improve performance. We found that the results obtained from the salient sentences only show mixed results. For MS^S, extracting the results sentences only seems to be the most promising method. For the Cochrane dataset, all extractive methods show small improvements over the baseline. LexRank seems to be the most promising, as it slightly improves the results, both in terms of ROUGE and factuality metrics.

In addition to ours, other strategies could be explored to sort the input abstract: DeYoung et al. (2021), for example, sorts abstracts by some measures of quality; it would be interesting to see how this compares to our proposed strategies. We also plan to explore different input representations that go beyond the simple concatenation of abstract and data augmentation techniques. Another possible route could be that of extracting domain-specific concepts, through, e.g., PubTator (Wei et al., 2013), to enrich abstracts.

References

Waleed Ammar, Dirk Groeneveld, Chandra Bhagavatula, Iz Beltagy, Miles Crawford, Doug Downey, Jason Dunkelberger, Ahmed Elgohary, Sergey Feldman, Vu Ha, Rodney Kinney, Sebastian Kohlmeier, Kyle Lo, Tyler Murray, Hsu-Han Ooi, Matthew Peters, Joanna Power, Sam Skjonsberg, Lucy Wang, Chris Wilhelm, Zheng Yuan, Madeleine van Zuylen, and Oren Etzioni. 2018. Construction of the literature graph in semantic scholar. In *Proceedings of the 2018 Conference of the North American Chapter of the Association for Computational Linguistics: Human Language Technologies, Volume 3 (Industry Papers)*, pages 84–91, New Orleans - Louisiana. Association for Computational Linguistics.

Arman Cohan, Franck Dernoncourt, Doo Soon Kim, Trung Bui, Seokhwan Kim, Walter Chang, and Nazli Goharian. 2018. A discourse-aware attention model for abstractive summarization of long documents. *Proceedings of the 2018 Conference of the North American Chapter of the Association for Computational Linguistics: Human Language Technologies, Volume 2 (Short Papers)*.

Jacob Devlin, Ming-Wei Chang, Kenton Lee, and Kristina Toutanova. 2019. BERT: Pre-training of deep bidirectional transformers for language understanding. In *Proceedings of the 2019 Conference of the North American Chapter of the Association for Computational Linguistics: Human Language Technologies, Volume 1 (Long and Short Papers)*, pages 4171–4186, Minneapolis, Minnesota. Association for Computational Linguistics.

Jay DeYoung, Iz Beltagy, Madeleine van Zuylen, Bailey Kuehl, and Lucy Wang. 2021. MS^2: Multi-document summarization of medical studies. In *Proceedings of the 2021 Conference on Empirical Methods in Natural Language Processing*, pages 7494–7513, Online and Punta Cana, Dominican Republic. Association for Computational Linguistics.

Günes Erkan and Dragomir R. Radev. 2004. Lexrank: Graph-based lexical centrality as salience in text summarization. *J. Artif. Int. Res.*, 22(1):457–479.

Si Huang, Rui Wang, Qing Xie, Lin Li, and Yongjian Liu. 2019. An extraction-abstraction hybrid approach for long document summarization. *2019 6th International Conference on Behavioral, Economic and Socio-Cultural Computing (BESC)*, pages 1–6.

Mike Lewis, Yinhan Liu, Naman Goyal, Marjan Ghazvininejad, Abdelrahman Mohamed, Omer Levy, Veselin Stoyanov, and Luke Zettlemoyer. 2020. BART: Denoising sequence-to-sequence pre-training for natural language generation, translation, and comprehension. In *Proceedings of the 58th Annual Meeting of the Association for Computational Linguistics*, pages 7871–7880, Online. Association for Computational Linguistics.

Chin-Yew Lin. 2004. ROUGE: A package for automatic evaluation of summaries. In *Text Summarization Branches Out*, pages 74–81, Barcelona, Spain. Association for Computational Linguistics.

Rada Mihalcea and Paul Tarau. 2004. TextRank: Bringing order into text. In *Proceedings of the 2004 Conference on Empirical Methods in Natural Language Processing*, pages 404–411, Barcelona, Spain. Association for Computational Linguistics.

Lawrence Page, Sergey Brin, Rajeev Motwani, and Terry Winograd. 1999. The pagerank citation ranking : Bringing order to the web. In *WWW 1999*.

Byron C Wallace, Sayantan Saha, Frank Soboczenski, and Iain J Marshall. 2021. Generating (factual?) narrative summaries of RCTs: Experiments with neural multi-document summarization. *AMIA Summits Transl. Sci. Proc.*, 2021:605–614.

Chih-Hsuan Wei, Hung-Yu Kao, and Zhiyong Lu. 2013. Pubtator: a web-based text mining tool for assisting biocuration. *Nucleic acids research*, 41(W1):W518–W522.

Tianyi Zhang*, Varsha Kishore*, Felix Wu*, Kilian Q. Weinberger, and Yoav Artzi. 2020. Bertscore: Evaluating text generation with bert. In *International Conference on Learning Representations*.

Abstractive Approaches To Multidocument Summarization Of Medical Literature Reviews

Rahul Tangsali *
rahuul2001@gmail.com

Aditya Vyawahare *
aditya.vyawahare07@gmail.com

Aditya Mandke †
amandke@ucsd.edu

Onkar Litake †
olitake@ucsd.edu

Dipali Kadam ‡
ddkadam@pict.edu

Pune Institute of Computer Technology, India

Abstract

Text summarization has been a trending domain of research in NLP in the past few decades. The medical domain is no exception to the same. Medical documents often contain a lot of jargon pertaining to certain domains, and performing an abstractive summarization on the same remains a challenge. This paper presents a summary of the findings that we obtained based on the shared task of Multidocument Summarization for Literature Review (MSLR). We stood fourth in the leaderboards for evaluation on the MS^2 and Cochrane datasets. We finetuned pre-trained models such as BART-large, DistilBART and T5-base on both these datasets. These models' accuracy was later tested with a part of the same dataset using ROUGE scores as the evaluation metrics.

1 Introduction

The last few decades have witnessed a wide range of research applications in the field of natural language processing, especially text summarization. Text summarization has been applied in a number of domains including healthcare and medicine. With the tremendous amounts of big data getting generated in the medical industry each day, there is a need realized for effective techniques to summarize the data for further purposes. With the exponential rise in data getting accumulated in hospital databases and medical research labs, the need is increasing correspondingly. Text summarization in the healthcare domain has enabled far-reaching benefits for medical professionals. Effective summarization techniques help researchers and other individuals to parse long documents effectively, and gain valuable insights in shorter time periods.

The history of text summarization in NLP dates back to 1958, when the first paper on text summarization was published. Since then, its incorporation in healthcare has been widely done. Text mining and NLP methods have played an essential role in developing automatic text processing tools (Fleuren and Alkema, 2015). Automatic text summarization, thus proves to be an effective means of gaining valuable information from large documents and reports. In the medical domain, many approaches have been proposed for effective document summarization(Mishra et al., 2014) (Moradi and Ghadiri, 2019). Subfields in the biomedical domain where summarization is used include medical literature(Moradi and Ghadiri, 2016), evidence-based medical care (Fiszman et al., 2009), clinical notes(Moen et al., 2016), and drug information extraction(Fiszman et al., 2006).

Summarization approaches are broadly classified as abstractive and extractive. In extractive summarization(Gupta and Lehal, 2010), important sentences from the text are directly extracted and put into the summary, whereas for abstractive summarization(Moratanch and Chitrakala, 2016), new sentences depicting the summary of the topic are formed. Summarization approaches based on the number of documents can be classified as single document and multi-document(more than one documents are searched). In this paper, we present our findings obtained from performing multi-document summarization on the MS^2(DeYoung et al., 2021a) and Cochrane(Wallace et al., 2020a) datasets.

We finetune a few models on the MS^2 and Cochrane datasets, and research upon the best possible hyperparameters that could give us good results. We experimented with the BART-large model (Lewis et al., 2020) provided by Facebook AI on HuggingFace, the CNN version of the DistilBART model (Shleifer and Rush, 2020), and T5-base model (Raffel et al., 2020a) for text summarization. We preprocessed the inherently messy data provided, and generated summariza-

* equal contribution
† equal contribution
‡ equal contribution

Proceedings of the Third Workshop on Scholarly Document Processing, pages 199–203
October 12–17, 2022.

MS^2 (Provided Dataset)	Total input studies	Target summaries
Train	323608	14191
Validation	49002	2021
Test	42723	-
Cochrane (Provided Dataset)	**Total input studies**	**Target summaries**
Train	40497	3752
Validation	5033	470
Test	5678	-

Table 1: Statistics of the dataset used for training

tions on the same. We have experimented and compared the results of the aformentioned models. The datasets were provided by AllenAI. We have used the ROUGE evaluation metric (Lin, 2004) for comparing summarization accuracies.

2 Dataset Description

2.1 MS^2 (Multi-Document Summarization of Medical Studies)

The MS^2 (Multi-Document Summarization of Medical Studies) dataset (DeYoung et al., 2021b) is derived from documents and summaries from systematic literature reviews constructed from the papers in the Semantic Scholar literature Corpus (Ammar et al., 2018). Systematic literature reviews are a type of biomedical paper that compiles results from many different studies. The MS^2 dataset uses clustering before splitting into train, validation and test to avoid the learning of the test data during training. For each review, sentences were classified into 2 categories: Target sentences which contained information about the findings or summary of the paper and background sentences which described the research question. The statistics of the data provided are given in Table 1.

2.2 Cochrane Dataset

The Cochrane dataset (Wallace et al., 2020b) consists of the systematic reviews, created by the Cochrane collaboration, along with the title and abstract of the trials summarized by these reviews. The reviews summarized about 10 trials on average. The abstracts of the systematic reviews contained an average length of 75 words. The dataset statistics provided by the organizers are given in Table 1.

3 Data Preparation

The MS^2 and Cochrane datasets were provided to us in the CSV format. The input dataset consisted of the following columns: "ReviewID", "PMID", "Title" and "Abstract", whereas the target dataset consisted of the following columns: "ReviewID" and "Target". For the MS^2 dataset, additional 'Reviews-Info' files were included, which consisted of background information associated with the review. However, we didn't utilize them for training purposes.

In data preprocessing, the reviews present in the MS^2 and Cochrane datasets contain unnecessary delimiters and redundant line breakers, which made it necessary to clean them, before they could be passed to the model. We used simple Pandas preprocessing(Mckinney, 2011) on the CSV files, and cleaned these reviews into simple plain text which could be passed to the model.

We mapped each of the documents corresponding to a particular review ID, to the corresponding target summary in the target dataset, thus establishing a many-to-one relationship between the abstracts and the targets. We then removed all the other columns which were unnnecessary for summarization ("Background", "Title", etc). Newly formed dataframes, consisting of the source texts (multiple documents merged together for each review ID) and the target text (target summaries) were formed and passed for preprocessing.

We used the pretrained BART-base tokenizer provided by Facebook AI for the BART-large and DistilBART models, whereas for the T5-base model training, the t5-base tokenizer was used. Both of these tokenizers are available open-source on the HuggingFace[1] model hub.

4 Experiments

4.1 Training Details

For training the models we used the Simple Transformers [2] library, an API used for transformer mod-

[1]https://huggingface.co

[2]https://simpletransformers.ai/

System/Model	rougeL	rouge1	rouge2	RougeLsum
facebook/bart-large	0.1449	0.2139	0.0349	0.172
sshleifer/distilbart-cnn-12-6	0.1377	0.2082	0.0298	0.1347
t5-base	0.1139	0.1762	0.1830	0.1179

Table 2: Scores recorded on the MS^2 dataset.

System/Model	rougeL	rouge1	rouge2	RougeLsum
facebook/bart-large	0.1751	0.2638	0.0576	0.1775
sshleifer/distilbart-cnn-12-6	0.1821	0.2898	0.0503	0.1820
t5-base	0.1549	0.2278	0.0319	0.1549

Table 3: Scores recorded on the Cochrane dataset.

els (Vaswani et al., 2017), which provides built-in support for various natural language processing tasks including text summarization.

We trained our models on the Nvidia K80 GPU which has a GPU RAM of 15 gigabytes. CUDA was utilized for effective computing, and making the training and evaluation processes faster. All the models were trained on 10 epochs, with training and validation losses measured over time for each epoch.

We trained the BART-large and the DistilBART-CNN models on the datasets, by instantiating Seq2Seq models (Sutskever et al., 2014) and arguments provided by Simple Transformers. We later modified some of the arguments by making the maximum length for each sequence equal to 140. Due to limited RAM available on the CUDA used, we faced memory errors. Hence, after each epoch, the weights directory was overwritten for memory availability. Maximum sequence length for the tokenized sequences of each input document was set to 512. For T5 (Text-To-Text Transfer Transformer), we used the t5-base models (Raffel et al., 2020b), after providing t5-base tokenization, and trained them with the same aforementioned hyperparameters.

All the above mentioned hyperparameters were giving the best possible results, and hence we proceeded with the use of the same. We finetuned the basic configurations specified in the Fairseq documentation. [3]

4.2 Evaluation Metrics

ROUGE Score (Lin, 2004), which stands for Recall-Oriented Understudy for Gisting Evaluation, was used as the evaluation metric. To calculate the rouge score we used the rouge metric provided by HuggingFace library [4]. We recorded rouge1, rouge2, rougeL and RougeLsum scores for our summaries. Rouge1 measured the overlap of unigram between the candidate and the reference summaries whereas rouge2 compared the bigram similarities between the summaries. RougeL and RougeLsum measured the Longest Common Subsequence (LCS)(Lin and Och, 2004) words between predicted and target summaries. All the Rouge scores recorded are scored out of 1; where, closer to 1 means more accurate summaries.

5 Results

For the results please refer to Table 2 and Table 3. The table contains different models which we tried for the summarization task and the ROUGE recorded on those models. For the submission of the summarization task on both datasets, we used the BART-base tokenizer and trained BART-large model provided by Facebook AI.

6 Competition Results

We obtained high rouge1 and deltaEi-macrof1 scores for the multi-document summarization task on the Cochrane dataset. We stood 5th when ranked according to rougeL metric.

For the MS^2 data summarization subtask, we stood 4th when ranked according to the rougeL metric. We attained high delta EI-avg scores for the summarization subtask.

The scores obtained in the MSLR MS^2 and Cochrane subtask are given in Table 4

[3] https://fairseq.readthedocs.io/en/latest/index.html

[4] https://huggingface.co/spaces/evaluate-metric/rouge

MSLR Subtask	rougeL	rouge1	rouge2	BERTScore	DeltaEI-avg	DeltaEI-macrof1
MS^2	0.1439	0.2060	0.0350	0.8479	0.5319	0.3558
Cochrane	0.1725	0.2468	0.0545	0.8591	0.2707	0.3789

Table 4: Rouge and BERT scores of the summarizations submitted to MSLR MS^2 and Cochrane Subtasks.

7 Conclusion

Thus, we implemented multi-document summarization of different clinical studies and their literature surveys in the medical field. We implemented various architectures and analysed their performance. Finally, we evaluated the models using ROUGE metric. We plan to explore other models and tokenization methods to provide more accurate summarizations. Also, we plan to train the models on different medical survey datasets for better results in our summarizations.

References

Waleed Ammar, Dirk Groeneveld, Chandra Bhagavatula, Iz Beltagy, Miles Crawford, Doug Downey, Jason Dunkelberger, Ahmed Elgohary, Sergey Feldman, Vu Ha, Rodney Kinney, Sebastian Kohlmeier, Kyle Lo, Tyler Murray, Hsu-Han Ooi, Matthew Peters, Joanna Power, Sam Skjonsberg, Lucy Wang, Chris Wilhelm, Zheng Yuan, Madeleine van Zuylen, and Oren Etzioni. 2018. Construction of the literature graph in semantic scholar. In *Proceedings of the 2018 Conference of the North American Chapter of the Association for Computational Linguistics: Human Language Technologies, Volume 3 (Industry Papers)*, pages 84–91, New Orleans - Louisiana. Association for Computational Linguistics.

Jay DeYoung, Iz Beltagy, Madeleine van Zuylen, Bailey Kuehl, and Lucy Lu Wang. 2021a. Ms2: Multi-document summarization of medical studies.

Jay DeYoung, Iz Beltagy, Madeleine van Zuylen, Bailey Kuehl, and Lucy Lu Wang. 2021b. Ms^2: Multi-document summarization of medical studies. In *EMNLP*.

Marcelo Fiszman, Dina Demner-Fushman, Halil Kilicoglu, and Thomas C. Rindflesch. 2009. Automatic summarization of medline citations for evidence-based medical treatment: A topic-oriented evaluation. *J. of Biomedical Informatics*, 42(5):801–813.

Marcelo Fiszman, Thomas C Rindflesch, and Halil Kilicoglu. 2006. Summarizing drug information in medline citations. *AMIA ... Annual Symposium proceedings. AMIA Symposium*, page 254—258.

Wilco W. M. Fleuren and Wynand Alkema. 2015. Application of text mining in the biomedical domain. *Methods*, 74:97–106.

Vishal Gupta and Gurpreet Lehal. 2010. A survey of text summarization extractive techniques. *Journal of Emerging Technologies in Web Intelligence*, 2.

Mike Lewis, Yinhan Liu, Naman Goyal, Marjan Ghazvininejad, Abdelrahman Mohamed, Omer Levy, Veselin Stoyanov, and Luke Zettlemoyer. 2020. Bart: Denoising sequence-to-sequence pre-training for natural language generation, translation, and comprehension. In *ACL*.

Chin-Yew Lin. 2004. ROUGE: A package for automatic evaluation of summaries. In *Text Summarization Branches Out*, pages 74–81, Barcelona, Spain. Association for Computational Linguistics.

Chin-Yew Lin and Franz Josef Och. 2004. Automatic evaluation of machine translation quality using longest common subsequence and skip-bigram statistics. In *Proceedings of the 42nd Annual Meeting of the Association for Computational Linguistics (ACL-04)*, pages 605–612, Barcelona, Spain.

Wes Mckinney. 2011. pandas: a foundational python library for data analysis and statistics. *Python High Performance Science Computer*.

Rashmi Mishra, Jiantao Bian, Marcelo Fiszman, Charlene R Weir, Siddhartha Jonnalagadda, Javed Mostafa, and Guilherme Del Fiol. 2014. Text summarization in the biomedical domain: a systematic review of recent research. *Journal of biomedical informatics*, 52:457—467.

Hans Moen, Laura-Maria Peltonen, Juho Heimonen, Antti Airola, Tapio Pahikkala, Tapio Salakoski, and Sanna Salanterä. 2016. Comparison of automatic summarisation methods for clinical free text notes. *Artificial Intelligence in Medicine*, 67:25–37.

Milad Moradi and Nasser Ghadiri. 2016. Different approaches for identifying important concepts in probabilistic biomedical text summarization.

Milad Moradi and Nasser Ghadiri. 2019. Text summarization in the biomedical domain. *ArXiv*, abs/1908.02285.

N. Moratanch and S. Chitrakala. 2016. A survey on abstractive text summarization. In *2016 International Conference on Circuit, Power and Computing Technologies (ICCPCT)*, pages 1–7.

Colin Raffel, Noam Shazeer, Adam Roberts, Katherine Lee, Sharan Narang, Michael Matena, Yanqi Zhou, Wei Li, and Peter J. Liu. 2020a. Exploring the limits of transfer learning with a unified text-to-text transformer. *Journal of Machine Learning Research*, 21(140):1–67.

Colin Raffel, Noam Shazeer, Adam Roberts, Katherine Lee, Sharan Narang, Michael Matena, Yanqi Zhou, Wei Li, and Peter J. Liu. 2020b. Exploring the limits of transfer learning with a unified text-to-text transformer. *Journal of Machine Learning Research*, 21(140):1–67.

Sam Shleifer and Alexander M. Rush. 2020. Pre-trained summarization distillation.

Ilya Sutskever, Oriol Vinyals, and Quoc V Le. 2014. Sequence to sequence learning with neural networks. In *Advances in Neural Information Processing Systems*, volume 27. Curran Associates, Inc.

Ashish Vaswani, Noam Shazeer, Niki Parmar, Jakob Uszkoreit, Llion Jones, Aidan N. Gomez, Łukasz Kaiser, and Illia Polosukhin. 2017. Attention is all you need. In *Proceedings of the 31st International Conference on Neural Information Processing Systems*, NIPS'17, page 6000–6010, Red Hook, NY, USA. Curran Associates Inc.

Byron C. Wallace, Sayantan Saha, Frank Soboczenski, and Iain J. Marshall. 2020a. Generating (factual?) narrative summaries of rcts: Experiments with neural multi-document summarization.

Byron C. Wallace, Sayantani Saha, Frank Soboczenski, and Iain James Marshall. 2020b. Generating (factual?) narrative summaries of rcts: Experiments with neural multi-document summarization. *AMIA Annual Symposium*, abs/2008.11293.

An Extractive-Abstractive Approach for Multi-document Summarization of Scientific Articles for Literature Review

Kartik Shinde, Trinita Roy, Tirthankar Ghosal
SciSpace, US
(kartik,trinita,tirthankar)@typeset.io

Abstract

Research in the biomedical domain is constantly challenged by its large amount of ever-evolving textual information. Biomedical researchers are usually required to conduct a literature review before any medical intervention to assess the effectiveness of the concerned research. However, the process is time-consuming, and therefore, automation to some extent would help reduce the accompanying information overload. Multi-document summarization of scientific articles for literature reviews is one approximation of such automation. Here in this paper, we describe our pipelined approach for the aforementioned task. We design a BERT-based extractive method followed by a BigBird PEGASUS-based abstractive pipeline for generating literature review summaries from the abstracts of biomedical trial reports as part of the Multi-document Summarization for Literature Review (MSLR) shared task[1] in the Scholarly Document Processing (SDP) workshop 2022[2]. Our proposed model achieves the *best performance* on the MSLR-Cochrane leaderboard[3] on majority of the evaluation metrics. Human scrutiny of our automatically generated summaries indicates that our approach is promising to yield readable multi-article summaries for conducting such literature reviews.

1 Introduction

The effectiveness of medical treatments following medical diagnosis can have both acknowledgments and contradictions with respect to various studies conducted. Prior to any medical treatment, evidence synthesis is essential to understand and stay up-to-date with medical advances from different clinical studies. A literature survey provides high-quality evidence for healthcare. However, such a task is very time-consuming if done manually.

To mitigate these issues high-quality largescale multi-document summarization datasets, e.g., The Cochrane Dataset (Wallace et al., 2021) and Multi-Document Summarization of Medical Studies (MS2) Dataset (DeYoung et al., 2021) were developed. Both the datasets consists of a wide variety of task-oriented summaries from clinical trials. To further encourage community research in multi-document summarization of biomedical reviews, the Allen Institute for Artificial Intelligence (or "AI2" for short) proposed a shared task named Multi-document Summarization for Literature Review (MSLR) 2022[4].

The MSLR shared task aims at summarizing and analyzing medical evidence from different clinical studies. The task consists of two datasets - Cochrane and MS2, which provide a brief narrative summary from the abstracts of different clinical studies communicating the main findings.

In this paper, we describe our system submission for the task. We participated in the Cochrane subtask. In our system submission, we design a pipelined approach leveraging state-of-the-art neural extractive and abstractive summarization models. Our system first extracts the vital information from the abstracts of all papers under a particular review ID and then generates an abstractive summary, with the help of pre-trained BigBird PEGASUS model (Zaheer et al., 2020), as the literature review test for that review ID.

2 Related Work

The concerned task in MSLR is a novel one and hence not much prior works were conducted except the papers that proposed the datasets. However, in this section we discuss some relevant recent works on multi-document summarization. Agarwal et al. (2011) propose an unsupervised method of using topic based clustering of fragments extracted from

[1]https://github.com/allenai/mslr-shared-task
[2]https://sdproc.org/2022/
[3]https://leaderboard.allenai.org/mslr-cochrane/submissions/public

Proceedings of the Third Workshop on Scholarly Document Processing, pages 204–209
October 12–17, 2022.

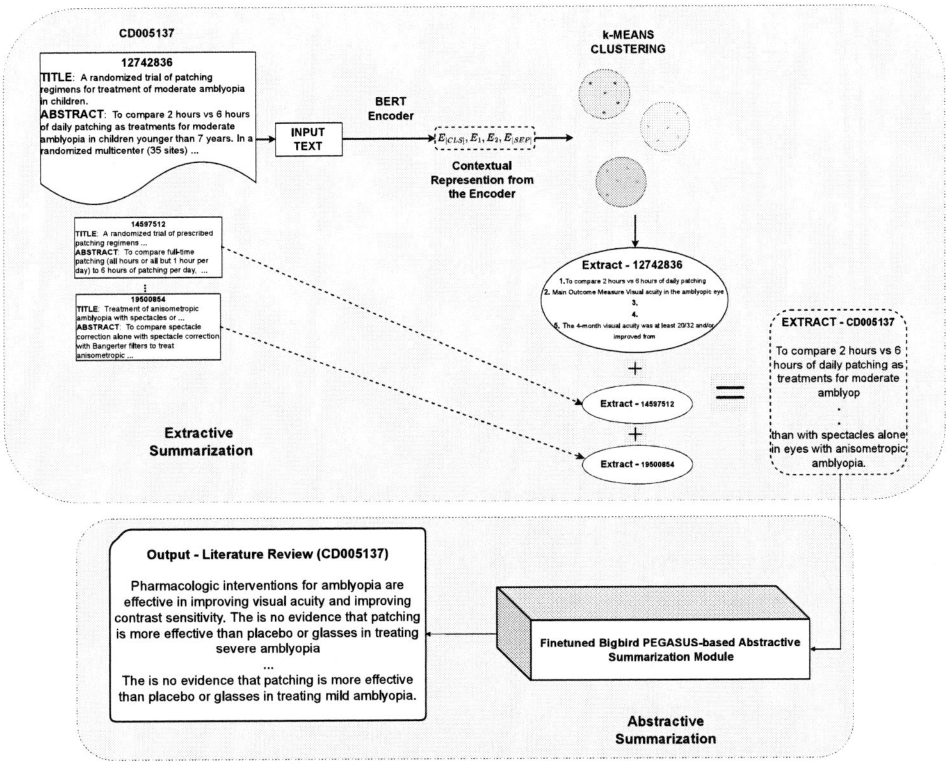

Figure 1: Workflow of the hybrid model - Original Abstracts from different PMIDs under a Review ID (*Top Left*), Combined Extractive summary being used as input for the abstractive summarizer (*Right*), Generated Output as a Literature Review Text (*Bottom*).

each co-cited article.

These fragments are ranked by relevance via a query generated from the context surrounding the co-cited list of papers. Multi-document summarization techniques can be broadly categorized into graph based (Mihalcea and Tarau, 2004; Meena et al., 2014; Hariharan and Srinivasan, 2009; Ge et al., 2011; Nguyen-Hoang et al., 2012), cluster based (Schlesinger et al., 2008; Meena et al., 2014; Gupta and Siddiqui, 2012) term frequency based (Salton, 1989; Fukumoto and SUGIMURA, 2004), context based (Sonawane et al., 2019), and latent semantic analysis based methods (Varma, 2019; Steinberger et al., 2004). Zakowski et al. (2004) describes a PICO (**P**opulation, **I**ntervention, **C**omparator and **O**utcome) framework for systematic review research. The study gives an account of the population that is being studies, what intervention was studied, what the intervention was compared to and what was the outcome. As an extension of PICO, DeYoung et al.; Fabbri et al. groups and identifies overall findings in reviews. However, multi document summarization needs expansion in the biomedical domain so as to reduce time and cost for addressing the delay in creating and updating reviews, thereby needing automation (DeYoung et al., 2021). Studies like (Marshall et al., 2016; Tsafnat et al., 2014) make an attempt at such automation tasks. Further, DeYoung et al. explore the use of Bi-directional and Auto-Regressive Transformers (Lewis et al., 2019) based approach on the MS2 Dataset. Pertaining to the peculiarities of the task, we formulate a hybird extractive-abstractive approach using a BERT-based extractive summarizer with K-means Clustering and a BigBird-PEGASUS based abstractive summarizer. Our system achieved the best performance among all the participating systems with a ROUGE-L score of 0.1969.

3 Dataset Description

The MSLR2022 shared task consists of two subtasks based on the Cochrane dataset (Wallace et al., 2021) and the MS2 dataset (DeYoung et al., 2021). In the Cochrane dataset there are approximately 4.5K systematic reviews of all trials relevant to a given clinical question, compiled by members of the Cochrane Collaboration. The dataset consists of the summarized systematic reviews along with the titles and abstracts of, on an average, 10 clinical trials each. The average length of the abstracts of

Model	ROUGE-L	ROUGE-1	ROUGE-2	BERTscore F1	Delta EI Avg. Divergence	Delta EI Macro F1
BERT+PEGASUS	**0.1969**	**0.2622**	0.0574	0.8590	0.2234	0.3011
ittc2	0.1837	0.2464	**0.0692**	**0.8762**	0.2195	0.3089
ittc1	0.1787	0.2413	0.0643	0.8729	0.2880	0.3375
BART	0.1760	0.2397	0.0671	0.8632	0.2081	0.3348
Longformer BART	0.1755	0.2387	0.0655	0.8641	0.2345	0.3316

Table 1: Evaluation Scores of different models in the MSLR2022 Cochrane Subtask.

the included trials is 245 words and the target summary is of the average length of 75 words. MS2 is a dataset containing 20K medical systematic reviews from approximately 470K studies collected from PubMed, created as an annotated subset of the Semantic Scholar research corpus. The MS2 dataset is much larger than the Cochrane dataset, but the latter contains cleaner data. For this shared task, the inputs and the target summaries are oriented in the same format which is then split into train, dev and test.

4 Methodology

Multi-document summarization aims to have a summary with maximum coverage and cohesiveness with less redundant data from the given set of papers pertaining to a topic. Sequence-to-sequence models do not perform well with large input sizes (Zaheer et al., 2020). Hence, we choose to leverage an extractive-abstractive summarization technique in our approach, to summarize biomedical reviews of correlated papers. In extractive summarization, we select a pre-decided number of statements from a given text as a relatively shorter representation of the entire text. We choose the Lecture Summarizer model in order to extract the most important sentences. This extraction is done by using a clustering algorithm on a set of embeddings, which are basically the contextual representations of sentences obtained from a BERT encoder. Hence, this also assists in maintaining some sort of coherence withing the input text.

We primarily use the provided abstracts as inputs to the extractive summarizer. For the titles that do not have any abstract, we use the titles as the inputs instead. We shorten these inputs to have at most five sentences from every different paper within a given Review_Id. We use BERT Extractive Summarizer (Miller, 2019), a model that performs extractive text summarization on lecture transcripts. We pass the abstracts separately to this model. The model first generates the contextual embeddings of the the input sentences. Further, the K-means clustering algorithm is used to find the k-sentences closest to the cluster's centroids. We proceed with the top 5 sentences from the cluster. The workflow of the model is provided in Figure 1.

For every Review_Id, we join the short extracts from different papers under that particular ID, and use the resulting sequence as the input sequence for training the abstractive summarization module. These shortened extracts, put together with the target summaries from original Cochrane dataset, give us a new data. We choose the BigBird PEGASUS model from (Zaheer et al., 2020), and finetune it on this newly obtained dataset. This model uses global attention and random attention on the input sequences apart from sparse-attention, which theoretically approximates to full attention. This sparse-attention mechanism can handle sequences of length up to 8x compared to what was possible prior to this and simultaneously reduces the quadratic dependency to linear, hence making the model suitable to learn using longer input sequences.

We finetune the model from the checkpoint '*google/bigbird-pegasus-large-pubmed*' using the newly created data for 6 epochs with a batch size of 4 and an initial learning rate of 2e-5 accompanied by FP16 precision training. The final output of the abstractive summarization module is the 'Related Works' text corresponding to the research topic aligned with a particular Review_Id. Figure 1 shows the workflow of our hybrid extractive-abstractive system.

5 Result and Analysis

The task realizes ROUGE (-1,2,L) (Lin, 2004), BERTScore F1 (Zhang et al., 2019), along with Delta EI Average Divergence and Macro F1 to be best suitable metrics for evaluation. Hence, to monitor the training, we use ROUGE as the basis of evaluation. Table 1 shows the comparison among all the participant teams on the Cochrane subtask where our best submission ranks first in ROUGE-L (0.1969) and ROUGE-1 (0.2622) scores.

ROUGE scores do not sufficiently measure the factual correctness of statements. Table 2 shows a

Review ID	Model Generated Summary
CD007066	There is some evidence that aliskiren 300 mg is superior to placebo in lowering blood pressure in patients with hypertension. The data are based on a single study and therefore we can not draw any conclusions about the relative efficacy of aliskiren 300 mg versus placebo.
CD005616	Devain disease is a common cause of pain in women of childbearing age. The evidence is limited and the use of cortisone injections in devain disease is not currently recommended.
CD007926	Menopausal hormone therapy is effective in the treatment of women with advanced or recurrent endometrial cancer. The is insufficient evidence to recommend the use of hormonal therapy alone or in combination with other hormonal agents.
CD002869	There is insufficient evidence to support or refute the effectiveness of any intervention to improve maternal and neonatal outcomes. The evidence is limited, and the results are not consistent across studies. The evidence is limited, and the results do not support the use of any intervention to improve maternal and neonatal outcomes.

Table 2: Example outputs of the hybrid model on the Cochrane dataset.

Review ID	Error outputs
CD004366	There is insufficient evidence to support the use of exercise as a treatment for depression. The is insufficient evidence to support the use of exercise as a treatment for depression. The is insufficient evidence to support the use of exercise as a treatment for depression.
CD010256	There is no evidence to support the use of aminophylline in the treatment of acute asthma. The is no evidence to support the use of salbutamol in the treatment of acute asthma. The is no evidence to support the use of aminophylline in the treatment of acute asthma.

Table 3: Observed erroraneous outputs from the model on the Cochrane dataset.

few instances with the review IDs and the generated literature review text. We can see that the generated text is coherent and does not contradict within itself. We observe that all the summaries were factually true and matched with the statements from input abstracts. Although the model generates better among other systems, a few issues still persist. Table 3 shows the most observed error case in the generation of model. We see that the model repeats the same statements multiple times. This might be attributed to the fact that a *Literature Review* OR *Related Works* section from a paper often consists of statements that are very coherent, and reinforce each other in order to establish an overall review of literature from a particular research topic. They highlight different findings, and more often than not, they have a similar gist.

For instances, consider a) "*We found only low quality evidence comparing ultra-radical and standard surgery in women with advanced ovarian cancer and carcinomatosis.*", b) "*It was unclear whether there were any differences in progression-free survival, QoL and morbidity between the two groups.*", and c) "*We are, therefore, unable to reach definite conclusions about the relative benefits and adverse effects of the two types of surgery.*". All these statements are very closely related in terms of the message they deliver. Hence, the finetuned summarizer does not account for facts, instead repeats the overall gist of the literature review.

6 Limitations

There are no ground truth summaries for lecture summarizer and therefore no metric for evaluating the outputs that we receive from the model. Due to the use of a clustering algorithm, the extractive part of out system is not readily trainable. We notice that the same model could not perform well in the subtask using the MS2 dataset. This can pertain to the long input sequences which is much greater than the Cochrane input sizes. Sequence-to-sequence models tend to not perform well with larger input sizes. Even if we shorten the input sequences, we would be losing out of essential information from the original data.

7 Conclusion

With the increasing rate of research and publications, literature reviews help keep track of the various advancements in the respective domains. Automation, although essential, also opens up new challenges including summarization over contradictory information present in different studies over a particular topic and summarization quality. Although our results show that our hybrid approach can be used for generating fluent high-quality literature review summaries, there is still significant scope for improvement. Additionally, ethical concern involving the factuality of the summaries also comes into play because deploying such a system without proper monitoring is speculative when it comes to such a high-impact domain as healthcare. This task helps us understand the challenges in multi-document summarization in the high-impact biomedical domain. The future scope of research can include trying real-world applications of such systems having proper evaluation and monitoring strategies to test the correctness of the summaries.

References

Nitin Agarwal, Ravi Shankar Reddy, GVR Kiran, and Carolyn Rose. 2011. Towards multi-document summarization of scientific articles: making interesting comparisons with scisumm. In *Proceedings of the Workshop on Automatic Summarization for Different Genres, Media, and Languages*, pages 8–15.

Jay DeYoung, Iz Beltagy, Madeleine van Zuylen, Bailey Kuehl, and Lucy Lu Wang. 2021. Ms2: Multi-document summarization of medical studies. *arXiv preprint arXiv:2104.06486*.

Jay DeYoung, Eric Lehman, Ben Nye, Iain J Marshall, and Byron C Wallace. 2020. Evidence inference 2.0: More data, better models. *arXiv preprint arXiv:2005.04177*.

Alexander R Fabbri, Irene Li, Tianwei She, Suyi Li, and Dragomir R Radev. 2019. Multi-news: A large-scale multi-document summarization dataset and abstractive hierarchical model. *arXiv preprint arXiv:1906.01749*.

Jun-ichi Fukumoto and Tomoya SUGIMURA. 2004. Multi-document summarization using document set type classification. In *NTCIR*.

Shuzhi Sam Ge, Zhengchen Zhang, and Hongsheng He. 2011. Weighted graph model based sentence clustering and ranking for document summarization. In *The 4th International Conference on Interaction Sciences*, pages 90–95. IEEE.

Virendra Kumar Gupta and Tanveer J Siddiqui. 2012. Multi-document summarization using sentence clustering. In *2012 4th International Conference on Intelligent Human Computer Interaction (IHCI)*, pages 1–5. IEEE.

Shanmugasundaram Hariharan and Rengaramanujam Srinivasan. 2009. Studies on graph based approaches for single and multi document summarizations. *International Journal of Computer Theory and Engineering*, 1(5):1793–8201.

Mike Lewis, Yinhan Liu, Naman Goyal, Marjan Ghazvininejad, Abdelrahman Mohamed, Omer Levy, Ves Stoyanov, and Luke Zettlemoyer. 2019. Bart: Denoising sequence-to-sequence pre-training for natural language generation, translation, and comprehension. *arXiv preprint arXiv:1910.13461*.

Chin-Yew Lin. 2004. Rouge: A package for automatic evaluation of summaries. In *Text summarization branches out*, pages 74–81.

Iain J Marshall, Joël Kuiper, and Byron C Wallace. 2016. Robotreviewer: evaluation of a system for automatically assessing bias in clinical trials. *Journal of the American Medical Informatics Association*, 23(1):193–201.

Yogesh Kumar Meena, Ashish Jain, and Dinesh Gopalani. 2014. Survey on graph and cluster based approaches in multi-document text summarization. In *International Conference on Recent Advances and Innovations in Engineering (ICRAIE-2014)*, pages 1–5. IEEE.

Rada Mihalcea and Paul Tarau. 2004. Textrank: Bringing order into text. In *Proceedings of the 2004 conference on empirical methods in natural language processing*, pages 404–411.

Derek Miller. 2019. Leveraging bert for extractive text summarization on lectures. *arXiv preprint arXiv:1906.04165*.

Tu-Anh Nguyen-Hoang, Khai Nguyen, and Quang-Vinh Tran. 2012. Tsgvi: a graph-based summarization system for vietnamese documents. *Journal of Ambient Intelligence and Humanized Computing*, 3(4):305–313.

Gerard Salton. 1989. Automatic text processing: The transformation, analysis, and retrieval of. *Reading: Addison-Wesley*, 169.

Judith D Schlesinger, Dianne P O'leary, and John M Conroy. 2008. Arabic/english multi-document summarization with classy—the past and the future. In *International Conference on Intelligent Text Processing and Computational Linguistics*, pages 568–581. Springer.

Sheetal Sonawane, Archana Ghotkar, and Sonam Hinge. 2019. Context-based multi-document summarization. In *Contemporary advances in innovative and applicable information technology*, pages 153–165. Springer.

Josef Steinberger, Karel Jezek, et al. 2004. Using latent semantic analysis in text summarization and summary evaluation. *Proc. ISIM*, 4(93-100):8.

Guy Tsafnat, Paul Glasziou, Miew Keen Choong, Adam Dunn, Filippo Galgani, and Enrico Coiera. 2014. Systematic review automation technologies. *Systematic reviews*, 3(1):1–15.

Rashmi Varma. 2019. A hybrid approach for multi-document text summarization.

Byron C Wallace, Sayantan Saha, Frank Soboczenski, and Iain J Marshall. 2021. Generating (factual?) narrative summaries of rcts: Experiments with neural multi-document summarization. *AMIA Summits on Translational Science Proceedings*, 2021:605.

Manzil Zaheer, Guru Guruganesh, Kumar Avinava Dubey, Joshua Ainslie, Chris Alberti, Santiago Ontanon, Philip Pham, Anirudh Ravula, Qifan Wang, Li Yang, et al. 2020. Big bird: Transformers for longer sequences. *Advances in Neural Information Processing Systems*, 33:17283–17297.

Laura Zakowski, Christine Seibert, and Wisconsin Selma VanEyck. 2004. Evidence-based medicine: answering questions of diagnosis. *Clinical medicine & research*, 2(1):63–69.

Tianyi Zhang, Varsha Kishore, Felix Wu, Kilian Q Weinberger, and Yoav Artzi. 2019. Bertscore: Evaluating text generation with bert. *arXiv preprint arXiv:1904.09675*.

Overview of the DagPap22 Shared Task on Detecting Automatically Generated Scientific Papers

Yury Kashnitsky[1] **Drahomira Herrmannova**[1] **Anita de Waard**[1]
Georgios Tsatsaronis[1] **Catriona Fennell**[1] **Cyril Labbé**[2]
Elsevier, USA[1] Université Grenoble Alpes, France[2]
{d.herrmannova, a.dewaard, y.kashnitskiy
g.tsatsaronis, c.fennell}@elsevier.com,
cyril.labbe@imag.fr

Abstract

This paper provides an overview of the 2022 COLING Scholarly Document Processing workshop shared task on the detection of automatically generated scientific papers. We frame the detection problem as a binary classification task: given an excerpt of text, label it as either human-written or machine-generated. We shared a dataset containing excerpts from human-written papers as well as artificially generated content and suspicious documents collected by Elsevier publishing and editorial teams. As a test set, the participants were provided with a 5x larger corpus of openly accessible human-written as well as generated papers from the same scientific domains of documents. The shared task saw 180 submissions across 14 participating teams and resulted in two published technical reports. We discuss our findings from the shared task in this overview paper.

1 Introduction

There are increasing reports that research papers can be written by computers, which presents a series of concerns (e.g., see Cabanac et al. (2021)). For scientific publishers, the problem of automatic detection of generated scientific content provides a technical and ethical challenge. Technically, any detector of automatically generated content is hard to remain effective for long: e.g., if a new language or summarization model is developed to generate text, the detector no longer works (for more details see the paper by (Rosati, 2022)). In terms of ethics, it is important to distinguish malicious and benign scenarios of generated content appearing in submitted scientific manuscripts. It is possible that authors might resort to translation systems to aid their writing process, e.g. helping to translate some excerpts from their native language into English. However, there is increased evidence of fraudulent papers, partially or entirely artificially generated, that have passed the peer-review process and were published. Most notoriously, there has been an experiment called SCIgen[1] where an entire conference workshop was generated comprised of gibberish talks. See (Noorden, 2021) and (Labbé and Labbé, 2012) for more details on SCIgen's impact on science, SCIgen detectors, and other examples of gibberish papers lurking into scientific literature. Recently, "paper mills" (Else, 2021) have caught increased attention as the main source of potentially fabricated research content. In (Cabanac et al., 2021), the authors found traces of GPT2-generated content in scientific literature, along with "tortured phrases" appearing as a side effect of using generating models and paraphrasing tools like SpinBot[2].

Partly driven by this work, we have organised a competition to encourage the NLP community to detect automatically generated papers. This project is a collaboration between a publisher (Elsevier) and the research community to attempt a resolution through technical means. To build on the excellent detective work by the (Cabanac et al., 2021) team, excerpts from the papers in their paper were added as examples of "fake" text to the dataset in this competition.

2 Corpus creation

The data provided for this competition contains text excerpts from scientific papers and an indication of whether these texts are "fake" (probably generated) or "real", i.e. human-written. The data comes from both published and retracted Scopus papers with 5,327 records in the training set and

[1] https://pdos.csail.mit.edu/archive/scigen/

[2] https://spinbot.com

Proceedings of the Third Workshop on Scholarly Document Processing, pages 210–213
October 12–17, 2022.

21,310 records in the test set. Around 69% of all texts in both sets are "fake". The code reproducing some steps of the data generation process is publicly available (Kashnitsky, 2022).

The data comes from the following sources:

1. MICPRO retracted papers ("fake"). These are excerpts from a set of retracted papers of the "Microprocessors and microsystems" journal (MICPRO). Some of those are explored in (Cabanac et al., 2021) in the context of "tortured phrases";

2. Good MICPRO papers ("real"). Similar excerpts from earlier issues of the "Microprocessors and microsystems" journal;

3. Abstracts of papers related to UN's Sustainable Development Goals[3] ("real"). Sustainable Development Goals (SDGs) cover a wide range of topics, from poverty and hunger to climate action and clean energy;

4. Summarized SDG abstracts ("fake"). These texts were generated using "pszemraj/led-large-book-summary" model;

5. Summarized MICPRO abstracts ("fake"). The same model as above was applied to MICPRO abstracts;

6. Generated SDG abstracts (fake). These texts were generated using the "EleutherAI/gpt-neo-125M" model with the first sentence of the abstract being a prompt;

7. Generated MICPRO abstracts (fake). The same model as above was applied to MICPRO abstracts;

8. SDG abstracts paraphrased with Spinbot ("fake");

9. GPT-3 few-shot generated content with the first sentence of the abstract as a prompt ("fake").

We also experimented with back-translated content, e.g. when the original excerpt is translated to, say, German and then back to English. We found that modern translation systems are so advanced that the back-translated snippets look almost identical to the originals, hence we rejected the idea of including such content as "fake". Repeated back-translation, especially with under-represented languages (say, En -> Swahili -> Korean -> En) might introduce some artefacts and help the back-translated snippets look "more fake", but we didn't conduct such experiments.

Source N	Source	Acc, %
4	summarized_sdg	100
5	summarized_micpro	99.9
8	spinbot_paraphrased	98.9
1	micpro_retracted	97
9	generated_gpt3	95.5
7	generated_micpro	87.3
6	generated_sdg	74
3	sdg_abstracts_original	57.4
2	micpro_original	57.3

Table 1: Validation accuracy split by data provenance type from Sec. 2. Model: logistic regression with Tf-Idf text representation.

3 Competition setup

3.1 Metric and data split

The metric chosen in the competition is average F1-score. We merged all data sources described in Sec. 2 (skipping only back-translated content as almost identical to the original), and performed a stratified 20/80 train-test split intentionally leaving a small train set. This resulted in 5327 training records and 21310 test records forming the datasets described on the competition page[4].

3.2 Baselines

As organizers, we provided 2 baselines: Tf-Idf & logistic regression[5] and fine-tuned SciBERT achieving 82% and 98.3% test set F1 score, respectively.

4 Experiments with data provenance

Given one of the simplest possible baseline models, namely, Tf-Idf & logistic regression, we explored model accuracy w.r.t. to data provenance, i.e. types of content described in Sec. 2.

Table 1 shows validation accuracy for the test set split by data provenance type, see Sec. 2 for details. The Tf-Idf & logistic regression model

[3] https://sdgs.un.org/2030agenda

[4] https://www.kaggle.com/competitions/detecting-generated-scientific-papers/

[5] Kaggle Notebook: https://bit.ly/3dJR9m0

was trained with 5,327 training records (containing data from all 9 sources listed in Sec. 2), and then the predictions were evaluated separately for each data source, i.e. first for excerpts from retracted MICPRO papers, then for excerpts from good MICPRO papers, and so on, up to excerpts of text generated with GPT-3.

We see that summarized content was easily detected, probably due to peculiarities of the "pszemraj/led-large-book-summary" summarization model, e.g. most of the summaries are opened with "This paper is focused on..." or "In this paper, the authors ...". Likewise, SpinBot-generated content is easily detected, probably because SpinBot was found to introduce "tortured phrases" (Cabanac et al., 2021) and those can be spotted even with Tf-Idf. Somewhat surprisingly, the model had no problem with retracted MICPRO content.

The model had most trouble identifying original human-written content, a possible reason is that with all the generated content due to class imbalance (70% of the data is "fake"), it's easy to get false positives when a normal human-written text is easy to be confused with fake content.

5 Systems Overview

14 teams participated in the task this year, with a total of 180 submissions. Out of these, 11 teams managed to beat the publicly shared Tf-Idf & logreg baseline, and 5 teams managed to beat the fine-tuned SciBERT baseline which was not publicly shared. Three teams submitted peer-reviewed technical reports, of which two are published as part of the workshop proceedings. Both teams managed to achieve >99% test set F1-score.

In "Detecting Generated Scientific Papers using an Ensemble of Transformer Models" (Glazkova and Glazkov, 2022) the authors describe an ensemble of SciBERT, RoBERTa, and DeBERTa fine-tuned using random oversampling technique.

The winning team led by Domenic Rosati "SynSciPass: detecting appropriate uses of scientific text generation" (Rosati, 2022) generates a partially synthetic dataset similar to what we as competition organizers had done. Then Rosati shows that the models trained with the DAGPap22 generalize badly to a new data source. Ablations studies show that generalization to unseen text generation models might not be possible with current approaches. Rosati concludes that the results in his paper should make it clear that at this point machine generated text detectors should not be used in production because they do not perform well on distribution shifts and their performance on realistic full-text scientific manuscripts is currently unknown.

6 Discussion

It turned out that the task turned was very easy to solve, with winners' models hitting >99% of the test set F1 scores. Although this suggests that the task of detecting machine-generated content is easy, both work done at Elsevier and as reported by the team led by Rosati convinces us that we are far from developing a general detector of generated content. Each new model (say, GPT-4) for which we don't have training data poses a new challenge, and any detector is likely to fail at identifying content generated with such a model due to a data shift. In summary, the problem is far from being solved: at this point we can not rely on detectors of generated content to support our production systems. However, the DAGPap22 shared task did offer a step forward to explore this challenging problem, and we hope to work together with the community on resolving this pernicious issue.

References

Guillaume Cabanac, Cyril Labbé, and Alexander Magazinov. 2021. Tortured phrases: A dubious writing style emerging in science. evidence of critical issues affecting established journals. *arXiv preprint arXiv:2107.06751*.

Holly Else. 2021. 'tortured phrases' give away fabricated research papers. *Nature*.

Anna Glazkova and Maksim Glazkov. 2022. Detecting generated scientific papers using an ensemble of transformer models. In *Proceedings of the Third Workshop on Scholarly Document Processing*. Association for Computational Linguistics.

Yury Kashnitsky. 2022. Source code for the coling workshop competition "detecting automatically generated scientific papers". `https://github.com/Yorko/fake-papers-competition-data`.

Cyril Labbé and Dominique Labbé. 2012. Duplicate and fake publications in the scientific literature: how many SCIgen papers in computer science? *Scientometrics*, pages 10.1007/s11192–012–0781–y.

Richard Van Noorden. 2021. Hundreds of gibberish papers still lurk in the scientific literature. *Nature*.

Domenic Anthony Rosati. 2022. Synscipass: detecting appropriate uses of scientific text generation. In *Proceedings of the Third Workshop on Scholarly Document Processing*. Association for Computational Linguistics.

SynSciPass: detecting appropriate uses of scientific text generation

Domenic Rosati
scite / Brooklyn, NY
dom@scite.ai

Abstract

Approaches to machine generated text detection tend to focus on binary classification of human versus machine written text. In the scientific domain where publishers might use these models to examine manuscripts under submission, misclassification has the potential to cause harm to authors. Additionally, authors may appropriately use text generation models such as with the use of assistive technologies like translation tools. In this setting, a binary classification scheme might be used to flag appropriate uses of assistive text generation technology as simply machine generated which is a cause of concern. In our work, we simulate this scenario by presenting a state-of-the-art detector trained on the DAGPap22 with machine translated passages from Scielo and find that the model performs at random. Given this finding, we develop a framework for dataset development that provides a nuanced approach to detecting machine generated text by having labels for the type of technology used such as for translation or paraphrase resulting in the construction of SynSciPass. By training the same model that performed well on DAGPap22 on SynSciPass, we show that not only is the model more robust to domain shifts but also is able to uncover the type of technology used for machine generated text. Despite this, we conclude that current datasets are neither comprehensive nor realistic enough to understand how these models would perform in the wild where manuscript submissions can come from many unknown or novel distributions, how they would perform on scientific full-texts rather than small passages, and what might happen when there is a mix of appropriate and inappropriate uses of natural language generation.

1 Introduction

While estimated submission rates of machine generated scientific papers are still small (Cabanac and Labbé, 2021), contemporary text generation models can generate highly fluent scientific text (Generative Pretrained Transformer et al., 2022) and manuscripts constructed this way could easily be produced en masse potentially introducing an unprecedented threat to scientific publishing and research integrity. Despite this risk, machine generated text in scientific settings have appropriate uses such as with assistive technology like translation, paraphrasing, and speech-to-text (Li et al., 2022). [1] Scientific manuscripts may increasingly use both appropriate and inappropriate text generation technologies. If appropriate uses of text generation cause a manuscript to be flagged or rejected this could harm populations that might already struggle with manuscript writing and submission. For instance, even if publisher's intention is only to guide editors, misclassified manuscripts can unintentionally bias editors decisions. Inspired by Schuster et al. (2020), we ask whether we can develop a method that could adequately distinguish between appropriate and inappropriate uses of text generation by identifying the category of tool being used such as for translation or paraphrase.

	DAGPap22	SynSciPass	Scielo
DAGPap22	99.6	31.4	52.0
SynSciPass	81.3	98.6	65.6
SciBERT	98.3		
TF-IDF	82.0		

Table 1: F1 scores on the DAGPap22, SynSciPass, and Scielo datasets including baselines for DAGPap22 (see Appendix B for model details)

Alarmingly, our study finds that a DeBERTa v3 (He et al., 2021) detector that achieves state-of-the-art performance when finetuned on a dataset designed for detecting generated academic text (DAGPap22 kag (2022)) does poorly on flagging

[1] This is not to say that other malicious applications of these technologies such as disguising plagarism do not exist or that use of poor quality text generation technologies don't introduce problems such as nonsensical phrases (see Cabanac et al. (2021))

Proceedings of the Third Workshop on Scholarly Document Processing, pages 214–222
October 12–17, 2022.

machine generated text under realistic scenarios of appropriate text generation (see Table 1 which shows SciBERT and logistic regression with TF-IDF baselines trained on DAGPap22 as well as DeBERTa v3 trained on DAGPap22 and SynSciPass). Since misflagging a manuscript as machine generated is harmful to the submitting author, we reframe the problem as detecting the type of tool used for generating text so that authors and publishers can have a more nuanced and neutral approach to understanding flagged texts and guiding editorial decisions. We develop a framework to generate academic texts including labels of the type of technology being used resulting in our dataset of synthetic scientific passages (SynSciPass). Section 2 explores how this dataset was constructed and how it could be extended to further improve robustness under domain shifts. In section 3, we show training on SynSciPass results in being able to distinguish the type of technology and how our reframed task helps us move beyond brittle attribution tasks that rely on having access to particular models or the less informative and potentially misleading binary detection task. Finally in section 4, we show that while models trained on our dataset are able to improve robustness under domain shifts for machine generated scientific texts, models for detecting machine generated scientific text are far from ready for safe use by publishers. We provide a roadmap for how to close the gap by focusing on realistic dataset construction that is designed to test detectors ability to robustly generalize across domain shifts.

2 A framework for robust and granular detection datasets

Previous work on detecting machine generated text has focused on attribution of text to particular models (Uchendu et al., 2020; Munir et al., 2021). These approaches have shown the utility of having knowledge of the underlying models for text generation since by having access to those models synthetic corpora can be built for the detection of synthetic text (Liyanage et al., 2022). However those approaches are limited to attributions on specific models trained on particular datasets and do not present a realistic or comprehensive scenario where models may be trained on different datasets or models might be unknown. Our framework improves upon model attribution methods by creating corpora from a variety of distributions with a hierarchy of labels including parent labels based on the type of tool used such as for paraphrasing, translation, or novel text generation. By having access to the type of tool used, we are able to make more sophisticated judgments about machine generated text such as allowing translation and paraphrase as appropriate uses of text generation while requiring more scrutiny for fully generated passages. Our framework consists of (1) proposing a taxonomy of approaches, model families, and models with a variety of pretraining or finetuning datasets that might be used for text generation and (2) sampling machine generated text from each model in the taxonomy so that each text can be labeled with a granular labeling scheme according to (1). By doing so, we hope to be able to attribute generated text not only to specific models but also model families and types of technology. With these more generic labels we are able to determine if models generalize detection across model families or across approaches used like if an unseen model for translation were to be introduced.

2.1 SynSciPass

In order to address these issues we constructed SynSciPass. For our dataset, we theorized three potential sources of machine generated text (1) free-form text generation using generative models like GPT-2 (2) paraphrase models and (3) translation models. While other approaches like speech-to-text or summarization are also likely used in practice, we restricted to the previously mentioned three. We also did not consider the use of multitask models like GPT-3 that are able to use in-context learning to also do paraphrase and translation (Brown et al., 2020) which future work should follow up on to understand if different uses of the same model can be properly distinguished. For each approach, we selected a variety of models from different model families in order to try to synthesize a distribution of text generations that might be found in manuscripts (as have been identified by Cabanac et al. (2021) and Cabanac and Labbé (2021)). These included common services a user might have access to like GPT-2, Spinbot, SCIgen (cf. Cabanac et al. (2021)) and Google translate as well state of the art approaches for each source such as BLOOM for text generation (BigScience, 2022). For each technology type, we also included at least one model that was trained on a distribution of scientific text. The final dataset consisted of

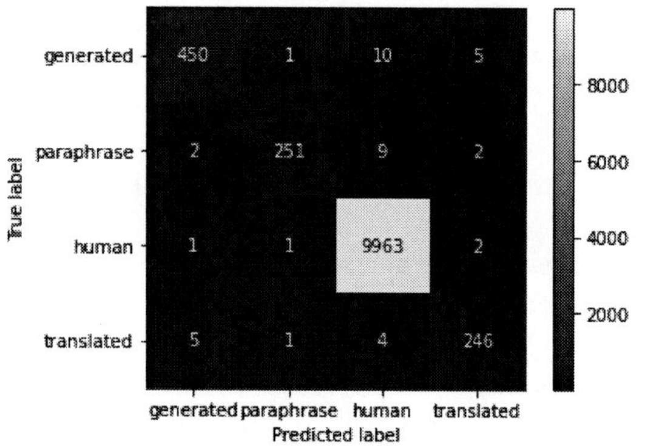

Figure 1: Confusion matrix for multi-class prediction on SciSynPass test set

110,474 passages of which 99,989 (90.5%) were not synthetic to introduce more realistic class imbalance given the estimation that only a few papers per million are machine generated (Cabanac and Labbé, 2021). Please reference Appendix A and B for construction details and Table 4 for full details on dataset construction including the models used to generate data and which model family and technology type they belong to.

3 Reframing synthetic text detection as multi-class classification for understanding appropriate use

Beyond making models more robust through producing a more comprehensive dataset, our framework reframes binary synthetic text detection as multi-class classification that asks not "Is this passage of text synthetic?" but asks "If this passage is synthetic, how was it created?". Given that there are several legitimate uses of text generation tools in the scientific writing process such as using assistive technology, in practice this reframing could allow journal editors to make a more nuanced assessment of potentially synthetic text. For example, if a passage of text was detected as using a translation tool, an editor or submitting author can assess if the translation tool was adequate in conveying meaning or if professional translation services should be employed during revisions. If a paraphrase tool was used, editors can assess whether it might have been used to disguise plagiarism or be the result of a poor quality tool such as Spinbot which is known to introduce non-idiomatic phrases (Cabanac et al., 2021).

Using this approach we trained a multi-class classifier resulting in a micro-averaged F1 score of 99.6% (97.4%, 96.9%, 99.8%, and 96.2% per class F1 for generation, paraphrase, human written, and translation classes respectively) on our held-out test set. To illustrate the models performance we present the confusion matrix in Figure 1 showing that our model does quite well across classes even with the large class imbalance. Additionally as seen in Table 1, the model achieves a F1 score of 81.3% on DAGPap22 which is quite good considering the different domains and notably is about the same as logistic regression with TF-IDF *despite not being trained on the DAGPap22 dataset*. However, this might simply be that DAGPap22 contains a similar underlying distribution. Unfortunately the distribution of DAGPap22 was not known at the time of writing preventing us from providing a nuanced picture of the differences and overlap between DAGPap22 and SynSciPass.

In order to see how our multi-class model might generalize across families of text generation models, we performed an ablation study (Table 2) measuring the performance of DeBERTa v3 trained on SynSciPass as a whole, DeBERTa v3 trained on SynSciPass with texts generated by gpt2-arxiv removed and finally DeBERTa v3 trained on SynSciPass with texts generated by BLOOM removed. F1 scores were reported on model performance on each text generate dataset (see Appendix A and B for details on dataset and model names). In Table 2 we see that removing gpt2-arxiv samples results in a small drop in average performance from the model trained on SynSciPass as a whole (96.5 F1 down from 97.0 F1) indicating that *when we test against a seen model trained on a new dataset detectors may still be effective at detecting the type of technology used.* Interestingly removing gpt2-arxiv samples causes the model to do better on gpt2 than SynSciPass as a whole (94.4 F1 up from 90.7 F1). This indicates that having access to the model on a generic domain might be more important than having access to a model pretrained on a specific distribution as has been studied in Rodriguez et al. (2022). Along these lines we see that removing BLOOM drops performance dramatically on BLOOM from 96.3 to 28.0 F1 score further indicating that having access to underlying models are particularly important and that unseen models may cause detectors to fail. Future work should try to analyze detection models trained to generalize across tools with a wider variety of models including more shifts in underlying pretraining

	BLOOM	distilgpt2	gpt2-arxiv	gpt2	SCIgen	average
SynSciPass	**96.3**	**100.0**	**97.9**	90.7	**100.0**	**97.0**
-gpt2-arxiv	93.5	96.6	**97.9**	**94.4**	**100.0**	96.5
-BLOOM	28.0	97.8	96.8	91.7	**100.0**	82.9

Table 2: Ablation study reporting F1 scores on each text generation subset using DeBERTa v3 trained on SynSciPass as a whole, SynSciPass without the samples generated by gpt2-arxiv and SynSciPass without samples generated by BLOOM. See Appendix A and B for more details.

distribution, a variety of model sizes, different sampling procedures, and introducing unseen models.

4 Out-of-domain Synthetic Passage Detection

Following poor performance of models trained only on DAGPap22 on SynSciPass and vice versa (See Table 1). We wanted to investigate additional domain shifts to understand how robust these models could be in realistic scenarios like seeing new subject domains or new models as this might give us a better picture of how these models might perform in practice. To test robustness over domain shift, we created an additional dataset by sampling human written English passages from Scielo (using Soares et al. (2019)) aligned with human written Spanish passages that were translated back into English. This was done to (1) simulate detection where manuscripts might have used translation and (2) simulate where the underlying distribution from Scielo represents a potential stylistic and disciplinary shift from the Pubmed and arXiv domains which have been seen in SynSciPass.

We sampled 1,000 bilingual English-Spanish human written passages from the Scielo bilingual scientific texts dataset (Soares et al., 2019). We kept the human written English passages labeled as human generated. Then we translated the aligned human written Spanish passages into English using Google translate and labeled these as machine generated. To get a sense of the resulting lexical overlap between the human and machine translated passages, the BLEU score was 40.9 where the overlap between the English passages with themselves is a BLEU score of 100.0. We tested the resulting dataset of 2,000 passages using (1) DeBERTa v3 trained on DAGPap22 only (DAGPap22) (2) DeBERTa v3 pretrained on the Pubmed split of scientific papers and pretrained on the test and train texts from DAGPap22 and then finetuned on DAGPap22 only (DAPT-TAPT) (3) DeBERTa v3 trained on SynSciPass only (SynSciPass) (4) DeBERTa v3 trained on only translations from SynSciPass (SynSciPass (Translation)) (5) DeBERTa v3 trained with potential confounding factors removed (passages generated by google translate and passages generated by a model finetuned on scielo) SynSciPass (SynSciPass (Removed)) (6) DeBERTa v3 trained on both SynSciPass and DAGPap22 (SynSciPass+DAGPap22) (See Appendix B for full training details). In order to compare the results fairly, we should be clear that SynSciPass uses 1 translation model that was finetuned on the same Scielo dataset (Soares et al., 2019) to back translate between English and Spanish as well as Google translate to back translate between English and Chinese so there may be some confounding effect of having samples produced by these models. SynSciPass does not contain any samples from Scielo itself. In order to address this potential confounding factor readers should reference the results from SynSciPass (Removed) where both of those sample sets are removed.

In Table 3, we see that DAGPap22 does quite poorly with an F1 score of 52%, mostly due to poor recall indicating that a state-of-the-art model trained on DAGPap22 would perform as if it's randomly assigning a human generated or machine generated label on translated material mixed in with human written passages from the Scielo domain. Even though this is somewhat expected given that DAGPap22 does not contain information about translations, it is alarming that this is what performance would look like in real life manuscript flagging systems if manuscripts used translators.

A standard approach to improving robustness is pretraining on in-domain and expected task datasets (Gururangan et al., 2020), when utilizing this (DAPT-TAPT) the model does not do too much better (57% F1) than the one trained on DAGPap22 only. Models trained on SynSciPass do improve (up to 66.5 F1 for SynSciPass (Translation)) but do not perform well enough to be considered safe. These results indicate that common approaches for

	AURC ↓	F1 ↑	Precision ↑	Recall ↑
DAGPap22	47.9	52.0	49.6	54.6
DAPT-TAPT	49.3	57.0	50.4	65.7
SynSciPass	51.3	65.6	50.2	94.5
SynSciPass (Translation)	41.3	66.5	50.0	99.1
SynSciPass (Removed)	49.6	66.5	50.1	99.1
SynSciPass+DagPap22	45.6	65.6	50.4	93.9

Table 3: Performance of models presented in Section 4 on an out of distribution translation dataset (Scielo Translations) showing a more than 13 point increase over a model trained on DAGPap22 when using SynSciPass.

machine generated text detection are not robust against shifts in domain and result in dismal performance under a realistic scenario. We also measured the area under risk-coverage (AURC) (El-Yaniv and Wiener, 2010) to present what it might be like if we calibrated our models to only select answers they are most confident in. For AURC, DAGPap22 actually does better than SynSciPass and DAPT-TAPT indicating that it's selective predictions can be made safer. Not surprisingly SynSciPass (Translation) achieves the best AURC of 41.3 indicating that its confidence scores are more meaningful than the others and would perform best at selective prediction, however this requires knowing where the test distribution comes from.

5 Limitations

Given the above results it should be clear that machine generated text detectors in the scientific domain are not very robust to realistic domain shifts. While adding nuance to classifications with the multi-class classifier and providing a more comprehensive dataset enables enhanced robustness, the approach is still sensitive to even small shifts in distribution such as using a known model, google translate in the Scielo case, trained on an unseen dataset, Spanish to English scientific passage translation. The major limitation with our framework is that in order to become more robust we will have to continue to collect more distributions to synthesize from and even as we collect a critical mass of potential distributions of machine generated text, our results are inconclusive as to whether models will continue to be more robust to distributions shifts. Our results with BLOOM removed indicate that generalization to unseen text generation models might not be possible with current approaches. Since machine generated text will continue to approach human-level fluency and new approaches will continue to be developed, it will not be tractable to develop a comprehensive dataset that is representative of the underlying distribution of machine generated text. Additionally, since these models are still sensitive to slight shifts in distribution, we suggest that future work should shift focus to improving robustness of detection on out of domain samples such as with selective prediction or more sample efficient approaches of collecting data to become robust as in Rodriguez et al. (2022). In order to accomplish this, future work should develop a comprehensive suite of tests to evaluate the effects of domain shifts on detectors.

While a multi-class labeling approach might help human evaluators of texts understand why a passage was flagged, this approach should additionally be extended to provide interpretability on why particular passages of texts were flagged. This can be with generating human-like rationales or using methods similar to GLTR (Gehrmann et al., 2019) to assist authors and journal editors in understanding places their manuscript might be improved.

Another limitation of both SynSciPass and DAGPap22 is that they both consist of small passages extracted from scientific texts. Since most manuscripts are submitted as long texts, we are not sure how these results would apply to realistic scientific full-texts, especially when those full-texts include tables, figures, and other non-textual items. While Rodriguez et al. (2022) does provide approaches to address this with passage-based models, future work should still aim to construct datasets that are more realistic and close to the task by providing full-text scientific documents that include layout, figures, and tables. Finally, these datasets should aim to match the extreme class imbalance that has been observed in real world distribution of machine generated texts identified in Cabanac and Labbé (2021).

6 Related Works

Jawahar et al. (2020) outlines many recent approaches to detecting machine generated text in a variety of domains. The closest to our approach is attribution models that attempt to use a stylometric approach for uncovering the authorship of a text where the author is a particular model or particular model using a particular dataset (Jones et al., 2022; Munir et al., 2021). Our approach is unique in that it focuses on attribution of general classes of tools such as translation, paraphrase, and generation rather than specific models.

While we agree in principal with criticisms of the stylometric approaches that seek to center the veracity and coherence of texts (Dou et al., 2022; Schuster et al., 2019), as text generation models improve, the factuality and fluency gap between machine and human generated text will get smaller and smaller and methods that utilize veracity and coherence will no longer work [2]. Additionally, many humans make errors and write poor quality manuscripts so we do not feel like this is a good criterion for detecting machine generated texts but should be clearly separated as an equally important but orthogonal task of understanding the quality of scientific texts. Similarly, we are skeptical of approaches like MAUVE (Pillutla et al., 2021) that rely on distributional artifacts produced by machine generated texts since as text generation models mature the gap between human and machine distributions will also close.

Rodriguez et al. (2022) is the closest to our work in examining the effects of domain shifts in detecting machine generated scientific texts showing that detectors do not generalize well when subject domains shift from physics to biomedicine. While they show that generating even a small number of samples in another domain improves detection, their work is limited to only GPT-2 making their findings reliant on having access to the underlying models. Data augmentation like we used is a common strategy shown to improve the robustness of models in NLP (Wang et al., 2022) and is common for examining text generation model attribution in detecting machine generated text since we have access to the underlying text generation models during analysis (Uchendu et al., 2020). Finally, recent work has examined the robustness of these models (Gagiano et al., 2021; Wolff, 2020) but these methods focus on robustness to adversarial attacks such as homoglyphs and misspellings rather than robustness to domain shifts and generalization to unseen models which is studied in this work and which we understand as area with the most promise for both understanding and improving detectors.

7 Ethics Statement

The results in this paper should make it clear that at this point machine generated text detectors should not be used in production because they do not perform well on distribution shifts and their performance on realistic full-text scientific manuscripts is currently unknown. Further development is needed on both interpretable and robust detection methods as well as better datasets that are both realistic (such as including full-texts rather than passages) and varied (including comprehensive samples across scientific disciplines). Because erroneously detecting a manuscript as machine generated is a high harm activity, future work should continue more nuanced harm-reduction approaches to synthetic paper detection like the ones introduced in this paper.

8 Data Availability

The final constructed dataset, SynSciPass, source code, and models are available at `https://github.com/domenicrosati/synscipass`.

9 Conclusion

Given our findings, we envision future work along three lines (1) developing machine generated text detectors that are robust across domain shifts and developing realistic datasets that test this robustness comprehensively (2) developing methods of interpretability that help editorial teams detect and manage the use of both appropriate and inappropriate use of text generation models (3) discussion about the safe and ethical application of these technologies and the potential harm involved in their deployment when use cases such as assistive technology are not considered.

We introduced a framework for collecting datasets to improve the robustness and interpretability of detecting machine generated text in the scientific domain. By developing a comprehensive dataset, SynSciPass, we were able to show that

[2] Clark et al. (2021) find that humans already cannot reliably distinguish between human and machine generated text produced by GPT-3)

models trained on it were not only more robust under domain shifts but also that those models were able to detect the generic type of text generation technology such as for translation, paraphrase, or novel generations which could help understand if a passage was generated by appropriate or inappropriate means. Despite these findings, our work has also shown that current models, including our own, do not perform well in realistic scenarios that change the distribution of text seen. Because of this lack of robustness, we suggest that future work concentrate on formulating both datasets and approaches that comprehensively test machine generated text detectors in a wide variety of realistic and unseen scenarios.

References

2022. Detecting generated scientific papers.

BigScience. 2022. Bigscience large open-science openaccess multilingual language model.

Tom B. Brown, Benjamin Mann, Nick Ryder, Melanie Subbiah, Jared Kaplan, Prafulla Dhariwal, Arvind Neelakantan, Pranav Shyam, Girish Sastry, Amanda Askell, Sandhini Agarwal, Ariel Herbert-Voss, Gretchen Krueger, Tom Henighan, Rewon Child, Aditya Ramesh, Daniel M. Ziegler, Jeffrey Wu, Clemens Winter, Christopher Hesse, Mark Chen, Eric Sigler, Mateusz Litwin, Scott Gray, Benjamin Chess, Jack Clark, Christopher Berner, Sam McCandlish, Alec Radford, Ilya Sutskever, and Dario Amodei. 2020. Language Models are Few-Shot Learners. ArXiv:2005.14165 [cs].

Guillaume Cabanac and C. Labbé. 2021. Prevalence of nonsensical algorithmically generated papers in the scientific literature. *J. Assoc. Inf. Sci. Technol.*

Guillaume Cabanac, Cyril Labbé, and Alexander Magazinov. 2021. Tortured phrases: A dubious writing style emerging in science. Evidence of critical issues affecting established journals. ArXiv:2107.06751 [cs].

Elizabeth Clark, Tal August, Sofia Serrano, Nikita Haduong, Suchin Gururangan, and Noah A. Smith. 2021. All That's 'Human' Is Not Gold: Evaluating Human Evaluation of Generated Text. In *Proceedings of the 59th Annual Meeting of the Association for Computational Linguistics and the 11th International Joint Conference on Natural Language Processing (Volume 1: Long Papers)*, pages 7282–7296, Online. Association for Computational Linguistics.

Arman Cohan, Franck Dernoncourt, Doo Soon Kim, Trung Bui, Seokhwan Kim, Walter Chang, and Nazli Goharian. 2018. A Discourse-Aware Attention Model for Abstractive Summarization of Long Documents. In *Proceedings of the 2018 Conference of the North American Chapter of the Association for Computational Linguistics: Human Language Technologies, Volume 2 (Short Papers)*, pages 615–621, New Orleans, Louisiana. Association for Computational Linguistics.

Yao Dou, Maxwell Forbes, Rik Koncel-Kedziorski, Noah A. Smith, and Yejin Choi. 2022. Is GPT-3 Text Indistinguishable from Human Text? Scarecrow: A Framework for Scrutinizing Machine Text. In *ACL*.

Ran El-Yaniv and Yair Wiener. 2010. On the foundations of noise-free selective classification. *Journal of Machine Learning Research*, 11(53):1605–1641.

Rinaldo Gagiano, Maria Kim, Xiuzhen Zhang, and J. Biggs. 2021. Robustness Analysis of Grover for Machine-Generated News Detection. In *ALTA*.

Sebastian Gehrmann, Hendrik Strobelt, and Alexander M. Rush. 2019. GLTR: Statistical Detection and Visualization of Generated Text. In *ACL*.

Gpt Generative Pretrained Transformer, Almira Osmanovic Thunström, and Steinn Steingrimsson. 2022. Can GPT-3 write an academic paper on itself, with minimal human input?

Suchin Gururangan, Ana Marasović, Swabha Swayamdipta, Kyle Lo, Iz Beltagy, Doug Downey, and Noah A. Smith. 2020. Don't Stop Pretraining: Adapt Language Models to Domains and Tasks. In *Proceedings of the 58th Annual Meeting of the Association for Computational Linguistics*, pages 8342–8360, Online. Association for Computational Linguistics.

Pengcheng He, Jianfeng Gao, and Weizhu Chen. 2021. DeBERTaV3: Improving DeBERTa using ELECTRA-Style Pre-Training with Gradient-Disentangled Embedding Sharing. ArXiv:2111.09543 [cs].

Ganesh Jawahar, Muhammad Abdul-Mageed, and L. Lakshmanan. 2020. Automatic Detection of Machine Generated Text: A Critical Survey. In *COLING*.

Keenan I. Jones, Jason R. C. Nurse, and Shujun Li. 2022. Are You Robert or RoBERTa? Deceiving Online Authorship Attribution Models Using Neural Text Generators. *ArXiv*.

Pengcheng Li, Wei Lu, and Qikai Cheng. 2022. Generating a related work section for scientific papers: an optimized approach with adopting problem and method information. *Scientometrics*, 127(8):4397–4417.

Vijini Liyanage, Davide Buscaldi, and Adeline Nazarenko. 2022. A Benchmark Corpus for the Detection of Automatically Generated Text in Academic Publications. ArXiv:2202.02013 [cs].

Shaoor Munir, Brishna Batool, Zubair Shafiq, P. Srinivasan, and Fareed Zaffar. 2021. Through the Looking Glass: Learning to Attribute Synthetic Text Generated by Language Models. In *EACL*.

Krishna Pillutla, Swabha Swayamdipta, Rowan Zellers, John Thickstun, S. Welleck, Yejin Choi, and Z. Harchaoui. 2021. MAUVE: Measuring the Gap Between Neural Text and Human Text using Divergence Frontiers. In *NeurIPS*.

Juan Rodriguez, Todd Hay, David Gros, Zain Shamsi, and Ravi Srinivasan. 2022. Cross-Domain Detection of GPT-2-Generated Technical Text. In *Proceedings of the 2022 Conference of the North American Chapter of the Association for Computational Linguistics: Human Language Technologies*, pages 1213–1233, Seattle, United States. Association for Computational Linguistics.

Tal Schuster, R. Schuster, Darsh J. Shah, and R. Barzilay. 2019. Are We Safe Yet? The Limitations of Distributional Features for Fake News Detection. *undefined*.

Tal Schuster, R. Schuster, Darsh J. Shah, and R. Barzilay. 2020. The Limitations of Stylometry for Detecting Machine-Generated Fake News. *Computational Linguistics*.

Felipe Soares, Viviane Pereira Moreira, and Karin Becker. 2019. A Large Parallel Corpus of Full-Text Scientific Articles. ArXiv:1905.01852 [cs].

Adaku Uchendu, Thai Le, Kai Shu, and Dongwon Lee. 2020. Authorship Attribution for Neural Text Generation. In *Proceedings of the 2020 Conference on Empirical Methods in Natural Language Processing (EMNLP)*, pages 8384–8395, Online. Association for Computational Linguistics.

Xuezhi Wang, Haohan Wang, and Diyi Yang. 2022. Measure and Improve Robustness in NLP Models: A Survey. In *Proceedings of the 2022 Conference of the North American Chapter of the Association for Computational Linguistics: Human Language Technologies*, pages 4569–4586, Seattle, United States. Association for Computational Linguistics.

Max Wolff. 2020. Attacking Neural Text Detectors. *ArXiv*.

A Construction of SynSciPass

SynSciPass was constructed using 100,000 passages that were randomly sampled from the scientific papers dataset (Cohan et al., 2018). Each passage was between 2 and 10 sentences randomly sampled from the full-text of single publication from both the arXiv and Pubmed training splits with a resulting mean token length of 142 tokens roughly matching the 140 token mean of the DAGPap22 dataset. From these passages 1,000 items were randomly sampled (with replacement) for each model found in Table 4. Passages that were constructed using BLOOM and GPT-2 proceeded following the approach of (Liyanage et al., 2022) where the first sentence of the real passage was used as the prompt to construct the synthetic passage, subsequent generations were used to re-prompt the model to sample passages between 2 and 10 sentences. The first sentence from the real passage was then removed. For these models greedy decoding with a temperature of 1.0 was used. For SCIgen, 1,000 papers were generated and then a random passage of between 2 and 10 sentences was extracted from each one. For the paraphrase models, a randomly sampled passage from the human written passages were sent through a paraphrase tool. For the translation models, a human written passage was sent through the translation tool into a target language and then back translated into english. For all models generations, text similarity was measured between the original passage and the synthesized example, if the sample was more than 10% similar it was not kept. This does simplify the problem and make the data less realistic as it removes synthetic passages that have a high lexical overlap with reference passages which might be common with inapporiate uses such as masking plagarism. The final dataset consisted of 110,474 passages of which 99,989 (90.5%) were human written. This was done to try to match the extreme class imbalance that has been observed on synthetic scientific papers in the wild (Cabanac and Labbé, 2021). The final dataset was split by 80%/10%/10% into train, validation, and test sets.

B Training details on models used

For this work, all of our classification models were trained by finetuneing DeBERTa v3 large (He et al., 2021) using the following hyperparameters: adamW optimizer, learning rate of 6e-6, batch size of 8, weight decay of 0.01 with warmup steps of 50. All classification models were trained for 3 epochs. For the domain adaptive pretraining (DAPT) model, we further pretrained using the parameters mentioned above with a masked language modeling objective on the Pubmed train split from the scientific papers dataset (Cohan et al., 2018) using 128 token chunks for 5 epochs. For the task adaptive pretraining (TAPT) model, we used the same approach with 5 epochs on the DAGPap22 dataset. Details of the SciBERT and logistic regression TF-

type	model family	model	passages
generate	bloom	bloom	1073
	gpt2	GPT-2-arxiv_generate	998
		distilgpt2	998
		gpt2-medium	998
	SCIgen	SCIgen	822
paraphrase	pegasus	pegasus-xsum-finetuned-paws*	1000
		pegasus-xsum-finetuned-paws-parasci*	1000
	spinbot	spinbot	990
real	real	real	99064
translate	google_translate	google_translate	901
	opus	opus-es-en	794
		opus-es-en-scielo*	901

Table 4: Approaches used for data augmentation and number of passages generated. Models with an asterisk were trained by the authors. Spinbot, SCIgen, and google translate are the names of the services used available online. The rest of the models are or will be made available on the huggingface repository under those names.

IDF model baselines were not made available at the time of writing this paper.

Detecting Generated Scientific Papers using an Ensemble of Transformer Models

Anna Glazkova
University of Tyumen
Tyumen, Russia
a.v.glazkova@utmn.ru

Maksim Glazkov
Voctiv RnD d.o.o. Beograd
Belgrade, Serbia
my.eye.off@gmail.com

Abstract

The paper describes neural models developed for the DAGPap22 shared task hosted at the Third Workshop on Scholarly Document Processing. This shared task targets the automatic detection of generated scientific papers. Our work focuses on comparing different transformer-based models as well as using additional datasets and techniques to deal with imbalanced classes. As a final submission, we utilized an ensemble of SciBERT, RoBERTa, and DeBERTa fine-tuned using random oversampling technique. Our model achieved 99.24% in terms of F1-score. The official evaluation results have put our system at the third place.

1 Introduction

State-of-the-art natural language processing (NLP) tools generate high-quality texts that could hardly be distinguished from human-written texts. This represents a remarkable achievement in modern science, but raises challenges in terms of detecting machine-generated texts. Detection of automatically generated texts is crucial for many NLP tasks, in particular, for prevention of spreading fake scientific publications and citations (Else et al., 2021). Here we focus on the task of detecting automatically generated scientific excerpts as a part of the Third Workshop on Scholarly Document Processing shared tasks. The source code that we used for fine-tuning our models as well as additional data generated by us are freely available[1].

The work is based on the participation of our team in the DAGPap22 shared task. The objective of the task is to detect automatically generated papers in terms of a binary classification task. This task is challenging due to the developing models for text generation and wide spreading of untruthful content on the internet. To date, language models for generating texts are widely used in the scientific domain, for example for producing long and short summaries (Gharebagh et al., 2020; Cachola et al., 2020; Takeshita et al., 2022), citation texts (Xing et al., 2020; Ge et al., 2021), keyphrases (Glazkova and Morozov, 2022; Chowdhury et al., 2022), peer reviews (Yuan et al., 2021). The scientific community has held several machine learning competitions to identify machine-generated texts in different domains (Uchendu et al., 2021; Shamardina et al., 2022).

The paper is organized as follows. We provide the dataset and task description in Section 2. In Section 3, we describe our experiments during the development phase and report the official results. Section 4 concludes this paper.

2 Task Overview

2.1 Task Definition

The objective of the task is to identify whether a text is automatically generated. Therefore, the task represents a binary classification problem, the purpose of which is to split the given texts into two mutually exclusive classes. Formally, the problem is described as follows.

- **Input.** Given a scientific excerpt.
- **Output.** One of two different labels, such as "human-written" or "machine-generated".

2.2 Data

The original training set contains 5350 excerpts from a scientific papers, among which 1686 are human-written and 3664 are machine-generated. The test set includes 21403 excerpts. The text corpus is based on the work by Cabanac et al. (2021), as well as fragments collected by Elsevier publishing and editorial teams. The statistics is presented

[1] https://github.com/oldaandozerskaya/DAGPap22

Proceedings of the Third Workshop on Scholarly Document Processing, pages 223–228
October 12–17, 2022.

in Table 1[2]. Table 2 contains some examples of automatically generated texts.

Characteristic	Train	Test
Avg number of words	157.4	158.37
Min number of words	51	51
Max number of words	1895	1784
Avg number of sentences	5.8	5.75
Min number of sentences	1	1
Max number of sentences	63	68

Table 1: Data statistics.

ID	Excerpt
23	Electronic nose or machine olfaction are systems used for detection and identification of odorous compounds and gas mixtures Electronic nose or machine olfaction are systems used for detection and identification of odorous compounds and gas mixtures. Olfactors, e.g. motorbikes, are used for odor detection. These devices do not detect volatile agents or gas mixtures, and cannot be used for quantitative odor determination.
55	For the low price of coal and ineffective environmental management in mining area, China is in the dilemma of the increasing coal demand and the serious environmental issues in mining area For the low price of coal and ineffective environmental management in mining area, China is in the dilemma of the increasing coal demand and the serious environmental issues in mining area.
242	The motivation behind this paper is to answer analysis of the past portrayals of Sandler and Smith of the numeraire in an intertemporal investigation of Pareto effectiveness conditions. This reevaluation recommends that the job of the numeraire is demonstrated to be less obvious than Cabe infers. In addition, the examination shows that the prior ends are not critically subject to the numeraire presumption.

Table 2: Examples of generated texts from the official training set.

[2]The number of words and sentences was defined using NLTK (Bird, 2006)

3 Our Work

3.1 Models

Model	Value
Vocabulary (K)	
SciBERT	30
RoBERTa	50
DeBERTa	50
Backpone Parameteres (M)	
SciBERT	110
RoBERTa	355
DeBERTa	350
Hidden Size	
SciBERT	768
RoBERTa	1024
DeBERTa	1024
Layers	
SciBERT	12
RoBERTa	16
DeBERTa	24

Table 3: Hyperparameteres of the considered BERT-based models (SciBERT$_{base-cased}$, RoBERTa$_{large}$, and DeBERTa$_{large}$).

In this work, we used neural models based on Bidirectional Encoder Representations from Transformers (BERT) (Devlin et al., 2019) because they showed high results in the scientific domain (Glazkova, 2021; Pan et al., 2021; Zhu et al., 2021). We experimented with the following models, the overview of which is presented in Table 3:

- SciBERT$_{base-cased}$ (Beltagy et al., 2019), a BERT-based model that is pretrained on the texts of papers taken from Semantic Scholar.
- RoBERTa$_{large}$ (Liu et al., 2019), a modification of BERT that is pretrained using dynamic masking.
- DeBERTa$_{large}$ (He et al., 2020), a model that is pretrained using disentangled attention and enhanced mask decoder.

To evaluate our models during the development phase, we performed 3-fold cross-validation on the training set. The results were evaluated in terms of macro-averaged F1-score (F1), precision (P), and recall (R).

Model	P	R	F1
$SciBERT_{128}$	96.19	94.69	95.38
$SciBERT_{256}$	97.58	96.49	96.99
$SciBERT_{512}$	97.84	97.16	97.49
RoBERTa	96.54	94.89	95.65
DeBERTa	97.35	97	97.17
$SciBERT_{512}$ + oversampling	**98.2**	97.92	**98.06**
$SciBERT_{512}$ + undersampling	97.07	95.42	96.15
$SciBERT_{512}$ + class weighting	98.05	97.81	97.93
RoBERTa + oversampling	96.92	96.5	96.7
RoBERTa + undersampling	95.55	92.83	93.89
RoBERTa + class weighting	96.62	96.49	96.56
DeBERTa + oversampling	97.51	96.61	97.04
DeBERTa + undersampling	95.62	93.04	94.13
$SciBERT_{512}$ + KP20K (BT) + oversampling	97.65	**98.18**	97.91
$SciBERT_{512}$ + KP20K (GPT-2) + oversampling	97.16	97.03	97.07
$SciBERT_{512}$ + original (BT) + oversampling	97.44	97.75	97.59
$SciBERT_{512}$ + original (GPT-2) + oversampling	97.56	98.15	97.84
RoBERTa + KP20K (BT) + oversampling	96.86	96.48	96.66
RoBERTa + KP20K (GPT-2) + oversampling	96.49	95.2	95.8
RoBERTa + original (BT) + oversampling	96.56	95.99	96.26
RoBERTa + original (GPT-2) + oversampling	96.12	96.12	96.12
DeBERTa + KP20K (BT) + oversampling	96.76	97.03	96.89
DeBERTa + KP20K (GPT-2) + oversampling	94.16	95.86	94.95
DeBERTa + original (BT) + oversampling	96.51	96.7	96.59
DeBERTa + original (GPT-2) + oversampling	96.58	96.94	96.76

Table 4: Results (%, development phase).

3.2 Experiments

We adopted pretrained models from HuggingFace (Wolf et al., 2020) and fine-tuned them using SimpleTransformers[3]. We fine-tuned each pre-trained language model for three epochs with the learning rate of 2e-5 using the AdamW optimizer (Loshchilov and Hutter, 2017). We set batch size to 16 and used the sliding window technique to prevent truncating longer sequences. We utilized the maximum sequence length equal to 128, 256, and 512 for SciBERT ($SciBERT_{128}$, $SciBERT_{256}$, and $SciBERT_{512}$ respectively) and 128 for RoBERTa and DeBERTa due to the limited computing resources. Similar to our previous work (Glazkova et al., 2021), we used raw texts as an input.

Since the corpus provided by the organizers is imbalanced, we explored several techniques to handle imbalanced data. Namely, we used a) random oversampling, b) random undersampling, c) class weighting, d) generating new data. Random oversampling and undersampling are implemented using the Imbalanced-learn library[4]. To generate new data, we experimented with the original corpus and the fragment of the KP20K dataset (Meng et al., 2017). KP20K is a large-scale scholarly papers dataset for keyphrase extraction containing 568K papers with their abstracts. To produce new machine-generated data, we utilized two techniques for text generation: a) Back Translation (BT)[5] through Googletrans[6], and b) zero-shot generation by prompting GPT-2 (Radford et al.) and specifying the maximum number of generated tokens equal to the number of tokens in the source text (see Figure 1 for example).

The results are presented in Table 4. In our experiments, the model fine-tuned on longer input sequences ($SciBERT_{512}$) performed better than other baselines despite the use of the sliding win-

[3]https://simpletransformers.ai

[4]https://imbalanced-learn.org

[5]https://github.com/hhhwwwuuu/BackTranslation

[6]https://py-googletrans.readthedocs.io/en/latest

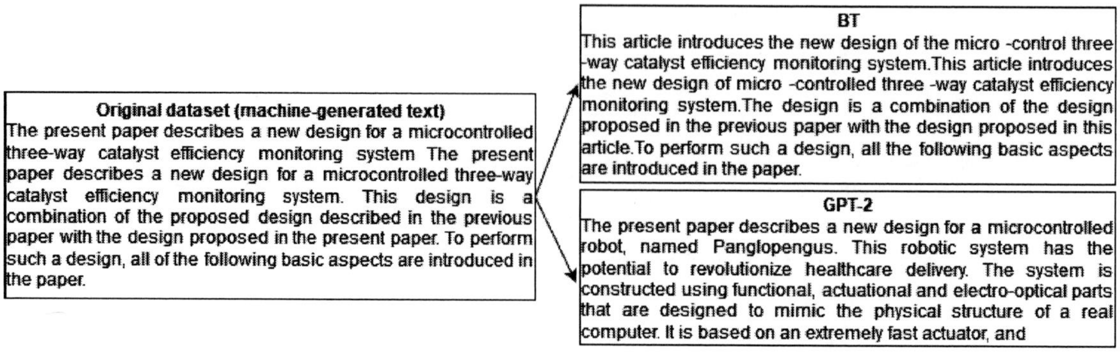

Figure 1: Example of generating new data using BT and GPT-2.

dow technique. Due the processing of class imbalance, we found that oversampling and class weighting increase the performance of the models while undersampling produces lower results. Further, we experimented with using additional data. First, we made an attempt to add scientific abstracts from KP20K utilizing texts of 1000 random abstracts and 1000 texts generated by BT or GPT-2 and than perform oversampling. Second, we tried to produce new examples of machine-generated excerpts from the dataset provided by the organizers of the competition. We generated 1000 examples using BT and GPT-2, added them to the training set, and finally performed oversampling. The use of additional data showed no increase compared to the models fine-tuned with oversampled texts.

3.3 Results

During the evaluation phase, we experimented with the hard and soft voting ensembles of transformer-based models. The results were evaluated on the official test set. Our best submission is an ensemble of SciBERT, RoBERTa, and DeBERTa fine-tuned using random oversampling technique. The confusion matrix for this solution is presented in Figure 2. The ensembling of predictions was performed at two levels:

1. Model level, i. e. soft voting calculated for three models of the same type fine-tuned with different random seeds.

2. Ensemble level, i. e. hard voting for the labels produced by the models of different type.

Table 5 shows the comparison of our best solution to the official scores from the private leader-

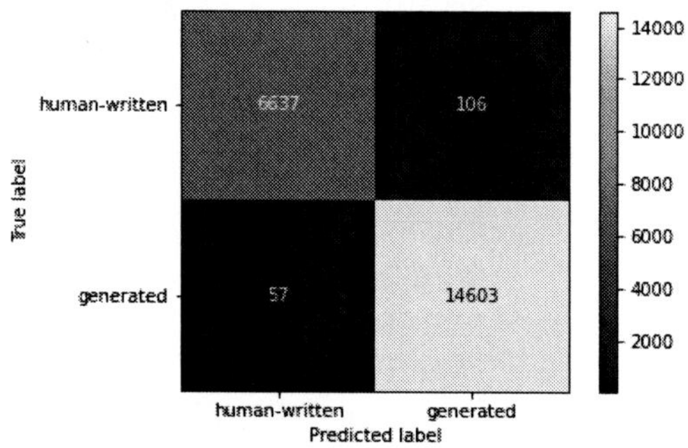

Figure 2: Confusion matrix for our model.

board of the competition[7]. In this competition, only five models outperformed the baseline provided by the organizers. Our model achieved 99.24% of F1-score and ranked the third place of the leaderboard for this task.

Run name	F1
Our solution	99.24
Stronger benchmark	98.32
Tf-Idf & logreg benchmark	82.04
Average scores	92.96

Table 5: Official results (%, private leaderboard).

4 Conclusion

In this work, we have explored the application of BERT-based models to the task of detecting machine-generated scientific texts. We have evaluated several techniques for handling imbalanced data and compared three models in a variety of settings. Our results on the test data showed that

[7]https://www.kaggle.com/competitions/detecting-generated-scientific-papers

the ensemble of different transformer-based models outperforms other our submissions and strong baselines. Moreover, our final model ranked third in this task.

A further study could explore the state-of-the art-in detecting automatically generated papers for other languages and multilingual corpora. Another future direction is to continue our experiments with generating new data to improve the classification performance.

References

Iz Beltagy, Kyle Lo, and Arman Cohan. 2019. Scibert: A pretrained language model for scientific text. In *EMNLP*. Association for Computational Linguistics.

Steven Bird. 2006. Nltk: the natural language toolkit. In *Proceedings of the COLING/ACL 2006 Interactive Presentation Sessions*, pages 69–72.

Guillaume Cabanac, Cyril Labbé, and Alexander Magazinov. 2021. Tortured phrases: A dubious writing style emerging in science. evidence of critical issues affecting established journals. *arXiv preprint arXiv:2107.06751*.

Isabel Cachola, Kyle Lo, Arman Cohan, and Daniel S Weld. 2020. TLDR: Extreme summarization of scientific documents. In *Findings of the Association for Computational Linguistics: EMNLP 2020*, pages 4766–4777.

Md Faisal Mahbub Chowdhury, Gaetano Rossiello, Michael Glass, Nandana Mihindukulasooriya, and Alfio Gliozzo. 2022. Applying a generic sequence-to-sequence model for simple and effective keyphrase generation. *arXiv preprint arXiv:2201.05302*.

Jacob Devlin, Ming-Wei Chang, Kenton Lee, and Kristina Toutanova. 2019. BERT: Pre-training of deep bidirectional transformers for language understanding. In *Proceedings of the 2019 Conference of the North American Chapter of the Association for Computational Linguistics: Human Language Technologies, Volume 1 (Long and Short Papers)*, pages 4171–4186, Minneapolis, Minnesota. Association for Computational Linguistics.

Holly Else et al. 2021. 'tortured phrases' give away fabricated research papers. *Nature*, 596(7872):328–329.

Yubin Ge, Ly Dinh, Xiaofeng Liu, Jinsong Su, Ziyao Lu, Ante Wang, and Jana Diesner. 2021. BACO: A background knowledge-and content-based framework for citing sentence generation. In *Proceedings of the 59th Annual Meeting of the Association for Computational Linguistics and the 11th International Joint Conference on Natural Language Processing (Volume 1: Long Papers)*, pages 1466–1478.

Sajad Sotudeh Gharebagh, Arman Cohan, and Nazli Goharian. 2020. Guir@ longsumm 2020: Learning to generate long summaries from scientific documents. In *Proceedings of the First Workshop on Scholarly Document Processing*, pages 356–361.

Anna Glazkova. 2021. Identifying topics of scientific articles with bert-based approaches and topic modeling. In *Pacific-Asia Conference on Knowledge Discovery and Data Mining*, pages 98–105. Springer.

Anna Glazkova, Maksim Glazkov, and Timofey Trifonov. 2021. g2tmn at constraint@AAAI2021: exploiting CT-BERT and ensembling learning for COVID-19 fake news detection. In *International Workshop on Combating Online Hostile Posts in Regional Languages during Emergency Situation*, pages 116–127. Springer.

Anna Glazkova and Dmitry Morozov. 2022. Applying transformer-based text summarization for keyphrase generation. *arXiv preprint arXiv:2209.03791*.

Pengcheng He, Xiaodong Liu, Jianfeng Gao, and Weizhu Chen. 2020. DeBERTa: Decoding-enhanced BERT with disentangled attention. *arXiv preprint arXiv:2006.03654*.

Yinhan Liu, Myle Ott, Naman Goyal, Jingfei Du, Mandar Joshi, Danqi Chen, Omer Levy, Mike Lewis, Luke Zettlemoyer, and Veselin Stoyanov. 2019. RoBERTa: A robustly optimized BERT pretraining approach. *arXiv preprint arXiv:1907.11692*.

Ilya Loshchilov and Frank Hutter. 2017. Decoupled weight decay regularization. *arXiv preprint arXiv:1711.05101*.

Rui Meng, Sanqiang Zhao, Shuguang Han, Daqing He, Peter Brusilovsky, and Yu Chi. 2017. Deep keyphrase generation. In *Proceedings of the 55th Annual Meeting of the Association for Computational Linguistics (Volume 1: Long Papers)*, pages 582–592.

Chunguang Pan, Bingyan Song, Shengguang Wang, and Zhipeng Luo. 2021. BERT-based acronym disambiguation with multiple training strategies. In *Scientific Document Understanding 2021*.

Alec Radford, Jeffrey Wu, Rewon Child, David Luan, Dario Amodei, Ilya Sutskever, et al. Language models are unsupervised multitask learners.

Tatiana Shamardina, Vladislav Mikhailov, Daniil Chernianskii, Alena Fenogenova, Marat Saidov, Anastasiya Valeeva, Tatiana Shavrina, Ivan Smurov, Elena Tutubalina, and Ekaterina Artemova. 2022. Findings of the the RuATD shared task 2022 on artificial text detection in Russian. *arXiv preprint arXiv:2206.01583*.

Sotaro Takeshita, Tommaso Green, Niklas Friedrich, Kai Eckert, and Simone Paolo Ponzetto. 2022. X-scitldr: cross-lingual extreme summarization of scholarly documents. *arXiv preprint arXiv:2205.15051*.

Adaku Uchendu, Zeyu Ma, Thai Le, Rui Zhang, and Dongwon Lee. 2021. Turingbench: A benchmark environment for turing test in the age of neural text generation. In *Findings of the Association for Computational Linguistics: EMNLP 2021*, pages 2001–2016.

Thomas Wolf, Lysandre Debut, Victor Sanh, Julien Chaumond, Clement Delangue, Anthony Moi, Pierric Cistac, Tim Rault, Rémi Louf, Morgan Funtowicz, et al. 2020. Transformers: State-of-the-art natural language processing. In *Proceedings of the 2020 conference on empirical methods in natural language processing: system demonstrations*, pages 38–45.

Xinyu Xing, Xiaosheng Fan, and Xiaojun Wan. 2020. Automatic generation of citation texts in scholarly papers: A pilot study. In *Proceedings of the 58th Annual Meeting of the Association for Computational Linguistics*, pages 6181–6190. Association for Computational Linguistics.

Weizhe Yuan, Pengfei Liu, and Graham Neubig. 2021. Can we automate scientific reviewing? *arXiv preprint arXiv:2102.00176*.

Danqing Zhu, Wangli Lin, Yang Zhang, Qiwei Zhong, Guanxiong Zeng, Weilin Wu, and Jiayu Tang. 2021. AT-BERT: Adversarial training BERT for acronym identification winning solution for SDU@ AAAI-21.

Overview of the SV-Ident 2022 Shared Task on Survey Variable Identification in Social Science Publications

Tornike Tsereteli[1], Yavuz Selim Kartal[2], Simone Paolo Ponzetto[1], Andrea Zielinski[3], Kai Eckert[4], Philipp Mayr[2]

[1]Data and Web Science Group, University of Mannheim, Germany

[2]GESIS – Leibniz Institute for the Social Sciences, Germany

[3]Fraunhofer ISI, Germany

[4]Web-based Information Systems and Services, Stuttgart Media University, Germany

{tornike.tsereteli, ponzetto}@uni-mannheim.de

{yavuzselim.kartal, philipp.mayr}@gesis.org

andrea.zielinski@isi.fraunhofer.de

eckert@hdm-stuttgart.de

Abstract

In this paper, we provide an overview of the SV-Ident shared task as part of the 3rd Workshop on Scholarly Document Processing (SDP) at COLING 2022. In the shared task, participants were provided with a sentence and a vocabulary of variables, and asked to identify which variables, if any, are mentioned in individual sentences from scholarly documents in full text. Two teams made a total of 9 submissions to the shared task leaderboard. While none of the teams improve on the baseline systems, we still draw insights from their submissions. Furthermore, we provide a detailed evaluation. Data and baselines for our shared task are freely available at `https://github.com/vadis-project/sv-ident`.

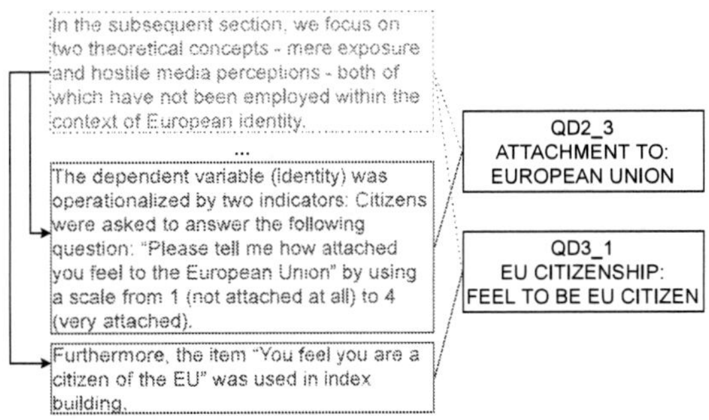

Figure 1: Example of explicit (blue) and implicit (red) variable mentions in sentences from a social science article (source: Ejaz et al. (2017)) mapped to survey variables. Lines with arrows show contextual dependence. Linked variables: QD2_3 and QD3_1.

1 Introduction

Social science publications often use and reference survey datasets, containing hundreds or thousands of questions, using so-called *survey variables*.[1] While publications may focus only on a specific subset of these variables, explicit references are usually missing: the lack of explicit links between survey variables and publications, in turn, limits access to research along the FAIR principles (Wilkinson et al., 2016). To address this issue, we propose a task where variable mentions in unstructured documents are linked to items from a catalog of survey research datasets using Natural Language Processing (NLP) methods. Automatically identifying which variable is mentioned in a given text is challenging due to the diverse linguistic realizations of variables (Zielinski and Mutschke, 2018). A short example text is shown in Figure 1. All three sentences mention and are linked to relevant variables. The first sentence mentions three concepts:[2] *mere-exposure effect*, *hostile media perceptions*, and *European identity*. The first two concepts are defined later in the text (we omit their links in this example), while the latter is defined in the bottom two sentences in the figure. The second and third sentences both are explicit mentions, as they include direct quotations of variable questions. Ideally, a system should link relevant variables to each of the sentences in the example. Specifically, when only provided the given context, it should link the first sentence to the variables `QD2_3` and `QD3_1`, the second sentence to `QD2_3`, and the third sentence to `QD3_1`. A larger variant of the example is provided in Figure 3 in the Appendix.

The Survey Variable Identification[3] (henceforth,

[1]In the following, we use the terms *survey variable* and *variable* interchangeably.

[2]Concepts that have been operationalized by variables are also treated as variables throughout this work.

[3]`https://vadis-project.github.io/sv-ident-sdp2022/`

Proceedings of the Third Workshop on Scholarly Document Processing, pages 229–246
October 12–17, 2022.

SV-Ident) shared task aims at promoting the developing of systems that can identify variables within the text of scholarly publications from the social sciences in different languages (initially, we focus here on English and German). The shared task is divided into two sub-tasks: a) Variable Detection and b) Variable Disambiguation. The former deals with identifying sentences that contain variable mentions, while the latter focuses on linking the correct variables mentioned in a sentence. Variable mentions are often implicit (e.g., sentences 1 and 3 in Figure 1), and understanding when a variable is mentioned may require contextual information as well as knowledge from external sources (e.g., a variable vocabulary). Since annotating scientific texts requires domain knowledge, training data is costly to create and thus scarce. To overcome these limitations, NLP systems, e.g., models using pre-trained language models (PLMs) and transfer learning are promising technologies to use.

In this paper, we report the results on the first edition of the SV-Ident shared task. Two teams made a total of 9 submissions to the leaderboard. One of the teams developed systems for both sub-tasks and submitted a system description paper. While none of the teams improve on the baselines, we use the submissions provided by the teams to collect a few initial findings on the difficulties and challenges of the SV-Ident task. Crucially, we find that there is a difference between the performance on two types of variable mentions: explicit and implicit. Implicitly mentioned variables (sentence 1 in Figure 1) are significantly more difficult to detect and disambiguate, as they require contextual knowledge. This opens up new research questions for future work, such as, for instance: can implicit mentions of survey variables be further categorized into finer-grained classes or can co-reference resolution be used to link variable mentions across different parts of a document? In order to foster future research on this task, we release all of our code to reproduce the analysis results and the annotation guidelines for creating the dataset at `https://github.com/vadis-project/sv-ident`.

The remainder of this paper is organized as follows: we provide an overview of the dataset used in §2. In §3, we describe the task definition and evaluation metrics. We present the submitted systems in §4 and provide a detailed analysis of the results in §5. We briefly discuss related work in §6 and frame the shared task into a broader context in §7. Finally, we summarize the shared task and propose future work in §8.

2 Data

The SV-Ident 2022 shared task has been conceived in the context of the VADIS project[4] and organized as part of the third Workshop on Scholarly Document Processing (SDP) (Chandrasekaran et al., 2020), co-located at the 2022 International Conference on Computational Linguistics. In the following, we describe the data collection process and the dataset used for the shared task.

2.1 SV-Ident Corpus

The SV-Ident Corpus contains publicly-available scientific publications from the Social Science Open Access Repository (SSOAR)[5] in full text. To collect the corpus, we first filter the 5,000 most popular research datasets using search logs from GESIS Search.[6] We then retrieve the publications linked to these datasets as our candidate set. Finally, only those publications that had at least one associated research dataset with indexed variables on the GESIS Search platform are retained. This results in 285 documents from the original set of 120k publications. For this set of candidates, we then select 44 documents for annotation, which include the most popular ones as well as publications linked to variable vocabularies of different sizes.

Each document in our dataset has been annotated in PDF format using the INCEpTION software (Klie et al., 2018) by two domain experts (graduate students trained in the social sciences). Annotators are provided with the whole document and asked to label all sentences that contained variables, including the variables the sentences mentioned. We first conduct two calibration rounds, for which annotators are given 50 two-page documents from the dataset collected by Zielinski and Mutschke (2018). Afterwards, the selected 44 documents are annotated in three annotation rounds over a period of 8 weeks (on average, each annotator spent between 1-2 hours on each document). Texts are then extracted, and all parsing errors are manually corrected. Common errors include sentence breaks (due to incorrect splitting of abbreviations, such as *et al.* or *i.e.*), page breaks (due to improper handling of footnotes), and missing spaces between

[4] `https://vadis-project.github.io/`
[5] `https://www.gesis.org/ssoar/home`
[6] `https://search.gesis.org/`

```
{'doc_id': '55534',
 'is_variable': 1,
 'lang': 'en',
 'research_data': ['ZA5876'],
 'sentence': 'The respondents were asked, "Do
             you think that the [national]-
             television present(s) the EU to
             opositively, objectively, or too
             negatively?"',
 'uuid': '39238aee-2d44-4aa9-999f-eb597a1f0da9',
 'variable': ['exploredata-ZA5876_Varqc3b',
              'exploredata-ZA5876_Varqe11_1',
              'exploredata-ZA5876_Varqc3a',
              'exploredata-ZA5876_Varqe11_3']}
```

Figure 2: Example sentence with provided metetadata and labels.

words. Because annotators have access to all parts of the document at once, the annotation setup allows the use of document-level knowledge to infer sentence-level labels.

The annotations include the variable IDs that are mentioned in a text from a set of possible candidates, confidence scores for the annotations, and, for the test set, annotators also classified each mentioned variable into an *explicit* or an *implicit* mention (examples of explicit and implicit mentions were both found in the annotation guidelines). We generally define explicit mentions as those which do not require contextual information to be labeled correctly. The opposite is true for implicit mentions.

2.2 SV-Ident Shared Task Dataset

When annotating, the set of candidate variables is potentially made up of all variables from the research datasets linked to a publication on the GESIS platform: this set usually contains hundreds or thousands of variables, thus making the annotation task impractical and hard to scale. To help reduce the size of the set of possible survey variable labels, annotators are provided with a tool to find matches using different methods. The first method uses an ensemble of four sentence-transformer models to predict the top 20 variables that are semantically most similar to the reference sentence for each model. The annotators receive recommendations for variables for which at least two models predict them to be in the top 20 results. The second method allows annotators to search using a method of matching strings approximately rather than exactly: specifically, we use the *Token Set Ratio* metric, which compares the number of insertion and deletion operations for unique and common words between the strings to be compared.[7] The last method simply provides annotators with the full list of variables to manually search through. All three methods have their drawbacks. The first two might fail to recommend valid variables for cases with high linguistic variation, vagueness, or infrequent words, while the last may provide annotators with a search space that is too large. While we do not control for such possible failures, future work may draw insights from the analysis of the annotations.

	English	German	Total
Train	1,882	1,941	3,823
Dev	209	216	425
Test	944	780	1,724
Total	3,035	2,937	5,972

Table 1: Total number of sentences in the SV-Ident shared task dataset per language for each dataset split.

The dataset for the shared task is a subset of the SV-Ident corpus. More specifically, 14 out of the 44 annotated documents from the SV-Ident Corpus are additionally filtered out due to missing links to research data, incorrect annotations, or PDF parsing errors, leaving 30 documents in total. The dataset consists of 18 documents (7 English and 11 German) for the training and development sets and 12 documents (6 for each English and German) for the blind test set.

An example of a sentence and its metadata, including annotated labels from the dataset, is shown in Figure 2. Each instance in our dataset contains: a document ID (*doc_id*); a binary label (*is_variable*), where a value of *1* implies that the sentence contains a variable; the language of the sentence (*lang*); a list of document-level linked research datasets (*research_data*); the sentence (*sentence*); a unique ID (*uuid*); and a list of annotated variables (*variable*). Raw sentence counts for each of the dataset splits are provided in Table 1. Since the test set contains more English sentences, during evaluation, we compute the mean of the scores for each language for the competing systems (see §5 for more details). In total, there are 3,823 training, 425 validation, and 1,724 test sentences. English and German sentences are roughly evenly distributed at 3,035 and 2,937 instances for each language, respectively.

[7]We use the RapidFuzz library (`https://github.com/maxbachmann/RapidFuzz`) to match relevant variables given a search query.

Task / Metric	English	German
Detection (Cohen's κ)	0.48	0.46
Disambiguation (Krippendorff's α)	0.08	0.08

Table 2: Inter-annotator agreement scores. We use Cohen's Kappa for Task 1 (detection), while Krippendorff's Alpha is used for Task 2 (disambiguation).

Type	Count
Total # variables (vocab. size)	27,365
# annotated variables (tokens)	11,356
# uniquely used Variables (types)	1,165

Table 3: Vocabulary size, variable types, and tokens in our SV-Ident dataset.

Because of the challenging nature of the annotation task, we join the annotated instances of variable mentions and link variables of each annotator. We provide agreement scores between annotators for English and German instances separately (Table 2). We calculate the Cohen's Kappa score for agreement on Variable Detection. The scores for both English and German range between 0.46 and 0.48, which indicate that there is a moderate agreement. For Variable Disambiguation, we use Krippendorff's Alpha. Both languages have an agreement score of 0.08, which implies that the agreement is close to random. One reason for such low agreement is the large number of possible variables to choose from, given that the total vocabulary size for all the documents is very large (27,365 variables that are often similar). The annotators labeled 1,165 unique variables (around 4% of the vocabulary) a total of 11,356 times (Table 3). In the future, we plan to analyze this disagreement with respect to the choice of variables further.

Looking at the document-level, variables occur with different frequency in different documents (shown in Table 4). The size of the variable vocabulary (i.e., the subset of all variables, containing only the variables from the research datasets that are linked to a publication) related to a publication ranges from 64 to 5,733. The number of annotated variables is at least 13 and at most 1,204 for English, and for German 20 and 1,143, respectively. The number of uniquely annotated variables is at most 153. In the final analysis, we investigate at which ratio sentences of a document are annotated. While the annotation ratio is at least 7%, it is at most 86% for relatively dense documents.[8]

Type	English		German	
	Min	Max	Min	Max
Rel. Variables	134	3,062	64	5,733
Variable tokens	13	1,204	20	1,143
Variable types	4	153	5	54
(%) Annt. Sent.	7	80	12	86

Table 4: Maximum and minimum number of related variables, annotated variables, and the ratio of annotated sentences for each document in English and German.

In addition to document-level differences, variables may require contextual knowledge to be disambiguated. Based only on the test set, annotators agree that 242 sentences had explicit, 13 implicit, and 18 both types of mentions. At the fine-grained annotator-level, the first annotator labeled close to 37% more implicit than explicit mentions, while the second labeled nearly thirteen times as many explicit as implicit mentions. Given that we did not conduct calibration rounds on this specific concept, annotators may not have shared the same understanding, since this distinction was introduced only in the third round of annotations. Future work will focus on further analyzing and validating the annotations. We make our dataset available on GitHub as well as on HuggingFace.[9] In addition, we also release, as the trial dataset, the data that were originally created by Zielinski and Mutschke (2018) (while the annotation procedure does not follow the same guideline, the data can be used as additional training data). Notably, consecutive sentences mentioning the same variable as well as vague variable mentions were not annotated in the trial data. We manually filter the trial data, after which, 446 English and 573 German sentences remain in the training set and 87 and 111 in the test set for each language, respectively.

3 Experimental Setup

The task of SV-Ident deals with identifying variable mentions in a text. For simplicity, the task is formulated as a sentence-level task, but can also be solved using document-level information (inline with the data annotation process). The shared task is decomposed into two sub-tasks: Variable Detection and Variable Disambiguation, where the

[8] Variable-dense documents are usually short in our dataset.

[9] https://huggingface.co/datasets/vadis/sv-ident

former task can be used to help filter candidate sentences for the latter.

3.1 Tasks

Task 1: Variable Detection. The first task can be seen as a binary text classification task. More formally, given a set of texts T (in our case, sentences), for each t, where $t \in T$, systems should predict the binary label $l \in [0, 1]$ for t, where a value of 1 implies that t mentions a variable.

Task 2: Variable Disambiguation. The second task can be viewed as an information retrieval (IR) task, where the goal is to identify all relevant documents (i.e., variables) for a given query (i.e., input sentence). More formally, given a set of queries Q that mention variables, where $Q \subseteq T$, and the set of all documents D (in our case, variables), for each q, where $q \in Q$, systems should predict the subset of documents D' that are mentioned in q, where $D' \subseteq D$.

3.2 Evaluation Metrics

To evaluate systems, we use standard text classification and information retrieval evaluation metrics. For the first task, systems are evaluated using the standard $F1 - macro$ score averaged across languages and documents. $F1 - macro$ is defined as follows:

$$F1 = \frac{1}{N}\sum_{n\in N}^{n} F1_n = \frac{1}{N}\sum_{n\in N}^{n} \frac{2P_nR_n}{P_n + R_n}, \quad (1)$$

where P and R are the precision and recall scores, respectively. The $F1 - macro$ averages the scores for P and R across classes (i.e., scores are computed for each class separately and each is weighted equally). For the second task, systems were evaluated using the (Mean) Average Precision (MAP) score with a recall cutoff value of 10 (denoted as MAP@10). Average Precision (AP) measures the average of the precision scores at each relevant item returned (i.e., recall level) in a search result set. MAP is the mean of the AP scores when computed across more than one query. MAP considers the ranking position of each relevant document. It further assumes that a user desires to retrieve many relevant documents. MAP is defined as follows:

$$\text{MAP}@K = \frac{1}{N}\sum_{n\in N}^{n} AP@K_n = \frac{1}{N}\sum_{n\in N}^{n}\frac{1}{K}\sum_{k\in K}^{k} P@k, \quad (2)$$

where P is the precision score, K the recall level, and N the number of queries. We choose MAP over accuracy, because MAP incorporates the rank of the predicted document, which accuracy ignores. In a realistic use-case, a user may be interested in being recommended up to K relevant variables per sentence. While we did not empirically test what value of K would be most suitable for a user, we choose K to equal 10, since 95% of all sentences are labeled with up to 10 variables. In addition to $F1 - macro$ and MAP@10, we provide secondary metrics, which are not used for ranking the submitted systems, but can provide additional insights into the results. These include precision (P), recall (R), different values of K for MAP, and R-precision, which is the precision at recall R, where R is the number of relevant documents for a query.

In order to account for dataset imbalance during evaluation, for each score function f (i.e., evaluation metric), we compute the average score across languages and documents. The intuition is that languages and documents are equally important, and a model should perform well on all. The average score is computed as follows:

$$\text{average score} = \frac{1}{L}\sum_{l\in L}^{l}\frac{1}{D_l}\sum_{d\in D_l}^{d} f(d), \quad (3)$$

where L is the set of languages, D the set of documents, and D_l the set of documents for a given language, for $l \in L$ and $D_l \subseteq D$.

3.3 Shared Task Setup

The shared task was hosted on CodaLab.[10] After registering for the shared task, participants could download the test set and were asked to submit their predictions on CodaLab as a single file for each task (submissions were allowed from July 18th through August 1st, 2022). Submissions were limited to 20 for each task. For each submission, an automated evaluation system would upload the computed scores to the public leaderboard.

[10] https://codalab.lisn.upsaclay.fr/competitions/6400

4 Participating Systems

Two teams participated in our challenge on CodaLab, and one of the teams submitted a system description, which is included in the proceedings. We summarize the report here. The participant (Hövelmeyer and Kartal, 2022) treated both tasks, at least partly, as a problem of semantic textual similarity (Agirre et al., 2013). For Task 1, sentences were first preprocessed by randomly undersampling in order to balance the data, removing stopwords, lemmatizing the data, and using only a subset of the fields from the vocabulary metadata based on preliminary experiments. Then, test sentences and vocabulary data were converted into dense sentence representations using Sentence-T5 (Ni et al., 2022) for English and `Sahajtomar/German-semantic`[11] (henceforth, GS) for German. Similarity scores were computed for those test sentence and vocabulary item pairs. Pairs with a score greater than a predetermined threshold were classified as sentences containing variables. For Task 2, the same sentence representations were used, but for all test sentences. The variables were then ranked based on their scores, with a higher score implying a greater similarity. While other methods were also implemented, such a Logistic Regression and Multinominal Naive Bayes classifiers, the best performing systems used Sentence-T5.

5 Evaluation

This section first describes the baseline systems for each task and later provides the results of the shared task.

5.1 Baselines

We train a transformer-based model for Variable Detection and implement lexical and neural zero-shot baselines for Variable Disambiguation.

The baseline system for the first task uses a transfer learning approach by fine-tuning a pre-trained language model (PLM) on the training and validation datasets. We use a PLM that was further pre-trained on a corpus of English social science abstracts, SsciBERT (Shen et al., 2022), which outperforms BERT (Devlin et al., 2019) and SciBERT (Beltagy et al., 2019) models on the SV-Ident test set. Because no multilingual or German PLM counterparts exist that have been pre-trained on scientific texts, we use the specialized monolingual SsciBERT for both English and German data.

For the second task, we implement three baseline systems in a zero-shot setting: a lexical as well as sparse and dense retrieval models. We choose BM25 as our lexical baseline, using Elasticsearch.[12] For the sparse model, we use SPARTA (Zhao et al., 2021) and a multilingual sentence-transformer[13] (Reimers and Gurevych, 2019, 2020) as the dense retriever. Rather than training the models on the data, we use them to first encode the query and documents (i.e., variable metadata) and later rank those which are most semantically similar to a query by computing the cosine similarity between query-document pairs. The similarity computation assumes that instances that are closer together in vector space are semantically more similar. While participant 2 conducts an ablation study on the choice of metadata to use for matching the variables, we choose to include all metadata and leave finding the the optimal combination of metadata to future work.

5.2 Results

Task 1 had two participants and a single baseline system, while Task 2 had one participant and three baseline systems. In the tables below, the systems are denoted as follows: participant 1 as Unk, participant 2 as S-T5/GS (or S-T5 for English and GS for German), the baseline for Task 1 as SSBert*, and the baselines for Task 2 as BM25*, Sparse* for the SPARTA model, and Dense* for the multilingual sentence-transformer (all baselines across text and tables are always marked with a * asterisk).

Variable Detection. For this task, none of the participating systems are able to beat the average score of the baseline. Unk scores lower than chance likelihood, while, with a score of 60.17, S-T5/GS comes close to SSBert*, which has a score of 66.10 (Table 5). Breaking the scores down into the average scores across documents for each language, S-T5 outperforms the baseline for English. Thus, Task 1 can also be solved in a zero-shot setting, given that the Sentence-T5 model was not fine-tuned on the provided data. Similar large PLMs may show further improvements.

[11] `https://huggingface.co/Sahajtomar/German-semantic`

[12] `https://www.elastic.co/`

[13] `https://huggingface.co/sentence-transformers/distiluse-base-multilingual-cased-v1`

Language	System	P	R	F1
English	Unk	65.03	55.24	38.64
	S-T5	68.38	67.77	**66.96**
	SSBert*	**70.94**	**70.04**	64.28
German	Unk	51.66	52.66	30.88
	GS	59.18	56.04	53.37
	SSBert*	**68.38**	**68.53**	**67.91**
Average	Unk	58.35	53.95	34.76
	S-T5/GS	63.78	61.91	60.17
	SSBert*	**69.66**	**69.29**	**66.10**

Table 5: Results for task 1 (detection).

At the document-level, systems show varying performance (see Table 8 in the Appendix). For the document with the ID 21357, participants' systems have low scores, while SSBert* has the highest score across all documents. Furthermore, for 7 out of the 12 documents, the baseline system has the highest score. In addition to the number of positive and negative instances, we also report the number of variables associated with a document as well as the year of the publication. When computing the Pearson correlation coefficient, we find a weak correlation between the $F1$ scores and the size of the search space (i.e., vocabulary size) for Unk ($r = 0.132$, $p = 0.68$), S-T5/GS ($r = 0.266$, $p = 0.26$), and SSBert* ($r = 0.152$, $p = 0.64$). With respect to the year of the document, we find a moderate correlation for Unk ($r = 0.272$, $p = 0.39$), S-T5/GS ($r = 0.274$, $p = 0.39$), and SSBert* ($r = 0.392$, $p = 0.21$). However, these correlations may not generalize due to the small number of documents.

Given the low annotator agreement with respect to the fine-grained labels, explicit and implicit, we report scores for the cases where both annotators agree on the label (see Table 9 in the Appendix) as well as for each annotator independently (see Tables 10 and 11 in the Appendix). We divide the labels into *explicit*, *implicit*, and *mixed* classes, where sentences that contain explicit and implicit variables are labeled as mixed. In cases where both annotators agree on the label, systems perform better on explicit than on implicit or mixed mentions. The same is true for annotator 1, except for S-T5/GS. This implies that explicit mentions are easier to detect and disambiguate. This is not the case for annotator 2. A possible explanation could be the low number of implicit annotations, which may be due to a difference in understanding of the labels. Unk outperforms all systems for the cases when both annotators agree on the label. This is surprising given the low average performance of the system (unfortunately, no system description was provided).

Variable Disambiguation. For the second task, we report only a single submission together with the results for three baselines (Table 6). As described in Section 5, the baselines include BM25, SPARTA (henceforth, Sparse*), and a multilingual sentence-transformer (henceforth, Dense*). While we provide participants all the test sentences, we only evaluate performance on the subset of instances that contain variable mentions, as Task 1 already validates Variable Detection performance (this setup ignores false positive queries submitted by the participants). Unless explicitly stated, the following discussion mainly focuses on the MAP@10 scores. While the participant's system performs close to Dense* for English, Dense* scores twice as high for German. Sparse* outperforms all systems on English data. This is likely due to the system having been trained on a large English retrieval corpus.[14] BM25* and Sparse* perform worse on German. Lexical models, such as BM25*, are prone to perform worse for languages that have many rare words, such as German, which allows compound nouns. Furthermore, because Sparse* is only specialized for English, it does not perform well for data in a different language. Overall, Dense* outperforms all systems by at least 0.5 points for English, except for Sparse*, and by at least around 10 points for German.

At the document-level, scores vary significantly (see Table 12 in the Appendix). Scores across different values of K improve as K increases. For dense documents (i.e., documents with a high ratio of variable mention sentences), scores increase significantly when going from $k = 1$ to $k = 5$, such as for the IDs 21357, 57204, and 66324. Furthermore, while some systems perform well on a document, others perform poorly. For example, the document with ID 66324 shows the lowest performance by all systems except for BM25*, which has a score of 22.01 and is the second-highest document score for BM25*. For 57561, BM25* achieves only a score of 1.60, while all other systems score higher than 16. S-T5/GS outperforms all baselines only once and twice when compared

[14] https://github.com/microsoft/MSMARCO-Passage-Ranking

Language	System	MAP@10	R-Prec
English	S-T5	16.27	14.83
	BM25*	12.39	12.10
	Sparse*	**19.02**	**18.87**
	Dense*	16.96	15.34
German	GS	10.91	10.35
	BM25*	6.46	7.02
	Sparse*	3.52	3.69
	Dense*	**20.89**	**17.96**
Average	S-T5/GS	13.59	12.59
	BM25*	9.43	9.56
	Sparse*	11.27	11.28
	Dense*	**18.93**	**16.65**

Table 6: Results for task 2 (disambiguation).

	OM	SV-Ident
Documents	64	44
Research Datasets	1	76
Total # variables (vocabulary size)	406	27,365
# annotated variables (tokens)	414	8,721
# uniquely used variables (types)	243	851
Instances annotate (# annotated sentences)	1,217	5,972

Table 7: Comparison between the OpenMinTeD and SV-Ident datasets.

to only Dense*. Such exceptions may be caused by a larger overlap between the tokens in the document and the underlying data used to train the models. In addition, we find a moderate correlation between MAP@10 scores and the vocabulary size (and a strong correlation for Dense*) for S-T5/GS ($r = 0.395.p = 0.20$), BM25* ($r = 0.465.p = 0.13$), Sparse* ($r = 0.427.p = 0.17$), and Dense* ($r = 0.623.p = 0.03$). As the search space increases, performance goes down. Finally, we find that MAP@10 is highly correlated with R-Precision ($r = 0.941, p = 4.99$), which implies that MAP is a good metric in the absence of the ground truth number of relevant variables.

Performance on the annotator-level is similar to that of Task 1: scores are highest when both annotators agree on the label (see Table 13 in the Appendix). For both annotators, scores for the explicit class are consistently higher than for either implicit or mixed classes (see Tables 14 and 15 in the Appendix). This means that for the task of Variable Detection, knowing whether a variable is mentioned explicitly or implicitly can mean a 10 to 20 point absolute difference in performance. In the case when either both annotators agree on the label or when looking only at annotator 1, Sparse* outperforms all systems. Exploring other sparse models is a promising future direction for disambiguating implicit variable mentions.

6 Related Work

Identifying mentions of survey variables in text was first introduced by Zielinski and Mutschke (2017, 2018) in the OpenMinTeD project (OM).[15] As the predecessor of our task, they created the first dataset for the problem of SV-Ident. Table 7 shows the statistical differences between the OM and SV-Ident datasets. Although fewer documents are annotated in SV-Ident, the number of instances in SV-Ident is almost 5 times that of OM. To have a greater diversity of survey variables, SV-Ident corpus uses 76 datasets with more than 27k variables from different research studies, such as ALLBUS, ISSP, and Eurobarometer, whereas OM only used a single dataset. Moreover, the SV-Ident corpus comes up with modified and additional annotation features: the unknown (UNK) token was used for ambiguous variable mentions; consecutive mentions of the same variable were included; confidence levels of the annotations and variable mention types were labeled; and variables were linked across languages. As a result, our corpus is much larger and more diverse.

Given that identifying variables requires semantic relations, other NLP tasks deal with a fundamentally similar perspective, such as entity linking (EL), recognizing textual entailment (RTE), semantic textual similarity (STS), plagiarism detection, and detecting previously fact-checked news. EL can be conceptualized as linking mentions to variables in a knowledge base (Rao et al., 2013). Since there are many similar survey variables in research datasets, disambiguating the right variable for a sentence is similar to determining the identity of an entity from a knowledge base. The RTE task is to identify whether a sentence entails a given candidate hypothesis or not (Dzikovska et al., 2013). A question answering adaptation of RTE (Dagan et al., 2013) is similar to SV-Ident, as the question and each answer form a hypothesis, which then re-

[15] http://openminted.eu/

quires the system to determine whether a sentence entails a given candidate hypothesis. STS is yet another similar task, which aims to find the similarity level between given texts (Agirre et al., 2013). STS was organized as a shared International Workshop on Semantic Evaluation between 2012 and 2017, and STS models have been developed for various domains (Wang et al., 2020; Yang et al., 2020; Guo et al., 2020). In the task of Plagiarism Detection of PAN,[16] a system should extract all plagiarized passages from a given set of candidate documents with (external) or without (intrinsic) comparing them to potential source documents (Potthast et al., 2013). Lastly, Detecting Previously Fact-Checked Claims, a shared task by the CheckThat! Lab (Nakov et al., 2022), aims to match the most similar claims — text fragments from social media or political debate scripts — to a corpus of verified claims. The corpus is used to find the most similar claims, which does not require direct linking, as is done in SV-Ident Task 2, because implicit links are inferred.

7 Why SV-Ident?

Today's search engines are the core elements of information access for social scientists. While search engines have seen many improvements in terms of keyword search and text understanding, they suffer from a limited capability of retrieving information from interconnected data sources, such as academic literature and research datasets. Nonetheless, they show outstanding performance on retrieving such documents individually. Current interlinking infrastructures typically only link research datasets to publications on the citation-level. Such systems do not yet consider fine-grained linking of publications to individual survey variables from research datasets. As demonstrated in the SV-Ident shared task, survey variables may be mentioned implicitly, which makes their manual or automatic identification non-trivial. Currently, social scientists have to manually identify such variables, which is time-consuming. In addition to these limitations, search engines do not yet support queries specific to social science topics, concepts, or relations. Yet, keyword search, which is widely used, has many known problems (e.g., vocabulary mismatch or complex queries). As a result, social scientists are unable to access interlinked publications and research data. Thus, the re-use and reproducibility of research is limited.

SV-Ident, and more generally the VADIS project, plays an important role in filling the gap in the lack of infrastructure for social scientists (Kartal et al., 2022). SV-Ident aims to build automatic models for identifying survey variables in social science publications. This directly enables a more fine-grained interlinking of publications and research datasets. More specifically, variables can be linked on the sentence-level, which allows new features to be developed. Within the VADIS project, we aim to develop variable-based automatic summarization, which will allow scientists to quickly get an overview of a publication with respect to the variables used. Furthermore, we plan to incorporate variable recommendation algorithms into the GESIS Search platform to enable scientists to find relevant variables outside the scope of variables they are already familiar with.

8 Conclusion

This overview reports on the results of the SV-Ident 2022 shared task. We introduce two subtasks relevant for SV-Ident, namely, Variable Detection and Variable Disambiguation. We report on data, which is currently the largest of its kind, that was collected, annotated, and made publicly available for this challenge. Baseline as well as participants' systems are described and evaluated. We find that nearly all systems perform better on explicit variable mentions, opening up new directions of research. Finally, we contextualize the shared task into related work and highlight its importance within a broader context. Future work will further analyze the distinction between different variable mention types. In addition, multi-task learning could solve both tasks jointly or in combination with adjacent tasks. Co-reference resolution could be used to help disambiguate implicit variable mentions. Finally, evaluating systems on more diverse metrics, such as fairness or robustness, is critical for applied research.

Acknowledgement The SV-Ident 2022 shared task is organized by the VADIS project (Kartal et al., 2022). This work is supported by DFG project VADIS, grant numbers ZA 939/5-1, PO 1900/5-1, EC 477/7-1, KR 4895/3-1. We would like to also thank Jan Hendrik Blaß and Joudie Mekky for their contributions.

[16]`https://pan.webis.de/`

References

Eneko Agirre, Daniel Cer, Mona Diab, Aitor Gonzalez-Agirre, and Weiwei Guo. 2013. *SEM 2013 shared task: Semantic textual similarity. In *Second Joint Conference on Lexical and Computational Semantics (*SEM), Volume 1: Proceedings of the Main Conference and the Shared Task: Semantic Textual Similarity*, pages 32–43, Atlanta, Georgia, USA. Association for Computational Linguistics.

Iz Beltagy, Kyle Lo, and Arman Cohan. 2019. SciBERT: A pretrained language model for scientific text. In *Proceedings of the 2019 Conference on Empirical Methods in Natural Language Processing and the 9th International Joint Conference on Natural Language Processing (EMNLP-IJCNLP)*, pages 3615–3620, Hong Kong, China. Association for Computational Linguistics.

Muthu Kumar Chandrasekaran, Guy Feigenblat, Dayne Freitag, Tirthankar Ghosal, Eduard Hovy, Philipp Mayr, Michal Shmueli-Scheuer, and Anita de Waard. 2020. Overview of the first workshop on scholarly document processing (SDP). In *Proceedings of the First Workshop on Scholarly Document Processing*, pages 1–6, Online. Association for Computational Linguistics.

Ido Dagan, Dan Roth, Mark Sammons, and Fabio Massimo Zanzotto. 2013. Recognizing textual entailment: Models and applications. *Synthesis Lectures on Human Language Technologies*, 6(4):1–220.

Jacob Devlin, Ming-Wei Chang, Kenton Lee, and Kristina Toutanova. 2019. BERT: Pre-training of deep bidirectional transformers for language understanding. In *Proceedings of the 2019 Conference of the North American Chapter of the Association for Computational Linguistics: Human Language Technologies, Volume 1 (Long and Short Papers)*, pages 4171–4186, Minneapolis, Minnesota. Association for Computational Linguistics.

Myroslava Dzikovska, Rodney Nielsen, Chris Brew, Claudia Leacock, Danilo Giampiccolo, Luisa Bentivogli, Peter Clark, Ido Dagan, and Hoa Trang Dang. 2013. SemEval-2013 task 7: The joint student response analysis and 8th recognizing textual entailment challenge. In *Second Joint Conference on Lexical and Computational Semantics (*SEM), Volume 2: Proceedings of the Seventh International Workshop on Semantic Evaluation (SemEval 2013)*, pages 263–274, Atlanta, Georgia, USA. Association for Computational Linguistics.

Waqas Ejaz, Marco Bräuer, and Jens Wolling. 2017. Subjective evaluation of media content as a moderator of media effects on european identity: Mere exposure and the hostile media phenomenon. *Media and Communication*, 5(2):41–52.

Xiao Guo, Hengameh Mirzaalian, Ekraam Sabir, Ayush Jaiswal, and Wael Abd-Almageed. 2020. CORD19STS: Covid-19 semantic textual similarity dataset. *arXiv preprint arXiv:2007.02461*.

Alica Hövelmeyer and Yavuz Selim Kartal. 2022. Varanalysis@sv-ident 2022: Variable detection and disambiguation based on semantic similarity. In *Proceedings of the Third Workshop on Scholarly Document Processing*. Association for Computational Linguistics.

Yavuz Selim Kartal, Sotaro Takeshita, Tornike Tsereteli, Kai Eckert, Henning Kroll, Philipp Mayr, Simone Paolo Ponzetto, Benjamin Zapilko, and Andrea Zielinski. 2022. Towards Automated Survey Variable Search and Summarization in Social Science Publications. *arXiv preprint arXiv:2209.06804*.

Jan-Christoph Klie, Michael Bugert, Beto Boullosa, Richard Eckart de Castilho, and Iryna Gurevych. 2018. The INCEpTION platform: Machine-assisted and knowledge-oriented interactive annotation. In *Proceedings of the 27th International Conference on Computational Linguistics: System Demonstrations*, pages 5–9, Santa Fe, New Mexico. Association for Computational Linguistics.

Preslav Nakov, Alberto Barrón-Cedeño, Giovanni da San Martino, Firoj Alam, Julia Maria Struß, Thomas Mandl, Rubén Míguez, Tommaso Caselli, Mucahid Kutlu, Wajdi Zaghouani, et al. 2022. Overview of the clef–2022 checkthat! lab on fighting the covid-19 infodemic and fake news detection. In *International Conference of the Cross-Language Evaluation Forum for European Languages*, pages 495–520. Springer.

Jianmo Ni, Gustavo Hernandez Abrego, Noah Constant, Ji Ma, Keith Hall, Daniel Cer, and Yinfei Yang. 2022. Sentence-t5: Scalable sentence encoders from pre-trained text-to-text models. In *Findings of the Association for Computational Linguistics: ACL 2022*, pages 1864–1874, Dublin, Ireland. Association for Computational Linguistics.

Martin Potthast, Matthias Hagen, Tim Gollub, Martin Tippmann, Johannes Kiesel, Paolo Rosso, Efstathios Stamatatos, and Benno Stein. 2013. Overview of the 5th international competition on plagiarism detection. In *CLEF Conference on Multilingual and Multimodal Information Access Evaluation*, pages 301–331. CELCT.

Delip Rao, Paul McNamee, and Mark Dredze. 2013. Entity linking: Finding extracted entities in a knowledge base. In *Multi-source, multilingual information extraction and summarization*, pages 93–115. Springer.

Nils Reimers and Iryna Gurevych. 2019. Sentence-BERT: Sentence embeddings using Siamese BERT-networks. In *Proceedings of the 2019 Conference on Empirical Methods in Natural Language Processing and the 9th International Joint Conference on Natural Language Processing (EMNLP-IJCNLP)*, pages 3982–3992, Hong Kong, China. Association for Computational Linguistics.

Nils Reimers and Iryna Gurevych. 2020. Making monolingual sentence embeddings multilingual using knowledge distillation. In *Proceedings of the*

2020 Conference on Empirical Methods in Natural Language Processing (EMNLP), pages 4512–4525, Online. Association for Computational Linguistics.

Si Shen, Jiangfeng Liu, Litao Lin, Ying Huang, Lin Zhang, Chang Liu, Yutong Feng, and Dongbo Wang. 2022. SsciBERT: A pre-trained language model for social science texts. *arXiv preprint arXiv:2206.04510*.

Yanshan Wang, Naveed Afzal, Sunyang Fu, Liwei Wang, Feichen Shen, Majid Rastegar-Mojarad, and Hongfang Liu. 2020. MedSTS: a resource for clinical semantic textual similarity. *Language Resources and Evaluation*, 54(1):57–72.

Mark D. Wilkinson, Michel Dumontier, IJsbrand Jan Aalbersberg, Gabrielle Appleton, Myles Axton, Arie Baak, Niklas Blomberg, Jan-Willem Boiten, Luiz Bonino da Silva Santos, Philip E. Bourne, Jildau Bouwman, Anthony J. Brookes, Tim Clark, Mercè Crosas, Ingrid Dillo, Olivier Dumon, Scott Edmunds, Chris T. Evelo, Richard Finkers, Alejandra Gonzalez-Beltran, Alasdair J.G. Gray, Paul Groth, Carole Goble, Jeffrey S. Grethe, Jaap Heringa, Peter A.C 't Hoen, Rob Hooft, Tobias Kuhn, Ruben Kok, Joost Kok, Scott J. Lusher, Maryann E. Martone, Albert Mons, Abel L. Packer, Bengt Persson, Philippe Rocca-Serra, Marco Roos, Rene van Schaik, Susanna-Assunta Sansone, Erik Schultes, Thierry Sengstag, Ted Slater, George Strawn, Morris A. Swertz, Mark Thompson, Johan van der Lei, Erik van Mulligen, Jan Velterop, Andra Waagmeester, Peter Wittenburg, Katherine Wolstencroft, Jun Zhao, and Barend Mons. 2016. The fair guiding principles for scientific data management and stewardship. *Scientific Data*, 3(1):160018.

Xi Yang, Xing He, Hansi Zhang, Yinghan Ma, Jiang Bian, Yonghui Wu, et al. 2020. Measurement of semantic textual similarity in clinical texts: comparison of transformer-based models. *JMIR medical informatics*, 8(11):e19735.

Tiancheng Zhao, Xiaopeng Lu, and Kyusong Lee. 2021. SPARTA: Efficient open-domain question answering via sparse transformer matching retrieval. In *Proceedings of the 2021 Conference of the North American Chapter of the Association for Computational Linguistics: Human Language Technologies*, pages 565–575, Online. Association for Computational Linguistics.

Andrea Zielinski and Peter Mutschke. 2017. Mining social science publications for survey variables. In *Proceedings of the Second Workshop on NLP and Computational Social Science*, pages 47–52, Vancouver, Canada. Association for Computational Linguistics.

Andrea Zielinski and Peter Mutschke. 2018. Towards a gold standard corpus for variable detection and linking in social science publications. In *Proceedings of the Eleventh International Conference on Language Resources and Evaluation (LREC 2018)*, Miyazaki, Japan. European Language Resources Association (ELRA).

Appendix

This section contains a figure with example sentences mapped to variables and additional detailed evaluation results for both SV-Ident tasks. More specifically, Tables 8 and 12 provide results for each document, while Tables 9–11 and Tables 13–15 provide results for explicit, implicit, and mixed mention types for each annotator individually as well as for the case when both annotators agreed on the labels.

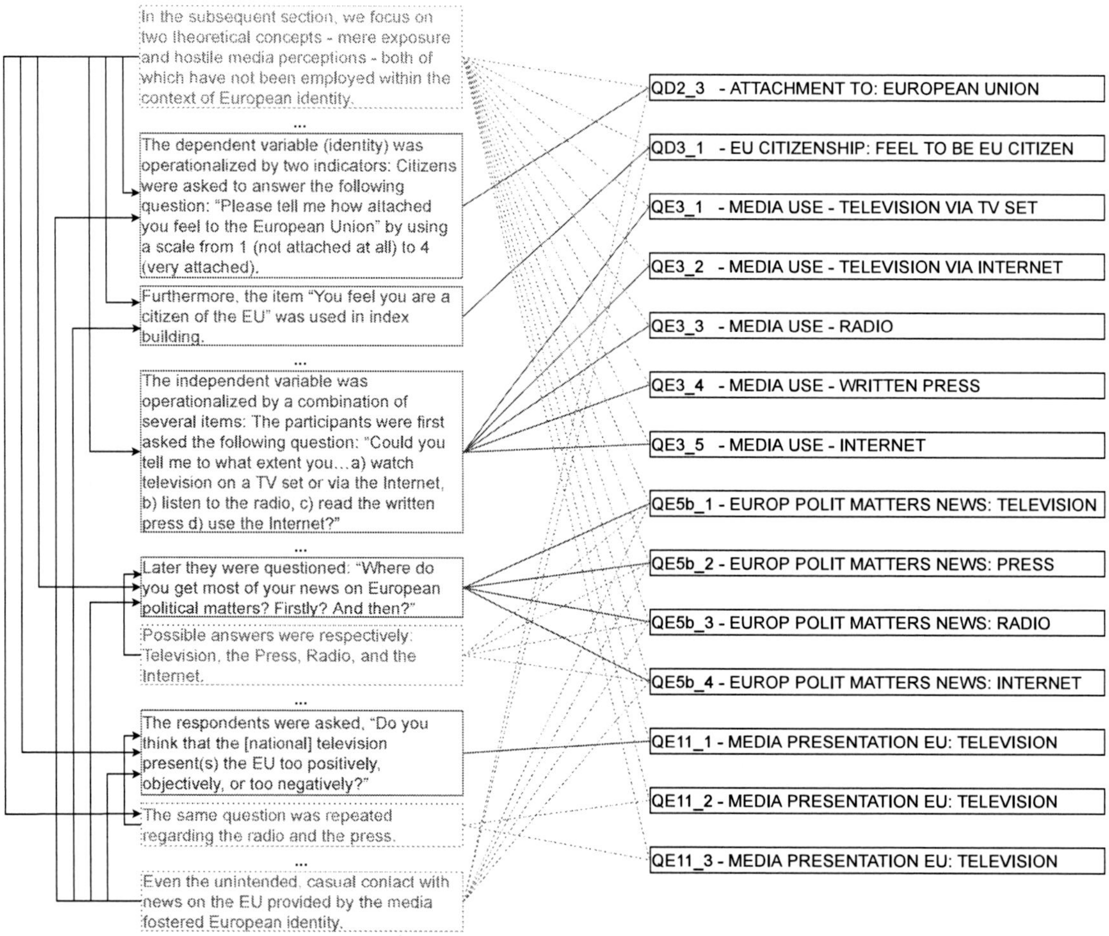

Figure 3: Example explicit (blue) and implicit (red) sentences from a social science article (source: Ejaz et al. (2017)) mapped to survey variables. Lines with arrows show contextual dependence. Linked variables: QD2_3, QD3_1, QE3_1, QE3_2, QE3_3, QE3_4, QE3_5, QE5b_1, QE5b_2, QE5b_3, QE5b_4, QE11_1, QE11_2, and QE11_3.

ID	System	F1	P	R	# p/n	Vars	Lang	Year
16547	Unk	33.47	25.16	50.00	160/162	209	de	2003
	S-T5/GS	**65.77**	**69.20**	**66.88**				
	SSBert*	65.50	65.61	65.55				
19944	Unk	33.54	73.27	50.91	110/94	457	de	1999
	S-T5/GS	51.95	**67.05**	57.38				
	SSBert*	**63.16**	63.20	**63.28**				
21279	Unk	22.22	60.00	52.94	51/12	477	de	1993
	S-T5/GS	42.61	42.85	42.40				
	SSBert*	**67.56**	**67.08**	**68.14**				
21357	Unk	24.68	16.38	50.00	39/19	239	de	2002
	S-T5/GS	45.96	47.07	46.69				
	SSBert*	**79.20**	**81.86**	**77.73**				
21622	Unk	30.43	59.80	58.16	49/10	142	de	1991
	S-T5/GS	63.39	62.30	65.82				
	SSBert*	**75.70**	**73.66**	**78.88**				
56983	Unk	40.96	75.35	53.95	38/36	367	de	2018
	S-T5/GS	50.51	**66.58**	57.09				
	SSBert*	**56.31**	58.87	**57.60**				
49163	Unk	26.12	64.23	52.06	97/37	211	en	2005
	S-T5/GS	**63.20**	**63.06**	**65.62**				
	SSBert*	54.27	62.75	64.38				
49734	Unk	54.73	78.39	61.36	66/67	148	en	1998
	S-T5/GS	**71.94**	76.37	**72.80**				
	SSBert*	69.30	**79.05**	71.23				
57204	Unk	31.29	53.07	50.38	119/77	134	en	2017
	S-T5/GS	66.45	67.89	66.08				
	SSBert*	**66.82**	**71.17**	**70.63**				
57561	Unk	25.51	62.13	53.18	110/33	134	en	2017
	S-T5/GS	**61.81**	61.47	64.70				
	SSBert*	56.49	**65.34**	**70.15**				
61603	Unk	52.92	66.16	61.92	71/42	336	en	2016
	S-T5/GS	**77.90**	**80.75**	76.73				
	SSBert*	76.84	78.51	**80.23**				
66324	Unk	41.26	66.20	52.50	105/120	775	en	2020
	S-T5/GS	60.44	60.71	60.71				
	SSBert*	**61.96**	**68.84**	**63.63**				

Table 8: Fine-grained results across documents for Task 1. Sys = system, P = precision, R = recall, # p/n = number of positive/negative sentences, Vars = total number of variables, Lang = language of the document.

Type	System	F1	P	R	#
A1+2exp	Unk	**59.45**	**66.96**	57.49	242
	S-T5/GS	38.16	53.99	58.73	
	SSBert*	53.62	58.51	**70.52**	
A1+2imp	Unk	**48.58**	49.60	47.60	13
	S-T5/GS	25.96	49.92	47.72	
	SSBert*	36.28	**50.02**	**50.72**	
A1+2mix	Unk	**48.51**	49.45	47.60	18
	S-T5/GS	26.18	49.88	47.50	
	SSBert*	36.97	**50.35**	**58.28**	
Average	Unk	**52.18**	**55.34**	50.90	
	S-T5/GS	30.10	51.27	51.31	
	SSBert*	42.29	52.96	**59.84**	
A1+2	Unk	**57.66**	**66.01**	56.25	273
	S-T5/GS	39.08	53.80	57.34	
	SSBert*	54.70	58.88	68.92	

Table 9: Fine-grained results across types of variable mentions for Task 1. Sys = system, P = precision, R = recall, # = number of (positive) sentences.

Type	System	F1	P	R	#
A1exp	Unk	**57.51**	**69.06**	56.39	339
	S-T5/GS	41.11	54.31	57.15	
	SSBert*	57.05	60.17	**68.59**	
A1imp	Unk	46.00	47.67	49.37	403
	S-T5/GS	44.86	**55.42**	**57.19**	
	SSBert*	**50.77**	53.41	54.99	
A1mix	Unk	49.06	49.15	49.53	166
	S-T5/GS	36.33	53.91	60.79	
	SSBert*	**49.40**	**56.00**	**68.23**	
Average	Unk	50.85	55.29	51.76	
	S-T5/GS	40.77	54.55	58.38	
	SSBert*	**52.40**	**56.53**	**63.94**	
A1	Unk	42.31	65.88	52.89	908
	S-T5/GS	60.51	63.65	62.29	
	SSBert*	**69.49**	**69.58**	**69.45**	

Table 10: Fine-grained results across types of variable mentions for annotator 1 for Task 1. Sys = system, P = precision, R = recall, # = number of (positive) sentences.

Type	System	F1	P	R	#
A2exp	Unk	47.38	**70.97**	54.03	864
	S-T5/GS	58.40	63.71	63.03	
	SSBert*	**65.45**	65.39	**66.13**	
A2imp	Unk	**48.82**	49.15	48.60	74
	S-T5/GS	27.95	**50.08**	**50.66**	
	SSBert*	37.60	49.78	47.99	
A2mix	Unk	**50.51**	50.49	50.59	74
	S-T5/GS	28.93	50.14	50.82	
	SSBert*	39.59	**50.66**	**54.28**	
Average	Unk	**48.91**	**56.87**	51.07	
	S-T5/GS	38.43	54.64	54.84	
	SSBert*	47.55	55.27	**56.13**	
A2	Unk	44.21	**70.61**	53.77	1012
	S-T5/GS	60.37	63.93	62.62	
	SSBert*	**65.81**	65.82	**65.81**	

Table 11: Fine-grained results across types of variable mentions for annotator 2 for Task 1. Sys = system, P = precision, R = recall, # = number of (positive) sentences.

ID	System	M@1	M@5	M@10	M@20	R-Prec	#	Vars	Lang	Year
16547	S-T5/GS	11.55	14.12	15.20	16.72	16.55	160	209	de	2003
	BM25*	2.98	3.30	3.49	3.57	3.52				
	Sparse*	0.03	0.24	0.51	0.86	1.34				
	Dense*	**20.50**	**27.88**	**30.41**	**32.06**	**31.73**				
19944	S-T5/GS	9.47	14.07	15.75	16.85	13.03	110	457	de	1999
	BM25*	9.09	14.64	15.50	15.92	14.02				
	Sparse*	8.03	10.37	10.77	11.49	10.30				
	Dense*	**11.74**	**18.41**	**19.16**	**19.96**	**15.68**				
21279	S-T5/GS	6.65	11.87	14.47	16.08	15.94	51	477	de	1993
	BM25*	4.92	6.96	7.04	7.24	7.93				
	Sparse*	0.00	1.16	1.63	2.01	1.91				
	Dense*	**14.12**	**18.17**	**19.88**	**21.09**	**18.06**				
21357	S-T5/GS	1.28	3.85	4.13	4.95	2.56	39	239	de	2002
	BM25*	0.00	0.00	0.00	0.00	0.00				
	Sparse*	0.00	0.00	0.26	0.26	0.00				
	Dense*	**7.69**	**15.15**	**16.71**	**17.12**	**7.69**				
21622	S-T5/GS	3.69	7.05	9.00	10.15	7.80	49	142	de	1991
	BM25*	0.34	3.67	4.01	4.01	6.07				
	Sparse*	1.31	3.49	3.82	4.21	4.23				
	Dense*	**6.63**	**13.01**	**14.67**	**15.83**	**11.18**				
56983	S-T5/GS	1.02	6.19	6.88	7.19	6.23	38	367	de	2018
	BM25*	5.95	7.48	8.72	10.11	10.57				
	Sparse*	1.32	3.33	4.13	4.75	4.37				
	Dense*	**18.79**	**24.06**	**24.54**	**25.11**	**23.44**				
49163	S-T5/GS	4.33	8.84	10.28	11.46	9.16	97	211	en	2005
	BM25*	1.96	4.32	5.52	6.05	3.49				
	Sparse*	3.89	7.87	8.92	9.73	6.61				
	Dense*	**8.12**	**13.96**	**15.46**	**16.49**	**11.55**				
49734	S-T5/GS	9.03	12.71	15.47	16.80	12.88	66	148	en	1998
	BM25*	19.41	21.49	23.80	24.99	23.50				
	Sparse*	**23.57**	**29.06**	**33.57**	**36.03**	**30.49**				
	Dense*	17.14	22.71	24.08	25.18	21.69				
57204	S-T5/GS	7.48	22.12	31.73	34.41	31.10	119	134	en	2017
	BM25*	1.21	5.11	8.51	13.06	8.80				
	Sparse*	**8.93**	**28.77**	**36.32**	**39.48**	**38.26**				
	Dense*	7.09	16.73	24.90	30.11	23.82				
57561	S-T5/GS	6.96	12.06	14.61	16.47	10.60	110	134	en	2017
	BM25*	0.76	1.04	1.30	1.60	1.12				
	Sparse*	**9.33**	13.04	14.82	16.58	15.70				
	Dense*	7.47	**16.80**	**19.20**	**20.93**	**16.14**				
61603	S-T5/GS	**14.82**	**21.32**	**22.57**	**23.19**	**20.68**	71	336	en	2016
	BM25*	10.62	14.45	14.87	15.30	12.51				
	Sparse*	12.81	16.96	17.98	18.61	19.34				
	Dense*	12.16	15.47	16.69	17.19	16.92				
66324	S-T5/GS	0.58	1.95	2.95	3.81	4.55	105	775	en	2020
	BM25*	**8.17**	**16.22**	**20.34**	**22.01**	**23.18**				
	Sparse*	0.25	1.92	2.51	3.15	2.81				
	Dense*	0.12	0.58	1.44	2.21	1.95				

Table 12: Fine-grained results across documents for Task 2. Sys = system, M = MAP, R-Prec = R-Precision, # = number of (positive) sentences, Vars = total number of variables, Lang = language of the document..

Type	System	M@1	M@5	M@10	M@20	R-Prec	#
A1+2exp	S-T5/GS	14.38	21.62	22.99	24.18	19.77	242
	BM25*	13.49	16.00	16.78	17.17	16.34	
	Sparse*	11.56	14.57	15.57	16.23	14.82	
	Dense*	**24.90**	**32.43**	**34.31**	**35.11**	**30.29**	
A1+2imp	S-T5/GS	0.00	5.85	9.62	14.21	11.70	13
	BM25*	0.00	4.72	7.79	9.82	8.46	
	Sparse*	**5.13**	**18.07**	**25.97**	**27.73**	**24.90**	
	Dense*	1.54	6.22	11.85	15.15	9.42	
A1+2mix	S-T5/GS	6.07	11.10	13.74	15.55	16.13	18
	BM25*	0.00	1.73	1.94	2.72	4.48	
	Sparse*	4.03	11.63	15.14	18.51	18.31	
	Dense*	**8.05**	**14.60**	**15.84**	**18.66**	**20.09**	
Average	S-T5/GS	6.81	12.85	15.45	17.98	15.87	
	BM25*	4.50	7.48	8.84	9.91	9.76	
	Sparse*	6.90	14.75	18.89	20.82	19.34	
	Dense*	**11.50**	**17.75**	**20.67**	**22.97**	**19.93**	
A1+2	S-T5/GS	12.92	19.91	21.52	22.95	19.03	273
	BM25*	11.68	14.25	15.12	15.63	14.97	
	Sparse*	10.61	14.53	16.12	17.05	15.66	
	Dense*	**22.27**	**29.57**	**31.60**	**32.70**	**28.32**	

Table 13: Fine-grained results across types of variable mentions for Task 2. Sys = system, M = MAP, R-Prec = R-Precision, # = number of (positive) sentences.

Type	System	M@1	M@5	M@10	M@20	R-Prec	#
A1exp	S-T5/GS	14.14	20.47	21.87	22.77	16.97	271
	BM25*	13.91	15.98	16.76	17.22	15.27	
	Sparse*	11.77	14.84	15.61	16.25	13.92	
	Dense*	**25.28**	**31.48**	**32.60**	**33.30**	**28.05**	
A1imp	S-T5/GS	3.44	7.65	10.83	12.33	9.23	370
	BM25*	2.23	4.73	5.98	7.27	4.93	
	Sparse*	**4.79**	**10.63**	**13.06**	**14.15**	**12.55**	
	Dense*	3.89	8.97	11.82	13.78	10.20	
A1mix	S-T5/GS	2.41	5.20	7.24	8.59	7.69	153
	BM25*	3.63	6.10	6.98	7.87	6.80	
	Sparse*	3.16	6.64	7.45	8.68	8.32	
	Dense*	**4.85**	**10.12**	**11.88**	**13.60**	**11.89**	
Average	S-T5/GS	6.66	11.10	13.32	14.57	11.30	
	BM25*	6.59	8.94	9.91	10.79	9.00	
	Sparse*	6.57	10.70	12.04	13.03	11.60	
	Dense*	**11.34**	**16.86**	**18.77**	**20.23**	**16.71**	
A1	S-T5/GS	6.89	11.55	13.91	15.18	11.58	794
	BM25*	6.49	8.83	9.85	10.78	8.82	
	Sparse*	6.86	11.30	12.85	13.81	12.20	
	Dense*	**11.37**	**16.87**	**18.93**	**20.41**	**16.62**	

Table 14: Fine-grained results across types of variable mentions for annotator 1 for Task 2. Sys = system, M = MAP, R-Prec = R-Precision, # = number of (positive) sentences.

Type	System	M@1	M@5	M@10	M@20	R-Prec	#
A2exp	S-T5/GS	10.38	16.74	19.48	20.89	16.57	637
	BM25*	7.73	11.14	12.74	13.81	11.12	
	Sparse*	7.29	12.55	14.17	15.02	12.24	
	Dense*	**15.90**	**23.47**	**26.25**	**27.66**	**21.65**	
A2imp	S-T5/GS	0.00	3.22	5.41	6.38	4.30	48
	BM25*	1.04	3.39	4.50	5.89	4.09	
	Sparse*	3.24	7.61	9.20	10.47	6.91	
	Dense*	**7.52**	**12.87**	**14.43**	**14.98**	**10.14**	
A2mix	S-T5/GS	3.99	9.58	13.96	15.11	13.90	74
	BM25*	2.44	4.65	5.26	6.62	6.42	
	Sparse*	5.24	13.03	15.93	17.54	16.35	
	Dense*	**7.94**	**13.35**	**15.91**	**18.28**	**18.00**	
Average	S-T5/GS	4.79	9.85	12.95	14.13	11.59	
	BM25*	3.74	6.39	7.50	8.77	7.21	
	Sparse*	5.26	11.06	13.10	14.34	11.83	
	Dense*	**10.45**	**16.56**	**18.86**	**20.31**	**16.59**	
A2	S-T5/GS	9.14	15.23	18.09	19.44	15.55	753
	BM25*	6.82	10.06	11.54	12.65	10.25	
	Sparse*	6.85	12.28	14.01	14.96	12.27	
	Dense*	**14.65**	**21.88**	**24.56**	**26.01**	**20.58**	

Table 15: Fine-grained results across types of variable mentions for annotator 2 for Task 2. Sys = system, M = MAP, R-Prec = R-Precision, # = number of (positive) sentences.

Varanalysis@SV-Ident 2022: Variable Detection and Disambiguation Based on Semantic Similarity

Alica Hövelmeyer, Yavuz Selim Kartal*
GESIS – Leibniz Institute for the Social Sciences, Germany
{alica.hoevelmeyer,yavuzselim.kartal}@gesis.org

Abstract

This paper describes an approach to the *SV-Ident* Shared Task which requires the detection and disambiguation of survey variables in sentences taken from social science publications. It deals with both subtasks as problems of semantic textual similarity (STS) and relies on the use of sentence transformers. Sentences and variables are examined for semantic similarity for both detecting sentences containing variables and disambiguating the respective variables. The focus is placed on analyzing the effects of including different parts of the variables and observing the differences between English and German instances. Additionally, for the variable detection task a bag of words model is used to filter out sentences which are likely to contain a variable mention as a preselection of sentences to perform the semantic similarity comparison on.

1 Introduction

One important way of improving reproducibility and reusability of research is to make its results accessible and comparable. Besides the interlinking of scientific papers, researchers of different disciplines can also benefit from the interlinking of publications and primary data (Boland et al., 2012).

Social scientists often refer to the same survey datasets. Unfortunately, these are seldom properly linked in the publications and if they are, the different surveys and studies often contain a large amount of single questions, called variables which need to be found in the respective corpus (Zielinski and Mutschke, 2017). It would be really helpful to have an automized way of detecting and disambiguating survey variables in scientific papers. For this reason, the very first shared task for survey variable identification is organized as SV-Ident (Tsereteli et al., 2022) at the 3rd Scholarly Document Processing (SDP) workshop at COLING 2022.

We mainly approached the task as a problem of semantic textual similarity (STS) and used language-dependent sentence embedding models to detect and disambiguate variables. For variable detection we additionally used a *Bag of Words* (BoW) model. Although the results did not exceed the baselines, our approach gives insights into which parts of the variables provide the most useful information for semantic similarity based disambiguation.

This paper is structured as follows. In section 2, we present the task and the related data. In section 3, we describe our approach to both tasks. This section starts with an introduction on how the semantic similarity comparison is done, which is the same for both subtasks. Section 4 contains a presentation of experiments performed to find the best parameters for our system. In section 5 and 6 we present our results and we discuss lessons learned, respectively. The paper is concluded in section 7.

2 Task Description and Data

The shared task consists of two subtasks: variable detection (Task 1) and variable disambiguation (Task 2). Both subtasks relate to the same dataset consisting of examples of sentences taken from social science publications[1].

The provided training set consists of 3,823 sentences with labels that indicate whether they contain a variable or not. Each sentence has a document id referring to its source document and an unique id. If the sentence contains one or more variables, ids of these variables are also given, together with a research id which refers to the specific corpus or corpora the variables were taken from.

*As an organizer of SV-Ident, this author contributed to the model discussion and the preparation of the system description under the terms and conditions of this task.

[1] https://vadis-project.github.io/sv-ident-sdp2022/

Proceedings of the Third Workshop on Scholarly Document Processing, pages 247–252
October 12–17, 2022.

Moreover, the sentences have a language label (see Table 1). There are 1,882 English and 1,941 German sentences in the training set. Additionally, a validation set containing 425 sentences (209 English and 216 German) was released. The test set consists of 1,724 sentences (944 English and 780 German). The test set was in the same format as the training set and it is expected to predict the value of the label indicating whether a sentence contains a variable or not for **Task 1** and the respective variables to the corresponding sentence for **Task 2**.

Attribute	Value
sentence	The probability of 'never-membership' is substantially lower if there is a union at the workplace.
is variable	1
variable	exploredata-ZA3700_VarV519
research data	ZA3700
document id	35933
uuid	e2428b76-28de-4b78-aa3f-6055c7d71a1e
lang	en

Table 1: Example of an instance from SV-Ident dataset.

For Task 2, a corpus of variables is also provided. It is divided into 329 sub-corpora labeled with different research ids. They contain variables with their unique ids. Each variable consists of the respective study title, a variable name, the question text in its original language, the question text in English, sub-questions, item categories, answer categories, the variable's topic in its original language and the variable's topic in English (see Table 2). Not every item is available for every variable. For 108,374 variables in total, the study titles, variable labels, variable names, topics in the original language and topics in English are missing 25 times. Question texts in the original language are missing 27,705 times, question texts in English 50,319 times, sub-questions 58,294 times, item categories 58,079 times and answer categories 8,783 times.

3 Approach and System Description

The task dataset features several difficulties. One of them is that it is multi-lingual containing both German and English sentences. The fact that the variables consist of different parts with different semantic structures which are not available for all of the variables is another one. Our approach focuses on the analysis of how the diverse information available can be beneficial for semantic similarity comparison.

Attribute	Value
research id	ZA3950
variable id	exploredata-ZA3950_VarV31
study title	International Social Survey Programme: Citizenship - ISSP 2004
variable label	Q7b Rights in democr: Gov respect minorities
variable name	V31
question text	There are different opinions about people's rights in a democracy. On a scale of 1 to 7, where 1 is not at all important and 7 is very important, how important is it:
question text en	There are different opinions about people's rights in a democracy. On a scale of 1 to 7, where 1 is not at all important and 7 is very important, how important is it:
sub question	Q.7b - ... that government authorities respect and protect the rights of minorities
item category	... that all citizens have an adequate standard of living;... that government authorities treat everybody equally regardless of their position in society;... that politicians take into account the views of citizens before making decisions;... that people be given more opportunities to participate in public decision-making
answer category	Not at all important;2;3;4;5;6;Very important;Can't choose, don't know;No answer, refused
topic	['Soziales Verhalten und soziale Einstellungen', 'Internationale Politik und Institutionen', 'Politische Verhaltensweisen und Einstellungen/Meinungen', 'Regierung, politische Systeme, Parteien und Verbände']
topic en	['Social behaviour and attitudes', 'International politics and organisation', 'Mass political behaviour, attitudes/opinion', 'Government, political systems and organisation']

Table 2: Example of a survey variable.

3.1 Semantic Textual Similarity

We treated Task 1 partly and Task 2 fully as a problem of semantic textual similarity (Agirre et al., 2013). We used language-dependent sentence encoders (Conneau et al., 2017; Reimers and Gurevych, 2019) to create fixed-sized vector representations of the input sentences and some parts of the variables. For this purpose, we experimented with different sentence embedding models.

For the English data, we used *Sentence T5* (Ni et al., 2021) as a sentence embedding model. The variable parts that led to the best results for the English variables were the label, the question text, the question text in English and the topic in English. For the German data, we used the sentence embedding model *"Sahajtomar/German-semantic"* [2]. It is one of the few available German sentence embedding models hosted by HuggingFace to be used out of the box and the one we achieved the best results with[3]. We applied it on all variable parts, except the English translation ones.

We then computed the cosine similarity of all possible pairs of sentences and variables with the same research id. Afterwards the sentence-variable pairs were ranked by their similarity scores. This procedure was the same for both Task 1 and Task 2.

3.2 Task 1 – Variable Detection

The Variable Detection Task basically is a binary classification task. Since this task aims to detect only sentences containing any survey variable, the vocabulary of variables is not essential to use. We tried out two different approaches: one that is independent of the vocabulary and focuses on lexical features of the input sentences only (**BOW Model**) and one that is dependent on the vocabulary and focuses on semantic similarity (**STS Model**). A variation of the first one is used as a preparation for the latter.

3.2.1 BOW Model

For the vocabulary-independent approach, we trained a BoW model similar to (Zielinski and Mutschke, 2017). The input sentences were cleaned of special characters, converted to lowercase, tokenized and stop words were removed using *Natural Language Toolkit* (Bird et al., 2009). Then they were lemmatized.[4]

We used Logistic Regression for the English sentences and Multinomial Naive Bayes for the German sentences to predict whether a sentence contains a variable or not.

[2]https://huggingface.co/Sahajtomar/German-semantic

[3]The model is based on *German BERT large* (https://huggingface.co/deepset/gbert-large), but unfortunately we could not contact the author to find out which dataset it was further trained on.

[4]This approach is strongly aligned with the BOW Jupyter Notebook, which has been made available in the GitHub repository of the Shared Task as a starting point. https://github.com/vadis-project/sv-ident/tree/main/notebooks/variable_detection

3.2.2 STS Model

The variable-independent approach relies partly on a variation of the vocabulary-dependent approach. We tried to increase the recall to ensure to classify all true positives. This way we got a candidate list to further exclude false positives from (similar to (Zielinski and Mutschke, 2017)).

In order to increase the number of true positives in the training data we used *random undersampling* and balanced the distribution of positive and negative instances as explained in section 4.1.1.

We used the STS settings described above to get the similarity scores for the positively labeled sentences and all possible variables. We discarded all sentences that did not exceed a certain threshold. This threshold was computed taking the mean of all true sentence-variable pairs of the training data which showed to be more successful than considering the mean subtracted by the standard deviation of the pairs.

3.3 Task 2 – Variable Disambiguation

Task 2 aims to provide the id of the variable which is referenced in a given sentence. So for this task we directly computed the most similar variables for each input sentence. We used the setup described in 3.1 using language-dependent sentence embedding models to encode the input sentences and specified parts of the variables and then ranked the most similar pairs based on cosine similarity.

4 Experiments

Most of the settings described above were chosen because they proved to be successful in experiments on the validation data. This section provides the results of different experimental setups for BOW and STS models, respectively.

4.1 BOW Model

4.1.1 Random Undersampling

For the preselection of sentences likely to contain a variable, the aim was to exclude false negatives from the prediction by decreasing the number of negative instances in the training data. This was achieved by undersampling negative samples such that the ratio of negative ones to positives decreased from *3.865 to 1* (see Table 3).

4.1.2 Classifier Selection

We treated the languages separately since the lexical distribution of the English and the German

Class Balance	F. Negatives	F. Positives
0: 400, 1: 773	7	63
0: 300, 1: 773	4	75
0: 200, 1: 773	0	81

Table 3: False negatives and false positives for different ratios of positive (1) and negative samples (0) in the training set using Multinomial Naive Bayes.

language differ significantly. The best predictions for variable detection were made using Logistic Regression for the English data and Multionomial Naive Bayes for the German data (see Table 4).

Classifier	English	German
Logistic Regression	**0.780**	0.703
Multinomial Naive Bayes	0.749	**0.745**
KNN	0.520	0.501
Linear SVM	0.757	0.701

Table 4: F1 Scores for Different Classifiers

4.2 STS Model

4.2.1 Variable Parts

Some parts of the variables, like the variable label and name, at first glance do not seem to contain a lot of useful semantic information. Thus, we experimented with using different parts of the variables. Tables 5 and 6 show the impact of these experiments. While using only some parts is effective for the English data, using all parts without English ones yields the best results for the German data.

4.3 Pre-Processing

Different methods of pre-processing were used for both subtasks (see Table 7 and 8, 9). For Task 2, we differentiated between pre-processsing all variable parts and pre-processing only those that do not consist of natural language sentences. Sentence transformers are designed to encode the meaning of whole sentences and pre-processing destroys their syntactical structure. Interestingly, the best result was achieved pre-processing all variable parts, including full sentences.

Variable Parts	Map@10
All	0.127
variable label + question text + question text en + topic en	**0.167**
variable label + question text + topic en	0.143

Table 5: Impact of including different parts of the variables for the English data. The variable parts 'question text' and 'question text en' are the same in this setting.

Variable Parts	Map@10
All (except from English)	**0.091**
variable label + question text + question text en + topic en	0.050
variable label + question text	0.077

Table 6: Impact of including different parts of the variables for the German data.

Pre-Processing Method	F1
No Pre-Processing	0.756
Pre-Processing without Lemmatization	0.761
Pre-Processing with Lemmatization	**0.765**

Table 7: Impact of pre-processing the English sentences for Task 1. The pre-processing with lemmatization is described in section 3.2.1

Pre-Processing Method	MAP@10
No Removal	0.163
Stop Words *	**0.169**
Duplicates *	0.114
Stop Words and Duplicates *	0.108
Stop Words †	0.164
Duplicates †	0.146
Stop Words and Duplicates †	0.136

Table 8: Impact of removing stop words and duplicates from every part of the variable * and from every part except those including full sentences † for the English instances of Task 2.

Pre-Processing Method	MAP@10
No removal	0.092
Stop Words *	0.081
Duplicates *	0.095
Stop Words and Duplicates *	**0.140**
Stop Words and Duplicates †	0.116

Table 9: Impact of removing stop words and duplicates from every part of the variable * and from every part except those including full sentences † for the German instances of Task 2.

4.4 Trial Data

Additional to the training and validation data, some trial data was released by the organizers [5]. This data set contains a smaller vocabulary of variables. Results on this data were overall better for both subtasks and significantly better for Task 2. Using a similar setup as described above, we achieved an F1 score of **0.823** for the English data on Task 1 and a MAP@10 score above **0.674** for Task 2.

5 Results

While the official evaluation metric for Task 1 is F1-macro, or averaged F1 (averaged harmonic mean of precision and recall), it is MAP@10 (mean average precision of the ten top ranked items) for Task 2.

We achieved the best results using the STS model for Task 1. It scored *0.6016* on the test data (compared to *0.58* for the BOW model) which is still beneath the baseline[6] of *0.6609*, but the best result provided by participants.

In Task 2, our model achieved a result of *0.1359*, which is also beneath the baseline[7] of *0.1893* and it was the only submission made by participants.

6 Lessons Learned

The task proved to be challenging. This can partly be explained by the challenging nature of the data in general. Variable mentions in social science publications typically vary a lot on the linguistic level (Zielinski and Mutschke, 2018). Additionally, dealing with a very large corpus of variables might explain why the results on the test data were so much worse than the results on the trial data..

Since the pre-processing and evaluation of taking into account different variable parts were the main factors improving the results, it would be beneficial to further concentrate on these approaches for future work.

One step into this direction could be the use of data augmentation. This already showed to be successful implicitly, since for the English data better results were achieved including the *question text* and *question text en*, which are the same sentences (see Table 2 and Table 5).

[5]`https://github.com/vadis-project/sv-ident/tree/main/data/trial`

[6]The baseline model is the fine-tuned SciBERT model *SSCI-SciBERT* that was further trained on English Social Science abstracts.

[7]The baseline model is a pre-trained multilingual sentence representation model in a zero-shot setting.

The sentence embedding models used in our approach have the advantage of being suitable for general STS tasks and perform competitively for a variety of such tasks without further fine-tuning (Hövelmeyer et al., 2022). Nevertheless, the baseline models of which one is fine-tuned on social science literature and the other is multilingual achieved better results for this task. For future work, it therefore would be interesting to experiment with models fine-tuned on data similar to the data at hand and multilingual models.

7 Conclusion

We presented a solution to the *SV-Ident* Shared Task relying on semantic similarity and basically treating the subtasks of variable detection and variable disambiguation as the same problem. We encoded the input sentences and parts of the variables using sentence transformer models and treating English and German sentences separately. For Task 1, we used a BOW model with random undersampling in order to create a preselection of likely candidates to contain a variable and then looked for sufficiently similar variables to decide whether a sentence contains a variable or not. For Task 2, we ranked the most similar variables to every input sentence. Throughout, we experimented with different pre-processing methods and different variable parts which proved to be beneficial. It showed that a promising approach for future work could be the consideration of data augmentation techniques.

References

Eneko Agirre, Daniel Cer, Mona Diab, Aitor Gonzalez-Agirre, and Weiwei Guo. 2013. *sem 2013 shared task: Semantic textual similarity. *Proceedings of *sEM*, pages 32–43.

Steven Bird, Ewan Klein, and Edward Loper. 2009. *Natural language processing with Python: analyzing text with the natural language toolkit.* " O'Reilly Media, Inc.".

Katarina Boland, Dominique Ritze, K. Eckert, and Brigitte Mathiak. 2012. Identifying references to datasets in publications. In *TPDL*.

Alexis Conneau, Douwe Kiela, Holger Schwenk, Loic Barrault, and Antoine Bordes. 2017. Supervised learning of universal sentence representations from natural language inference data.

Alica Hövelmeyer, Katarina Boland, and Stefan Dietze. 2022. Simba at checkthat! 2022: Lexical and semantic similarity based detection of verified claims in an unsupervised and supervised way. In *Working Notes of CLEF 2022—Conference and Labs of the Evaluation Forum*, CLEF '2022, Bologna, Italy.

Jianmo Ni, Gustavo Hernández Ábrego, Noah Constant, Ji Ma, Keith B. Hall, Daniel Cer, and Yinfei Yang. 2021. Sentence-t5: Scalable sentence encoders from pre-trained text-to-text models. *CoRR*, abs/2108.08877.

Nils Reimers and Iryna Gurevych. 2019. Sentence-bert: Sentence embeddings using siamese bert-networks.

Tornike Tsereteli, Yavuz Selim Kartal, Simone Paolo Ponzetto, Andrea Zielinski, Kai Eckert, and Philipp Mayr. 2022. Overview of the SV-Ident 2022 Shared Task on Survey Variable Identification in Social Science Publications. In *Proceedings of the Third Workshop on Scholarly Document Processing*. Association for Computational Linguistics.

Andrea Zielinski and Peter Mutschke. 2017. Mining social science publications for survey variables. In *Proceedings of the Second Workshop on NLP and Computational Social Science*, pages 47–52. Association for Computational Linguistics (ACL).

Andrea Zielinski and Peter Mutschke. 2018. Towards a gold standard corpus for variable detection and linking in social science publications. In *Proceedings of the 11th International Conference on Language Resources and Evaluation (LREC)*. European Language Resources Association (ELRA).

Benchmark for Research Theme Classification of Scholarly Documents

Óscar E. Mendoza[1] Wojciech Kusa[2] Alaa El-Ebshihy[2]

Ronin Wu[3] David Pride[4] Petr Knoth[4] Drahomira Herrmannova[5]

Florina Piroi[2] Gabriella Pasi[1] Allan Hanbury[2]

[1]University of Milano-Bicocca, Milan, Italy
oscar.espitiamendoza@unimib.it
[2]TU Wien, Vienna, Austria
[3]IRIS.ai, Stabekk, Norway
[4]Knowledge Media institute, The Open University, Milton Keynes, U.K.
[5]Elsevier, U.S.

Abstract

We present a new gold-standard dataset and a benchmark for the *Research Theme Identification* task, a sub-task of the Scholarly Knowledge Graph Generation shared task, at the 3rd Workshop on Scholarly Document Processing. The objective of the shared task was to label given research papers with research themes from a total of 36 themes. The benchmark was compiled using data drawn from the largest overall assessment of university research output ever undertaken globally (the Research Excellence Framework - 2014).

We provide a performance comparison of a transformer-based ensemble, which obtains multiple predictions for a research paper, given its multiple textual fields (e.g. title, abstract, reference), with traditional machine learning models. The ensemble involves enriching the initial data with additional information from open-access digital libraries and Argumentative Zoning techniques (Teufel et al., 1999b). It uses a weighted sum aggregation for the multiple predictions to obtain a final single prediction for the given research paper.

Both data and the ensemble are publicly available on https://www.kaggle.com/ and https://github.com/ProjectDoSSIER/sdp2022, respectively.

1 Introduction

With the recent demise of the widely used Microsoft Academic Graph (MAG) (Sinha et al., 2015), the scholarly document processing community is facing a pressing need to replace MAG with an open-source community-supported service. In order to create a comprehensive scholarly graph, it is challenging to correctly represent each paper as a node on the graph. This requires condensing meta-information, such as authorship, research organizations, research themes etc., of research papers to one node.

So far, the task of identifying research themes for a given scholarly document has been challenging due to the lack of large high-quality labelled data. This made it difficult both to train high-performance classification models as well as to compare models' performance across studies.

This paper provides a benchmark for research theme classification based on a large human-annotated corpus of scholarly papers across 36 themes defined by the UK Research Excellence Framework, the largest overall assessment of university research outputs ever undertaken globally (the Research Excellence Framework - 2014)[1] (Cressey and Gibney, 2014). The outcome of this paper is the product of the Scholarly Knowledge Graph Generation shared task which was part of the Scholarly Document Processing (SDP) workshop at COLING2022.

We started with a labelled dataset containing publications and subjects to which they belong (Section 3), which contains descriptions or abstracts, the first author, DOI, year of publication, and identifier to link the publication to the CORE (Knoth and Zdrahal, 2012) aggregator. We later enriched this dataset with further information including the full text, where available. This represents a new gold-standard dataset for theme classification of scholarly documents.

To establish a benchmark for research theme classification, we present experiments and evaluation results with traditional machine learning models and compare them to a more sophisticated transformer-based ensemble model.

Our transformer-based ensemble model exploits

[1]https://ref.ac.uk/2014/

Proceedings of the Third Workshop on Scholarly Document Processing, pages 253–262
October 12–17, 2022.

all textual fields for each scholarly document and maps these documents to CORE and Semantic Scholar (Fricke, 2018) to gather further external information. Thus, the ensemble consists of a transformer-based classifier used to produce multiple predictions for individual publications (split into multiple textual fields) that are aggregated to produce a single final prediction. We aggregate predictions from titles, abstracts, references, citations, and related titles for every publication, when available. Furthermore, we use abstracts, PDFs and full texts available to identify argumentative zones (Teufel et al., 1999b) to use them as additional fields. We report on the results of using aggregation for different combinations of these predictions.

The rest of the paper is organized as follows: Section 2 presents a discussion of the related work, focusing mainly on scientific document classification approaches and their evaluation. Section 3 describes details of building the new benchmark for theme classification. Section 4 discusses the ensemble we propose as a baseline and the system components in more detail. In Section 5, we describe the experimental settings. In Section 6, we discuss the evaluation results from a diverse set of experiments. Finally, we discuss the conclusion and the potential direction of future work in Sections 7 and 8.

2 Related Work

Classifying scholarly documents is an important task, whether for understanding the dynamics of scientific fields or simply for organizing scientific literature more effectively. In previous literature, it typically relies on textual features such as titles, author keywords, and abstracts, as well as the interrelationships between the documents (i.e., citations and co-authorship). Full texts are frequently not available and processing a large amount of text can be computationally expensive.

A wide variety of classification features have been proposed at different levels of granularity, e.g., themes, topics, and subjects. A large proportion of classification methods rely on semantic similarity (Wang and Koopman, 2017; Semberecki and Maciejewski, 2017; Salatino et al., 2022; Hande et al., 2021; Boyack and Klavans, 2018). Others include approaches for clustering documents based on keyword co-occurrence (Van Eck and Waltman, 2017; Kim and Gil, 2019). Further approaches leverage the relationship graph representation built from citations and co-authorship (Taheriyan, 2011; Shen et al., 2018; Hoppe et al., 2021).

One promising but unexplored approach to theme classification is using information about argumentative zoning (AZ) (Teufel et al., 1999b). AZ refers to the examination of the argumentative status of sentences in scientific articles and their assignment to specific argumentative zones. Its main goal is to collect sentences that belong to predefined zones, such as "claim" or "method". Annotated AZ corpora has been created by (Teufel et al., 1999a,b; Teufel and Moens, 2002; Teufel et al., 2009) with approaches to AZ identification reported in (Liu, 2017). In this work, we aim to test to what extent can the AZ signal support classification of scholarly documents into research themes.

Classification models previously appplied to this task include traditional machine learning models, such as k-Nearest Neighbours (Waltman and Van Eck, 2012; Łukasik et al., 2013), K-means (Kim and Gil, 2019) and Naïve Bayes (Eykens et al., 2021). It has been reported that these models encounter performance challenges related to overly coarse classifications and low accuracy (Daradkeh et al., 2022). There are applications of deep neural networks (NN) models as well, such as convolutional NN (Rivest et al., 2021; Daradkeh et al., 2022) and recurrent NN (Semberecki and Maciejewski, 2017; Hoppe et al., 2021). More recent deep learning approaches take advantage of pretrained language models (Kandimalla et al., 2021; Hande et al., 2021).

One of the common practices to evaluate approaches for classifying scientific text is to use classification systems from digital libraries (Kandimalla et al., 2021; Gialitsis et al., 2022; Taheriyan, 2011; Gündoğan and Kaya, 2020), such as the ACM Computing Classification System[2], the Web of Science Categories[3] and Science-Metrix[4]. Other practices involve generating automatic annotations for scientific collections that can be completely synthetic (Waltman and Van Eck, 2012) or curated by experts (Salatino et al., 2022; Eykens et al., 2021; Daradkeh et al., 2022; Hande et al., 2021; Pech et al., 2022). However, to date, there has been no established benchmark to evaluate these approaches.

We present a new high-quality benchmark for evaluating research theme classification, used for

[2]ACM Computing Classification System
[3]Web of Science Categories
[4]Science-Metrix

the first time in the Scholarly Knowledge Graph Generation Shared Task.

3 Inital Dataset Creation

As previously discussed, one of the significant challenges faced in the domain is the lack of large-scale labelled data for research theme classification. For the shared task, a completely new gold-standard dataset was compiled using data drawn from the U.K.'s Research Excellence Framework (REF) 2014 exercise (Cressey and Gibney, 2014). In total, 191,000 research outputs were submitted by 154 higher education and research institutions, and these were then peer-reviewed by experts from each domain. The REF divided research outputs into 36 'Units of Assessment' (UoA) or domain areas. The institutions themselves selected to which Unit of Assessment each output was submitted.

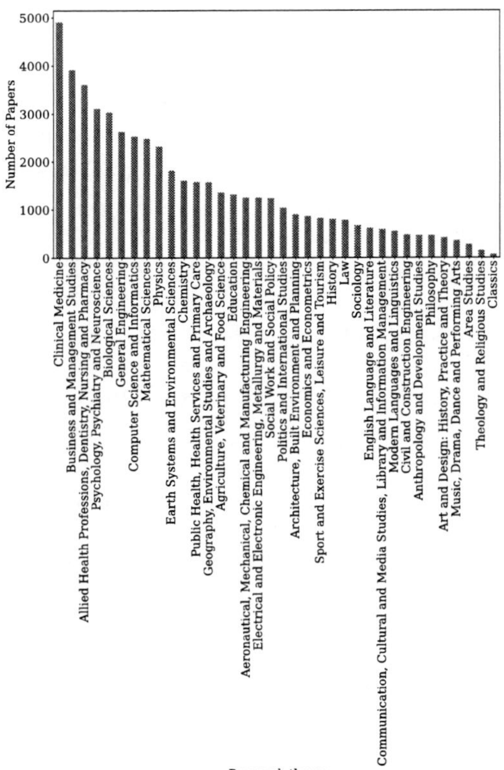

Figure 1: Breakdown of the dataset by theme.

The data from the REF exercise, therefore, provides a near-perfect starting point for the task of automatically identifying research themes as the UoA labels were manually assigned to each output by the expert academics responsible for its production.

For each output, the following were available from the REF data; publication title, publication year, publication venue, name of institution, and Unit of Assessment. These fields were fully populated for 190,628 out of 190,963 submissions to the outputs category of the REF process. We further enriched each record with the DOI, CORE id, and abstract (where available). The CORE id is used to identify the actual research article held by the CORE service[5]. Not all papers in the dataset are open access, therefore the full-text content of all papers is not available. For non-open access papers, CORE often still has the metadata for these articles.

For the data used in this shared task, separate test and train datasets were generated. From the full REF dataset, 51,560 randomly selected records were used for the train set, and a separate 10,000 were selected for the test set. The datasets were then verified to ensure that there was no overlap between the two sets. Figure 1 shows the cross-domain (theme) breakdown of all records used for this task.

4 Classification Ensemble

This section depicts the approach we used to estimate probabilities of academic publications belonging to specific theme and the heuristics we follow for classification. In general, we want to exploit all the information available for the scholarly documents that need to be classified. Academic publications are typically well-structured documents with multiple textual fields and metadata. We rely on open-access platforms to enrich the data with additional information (Section 4.2).

Currently, Transformer-based contextual language models like ELMo (Peters et al., 2018) or BERT (Devlin et al., 2019) outperform most feature-based representation methods. We use a classifier based on contextual word embeddings to evaluate the utility of individual textual fields in the classification of Academic publications.

4.1 Transformer-based Classifier

We rely on the pre-trained general language model BERT (Devlin et al., 2019), which achieves outstanding performance on different NLP tasks through fine-tuning for the downstream tasks (Acheampong et al., 2021), in this case, multiclass classification.

[5]https://core.ac.uk

We allow all layers of BERT to be updated as we are learning the relevant context from the training data. A custom operation is added on top of the model, which takes the last hidden state tensor from the encoder and then passes it to a linear layer. At the end of the linear layer, we have a vector with a size equal to the number of classes, and each element corresponds to a category of the provided labels. Specifically, we use the following setting to build the model base:

Input layer. It builds the model's input sequence. The input sequence is segmented according to the WordPiece embeddings and the token vocabulary. The final input representations are then produced by adding the position embeddings, word embeddings, and segmentation embeddings for each token.

BERT encoder. It consists of multiple Transformer blocks and multiple self-attention heads that take an input of a sequence of a limited number of tokens and output the representations of the sequence. The representation can be a specific hidden state vector or a time-step sequence of hidden state vectors.

Output layer. It consists of a simple linear layer with a Softmax classifier on top of the encoder for computing the conditional probability distributions over predefined categorical labels.

The cross-entropy loss is used to optimize the model with the Adam optimizer.

4.2 Data Enrichment

Taking advantage of the open access libraries available for scientific publications, we search for complementary data for each example provided for the task. Specifically, we use the CORE (Knoth and Zdrahal, 2012) and the Semantic Scholar (Ammar et al., 2018) APIs to map publication titles to the various fields available for each publication.

The original task dataset includes mainly titles with metadata. Our goal with the enrichment is to collect more information related to the publication to better match the themes. After mapping the papers to results from the search using the APIs, we add a list of references and citations, full papers, abstracts, and PDFs, for the cases when they are available. Moreover, we search for five recommended papers using the title for every publication using the CORE API.

We believe that regardless of the performance of the classification model, if there is enough evidence for a publication to belong to a specific theme, we should be able to classify it with enough certainty. For instance, given a publication title, which can be ambiguous, we hypothesize that considering the multiple references or citations leads to disambiguation and deciding effectively to which topic this publication should belong. The list of references or citations can be classified the same way as single inputs, and the classification result can consider the multiple corresponding outputs for the final decision.

Since there is no guarantee that this data is available for all the original samples, we exploit all available sections, including the full text and PDFs. However, since processing such an amount of text is expensive, we use AZ (Teufel et al., 1999b). Here, we define four zones that cover the main components of scientific articles, namely: *Claim*, *Method*, *Result* and *Conclusion*.

In order to extract sentences that cover the four zones from the available PDF scientific articles, we follow an approach similar to a previously proposed approach by El-Ebshihy et al. (2020), which generates an article summary by expanding the article abstract. To sum up, the sentence selection and labeling with zones process goes as follows: (1) we convert the PDF papers to an XML format using the GROBID PDF parser (Lopez, 2009), which identifies the paragraphs of the article, (2) the paragraphs are fed into a Solr[6] index, (3) the sentences in the article's abstract are passed as queries to the Solr index in order to find the top most similar paragraphs to the abstract sentences, (4) sentences of the retrieved paragraphs, as well as the sentences of the abstract, are labeled to zones using a pre-trained BERT model based on the approach proposed by Accuosto et al. (2021), and (5) we use the labeled sentences to extend our training data with four extra text fields that represent the *Claim*, the *Method*, the *Result* and the *Conclusion* — we refer to these extra fields as Argumentative Zones. In case we cannot find the PDF source of the article, we use the article abstract, if found, to generate these fields.

4.3 Extending Labels to Enriched Data

During training, the model takes text examples together with the labels associated with them. Since examples for this task are academic publications,

[6]https://lucene.apache.org/solr/

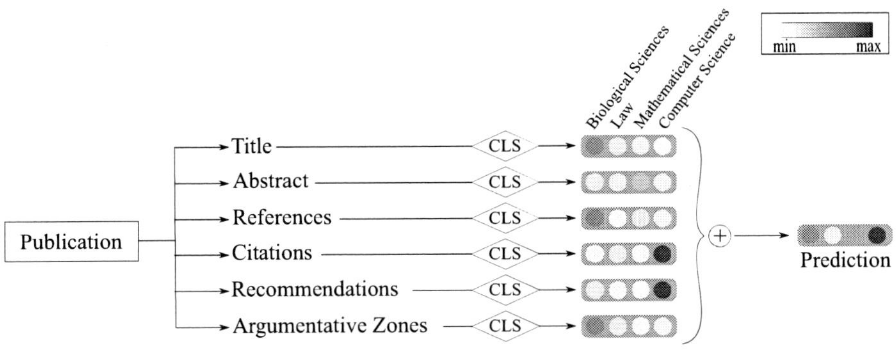

Figure 2: Ensemble for research theme classification. CLS stands for classifier.

and we want to use different sections independently, we rebuild the dataset considering each section as a single sample but associated with the same publication, and we use the same label for all samples of the same publication.

In this way, we end up with an extended version of the initial dataset, in which new samples are created for titles, abstracts, citations, references, and recommendations.

	Train	Test
Size	51,560	10,000
% of Publications		
- available via CORE API	91.6%	92.4%
- with abstract	31.8%	31.7%
- with PDF	24.6%	25.6%
- with full text	6.3%	6.4%
- with references	8.4%	7.6%

Table 1: Dataset statistics.

4.4 Aggregating Predictions from Enriched Data

During inference time, we compute multiple predictions associated with the same publication. These predictions can either agree or disagree, so we formulate the final prediction as the aggregation of the different predictions. Figure 2 illustrates the prediction procedure used to obtain the final theme prediction for a publication in which various sections are evaluated as independent samples with the classifier. Section 5 describes how this aggregation is parameterized for the experiments.

5 Experimental setup

5.1 Dataset

Statistics for the initial dataset are provided in Table 1. Most of this dataset's publications do not contain abstracts, additional metadata, or PDFs. Theme identification algorithms should be robust to these missing features and work well when only titles are available.

5.2 Training Settings

Given the labelled training samples, we train the model using two different sets. The first training set consists of the list of titles, while the second takes both titles and available abstracts. We argue that although more information can be available per publication, the labels provided match only titles and abstracts, and further assumptions can hurt the model's performance. However, we define an additional training set under our data enrichment procedure. We refer to the first model as BERT_T and to the second one as BERT_{T+A}.

We train the model for 10 epochs, with early stopping based on the performance measured using the evaluation metric (see Section 6.1) and patience of 3 epochs. The training samples are picked randomly, searching for a uniform distribution over the classes per batch. To prevent overfitting in case of unbalanced batches, we use the weighted cross-entropy loss, and assign the weights dynamically, according to the result of the random selection of samples in the batch. We use 16384 samples from the training set per epoch divided into batches of 64 samples, and train the models on an Nvidia Quadro RTX 8000 GPU.

5.3 Prediction Settings

As well as the training strategy, we evaluate the utility of having multiple predictions per publication in the test set compared to a single prediction. To do so, we prepare different evaluation sets, following the same training set schema. Thus, we evaluate the model using only titles, then using titles and abstracts, and finally, using the set created under our data enrichment procedure.

Since we have to produce a single prediction per publication, and the sets are not uniform, in the sense that certain publications may not have extra fields (see Table 1, for instance, abstracts are available for only 32% of publications), we parameterise the prediction aggregation based on the different sets of fields. We consider the aggregation to be a weighted sum. The motivation for selecting a weighted sum, instead of just summing up the outputs is that we can introduce offsetting through the weights. Thus, we give an advantage to the labelled fields in the original dataset over the extended data.

For our experiments, in the case of the set with titles and abstracts, we use uniform weighting. In the case of the extended set, we assign weights such that: 0.5 is distributed uniformly between title and abstract, and 0.5 is uniformly distributed between all the additional fields available per publication. This setting is compared experimentally to a uniform weighting across all the fields.

6 Results

6.1 Evaluation metrics

The evaluation metric used for evaluating classification results is micro F1-Score. The F1 score, commonly used in machine learning, measures accuracy using the statistics precision and recall.

The F1 metric weighs recall and precision equally, and a good classification algorithm will maximize both precision and recall simultaneously. Thus, moderately good performance on both will be favored over extremely good performance on one and poor performance on the other.

6.2 Baseline Models

We implement several baseline models for comparison to the ensemble described in Section 4:

K-nearest neighbours classifier with Tf-idf representation

Logistic Regression classifier with Tf-idf representation

Naïve Bayes classifier with Tf-idf representation

Support Vector Machine classifier with Tf-idf representation

fastText classifier (Joulin et al., 2016) with word vectors pretrained on wikipedia[7]

We also present scores using two dummy classifiers: selecting the most frequent category and sampling from a multinomial distribution parameterised by prior probabilities. All classifiers except for fastText are implemented using scikit-learn (Pedregosa et al., 2011).

6.3 Validation Results

Given the provided training data, we create balanced splits such that 60% is used for train, 10% for early stopping and 30% for validation. All the sets are enriched following the process described earlier. Table 2 shows some preliminary results for experiments we perform to select the model and the training setup. We compare the two different BERT models with traditional models. The performance of the model trained using titles and abstracts is slightly better, and we use it for further experiments.

Model name	Titles	Titles and abstracts
Dummy: most frequent	— 0.095 —	
Dummy: stratified random	— 0.048 —	
K-nearest Neighbours	0.132	0.468
Logistic Regression	0.457	0.498
Naïve Bayes	0.460	0.493
Support Vector Machine	0.474	0.506
fastText	0.454	0.473
BERT_T	0.498	–
BERT_{T+A}	**0.500**	**0.512**

Table 2: Micro F1-score results comparison using different input features for prediction. BERT_T stands for BERT model trained on titles only, BERT_{T+A} means model trained on both titles and abstracts.

Furthermore, we evaluated the utility of enriching the dataset by comparing predictions from titles only with aggregated predictions using titles and additional available fields. Table 3 shows that adding information improves the classification for all three experiments. Notice that the experiments are not comparable to each other because the dataset samples are different. Subsamples are selected such that corresponding sections are available for all documents.

Table 4 shows the results obtained for the validation set using different variants of ensemble. In general, we are able to improve the performance of the classification while adding more data, although the difference between the experiments is small. The best score reached is 0.526, using titles, abstracts, citations, references and the argumentative

[7] https://dl.fbaipublicfiles.com/fasttext

Sections	Sample size	F1-score (title)	F1-score (all sections)
Title + Abs.	31.3%	0.503	0.539
Title + Cit. + Refs	25.4%	0.492	0.541
Title + AZ	1.6%	0.548	0.552

Table 3: Three experiments testing the utility of individual sections on BERT_{T+A}. The augmentation is evaluated by independent sections combined with titles. Samples are selected such that corresponding sections are available for all documents.

Title	Abs.	Cit.	Refs	AZ	Recs.	F1
×	–	–	–	–	–	0.500
×	×	–	–	–	–	0.512
×	×	×	×	–	–	0.523
×	×	×	×	×	–	**0.526**
×	×	×	×	×	×	0.525

Table 4: Validation results using different fields for BERT_{T+A}. The experiments vary in the prediction and aggregation settings. The aggregations we use are simply weighted sums with uniform weights and assigned arbitrarily according to Section 5.3.

zones.

For the best configuration, we also show the confusion matrix (see Figure 3). For convenience, we show the results for only the 25 most frequent classes and we group the rest of them in a single class. It should be noted that for Clinical Medicine, most of the examples where the model's prediction is incorrect are classified as Allied Health Professions, Dentistry, Nursing and Pharmacy, and Biological Sciences. Similar behaviour can be observed with related fields of study. Further analysis must be done to evaluate overlapping between disciplines.

6.4 Test Results

In this section, we show the results for the test set (see Table 5). In general, we see a positive impact with our approach considering that we could not get additional information for all the items in the original dataset.

In this set of experiments, we evaluate a different aggregation setting, uniform weighting through all the fields (run 4), and the result is the best score for the set of runs. Furthermore, we also evaluate an additional model trained with all the fields available (run 5), and we see no improvements.

7 Discussion

In this work, we first released a new gold-standard human-annotated dataset of over 60k papers complete with paper metadata, research themes and additional textual information including the papers' abstract and full-text where available. In future, it would be possible to further extend the size of the presented dataset to include all REF2014 and now the recently finalised REF2021 papers, which both used the same research themes classifications. This would result in an annotated dataset of over quarter of a million papers. To our knowledge, our work was the first to utilise REF research evaluation for the purposes of building machine learning models for themes classification and highlighted the significant potential of this dataset for developing state-of-the-art models.

Run	Title	Abs.	Cit.	Refs	AZ	Recs.	Agg.	F1
1	T+P	T+P	–	–	–	–	U	0.569
2	T+P	T+P	P	P	P	–	C	0.575
3	T+P	T+P	P	P	P	P	C	0.571
4	T+P	T+P	P	P	P	P	U	**0.577**
5	T+P	T+P	T+P	T+P	–	T+P	C	0.556

Table 5: Test results with different experimental (Run) settings. The experiments vary in the training (T), prediction (P) and aggregation (Agg.) settings. The aggregations we use are simply weighted sum with uniform weights (U) and compensation weights (C) assigned according to section 5.3.

Second, we use this dataset to establish a new benchmark for research theme classification, testing a range of classic machine learning models under the same laboratory conditions. Unsurprisingly, our results confirm that models trained with both titles and abstracts as input features consistently achieve higher results than when using titles alone. These results hold both for baseline models and our newly introduced ensemble BERT model. While the results confirm that the BERT-based ensemble model outperforms traditional models, the performance of SVMs is only marginally worse.

It is interesting to note that using all available features for training (run 5) decreases the score compared to the model trained on titles and abstracts only. We hypothesise that a large proportion of false negatives can be attributed to noise introduced by reference sections within the full texts, especially for closely aligned domains. The confusion matrix (Figure 3) shows that many of the incorrect classifications happened in closely related domains (Clinical Medicine / Biological Science for example).

This is indicative of the difficulty of this task, particularly when presented with closely matched

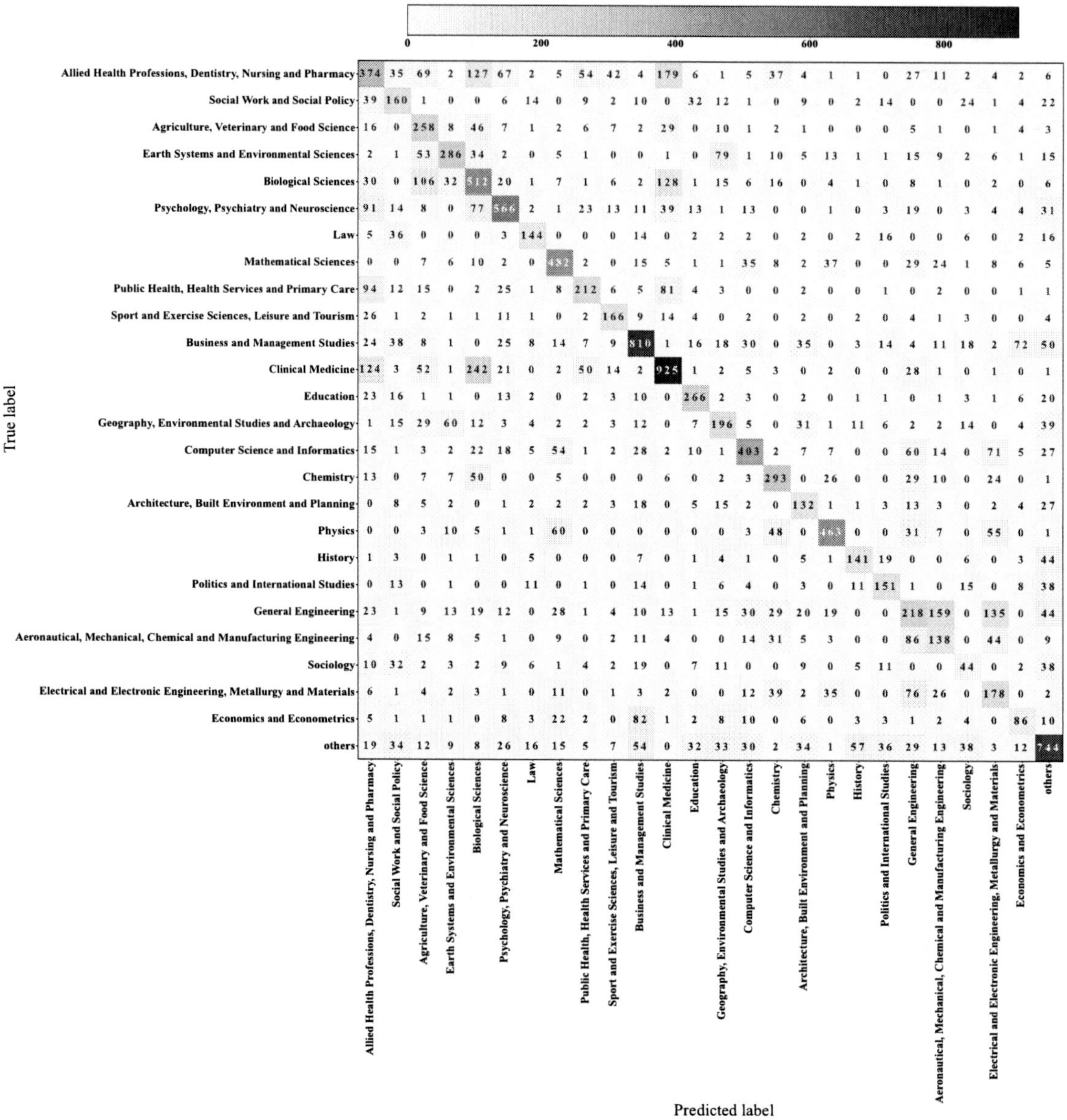

Figure 3: Confusion Matrix for validation results for 25 most frequent classes. The remaining 11 classes are grouped in the 'others' category.

or overlapping domains. Indeed, one limitation of our approach may be the classification of each paper into a single research field. In real-world examples, a paper could often be classified into multiple domains. Another limitation is that our ensemble model requires the availability of both title and abstract, which are necessary for the AZ approach, which we have seen contributes to the performance.

Assigning research themes to scholarly documents has wide-ranging applications. These include enhanced domain-specific search, for instance search in Chemistry is a complex task due to the need to index chemical compounds, and identifying emerging research trends. Further, a significant problem with current bibliometric methodologies is accounting for cross-disciplinary differences in both publishing and citation practices. Identifying the research theme enables accounting for disciplinary differences by, for instance, calculating normalised citation counts.

In future work, we would like to measure the importance of weight assignments for augmented predictions and consider the overlap between disciplines to evaluate ways of disambiguating predictions falling into related themes.

8 Conclusion

We have introduced a new large human annotated gold-standard dataset and a benchmark for research theme classification of scholarly documents. The work was conducted in the context of the *Extracting Research Themes* task from the 2022 edition of the Scholarly Knowledge Graph Generation shared task. The task was to identify the main research theme from a taxonomy of 36 classes, introduced by the UK Research Excellence Framework.

Our experiments addressed the effect of using a variety of textual fields on the prediction performance. Enriching the supplied training and testing data with external textual information (e.g., PDF source, full-text article, references) using open-access sources improved the results of our models. However, we have demonstrated that this enrichment might also introduce additional noise.

We presented a new transformer-based classifier model based on BERT and used it to obtain multiple predictions for a given research article for each textual field. We experimented with a variety of aggregation functions to produce the final prediction. Despite incomplete and noisy data, the results show that our ensemble model has a small positive impact on the classification performance.

Acknowledgements

This work was supported by the EU Horizon 2020 ITN/ETN on Domain Specific Systems for Information Extraction and Retrieval – DoSSIER (H2020-EU.1.3.1., ID: 860721).

References

Pablo Accuosto, Mariana Neves, and Horacio Saggion. 2021. Argumentation mining in scientific literature: from computational linguistics to biomedicine. In *Frommholz I, Mayr P, Cabanac G, Verberne S, editors. BIR 2021: 11th International Workshop on Bibliometric-enhanced Information Retrieval; 2021 Apr 1; Lucca, Italy. Aachen: CEUR; 2021. p. 20-36.* CEUR Workshop Proceedings.

Francisca Adoma Acheampong, Henry Nunoo-Mensah, and Wenyu Chen. 2021. Transformer models for text-based emotion detection: a review of bert-based approaches. *Artificial Intelligence Review*, 54(8).

Waleed Ammar, Dirk Groeneveld, Chandra Bhagavatula, Iz Beltagy, Miles Crawford, Doug Downey, Jason Dunkelberger, Ahmed Elgohary, Sergey Feldman, Vu Ha, et al. 2018. Construction of the literature graph in semantic scholar. *arXiv preprint arXiv:1805.02262*.

Kevin W Boyack and Richard Klavans. 2018. Accurately identifying topics using text: Mapping pubmed. In *STI 2018 Conference Proceedings*, pages 107–115. Centre for Science and Technology Studies (CWTS).

Daniel Cressey and Elizabeth Gibney. 2014. Uk releases world's largest university assessment. *Nature*.

Mohammad Daradkeh, Laith Abualigah, Shadi Atalla, and Wathiq Mansoor. 2022. Scientometric analysis and classification of research using convolutional neural networks: A case study in data science and analytics. *Electronics*, 11(13):2066.

Jacob Devlin, Ming-Wei Chang, Kenton Lee, and Kristina Toutanova. 2019. BERT: Pre-training of Deep Bidirectional Transformers for Language Understanding. In *Proceedings of the 2019 Conference of the North American Chapter of the Association for Computational Linguistics: Human Language Technologies, Volume 1 (Long and Short Papers)*, pages 4171–4186.

Alaa El-Ebshihy, Annisa Maulida Ningtyas, Linda Andersson, Florina Piroi, and Andreas Rauber. 2020. ARTU / TU Wien and artificial researcher@ LongSumm 20. In *Proceedings of the First Workshop on Scholarly Document Processing*, Online. Association for Computational Linguistics.

Joshua Eykens, Raf Guns, and Tim CE Engels. 2021. Fine-grained classification of social science journal articles using textual data: A comparison of supervised machine learning approaches. *Quantitative Science Studies*, 2(1):89–110.

Suzanne Fricke. 2018. Semantic scholar. *Journal of the Medical Library Association: JMLA*, 106(1):145.

Nikolaos Gialitsis, Sotiris Kotitsas, and Haris Papageorgiou. 2022. Scinobo: A hierarchical multi-label classifier of scientific publications. *arXiv preprint arXiv:2204.00880*.

Esra Gündoğan and Mehmet Kaya. 2020. Research paper classification based on word2vec and community discovery. In *2020 International Conference on Decision Aid Sciences and Application (DASA)*, pages 1032–1036. IEEE.

Adeep Hande, Karthik Puranik, Ruba Priyadharshini, and Bharathi Raja Chakravarthi. 2021. Domain identification of scientific articles using transfer learning and ensembles. In *Pacific-Asia Conference on Knowledge Discovery and Data Mining*, pages 88–97. Springer.

Fabian Hoppe, Danilo Dessì, and Harald Sack. 2021. Deep learning meets knowledge graphs for scholarly data classification. In *Companion proceedings of the web conference 2021*, pages 417–421.

Armand Joulin, Edouard Grave, Piotr Bojanowski, and Tomas Mikolov. 2016. Bag of tricks for efficient text classification. *arXiv preprint arXiv:1607.01759*.

Bharath Kandimalla, Shaurya Rohatgi, Jian Wu, and C Lee Giles. 2021. Large scale subject category classification of scholarly papers with deep attentive neural networks. *Frontiers in research metrics and analytics*, 5:600382.

Sang-Woon Kim and Joon-Min Gil. 2019. Research paper classification systems based on tf-idf and lda schemes. *Human-centric Computing and Information Sciences*, 9(1):1–21.

Petr Knoth and Zdenek Zdrahal. 2012. Core: three access levels to underpin open access. *D-Lib Magazine*, 18(11/12).

Haixia Liu. 2017. Automatic argumentative-zoning using word2vec. *CoRR*, abs/1703.10152.

Patrice Lopez. 2009. Grobid: Combining automatic bibliographic data recognition and term extraction for scholarship publications. In *International conference on theory and practice of digital libraries*, pages 473–474. Springer.

Michał Łukasik, Tomasz Kuśmierczyk, Łukasz Bolikowski, and Hung Son Nguyen. 2013. Hierarchical, multi-label classification of scholarly publications: modifications of ml-knn algorithm. In *Intelligent tools for building a scientific information platform*, pages 343–363. Springer.

Gerson Pech, Catarina Delgado, and Silvio Paolo Sorella. 2022. Classifying papers into subfields using abstracts, titles, keywords and keywords plus through pattern detection and optimization procedures: An application in physics. *Journal of the Association for Information Science and Technology*.

F. Pedregosa, G. Varoquaux, A. Gramfort, V. Michel, B. Thirion, O. Grisel, M. Blondel, P. Prettenhofer, R. Weiss, V. Dubourg, J. Vanderplas, A. Passos, D. Cournapeau, M. Brucher, M. Perrot, and E. Duchesnay. 2011. Scikit-learn: Machine learning in Python. *Journal of Machine Learning Research*, 12:2825–2830.

Matthew E. Peters, Mark Neumann, Mohit Iyyer, Matt Gardner, Christopher Clark, Kenton Lee, and Luke Zettlemoyer. 2018. Deep contextualized word representations. In *Proceedings of the 2018 Conference of the North American Chapter of the Association for Computational Linguistics: Human Language Technologies, Volume 1 (Long Papers)*, New Orleans, Louisiana. Association for Computational Linguistics.

Maxime Rivest, Etienne Vignola-Gagné, and Éric Archambault. 2021. level classification of scientific publications: A comparison of deep learning, direct citation and bibliographic coupling. *PloS one*, 16(5):e0251493.

Angelo Salatino, Francesco Osborne, and Enrico Motta. 2022. Cso classifier 3.0: a scalable unsupervised method for classifying documents in terms of research topics. *International Journal on Digital Libraries*, 23(1):91–110.

Piotr Semberecki and Henryk Maciejewski. 2017. Deep learning methods for subject text classification of articles. In *2017 Federated Conference on Computer Science and Information Systems (FedCSIS)*, pages 357–360. IEEE.

Zhihong Shen, Hao Ma, and Kuansan Wang. 2018. A web-scale system for scientific knowledge exploration. *arXiv preprint arXiv:1805.12216*.

Arnab Sinha, Zhihong Shen, Yang Song, Hao Ma, Darrin Eide, Bo-June Hsu, and Kuansan Wang. 2015. An overview of microsoft academic service (mas) and applications. In *Proceedings of the 24th International Conference on World Wide Web*, WWW '15 Companion, pages 243–246, Republic and Canton of Geneva, Switzerland. International World Wide Web Conferences Steering Committee.

Mohsen Taheriyan. 2011. Subject classification of research papers based on interrelationships analysis. In *Proceedings of the 2011 workshop on Knowledge discovery, modeling and simulation*, pages 39–44.

Simone Teufel, Jean Carletta, and Marc Moens. 1999a. An annotation scheme for discourse-level argumentation in research articles. In *Ninth Conference of the European Chapter of the Association for Computational Linguistics*.

Simone Teufel and Marc Moens. 2002. Summarizing scientific articles: experiments with relevance and rhetorical status. *Computational linguistics*, 28(4):409–445.

Simone Teufel, Advaith Siddharthan, and Colin Batchelor. 2009. Towards domain-independent argumentative zoning: Evidence from chemistry and computational linguistics. In *Proceedings of the 2009 conference on empirical methods in natural language processing*, pages 1493–1502.

Simone Teufel et al. 1999b. *Argumentative zoning: Information extraction from scientific text*. Ph.D. thesis, Citeseer.

Nees Jan Van Eck and Ludo Waltman. 2017. Citation-based clustering of publications using citnetexplorer and vosviewer. *Scientometrics*, 111(2):1053–1070.

Ludo Waltman and Nees Jan Van Eck. 2012. A new methodology for constructing a publication-level classification system of science. *Journal of the American Society for Information Science and Technology*, 63(12):2378–2392.

Shenghui Wang and Rob Koopman. 2017. Clustering articles based on semantic similarity. *Scientometrics*, 111(2):1017–1031.

Overview of the First Shared Task on Multi-Perspective Scientific Document Summarization (MuP)

Arman Cohan[1*] **Guy Feigenblat**[2] **Tirthankar Ghosal**[3] **Michal Shmueli-Scheuer**[4]

[1]Allen Institute for AI, Seattle, WA [2] Piiano Privacy Solutions
[3] ÚFAL, MFF, Charles University, CZ [4] IBM Research AI

armanc@allenai.org, guy@piiano.com
ghosal@ufal.mff.cuni.cz, shmueli@il.ibm.com

Abstract

We present the main findings of MuP 2022 shared task, the first shared task on multi-perspective scientific document summarization. The task provides a testbed representing challenges for summarization of scientific documents, and facilitates development of better models to leverage summaries generated from multiple perspectives. We received 139 total submissions from 9 teams. We evaluated submissions both by automated metrics (i.e., ROUGE) and human judgments on faithfulness, coverage, and readability which provided a more nuanced view of the differences between the systems. While we observe encouraging results from the participating teams, we conclude that there is still significant room left for improving summarization leveraging multiple references.[1]

1 Introduction

Generating summaries of scientific documents is known to be a challenging task as such documents are typically long and require domain expertise to fully comprehend them (Cohan et al., 2018; Cachola et al., 2020; Liu et al., 2022). The standard automated evaluation means in summarization compare system generated summaries with gold human written ones. At the same time, majority of existing work assumes only one single best gold summary for each given document. However, different readers of the same document can have different perspectives; therefore, there is often variability in human written summaries for a given document (Harman and Over, 2004). Having only one gold summary negatively impacts our ability to evaluate the quality of summarization systems through automated metrics (Harman and Over, 2004; Zechner, 1996). Also at training time this potentially prevents the model from capturing salient points with respect to different facets in the document (Hirsch et al., 2021). This is specially the case for longer documents where the summary compression ratio (ratio of length of the input document to the length of summary) is high (Cachola et al., 2020). While having multiple reference summaries for each document is desirable, human data collection can be expensive especially for long scientific documents.

To address this challenge, we introduce a new dataset and a new shared task to explore methods for generating multi-perspective summaries. We introduce a novel summarization corpus, MUP, leveraging data from scientific peer reviews to capture diverse perspectives from the reader's point of view. Our shared task similarly encourages development of methods to leverage multiple references. The dataset is collected from OpenReview,[2] an open publishing platform where peer reviews for some machine learning venues are publicly available. Peer reviews in various scientific fields often include an introductory paragraph that summarizes the main points and key contributions of a paper from the reviewer standpoint. For example, the first guideline to the reviewers in ACL review form[3] is to provide a "summary of the paper". In addition, each paper usually receives multiple reviews. Based on peer reviews, we collect a corpus of papers and their reviews from AI related venues such as ICLR, NeurIPS, and AKBC. We use carefully designed heuristics to only include first paragraphs of reviews that are summary-like. We manually check the summaries obtained from this approach on a subset of the data and ensure the high quality of the summaries. The corpus contains a total of 12K papers, and 27K summaries (with average number of 2.57 summaries per paper).

We next introduce MuP 2022, the first shared

* All authors contributed equally. Order is alphabetical.

[1]Our dataset is available at https://github.com/allenai/mup

[2]openreview.net

[3]https://aclrollingreview.org/reviewform

Proceedings of the Third Workshop on Scholarly Document Processing, pages 263–267
October 12–17, 2022.

task on multi-reference summarization with the goal of encouraging the community to develop better summarization methods for leveraging multiple references. Nine teams participated in the task with the top scoring models leveraging a range of transformer-based and graph-based models. Automated evaluation results show that while we observe notable progress in the task, there is ample room left for future improvements. We also conduct human evaluation on submitted systems and found out that while most system outputs are readable, they often struggle with the coverage aspect of summarization and they tend to miss some important information in the document.

2 Task

This section describes the MuP 2022 shared task.

2.1 Definition

The MuP task is basically an standard document summarization task where the goal is to generate a summary $\mathcal{S}_{gen}$ given a document $\mathcal{D}$, capturing its salient points. Teams were instructed to generate a summary for each of the papers in the MUP test set. The input is the full text content of papers along with section information. For each paper, the generated summary $\mathcal{S}_{gen}$ is evaluated against the set of m gold references $\langle \mathcal{S}_{g_1}, ..., \mathcal{S}_{g_m} \rangle$.

2.2 Evaluation and System Submissions

Following standard practice in summarization evaluation, we use ROUGE (Lin, 2004) as the primary evaluation metric. The average of the ROUGE-F scores obtained against the multiple summaries and averaged over ROUGE-1, ROUGE-2, and ROUGE-L was used for final ranking for the leaderboard. We used the unlimited length ROUGE version. In addition, we conducted human evaluation on a sample of summaries submitted by systems to get better insights about faithfulness, readability and coverage. The training set was released 50 days prior to the release of the hidden test set (papers content). Codalab framework[4] was used for the evaluation against the hidden test set. Participants were allowed to submit up to 25 submissions and the evaluation period lasted a month.

[4] https://codalab.lisn.upsaclay.fr/competitions/5676

3 Dataset Description

The MuP summarization dataset is collected using the publicly available peer review data, sidestepping the significant costs associated with manually creating multiple summaries for each scientific document.

3.1 Dataset Collection and Creation

We use the OpenReview API[5], to extract reviews from publicly open AI related venues such as ICLR, NeurIPS and AKBC. We extract fields including the paper title, summary (if exists, under the field "Summary") and the main review (under "Review" field). In addition, we use Science-Parse[6] to extract full text of the paper from the PDF. Science-Parse outputs a JSON record for each PDF, which among other fields, contains the title, abstract text, metadata (such as authors and year), and a list of the sections of the paper. Participants could leverage any type of additional metadata to improve their models.

After collecting the reviews we use parts of the review as a candidate summary for the paper as follows. Some conferences provide a review form that explicitly ask for a summary section ("Summary"). For example, starting from 2020 NeurIPS[7] asks the reviewers to "Summarize the paper motivation, key contributions and achievements in a paragraph". Similarly, in the ACL rolling review[8] reviewers are asked for a separate summary of the paper "Summary of the paper - Describe what this paper is about.". For those, we simply extract the summary section. When a summary field does not exist, we assume a common methodology that asks to describe what is the paper about, and what contributions does it make, followed by the main strengths and weaknesses. For example in ICLR 2021[9] reviewers were asked to "Summarize what the paper claims to contribute. List strong and weak points of the paper.". Here, we need to extract only the part that discusses the main contributions. We assume that the reviewers followed the review guidelines, and started with summarizing the main contributions, followed by a detailed description on

[5] https://openreview-py.readthedocs.io/

[6] https://github.com/allenai/science-parse

[7] https://nips.cc/Conferences/2020/PaperInformation/ReviewerGuidelines

[8] https://aclrollingreview.org/reviewform

[9] https://iclr.cc/Conferences/2021/ReviewerGuide#step-by-step

#Summaries	1	2	3	4	5	>5
#Papers	2276	3039	2867	1827	225	257

Table 1: Statistics of the MUP dataset.

the strengths and weaknesses. Thus, we extracted the first paragraph of the review section. To ensure that those paragraphs are indeed summaries and not opinions nor criticism (i.e., strengths and weaknesses), we followed Keith Norambuena et al. (2019), and used a lexicon-based approach to determine whether the paragraph carries a sentiment or not, in addition, we also removed paragraphs that contained individual pronouns (I, me, mine, myself). After these filtering process, two organizers of this task went through a random sample of 300 paragraphs, and annotated whether they are qualified as summaries. In total, 95% of the paragraphs were annotated as summaries. Table 1 summarizes the characteristics of the MUP dataset, which includes 10,491 summaries with an average length of 100.1 words long (space tokenized).

4 Systems

In this section, we overview the systems participating in the MuP shared task.

4.1 Baseline

As a simple baseline we use the BART-Large model (Lewis et al., 2020) further trained on CNN-DM summarization dataset (Hermann et al., 2015).[10] This baseline was made available to participants prior to the evaluation period.

4.2 Participant System Description

Although 18 teams registered, 9 teams participated (submitted their system runs). Here we briefly describe the approaches of the participating systems that provided us with a system description paper.[11]

Graph Attention Networks (GATS) (Akkasi, 2022) This work employs a Graph Attention Network-based extractive summarization approach for the task in hand. The approach is based on ranking the sentences in each of the discourse facets of the paper. Using Graph Attention Networks (GATs), the authors create a graph for each article after choosing three sentences that are closest to the ground truth summary. They define the rank of the sentences as the normalized average cosine similarity score between each sentence and the ground truth summaries. Since the ground truth summaries were not available for the test data, the authors use the sentences in the abstract as ground truth in the graph sentence selection and graph creation process.

GUIR (Sotudeh and Goharian, 2022) explored two different approaches to generate multi-perspective summaries. Their first approach learns a latent topic distribution using neural topic modeling (NTM) in the fine-tuning stage of a state-of-the-art abstractive summarizer (Longformer-Encoder-Decoder (Beltagy et al., 2020)), and the knowledge is shared between the topic modeling and text summarization task for summary generation. Their second approach involves adding a two-step summarizer that first extracts the salient sentences from the document and then writes abstractive summaries from those sentences. The second approach performs better on the official test set.

LTRC (Urlana et al., 2022) Their best-performing model is a fine-tuned BART-Large-CNN model which is same as the official baseline. They also experiment with several pre-trained sequence-to-sequence models (T5, ProphetNet, SciTLDR, DANCER) that first divides the document into multiple sections to obtain section-wise summaries, and then aggregates all partial summaries to form the complete summary. They experiment with different combination of paper-sections and found that only introduction section for the training and abstract + introduction for test data outperforms all the rest for the MuP task.

AINLPML (Kumar et al., 2022) This system adopts a two-stage approach for the task. In the first step, an extractive summarization step is used to identify the essential part of the paper. Their extraction step includes utilizing a contributing sentence identification model. In the next step, the authors finetune a BART model on the extracted summary generated from the previous step.

5 Results and Analysis

We only report the results of the teams who submitted their system papers in this section. Table 2 shows the comparative performance of the systems in MuP. The performance of the systems which

[10] We also tried training BART on scientific summarization datasets such as arxiv but did not achieve better results.

[11] Unfortunately, for system submissions without any report there is no way for us to know the details of the method and thus we exclude them from this overview paper.

Team	R-1	R-2	R-L	Avg
BART (baseline)	40.8	12.3	24.5	25.9
GATS Akkasi (2022)	33.7	7.4	17.7	19.6
LTRC (Urlana et al., 2022)	40.7	12.5	25.0	26.0
GUIR (Sotudeh and Goharian, 2022)	**41.4**	12.5	24.8	26.2
AINLPML (Kumar et al., 2022)	41.1	**13.3**	**25.4**	**26.6**

Table 2: Main results from the MuP 2022 shared task. R represents the ROUGE F1 metric.

used abstractive methods are generally better. In terms of average F_1 scores, team AINLPML (Kumar et al., 2022) produced the best performance, although GUIR and LTRC were pretty close. Except one, other teams were able to surpass the MuP baseline, although with small margins. Since the results of all systems were pretty close, in the next section we conduct human evaluation to gain better insights.

5.1 Human Evaluation

We asked domain experts in NLP (researchers with 10+ years experience in the field) to annotated a set of 20 randomly selected papers along with all system submissions for those papers. We asked the experts to rate the systems on a Likert scale (1-5), w.r.t three main qualities: faithfulness, readability, coverage, and Boolean rating for style ("review" vs. "summary"[12]). The experts could access the paper PDF and the ground-truth reviews. To evaluate faithfulness we asked them to first find important terms or phrases in the generated summary (e.g., datasets names, algorithms, etc), and then to look for them in the original paper and evaluate them in context. For readability, we asked annotators to take into account fluency, coherence and grammatical correctness. Finally, to understand coverage, annotators analyzed ground-truth summaries, and noticed that they tend to follow some structure, often a sentence or two for introduction, followed by methodology, and results. Hence, we expect to see such content covered in the generated summary. Similarly, if one important point is covered in one of the summaries but the generated summary fails to mention it, it gets penalized. Overall, the annotation task was time consuming with each annotator spending about 40 minutes on average per paper. Table 3 summarizes the average scores for the systems. Consistent with the automated evaluation results, AINLPML outperforms the rest of the systems in readability and coverage (and very close to leading also in faithfulness). From readability perspective, GATS received the lowest score, mainly due to low coherence. This is somewhat expected as their approach is extractive, and seems like no order was enforced (e.g., sometimes the introduction section appears last). Also since this approach is extractive, it achieves the highest faithfulness score. From the abstractive approaches, The BART baseline mainly suffered from the last sentence being trimmed in the middle. Further postprocessing/decoding methods could address these issues. LTRC summaries were much shorter than the other systems (on average 89 tokens vs. an average of 105 tokens of the rest of the systems), leading to generally lower coverage, but higher faithfulness. It is worth noting that the style in all the systems was annotated as "summary" - showing that the generated output looks like an actually summary than a peer review. Overall, while systems are able to get high performance in terms of faithfulness and readability, coverage remains a challenge and systems often tend to miss some important aspect of the paper.

[12]To indicate that the generated output looks more like a peer review or like an actual summary.

Team	**Faithfulness**	**Readability**	**Coverage**
BART (baseline)	4.1	3.6	**3.9**
LTRC	4.4	4.6	3.6
GATS	5.0	2.7	2.4
GUIR	4.1	4.2	**3.9**
AINLPML	**4.4**	**4.7**	**3.9**

Table 3: Human evaluation (on a Likert scale 1-5).

6 Findings of MuP

Overall, our findings are summarized below:

- A general summarization baseline such as BART pretrained on news summarization dataset achieves decent results on the task.
- Combination of extractive and abstractive methods seem to work well for the task. This is inline

with how human summarize longer documents by first identifying salient pieces of information and then aggregating this information.

- While we saw high scores in terms of faithfulness and readability, coverage remained a challenge.
- None of the participating systems focused on the multi-perspective aspect of the dataset. Submissions instead focused on general aspects of scientific document summarization such as length and specialized domain. This was somewhat unfortunate because our goal was to provide a testbed for developing methods for utilizing multiple summaries per document. We hope to see more of such models in future iterations of this task.

7 Conclusion and Future Directions

We present MuP, a new shared task and dataset of 27K summaries, which attracted attention from the community with 18 registered teams and 9 active submitting teams. Automated and human evaluation results suggest promising progress towards the task but we conclude that additional research is required, especially around utilization of multi references per document in the training process. For future iterations, we plan to extend the dataset by collecting reviews from additional venues. In addition, we plan to incorporate automatic measures of faithfulness as part of the leaderboard metrics.

References

Abbas Akkasi. 2022. Multi perspective scientific document summarization with graph attention networks (gats). In *Proceedings of the Third Workshop on Scholarly Document Processing*, Online. Association for Computational Linguistics.

Iz Beltagy, Matthew E Peters, and Arman Cohan. 2020. Longformer: The long-document transformer. *arXiv preprint arXiv:2004.05150*.

Isabel Cachola, Kyle Lo, Arman Cohan, and Daniel S Weld. 2020. Tldr: Extreme summarization of scientific documents. *arXiv preprint arXiv:2004.15011*.

Arman Cohan, Franck Dernoncourt, Doo Soon Kim, Trung Bui, Seokhwan Kim, Walter Chang, and Nazli Goharian. 2018. A discourse-aware attention model for abstractive summarization of long documents. *arXiv preprint arXiv:1804.05685*.

Donna Harman and Paul Over. 2004. The effects of human variation in duc summarization evaluation. In *Text Summarization Branches Out*, pages 10–17.

Karl Moritz Hermann, Tomás Kociský, Edward Grefenstette, Lasse Espeholt, Will Kay, Mustafa Suleyman, and Phil Blunsom. 2015. Teaching machines to read and comprehend. In *NIPS*, pages 1693–1701.

Eran Hirsch, Alon Eirew, Ori Shapira, Avi Caciularu, Arie Cattan, Ori Ernst, Ramakanth Pasunuru, Hadar Ronen, Mohit Bansal, and Ido Dagan. 2021. ifacetsum: Coreference-based interactive faceted summarization for multi-document exploration. *arXiv preprint arXiv:2109.11621*.

Brian Keith Norambuena, Exequiel Lettura, and Claudio Villegas. 2019. Sentiment analysis and opinion mining applied to scientific paper reviews. *Intelligent Data Analysis*, 23:191–214.

Sandeep Kumar, Guneet Singh, Kartik Shinde, and Asif Ekbal. 2022. Team ainlpml @ mup in sdp 2022: Scientific document summarization by end-to-end extractive and abstractive approach. In *Proceedings of the Third Workshop on Scholarly Document Processing*, Online. Association for Computational Linguistics.

Mike Lewis, Yinhan Liu, Naman Goyal, Marjan Ghazvininejad, Abdelrahman Mohamed, Omer Levy, Veselin Stoyanov, and Luke Zettlemoyer. 2020. Bart: Denoising sequence-to-sequence pre-training for natural language generation, translation, and comprehension. In *ACL*.

Chin-Yew Lin. 2004. ROUGE: A package for automatic evaluation of summaries. In *Text Summarization Branches Out*, pages 74–81, Barcelona, Spain. Association for Computational Linguistics.

Yixin Liu, Ansong Ni, Linyong Nan, Budhaditya Deb, Chenguang Zhu, Ahmed H Awadallah, and Dragomir Radev. 2022. Leveraging locality in abstractive text summarization. *arXiv preprint arXiv:2205.12476*.

Sajad Sotudeh and Nazli Goharian. 2022. Guir @ mup 2022: Towards generating topic-aware multi-perspective summaries for scientific documents. In *Proceedings of the Third Workshop on Scholarly Document Processing*, Online. Association for Computational Linguistics.

Ashok Urlana, Nirmal Surange, and Manish Shrivastava. 2022. Ltrc @mup 2022: Multi-perspective scientific document summarization using pre-trained generation models. In *Proceedings of the Third Workshop on Scholarly Document Processing*, Online. Association for Computational Linguistics.

Klaus Zechner. 1996. Fast generation of abstracts from general domain text corpora by extracting relevant sentences. In *COLING 1996 Volume 2: The 16th International Conference on Computational Linguistics*.

Multi Perspective Scientific Document Summarization With Graph Attention Networks (GATS)

Abbas Akkasi
Computer Engineering Department,
Istanbul Gelisim University,
aakkasi@gelisim.edu.tr

Abstract

It is well recognized that creating summaries of scientific texts can be difficult. For each given document, the majority of summarizing research believes there is only one best gold summary. Having just one gold summary limits our capacity to assess the effectiveness of summarizing algorithms because creating summaries is an art. Likewise, because it takes subject-matter experts a lot of time to read and comprehend lengthy scientific publications, annotating several gold summaries for scientific documents can be very expensive. The shared task known as the Multi perspective Scientific Document Summarization (Mup) is an exploration of various methods to produce multi perspective scientific summaries. Utilizing Graph Attention Networks (GATs), we take an extractive text summarization approach to the issue as a kind of sentence ranking task. Although the results produced by the suggested model are not particularly impressive, comparing them with the state-of-the-arts demonstrates the model's potential for improvement.

1 Introduction

A summary is a clear and accurate representation of the input text that distills the main ideas from the source. It is important to maintain the text's inter-word and inter-sentence reliance. A novel method for ascertaining an article's main objective is text summarization. The article summary assists users in rapidly determining whether a paper is pertinent to their study areas and focusing on them. Regardless of the type of documents that need to be summarized, there are two methods for automatic text summarization: extractive and abstractive. While abstractive summarization attempts to recreate the key content in a fresh way after interpreting and analyzing the text with more sophisticated techniques, extractive summarization is based on identifying important sections of the text and producing a subset of the sentences from the original text (Kadriu and Obradovic, 2021; El-Kassas et al., 2021; Syed et al., 2021; Magdum and Rathi, 2021).

For news articles, automatic summary has recently produced impressive results; nevertheless, summarizing scholarly publications has gotten less attention (Yasunaga et al., 2019; Cohan and Goharian, 2018; Patil et al., 2022; Huang et al., 2021). Published papers differ from other sorts of material, including news, in a few key respects. They are typically longer and feature more complex subjects and technical jargon. Scientific publications are also citeable and contain citations. Additionally, these documents usually contain tables, charts, and figures, which complicates the summary process. Last but not least, another characteristic of scientific publications is that they may have unintended effects after being published.

The majority of the current research on scientific document summarization assumes only one optimal gold summary. Because creating summaries is a subjective process, having only one perfect summary makes it difficult to assess how well summarization systems are working. On the other hand, annotating several gold summaries for scientific publications can be quite expensive because it calls for specific topic experts to read and comprehend lengthy scientific documents.

As the first collaborative activity, Multi Perspective Scientific Document Summarization aims to investigate techniques for producing multi-perspective summaries. In this attempt, we proposed a model using Graph Attention Networks (GATs) with data preparation based on transformers to deal with the issue.

The remainder of this paper is organized as follows. Recent related work is presented in the next section. Sections 3 and 4 are dedicated to the model explanation and the experiments' results, respectively, and finally, the paper is ended by Section 5 as a conclusion.

Proceedings of the Third Workshop on Scholarly Document Processing, pages 268–272
October 12–17, 2022.

2 Related Work

Although scientific document summarization has been studied for a long time, there are still many outstanding questions about how to do it effectively Paice (1980); Elkiss et al. (2008); Lloret et al. (2013). Liu and Lapata (2019) has reported on the state-of-the-arts' results in abstractive and extractive summarization in the general text domain (news). The authors used pretrained encoders to build their summarizers and provided a two-stage technique in which the encoder is fine-tuned twice, once for extractive summarizing and once for abstractive summarizing. No official model that can provide a reasonable level of data independence has been mentioned (Kadriu and Obradovic, 2021).

By choosing important passages from a text and replicating them word for word, extractive summarization creates a subset of the original text's phrases. On the other hand, an abstractive summarizer recreates crucial content in a new way after reading and analyzing the text using sophisticated natural language algorithms to create a new shorter text that offers the most important information from the original one El-Kassas et al. (2021); Patil et al. (2022); Syed et al. (2021).

From another perspective, scientific paper summarization may be classified into two types: Summarization based on *Content* or *Citation* Sefid and Giles (2022); Khurana and Bhatnagar (2022). The summarizer just accepts the content of a document as input in content-based summarizing. In citation-based summarization, along with the original paper's content, external knowledge in the form of citations is also leveraged. The community has given those citations for the paper at hand. The majority of current studies in this domain are of the second category. Nevertheless, being cited by other research works is required here, which means that newly published papers may not be accurately summarized in their initial days of publication. Qazvinian and Radev (2008) proposed one of the first models for the scientific text summarization task. They suggest a clustering method where communities are generated in the lexical network of the citation summary and sentences are retrieved from various clusters. They claimed that , for this particular issue, their method outperforms LexRank, one of the most widely used multi-document summarizing algorithms. ScisummNet,(Yasunaga et al., 2019), is a large annotated corpus for scientific paper summarization considering the papers' citations. This dataset is suitable for data-driven approaches due to its size. Besides the corpus, the author presented a graph convolutional network for the paper summarization. An et al. (2021) used the citation graph to improve the work of summarizing scientific papers. In order to produce the final abstract, summarization algorithms specifically can find relevant data from the relevant research community from the citation graph, in addition to using the document information from the original publication. Additionally, they created a novel citation graph-based model that takes into account both the features of an article and its references. SciSummpip (Ju et al., 2020), is another unsupervised paper summarization pipeline which uses a transformer-based language model for contextual text representation and PageRank for sentence selection. Cachola et al. (2020), proposed a model to generate summaries for long papers. They used high source compression in their system for creating summaries, which entails complicated domain-specific language that needs to be understood by experts. SciBERTSUM (Sefid and Giles, 2022),is another model designed for summarizing lengthy texts, such as scientific publications with more than 500 sentences. By 1) incorporating a section embedding layer to include section information in the sentence vector and 2) employing a sparse attention mechanism, which allows each sentence to pay attention to nearby sentences locally while only a small number of sentences pay attention to all other sentences globally, SciBERTSUM extends BERTSUM to long documents. Another scientific document summarization system is proposed by Mishra et al. (2022). They introduced a new approach for summarizing scientific documents that makes use of multi-objective differential evolution. Making use of citation contextualization, different important sentences are first retrieved. The idea of multi-objective clustering is used to further group these sentences. Ibrahim Altmami and El Bachir Menai (2022), summarized almost all the recent works in the domain of scientific article summarization. They categorized the work based on different factors and reported the achieved results in terms of popular evaluation metrics.

3 Proposed Model

We adopted an extractive summary technique for the MuP shared task. For this, we generate a graph for each article after selecting the three sentences

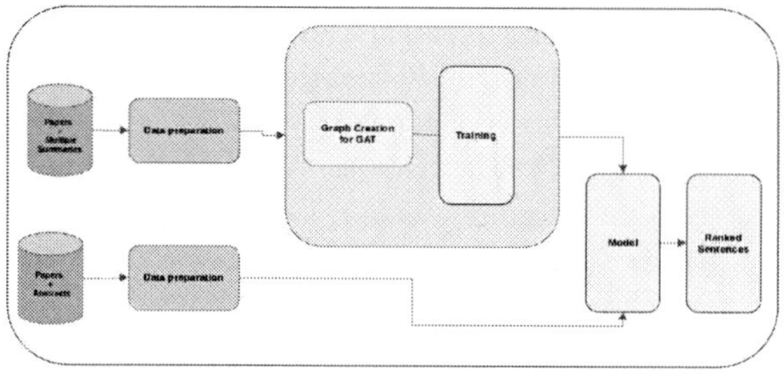

Figure 1: Suggested model for the Mup.

that are closest to the each summary sentences based on the cosine similarity between the their sentence embeddings. The oracle rank is defined as the normalized average cosine similarity score between each sentence and the provided summaries' embeddings. Figure 1 demonstrates the suggested model.

3.1 Graph Attention Networks

A particular kind of convolutional neural network called a "graph convolutional network" (GCN) may operate directly on graphs and benefit from their structural data. The fundamental tenet of GCN is that we gather feature information about each node from all of its neighbors as well as the feature itself. It resolves the issue of categorizing nodes in graphs (like citation networks) where labels are only accessible for a small portion of nodes (such as documents) (semi-supervised learning) (Zhang et al., 2019). The normalized sum of the node features of neighbors is what is produced for GCN by a graph convolution process as Formula 1.

$$h_i^{(l+1)} = \sigma\left(\sum_{j \in N(i)} \frac{1}{c_{ij}} W^{(l)} h_j^{(l)}\right) \quad (1)$$

Where $N(i)$ is the set of its one-hop neighbors , $c_{ij} = \sqrt{|N(i)|}\sqrt{|N(j)|}$is a normalization constant based on graph structure, σ is an activation function (e.g. ReLU), and $W(l)$ is a shared weight matrix for node-wise feature transformation.

The attention mechanism is a replacement for the statically normalized convolution operation in Graph Attention Networks (GATs) (Figure 2).

The equations to calculate the node embedding of layer l+1, h(l+1), from its layer l embeddings

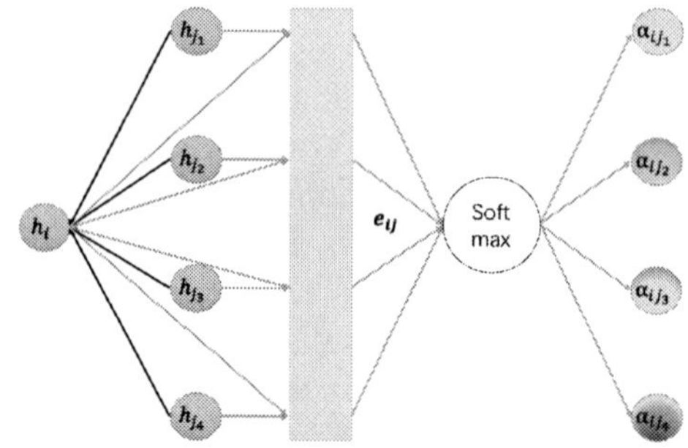

Figure 2: Graph Attention Networks, after (Veličković et al., 2018)

are listed below (Veličković et al., 2018).

$$\begin{aligned} z_i^{(l} &= W^{(l)} h_i^{(l)}, \\ e_{ij}^{(l)} &= LeakyReLU(\alpha^{(l)^T}(z_i^{(l)} || z_j^{(l)})), \\ \alpha_{ij}^{(l)} &= \frac{exp(e_{ij}^{(l)})}{\Sigma_{k \in N(i)} exp(e_{ik}^{(l)})}, \\ h_i^{(l+1)} &= \sigma(\Sigma_{j \in N(i)} \alpha_{ij}^{(l)} z_j^{(l)}) \end{aligned}$$

The main concept behind using GAT was to choose the most essential phrases based on inter-sentence relationships within the articles, using the attention mechanism to concentrate on more effective sentences.

3.2 Evaluation

ROUGE (Recall-Oriented Understudy for Gisting Evaluation) was presented as an automated evaluation approach in 2003. It is a series of metrics based on the similarity of n-grams[1]. Other ROUGE scores include ROUGE-L, which is a longest common sub-sequence measure , and ROUGE-SU4, which is a bigram measure that allows at most four unigrams inside bigram components to be skipped (ROUGE, 2004). In this task, the intrinsic evaluation using the ROUGE-1, -2, and -L metrics is applied. The final ranking also takes into account the average of the ROUGE-F scores achieved against the various summaries.

4 Experiments

The datasets made available by the task organizers were used for all of the experiments. We made use of two-layers GATs implemented with the Pytorch-Geometrics library with 10 epochs and a learning

[1]A sub-sequence of n words from a particular text is referred to as an n-gram.

rate of 0.0001 to train the suggested model. Applying the trained model on new data, the highly ranked sentences are selected as

4.1 Data preparation

In the first step, we prepared data to be used for graph generation. For this purpose, for each sentence of available summaries, the most similar 3 sentences to each summary sentence from the input article are taken as the graph nodes. The cosine similarity between the embeddings of body sentences and provided summary sentences is used as similarity metrics. Two pretrained transformer-based language models, SPECTER (Cohan et al., 2020) and all_mpnet_v2[2], are utilized to generate the sentence embeddings. The duplicate sentences are also ignored. The sentence embedding, which has a length of 768, is regarded as a node feature for each node. In addition, the dot product between the relevant pairs of nodes is used as a feature for the edges.

4.2 Results

Tables 1 and 2 demonstrate the obtained results by applying the trained model on development and test datasets respectively.

The tables show that the results on development data are marginally superior to the test data. Since for test data, there was no available summaries, we made use of the abstract's sentences as provided summaries in graph sentence selection and graph creation processes. Lower test data findings could be attributed to this. We experimented with SAGE, GCN, and other forms of graph neural networks in addition to GATs, but the results were not any better than those that had already been reported.

5 Conclusion

In this study, we used Graph Attention Networks to perform the Multi-Perspective Scientific Documents summary problem while adhering to the extractive summarization methodology. We first chose the three sentences from the input article that most closely resembled each summary sentence to produce the graphs for our node ranking task. Then, using each selected sentence as a node, the sentence embedding produced by the pretrained transformer-based language model is taken as the node features, and the dot product between the pairs of nodes is taken as the corresponding edge feature. Because of the discrepancy between the results published by other teams and the ones obtained by the suggested model , it can be inferred that preprocessing techniques and the use of external knowledge may improve the results.

[2]https://www.sbert.net/docs/pretrained_models.html

References

Chenxin An, Ming Zhong, Yiran Chen, Danqing Wang, Xipeng Qiu, and Xuanjing Huang. 2021. Enhancing scientific papers summarization with citation graph. In *Proceedings of the AAAI Conference on Artificial Intelligence*, volume 35, pages 12498–12506.

Isabel Cachola, Kyle Lo, Arman Cohan, and Daniel S Weld. 2020. Tldr: Extreme summarization of scientific documents. In *Findings of the Association for Computational Linguistics: EMNLP 2020*, pages 4766–4777.

Arman Cohan, Sergey Feldman, Iz Beltagy, Doug Downey, and Daniel S Weld. 2020. Specter: Document-level representation learning using citation-informed transformers. In *Proceedings of the 58th Annual Meeting of the Association for Computational Linguistics*, pages 2270–2282.

Arman Cohan and Nazli Goharian. 2018. Scientific document summarization via citation contextualization and scientific discourse. *International Journal on Digital Libraries*, 19(2):287–303.

Wafaa S El-Kassas, Cherif R Salama, Ahmed A Rafea, and Hoda K Mohamed. 2021. Automatic text summarization: A comprehensive survey. *Expert Systems with Applications*, 165:113679.

Aaron Elkiss, Siwei Shen, Anthony Fader, Güneş Erkan, David States, and Dragomir Radev. 2008. Blind men and elephants: What do citation summaries tell us about a research article? *Journal of the American Society for Information Science and Technology*, 59(1):51–62.

Luyang Huang, Shuyang Cao, Nikolaus Parulian, Heng Ji, and Lu Wang. 2021. Efficient attentions for long document summarization. *arXiv preprint arXiv:2104.02112*.

Nouf Ibrahim Altmami and Mohamed El Bachir Menai. 2022. Automatic summarization of scientific articles:: A survey.

Jiaxin Ju, Ming Liu, Longxiang Gao, and Shirui Pan. 2020. Monash-summ@ longsumm 20 scisummpip: An unsupervised scientific paper summarization pipeline. In *Proceedings of the First Workshop on Scholarly Document Processing*, pages 318–327.

Kastriot Kadriu and Milenko Obradovic. 2021. Extractive approach for text summarisation using graphs.

Alka Khurana and Vasudha Bhatnagar. 2022. Investigating entropy for extractive document summarization. *Expert Systems with Applications*, 187:115820.

Table 1: Results on Development data

	r1_f	r1_r	r2_f	r2_r	rL_f	rL_r	Average
	35.46	35.08	9.53	10.42	19.63	22.27	21.96

Table 2: Results on Test data

	r1_f	r1_r	r2_f	r2_r	rL_f	rL_r	Average
	33.85	38.05	7.40	8.33	17.74	20.13	19.66

Yang Liu and Mirella Lapata. 2019. Text summarization with pretrained encoders. *arXiv preprint arXiv:1908.08345.*

Elena Lloret, María Teresa Romá-Ferri, and Manuel Palomar. 2013. Compendium: A text summarization system for generating abstracts of research papers. *Data & Knowledge Engineering*, 88:164–175.

PG Magdum and Sheetal Rathi. 2021. A survey on deep learning-based automatic text summarization models. In *Advances in Artificial Intelligence and Data Engineering*, pages 377–392. Springer.

Santosh Kumar Mishra, Naveen Saini, Sriparna Saha, and Pushpak Bhattacharyya. 2022. Scientific document summarization in multi-objective clustering framework. *Applied Intelligence*, 52(2):1520–1543.

Chris D Paice. 1980. The automatic generation of literature abstracts: an approach based on the identification of self-indicating phrases. In *Proceedings of the 3rd annual ACM conference on Research and development in information retrieval*, pages 172–191.

Priyadarshini Patil, Chandan Rao, Gokul Reddy, Riteesh Ram, and SM Meena. 2022. Extractive text summarization using bert. In *Proceedings of the 2nd International Conference on Recent Trends in Machine Learning, IoT, Smart Cities and Applications*, pages 741–747. Springer.

Vahed Qazvinian and Dragomir Radev. 2008. Scientific paper summarization using citation summary networks. In *Proceedings of the 22nd International Conference on Computational Linguistics (Coling 2008)*, pages 689–696.

Lin CY ROUGE. 2004. A package for automatic evaluation of summaries. In *Proceedings of Workshop on Text Summarization of ACL, Spain.*

Athar Sefid and C Lee Giles. 2022. Scibertsum: Extractive summarization for scientific documents. *arXiv preprint arXiv:2201.08495.*

Ayesha Ayub Syed, Ford Lumban Gaol, and Tokuro Matsuo. 2021. A survey of the state-of-the-art models in neural abstractive text summarization. *IEEE Access*, 9:13248–13265.

Petar Veličković, Guillem Cucurull, Arantxa Casanova, Adriana Romero, Pietro Liò, and Yoshua Bengio. 2018. Graph attention networks. In *International Conference on Learning Representations*.

Michihiro Yasunaga, Jungo Kasai, Rui Zhang, Alexander R Fabbri, Irene Li, Dan Friedman, and Dragomir R Radev. 2019. Scisummnet: A large annotated corpus and content-impact models for scientific paper summarization with citation networks. In *Proceedings of the AAAI Conference on Artificial Intelligence*, volume 33, pages 7386–7393.

Si Zhang, Hanghang Tong, Jiejun Xu, and Ross Maciejewski. 2019. Graph convolutional networks: a comprehensive review. *Computational Social Networks*, 6(1):1–23.

GUIR @ MuP 2022: Towards Generating Topic-aware Multi-perspective Summaries for Scientific Documents

Sajad Sotudeh
IRLab, Georgetown University
sajad@ir.cs.georgetown.edu

Nazli Goharian
IRLab, Georgetown University
nazli@ir.cs.georgetown.edu

Abstract

This paper presents our approach for the MuP 2022 shared task—Multi-Perspective Scientific Document Summarization, where the objective is to enable summarization models to explore methods for generating *multi-perspective* summaries for scientific papers. We explore two orthogonal ways to cope with this task. The first approach involves incorporating a neural topic model (i.e., NTM) into the state-of-the-art abstractive summarizer (LED); the second approach involves adding a two-step summarizer that extracts the salient sentences from the document and then writes abstractive summaries from those sentences. Our latter model outperformed our other submissions on the official test set. Specifically, among 10 participants (including organizers' baseline) who made their results public with 163 total runs. Our best system ranks first in ROUGE-1 (F), and second in ROUGE-1 (R), ROUGE-2 (F) and Average ROUGE (F) scores.

1 Introduction

Scientific text summarization has received growing interest over the recent years (Cohan et al., 2018; Xiao and Carenini, 2019; Zerva et al., 2020; Cachola et al., 2020; Sotudeh et al., 2021; Cui and Hu, 2021; Pang et al., 2022; Sotudeh and Goharian, 2022), although it has been studied from years before (Teufel and Moens, 2002; Qazvinian and Radev, 2008; Nenkova et al., 2011; Qazvinian et al., 2013; Cohan and Goharian, 2015). Generating scientific summaries is deemed to be a challenging task, given the specific characteristics of scientific documents such as extreme document length, presence of complex domain-specific concepts, and specific structure, where the information is framed within sections. These characteristics of scientific papers, coupled with the aim of generating shorter or longer form summaries, call for special model considerations to deal with the challenging task of summarization. Researchers have looked into various approaches of unsupervised, supervised, neural, utilizing citations, knowledge, context, etc in generating the summaries in an extractive or abstractive way.

The existing evaluation systems in scientific summarization assume one signle gold summary for each scientific paper, based on which the summary generator optimizes the generation. The motivation of the MuP shared task (Cohan et al., 2022) is to provide multiple gold summaries per document so that the generated systems can be evaluated based on how well they captured various aspects of the paper into their summary. The assumption is that a single gold summary may not include multiple aspects expressed in the paper, as the writing of a summary is subjective. Specifically, the MuP organizers introduce a novel English summarization dataset collected from scientific peer reviews to reflect multiple perspectives from reviewers' standpoints. The participating teams are then asked to produce a scientific summary that can express diverse viewpoints on a given document.

In this study, we extend the Longformer Encoder-Decoder (LED) abstractive summarization model (Beltagy et al., 2020). In our experiments, we specifically explore two distinct approaches: (1) incorporating a neural topic modeling approach (Srivastava and Sutton, 2017) to the LED summarizer; and (2) proposing a two-step LED-based summarizer that first extracts the salient sentences and then performs abstraction over the extracted sentences to produce a *multi-perspective* summary. Our intuition of these extensions is that each *perspective* of a paper may focus on *specific sets of topics* which are discussed within specific *sets of sentences*, that should be taken into account by the summarizer. To benefit from the advantages of each of these approaches, we further combine them and propose a topic-aware two-step summarizer. Our combined model achieves the best results amongst the other settings on the validation and

Proceedings of the Third Workshop on Scholarly Document Processing, pages 273–278
October 12–17, 2022.

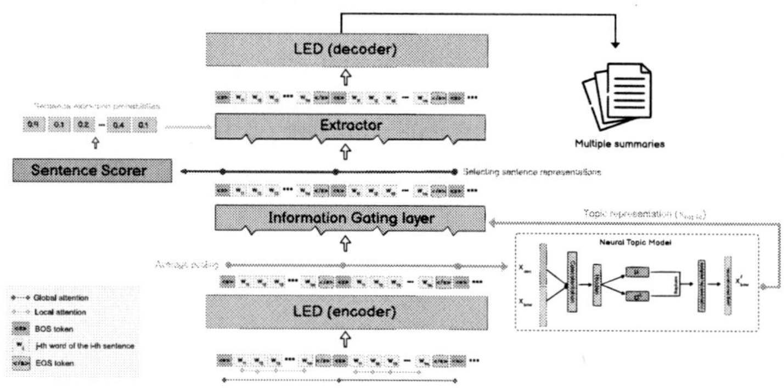

Figure 1: The overview of our proposed model. The LED encoder and decoder modules are expressed in blue boxes, the neural topic model takes in the contextualized representation of the document $\mathbf{x}_{\texttt{doc}}$ (average pooled from sentence representations), as well as the bow representation $\mathbf{x}_{\texttt{bow}}$ to generate topic representations $\mathbf{x}_{\texttt{topic}}$. The gating layer influences topic channels into the encoder outputs. The extractor picks the top sentences (in respect to the gold summaries) and passes their associated word representation to the decoder. The decoder attends to the top sentence representations for generating the summaries. In inference, we make the decoder generate only one summary.

official blind test sets. Specifically, it attains the first rank in ROUGE-1 (F), and second in ROUGE-1 (R), ROUGE-2 (F), and average ROUGE (F) scores, with 1.4% relative improvement over the baseline in terms of average ROUGE (F) scores.

2 Model

The general overview of our model is demonstrated in Figure 1. Our summarizer is composed of multiple components, including an LED encoder, a neural topic modeling layer, an information gating layer, and an extractor layer, followed by an LED decoder. In what follows, we explain the details of our proposed model.

2.1 Neural topic modeling for summarization

Topic modeling and text summarization can provide complementary features since both aim to distill salient information from a massive collection of textual data. With this intuition, we incorporate a *neural topic model* (NTM) (Miao et al., 2017; Srivastava and Sutton, 2017) into the summarization model (i.e., LED) to enrich the encoded word representations with topical information. We utilize the Combined Topic Model (Bianchi et al., 2021) as our topic modeling approach. This model is built around ProdLDA (Srivastava and Sutton, 2017), a neural topic modeling approach based on the Variational Autoencoders (VAE). VAE-based topic networks first infer a continuous latent representation $z \in \mathbb{R}^K$ (latent distribution over K topics) given the bag-of-words (bow) document representation $\mathbf{x}_{\texttt{bow}} \in \mathbb{N}^V$ (bow distribution over V distinct vocabulary). An NTM model assumes that z is generated from a prior distribution $p(z|x)$, which is estimated by the conditional distribution $q_\phi(z|x)$ modelled by a decoder ϕ. The NTM model aims to calculate the posterior $p(z|x)$, which is estimated by the variational distribution $q_\theta(z|x)$, modelled by an encoder θ. The NTM model optimizes the topic modeling network by defining the following loss criterion,

$$\mathcal{L}_{\texttt{topic}} = \max(\mathbb{E}_{q_\theta(z|x)}[\log p_\theta(x|z)] \\ -\mathbb{KL}[q_\theta(z|x)||p(z)]). \quad (1)$$

The first term is the reconstruction error, and the second one is Kullback-Leibler (KL) divergence that regularizes $q_\theta(z|x)$. We refer the readers to (Srivastava and Sutton, 2017) for more details.

2.2 Information gating layer

After obtaining the topic representations, we influence the topic channels into the encoder representations that are the outputs from LED encoder layer. To this end, we design an information gating layer in which multiple linear layers are used to transform and combine topic and encoder representations and pass them along to the next stage. Formally written, let $\mathbf{x}_{\texttt{topic}}$ be the topic representation from the NTM model, and $\mathbf{x}_{\texttt{encoder}}$ be the contextualized word representations from the LED encoder. Our gating layer combines $\mathbf{x}_{\texttt{topic}}$ with $\mathbf{x}_{\texttt{encoder}}$ to implement a filtering gate, and then produces a *fused* word representation that has the information of both NTM and LED encoder,

$$
\begin{aligned}
\mathbf{x}'_{\texttt{topic}} &= W_j \mathbf{x}_{\texttt{topic}} + b_j \\
g &= \sigma(W_i[\mathbf{x}_{\texttt{topic}}; \mathbf{x}_{\texttt{encoder}}] + b_i) \\
\mathbf{x}_{\texttt{fused}} &= (1-g)\mathbf{x}'_{\texttt{topic}} + (g)\mathbf{x}_{\texttt{encoder}}
\end{aligned} \tag{2}
$$

where W_i, W_j, b_i, and b_j are trainable parameters, g is the filtering gate ($g \in [0-1]$), and $\mathbf{x}_{\texttt{fused}}$ is the topic-aware contextualized word representations.

2.3 Two-step summarization

After obtaining the topic-aware word representation, we aim to implement a two-step summarizer to drop the unimportant sentences and retain the salient content of the scientific document. In this sense, we ensure that the LED decoder only attends to the salient content of source information. To consider the sentential importance, we take the representations associated with the BOS token as the sentence representations and define a classification task over the document's sentences to predict summary-worthy sentences using a Sigmoid classifier. We then minimize the cross-entropy loss function as follows,

$$
\mathcal{L}_{\texttt{sent}}(y, \hat{y}) = -\sum_{n=1}^{N}\sum_{i=1}^{|S|} y_i \log \hat{y}_i \tag{3}
$$

in which y is the probability output from the Sigmoid classifier, $\hat{y}$ is the gold label, $|S|_d$ is the set of sentences within the scientific document, and N is the number of gold summaries for the given document. Upon obtaining sentential probabilities, we sample the representations associated with top sentences until a fixed length (e.g., 3072 tokens) is reached and then pass the resulting word representations to the decoder for summary generation. Then the model minimizes the following generation loss for a θ-parameterized model.

$$
\mathcal{L}_{\texttt{gen}} = -\sum_{n=1}^{N}\sum_{t=1}^{T} \log P_\theta(\hat{y}_t)|\hat{y}_{<t}, x) \tag{4}
$$

where N is the number of ground-truth summaries for a given document, and T is the length of summary in tokens. We then optimize the whole network using multi-tasking heuristics as follows,

$$
\mathcal{L}_{\texttt{multi}} = \mathcal{L}_{\texttt{gen}} + (\alpha)\mathcal{L}_{\texttt{topic}} + (\beta)\mathcal{L}_{\texttt{sent}} \tag{5}
$$

where $\mathcal{L}_{\texttt{gen}}$ is the cross-entropy generation loss computed from the decoder's outputs and gold summaries, and α and β are regularizing hyper-parameters for topic modeling and sentence extraction tasks, respectively.

3 Experiments

Dataset. We use the dataset introduced by the organizers and fine-tune it on our model. The MuP dataset (Cohan et al., 2022) is composed of scientific documents, each with one or more summaries that are the submitted peer reviews hosted by OpenReview platform [1]. There are 8,734 (train) and 1,060 (validation) distinct documents with a total of 26.5K summaries (with an average number of 2.57 summaries per paper), with summaries being 100.1 words long on average. The official blind test set includes 1,052 documents.

Experimental setup. We use the Huggingface Transformers library (Wolf et al., 2020) to implement our model. Specifically, we fine-tune `allenai/led-large-16384-arxiv` (an LED large model fine-tuned on arXiv scientific dataset (Cohan et al., 2018)) on the MuP dataset. The learning rate of our summarization system is set to be $1e-3$ for parameters that we train from scratch (i.e., Sigmoid classifier and topic modeling), and $3e-5$ for the rest of the parameters. α and β hyper-parameters are tuned to be 0.1, and 0.2. We train the models for 5 epochs [2], and perform evaluation in each 0.5 epoch. The checkpoint that achieves the best validation scores is further used for inference on the official test set.

Automatic results. Table 1 reports the system performances in terms of ROUGE (Recall and F) metrics, as well as the average ROUGE (F) on validation and official test sets. Our best system (i.e., LED (topic-aware $\oplus$ two-step)) achieves the first rank on ROUGE-1 (F), and second in ROUGE-1 (R), ROUGE-2 (F) and average ROUGE. We also see a similar trend of model performance on the validation set. It is also clear that the addition of two-step summarizer results in a promising performance boost, indicating that the extractor can efficiently ease the information flow from the encoder to decoder for generating improved summaries grounded on the most important sentences of the document. Considering the performance of the BART baseline, it appears that feeding first 1024 tokens of the document to the summarizer leads to a promising performance in ROUGE Recall metrics, but degrades the performance in terms of ROUGE precision metrics as we see a large decrease in ROUGE (F) scores. Our best model improves upon the baseline by 1.4% relative improvement.

[1] https://openreview.net/

[2] Empirically determined.

	Recall			F-measure			
	R-1(%)	R-2(%)	R-L(%)	R-1(%)	R-2(%)	R-L(%)	Avg. RG-F (%)
Other systems							
guneetAI	42.96	**13.98**	26.62	41.08	**13.29**	**25.36**	**26.58**
ashokurlana	40.13	12.33	24.74	40.68	12.47	24.99	26.04
MuP baseline	**44.20**	13.50	**26.81**	40.80	12.33	24.48	25.87
sandeep.kumar82945	42.02	11.98	24.26	40.37	11.98	24.26	25.54
prachuryanath	35.83	10.88	22.43	38.74	11.73	24.21	24.89
This work							
LED (topic-aware)	42.15	12.46	25.21	40.62	11.96	24.18	25.59
LED (topic-aware ⊕ two-step)	43.29	13.20	26.21	**41.36**	12.52	24.83	26.24

(a) Top 5 Participating teams' (on Avg. ROUGE (F)) system performance on official blind test set.

	Recall			F-measure			
	R-1(%)	R-2(%)	R-L(%)	R-1(%)	R-2(%)	R-L(%)	Avg. RG-F (%)
LED	40.17	11.97	24.61	39.97	11.79	23.76	25.38
LED (topic-aware)	42.19	12.70	24.39	40.70	12.15	24.07	26.03
LED (topic-aware ⊕ two-step)	**42.82**	**12.80**	**25.86**	**41.05**	**12.18**	**24.61**	**26.55**

(b) Our systems' and LED baseline's (Beltagy et al., 2020) performance on validation set.

Table 1: ROUGE (F1) results of (a) our submissions compared to the other top 5 participating teams on the official blind test set of MuP challenge, and (b) our system's results on validation set. **Bold** scores show the top scores (in (a) and (b)), and underlined scores are the second top (in (a)). The table is sorted by the average RG-F score (last column). The MuP baseline is the BART (Lewis et al., 2020) summarizer, submitted by the challenge organizers.

Analysis. To explore the qualities and limitations of each system, we further perform a qualitative analysis over a random set of 15 test papers, comparing LED baseline with our submitted models. The percentage rate of our observations is also presented in parentheses. We found that: (1) in outperformed cases, detected topics by the NTM component fairly align with those discussed in gold summaries (i.e., gold topics); hence, the summarizer is guided to pick up on the paper information around the gold topics (47%), (2) addition of two-step summarizer has the most effect on refining the paper in terms of dropping unimportant/irrelevant information (66%), (3) in underperformed cases, our topic-guided summarizers focus more on the topics that are frequently mentioned in the paper; missing those topics that are less mentioned despite their saliency in gold summaries (72%). This might be addressed in future work by some heuristics such as saliency-aware (Zou et al., 2021), and hierarchical (Jin et al., 2021) topic-modeling.

4 Related work

While scientific document summarization has a long history, it has recently gained increasing attention from research communities. Previous works have approached this problem by either generating regular-length summaries, such as (Qazvinian et al., 2013; Cohan et al., 2018) among many, or very recently so-called extended summaries (Chandrasekaran et al., 2020; Sotudeh et al., 2020; Ghosh Roy et al., 2020; Gidiotis et al., 2020). These attempts include hierarchical sequence modeling (Xiao and Carenini, 2019; Rohde et al., 2021; Pang et al., 2022; Ruan et al., 2022), citation-context based approaches (Qazvinian and Radev, 2008; Cohan and Goharian, 2015; Zerva et al., 2020; An et al., 2021), using documents' structural information as saliency signals (Cohan et al., 2018; Sotudeh et al., 2020, 2021; Sotudeh and Goharian, 2022), two-phase summarization models (Ghosh Roy et al., 2020; Gidiotis and Tsoumakas, 2020). Up to recently, majority of existing work in scientific domain has evaluated the systems assuming that there is only one gold summary per paper. MuP challenge is the first attempt toward evaluation of summarization systems given multiple gold summaries, each of which captures a specific aspect of the paper.

5 Conclusion

In this study, we explore two summarization approaches to tackle the multi-perspective summary generation task, organized by the MuP challenge. Our first model learns a latent topic distribution using neural topic modeling (NTM) in the fine-tuning stage, and the knowledge is shared between the topic modeling and text summarization task for summary generation. Next, as our second model, we further incorporate a two-step summarization framework into the summarization model for yielding even more improvements. Our best submission ranks first in ROUGE-1 (F); and second in ROUGE-1 (R), ROUGE-2 (F), and average ROUGE (F) scores.

References

Chen An, Ming Zhong, Yiran Chen, Danqing Wang, Xipeng Qiu, and Xuanjing Huang. 2021. Enhancing scientific papers summarization with citation graph. *ArXiv*, abs/2104.03057.

Iz Beltagy, Matthew E. Peters, and Arman Cohan. 2020. Longformer: The long-document transformer. *ArXiv preprint*, abs/2004.05150.

Federico Bianchi, Silvia Terragni, and Dirk Hovy. 2021. Pre-training is a hot topic: Contextualized document embeddings improve topic coherence. In *Proceedings of the 59th Annual Meeting of the Association for Computational Linguistics and the 11th International Joint Conference on Natural Language Processing (Volume 2: Short Papers)*, pages 759–766, Online. Association for Computational Linguistics.

Isabel Cachola, Kyle Lo, Arman Cohan, and Daniel Weld. 2020. TLDR: Extreme summarization of scientific documents. In *Findings of the Association for Computational Linguistics: EMNLP 2020*, pages 4766–4777, Online. Association for Computational Linguistics.

Muthu Kumar Chandrasekaran, Guy Feigenblat, Eduard Hovy, Abhilasha Ravichander, Michal Shmueli-Scheuer, and Anita de Waard. 2020. Overview and insights from the shared tasks at scholarly document processing 2020: CL-SciSumm, LaySumm and LongSumm. In *Proceedings of the First Workshop on Scholarly Document Processing*, pages 214–224, Online. Association for Computational Linguistics.

Arman Cohan, Franck Dernoncourt, Doo Soon Kim, Trung Bui, Seokhwan Kim, Walter Chang, and Nazli Goharian. 2018. A discourse-aware attention model for abstractive summarization of long documents. In *Proceedings of the 2018 Conference of the North American Chapter of the Association for Computational Linguistics: Human Language Technologies, Volume 2 (Short Papers)*, pages 615–621, New Orleans, Louisiana. Association for Computational Linguistics.

Arman Cohan, Guy Feigenblat, Tirthankar Ghosal, and Michal Shmueli-Scheuer. 2022. Overview of the first shared task on multi-perspective scientific document summarization (mup). In *Proceedings of the Third Workshop on Scholarly Document Processing*, Online. Association for Computational Linguistics.

Arman Cohan and Nazli Goharian. 2015. Scientific article summarization using citation-context and article's discourse structure. In *Proceedings of the 2015 Conference on Empirical Methods in Natural Language Processing*, pages 390–400, Lisbon, Portugal. Association for Computational Linguistics.

Peng Cui and Le Hu. 2021. Sliding selector network with dynamic memory for extractive summarization of long documents. In *Proceedings of the 2021 Conference of the North American Chapter of the Association for Computational Linguistics: Human Language Technologies*, pages 5881–5891, Online. Association for Computational Linguistics.

Sayar Ghosh Roy, Nikhil Pinnaparaju, Risubh Jain, Manish Gupta, and Vasudeva Varma. 2020. Summaformers @ LaySumm 20, LongSumm 20. In *Proceedings of the First Workshop on Scholarly Document Processing*, pages 336–343, Online. Association for Computational Linguistics.

Alexios Gidiotis, Stefanos Stefanidis, and Grigorios Tsoumakas. 2020. AUTH @ CLSciSumm 20, LaySumm 20, LongSumm 20. In *Proceedings of the First Workshop on Scholarly Document Processing*, pages 251–260, Online. Association for Computational Linguistics.

Alexios Gidiotis and Grigorios Tsoumakas. 2020. A divide-and-conquer approach to the summarization of long documents. *IEEE/ACM Transactions on Audio, Speech, and Language Processing*, 28:3029–3040.

Yuan Jin, He Zhao, Ming Liu, Lan Du, and Wray L. Buntine. 2021. Neural attention-aware hierarchical topic model. In *EMNLP*.

Mike Lewis, Yinhan Liu, Naman Goyal, Marjan Ghazvininejad, Abdelrahman Mohamed, Omer Levy, Veselin Stoyanov, and Luke Zettlemoyer. 2020. BART: Denoising sequence-to-sequence pre-training for natural language generation, translation, and comprehension. In *Proceedings of the 58th Annual Meeting of the Association for Computational Linguistics*, pages 7871–7880, Online. Association for Computational Linguistics.

Yishu Miao, Edward Grefenstette, and Phil Blunsom. 2017. Discovering discrete latent topics with neural variational inference. In *Proceedings of the 34th International Conference on Machine Learning*, volume 70 of *Proceedings of Machine Learning Research*, pages 2410–2419. PMLR.

Ani Nenkova, Sameer Maskey, and Yang Liu. 2011. Automatic summarization. In *Proceedings of the 49th Annual Meeting of the Association for Computational Linguistics: Tutorial Abstracts of ACL 2011*, HLT '11, USA. Association for Computational Linguistics.

Bo Pang, Erik Nijkamp, Wojciech Kryscinski, Silvio Savarese, Yingbo Zhou, and Caiming Xiong. 2022. Long document summarization with top-down and bottom-up inference. *ArXiv preprint*, abs/2203.07586.

Vahed Qazvinian and Dragomir R. Radev. 2008. Scientific paper summarization using citation summary networks. In *Proceedings of the 22nd International Conference on Computational Linguistics (Coling 2008)*, pages 689–696, Manchester, UK. Coling 2008 Organizing Committee.

Vahed Qazvinian, Dragomir R. Radev, Saif M. Mohammad, Bonnie Dorr, David Zajic, Michael Whidby, and Taesun Moon. 2013. Generating extractive summaries of scientific paradigms. *J. Artif. Int. Res.*, 46(1):165–201.

Tobias Rohde, Xiaoxia Wu, and Yinhan Liu. 2021. Hierarchical learning for generation with long source sequences. *ArXiv preprint*, abs/2104.07545.

Qian Ruan, Malte Ostendorff, and Georg Rehm. 2022. HiStruct+: Improving extractive text summarization with hierarchical structure information. In *Findings of the Association for Computational Linguistics: ACL 2022*, pages 1292–1308, Dublin, Ireland. Association for Computational Linguistics.

Sajad Sotudeh, Arman Cohan, and Nazli Goharian. 2020. GUIR @ LongSumm 2020: Learning to generate long summaries from scientific documents. In *Proceedings of the First Workshop on Scholarly Document Processing*, pages 356–361, Online. Association for Computational Linguistics.

Sajad Sotudeh, Arman Cohan, and Nazli Goharian. 2021. On generating extended summaries of long documents. *The AAAI-21 Workshop on Scientific Document Understanding (SDU)*.

Sajad Sotudeh and Nazli Goharian. 2022. TSTR: Too short to represent, summarize with details! intro-guided extended summary generation. In *Proceedings of the 2022 Conference of the North American Chapter of the Association for Computational Linguistics: Human Language Technologies*, pages 325–335, Seattle, United States. Association for Computational Linguistics.

Akash Srivastava and Charles Sutton. 2017. Autoencoding variational inference for topic models. In *5th International Conference on Learning Representations, ICLR 2017, Toulon, France, April 24-26, 2017, Conference Track Proceedings*. OpenReview.net.

Simone Teufel and Marc Moens. 2002. Summarizing scientific articles: Experiments with relevance and rhetorical status. *Computational Linguistics*, 28:409–445.

Thomas Wolf, Lysandre Debut, Victor Sanh, Julien Chaumond, Clement Delangue, Anthony Moi, Pierric Cistac, Tim Rault, Remi Louf, Morgan Funtowicz, Joe Davison, Sam Shleifer, Patrick von Platen, Clara Ma, Yacine Jernite, Julien Plu, Canwen Xu, Teven Le Scao, Sylvain Gugger, Mariama Drame, Quentin Lhoest, and Alexander Rush. 2020. Transformers: State-of-the-art natural language processing. In *Proceedings of the 2020 Conference on Empirical Methods in Natural Language Processing: System Demonstrations*, pages 38–45, Online. Association for Computational Linguistics.

Wen Xiao and Giuseppe Carenini. 2019. Extractive summarization of long documents by combining global and local context. In *Proceedings of the 2019 Conference on Empirical Methods in Natural Language Processing and the 9th International Joint Conference on Natural Language Processing (EMNLP-IJCNLP)*, pages 3011–3021, Hong Kong, China. Association for Computational Linguistics.

Chrysoula Zerva, Minh-Quoc Nghiem, Nhung T. H. Nguyen, and Sophia Ananiadou. 2020. Cited text span identification for scientific summarisation using pre-trained encoders. *Scientometrics*, 125:3109–3137.

Yicheng Zou, Lujun Zhao, Yangyang Kang, Jun Lin, Minlong Peng, Zhuoren Jiang, Changlong Sun, Qi Zhang, Xuanjing Huang, and Xiaozhong Liu. 2021. Topic-oriented spoken dialogue summarization for customer service with saliency-aware topic modeling. In *AAAI*.

LTRC @MuP 2022: Multi-Perspective Scientific Document Summarization Using Pre-trained Generation Models

Ashok Urlana, Nirmal Surange, Manish Shrivastava
Language Technologies Research Center, KCIS
IIIT Hyderabad, India
{ashok.urlana,nirmal.surange}@research.iiit.ac.in,m.shrivastava@iiit.ac.in

Abstract

The MuP-2022 shared task focuses on multi-perspective scientific document summarization. Given a scientific document, with multiple reference summaries, our goal was to develop a model that can produce a generic summary covering as many aspects of the document as covered by all of its reference summaries. This paper describes our best official model, a fine-tuned BART_{large}, along with a discussion on the challenges of this task and some of our unofficial models including SOTA generation models. Our submitted model out performed the given, MuP 2022 shared task baselines on ROUGE-2, ROUGE-L and average ROUGE F1-scores. Code of our submission can be accessed here.

1 Introduction

With the rapidly growing research community, the volume of scientific papers being published every year is also going up. Which makes it nearly impossible for researchers to stay on top of the latest research. Scientific document summarization plays a crucial role in mitigating this problem. However, generating generic summaries for scientific documents is a non-trivial task due to their specific structure, varied content and inclusion of citation sentences. Scientific articles often represent salient information through tables, figures, and pseudo-codes (Altmami and Menai, 2020) and mathematical equations. And, generic text does not usually contain such elements.

The two widely used approaches for scientific document summarization are content-based (Collins et al., 2017; Nikolov et al., 2018) and citation-based (Nakov et al.; Abu-Jbara and Radev, 2011; Yasunaga et al., 2019). The former relies on traditional extractive and abstractive methods whereas, the latter locates the target paper by matching a portion of text with the citation sentences.

Almost all traditional summarization models, whether extractive or abstractive, follow supervised learning approach. That means, given a document the model learns to generate its summary based on its given gold (target) summary. However, in real world, summary writing is very subjective. For a given document, there could be multiple different yet valid summaries where each summary writer has written a summary of the same document from their perspective of the document. This subjectivity raises concerns about the evaluation ability of the model that is presented with only one gold summary. The MuP-2022 shared task is a novel attempt to address this concern. The goal of multi-perspective summarization task is to develop models that are capable of leveraging multiple gold summaries to generate one generic summary.

MuP-2022 shared task data contains a collection of scientific documents with multiple summaries. These summaries were collected by first taking (one or) multiple scientific peer reviews for each document and then extracting the introductory paragraph that summarizes the key contributions of the paper from the reviewer's perspective.

For this task, we explored several pretrained sequence-to-sequence models such as BART (Lewis et al., 2020), T5 (Raffel et al., 2020), and ProphetNet (Qi et al., 2020). We also experimented with: a two-stage fine-tuning approach using the SciTLDR dataset (Cachola et al., 2020) and the divide and conquer approach, by (Gidiotis and Tsoumakas, 2020), that first divides the document into multiple sections to obtain section-wise summaries, and then aggregates all partial summaries to form the complete summary.

For the MuP 2022 shared task dataset, our fine-tuned BART_{large} model remained the best among all our experiments by achieving 40.68 ROUGE-1 F1-score and 26.04 average ROUGE F1-score.

2 Related Work

Research on summarizing scientific documents has been widely explored in recent years. It is perti-

Proceedings of the Third Workshop on Scholarly Document Processing, pages 279–284
October 12–17, 2022.

	Train		Validation	
#Pairs	18934		3604	
#Unique Pairs	8382		1060	
	Text	Summary	Text	Summary
#Avg Words	2671.41	113.57	2671	115.13
#Avg Sentences	122.35	4.78	121.14	4.82

Table 1: MuP Data Statistics

nent to note that there is a great deal of variation in the density of information covered (Over and Yen, 2004), the level of details, and the organization of the content within the scientific document summaries. Recent work by (Fabbri et al., 2021) uses question threads from the Yahoo forum to build the multi-perspective answer summarization corpus. Meng et al., (2021) present FactSum that contains four summaries for each paper covers different aspects, they can provide summaries based on user requests.

A number of scholarly document summarization datasets, including PubMed and arXiv (Cohan et al., 2018), were used for training neural models ScisummNet (Yasunaga et al., 2019) and SciTLDR for extreme summarization (Cachola et al., 2020). Unlike these datasets, MuP2022 shared task organizers released a multi-perspective summarization dataset for scientific documents.

Various generation models, including BART, T5, ProphetNet, and PEGASUS, have shown great performance in summarization tasks. In particular, models like Big Bird (Zaheer et al., 2021) and Longformer (Beltagy et al., 2020) were released to handle long documents.

3 Corpus Description

The multi-perspective scientific document summarization task aims to generate a summary that covers various aspects of the document. Evaluating such a system with just one gold (or reference) summary negatively impacts the goal, as summaries are usually very subjective. Considering the fact that multiple summaries would help cover more different perspectives of the scientific document, which a single summary might have missed.

MuP2022 (Cohan et al., 2022) shared task data[1] contains multiple reference summaries for majority of the training set documents, and all of the development set documents also had a minimum of 3 reference summaries. The corpus consists of around 10K papers and 26.5K summaries. The average length of the summaries is 114.3 words long.

4 Methodology

Self-supervised pretrained models like BART (Lewis et al., 2020), T5 (Raffel et al., 2020), XLNet (Yang et al., 2019), ProphetNet (Qi et al., 2020), PEGASUS (Zhang et al., 2020) have been effective for many generative tasks. We experiment with these pre-trained models and fine-tune them on MuP dataset for this task.

BART is a transformer-based (Vaswani et al., 2017) standard sequence-to-sequence model modified to work as an auto-encoder (Lewis et al., 2020). A self-supervised autoencoder is trained on the corrupted text (addition of noise) and uses a language model to reconstruct the original text with the true replacement of corrupted tokens. BART uses five "noising" methods: token masking, token deletion, text infilling, sentence permutation, and document rotation.

T5 or **Text to Text Transfer Transformer** (Raffel et al., 2020) is a transformer-based approach that converts all the text-based language problems into the text-to-text format. This strategy allows the use of the same model architecture across a diverse set of tasks. T5 is pretrained on a multi-task mixture of supervised and unsupervised tasks using the common crawled corpus. We fine tune T5 base model on MuP corpus.

ProphetNet (Qi et al., 2020) is a sequence-to-sequence pretraining model. The unique objective of this model is to predict the future n-grams as the self-supervised training strategy. Unlike the traditional sequence-to-sequence models, ProphetNet is optimized by n-step ahead prediction instead of one-step-ahead prediction. We experimented with ProphetNet models with and without fine-tuned on the CNN/DailyMail dataset.

Utilizing SciTLDR The TLDR (Cachola et al., 2020) approach aims at creating extremely short summaries (TLDRs) for scientific documents. For this task, the authors introduced a SciTLDR dataset of 5400 TLDRs over 3200 papers.

DANCER (Gidiotis and Tsoumakas, 2020) Most of the extractive and abstractive methods for scientific document summarization typically consider the input as abstract and/or full text of the article to generate the abstract-like summary. In contrast, DANCER divides the source text into multiple sections, generates an individual summary for

[1] `https://github.com/allenai/mup`

Model	R-1	R-2	R-L	Avg R-f
Baseline	**40.8**	12.3	24.5	25.8
$BART_{large}$ cnn	40.68	**12.47**	**24.99**	**26.05**
DistilBART cnn	39.36	11.79	24.47	25.21
$BART_{base}$ cnn	39.12	11.42	23.8	24.78
$T5_{base}$	38.35	11.26	24.64	24.75
ProphetNet	38.15	11.45	24.25	24.62
$BART_{base}$	38.53	11.39	23.92	24.61
ProphetNet cnn	37.59	10.91	24.09	24.2
DANCER + BART	33.07	9.06	18.2	20.11
BART + Two-stage	32.51	6.82	20.64	19.99

Table 2: ROUGE scores for models fine-tuned on MuP2022 dataset

Parameters	BART	T5	ProphetNet
Max source length	1024	1024	512
Max target length	150	128	128
Min target length	56	30	56
Batch Size	1	1	1
Epochs	2	10	1
Vocab Size	50265	32128	30522
Beam Size	4	4	5
Learning Rate	5e-5	1e-4	5e-5

Table 3: Experimental Setup and Parameters Settings

each section, and aggregates the partial summaries to form the target summary.

5 Experiments

All of our experiments were performed on the same splits of train, validation and test sets as provided by the organizers. Table 1 shows the data statistics. We used NLTK tokenizer and the simplified version data released by the task organizers to report all the counts mentioned in Table 1.

The following subsections detail various categories of experiments. We hypothesise that various sections of the source document may contribute in multi-perspective reviews of the document reviews. The subsection 5.3 and 5.4 detail the experiments conducted, specifically, to capture various sections of the document.

5.1 Existing Pre-trained Generation models

We experimented with existing SOTA generation models like BART (Lewis et al., 2020), T5 (Raffel et al., 2020) and ProphetNet (Qi et al., 2020). Table 3 details the general experimental setup for each.

Experiments were conducted with different versions of these models, such as DistilBART-cnn, $BART_{base}$, $BART_{base}$-cnn (base model of BART fine-tuned on CNN dataset), and ProphetNet-cnn.

Among all these, $BART_{large}$ achieved better performance for the MuP task. We use the $BART_{large}$ model fine-tuned on the CNN/DailyMail dataset (Hermann et al., 2015) to initialize our model.

5.2 Two Stage Fine-tuning

In order to follow TLDR (Cachola et al., 2020) approach, we attempted two stage fine tuning. Using the available checkpoints in the Hugging Face Transformers Library (Wolf et al., 2020), first we fine-tune the BART model on the SciTLDR dataset for 10 epochs with the max source and target token lengths of 1024 and 150 respectively. In the second stage, we fine-tune this model on the MuP dataset, with the same settings. However, as the bottom line of the Table 2 shows, this approach did not help with this MuP task.

5.3 Data Variation

The entire MuP dataset was released in two formats: one that consisted of the full-text of the scientific document along with meta-data and second, a simplified version of the source document. This simplified content is basically the pre-processed initial 2000 tokens of the documents' introduction sections.

We conducted a few experiments, with our submitted model, to investigate the contribution of various sections of these documents in the target summaries. For this, we created four categories of training, validation and test sets such that each category's source content consisted of one of the following combinations of sections of the source document:

1. ***Introduction***: Only the introduction section of the document was used as the input to the BART model.

2. ***Abstract + Introduction***: Both abstract and introduction sections, in concatenation, were utilized as the input for the BART model.

3. ***Abstract + Introduction + Conclusion***: The BART model was fed with a combination of abstract, introduction and conclusion sections (if available) of the document.

4. ***Abstract + Conclusion***: A combination of abstract and conclusion section was used as the input to the BART model.

First, we separately fine-tuned our $BART_{large}$ model using the training and validation data of

				Train & Val Data				Test Data			
R-1	R-2	R-L	Avg R-f	1	2	3	4	1	2	3	4
40.68	**12.47**	**24.99**	**26.05**	✓					✓		
40.67	12.5	24.93	26.03	✓						✓	
40.47	12.29	24.76	25.84			✓			✓		
40.34	12.28	24.79	25.8				✓				✓
40.33	12.28	24.75	25.79		✓				✓		
40.39	12.25	24.73	25.79			✓				✓	
40.23	12.32	24.77	25.77	✓							✓
40.23	12.17	24.6	25.67				✓		✓		
40.1	12.25	24.63	25.66		✓			✓			
40.22	12.13	24.54	25.63	✓				✓			

Table 4: Impact of Data Variations

each of these categories. Next, in each of these experiments all 4 models were tested with all 4 categories of test data. Table 4 shows the respective ROUGE f1-scores. Where, the checkmarks (✓) indicate the selected combination of training and test data category.

As shown in Table 4, the combination of '1' & '2' (i.e. only-introduction section for the training data and abstract + introduction for test data) outperforms all the rest. All these models were fine-tuned for two epochs and with the max source and target lengths of 1024 and 150, respectively.

Epochs	R-1	R-2	R-L	Avg R-f
1	40.5	12.48	24.88	25.95
2	**40.57**	**12.49**	**24.98**	**26.01**
3	40.31	12.23	24.8	25.78
5	40.35	12.02	24.59	25.65

Table 5: Impact of number-of-Epochs Variation

Epochs	Max Target Length	R-1	R-2	R-L	Avg R-f
2	128	40.57	**12.49**	24.98	26.01
	150	**40.68**	12.47	**24.99**	**26.05**
	200	40.67	12.47	24.99	26.04
5	128	**40.35**	12.02	24.59	25.65
	150	40.31	**12.1**	**24.66**	**25.69**

Table 6: Impact of Max-Target-Length Variation

5.4 Divide and Conquer Approach

Following the DANCER approach, we prepare the training, validation and test inputs by dividing each corresponding source documents into four sections: **Abstract, Introduction, Results and Discussion, and Conclusion**. We fine-tuned the BART model on each section of information separately and combined all the summaries at the end to get the final generated summary.

5.5 Impact of Hyperparameters

In order to find the optimal architecture for our BART_{large} model, we experimented with number-of-epochs (1, 2, 3, 5) with default max-target-length of 128, where fine-tuning with 2 epochs showed better performance. We then tested for max-target-lengths (128, 150, 200) with 2 epochs. Where max-target-length 150 gave slightly better performance than the remaining. Tables 5 and 6 detail the corresponding ROUGE f1-scores.

6 Results & Discussion

For the MuP task, we experimented with various pre-trained generation models, a couple of scientific document summarization approaches, methods to cover different sections of the document and parameter settings. As shown in Table 2, among all of these the BART_{large}cnn (our submitted) model performed the best. This model was fine-tuned for 2 epochs with max-target-length 150 and data combination 1-2 (as mentioned in section 5.3). With this model, we secured 3rd rank in the MuP-2022 shared task.

While the MuP task considers summaries from multiple reviewers as different "perspectives", most of these summaries cover only the major contributions of the paper. These summaries, though diverse in their construction, do not look at the research paper from different points-of-view. We see a validation of this claim from the results in table 4, where model trained on "introduction" section alone outperforms all other combinations.

References

Amjad Abu-Jbara and Dragomir Radev. 2011. Coherent citation-based summarization of scientific papers. In *Proceedings of the 49th annual meeting of the association for computational linguistics: Human language technologies*, pages 500–509.

Nouf Ibrahim Altmami and Mohamed El Bachir Menai. 2020. Automatic summarization of scientific articles: A survey. *Journal of King Saud University-Computer and Information Sciences*.

Iz Beltagy, Matthew E. Peters, and Arman Cohan. 2020. Longformer: The long-document transformer. *arXiv:2004.05150*.

Isabel Cachola, Kyle Lo, Arman Cohan, and Daniel Weld. 2020. TLDR: Extreme summarization of scientific documents. In *Findings of the Association for Computational Linguistics: EMNLP 2020*, pages 4766–4777, Online. Association for Computational Linguistics.

Arman Cohan, Franck Dernoncourt, Doo Soon Kim, Trung Bui, Seokhwan Kim, Walter Chang, and Nazli Goharian. 2018. A discourse-aware attention model for abstractive summarization of long documents. *arXiv preprint arXiv:1804.05685*.

Arman Cohan, Guy Feigenblat, Tirthankar Ghosal, and Michal Shmueli-Scheuer. 2022. Overview of the first shared task on multi-perspective scientific document summarization (mup). In *Proceedings of the Third Workshop on Scholarly Document Processing*, Online. Association for Computational Linguistics.

Ed Collins, Isabelle Augenstein, and Sebastian Riedel. 2017. A supervised approach to extractive summarisation of scientific papers. *arXiv preprint arXiv:1706.03946*.

Alexander R Fabbri, Xiaojian Wu, Srini Iyer, and Mona Diab. 2021. Multi-perspective abstractive answer summarization. *arXiv preprint arXiv:2104.08536*.

Alexios Gidiotis and Grigorios Tsoumakas. 2020. A divide-and-conquer approach to the summarization of long documents. *IEEE/ACM Transactions on Audio, Speech, and Language Processing*, 28:3029–3040.

Karl Moritz Hermann, Tomas Kocisky, Edward Grefenstette, Lasse Espeholt, Will Kay, Mustafa Suleyman, and Phil Blunsom. 2015. Teaching machines to read and comprehend. *Advances in neural information processing systems*, 28.

Mike Lewis, Yinhan Liu, Naman Goyal, Marjan Ghazvininejad, Abdelrahman Mohamed, Omer Levy, Veselin Stoyanov, and Luke Zettlemoyer. 2020. BART: Denoising sequence-to-sequence pre-training for natural language generation, translation, and comprehension. In *Proceedings of the 58th Annual Meeting of the Association for Computational Linguistics*, pages 7871–7880, Online. Association for Computational Linguistics.

Rui Meng, Khushboo Thaker, Lei Zhang, Yue Dong, Xingdi Yuan, Tong Wang, and Daqing He. 2021. Bringing structure into summaries: a faceted summarization dataset for long scientific documents. *arXiv preprint arXiv:2106.00130*.

Preslav Nakov, Ariel Schwartz, and M Hearst. Citation sentences for semantic analysis of bioscience text. In *Proceedings of the SIGIR'04 workshop on Search and Discovery in Bioinformatics*.

Nikola I Nikolov, Michael Pfeiffer, and Richard HR Hahnloser. 2018. Data-driven summarization of scientific articles. *arXiv preprint arXiv:1804.08875*.

Paul Over and James Yen. 2004. An introduction to duc-2004. *National Institute of Standards and Technology*.

Weizhen Qi, Yu Yan, Yeyun Gong, Dayiheng Liu, Nan Duan, Jiusheng Chen, Ruofei Zhang, and Ming Zhou. 2020. ProphetNet: Predicting future n-gram for sequence-to-SequencePre-training. In *Findings of the Association for Computational Linguistics: EMNLP 2020*, pages 2401–2410, Online. Association for Computational Linguistics.

Colin Raffel, Noam Shazeer, Adam Roberts, Katherine Lee, Sharan Narang, Michael Matena, Yanqi Zhou, Wei Li, Peter J Liu, et al. 2020. Exploring the limits of transfer learning with a unified text-to-text transformer. *J. Mach. Learn. Res.*, 21(140):1–67.

Ashish Vaswani, Noam Shazeer, Niki Parmar, Jakob Uszkoreit, Llion Jones, Aidan N Gomez, Łukasz Kaiser, and Illia Polosukhin. 2017. Attention is all you need. *Advances in neural information processing systems*, 30.

Thomas Wolf, Lysandre Debut, Victor Sanh, Julien Chaumond, Clement Delangue, Anthony Moi, Pierric Cistac, Tim Rault, Remi Louf, Morgan Funtowicz, Joe Davison, Sam Shleifer, Patrick von Platen, Clara Ma, Yacine Jernite, Julien Plu, Canwen Xu, Teven Le Scao, Sylvain Gugger, Mariama Drame, Quentin Lhoest, and Alexander Rush. 2020. Transformers: State-of-the-art natural language processing. In *Proceedings of the 2020 Conference on Empirical Methods in Natural Language Processing: System Demonstrations*, pages 38–45, Online. Association for Computational Linguistics.

Zhilin Yang, Zihang Dai, Yiming Yang, Jaime Carbonell, Russ R Salakhutdinov, and Quoc V Le. 2019. Xlnet: Generalized autoregressive pretraining for language understanding. *Advances in neural information processing systems*, 32.

Michihiro Yasunaga, Jungo Kasai, Rui Zhang, Alexander R Fabbri, Irene Li, Dan Friedman, and Dragomir R Radev. 2019. Scisummnet: A large annotated corpus and content-impact models for scientific paper summarization with citation networks. In *Proceedings of the AAAI conference on artificial intelligence*, volume 33, pages 7386–7393.

Manzil Zaheer, Guru Guruganesh, Avinava Dubey, Joshua Ainslie, Chris Alberti, Santiago Ontanon, Philip Pham, Anirudh Ravula, Qifan Wang, Li Yang, and Amr Ahmed. 2021. Big bird: Transformers for longer sequences.

Jingqing Zhang, Yao Zhao, Mohammad Saleh, and Peter Liu. 2020. Pegasus: Pre-training with extracted gap-sentences for abstractive summarization. In *International Conference on Machine Learning*, pages 11328–11339. PMLR.

Team AINLPML @ MuP in SDP 2021: Scientific Document Summarization by End-to-End Extractive and Abstractive Approach

Sandeep Kumar†, Guneet Singh Kohli*, Kartik Shinde†, Asif Ekbal†
†Indian Institute of Technology Patna, India
*Thapar Institute of Engineering and Technology, India
†(sandeep_2121cs29,kartik_1901ce16,asif)@iitp.ac.in
*guneetsk99@gmail.com

Abstract

This paper introduces the proposed summarization system of the AINLPML team for the First Shared Task on Multi-Perspective Scientific Document Summarization at SDP 2022. We present a method to produce abstractive summaries of scientific documents. First, we perform an extractive summarization step to identify the essential part of the paper. The extraction step includes utilizing a contributing sentence identification model to determine the contributing sentences in selected sections and portions of the text. In the next step, the extracted relevant information is used to condition the transformer language model to generate an abstractive summary. In particular, we fine-tuned the pre-trained BART model on the extracted summary from the previous step. Our proposed model successfully outperformed the baseline provided by the organizers by a significant margin. Our approach achieves the best average Rouge F1 Score, Rouge-2 F1 Score, and Rouge-L F1 Score among all submissions.

1 Introduction

Automatic summarization involves distilling a document down to its essentials. There are two types of summarization techniques: abstractive summarization and extractive summarization. Abstractive summarization examines a document and creates a summary from it that may contain phrases that do not present in the original text. The more challenging goal is abstractive summarization, which is beneficial in fields like novels where phrases taken out of context are not a good foundation for producing a grammatical and cohesive summary. We are interested in summarizing scientific literature in this instance. Summarization of research papers can help in obtaining core ideas instantly and would help researchers all around the world in fastening the process of literature surveys.

It is well recognized that creating summaries of scientific papers is a difficult endeavour. The main question is why the article's abstract doesn't suffice since it summarizes the scientific article. Although an abstract has been written, there are many reasons for generating article summaries. First, one of the main problems with abstracts is that they do not include relevant information from the full text. Second, it presents the author's viewpoint on the unique characteristic in an incomplete and biased manner (Yang et al., 2016). Thirdly, no single summary meets all the user's needs (Reeve et al., 2007). In addition, the abstract does not cover all the impacts and contributions of the article (Elkiss et al., 2008) but rather what the author wishes to emphasize. As a result, the summary generated by such a system should be informative enough, cover all the critical sections of the input article, and provide the reader with essential information. Furthermore, (Yasunaga et al., 2019) discuss the impact factor of a scientific article. Summarization systems should accommodate the viewpoints of other researchers (i.e., citations) and the significant aspects highlighted by the article's authors in the abstract since the significance of papers may change over time.

Most existing summarizing research assumes only one best gold summary for each given material. Having just one gold summary limits our capacity to assess the effectiveness of summarizing algorithms because creating summaries is important to derive the significant aspects of any long document. Furthermore, because it takes subject matter experts a lot of time to read and comprehend lengthy scientific publications, annotating several gold summaries for scientific documents can be very expensive. The workshops aimed to promote the exploration of strategies for producing multi-perspective summaries. A novel summarizing corpus was provided that used information from peer-reviewed scientific articles to capture various viewpoints from the reader's perspective. In many different branches of science, peer reviews typi-

Proceedings of the Third Workshop on Scholarly Document Processing, pages 285–290
October 12–17, 2022.

cally begin with a paragraph that summarizes the most important contributions made by a work from the perspective of the reviewer, and each paper typically undergoes a number of different reviews.

This paper presents our approach to the MuP shared task(Cohan et al., 2022). We present an end-to-end approach to generate summaries of long scientific documents that uses the advantages of both extractive and abstractive approaches. Before producing a summary in an abstractive manner, we perform the extractive step, which is then used for conditioning the abstractor module. We first determined the section of a research paper. We took the Abstract, and the last few sentences of the introduction section as mostly authors summarize a few critical questions about the paper in these, such as, 'What is the contribution in the paper?', 'What is the novelty?', 'How is it different from previous works?'. From the rest of the portion of the document, we extracted the contributing sentences using a Large Language Model named ContriSci(Gupta et al., 2021). ContriSci is a BERT fine-tuned over sectional data from a research paper, capable of generating binary labels for a given sentence in that section which tells us if the sentence is contributing to the understanding of the section or not. After performing these extractive steps, we trained an abstractive model to form a final summary. Our experiments showed that jointly using extractive and abstractive models improves the summarization results.

2 Methodology

We propose an end-to-end pipeline approach to generate summaries automatically from scientific documents. Figure 1 shows an overview of our approach. We describe each component briefly as follows:

2.1 Extractive Model

The input to this model is the full text of the paper. Extractive Summarization deals with extracting pieces of text directly from the input document. Extractive Summarization can also be seen as a text classification task where we try to predict whether a given sentence will be part of the summary or not(Liu, 2019).

2.1.1 Section Identification

Section information is essential as the reviewer often focuses on a few sections, such as the abstract and conclusion, more than other sections (Ghosh Roy et al., 2020). Section identification for any full scientific paper is not straightforward as there is no fixed pattern through which a template of a research paper is generalized. On close observation of the training data, We found that in training, only 60% of the data had a section named 'Conclusion' explicitly. Similarly, for 'Conclusion' similar problem was seen for generic sections such as 'Methodology' and 'Results'. Moreover, the section 'Conclusion' is not necessary the last section or the second last section of the paper. So, we found that the only sections uniformly available in each research paper were 'Introduction' and 'Abstract.'

2.1.2 Contributing Sentence Identification

Apart from the 'Abstract' and last n[1] sentences of the introduction section, we also extract the contributing sentences using an attention-based deep neural model named ContriSci. ContriSci is a deep neural architecture that leverages Multi-task Learning to identify statements from a given research article that mention a contribution of the study. The model makes use of two auxiliary tasks: 1) Section Classification - classifying a given statement as belonging to a specific section of the paper, 2) Citation Classification - classifying whether a given statement consists of a citation within itself.

The authors generalize the specific sections of a conventional research paper into six categories - '*Title*', '*Abstract*', '*Introduction*', '*Background*', '*Method*', and '*Result*'. The study makes use of the NLPContributionGraph (NCG) data set (D'Souza et al., 2021) from Sem-Eval 2021 Task A [2]. The authors use set of predefined rules to annotate the dataset for the task of Section Classification. A specific research statement is fed into model together with the name of the section to which it belongs and the statements that surround it. Intuitively, this means that the model trains on more knowledge about the context in which a given research statement has been written. Given the peculiarities of the model and it's relevance to SDP, we choose to leverage it to enrich the extraction of textually salient statements.

[1] n=5. It was set empirically. We analyzed various values of n between 1 to 10 and chose the one that resulted in the best Rouge-1 F1 score

[2] https://ncg-task.github.io

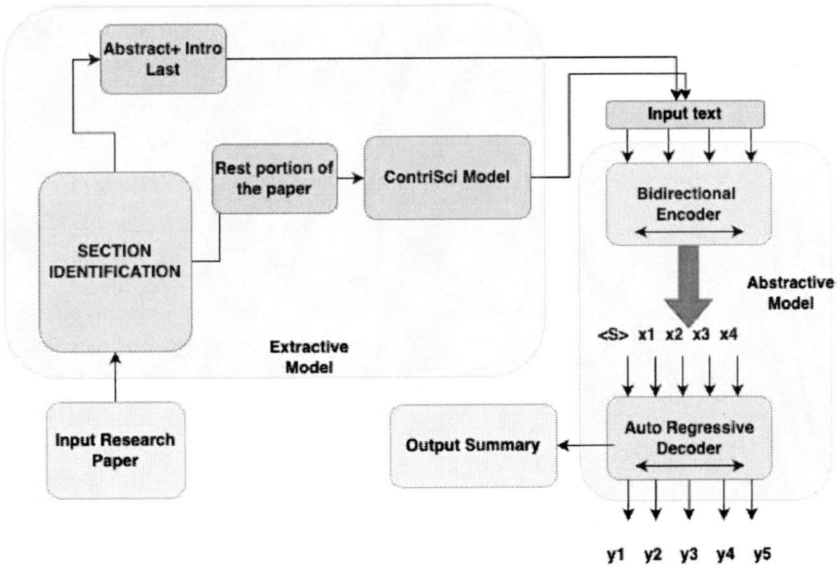

Figure 1: Architecture diagram of our proposed methodology.

System	Rouge1 F	Rouge1 R	Rouge2 F	Rouge2 F	RougeL R	RougeL R	Avg Rouge F
Baseline	40.80	44.20	12.33	13.50	24.48	26.81	25.87
Other System	**41.36**	**43.29**	12.52	13.20	24.83	26.21	26.24
Our System	41.08	42.96	**13.29**	**13.98**	**25.36**	26.62	**26.58**

Table 1: Experimental results of our model.(R:Recall, F:1 Score, Other System: Refers to the system with highest Rouge F1 in the leaderboard)

2.2 Abstractive Model

We use the BART autoencoder for pretraining sequence-to-sequence models. The structure of BART consists of two parts: an encoder and a decoder. The encoder part is a bidirectional encoder that corresponds to the structure of BERT (Vaswani et al., 2017), and the decoder part is an auto-regressive decoder following the settings of GPT. During the pretraining process, BART receives the corrupted document as input and performs the task of predicting the original uncorrupted document. In this way, BART can effectively learn contextual representations. When fine-tuned for the summarization task, the bidirectional encoder part encodes the original document, and the decoder part predicts the reference summary. BART obtains excellent performance on the summarization task. We gave the input to BART as follows:
Input text: Abstract $[SEP]$ INTRO_LAST $[SEP]$ Contributing sentences

Here the input to the BART model is Abstract, the last n sentences of the introduction(INTRO_LAST) and the contributing sentences separated by a token $[SEP]$. We use the BART fine-tuned on CNN/DailyMail dataset (Hermann et al., 2015) to initialize our model.

3 Experiments

In this section we discuss our results and analysis. The data set description (A) and experimental settings (B) can be found in the Appendix section.

3.1 Results and Discussion

In Table 1 the comparison of our best-submitted system has been made with the organizer's baseline model as well as the best performing system (based on Rouge1_f score (Lin, 2004)). Our methodology outperforms the baseline by a significant margin of 0.28 Rouge1_f score and 0.71 Avg Rouge F scores. Comparing our submission with the 'best leader board submission' shows that the submitted system performs well in Rouge2, RougeL, and overall avg Rouge F scores.

3.1.1 Different inputs to the model

The submitted system had varied inputs passed through BART for summary generation. We report the result on the following combinations:

Submitted Systems [Input to the BART while fine tuning]	Rouge1_F	Rouge2_F	RougeL_F	Avg Rouge F
Abstract + Full Paper	40.53	12.02	24.32	25.62
Abstract + Rule based selection from Intro	40.62	12.22	24.22	25.74
Abstract + Rule based selection from Full Paper	40.78	12.19	24.27	25.79
Abstract + Full Intro + ContriSci	40.73	12.25	26.01	26.33
Abstract + Intro Last + ContriSci	**41.08**	**13.29**	**25.36**	**26.58**

Table 2: Ablation Study of our model.(F in the Rouge metrics refer to Rouge F1 Score)

- We performed the first set of experiments by tuning BART on Abstract + Full paper contents.
- Then we performed experiments by selecting contributing sentences from Abstract + Introductions of the paper and Abstract + Full paper. These contributing sentences were selected by defining rules to select sentences that contained words like 'propose,' 'demonstrate,' 'formulate,' 'contributes,' etc.
- The final set was formulating the approach of selecting contributing sentences using a ContriSciBERT(a pre-trained model used to identify whether a given sentence was a contributing sentence or not).

3.1.2 Performance Analysis

We show the result of the experiments in Table 2. One of our significant experiments focused on exploiting sectional knowledge and selecting only sentences that concentrated on the substantial understanding of the paper. In particular, selecting contributing sentences helped to comprehend the paper's contribution. It assisted the subsequent model in generating a better-focused summary than other systems. Due to this we surpassed the baseline scores the organizers provided. In particular, we achieved an average Rouge F score of 26.58 when the Abstract + Intro Last + ContriSciBERT which is best among all the submissions made to the task. We also tested our result by passing the whole text of the introduction section as input. We achieved an avg Rouge F score of 26.33, which shows that it is better to give only the last portion of the introduction as it generally summarises the paper's contribution rather than proving the entire introduction to the subsequent summarization model. We also reported the result from extracting contributing sentences using generated rules. The result indicates that extracting contributing sentences from full papers is better than extracting them from only introduction section. We also report our system's scores on the Abstract + Full paper. The organizer used the same model as the baseline. The model produced a lower score than the baseline, perhaps because the organizers used better hyperparameters.

These analyses show the importance of the two-step approach to our proposed system. The first extractive summarization step ie: extracting the contributing sentences, the last part of the introduction section and the abstract written by the author assist the next abstractive step. It finally creates a focused summary highlighting the paper's contribution, motivation, etc of the paper. We perform a human evaluation of our summaries by hiring four human experts pursuing their masters in engineering and technology. They are well versed in NLP and machine learning. The ten summaries appear in entirely random order. We asked the responders to evaluate the summaries by rating them between 1 to 9 on the Likert Scale. The summaries generated by our model achieve the 7.5 Informativeness and 7 Coverage scores (described in Appendix Section C) compared to the golden summaries.

4 Conclusions

In this paper, we studied the Multi-Perspective Scientific Document Summarization task. We experimented with a joint model using extractive and abstractive approaches. The extractive approach supports the modelling of the document structure with a strong focus on which parts/sentences of a research paper to attend to while composing a summary, which significantly boosts the quality of the resultant output. On blind test corpora, our system ranks first wrt. to average Rouge F1 score. The results motivate towards experimenting with better extractive approaches in future which can improve the generation of abstractive summaries by feeding them ideal input data.

5 Acknowledgment

Sandeep Kumar acknowledges the Prime Minister Research Fellowship (PMRF) program of the Govt of India for its support.

References

Arman Cohan, Guy Feigenblat, Tirthankar Ghosal, and Michal Shmueli-Scheuer. 2022. Overview of the first shared task on multi-perspective scientific document summarization (mup). In *Proceedings of the Third Workshop on Scholarly Document Processing*, Online. Association for Computational Linguistics.

Jennifer D'Souza, Sören Auer, and Ted Pedersen. 2021. Semeval-2021 task 11: Nlpcontributiongraph–structuring scholarly nlp contributions for a research knowledge graph. *arXiv preprint arXiv:2106.07385*.

Aaron Elkiss, Siwei Shen, Anthony Fader, Günes Erkan, David J. States, and Dragomir R. Radev. 2008. Blind men and elephants: What do citation summaries tell us about a research article? *J. Assoc. Inf. Sci. Technol.*, 59(1):51–62.

Sayar Ghosh Roy, Nikhil Pinnaparaju, Risubh Jain, Manish Gupta, and Vasudeva Varma. 2020. Summaformers @ LaySumm 20, LongSumm 20. In *Proceedings of the First Workshop on Scholarly Document Processing*, pages 336–343, Online. Association for Computational Linguistics.

Komal Gupta, Ammaar Ahmad, Tirthankar Ghosal, and Asif Ekbal. 2021. Contrisci: A bert-based multitasking deep neural architecture to identify contribution statements from research papers. In *International Conference on Asian Digital Libraries*, pages 436–452. Springer.

Karl Moritz Hermann, Tomás Kociský, Edward Grefenstette, Lasse Espeholt, Will Kay, Mustafa Suleyman, and Phil Blunsom. 2015. Teaching machines to read and comprehend. *CoRR*, abs/1506.03340.

Chin-Yew Lin. 2004. ROUGE: A package for automatic evaluation of summaries. In *Text Summarization Branches Out*, pages 74–81, Barcelona, Spain. Association for Computational Linguistics.

Yang Liu. 2019. Fine-tune BERT for extractive summarization. *CoRR*, abs/1903.10318.

Lawrence H. Reeve, Hyoil Han, and Ari D. Brooks. 2007. The use of domain-specific concepts in biomedical text summarization. *Inf. Process. Manag.*, 43(6):1765–1776.

Ashish Vaswani, Noam Shazeer, Niki Parmar, Jakob Uszkoreit, Llion Jones, Aidan N. Gomez, Lukasz Kaiser, and Illia Polosukhin. 2017. Attention is all you need. *CoRR*, abs/1706.03762.

Shansong Yang, Weiming Lu, Zhanjiang Zhang, Baogang Wei, and Wenjia An. 2016. Amplifying scientific paper's abstract by leveraging data-weighted reconstruction. *Inf. Process. Manag.*, 52(4):698–719.

Michihiro Yasunaga, Jungo Kasai, Rui Zhang, Alexander R. Fabbri, Irene Li, Dan Friedman, and Dragomir R. Radev. 2019. Scisummnet: A large annotated corpus and content-impact models for scientific paper summarization with citation networks. In *The Thirty-Third AAAI Conference on Artificial Intelligence, AAAI 2019, The Thirty-First Innovative Applications of Artificial Intelligence Conference, IAAI 2019, The Ninth AAAI Symposium on Educational Advances in Artificial Intelligence, EAAI 2019, Honolulu, Hawaii, USA, January 27 - February 1, 2019*, pages 7386–7393. AAAI Press.

A Data

The information from OpenReview[3], a platform for open and public publication of scientific research was provided. The corpus is composed of publications from venues including ICLR, NeurIPS, and AKBC. There are around 10,000 publications and 26.5 thousand summaries in the corpus (with an average number of 2.57 summaries per paper). Average word count for the summaries is 100.1. (space tokenized).

B Experimental Settings

To train the ContriSci, we use an 80:10:10 split. We use the default hyperparameters with which ContriSci is trained. We use a learning rate of 1e-5 and an LR scheduler with Polynomial Decay and train the model for 5 epochs.

There are multiple summaries for a paper, so we have taken each paper's content and each summary as one instance to train the model[4]. We use a dynamic learning rate for the BART-based summarization, warm up 1000 iterations, and decay afterward. We set the batch size to 4. The gradient will accumulate every ten iterations, and we train all models for 6000 iterations on 1 GPU (NVIDIA A100 16GB). We save the best model with the highest Rouge1-F1 score based on the validation set. For the BART model, we use the implementation from the huggingface [5]. We use the BART large model pre-trained on CNN/DailyMail dataset.

C Human Evaluation

We used the human evaluation as specified below :-

- Q1 (Readability): determines which of the summaries are most readable?
- Q2 (Informativeness): determines how much useful information about the reviews does the

[3]https://openreview.net/

[4]For example, if there are k summary of a paper, then we will create k instances of the paper.

[5]https://huggingface.co/

summary provide? You need to skim through the original reviews to answer this.

Author Index

Association for Computational Linguistics
209 N. Eighth Street
Stroudsburg, Pennsylvania 18360

ISBN 978-1-7138-6194-2

CURRAN ASSOCIATES INC.
proceedings.com